OXFORD UNDERGRADUATE

1960-3

Alan Macfarlane

Contents

First year: 1960-1961

1961

Second Year 1961-1962

1961

1962

Third year 1962-1963

1962

1963

PRELUDE

When I went to Oxford University in October 1960 I was still in the tiny minority who were attending one of the two old collegiate universities. So there is a real question as to why I went to Oxbridge at all, especially as it caused my parents extra financial difficulties. There is the further question of why I went to Oxford rather than Cambridge, and to Worcester College in particular.

Part of the explanation lies in a long family history. Previous generations of my family along four family lines had been sending their children into tertiary education, though not necessarily to Oxford.

I can think of a dozen or so who went to Oxbridge, and the same number who went to other higher educational institutions. In the generation above me, my mother's middle and younger brothers, Richard and Robert Rhodes James, both went to Oxford to read history. Robert went to Worcester College and it was his contacts with my future teachers that sent me in that direction. Yet he was not the first of the family at Worcester, for in the nineteenth century my great-grandfather's brother John Rhodes James also went to that College. A number of my Jones ancestors went to Oxford, two brothers going to Oriel and another to Magdalen, while their other brother went to University College London. Two of my Stirling ancestors in the nineteenth century, Charles and his brother Waite, a future bishop, went to Exeter College. A century earlier a distant ancestor, Haughton James also went to Oxford. In terms of my family background, on my mother's side there were lawyers, soldiers, doctors, school and university teachers, diplomats, naturalists, clergymen and earlier on plantation owners in Jamaica. On my father's side there were engineers, tea planters and Scottish ministers.

*

My own life and earlier education also provided a set of conditions which nudged me in the direction of Oxbridge. I was born in Shillong, Assam (India) in December 1941. Elsewhere I describe my first five years living through the war and beyond as my father, Donald, a tea planter, became an officer in the Assam regiment, my uncles fought in Burma and my maternal grandfather ended his many years as a Colonel in the Indian army. At the end of the war my father returned to the life of a tea planter and my two sisters, Fiona (born 1944) and Anne (born 1946), were added to the family.

We all came home on leave in April 1947 where we joined my recently retired grandparents in north Oxford for six months. This was my first association with Oxford, and some of my earliest memories are of the tall house in St. Margaret's road, swimming in the river Cherwell next to the Dragon School, watching cricket, fishing in the small canal near our home.

We then went to live in Dorset, where my mother left my sister Fiona and me with my grandparents towards the end of 1948. A detailed account of our life there until we left in 1954 is contained in *Dorset Days*. I was sent to the Dragon School in north Oxford, a boarding preparatory school where I arrived in October 1950. The detailed account of the next five years there until 1955 as told elsewhere, in *Becoming a Dragon*. My parents came home to visit in 1951 and 1954, and I went out to see them in Assam in 1952.

The time at the Dragon school re-introduced me to Oxford and the memories are stronger. I came to know the city and some of the Colleges, in particular the river Cherwell where we boated, the Parks and cricket, the hotels, especially the Randolph, the Playhouse and drama, the churches, the shops and the gardens of Colleges, including Worcester with its lake and ducks. Oxford by the age of thirteen was in my blood.

The family moved north to Windermere in the Lake District in the autumn of 1954 and then my parents bought our first house in Esthwaite Dale, near where Wordsworth had been at school in Hawkshead. This was partly connected to the fact that I would be going to public school some miles away in the Yorkshire Dales at Sedbergh, where my three uncles Billy, Richard and Robert had been before me. My sisters meanwhile went to a local boarding school in Ambleside, run by the P.N.E.U., which made it easier later on for my mother to educate my younger sister in India for her 'O' levels through distance education.

My life over the five years growing up in Wordsworth's valley and in the beautiful Yorkshire moors at Sedbergh is described in detail in *Lakeland Life* and *Sedbergh Schooldays*. There I record the change from child to adolescent to the verge of adulthood. The Robin Hood and King Arthur fantasies and games with soldiers and trains gave way to trout fishing and motorbikes and a skiffle group. The world changed dramatically around us as the post-war austerity gave way to renewed affluence. My parents visited us twice in this period and I went to Assam once when I was sixteen.

It was around the same age of sixteen, as I entered the lower sixth, that various factors - the influence of William Wordsworth and his 'Prelude', my grandparents' and parents' interest in writing and keeping letters, my own need to establish a separate identity – meant that I started to keep as much as I could about what was happening to me. I began to fill empty tomato boxes with different kinds of material – cards, programmes, photos, copies of letters I sent or received, school work and occasional diaries. This has continued throughout my life and it is upon this accumulated hoard that I have based the accounts of my earlier life and the book to which this is a prelude.

*

Although Sedbergh and the Lake District are at the other end of England from Oxford and Cambridge, in fact the connections have always been strong. Wordsworth went from Hawkshead School to St John's College, Cambridge. Trinity College owned land and the presentation to the Church in Sedbergh. Sedbergh itself had been founded in 1525 by a Fellow of King's College, Cambridge, Roger Lupton (who was also Provost of Eton). The ties to Cambridge and Oxford were built up through various scholarships, one of which, the Hastings, my uncle Richard had won to Queen's College, Oxford.

Queen's where Richard had read history was also where my senior history teacher, Andrew Morgan had studied. My equally influential English master, David Alban, had been at Cambridge. In fact, the whole staff (except for one educated in Paris) were educated at Oxford and Cambridge and they imparted to the school the ethos and identity of an offshoot of Oxbridge. Both the content of what we were taught and the way we were taught through an Oxbridge supervision or tutorial system was based on their recent experience of Oxbridge. In Oxford, the face to face teaching with one or two students was called a tutorial, but I also referred to it as supervision.

Although my parents were away for most of this period in India, my grandparents having had two sons at Oxford provided encouragement and experience, as did my uncles. As I showed some academic ability and started to work hard and carefully from about the age of sixteen, there was a growing realization that, although I was not a high flyer and unlikely to win an award, I might get to Oxbridge. The process of doing so is described in the volume on Sedbergh, but basically I failed to get in to Cambridge and did not get a Trevelyan scholarship to Oxford, but was accepted by Worcester College in April 1960 to read history on the basis of my 'A' level results.

My parents were delighted that I had been accepted. My mother had always dreamt of such a chance for herself, and lived her dreams a little through me. My father had rebelled at his public school, Dollar Academy, and left without qualifications, then trained as an engineer on the Clyde and went out in his early twenties to a tea plantation. Yet his mother and younger brother had both been to university; his grandfather and an uncle had graduated from Glasgow University and become ministers. So, he always respected education and was a bright and gifted man, good at mathematics, painting and interested in things of the mind.

That my parents supported me in this final stage of my education was clearly crucial and not to be taken for granted. Although I had grants, there were still large costs and their struggle to help me is chronicled below. They had already spent a large amount on my boarding education for ten years and were now faced with another three years at a time when my father was in debt in Assam. Yet I never knew in any detail of the sacrifice they were making for me; learning about it has been one of the revelations of writing this account.

*

When I arrived at Oxford University in October 1960, shortly before my nineteenth birthday, I was re-entering the city I had left at the age of thirteen. As I recall we were not given any formal advice or information about either the city, the University or the College.

In relation to the City and University, there was a rough map in the useful publication *Vade Mecum*, showing the inner Colleges, but it did not cover a good deal even of the following map. This map does not show my preparatory school, the Dragon, which was located on the top left above 'Park Town'.

The map shows the way in which the city was flanked by two rivers and a canal, and how the Colleges tended to crowd into the middle, with Worcester as an outlier by its lake half way down, on the left.

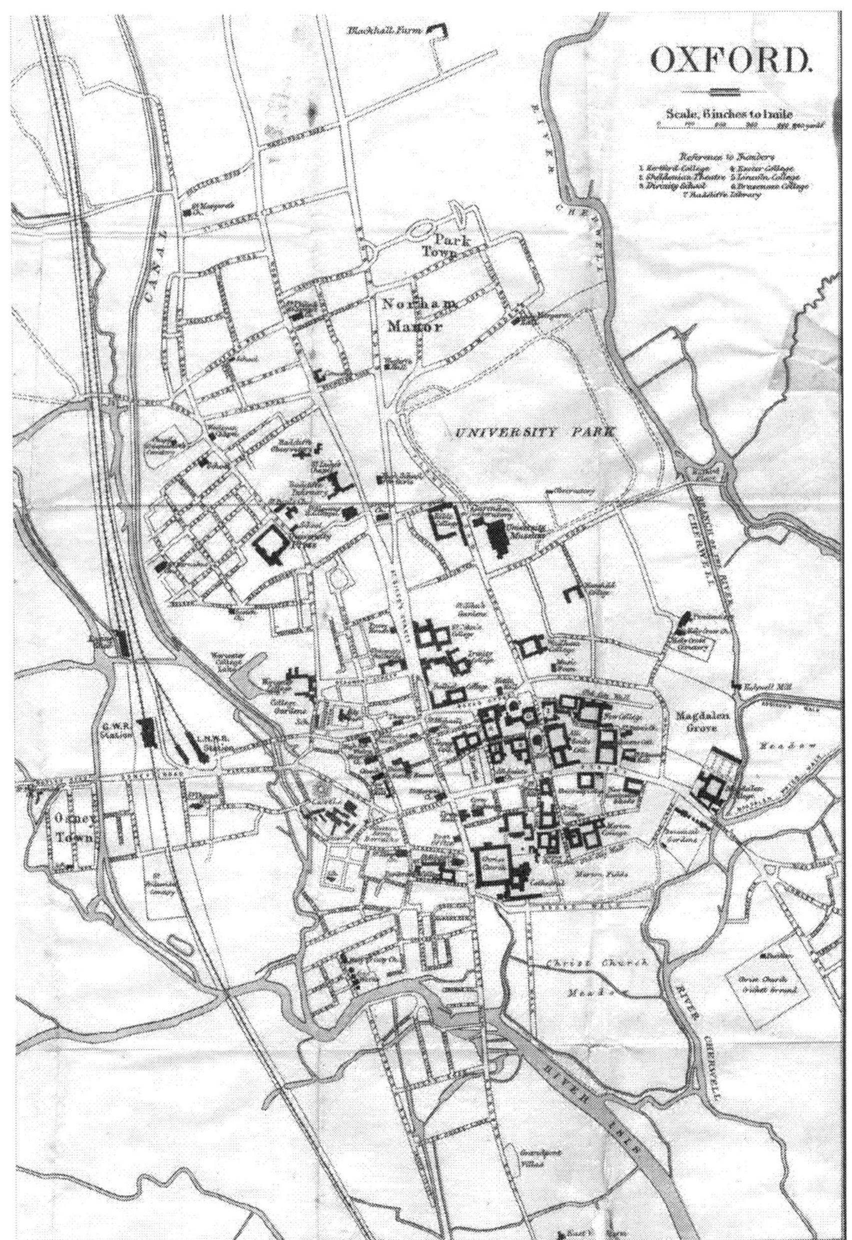

Nor were we told anything about the University. I do not recall that we were informed that Oxford University was the second oldest University in continuous occupation in the world, having been founded formally in 1167 A.D. The unique College-based university system, only now found in Oxford and Cambridge, was not explained to us. It was only many years later, as I retired from my life as a Professor at Cambridge and was writing my book *Reflections on Cambridge* (2009) that I really came to explain to myself how it evolved. Much of what I wrote there about how Cambridge works also applied to my life at Oxford.

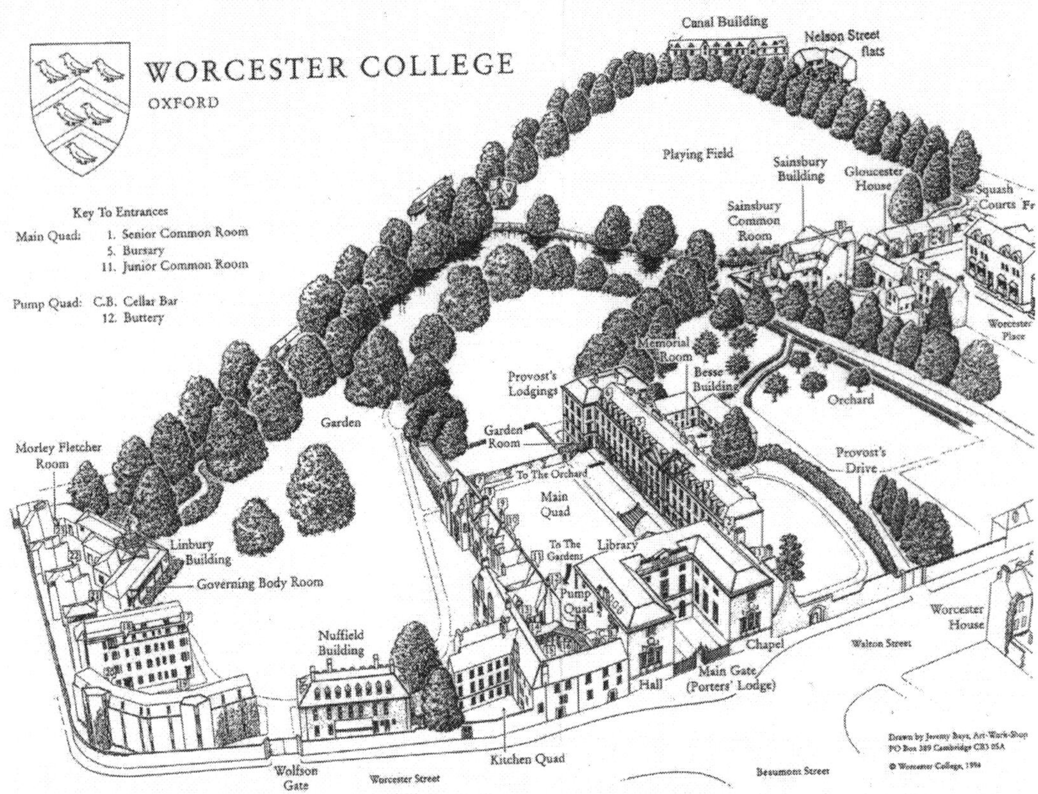

[The buildings on the far left (beyond the Wolfson gate) , and the far right (top) were not there during my time]

Nor was I told anything much about the College which would be my main institutional contact for what turned out to be the next six years. So the following short outline from the current College website was not something available to us.

> Worcester College was founded in 1714, but there has been an institution of learning on the site since the late 13th century. Its predecessor, Gloucester College, was founded in 1283 by the Benedictine Abbey of St Peter at Gloucester as a place of study for 13 monks. The other Benedictine Houses recognised the advantages of bringing their students together and obtained permission from the Abbey at Gloucester to share the House, adding several lodgings to the existing buildings. Fifteen abbeys in total had lodgings in Gloucester College. The dissolution of the monasteries in about 1539 ended the existence of Gloucester College, but the buildings remaining from this period include the row of medieval 'cottages' on the south side of the main quad, Pump Quad and Staircases 1 and 2 ... In 1560 the buildings were purchased by Sir Thomas White, the founder of St John's College, and they became Gloucester Hall... In 1714 the Hall was re-founded as Worcester College after a Worcestershire baronet, Sir Thomas Cookes, left a benefaction for the foundation of a new college. Building began in 1720, but because of a lack of funds proceeded in fits and starts. Sir George Clarke, together with his friend Nicholas Hawksmoor, designed the central group comprising the Hall, Chapel and a magnificent Library, to which Sir George left his collection of books and manuscripts.

Instead of any formal orientation, when I arrived I walked round the College and savoured the stage upon which my life would be mainly enacted in the following years. I entered by the front gate, which is at the end of Beaumont Street, and in its soot-covered stone in the 1960s it was not impressive, especially when compared to other Oxford or Cambridge Colleges.

Oxford, Worcester College, founded A.D. 1714.

Yet the moment I entered, I was met with the splendid view from the cloisters.

Oxford, Worcester College Quadrangle. (Founded A. D. 1714).

The building I entered by, with the fine library above and the cloisters below, can be seen in another postcard of my time.

On one side of the quadrangle were the medieval Benedictine 'Mansions'. My room in the second year was through the second door from the left. My tutor Harry Pitt's room was at the far end of the row.

Worcester College. (Founded A. D. 1714.)

When I was there the back of the 'Mansions' to the right was covered with foliage, as follows. One of the original parts of the old mansions were the Benedictine kitchens, with their huge chimney. My room was on the second floor, the window just behind the chimney.

On the right of the front quadrangle was the grand Hawksmoor terrace looking down on the grass, with the Provost's Lodging at the end and my first tutor's rooms on the second floor at this end.

The Dining Hall on the left as one entered the cloisters, where I ate three times a day for my first two years, was also where we had lectures and did College exams.

Balancing it on the right was the College Chapel which became an important part of my life. This had been originally built in the eighteenth century, but was redecorated in 1864-6 by William Burgess. It is, as described by *Wikipedia*, 'highly unusual and decorative; being predominantly pink, the pews are decorated with carved animals, including kangaroos and whales, and the walls are riotously colourful, and include frescoes of dodos and peacocks.'

The part which most entranced me was the College garden. These were unique in Oxford, comprising more than 26 acres. I entered them by one of the two small tunnels, the further one being reputedly an inspiration for Lewis Carroll's *Alice in Wonderland*. I spent many hours over the years walking through the imposing trees, beside the glorious herbaceous border, alongside the lake complete with ducks and sometimes swans, and playing on or walking round the large playing fields. In sum, the College resembled a country house and estate, where we, as trainee gentlemen and sons of the gentry, would feel at home.

Nothing was explained to us when we arrived because it was assumed that we would understand how Oxford worked on the basis of our previous education. The majority of us had been to public schools and the rest to grammar schools. The principles upon which these schools were based were continued, but magnified. The House at school, was now the College. It was the place where your social, intellectual and spiritual life was centred – a total institution where you went to the library, lectures, tuitions, where you ate and drank and talked. You lived in a room within it for a year or more and in nearby hostels or digs with other students for the rest of your course. The overarching institution, the School at Sedbergh, Oxford University now, was far less important in our daily lives. My loyalty and emotion were tied to the sub-unit of House and College.

We did not need to be given any detailed introduction to the culture and social structure of this institution for they were a continuation of what we already knew. There might be some new specific words and slang - the terms were now called Michaelmas (Winter), Hilary (Spring) and Trinity (Summer), you 'came up' to Oxford. The holidays were 'vacations' or 'vacs'. You were *in statu pupillari* (in the status of pupils) and the College acted *in loco parentis* (in the place of parents). Your teachers were Tutors and your sessions with them were tutorials. The exams were now called 'Prelims' (Preliminary exams after a term) and 'Finals' at the end of our course. We learnt about *exeats* (permission to be absent), about *sub fusc* (full academic dress), about 'Commems' (Commemoration Balls, or Summer Balls) about bedels and proctors and Deans and Provosts. Yet all the more important part of the culture was just a continuation of what we had known at school.

The humour, language, games, friendship patterns, and even the ways of working on one's own in libraries to write weekly essays were things we had learnt at school.

The boys around us (and this was at that time an all-male College, as my school had been) might on average be more skilled and talented in various ways than the average at Sedbergh, and the teachers expected a higher standard of work. Yet it was a change in scale, not in form.

Already I was used to the procedure of entering at the bottom, being a novice who was learning and of a lower status, then moving through the middle ranks, and ending up at the top of the institutions. This had happened at the Dragon School, and then Sedbergh. It happened again twice at Oxford. In the first three years I started as a 'Fresher' or 'Freshman' and then graduated with my degree as an adult after three years. I then returned and started as novice in research, gradually learning the tools of a higher level of search for original discoveries and ending up as a doctor of philosophy, on the level of my teachers.

FIRST YEAR AT OXFORD
1960-61

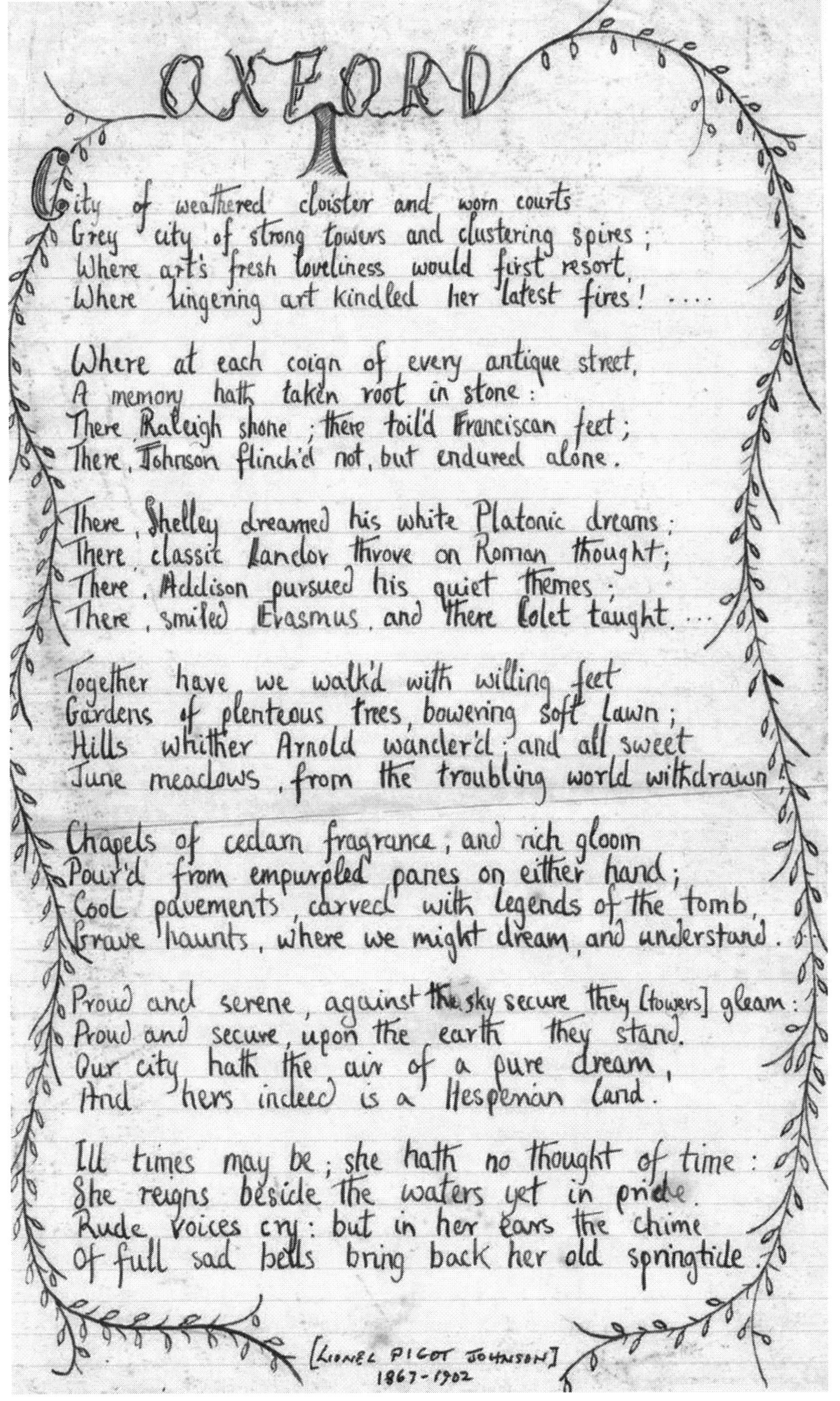

OXFORD

City of weathered cloister and worn courts
Grey city of strong towers and clustering spires;
Where art's fresh loveliness would first resort,
Where lingering art kindled her latest fires! ....

Where at each coign of every antique street,
A memory hath taken root in stone:
There Raleigh shone; there toil'd Franciscan feet;
There, Johnson flinch'd not, but endured alone.

There, Shelley dreamed his white Platonic dreams;
There classic Landor throve on Roman thought;
There, Addison pursued his quiet themes;
There, smiled Erasmus, and there Colet taught. ...

Together have we walk'd with willing feet
Gardens of plenteous trees, bowering soft lawn;
Hills whither Arnold wander'd; and all sweet
June meadows, from the troubling world withdrawn;

Chapels of cedarn fragrance, and rich gloom
Pour'd from empurpled panes on either hand;
Cool pavements, carved with legends of the tomb,
Grave haunts, where we might dream, and understand.

Proud and serene, against the sky secure they [towers] gleam:
Proud and secure, upon the earth they stand.
Our city hath the air of a pure dream,
And hers indeed is a Hesperian land.

Ill times may be; she hath no thought of time:
She reigns beside the waters yet in pride.
Rude voices cry: but in her ears the chime
Of full sad bells bring back her old springtide.

[LIONEL PIGOT JOHNSON]
1867-1902

Winter Term and Vacation 1960

My mother and sisters left England for Assam on 30th September 1960. They went by boat and must have reached Gibraltar in early October, where my mother wrote a short (undated) letter from the 'Chusan'.

My dear Alan,

We're just stopping here, very impressive but cloudy & not warm as I'd thought. Everything has gone well so far… I'm sharing with a nice missionary going to Sarawak. I've told her about Geoffrey but I don't suppose they'll meet as she's going into the depths of the jungle.[1]

I do wonder how you are settling. Have cosy visions of you & the Provost dressed in Terylene trousers sharing tea from the black tea-pot but don't fancy it will turn out quite like that. I'm longing to hear anyway, don't work too hard and write soon – at Bombay I hope …

All our love & thoughts, Mummy

My father was flying back to India so was able to take me and my luggage part-way to Oxford on Wednesday 5th October, leaving me to spend the night at Haileybury with my uncle Richard who was a master there. I struggled on to Oxford the next day with, among other things, the black teapot.

Basically the idea was that we would spend the first years outside the College in a college hostel (in my case 5 Beaumont Street, between the Arts Theatre and the Randolph Hotel), the middle year within the College itself, and the last year in a College-owned room just outside the College.

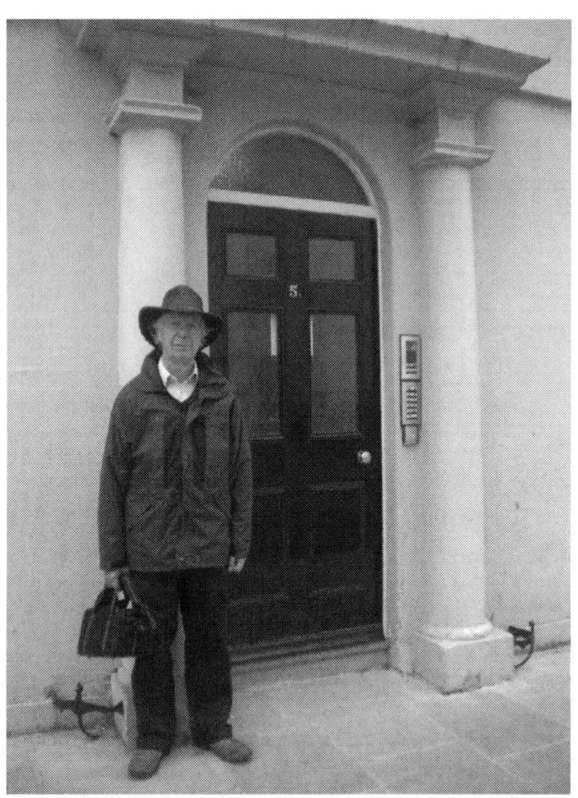

Many years later, returning to 5 Beaumont Street

[1] Geoffrey Bromley was a Sedbergh school friend who had also gone to Sarawak as a trainee missionary and teacher.

As in school days, I wrote my first family letter on a Sunday [9th October], on Worcester College headed notepaper.

Dear Mummy, Fiona and Annie,

I trust this will reach you at Bombay and find you full of vigour and health. Thank you very much for your letter which cheered me up on my arrival here. I have just about settled down now and the first strangeness is almost gone.

I do hope everything has gone off well on your trip and you have enjoyed it. I won't ask the obvious questions about Fiona's affairs – but I don't expect that she will be interested to hear that I gave her message to Steve just before I left. Anyhow you will be seeing Daddy soon after you read this so good travelling 'till then.

I spent a very pleasant evening with Richard at Hayleybury [sic] *when Daddy dropped me. I looked around the school, listened to his stereophonic records and later went out to dinner in Hertford.*

After a <u>*fairly*</u> *hectic journey over here I arrived at about 1.0 at Oxford station and waited about ¾ of an hour for a taxi! When the "scout" (a Mrs Smith – a* <u>*very*</u> *nice and helpful person) showed me my room she said it was the best in the hostel – and I think she was right. The hostel itself is between the "theatre" and the Randolph Hotel – about 3 minutes walk (at the far end of the street) from Worcester.*

My room is quite large – a bit smaller than the drawing room but slightly higher-ceilinged. It has two built in clothes cupboards etc. I enclose a drawing which will save much description.

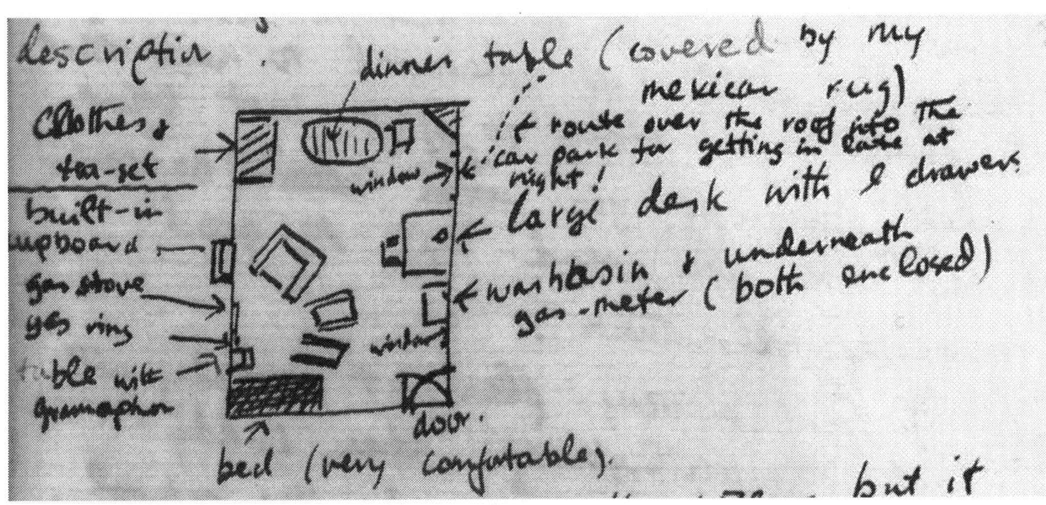

I expect you are none the wiser – but it is a lovely room – with a nice carpet – a very comfortable armchair – and you can imagine the picture as I was this afternoon – discussing "life" with a friend – lounging back (<u>*not*</u> *in my "terylene" trousers I'm afraid as it was Sunday and I had my suit trousers on) – the gas fire aglow – the sidelight painting gentle shadows on the large "Goya" reprint above my bed and the kettle murmuring and whistling contentedly to itself – the only thing missing was the Provost!*

So far I have only seen him twice – once when we were all formally admitted to the college one by one in the main hall – and once in a 3 minute chat at an arranged time.

In the work line I have already been set quite a bit to do (there is hardly <u>*any*</u> *supervision – apart from half an hour a week we are left alone) – but I seem to have done more work in the holidays than most of the others. I am just awaiting the result of a Latin & French unseen to see whether I will have to have extra 'unseen' tuition!*

I have made friends (or am on first name terms with) about 9 or ten boys of which there are two who I especially like – one from Manchester [John Munks?] and another from Spain!

Already I am being caught up in the whirl of things – for instance today after Communion I went almost straight in to St Aldate's church where I was practically forced into joining some discussion classes – and then to go on to a Buffet lunch at the Rectory, and I only just escaped to go to the "Freshman's meeting" of the "Union". Here they tried to persuade us to join – and I might do if I have enough money – for there is a very good library – a dance hall in the cellars – and of course the debating hall. Among the speakers this term are about 8 MP's and in the last debate Vic Oliver & Jimmie Edwards!

I have been approached by about 10 different clubs so far but am manfully resisting. As you can see everything is in a whirl but I am enjoying myself thoroughly. At present I am just about to go to a J.C.R. meeting (Junior Common Room & going to a debate after that). I am playing for the college 2nd XI (football)

on Tuesday – and have been invited to coffee with an ex-Dragon. Must finish now. Please keep this & show to Daddy (& keep it for me – it will save me writing a diary),
All my love & best wishes, Alan xx

Worcester football team, I am second from right in back row

My mother arrived at the Assam tea garden in October and in an undated letter of that month described the journey and arrival.

We were delighted to get your letter a few days ago, your life sounds incredibly gay and I can understand your difficulty in fitting in any work, particularly as its all left to you. When do these beastly Prelims come off? How is the grant working out? Have you met any old Dragon friends, or been to the school? A barrage of questions and I don't really expect too many letters as time must be a problem but we're all panting for information – Fiona with jealousy too at the thought of the dives and the dozens of extra CHAPS.

The next letter is an airmail letter from 5 Beaumont Street, dated from the postmark in Oxford as 11 November (a Friday).

Dear Mummy, Daddy, Fiona, and Anne,
I hope the absence of a letter this week doesn't mean that the arrival of my estimate of the fees was such a shock that you decided you couldn't afford the stamps! Anyhow – seriously, I hope you are alright and happy and not working as hard as I <u>*should*</u> *be doing. The pressure is really beginning to increase now, and I find I haven't much time for anything else except work, for although cutting entertainment down to a minimum and not indulging in having cups of coffee with people I still don't get much done. All my "history" friends are very depressed and each seems certain that he will fail so if they want* <u>*any*</u> *of us to pass they will have a pretty low pass-mark. Next week for instance I have got to write an essay on Bede [and] on Macaulay and have to do a 2½ hour exam paper on "de Tocqueville" – still I won't bore you any further with this.*

If at times in my letter I sound dispirited it is only because I had a very exhausting day yesterday. After a French tutorial and Latin unseen in the morning it was pleasant to have a mental rest in the afternoon and play a match of football v New College. This week one of the 1st XI full-backs has been away so I have been playing in his place. We have played 3 times and been fairly fortunate in winning all three – 3-2, 3-1, 1-0. After cycling speedily back from the soccer and rushing through a bath into my clothes (not literally!) I arrived at

Keble College to find that the O.D [Old Dragon] *with whom I was meant to be having tea and going to the Dragon performance of the "Mikado" had left me a note saying he had 'flu! Anyhow his mother teaches at the Dragon so I went on there and met her and got the best seat in the hall – right at the top at the back.*[1]

Surprisingly I wasn't overcome by nostalgia or amazed at the shrinkage of everything – perhaps I was prepared for it. Anyhow things didn't seem to have changed much – there were still boys sitting on the pillar-box and languidly waiting for their parents – I must say I see what you mean by saying that the boys were pretty offhand and cheeky – I just can't imagine how I was ever like that! "Nasty little specimens!" (to quote my old form-master's opinion – I met him over a drink in the interval). Anyhow I must say – though one could see the limitations – that the operetta was exceedingly good – the "Lord High Executioner" – obviously the form funny-man – was especially good. Just to add a touch of class to the performance I had a little fat boy of about 6 yrs next to me who spent his time either making remarks – or more generally snivelling – shades of Anne! (in the former part at least).

After that I came straight back to improve my spoken French – in other words to meet a French friend (female) who can only speak about 3 words of English. You can imagine the highly intelligent conversation we had!!! – anyhow we went on to the Saturday "hop" at the Union cellars which included some real "cool" cha-cha-cha etc – after seeing Nicole home I set out purposefully for 5 Beaumont Street at about 12.15 – with my college scarf slung around my neck (it is a revolting pink & black affair – which Fiona will love -) after about 6 people had gazed at me as if I was mad and looked at their watches I suddenly realised that with my scarf round my neck I was very likely to have my name taken by a 'proctor' ("prog" in "Oxonian") or his bulldog – I hid it therefore. Then having bought some delicious hot-dogs, smothered in chutney, onions & mustard I climbed in through a bottom-floor window (by an arrangement with the owner) and collapsed on my bed worn out.

I tried my bottle of "Merrydown" cider out during the course of the evening and it certainly is powerful stuff! Nicole although coming from Montpellier and having a father who owned some vinyards was made pretty happy by ¼ pint and half a small glass of ordinary wine! I was also feeling pretty dizzy. If I have some sort of a party this holidays – as I hope to do if there are any young people left around (Martin I hear is going for good – although I haven't heard what he's doing) I'll mix some of this stuff in the "punch"!

By the way I want to send the new Peter Sellers record out as a christmas present to one of you – its called "My Goodness Me" (with Sophie Loren) – other side 'Grandpa's Grave' and is only a single (3 mins each side) "45" – but I'm not sure if I can

a) Because of the customs?
b) have you a gramophone?
c) it is a wonderful "take-off" again of an Indian doctor and might not be appreciated at the club?! – anyhow its his best yet.

Hoping to hear all the news soon – look after yourselves and be <u>happy</u>!
With all my love to you all, Alan

As a footnote to the French lessons, I have two short notes from Nicole. The first was probably written a week after the events described above, from Westbury Lodge, Marham Road.

Dear Alan,
Thank you very much for your letter – I shall be allowed to go to your house, to-morrow, Saturday at "five o'clock" – Your letter was written in a very good French and I am very sorry for my bad English. Missis Middlemiss went on Monday to the hospital, and I must do all the work by myself, but to-morrow I shall be free after the Lunch and it is very kind of you, to invite me –

I thank you, also, for the nice evening, on the last Saturday.

I hope that you shall receive my letter in good time –

Amicalement,
Nicole

Nicole obviously also dropped in at some point at the end of term and wrote:

---

[1] This was probably Anthony Escritt, whose mother taught at the Dragon.

Dear Alan,
I am spending Christmas Holidays in France and I came to wish you have very good holidays – Have you pass your exam?
I send you all my best wishes for the new year –
Very sincerely – Nicole[1]

There are only two surviving letters from me at Oxford that term, but some of the missing news is supplied by my mother's letters to me.

On November 13, my mother wrote from Assam:

My dear Alan,
I'm afraid this is a couple of days late as Fiona used the last Airgraph, I don't suppose in your crowded life you will notice. We got a very nice letter yesterday which cheered us up no end, I was afraid my last one might have depressed you. We were most amused to read about the Queens visit, specially as we'd read the sequel about the foundation stone having been stolen, any of your pals?[2] *Its hard to think about floods when we're having such perfect weather here, day after golden day….*

The last page is largely a short piece by my father. It starts…

At long last I have managed to get a little space to write a word. Very pleased indeed with your letter and hearing about your goings-on. I would love to be there and wish I had worked a bit harder when I was younger!

On the outside in my hand are some words which were obviously things I would include in my reply: Collecting, Christmas, reading, Daddy, Fiona, Drink & parties, Work, Plays, Tea-party, Squash etc, Tea – Anthony, heard Geoffrey/Ian (old Sedbergh friends)

My mother wrote again on November 19:

My dear Alan,
A nice letter to thank you for, though I'm sorry mine depressed you. Don't worry about the finances, we shall manage somehow and it will get easier when we've paid off the girls' passages. We can get the Battels home before mid Jan. I don't doubt, and will then repay what you have had to fork out of your grant, let us know how this is going though. Your main worry at the moment will be Prelims, what a bore and so much a matter of luck in things like Latin Unseens. I hope you'll continue to hold out against the militant (and un-Christian!) Christians. You seem to have reached a stage beyond them, that hammering of ones ideas into other people is usually replaced by a mature, more tolerant un-anxious certainty that God can be all things to all people, and how they worship him is their own affair. Horrible grammar but you know what I mean. That devastating narrowness is surely a contradiction of every Christian precept! To more mundane topics…
"The 7th Seal" sounds a wonderful film, I'll see if I cant get them to get it here though perhaps it's a bit beyond Nazira P.O. [Post Office] [So, this was the time I saw my first Bergman, which I still remember so vividly.] …
[Teaching my sister history etc] We're just through the Anglo Saxons and I thought of you when we dismissed the Ven. Bede in one sentence! …
I hear from Granny that Martin has been finally thrown out, I wonder how long it will last, the gang will be dispersed without his room to gather in but perhaps after Oxford you will find them puerile anyway. Have you met anyone you like particularly? Have you heard from Ian or Geoffrey? Tell the latter to send any stamps he has, for Anne!

---

[1] Written on a small Xmas card.

[2] There is a five minute clip of the Queen's visit on Youtube which can be found by searching for 'Queen's visit to Oxford 1960'.

Again I have scribbled some words which would give me clues to my next letter. Tessa, Tea-party (?memories of By-the-Way), Spree, Teaching History – when I send note – friends – party – M, Prelims – Collections & Work, Party – Well, Film – Brigitte, Midwitch Cuckoo, Today, Lonely , packing, Christmas, Martin, Pens

*

There are few other remains of this first term. The only letters I have are as follows. The first is dated December 3rd and appears to be written by one of my connections through the Christian fellowship. It is addressed from Reading, though the writer was clearly a teacher. I shall just give an extract.

Dear Alan,
.... It was good to get to know you better at Oxford. I imagine you must have felt that your movements were very constricted by your having to work for an exam: but thank you for inviting me to tea, and for treating me to your records. You must come round again next term when you have more time.

This vac. means work for me (the vision of you just sleeping won't be very inspiring, but I suppose you'll keep the wheels turning) with the occasional game of rackets in the school courts.

I hope I'll see you at Eastbourne as I am planning to come on the 8th and catch the end of the 'Leadership Course'. I look forward to hearing your news then. Finally, all power to your elbow in the next three days.[1]
Yours sincerely, Mark

The next is perhaps from my Worcester friend John Munks, and alludes to a visit to the Langdales. It is sent from 14, Granary Lane, Worsley, Walkden, Lancs., on 12 December.

Dear Alan,
Look, do you want to have three nights holiday over New Year in the Langdales with our mob from Worsley? If you came you would have a good time – especially if there aren't many folk up your way. We are going to the Holiday Fellowship Home, Wall End Youth Club, Langdale, Ambleside – from Friday night 30th December to Monday morning 2nd January. If you can come you would be most welcome; seriously thinking of coming? If so could you send me (wait for it) £3 and I'll see it is all squared right with the booking at this end. If you can't make it, Alan, do you think we could see each other some time between those dates while I'm up there? Let me know how places & times suit you most.

How did the exams go? I hope all went well – let me know when you get the results?
.... Best wishes, John

The letters above give few hints of what I did during the first term. In terms of societies and clubs, I have cards for the opera club, but the only one of their productions I went to (I have the programme) was the 'Gondoliers' on November 9. I also have the programmes for two plays at the Oxford Playhouse, 'Naked' by Luigi Pirandello and 'The Apple Cart' by Bernard Shaw. I also have a card for the Carols at Worcester College on Sunday December 4th. I joined the Heritage Society, the folk song society, for which I have the card, and have a card stating that I had paid my subscription for Michaelmas term 1960 for the Oxford Union Society. I also have the match card for the Worcester College R.F.C. (Rugby Football Club), but don't remember ever playing or attending any matches.

Sample of the range of entertainment of every sort can be seen in the following university diary, and a programme for the local cinema.

---

[1] A reference to the Prelims examination.

FIRST WEEK DIARY

Scala Cinema : Vittorio de Sica and Sophia Loren in "L'oro di Napoli" and "The Lost Continent."
Ritz Cinema : "A French Mistress."
Super Cinema : "Green Mare's Nest" and "Wages of Fear."
Regal Cinema : "The Young have no time" and "More Deadly than the Male."

SUNDAY, 9th OCTOBER

OI CCU : Rev. J. A. Motyer, Freshmen's Sermon. Wesley Memorial Church, 8.30.
Friends' Society : Harold Loukes' "Lost Causes and Screaming Tyres." 43 St. Giles, 12.45.

MONDAY, 10th OCTOBER

Humanist Group : Social, Union Cellars, 8.15.
Labour Club : Open Meeting. Ralph Samuel "Can Socialism Survive?" Ruskin, 4.30.
Badminton Club : Trials. Manor Road Court.

TUESDAY, 11th OCTOBER

SCM : Canon T. R. Milford (Master of the Temple) "Why Christianity?" Wesley Mem. Church, 8.15.
OU Cross Country : University Trials.
Humanist Group : F. A. Ridley (Pres. Nat. Secular Soc.) "On Rome." Taylor Institute, 8.15.
Badminton Club : Trials. Manor Road Club.

WEDNESDAY, 12th OCTOBER

Cosmos : Sir William Hayter "Soviet Foreign Policy." Rhodes House, 8.15.
Medical Society : Prof. Sir Alistair Hardy "Did Man have a more Aquatic Past?" Radcliffe Infirmary, 8.15.
CND : Social. Union Cellars. 8.15.
French Club : "Vive! Monsieur Blaireau." School of Botany, South Parks Road, 8.
Crime—A Challenge : Open Meeting. Prof. Radzinowicz "The Study of Criminology." Rhodes House, 8.15.
Opera Club : "Il Seraglio." Holywell Music Room, 8.
E.T.C. : Dame Peggy Ashcroft. 8.15.

Monday, October 15 - - - - Six Days

One of the Cinema's Ten Best Films
KENJI MIZOGUCHI's
***UGETSU MONOGATARI** (x)
2.2, 5.15, 8.30

JAMES STEWART
KIM NOVAK
JACK LEMMON
ERNIE KOVACS
BELL, BOOK AND CANDLE (a)
(Eastman Colour)
3.31, 6.47

ADULTS ONLY
F.P. 2.0 L.P. 6.45 E. 10.0

Monday, October 22 - - - - Six Days

SANDRO PANZERI
LOREDANA DETTO
TULLIO KEZICH
in Ermanno Olmi's
***IL POSTO** (u)
(The Job)
1.55, 5.12, 8.33

TREVOR HOWARD
JOSEPH COTTEN
ORSON WELLES
in Carol Reed's
THE THIRD MAN (a)
3.25, 6.47

F.P. 1.55 L.P. 6.47 E. 10.5

Monday, October 29 - - - - Six Days

TADEUSZ LOMNICKI
KRYSTYNA STYPULKOWSKA
in Andrzej Wajda's
***NIEWINNI CZARODZIEJE** (a)
(Innocent Sorcerers)
2.6, 5.16, 8.30

STANLEY BAKER
SAM WANNAMAKER
MARGIT SAAD
in Joseph Losey's
THE CRIMINAL (x)
3.36, 6.50

ADULTS ONLY
F.P. 2.6 L.P. 6.50 E. 10.1

Monday, November 5 - - - - Six Days

MAI ZETTERLING
ALF KJELLIN STIG JARREL
in Alf Sjöberg's
***FRENZY**
Script : Ingmar Bergman
1.55, 5.5, 8.20

GEORGES POUJOULY
BRIGITTE FOSSEY
in René Clements'
***LES JEUX INTERDITS** (x)
3.35, 6.50

ADULTS ONLY
F.P. 1.55 L.P. 6.50 E. 10.3

F.P. = First Programme
* English Titles

Monday, November 12 - - - - Six Days

FARLEY GRANGER
ROBERT WALKER
RUTH ROMAN
in Alfred Hitchcock's
STRANGERS ON A TRAIN (a)
1.53, 5.5, 8.22

JEAN ROUCH and
EDGAR MORIN's
***CHRONIQUE D'UN ETE** (a)
(Chronicle of a Summer)
3.30, 6.50

F.P. 1.50 L.P. 6.48 E. 10.4

Monday, November 19, Tuesday, Wednesday

STEVE COCHRAN
ALIDA VALLI
in Michelangelo Antonioni's
***IL GRIDO** (a)
(The Cry)
3.0, 5.35, 8.20

CHARLIE CHAPLIN
THE IMMIGRANT
——
WALT DISNEY CARTOON

F.P. 2.5 L.P. 7.19 E. 10.2

Thursday, November 22, Friday, Saturday

MARLON BRANDO FRANK SINATRA
JEAN SIMMONS
in Joseph L. Mankiewicz's
GUYS AND DOLLS (a)
(CinemaScope — Eastman Colour)
2.10, 4.53, 7.35

F.P. 2.5 L.P. 7.25 E. 10.4

Monday, November 26 - - - - Six Days

DANIEL GELIN
ANNIE GIRARDOT
CHRISTIAN MARQUAND
in Alexandre Astruc's
***LA PROIE L'OMBRE** (x)
(Dyaliscope)
1.56, 5.8, 9.25

BOB HOPE
DOROTHY LAMOUR
OTTO PREMINGER
EDUARD CIANNELLI
THEY GOT ME COVERED (u)
3.35, 6.50

ADULTS ONLY
F.P. 1.56 L.P. 6.50 E. 10.4

L.P. = Last Complete Programme
* English Titles

Monday, December 3 - - - - Six Day

DANNY KAYE VIRGINIA MAYO
FAY BAINTER BORIS KARLOFF
THE SECRET LIFE OF WALTER MITTY (u
(Technicolor) Approx. 2.0, 5.0, 8.10
Supporting programme to be announced

F.P. 2.0 L.P. 6.50 E. 10.

Monday, December 10 - - - - Six Day

LAURENCE OLIVIER's
RICHARD III (a
by William Shakespeare
Filmed in VistaVision and Eastman Colour
1.55, 4.39, 7.25

F.P. 1.55 L.P. 7.20 E. 10.

Monday, December 17 - - - - Six Day

PETER SELLERS
JEAN SEBERG
WILLIAM HARTNELL
THE MOUSE THAT ROARED (u)
(Eastman Colour)
2.30, 5.28, 8.30

A revival of a "Vintage" Comedy
WILL HAY
MOORE MARRIOTT
GRAHAM MOFFATT
CONVICT 99 (a
3.50, 6.54

F.P. 2.28 L.P. 6.50 E. 9.5

NEXT TERM—

LUIS BUNUEL's **LOS OLVIDADOS**
JOSEPH LOSEY's **BLIND DATE**
CHEKHOV's
THE LADY WITH THE LITTLE DOG

E = End
* English Titles

As regards the formal side of academic life, I have the card stating that I had made the Statutory Declaration not to 'abstract from the Library, nor to mark, deface, or injure in any way, any volume, document, or other object belonging to it; nor to bring into the Library or kindle therein any fire or flame, and not to smoke in the Library' and I promise to obey all regulations of the Library.' It was dated 8 October and stamped ‘Camera’, in other words the Radcliffe Camera. I had been through our admission ceremony, for I also have an admission ticket to the Sheldonian Theatre Quadrangle on 4 November, where ‘Academic Dress Must be Worn’, though I remember nothing about it.

I started my time at Oxford as a fairly devout and practising Christian of the evangelical church, and hence was attracted to St Aldate's, well known for its evangelical spirit. I remember attending some of the services there.

I also have the COSMOS card (U.N. Association) which states that I and Richard Smethurst (the future Provost of Worcester) were the College Representatives. Dick probably persuaded me to be involved as he was already rising in the organization and held various posts – and was a close friend.

Christmas Holidays 1961

There is a letter from my mother on December 6:

My dear Alan,
You will be home and dry by now – or maybe not so dry judging by the stories we hear of the weather. I do hope the exams weren't too bad and you're now enjoying the aftermath of released tension. It wont be a wildly exciting holiday probably, what with one thing and another (both the same thing in fact!) but I know it will cheer Granny and Granpa up having you and perhaps Richard will be there too for a bit. I just cant get any Christmas spirit together here….
Anne Johnson wrote yesterday with news of what she hoped was in store, I hope you'll find someone to partner at dances, judging by Anne's letter the selection doesn't seem to have widened much. Sad about Anne Hogg's father, so many people seem to be sickening suddenly. …
[note by my father at end:]
I join Mummy in hoping that the exams went well and that you didn't "fash" yourself over much. .. No fishing yet I am afraid… keep writing. We love getting your letters. Lots of love, Daddy[1]

The next letter was written from Cherideo on December 13:

My dear Alan,
I'm hoping this will arrive in time to wish you lots of Christmas cheer, but if you've already had it, I hope its not sitting too heavily on your solar plexus! We haven't heard from you since the Exam so I don't know whether to mention it or not, or when you're likely to be having results. I expect you've put the whole thing out of your mind for a week or two, and I hope you're getting some hops [dances] *and the weather is cheering up. Strange to think that on my nineteenth birthday I was a married woman with you on the way, and where will we all be in another nineteen years? Perched in front of the fire at Field Head I hope but we shall probably be atom dust, a cheering Yuletide thought for us but it doesn't bother me really as long as we get a year or two with our yew tree. One is always inclined to be nostalgic at this time of year and forget the fuss and fret of Christmas at home and the vast sense of relief when it's over, if only it could be a quiet and contented time instead of a financial worry.*

The last letter home from my mother this year is on December 27:

My dear Alan,
…. Your most amusing card arrived on Christmas Eve, plus letter, and we were glad to hear you had left your bed of sickness and ventured out into the slush. We do get a bit nostalgic for Yule logs and such like, but on the whole Christmas at home seems to have deteriorated into an orgy of eating and Telly and so I for one don't miss it all that much. Please don't think of sending us a present, partly because you will have little enough to spare, and partly because one has to pay 200% duty on anything that comes into the country and it just isn't worth it. When we next have a Christmas together we will make it a really slap up affair, for the present all we need to see us through the year is the knowledge that you are happy and well. …
I think you're right not to take your [driving] *lessons till the spring, what with the weather and lack of time. I believe you're going to Eastbourne* [religious camp] *for a few days, then straight back to Oxford I presume. Will you let us know about the battels, and who we are supposed to send the money to, also the state of the grant? I would like you to have a big coat, duffel or some such for this term, perhaps you could get it at Oxford or Eastbourne, or there's Penrice in Ambleside, they had some nice navy ones. We will reimburse! …*
And New Year greetings to all and sundry, that's the day of David's party I think?

According to my grandfather's diary, I arrived home on December 10 and David Porter, a Sedbergh friend, arrived on Monday 19, the day before my birthday. He left on the 21 and my uncle Richard arrived on Friday 23

[1] 'Fash' is to worry, perplex, make yourself anxious.

The last letter of that holidays between us was one I wrote from Field Head, with the Ambleside postmark of 31 December.

Dear Family, (It saves me saying Dear Mummy, Daddy, Fiona, Anne, etc!!)

"The time has come the Walrus said to talk of many things, of ships, and shoes and sealing-wax and cabbages and kings". The time has indeed come for me to unfold the next enthralling chapter in the life of Alan "Hancock" Macfarlane. But before that let me thank you very much indeed (if I haven't done so already) for both your letters and the telegram – all these just arrived on or before my birthday and cheered me up a great deal when I was just getting over my cold. An awful lot seems to have happened since then and that is why I am writing in this spidery fashion. I hope you can all read it.

I hope you had wonderful Christmas, though I don't suppose it was especially "Christmassy" under a hot sun. I haven't heard yet how things went, though probably our letters will cross as I am a bit late. We looked through the Indian slides yesterday and the pictures of Mummy trying to control the dogs and Miranda and smile sweetly at the same time brought back happy memories. Have you been fishing yet? And how are the boy friends – of Fiona of course!

Anyhow here we go.

I had a very enjoyable birthday as Granny was wonderful and we invited Vivien Chapman, Anne Johnson, Martin & David Porter over and had a super lunch and very enjoyable afternoon. The next but one evening we had one of our "parties". It was absolutely typical – as the organization broke down and of the 20 expected guests only 9 turned up for the whole evening – (Mike and Jill came for a short time). David, Anne J, Martin, Sally Atkinson etc all sat around fairly glumly, but I personally enjoyed myself having fallen (in a <u>very</u> small way) for Vivien Chapman. I won't bore you with the long narrative of our doings but we have had a pretty lively time with pony-club dances, cinema outings etc – this evening there is David's "New Year Eve" dance – I hope it isn't like last time – anyhow this time we are having it in the 'Old Farm House' and it is a jeans party. Fiona will be pleased to hear that everyone from Bill Critchley and "Milk Edward" (as Edward Acland is now known) to David M-F & Mike Bod[dington] have been inquiring after her. I must say everyone has grown up considerably and when we go to organized parties we are usually the largest and oldest gang there. Simon (M[amby]) always creates a stir with his new hair style – a <u>very</u> small tufted beard – a thin moustache and his hair very long and brushed forward over his ears – he completes the picture by going around in black jeans and a high, glossy top-hat – can you imagine him?! The gang is pretty much the same but the attachments have switched around a bit. Anne J. is mad over Simon (and he is fairly keen on her) – Anne Hogg who is up for a week likes Bill Critchley – Martin (surprise) is going quite steady with a very quiet girl – Sally Urquet (sister of Elspeth) – though he swears he never forgets Jacky for a moment. David is faintly pursuing Carol Hartwell, Digby is flirting with any girl who will play, John Atkinson is going steady with Wendy Babbington and I am supposed to be paired off with Vivien. We still roar around and I have been in after 3.0 about 3 times. Now having fulfilled my role as a sort of amateur Paul Tanfield I will get onto the other news.

Richard was up here over Christmas with his new car and Robert and Angela came over for lunch – then Richard and myself drove back to Cartmell and had <u>another</u> turkey there with them! We had a very pleasant day and thought of you all over our wine (given to Richard as a leaving present by a boy's parents!)

On Wednesday, as I think I told you, I had a carol service by candlelight at Greythwaite Chapel (in the Sandy's Estate). It was great fun and considering the obscurity of some of the carols the rest of the choir were pretty good. Then we retired to the Sandys mansion and in a wonderful old stone kitchen we drank mulled claret and ate hot mince-pies, and chatted informally to the squire – while the "merry firelight glowed warm on the brass pans hung along the ceiling" – all very cheery & Christmassy. We are having the proper carol service to-morrow on New Years Day and then going for another binge after that over to a Mrs Heaton at Coniston.

The weather has been absolutely miserable – out of 21 days this holidays only 1 has been completely fine – about two more were half fine. For the rest it has poured, hailed, sleeted and occasionally snowed – only to turn very quickly into slush. Vivien's brother is very keen on fishing and has been dragging the whole family down to the sea where they have spent days on end hurling plastic lugworms into the thundering waves with the hail beating down their neck – all to no avail. I can't think of anything more miserable. The roads up to now have been icy so I only got my mo-bike out yesterday – you will be surprised to hear it goes like a bird. Soon however I will have to go into the ghastly business of getting it insured etc. Tomorrow I have a group of friends coming up from Manchester to camp in a hostel in the Langdale valley and they have asked me over – unfortunately it is also the one day the Listers will be up. (Unfortunately in that I might have to meet Sally!)

Hope you are all very happy and busy, & beans, dogs, cooks etc surviving. Don't forget to tell me what you would like for Christmas!!
Lots of love to you all, Alan

Although it was written in 1961, the following letter describes events in the second half of the winter holidays. It is addressed Beaumont Street, Oxford, though, as explained, written elsewhere. It was posted in Oxford on January 11:

Dear Family,

I am writing a hurried letter from Eastbourne (not the above address) as I seem to have a bit of leisure and also because of pecuniary reasons which I will leave to the end of the letter.

I can't remember whether I answered and thanked you for your last letter which arrived a bit before I left the north – glad to hear all is going well and you had a happy – if chaotic, Christmas – already it seems a long time behind and we seem well into another year of unemployment, massacres in Africa and tension between East and West. I'm afraid I go around gloomily prophesying the destruction of the world in the near future – to me it seems inevitable (but perhaps not entirely final?)

The holidays ended in a real burst of gaiety & mad rushing about. I spent the last Monday and Tuesday afternoons over at the Chapmans – but in case you get any ideas Vivien and I are "just good friends" (although I had rather a row with her the last evening – when at her party (which was pretty debauched). My pride was rather shattered when she went off for the whole evening with Mike Boddington. Having escaped with relief from that whirl the whole thing seems terribly petty from down here. Thank goodness I can change my environment [three words torn] it gives you a chance to see the other place in a much better perspective.

Towards the end of the holidays I was getting rather worried about whether I would get my results before the end of the holidays – but when I arrived home the morning before I left Granpa threw his hands up in the air and said "You've passed!!"[1] *Up to a certain extent this was true as I had passed the exam as a whole = but failed <u>Latin</u>!! I don't think this is very serious as it means that I have got the two more detailed subjects out of the way and I don't suppose it will matter much if I just fail Latin. The only other historian I have met so far – here at Eastbourne – failed French, and he was fairly intelligent so I won't be the only one. Naturally I'm very relieved – but hope the fact that I have no exams for 8 terms won't make me <u>too</u> lazy. I'm afraid I didn't get as much history done in the holidays as I would like to have done!!*

This Reunion or "Christian Leadership Course" (as I have only just discovered it is called) is most refreshing and a welcome rest after an hectic holidays. We are situated in a very plush hotel just back from the sea-front – my ideas of a wind-swept and bleak stretch of wet and lovely sea-shore hasn't turned out at all – in fact it has been glorious weather and I have been for a very energetic walk up Beachy Head.

TUESDAY [10 Jan.]

I am dashing this off at about 11.30 in the evening over black coffee. I have arrived here safely after going to that party in London last night. It was good fun as quite a few of my college friends were there – very informal and just like all the others otherwise. When I arrived here I found a bill awaiting me – to be paid by 13 January!! Anyhow I will explain things to the bursar – if you could send the money – made payable to "Worcester College" "Oxford" as soon as possible. Also could you send <u>me</u> some money presto? As the first part of my grant is almost out and I wont have anything for this term. Here is a copy of the battels for last term – see what you can make of them.
[copied details]

- *could you send me £25 for the term please?! I will send full account soon & get organized!*
- *Sorry to end on this mercenary note.*
- *All my love to you all, Alan*
-

[1] Grandpa's diary: Wed 4 Jan 'Alan passed Oxford Prelims in 2 Subjects – History & French. Failed in Latin only which he must take again.'

	£	s	d.
Inclusive charge for Board and Lodging	59	4	0
Meals in Hall			
Guests Meals			
Guests Accommodation			
....			
....			
....			
Milk, Tea, Coffee and Stores ...			
Drinks		7	9
Coupons			
Gratuities	2	0	0
Laundry	1	9	11
Fuel		2	6
Gate Fines			
Postage and Messenger			2
J.C.R. Art Fund			
Damage			
Library—Book Fines			
Junior Common Room		15	0
College Clubs	3	5	0
University and College Dues ...	28	4	0
	95	8	4
Tuition Fee	25	0	0
Key Deposits			
B.U. Provident Association	1	1	0
Oxford Society			
Debtor Balance brought forward ...			
Prepayment for H.T. 1961	25	0	0
	146	9	4

Credit:	£	s.	d.
Prepayment for M.T. 1960...	25	0	0
Credit Balance of last account			
Scholarship			
Exhibition			
Ministry of Education ...			
Local Authority	58	4	0
Cash			
	83	4	0

Balance Due to the College £ 63 . 5 . 4

Among the surviving materials are cheque stubs for two out of the three years I was at Oxford. They give small indications of my expenses and will be included at appropriate points. The sums without further detail indicate the drawing of cash – 'Self' – for myself

For the first term and vacation the cheques are as follows:
6 Oct – £7
15 Oct – £3-10
15 Oct – Prelims Entrance Fee £5
22 Oct – Admission £45
22 Oct – £5

4 Nov – £5
17 Nov – £5
28 Nov – £5
28 Nov – £4-10

8 Dec – £8 (Travel)
17 Dec – £3
28 Dec – £4

4 Jan 1961 – £14

Thus, leaving on one side examination fees, I was drawing out between £15 and £20 in cash a month during this period. This covered everything except accommodation and main meals, which I had in College.

*

I had received a County University Scholarship from Lancashire County council in May 1960. They estimated the cost for attending an Oxford or Cambridge College, hostel or lodgings with tuition fees at £325 a year. They would pay a sum after deducting "parental contribution" calculated on parental income. As can be seen from the first Battels above, for the first term the total for the term was approximately £120 for board and lodging, sundries and University and College dues, and tuition fees. The Local Authority paid about half of this, leaving my parents with the other half, and also a voluntary amount (about £25 a term in the first year) for clothing and pocket money. So my parents were paying about £85 for each of the three terms, and my keep and pocket money for the three holidays, which were equal in length to the terms.

At a guess, they must have been paying between £400 and £500 a year for each of my three years. Thus, although my Oxford education was well supported by the local authorities, it was still very expensive for my parents, especially when they had to educate and support my two sisters as well.

Reading History at Oxford

One effect of the Oxford system of examinations at that time, where one was examined on the whole three-year course right at the end, was that it was essential to keep all one's notes and essays pretty carefully for the final revision. So, all my contemporaries must have done this. But what is perhaps unusual is that I should then have kept all the folders of work until now. There are over ten large folders and boxes of notes and essays and these will form the basis of an attempt to enrich the accounts of social and other life with some insight into how my thoughts were developing – as I have done with my Sedbergh writing.

It is worth putting on the record the experience of learning history of one undergraduate in the early 1960s at Oxford. As far as I know, noone has done this before. And the project is given some extra interest and perhaps authority by the fact that I became a professional historian later in my career. On the other hand, this is not easy to read, especially for non-academics and non-historians.

*

I was of average ability and had learnt at Sedbergh, and before that at the Dragon School, that only by hard and well-organized effort could I bring myself up to the level of naturally cleverer boys. So I put a great deal of effort into developing my abilities as a historian through hard work and organization. I greatly enjoyed the course, even if it was a considerable strain.

The nature of the course and our two most important teachers' characters can be sketched in briefly here so that the reader can imagine better the background of constant intellectual stimulation, and extended high level conversation with really well read and thoughtful teachers who later became friends.

I had been peculiarly fortunate both at the Dragon and in my last two years at Sedbergh in that I had outstanding teachers. When I went to Worcester it might have been thought that my luck would be over. Until the end of the 1940s Worcester was a relatively small, poor and intellectually undistinguished College, and this applied to history as to other subjects.

The situation began to change with the arrival of Harry Pitt in 1949, and then was consolidated when a young medievalist called James Campbell joined the College in 1957. Neither Harry nor James, as I shall now term them, ever attained international recognition except among specialists but they turned out to be as good a pair of tutors as one could possibly imagine.

Harry Pitt (centre back) and James Campbell (spectacles) three or so years before I arrived at Worcester, with the historians in formal dress

Harry Pitt around the time I first knew him

James Campbell when I interviewed him in 2009

Each was excellent and they complemented each other beautifully. Harry was one of the very best teachers of his generation. Robert Darnton, one of his pupils and later a distinguished historian, writes that 'I later discovered, he had won a reputation within the Faculty as the supreme master of that peculiar art, the Oxford tutorial.'[1] James also soon developed into a formidable teacher and it is unlikely that any other pair of historians in either Oxford or Cambridge could have been better. They worked together for thirty-three years and each of them must have supervised more than seven hundred students during their time at Worcester. Harry, in particular, put almost all of his energy and genius into his teaching and Alan Bullock rightly commented that 'Harry's books are his pupils'.[2] The enormous stimulus to my intellectual development, and the value of the Oxford tutorial teaching system can be seen through my time there. As the historian John Roberts said at Harry's memorial service, 'Like others of us here today, he was lucky enough to enjoy what now seems Oxford's golden age, and the Indian summer of a certain kind of academic society, one in which, as he once said, "Colleges and dons were masters of their own world".

*

The degree course was mainly concerned with the history of England between the end of the Roman occupation of Britain and 1914. There were also a few extra themes and topics. In the first term we prepared for the only formal university written exams we would take before our Final exams at the end of three years. These were

[1] Quoted in *For Harry* ed. Lesley Le Claire (2003)

[2] *Ibid.*

called 'Prelims' and consisted of the study of historiography as represented by Edward Gibbon, Thomas Babington Macaulay, Alexis de Tocqueville and the Venerable Bede. There were also Latin and French tests based on the latter two authors. Like several of my friends I failed a paper, the Latin unseen, but fortunately managed to pass on the retake. James Campbell told me that if I had failed again I would probably have been sent down (expelled) from Oxford.

In the subsequent years we moved gradually through the English history syllabus. Most of this was done with James and Harry, though I went to Lady Clay for the Tudors and Stuarts and Peter Dickson for late seventeenth and early eighteenth century history.

Lady Clay, probably about twenty years before I met her, reproduced with the kind permission of the Balliol College Archives, Oxford

In our third and fourth terms we chose a period of European history and I studied later medieval and the early modern period with Karl Leyser of Magdalen and Roger Howell, then a postgraduate student. In Spring and Summer terms of 1962 I studied political theory, basically Aristotle, Hobbes and Rousseau, with some J.S. Mill and Marx at the end, again with James.

In the last academic year we chose a special subject which was to introduce us to the use of original sources and I studied the Interregnum of Oliver Cromwell. We also chose a special theme, in my case Tudor and Stuart economic history, which I studied with G.D. Ramsay of St Edmund's Hall. In the spring term of our last year we did some wider general reading under the guidance of Harry Pitt and then some revision tutorials with both Harry and James in our last term.

There were several different ways in which we learnt. One was through writing a long essay roughly every week which we would take to an hour-long tutorial where, usually paired with another, we would either read it out or listen to the other essay and the comments of our tutor. These tutorials ('supervisions' with supervisors in Cambridge) were the really special part of my Oxford education. I had experienced them in a simpler form at Sedbergh, but my teachers were now expecting higher level work and the grilling was more intense.

Another teaching method was particularly important in the first term and in the special subjects – Cromwell and economic history – where there were set texts. These were the 'gobbets'. These consisted of short essays of less than a page each commenting on some quotations from our chosen authors. We were asked to set the passages in their proper context and explain the wider significance of the quoted extract. Again, this was something I had been introduced to in my last two years at Sedbergh but it was now more stringently marked.

In preparation for the essays and gobbets we were set a good deal of reading to do both before each essay and in the long vacations (over half the year) and were sometimes required to do an essay or two as well out of term. We were tested on this reading, as well as our previous term's work at the start of each new term in what were called 'Collections'. These were done on the first Friday and Saturday morning of the term, and consisted of two three-hour unseen exams, usually papers from a previous year. The marks did not count towards our final results, but prepared us for writing under pressure and they were again marked by our tutors. They kept our tutors informed of our progress and enabled them to see our strengths and weaknesses. Thus, although formally we only had exams at the end of our first and ninth terms, in fact we had them every term.

Most of what we learnt came either from our tutor's comments, or from articles or books. We would read in the undergraduate library at the top of the spiral steps in Worcester, but it was not well equipped with recent books, though I found some strange Victorian classics amidst the dusty shelves. We were not normally allowed into the rather grander old library looking out onto the back courtyard. Most of our books, therefore, were in the Bodleian library, and particularly in the beautiful round Radcliffe Camera, where I spent much of my work time. I had very little money to buy books and depended almost entirely on libraries.

We also went to some lectures, though these were not compulsory and some people hardly went to any. Our tutors would recommend a few lecture series, but many felt that it was a waste of precious time breaking up a morning for a lecture. As my fuller account shows, I tended to go to three or four sets of four or eight lectures a term, each lasting an hour. They were usually by good lecturers and sometimes I would indulge in the pleasure of going to hear a famous lecturer like A.J.P. Taylor or Isaiah Berlin even if it was not part of my course.

Finally there were seminars on two of the papers, the economic documents and Cromwell special subject. Between six and a dozen students met their teacher for an hour and a half or so and one or two would read out longer papers and we would be expected to comment.

At the end of all of this intense teaching, a mixture of coaxing, scolding, praising, criticising, with largely self-motivated and self-organized work within a careful framework of supervised study, we would be ready, in theory, for the exams.

Our progress through the course was monitored by our two College tutors. Unlike Cambridge, there were no instituted 'Directors of Studies' in Oxford. In my case, James told me that he and Harry shared the decisions about who should teach us. James did more of the teaching of College students in return for the fact that Harry dealt with the administration involved, contacting external tutors and arranging schedules.

The end of term report reading or 'Collections', as they were also confusingly called, used to be held in the Dining Hall of Worcester in front of all the dons. By my time they were held in the upper Senior Common Room. The Provost (Sir John Masterman in my first year, Lord Franks in my second and third) would sit at the end of a long table, with our two history tutors and the senior tutors, and one or two other tutors who might be awaiting their students. Written reports from those who had taught us for that term were read out and Harry and James might make further comments.

This is an account of the formal structure, a combination of teaching methods which I believe both supported and stretched me in an almost perfect way and which has remained with me in my own teaching at Cambridge over the years. But what was it actually like to be taught like this?

I have memories of a number of my teachers, and vivid flashes of particularly high and low points. I shall, however, mainly leave it to others to describe Harry and James, but I also remember the gentle and erudite Karl Leyser sliding out of his inner room like an over-grown school-boy to teach me in his outer room. And I remember summer afternoons sitting on Lady Clay's sofa in her beautiful north Oxford flat, looking out at the garden and hearing stories of an earlier Oxford and being entranced by her enthusiasm for the sixteenth and seventeenth century.

This apprenticeship-based teaching system is extremely difficult to describe or capture, especially at its best. I shall try to give a picture of it through a closer study of Harry Pitt and James Campbell who arranged my teaching and between them taught me for over half of my courses.

*

Harry Pitt was born in 1923, the son of a Herefordshire farmer, so he was 37, a year younger than my mother, when he started to teach me. He was a very small man, pugnacious and slightly heavy-jowled, a sort of over-grown hobbit in a way. I am not surprised now to learn that he was an effective tank commander towards the end of the war. Harry introduced me to the concept 'counter-suggestible', in other words he would argue with almost anything one said, but one could see that it was for the fun of it. He had a great sense of humour, I think I sensed dimly that he was at times an unhappy and depressed man, but he lit up when he was with people. He was fair, encouraging and immensely stimulating.

His contrary character, which reminds me very much of a robust Englishness whose archetype is Cobbett, is well caught by Lesley Le Claire, former librarian of Worcester, who worked closely with Harry for many years.

> He was very much a creature of paradox: he usually displayed a large tolerance but could be fierce and caustic when confronted with humbug; a youthful left-winger who later, like Clarendon, cherished England's 'old good manners, its old good humour and its old good nature'; a devoted Johnsonian and admirer of Gibbon who also loved Schubert and Keats; and Southron (southerner) who fell under the spell of the lone shieling and the misty island…

always remained something of an impish small boy himself… as Copper Le May puts it, 'many of the more amiable characteristics of Peter Pan.[1]

His teaching-companion over those years, James Campbell, wrote:

Harry was, indeed, an outstanding tutor… He was seriously interested in what he taught and in those whom he taught. He read widely and had a deep store of knowledge on which to call. His tutorial method was often sharp, though seldom abrasive. He sought to make his pupils think, often by means of provocative statements or questions. He did not mind particularly if they were not outstanding intellectuals… He *did* mind if they were intellectually dishonest. A great advantage of Harry's was that he was a genuinely cultivated man… He was concerned to educate his pupils as well as to instruct them.[2]

One of his pupils, who came up to Worcester to read history the year after me and became a distinguished medievalist at Oxford, was John Maddicott. He describes Harry's teaching methods as follows.

Harry was always a great encourager… Weekly sessions with him were educative in a broader and more humane way. His comments drew on literature and modern politics as well as history and, while inviting your opinion too, gave the impression of a cultivated intellect moving discursively but penetratingly, over a wide trace of historical country side, illuminating it with anecdotes, provocative asides and firm judgements, often moral ones, and acting in general, as a powerful stimulus to further thought and, above all, to interest. You left his tutorials as a near contemporary said to me, "fizzing".

That is exactly as I remember it – constant challenging, opening out new vistas, particularly in Victorian history, forcing one to think and rethink basic ideas. He was like a very good tennis or cricket coach, showing one new moves and how to have confidence in one self.

Part of the magic was his lovely set of rooms. We spent the first term with him learning in college teaching rooms of no great beauty. But in that last year we went for tutorials in the drawing room which opened out onto a magical garden. This was on the top of the wall at the far end of the 'mansions', the fifteenth century cottages which were among the oldest continuous college living accommodation in Oxford. Underneath this wall was Alice's passage into wonderland, and in his room above we explored our ideas together, sometimes over a sherry or beer in our last terms. The room, like James' or Lady Clay's room, was filled with special objects and many books. It is described by a colleague of his, the historian John Walsh. I now realize that the many years in which I tried to fill my room with strange anthropological treasures to intrigue and relax my students may have been based on his inspiration.

His tutorials were not only occasions for imparting information or technique; they were part of a civilising process, full of allusion to literature and music, unpretentiously offered, which pointed a pupil towards fascinating worlds which needed further investigation. In his appealingly furnished set of rooms he had an assortment of *objets trouvés* – a lump from the Parthenon, shards surreptitiously scraped off a Fort Sumner cannon, Gladstone's neck-tie – which he prized as physical contact with the past through which he could earth the electricity of his own historical imagination and arouse that of his pupils.

---

[1] *For Harry*, ed. Lesley Le Claire (2003), 3

[2] James Campbell, 'Memorial to Harry Pitt' – *Worcester College Record 2001*, 19-23

What was happening was that I was becoming an apprentice to a master – hence a Master of Arts. Someone the age of my parents was trying to tease out my mind through a prolonged and focused conversation. It is what is special about Oxford, and its quintessence is described by the distinguished historian Robert Darnton, who had come from America to do his D.Phil. with Harry.

I had no idea of … the Oxford way of handling such things [Essay writing] – something that goes by the name of empiricism in the outside world but that actually is quite different: a conception of history as argument, endless debate in a contest to win a case by rigorous use of evidence and a touch of rhetoric, nothing fancy, but enough plain English to drive the points home.[1]

I owe more than I can express to Harry and he remained someone to whom I wrote occasionally and visited much later, always continuing to take an interest in my career and showing considerable courage, not least when he stood up to one of his former pupils, the publisher Rupert Murdoch.

*

James Campbell was born in 1935 and was likewise from a non-academic background, being brought up by his grandparents in East Anglia. He was deeply myopic from early childhood and very scholarly, going from Lowestoft Grammar School to Oxford and then winning a Junior Research Fellowship after sharing the prestigious Gibbs History Scholarship with my future D.Phil. supervisor Keith Thomas. James came to Worcester in 1957, only three years before I arrived, and was only seven years older than me – the same age gap as that with my Worcester-trained historian uncle Robert.

I remember James as a wonderful teacher. I was in awe of his prodigious knowledge and mildly biting wit, but recognized the quirkiness, the real passion for originality and the deep scholarship. Again, I find it easier to see him through others' eyes as he is in many ways still too close. The following observations ring absolutely true to my memories of being taught by him.

Let us start with what the fellow teacher wrote about his colleague. Harry Pitt wrote a tribute:

James was just twenty-one when he arrived, and shy… very soon he grew into a formidable conversationalist and controversialist who loved learned talk and a good argument above all: he could never be accused of a predictable or rigid consistency in argument and he has at his disposal an almost polymathic expertise. … His astonishing range of knowledge and interests owed much to his skill as a fast reader and a Napoleonic capacity for doing without sleep.

From the beginning James quickly established his position as a deeply committed tutor and as a Fellow with a strong sense of collegiality. As a tutor he believes completely in the usefulness of his position: with undergraduates of ability he can stretch them far and deep and he has always shown great if stern patience with idlers. He takes infinite trouble with lame dogs, many of whom he has helped over the stile at the end of three years.

All this was true. Going to tutorials with James on Anglo-Saxon history changed my life, for it was his inspiration which set me on my most sustained work on English individualism and its deep roots.

---

[1] *For Harry*, 39-40

One of James Campbell's pupils, David Hargreaves, provides three delightful vignettes which bring back the voice and ambience. The first is of the tone and dry wit.

Most fascinating of all, and enduringly attractive, were his rhythms and idioms of speech, famous for their exactitude – occasionally pedantic, but never pompous. On this occasion, he took the leading role at interview, taking me to task for an essay on the decline of the Carolingian Empire.
"Well", he said, "you certainly make a jolly plausible case for its collapse." With a disarmingly regretful note in his voice (a device I later interpreted as a sure sign he was moving in for the kill), he went on "I just can't help feeling it's *so* jolly plausible, I'm just left wondering how it ever *staggered to its feet* in the first place".

A second is of the scene, so well-remembered, of the end of term collections in the Senior Common Room when the Provost, Harry, James and others would be seated with dimmed light behind a huge table and we would learn what they thought of our term's work. By David Hargreaves' time the Provost was no longer Lord Franks, but was Asa Briggs who had returned to the College.

At Provost's Collections at the end of term, I was introduced to yet another of Oxford's many oddities – a verbal report in the third person. Asa Briggs sat at the head of his table, smiling and nodding at me in a way I blithely interpreted as a mark of personal favour, rather than a part of his armoury of avuncular blandness.

Harry Pitt, in his wonderful staccato, dealt with me briskly and gently. There followed an extended, pregnant pause. Asa muttered questioningly in James's direction, but he was staring myopically at sheaves of paper and said nothing at all.
'James!', barked Harry.
He looked up, flustered.

'Oh, my apologies, Provost', he said, 'I'm afraid I was dreaming. *All too typical* of me.' Harry and Asa tried not to smile, and me also. After some preliminary courtesies, he warned: "He has yet to learn the difference between *speculation and fact*. And it's going to be someone's duty next term – indeed, I fear it will be mine – to make his life a total misery until he does so."

Most evocatively of all, David describes the room where I was taught and precisely catches the way in which a supervision was conducted.

James's rooms, for so many years on the first floor of Staircase Five, were another delight. There was a huge mahogany bookcase the entire width of the room, and an extended table on which endless papers, books and monographs lay scattered. The furniture was comfortable, and the whole impression that of somewhere whose owner cared for comfort, but not much for effect. Whatever reluctance he may have felt at either the first or the sixth tutorial of the day, he always greeted me warmly enough, staring as usual anywhere but directly at me, possibly fiddling with pipe or cigarette (he alternated between the two constantly). The famous black cat might also be putting in an appearance.

'Well then', he would say, sucking in his breath adenoidally, 'What have you got for me today?'

I would paraphrase whatever title it was he had set me the previous week.

'Good, good.' He would nod rapidly with his eyes tightly shut. 'Go on then, my dear fellow. *Edify me…*'

A tall order. Occasional hints of restiveness might penetrate if it became clear that I was enjoying my own declamation too much. Clicking of teeth or even spluttering might be provoked by a split infinitive, clumsy syntax or the pretentious pronunciation of a foreign name, but otherwise he was a restrained and polite audience.

The only eruption occurred during an essay on the legacy of King Stephen.

'If you ever write again about a monarch', he spluttered, 'medieval or other, having a track record – good, bad or otherwise – I'll break your bloody neck.' ...

I relished the résumé's above everything. He could hear my concluding paragraph from about three miles away as my voice and idiom moved into best Churchillian mode, but would hear me out patiently.

For a few seconds there would be silence.

'Now then', he might begin, eyes still closed in concentration, 'let me understand. What you are suggesting is...'

About twenty seconds of beautifully articulated and lucid exegesis would follow, and then his eyes would open and he would ask me with apparent anxiety: 'Now is that *about right?*'

I always thought so. It always sounded so frightfully plausible when he said it.

He then would settle back in his chair and close his eyes again.

'Well, that's not a bad essay... indeed, I think it's *probably rather a good one*. It's *not*, however, a *very good* one – and I'll tell you why.[1]

*

Given the importance of James in my education, and these colourful portraits, I asked whether I could talk to him about his teaching style. He kindly consented and in a long conversation in August 2012 at his home, he added some further points.

I asked him whether it was true that he and Harry could really be described as the best College history team in Oxford. He naturally doubted whether this was the case, citing his own experience of being taught at Magdalen by Karl Leyser, Bruce McFarlane, A.J.P.Taylor and John Stoye. He did concede, however that while some of these teachers were very keen, some were less so, while for many years he and Harry devoted almost all their energies into teaching.

I asked about what happened when two of us came to a supervision and James confirmed that only one would read the essay and it was uncommon for the other to be taken in to be read by the tutor. Part of the reason was sheer pressure. In the 1920s and 1930s tutors had often supervised for up to and more than 20 hours a week. James himself did between 12 and 18 hours a week. Supervising is exhausting work and if, on top of this, there had been a flow of a dozen or more essays to mark, it would have been too much.

I asked about what the main changes had been in teaching since those early days. He singled out two. One was that teaching was now regarded as less important than writing – indeed it is often spoken of and regarded as a 'burden'. James believed that this pressure towards research and writing and away from teaching undergraduates came as much from the German university tradition as the American.

A second change was in the sheer amount of secondary literature available. When I was an undergraduate, my tutors could expect me to read a dozen or so books or articles for an essay and this would cover most of what had been written in the last few decades. Now there are hundreds if not thousands of secondary sources for any essay. It is difficult to know how to handle this – and I have also noted this in my teaching and the simple device of some students, which is to ignore everything written more than, say, ten years ago.

A third change is in the quality of the students and their preparation. The tutorial system is based on the pupil already having the knowledge and training for there to be

---

[1] From *The Medieval State* eds. Maddicott and David Palliser: 'James Campbell as Tutor', xxiii–xxviii

a proper discussion. A few universities such as Keele have a four year course, in which the first year is spent getting the students up to the level where they are properly equipped to start on an undergraduate course. Yet in many universities, students are accepted who do not have any of the basic – they cannot spell, write, read intelligently and they know nothing in advance. This made me realize again how fortunate I was to have covered the whole of English history up to the end of the nineteenth century in some depth at Sedbergh before coming to Oxford. Even with this, I struggled. I cannot imagine what it would have been like to start with no previous knowledge and without the careful preparation in essay writing techniques I had received.

I quoted from some of the accounts of James' tutorials and he confirmed that they were substantially accurate, but added a few explanations and elaborations. He felt that tutorials were effective because they made sure that the student does a lot of work, when they might be disinclined to do so or under many competing pressures. But he admitted that the system could be pretty bad with a bad tutor and it was often very difficult to get rid of those who could not practise this art. He had learnt from a wonderful teacher at Lowestoft grammar school, Stuart Spalding, and put into practice his methods and those he had learnt from his tutors at Magdalen.

He remembered his technique of giving back a summary of the main argument of the essay. He thought it encouraged the student to know that the tutor had listened carefully and understood the argument. It then gave a basis for a discussion, a shared area for the backwards and forward of the debate. Reading the essay out loud was also good for the student as it revealed any weaknesses in the argument. Listening to oneself is an education in itself.

On the other hand, he admitted that supervising in this intense way for say 14 hours a week was very demanding indeed. Concentrating deeply to get the gist of an argument, and switching from subject to subject, takes huge effort. Thus he confessed that his habit of fiddling with the fire, of loading and lighting his pipe, and other habits was partly to cover up patches of thought. Without this, it would have been necessary to talk straight away and without a break and the quality of the comments would have deteriorated. Bad tutors often talk all the time, but one needs time to think. He also admitted that when he disappeared in pursuit of a reference around 12 o'clock in the morning after non-stop supervisions, he would sometimes be keener on a small glass of sherry to spur him on than the supposed book he was searching for. I found myself in my later years that sharing a cup of green tea, or a small glass of sherry, with my students was valuable in relaxing us and clearing the mind.

Finally, an important point made by James concerned the relationship between tutors and examiners. The tutors might be examiners from time to time, but mostly they were not official examiners – and, even if they were, only examined a very small part of the final exams. So they were basically on the side of their students, playing a kind of elaborate doubles against the wily examiners they would come to face. This, I can see, was the same with me in my teaching over the years and meant that there was a camaraderie, a shared task, between teacher and taught, which makes learning more pleasurable and equal.

*

The general shape of the work I did in my first term can be abstracted from my work notes and essays. The following does not include the frequent classes, language courses and other lectures.

October

Thursday 7 Arrive at Worcester College
Friday 8 Meet with Tutor James Campbell
Make notes on Gibbon's 'Autobiography'
Monday 10 First of nine lectures by Campbell on Bede
Tuesday 11 Take notes on Gibbon's Abridged 'Decline and Fall'
First set of 'gobbets' [short essays] on Tocqueville
Wednesday 12 Planning first essay on Gibbon
Thursday 12 Also planning first essay on Gibbon
Thursday 20 Second set of gobbets on Tocqueville
Friday 21 Planning second essay on Gibbon
Wednesday 26 Planning third essay on Gibbon
Thursday 27 Third set of gobbets on Tocqueville

November
Tuesday 1 Planning fourth essay on Gibbon
Monday 7 First essay on Bede
Tuesday 8 Plan first essay on Macaulay
Friday 11 Writing summary of Tocqueville's book from memory
Saturday 12 Writing summary of Tocqueville's book from memory
Fourth set of gobbets on Tocqueville
Monday 14 Second essay on Bede (approx. date)
Wednesday 16 Plan second essay on Macaulay
Friday 18 Writing summary of Tocqueville's book from memory
Friday 21 Third essay on Bede
Wednesday 23 (approx.) Plan third essay on Macaulay
Wednesday 30 (approx.) Plan essay comparing Gibbon and Macaulay
Two undated pieces towards the end of term – on Tocqueville

Finally, at the end of term, we were sent the following.

MODERN HISTORY

Gentlemen reading History should return into residence NOT LATER THAN THURSDAY, 12 JANUARY 1961.

Collections will be set on Friday and/or Saturday.

1st year: English History 400-1215

2nd year: General History Periods

3rd year: Special Subjects (Texts)
English History 1485-1660 or 1660-1914

H.G.P.
J.C.

1 December 1960

The organization of my work started off with high intentions. I have discovered a small black notebook which I clearly envisaged would be my work planning diary for my first term, but seems to have petered out quite quickly. I shall extract a few relevant bits indicating the start of work.

It starts with a quotation:

"He had been all things, and all was of little value." Emperor Severus.
Latin. Mr Campbell
Tuesday 5 p.m.

1. Stenton – A-S England
2. Vol I – Ox Hist of England
3. A-S Eng – Hunter Blair
4. Whitelock – Pelican
   Charles Plummer – essential notes. Bede Commentary.
   Lectures on Monday & Fridays
   By Tuesday.
   A-S History – Bede Book 3. (Read the text-books above)

Mr Hyde – Gibbon & Macaulay.
Friday Gr III. 6.0 Friday
5 St John's Street – middle flat (middle bell)
Thursday 5.0 Latin Class – Lecture Rm A. (Unseens)
1st Wk. Ch 1-15 Incl. – Gibbon.
Topic for Essays & Discussions.
Position of Gibbons' contribution to the historiography of his time. (short essays plan)
Momiliagno, Dawson, Young, Fuglum
There are some notes on what bits of Bede I should read and translate.
French. Wk 1. Comment & translate pieces given by Pitt – Tuesday (by Fri lunch). Unseen Gibbon & Macaulay.
Wk 1. Set (a) Read & study Ch 1-15 Gibbon (incl) (b) Essay plan.
Not set: Read the Vindication (if possible) (with special reference to the effects of his education & surroundings) – See Bury ed'n
Make a selection of his work (static & narrative)

- does G's title beg the question. (effects Byzantine Emp & Christianity)_ – fall from golden age.
- –why did he choose the fall?
- Isn't there too much characterisation of the Em's – too much detail – rather than institutions – consider his portrayal of m'ty govt
- -never made his mind up about the (benefit?) of bringing the barb's in to fight.
- He never says that the barb's fighting for were not as strong as those that fought against them (Ch 1-16)
- Make a collection of quotations
- Write on: "How does Gibbon convey his interpretation of Christianity" – The techniche [sic]
- Ch 15-21 inclusive
- Style, omission, emphasis, sarcasm, irony – see also the vindication.

There are also short lists of books to be read for De Tocqueville, Bede, Gibbon and Macaulay.

At the back are notes on when I should attend for tutorials and unseens. And right at the end a few biblical quotes, ending appropriately:

"Oh Lord enlighten and lead us in our study of thee And make us strong in thy faith".

Academic Work: Winter 1960

Edward Gibbon

As indicated in an essay at the end of the summer before I came up to Oxford I had already been thinking and writing about Gibbon, but we clearly went into his work with a bang. On the first Tuesday of term I was digesting the abridgement of the text. I describe this as 'Gibbon Text, Ch 1-15, and it consists of some 8 pages of notes.

To take a very small sample, I clearly found chapter 2 interesting.

Ch 2
Slaves – their number and condition
Roman Monuments
– what interests G is that many of the great works were erected at private expense, and almost all were intended for public benefit (a reflection on the "manners" of the time)
– gives an example of a private-citizen-builder – Herodes Atticus – interesting details
SCOPE

- gives extent number and size of the cities
- 300 cities in Africa
- 1197 cities in Ancient Italy etc
- Asia – 500 cities – many very rich. Pergamus. Smyrna, Ephesus ANTIOCH ALEXANDRIA etc

Improvement of Agriculture

- the introduction of various plants into the West. Especially grasses for cattle & vines & olives.
- the luxury market – a digression into economics & distribution of wealth!
- the unequal trading balance with India – unpopular

V.Imp. Last 2 pages. – Cause of decay.
"It was scarcely possible …
–similarly decline in the arts. Staleness.
"the decline of genius was soon followed by the corruption of taste."
"The Roman world was indeed peopled by a race of pigmies, when the first race of giants of the north broke in and mended the puny breed. They restored a manly spirit of freedom; and, after the revolution of ten centuries, freedom became the happy parent of taste and science".

This summary constitutes about one page of the eight pages of notes.

The next day I was starting to plan an essay. The heading was "The position of Gibbon's contribution to the historiography of his time". It is a complex plan of six pages. The first version of the plan is a page of headings with a few quotes from G.M. Young. There are then three and a half pages of detailed notes from the historians Christopher Dawson and A. Momiliagno on 'Gibbon's Contribution to Historical Method'. These are very thorough and are followed by a new and more succinct essay plan.

I do not have the essay I wrote, but I seem to have gone to a 'Mr Hyde' for the first tutorial I had, and made notes on his comments. There is a page of these notes which are quite detailed, linking Gibbons work to other philosophers and thinkers including Bayle and Montesquieu. Thus, within a week of arriving I had written my first essay and done my first tutorial.

The second essay was on 'How does Gibbon convey his interpretation of Christianity?' (A study of Ch 15-21). The essay plan is dated October 21 (Friday), and consists of seven pages of detailed notes, ending with a plan: Introduction, Irony – innuendo, Sarcasm, Ridicule, Omission, Emphasis (over?), Other methods.

Given the fact that I was a keen Christian, I wonder how I reacted to Gibbon's savage indictment of early Christian teaching.

For example, I note that on p.499 there is

> 'A withering attack'. Shows by his surprise that no one took any notice of the miracles that he did not believe that they happened. "The lame walked, the blind saw, the sick were healed, the dead were raised, daemons were expelled, and the laws of Nature were frequently suspended for the benefit of the church. But the sages of Greece & Rome turned aside from the awful spectacle… appeared unconscious of any alterations in the moral or physical govt of the world."

The third essay was on the subject 'Is Gibbon's view of human nature adequate?' There are eight pages of plans and notes for this essay on October 26, ending with the comment to myself 'Think out sentence before you write'. A piece of advice it took me some thirty years to overcome. The essay that resulted, four pages in quite a small hand, has survived.

A. Macfarlane. "Is Gibbon's view of human nature adequate?"

Edward Gibbon was no mystic and no poet. He was content to survey history from those Olympian heights which produce clarity and wideness of vision but tend to make intricate and sympathetic investigation difficult. Satisfied in knowing how the drama unfolded itself he did not delve deeply into the hearts and minds of those he studied except when they manifested their inner nature in their actions. Doubtless he was convinced of the centrality of man in history; in one of his essays he writes "L'objet de l'histoire, c'est l'homme;" but he was limited in his vision by the limitations of his age – an age in which human nature was considered uniform – underneath a varying exterior of 'accidental' features; where reason and moderation as the power of good fought against the corrupting influences of passion, enthusiasm, ambition and fanaticism. We will soon discern the result of this view on Gibbon's valuation of human nature.

There are three main sources from which we can find his real view of human nature – his general remarks on the subject, his particular observations on specific people or situations and in the application of his views to his study of the characters he surveys.

From the first source we can see the influence of his age with outstanding clearness. He speaks of the "uniform operation of human nature" (Dec II p 525); the "law of our imperfect nature" and the "immutable constitution of human nature" (Dec I p 555). The deductions which we can make from these statements, namely that he believes human nature is always the same, and that nothing can change it, are supported if we look at his writings. The standards on which he judges Trajan or Commodus are those on which he would have judged his contemporaries – and the virtues and vices of the Romans are no different from those of the inhabitants of the Byzantine Empire. Likewise his general view which makes him pessimistically exclaim "how little is man, how vain and imperfect" (I p 412) is amplified in his lengthy treatment of the vices of the Emperors and in his tendency to see goodness and purity as rare gifts especially in the reigns of such men as Caracalla, Caligula and Nero.

For Gibbon, though he lived in an age of considerable optimism, by the sheer weight of the descriptions of vice and the preponderance of evil characters over the good showed that he considered the balance tipped in favour of evil. This view of his may be taken by some as cause of his failure to recognise the goodness in such men as St Augustine, St John Chrysostom, Athanasius and later Bernard of Clairvaux. He relishes in his list of the dissolute Emperors "the dark, unrelenting Tiberius, the furious Caligula, the stupid Claudius, the profligate and cruel Nero, the beastly Vitellius, and the timid and inhuman Domitian ......" Where he has the choice between a salutary or damaging interpretation of character as in the cases of Constantine and Hadrian he usually favours the latter.

It is only in a very few of the reigns of the Emperor's that Gibbon sees sincere altruism, the most obvious examples being in those of the Antonines. Generally he strives to find the "mastering passion of the soul" of each personality for though a man may be clothed in benevolence and good works he is, according to the writer - only "so from fear or cunning." That "subtle tyrant" Augustus was prompted by "a cool head, an unfeeling heart, and a cowardly disposition ...... to assume the mask of hypocrisy, which he never afterwards laid aside ... his virtues and his vices were artificial." Hadrian, despite his "vast and active genius" had as the "ruling passions of his soul, curiosity and vanity" which made him in turns "an excellent prince, a ridiculous sophist and a jealous tyrant." Constantine suffered from "boundless ambition which .... appears as the ruling passion of his soul." It depends on our personal conception of the percentage of good and evil in each man whether we see Gibbon's pessimistic view of the baseness of the average man's motives as justified or showing a lack of understanding of human humanity. Nevertheless one deficiency in his view does appear, that is his over-simplification.

As I have illustrated, Gibbon in almost every historical portrait seeks for "the ruling passion" of a man's "soul." To take another example he states that Commodus' cruelty, which at first "obeyed the dictates of others" degenerated into habit, and at length became the ruling passion of his soul." This emphasis on one dominant sentiment may explain some personalities, but Gibbon seems in his attempt to clarify and regularise human nature to forget its complexity. The very fact that each character is so neatly pigeon-holed as "ruled by ambition", "ruled by pride" or "ruled by greed" shows an inadequate treatment if not conception of the great conflicts between contending passions which dictate the actions of most human beings.

A. Macfarlane. Is Gibbon's view of human nature adequate?

This may be the result of his detached viewpoint. He contemplates without fervour the pities, sufferings and actions of mankind, and rather from deduction than intuition tries to find the linking emotion which explains these external manifestations. Undoubtedly Gibbon's insight is amazingly rigorous, he seeks and finds the individual characteristics of each man and most of his creations are lifelike. But from the very simplification they lack fullness. For instance his description of Trajan's penetrating intelligence, sense of duty and above all stern vigour, of Augustus' cool, calculating character, slyness and subtlety show remarkable psychological insight, but we are faintly weary because each one is so squared, exhibiting three or four solid facets, and lacking the minor virtues and vices, details which often contribute more to our knowledge of a man than his outstanding assets or defects.

There is one field, however, where nearly everyone would agree that Gibbon's view of human nature is entirely inadequate. This is in its distrust for almost any kind of enthusiasm or passion. Moderation to Gibbon is practically synonimous with virtue, and passion with evil. The former contention, namely his emphasis on moderation is displayed by the fact that in almost every description of one of his heroes this is the quality most praised. Theodosius was praised because he was "chaste and temperate" and "the season of his prosperity was that of his moderation"; "the general tenor of his [Hadrian's] conduct deserved praise for its equity and moderation" Gibbon again repeats the virtues of Marcus Aurelius who had a "moderating influence" on the "zeal of the senate"; and of course in Julian we find that virtues which he conspicuously displayed at the end of his reign were "temperance and sobriety". This emphasis on moderation, a major product of reason is natural in a writer of Gibbon's time but the ensuing hatred of all enthusiasm was also natural.

Gibbon did not really attempt to understand or sympathize with religious or other kinds of enthusiasm. Religious asceticism was beyond his ken and we therefore find him almost always opposed to violent opinions or actions. He called the "outbursts of passion" and "hasty and choleric nature" of Theodosius "two essential imperfections." Or again Gibbon ascribed St Chrysostom's fall to the fact that "he was naturally of a choleric disposition" and his "ardour was not always exempt from passion." Gibbon seemed unaware that a great amount of the energy which produce great deeds stems from the emotions and that real feeling, emotion and enthusiasm can be beneficial. Here again we see the division between the "age of reason" personified by Johnson and that of "emotion" of the Romantics. This division is exaggerated in Gibbon by the very nature of his life. a life in which he seldom loved or liked, was infrequently subject to the turmoil, sorrows and agonies of real life. His disposition was averse to superstition, romanticism and mysticism and indeed to a considerable amount of the emotional and spiritual side of human nature.

Milman says of this deficiency that "Gibbons account of the early Christians is vitiated by his narrow and distorted conception of the emotional side of man's nature. Having no spiritual aspirations himself he could not appreciate or understand them in others." This is an extreme view but perhaps it contains some truth. Thompson's comments on him is fairer but enlightening "He (Gibbon) was not blind to the force of Christianity or to the simplicity of its appeal to the human soul, but these things left him personally cold." How often do we find him speaking of real, pure love, of exalted emotions, of altruism of imaginative perception and even of beauty? Gibbon may be a master in his description of the corruptions and powers of mind and body. but he is unwilling to leave even a corner for that mysterious essence we call the soul. He sees even conscience as a product of reason, and not as an independent force. The proof of this lies especially in his treatment of those who burn with religious fervour such as Saint Louis or Athanasius. Passions for him is nearly always of a darker kind, it consists of hatred, envy, cruelty, not of romantic love, adoration or sacrifice. He speaks of the "wild ambitions and black passions of Caracalla's soul" and blames Theodosius for being "sometimes inflamed by passion", while he praises Marcus Aurelius who had been taught by the Stoics "to submit his body to his mind, his passions to his reason". When does the historian praise in any of his heroes imagination, intuition, emotion, originality or when criticize the average, the merely sensible?

There are many excuses, or extenuating circumstances which can be offered in Gibbon's defence, and it is obvious that it is far easier to find faults in a great work of the nature of the "Decline and Fall" than in a more limited work. We may

Gibbon Essay (contd) liveliness

say therefore from the power and ~~lifelikeness~~ of his portraits and from the difficulty we find in criticising his analysis of such men as Augustus and Commodus; ~~and from~~ that Gibbon had a considerable knowledge of human nature. He may be limited by his pessimism, by his need and desire to explain symmetrically and with regularity the aspects of each character, by his lack of space, and by his natural emphasis on reason and moderation as opposed to emotion enthusiasm and spiritual qualities, but this lack of of warmth and humanity ~~which~~ and slightly one-sided approach is amply compensated by his detailed knowledge of certain aspects of human nature and by his wonderful power of dramatic presentation. He is like a painter who undertakes a great picture and while on close inspection we discover small faults and omissions the general impression from a distance is both splendid and accurate.

– ? essential imperfections of Theodosius "heresy & [illegible]"

– but many things make up for this one-sided approach.

The fourth and final essay plan was made on Tuesday November 1. The title was 'What was the value of the Decline and Fall in Gibbon's Day? And what is its value now?' There are two pages of notes from various books, by Edmund Blunden, A.H. Thompson, Christopher Dawson and others.

As well as this, I have a detailed chronological table of Emperors in Books 1-3 of "Decline and Fall", with their names, dates and a few facts about them – which I had constructed to help me through the maze.

Macaulay

I have found less of my work on Macaulay. A week after the last Gibbon essay I started to take notes on Macaulay, for an essay on 'What is the function of Macaulay's 3rd Chapter in relation to the rest of his history of England.' There are two pages of notes on Mark Thomson's Historical Association pamphlet on Macaulay, four pages of notes on J. Cotter Morison's work on Macaulay and one page of notes on 'Firth's commentary on Macaulay', all taken on that day. There is no essay surviving from these notes.

The second essay plan, in some detail, was written eight days later on 16 November, in relation to the following question: 'Macaulay in his Essay on Hallam said "History, at least in its state of ideal perfection, is a compound of poetry and philosophy. How did he attempt to achieve this combination – and was he justified in doing so?' There are four pages of notes and quotations from Macaulay as a preparation for an essay which again does not survive.

The third essay, presumably about a week later though there is no date, was on the question, 'What light does Macaulay's "Life" throw on the nature of his "History of England"?' There are some seven pages of notes from various sources, including one page from the "Life and Letters" of Macaulay. There is one longish essay in relation to this question. The relation between the writer's biography and his work has long interested me, so I shall include this as indication of my thoughts on this subject and my style and level of work towards the last two weeks of my first term at Oxford.

A. Macfarlane. — Bishop Kerr.

"What light does Macaulay's "Biography" throw upon his approach to the "History"?"

Many writers have struck an attitude of benevolence and magnanimity before the world, while in their domestic life they were selfish and mean. Thomas Macaulay was one of the few who practiced the reverse. The general impression we gain of the author from the "History" is of a highly intelligent yet dogmatical man, full of complacency and very ready to pass judgements on his subjects, even showing at times touches of conceit. But the "Biography" displays that as a son, a brother and an uncle he was a marvelous example of human virtue; kind, generous, affectionate and humble. Though we may say severe things about his writings; as a man he was effervescent if not profound, incorruptible and unselfish if prejudiced and humble if satisfied with his position and achievements.

These domestic characteristics though seemingly irrelevant are important because the interpretation and stress of history, especially the imaginative kind of history Macaulay was attempting to write is a result of the whole of a man's character and outlook. That is why every hint a biography gives of his very personality as well as his views on politics, religion, history and so on will contribute to our understanding of the writers approach to his work.

There are two gaps in the "Life and Letters of Macaulay" - the first is this lack of intellectual curiosity, the second the shallowness of the passions - passions which were almost always completely controled by Macaulay's common sense, in an age where feeling and enthusiasm were in vogue. With regard to the first we notice an amazing and almost voluptuous delight in reading but this is largely confined to the practical writings of the ancients. Their philosophy is soundly attacked in his essay on "Bacon" while we see that he shows no interest in the philosophic trends of his own time embodied largely in Coleridge and Bentham. This antipathy to abstract speculation spread so that hardly ever do we get observations in his letters on the fundamental difficulties of life, love, marriage, the education of children, religious doubt etc; even his references to politics in the letters were usually merely narratives of current affairs without any speculations on the great principles of government. This lack of interest in scientific, social or religious questions is even more apparent in his strange indifference to those who were attempting to pursue the very same historical approach as himself - men like de Barante, Augustin Thierry, or other contemporary historians like Michelet, like Ranke, Schlosser, Müller etc. This general antipathy to intellectual problems (it seems that throughout his life he was hardly ever faced with any intellectual difficulties - this paucity accounts for the confidence of his "History") resulted in an approach to history which fails largely to interpret the age he is studying. More particularly his disinterest in the contemporary revolution in historical criticism (he never speaks of Palgrave, Kemble or Mr Guest) means that he "investigated no obscure questions, cleared up no difficulties, reversed the opinion of scholars upon no important points." (Cotter Morison). in his History.

In one way Macaulay and Gibbon seem alike - neither of them were of a passionate nature. That this may be of general advantage to a historian can be argued - but it cannot really be maintained that a man who never fell in love, was never ruled by ambition, who never seems to have had strong temptations and who lived a blameless, spotless and prudent life can provoke the greatest heights of love, pity or passionate sympathy. Undoubtedly he was a sensitive, sweetly affectionate and sympathetic man but even in politics we can see his calm, reasonable and gentle nature. In his persecution by the Calcutta press he was not driven to fury as most men would have been - in the whole of his parliamentary career, we see zeal but never a breath of revolutionary fervour. This temperance prevented him from reaching the peaks sometimes reached by Michelet or Carlyle; but it also gave him his characteristic respect for toleration.

There are three outstanding examples of his desire for universal toleration, the aid he gave to the Jews to relieve them of the "absurd restrictions which lie on them - the last relic of the old system of intolerance." His willingness to sacrifice his popularity when

P.2 MACAULAY ESSAY (contd)

in his own constituency to support the R. Catholic cause at Maynooth and though bitterly attacked by the hostile Calcutta press an enthusiastic advocate of the freedom of the press. It is no wonder that we find in his History an attack on bigotry and support of toleration.

Before discussing the direct light the "Biography" throws on Macaulay's conception and methods of writing history there are two other important fields in which it explains the views of the historian – religion and politics.

Zachary Machaulay it seems failed to impart to his son a "vital religion" and his attempt may possibly be the indirect cause of the markedly unspiritual tone of his son's writing – and Thomas Macaulay's resolute silence on matters of ultimate belief. Whatever the cause, he shows, for example in his allusion to the minister at Dumbarton Castle in his journal, an inability to comprehend piety of mind. The prosaic tone of his mind is nowhere better demonstrated than in his comment on a service held by a friend – Guthrie. I will quote this in full as it shows his remarkable (because of his upbringing) scepticism and the predominant emphasis he puts on literary beauty as opposed to human emotion even in a church service.

He commences "I have just been to Guthrie's Church ... There was much appearance of devotion, and even of religious excitement, among the communicants; and the rite was decently performed, but, though Guthrie is a man of considerable powers, his prayers were at a prodigious distance from those of our Liturgy. There was nothing, which even for a moment, rose to the level of "Therefore with angels and archangels ... There were some fine passages amidst much that was bad, in his sermon." This was the man who had so little sympathy for Penn

We will soon gather from his "History" that Macaulay was a Whig and an Englishman – and proud of being both. The practical consequences of these political views and patriotism are easily discovered in the "Biography". The patriotism is shown in his pride and enthusiasm on hearing of the victory of "Inkermann"; or again in his own words "When I am travelling on the Continent, I like to

He puts back his idea of 2 organised parties to 1688 – in reality they were very loose terminology / why difficulty in calling Parlt of James in 1680's – conception of party irregular. "Namier" in 1685 – "country party".

think that I am a citizen of no mean city". His comments on the whole of the Crimean war are full of pride and enthusiasm and he was a sincere supporter of Palmerston's aggressive foreign policy.

Though not reared a Whig his swift conversion at Cambridge under the influence of Charles Austin was aided by his suitable temperament a temperament to which the common sense practical reforms of this party appealed. That he considered himself the spokesman of this party both in his writing and speaking is demonstrated by a sentence in a speech in defence of the Whigs in 1833. "The time will come" he says "when history will do justice to the Whigs of England, and will faithfully relate how much they did and suffered for Ireland." And again he said "Though a young member of the Whig party, I will venture to speak in the name of the whole ~~party~~ body."
But it is perhaps a mistake to think that in his history he consciously distorts the facts and interpretations to support Whiggery. The distortions came more as an unconscious result of his preconceived admiration for this party. Feelings v Tories 1830 very strong (: attack on James)

If we wish to get a wide vision of what Macaulay's stated principles were in writing History we would not go to the "Biography" but to his essays – especially those on "Hallam's Constitutional History" and "History". Yet occasional remarks in letters and the journal give us sudden glimpses into the mind of the writer which seem corroborated in his actual "History".

We have seen that he was not consciously part of that movement which were trying more and more to apply scientific techniques to the study of history. We first learn that the love Macaulay had for history was not of something which explained but which filled the imagination. He says that "with a person of my turn the minute touches are of as great interest, and perhaps greater, than the most important events .... I am no sooner in the streets than I am in Greece, in Rome." History is for him a very visual and living thing. Therefore his great objective was to make History popular and living so ~~that~~ he states his fears for the second part of his History are "Can it possibly come up to the first? Does the subject admit of such

MACAULAY ESSAY (contd) A. Macfarlane.

vivid description and such exciting narrative?" There is no doubt as to Macaulay's intentions in writing the history - he aimed at providing a popular work. Witness his letter in which are the oft quoted words "The materials for an amusing narrative is immense. I shall not be satisfied unless I produce something which shall for a few days supersede the last fashionable novel on the tables of young ladies." It seems that Macaulay was determined to produce an entertaining story. This need accompanied by Macaulay's oratorical approach to writing (a legacy of his parliamentary career) led him to write in a broad and clear way which enforced simple conclusions. In 1850 he wrote to Macvey Napier speaking metaphorically of the art of writing for a large public "It is not by his own taste, but by the taste of the fish, that the angler is determined in his choice of bait." This is by no means conclusive, but we can see in the History's simplicity and lack of elevated and intellectual tone that Macaulay was well aware of his audience.

There is one field in which the biography gives us an invaluable insight into the approach of the author, that is in its account of the method in which Macaulay worked. Firstly it shows us the writers desire to gain a visual and minute knowledge of the past. Talking of the plan for the reign of William III in his journal Macaulay says "I will first set myself to know the whole subject; to get by reading and travelling a full acquaintance with William's reign. I reckon that it will take me 18 months to do this. I must visit Holland, Belgium, Scotland, Ireland, France. I must turn over hundreds, thousands of pamphlets. ... When the materials are ready and the History mapped out in my mind, I ought easily to write on an average two of my pages daily." Here we come to the feature which was probably the secret of Macaulay's success and shows his emphasis on "History" as a "department of literature" (his own phrase) not of science. For Macaulay the prime difficulty lay in stating not finding the truth. Having spent

18 months in finding the facts Macaulay then spends 2 years in writing them down and another year in "polishing, retouching, and painting." A man who on his own admission "aims at interesting and pleasing readers whom ordinary histories repel" must spend tremendous energy in "ordering the parts of his history." Trevelyan gives an example of this concentration on stylistic problems in his extracts from Macaulay's diary during the nineteen days he spent on the massacre of Glencoe struggling over 30 octavo pages. Macaulay's own comment is "What trouble these few pages will have cost me! The great object is that, after all this trouble, they may read as if they had been spoken off, and may seem to flow as easily as table talk."

The Biography gives the picture of a virtuous family man – an incorruptible and able politician, an extremely intelligent administrator and an industrious worker. It also shows a man who is perhaps devoid of lasting and deep passion and intellectual curiosity, yet with an amazingly vivid imagination and a nimble intellect; a Whig, a secular-minded critic, and a historian who puts his emphasis on the literary side of his art.

MACAULAY.
– lawyer –: court-room scenes, putting pro's & con's.
(Trial of 7 bishops) – tremendous respect for law.

What are the qualities most valuable to a narrative historian X G + M

Much of what I wrote still interests me, particularly the comments on his method.

I then did a final essay comparing Gibbon and Macaulay, completing eight essays in eight weeks on these two.

De Tocqueville

I had come across Tocqueville at Sedbergh, but it was only when I started to work on him at Worcester did I really come under the influence of someone whose works have been a major influence on me ever since.

On the same day that I started work on Gibbon, Tuesday 12 October, I took a test of a kind on Tocqueville, what were known as 'Gobbets', or short commentaries on quoted passages from an author. There are two pages commenting on five quotations from Tocqueville. As a sample, I shall just give the first of these.

12/10/60. De Tocqueville. (1) S= Sound A. Macfarlane.

1. "Above all I have made great use of the "cahiers" (list of grievances, compiled by the three orders.."

De Tocqueville in his introduction to "L'Ancien Régime" gives us an account of the sources he used for the book, one such source were the 'cahiers', (also known as the 'cahiers de doléances") prepared at the time of the elections to the Estates General in 1789. In these documents each "order" in each district stated its grievances and recommended new policies to the king. De Tocqueville claims, probably justly, to be the first historian to examine critically the primary lists, especially from the rural parishes which show more fully than the final "bailiwick" petitions (those that actually reached the Estates-General) the wishes and state of mind of the population. It is indisputable that these 'cahiers' were an invaluable source and from them we learn the specific technical reforms which the people desired. The "cahiers" were unanimous in their attack on absolute royal power, in their silence in respect of freedom of conscience, in their support of monarchism, but radically divided into different 'orders' in their view of their order's own stations in society.

2. "The chief princes of Germany, reunited at Pilnitz in 1791 proclaimed... That the danger which threatened the royalty in France was common to all the ancient powers of Europe."

In the preceding passage the historian has maintained that those outside France were utterly unaware of the impending revolution, and that the "Declaration of Pilnitz" was nothing but a "clever pretext by which they masked their designs or made them plausible in the eyes of the crowd." De Tocqueville is probably right in saying "si par hasard, ils disent la vérité sur elle, c'est a leur insu," but it is a disputable fact whether the Declaration was merely the first stages in the hoped for division of France (which de Tocqueville implies) It seems unlikely that Leopold's intentions were warlike for he inserted in the manifesto a clause which made all aggressive action dependent on the formation of a coalition against France by the other powers of Europe, and he was aware that Pitt at that time would not accede to such a scheme. It was largely the warlike interpretation of the Count of Artois which aroused the fury of France. The truth in the Declaration has been proved by the event.

3. "The French Revolution then was a revolution which in its workings and its features was in some ways similar to a religious revolution."

De Tocqueville sees the similarity between the two both in the results and the causes of those results. He says that, unlike any other political or civil revolution in history, the new concepts and ideas

P.T.O.

I remember that we did Tocqueville with Harry Pitt and he was a considerable expert on the subject. At the top there is the enigmatic mark S minus minus and 'Sound'. In ink at the bottom it states that 'You should attend the class on Sat. mornings at 9.30' – the first indication I have that we had formal teaching on Saturdays. There is also a note 'Please get an unseen from one of the other freshmen – to be in by Monday noon'. Another part of the course, which would lead to an 'unseen' translation from French in Prelims.

As well as the Gobbets we started on lectures that very same day. The lectures were given by the distinguished expert on French culture and history who would later write many books, namely Theodore Zeldin, then some eight years older than me and a research fellow at St Antony's. I have ten pages of notes on six out of eight of the lectures. He described the practical politician, the life, the theoretical framework and many other aspects of Tocqueville's life and reputation.

Tocqueville then went on through the term, alongside the work on Gibbon and Macaulay. The second set of gobbets, four on this occasion, were done on October 20. Here is the first of them.

1 "It was enough to be connected to the administration by the slightest thread to have nothing to fear except from it." (p.64)
In de Tocqueville's times the representative of the central government were solely responsible to it. This principle, essential to the power of the government, was thought by many to be a product of the Revolution, but Tocqueville points out that this is merely another of the institutions which has its roots in the 'Old Order'. The monarchy he says guarded its officials from annoyance of rendering account to the common courts of law. The difference between pre and post revolutionary times was in the method in which the central government protected its servants.

The old monarchy could only protect its servants by irregular and arbitrary measures, in other words by "Evocations" which were every day issued to withdraw its officials from the common law courts and to try them before the government-controlled "Council". After the Revolution the civil servant's independence was put on a firmer and more legal footing by passing a law that no servant of the Government could even be tried in a common law court unless the Government gave preliminary authorization.

This evidence tends to support Tocqueville's important theory that there was a powerful centralized government before the Revolution.

At the top of the sheet I have noted comments, probably made to me, 'You must put yourself in the examiner's position. Quote an example. The mark at the end is again enigmatic – VS+ [vix satis - barely enough], with a comment 'Your examples are sometimes too general.'

The third set of Gobbets was done a week later, on 27 October. They are a little longer and more detailed, taking up three pages. Again the mark is slightly improved to VS++, but my attention may have been drawn to style since there is an enigmatic note at the top, 'Plain Words – Gowers' [the book by Sir Ernest Gowers]. There is also a page of notes, which were probably taken from the comments made by Harry Pitt.

A week later on November 3rd there was the fourth set of gobbets, again longer with five pages on four subjects. I was really becoming interested by now, as the end comment, 'You answer these with a sound sense of relevance', suggests. As this is a topic which would later interest me greatly, I shall again give just one of the four answers.

De Tocqueville was convinced that Centralization was directly opposed to liberty, or to define it more closely political liberty. He often exclaims that it was at the root of nearly all the vices which caused the fall of the monarchy and therefore he deplored it. He also saw that Centralization was a continuous process and not a Revolutionary or Napoleonic product. A considerable amount of his book concerns its secret growth – apparently with hardly any opposition from its rivals. But in the events of 1789-90 he is faced with the problems of the complete abolition of centralization. This he ascribes to a sudden, and unfortunately short-lived passion for Liberty – his love for this feeling can indeed be well seen in his romanticized picture of 1789 as a year "de générosité, d'enthousiasme, de virilité et de grandeur: temps d'immortelle mémoire…"[1]

---

[1] The fact that this is quoted in French suggest we were studying the text in the native language, perhaps.

Moved by some unexplained feeling, dormant until then, the revolutionaries shattered the laws which made the State their constant companion in everything they did. De Tocqueville does not elaborate any further but merely repeats the fact – that Centralization did fall with absolute government.

The historian seems almost to take it for granted that this love of liberty will not last. "Following the natural course of events of this kind the love of freedom … languished in the face of an anarchy and popular tyranny." [Tick in margin] The powerful centralized state was reborn more powerful than ever (for it was without any traditional checks) under Napoleon.

I seem to have been working ever harder on Tocqueville as my interest was aroused, for on Friday 11 November I decided to write down a summary of all the chapters of the book. I note that 'Each done in 10 minutes from memory', so presumably I read the chapter and then put it on one side and wrote what I could. On that first day I covered the preface and Book 1, chapters 1-5, and book 2, chapters 1-5. I shall give just one example of this test of memory and synthesis.

> Chapter 4 was "How almost all Europe had the same Institutions, and how these institutions fell into ruin everywhere."
> –in this chapter bare assertions by de T.
> - from the many split and divided nations which succeeded the Roman Empire arose a system of Uniform Law – this was in complete opposition to the Roman system – FEUDALISM
> - in the C14 – All Europe very alike – a single spirit animated all the institutions
> - through the centuries this old system weakened & decayed until throughout Europe in the C18 it had lost its vitality and was merely a hollow shell.
>   Old Institutions as opposed to the New
>   Old –they became more and more hated –especially as their [sic] was a new prosperous & enlightened & active spirit in the C18
>   New – powerful royalty, state administration, hierarchy of officials
>
> In England – the transition was completed in the C17 & C18 without revolution – gradually – there were no obstacles
> - C17 England quite a modern nation.
>   De Tocqueville convinced: – it is necessary to glance beyond the frontiers of France to see what is happening there.

I find this of great interest, since this framework is to a large extent the one which, fifty years later, I have fully adopted in my work. It was obviously internalized.

The following day, Saturday 12 November I continued with this exercise, covering Book II, chapters 6-12 in even more detail in a similar method, covering some eight pages of paper with detailed notes. I also wrote out a two page summary of the headings of all the three books . I then left the process for a week, resuming it on Friday 18 with Book 3, chapters 1-8, and a supplement, covered in five pages of notes.

The same Saturday 12 when I was summarizing the book, I also wrote another set of Gobbets, the answers to five more quotations. The mark was S minus minus and there are quite a few notes on the text which I obviously took from comments made by Harry Pitt.

Finally, there are two undated pieces which were probably done towards the end of term. One is a two-page essay on "To what extent did the "philosophes" contribute to the formation of a revolutionary temper in C18 France?" The mark was again S minus minus. Finally, there seems to have been a written exam where we chose questions. The first part consisted of 'Gobbets' once again, and I wrote three pages of comments on four gobbets. There were also two longer essays on 'To what extent was France unified before the Revolution' and 'How far was de Tocqueville biased in his personal predilections?' I shall give the last of these as an example of writing on Tocqueville towards the end of my first term.

movement of corn - a move which caused great suspicion among the peasants - these barriers were not removed until the revolution.

I have not dealt with the unity (as opposed to the unification) of the classes within France. As Tocqueville points out they were in wealth, thought and education (at least middle and upper classes) in many ways very alike - but because of the surface privileges, jealousies and envies they were unable to work together.

On the whole therefore we have a picture of a country which on the surface showed a multitude of local variations and differences but which was basically considerably unified both in administration, thought and in its ~~allegiance~~ dependence on Paris for a lead.

VP

5. How far was de Tocqueville biased in his personal predilections?

Alexis de Tocqueville claimed that "by no family interests" was he attached to the aristocracy. As the grandson of Malesherbes, the son of a man nearly ~~exe~~ guillotined in the revolution and related by marriage to Chateaubriand this seems unlikely. But though a progressive aristocrat in thought and perhaps regretting the Revolution we find that he ~~has~~ is far enough away from it to see many of the faults of the Old Régime.

As an aristocrat there is no doubt that Tocqueville was unable to see clearly the contribution of the middle class to the revolution. In parliament he hated the "petty passions, incomplete education and vulgar passions" of those like Guizot who merely sought ~~for~~ - in his opinion - for material comfort. The influence this has on his work is that he tends to ignore the economic factors - later stressed by Mathiez and Lefebvre - which created the revolution. Admittedly he does stress the growing wealth of 1780-80, but he never even mentions the grave economic crisis immediately preceding the revolution. As he himself says "A bourgeois may be a better man - but he is a stranger" and is "not one of us" (the aristocracy). He is constantly comparing the glory, genius and spirit of the pre-revolutionary nobility to the mundane values of his contemporaries.

We find that he is inclined to paint rather too glamorous a picture of the court of the Kings during the 18, a picture which completely omits the scandals (for instance Marie-Antoinette's necklace) the intrigues and the common hatred felt for the waste and corruption of Versailles. In his concluding chapter he eulogises on the Old Régime government as the "mildest, the most generous and the most benign the world has ever known" - a very questionable interpretation. But we must state here that he heartily condemns the nobility for not taking a more lively part in local government.

His exalted view of liberty, "that sublime passion" which he cannot "analyse", though praiseworthy tends at times to blind him to some of the evils of the Old Order. For instance he condemns the abolition of the Parlement, although it was probably the only way in which the King could carry out any reforms, because it destroyed one guardian of liberty. He is forced into a difficult position then the sale of offices also as though evil in itself it did in some measure help to safeguard his precious liberty.

De Tocqueville. A. Macfarlane

Therefore we see that in some ways he was slightly biased. But when we compare him to any of his forerunners, Thiers, Mignet, Carlisle, Burke or Michelet we will be amazed at the equitable view he takes of the whole. He realizes that the revolution was necessary, the culmination of a long process, but he wishes that it had been carried out by an intelligent monarch like Frederick the Great who by retaining the aristocracy and local institutions would not have destroyed liberty as completely as the revolution did. His penetration into art or literature is completely superficial, his examination of economic factors too limited, but his political and sociological study though slightly biased against the middle class is amazingly fair and able.

b+?+

VS+?+ A very sound paper

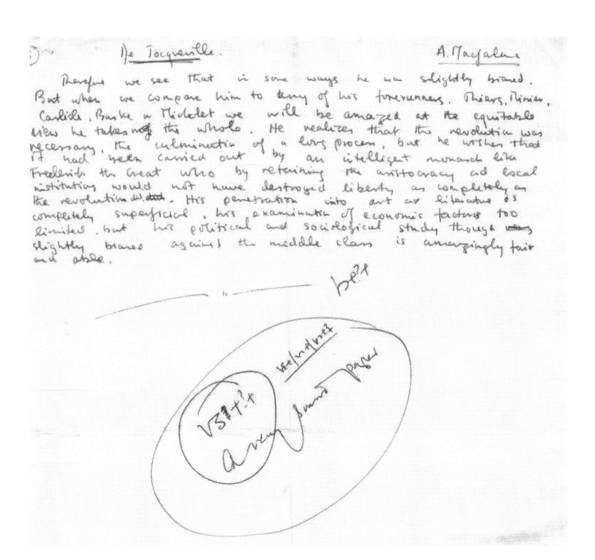

The mark on this question was 'b+?+' The overall mark on the paper was 'vs+?+', vs standing for very satisfactory, with the comment 'A very sound paper'.

I owe Harry Pitt a great deal for his careful induction into the work of this great thinker, to whose work, and wider writings, I would return again and again.

Latin: The Venerable Bede

We studied Bede over two terms. The first term was probably in relation to the Latin component of the Prelims. We went into his history of England in such depth partly because it was a solid foundation for the first part of our history of England course, Anglo-Saxon England, and partly, I suspect, because James Campbell, our main history tutor in the first year, was already a world expert on Bede.

We launched into Bede, whom I don't think I had ever read before, straight away. On the first Monday of term, 10 October, I have a set of notes headed 'P.H. Blair, Introduction to A–S England (Anglo-Saxon England) BEDE background', four pages of notes, with a map. The same day, James Campbell gave us the first of his nine lectures on Bede in Worcester College Hall. I took three pages of notes on this lecture, and my whole set of notes amounts to over 20 pages. In an index to the various essays and notes I was taking I summarized the lectures as follows: Political background; political events of Bk II & the political circumstances; contemporary factors – taxation, expansion etc.; King & nobility and the king in general; Economy of A-S –

plague, Church (this continued for lectures 5-7); Bede the man and historian. The ninth lecture was devoted to the Synod of Whitby.

As well as these lectures, I took notes from a number of books and articles. The notes are from A.H. Thompson 'Bede, His life, times and writings', Whitelock's 'The beginnings of English society', and a couple of other sources comprising eight pages of notes, as well as a few pages of notes on 'topics & people to study' which were presumably for revision.

I wrote three essays on Bede, all in the second half of the term. The first was written on Monday 7 November on the topic 'Account for the results of the Synod of Whitby'. This consisted of three pages of writing and a half page of notes to the essay. There are also five pages of notes for the essay, which show that I read a number of other books, including Stenton and Plummer. I noted in the mark S minus minus and the comment 'Good as far as it goes – clear & telling – good'. I suspect I read it out, since there are no notes on it, while at the bottom is the subject for the following essay with some suggested reading. This second essay, probably a week later on 14 November, was on 'Estimate the contribution made to political power by Christianity in the C7'. It is similar in length to the first essay, and with five pages of essay plan. There is no mark or comment.

The final essay was a week later on 21 November on "The Venerable Bede". Again there is no mark or comment, but a page of notes which I obviously made in the supervision. The essay shows something of my work on the fourth component of my first term and my humble offering to one of the greatest of Bede scholars.

21/11 "The Venerable Bede" H. Macfarlane

Bede was described by St Boniface as the "Candela Ecclesiae quam inluxit Spiritus Sanctus." But a candle to have any effect - especially in the dark night of seventh century England must be placed in a prominent yet sheltered position. His writings were the response of a great scholar to a great opportunity, and in understanding the nature of his success we must realise his singularily fortunate environment.

Benedict Biscop founded Wearmouth in 674 and Jarrow in 681 or 2. They were singularily fortunate in having a good librarys, largely formed by Biscop on his visits to Rome and later by Ceolfrid who donated among other books three copies of the Vulgate and one of the old version of the bible the Itala. From Bede's writings we can see that there were many Latin (for instance the younger Pliny and Virgil) a few Greek and other miscellaneous sources such as Orosius, Gildas, and Eusebius. Equally important was the fact that these two monasteries were blessed with a succession of pious and revered abbots among them Ceolfrid and after 716 Huaetberct. Bede therefore grew up among men who were ardent, hard-working and alive to the things of the spirit and mind. And at his desk in Jarrow he could collect evidence, letters, and stories either from his friends at other monasteries, for instance Abbot Esius who provided most of the information for his account of East Anglia, or from the many different kinds of people who visited Jarrow - celtic, Roman, Canterbury or Gaulish - Christian types as they might be. This central position and fusing of many different sources of information called forth his greatest gift in the words of Sir Frank Stenton an "astonishing power of co-ordinating the fragments of information which came to him through tradition, the relation of friends or documentary evidence. In an age where little was attempted beyond the registration of fact, he had reached the conception of history." coordination.

LIFE The opportunity was there, but what do we know of the life of the man who grasped it? Very little, and most of that is from the modest notice he gives of himself at the end of the Ecclesiastical History. The bones are there:- Born in either 672 or 3, traditionally at Monkton near Jarrow, he was given "by the care" of his relations to the Abbot Benedict to be educated at the age of seven. In 686 a severe outbreak of the plague destroyed most of the inhabitants of Jarrow and it seems likely that Bede was the "one little lad nourished and taught by him" (Ceolfrid) who outlined with the Abbot the devastation and helped to reintroduce the antiphons known by the new choristers. This belief is supported by the fact that though using the anonymous "History of the Abbots" which recounts this story Bede does not mention it.

At the age of nineteen he was advanced to the Diaconate by

John of Beverley; and as he was six years under the normal age for
this elevation it reflects something of his outstanding character.
Then in 702 or 3 at the age of thirty he was ordained priest.
Apart from his writings the only other recorded events to his death
were his visits to Lindisfarne and York in the last five years of
his life, a visit to Wicred in Yorkshire, perhaps to preach, the
sorrow of the departure of the revered Ceolfrid, and his probable influence
in converting the Ionan embassies and thence Iona to the Roman
observance of Easter. After some touching farewells including the
giving away of his small possessions he died, probably on Wednesday
the 25th of May 735 - just before Ascension day.

only other events

Clothe this with the flesh of a retired, studious and pious
life spent in teaching, writing, praying, performing the divine
services and perhaps even joining with the Abbot Ceolfrid in
performing his share of the manual labours on the monasteries land
or occasionally going out to preach to those around, and there lives
before one a simple and endearing person. A man who by both
his wisdom, and piety deserved the name "Venerable",
even if it is uncertain how he received it. It was within the
broad aim of increasing man's knowledge of the glory of God that
he wrote and within this framework there are roughly three main
divisions - his historical, scientific and theological works, though
his hagiographical writing is a mixture of the first and the last.

devout hardworking?

We do not know when he began writing, but probably the
two earliest were the "De Orthographia" and the "De Arte Metrica",
the first an alphabetically arranged glossary in which the meaning
or grammatical meanings of words are given, and the second a collection
of examples of verse forms intended in part to prove the superiority
of Christian poets. These "scientific" treatise were followed by his first
work elucidating the difficulties of calculating Easter - the "De Temporibus",
it also contains a condensed chronology of the six ages of the world.
After these Bede was for a time almost entirely occupied
in commentaries on the scripture, starting with books of the
New Testament, for example his "In Acta Apostolorum Expositio"
and possibly the greatest of the New Testament works of Bede the
"In Lucae Evangelium Exposito", in six books. These were all written
before Ceolfrid's departure in 716.

In 704 he had attempted a verse life of St Cuthbert
the "De Miraculis Sancti Cuthberti" but in this as in his other
two books of poetry though writing with ease and clarity he
did not achieve great success - and his second life, a prose
one written before 721, of St Cuthbert was better than the first.
From 721-725 he returned for a while to his "scientific" type
writings; his "De Natura Rerum" a kind of Cosmography which
though based on Isidore's similar work of 612 was not a blind
copy, and his second treatise on the calculation of Christian festivals -

21/11/60. The Venerable Bede (contd) A. Macfarlane

the "De Temporum Ratione."

The six years preceding the history were filled with expositions of the Old Testament - for instance the "De Templo Salominis" an allegorical explanation of 2 Chron ii - v, and with books of homilies, for instance the "Omeliarum Evangelii." In 731 he began and apparently completed the "Historia Ecclesiastica Gentis Anglorum" on which his fame rests. This was an almost totally original idea for he was the first man of his times to discover and relate the history of England, his only model being Eusebius' history.

This last work was the result of a really conscientious attempt at research and he sums up the sources as "prout vel ex litteris antiquorum vel ex traditione maiorum vel ex mea ipse cognitione scire potui." In this work we see in its maturity the "limpid and clear" latin style, the allegorical method of writing with its wonderful power of narrative, and a care to quote his sources which supports his belief that "vera historiae lex est." His style lacks the sententiousness and rhetorical artificiality of later writers in Latin for he wrote as he lived in a pure, simple and humble way.

" - social status of those in monasteries? - probably mostly higher class.

Why is Northumbria so learned.

i) Library.
ii) Aldfrith.
iii) Monastic discipline.
iv) Bede.

Lindisfarne. - Whitby. Anonymous life of Gregory the Gt.
Ripon or Hexham.. Eddius.

Innovation i)
ii) Form of eccl history. A.D. inception of -

A-S chronicle started to be written in 890.

Repton - a great lavishly endowed monastery - manuscripts not preserved.

- random destruction.

Spring Term and Holidays 1961

In my grandfather's diary there are just three entries for this period:

Tuesday 21 March 'Alan passes in Latin'
Wed 22 March 'Alan arrives back'
Sunday 2 April 'Alan leaves'

The first of my mother's letters has had the date and stamp torn off, but was clearly written early in January as it talks of New Year activities and also wonders whether I am back at Oxford yet. It is mostly about life in Assam but halfway through notes the arrival of a letter.

… got a letter from you to cheer me (us), you sound as if you've been having a gay time in spite of the weather and Fiona got very nostalgic reading about the gang though she feels now they're all Awfully Young!! … I think you'll be back at Oxford by now but we still haven't heard how much we should send for your battels, I think the best thing would be to transfer some money into your account at Oxford & hope for the best. …

My mother's first dated letter of 1961 is on 15th January from India.

My dear Alan,

Just got your letter from Oxford, and I'm glad you're safely back after a quiet period recuperating from the Gang! We were also delighted to hear you had passed the two more vital subjects in your Prelims, jolly good effort, as you say I don't suppose Latin is all that vital and I'm glad you haven't got to plod through Gibbon again. What are your books for this term? Actually I haven't quite fathomed what period you are doing, or don't you specialise yet? I'm sorry the finances are tricky, Daddy will send off the money to Worcester College pronto, and will write to the bank to-morrow asking them to transfer ten pounds to your account straight away and the other fifteen in a couple of weeks when he gets some advance commission. I'm sorry you've got to be bothered about finances, I know we still owe you a bit too, things should be easier when we have finished paying the girls' passages in three months time. I expect your bank will let you overdraw by a few pounds if you're absolutely out. I see you felt a bit like me about the promises of the new year, not a very thrilling world we brought you into but if one can be clear eyed about its muddles and disappointments and the vast confusion that is more than likely within our lifetimes, one can take the many small pleasures and add them into a reasonably contented life. The hardest thing is to reconcile it with the image of a just and loving God, although it should be easier for us who have so much more than the average … I get moods of deep depression and then Anne writes an essay that brightens my day. She is beginning to get the feel of words but I absolutely refuse to teach her to make rigid little plans of essays, I'm reading her model ones and telling her to leap right into her subject feet first without any introductory paragraphs, surely the whole point is to interest, or am I wrong?…
…I'm sorry Vivien treated you so offhandedly but girls are like that, as you must know by now, they must have their vanity tickled by constant fresh conquests. I hope you'll find one soon who can be a real friend, & not too Worthy either, let me know! Have a happy term – Much love Mummy

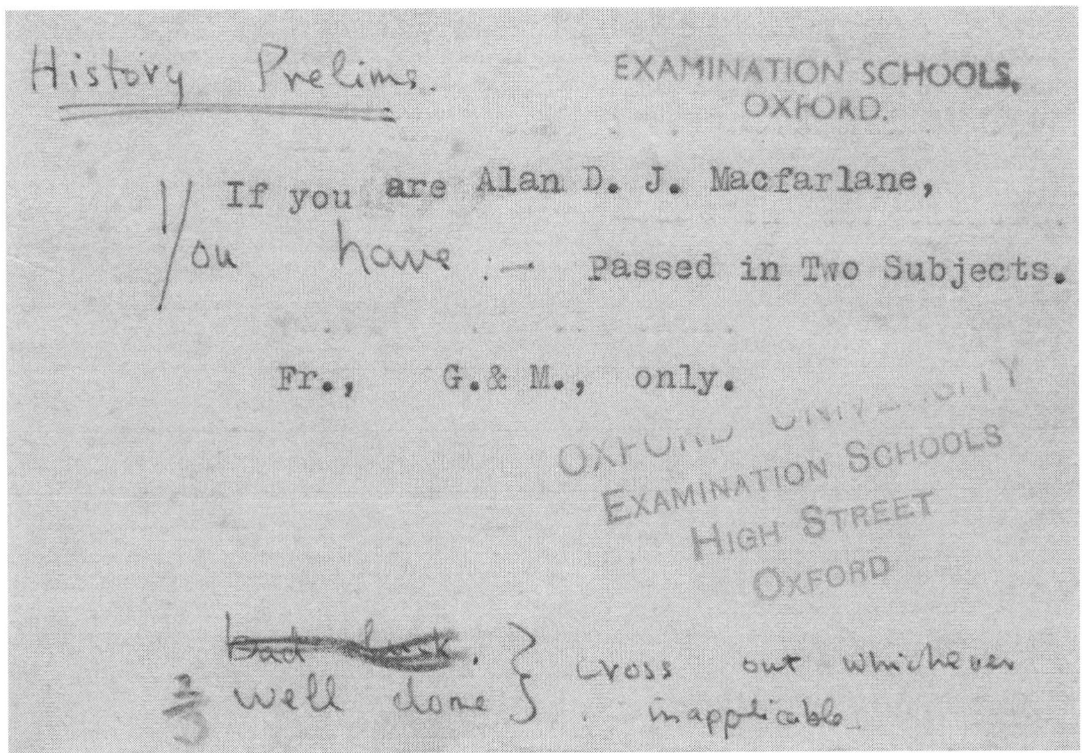
History Prelims.

EXAMINATION SCHOOLS,
OXFORD.

If you are Alan D. J. Macfarlane,
You have :— Passed in Two Subjects.

Fr., G.& M., only.

OXFORD UNIVERSITY
EXAMINATION SCHOOLS
HIGH STREET
OXFORD

~~bad luck~~. } cross out whichever
well done } inapplicable

I wrote on 17 January.

Dear Family,

Thank you (Mummy) very much for your letter which came shortly after I arrived here – I'm sorry all my letters have got behind – but I only got round to getting some air-letter forms this morning. I seem to be in my usual confusion – and haven't fully unpacked my trunk yet, although I have been back for over a week – I just scrabble about and get things out as I need them until the thing is empty!!

I am enjoying life immensely – although it seems to get fuller and fuller, both of work and social life. For instance having started to get down to this letter (on the first free evening I have had since I came back!!) I have been invaded by about 5 different people inviting themselves to coffee. One of them, the girlfriend of a friend of mine at this hostel – stayed from 8.0 – 10.0 nattering (fairly intelligently) about films (especially Alfred Hitchcock's film "Psycho" which is on at the moment) books etc. After that another friend came back and has been trying to arrange extra Latin tuition for me. He has a friend (now upstairs) who is a brilliant Latin scholar and who actually likes teaching people Latin!! Very useful as the usual fees as paid to some crusty old dame are exhorbitant – usually about 18/- bob an hour!

I am really beginning to get rather interested in my history at the moment – which is fortunate as I am being pretty hard-worked. Having just finished 15 large sides of notes and 6 of essay for a tutorial today I have 17 books to read and an essay to write on "The nature of King Offa's political power" before Saturday afternoon (I won't start 'till tomorrow – Thursday!) But fortunately I have got the good tutor who is very stimulating. If I don't watch out I will start writing history books – which I once imagined the dullest of occupations!

I can't remember whether I told you but I am doing quite a bit of reading (for me) – I have almost finished "Cider with Rosie" (which I have bought with a Christmas token) – I agree it is truly delightful. I am re-reading passages to all my friends – especially the first few pages – the "Grannies in the Wainscott" and the description of Winger – not to mention of course "the first bite"! I have just finished "Love me a little" an amusing book written by a 17-year-old American girl [Amanda Vail]; and François Sagain's "Bonjour Tristesse" will also be finished soon I hope. I have just opened "Chesterton's Essay's & Poems", a delightful book (so far), "Of Mice & Men" – Steinbeck. If you would like me to send any of these out to you (I bought them all in paper-back with my book-tokens) I will do so. I will try to get the "Green" aids (to history) soon.

I am being fairly social as I have said – and went out yesterday with a few friends to a girls hostel where we strummed guitars and listened to records. The day after tomorrow a friend is having a "birthday party" which should be fun – and on Sunday evening a Catholic friend is having a "Spanish Guitar" party. I would like to have got my new guitar by then – but I will see how things go.

I have not been out to much organised entertainment this week – just "Paris Holiday" in fact – last Saturday –Bob Hope and Fernandel – and quite good slapstick humour. The Ladykillers is on at the moment, I may see it on Saturday if I have the time and/or the money. "Charley's Aunt" which has been well reviewed is on next door (literally) at the "Playhouse" but I don't think I'll get to it.

Although I've managed to mislay your letter – as far as I remember everything is going alright. How is Fiona's art progressing? There [are] a lot of "arty" people here – she would love it. How did Anne's polo go – or is she still in hospital? I will have to refresh my memory of the game from Kipling's story – was it "The Siamese Cat"? – I can't remember.

Sorry for this hurried letter but it is getting late and I hope to be writing again in a few days.

Till then all my love and best wishes – look after yourselves!!

Alan

My mother's next letter is dated 24 January.

My dear Alan,

A cold misty morning, we had the coldest night of the year, 49 degrees!.... I haven't had a letter since I last wrote, don't bother, we don't expect one every week as I know you have far too much to do. Even here I find it hard to collect myself and my thoughts, I'm always so tired by the evening and the rest of the day too busy driving the girls into action. ..... and got back in time to hear Scotland being beaten at Rugger. Are you playing by the way? ... we're drawing to the end of the Middle Ages and about to start Our Period so if you know or see any cheap second hand volumes on Tudors or Stuarts would be most grateful for same, sea mail with the ends open you can get them out cheap. ... I wonder if Robert's book on Parliament is out yet, I must get him to send me a copy ... The big talking point is the Duke's twenty four hour visit to Jorhat next month. I must say I find it rather nauseating that the government should be able to find thousands of rupees to do up roads and buildings and make things pretty for the Queen when normally they don't seem to have a spare penny, also think it nasty of them to kill tigers for her amusement but my views hardly count needless to say! ... The Cowans sent me "Ring of Bright Water" for Christmas which has filled us with the urge to buy a broken down croft in the outer Hebrides, if you go there this summer look out for something suitable for us, no roads or electricity naturally, the trouble is one would probably find a rocket station as one's next door neighbour in a year or two. But its not a bad idea for our retirement all the same, there must still be derelict buildings we could retire to when we're letting Field Head at fifteen guineas a week.... I hope you are making ends come close if not actually meet, we will send the rest of the money at the beginning of next month.

Much love from us all – Mummy

The next letter from my mother is dated 1 February.

My dear Alan,

Four months to-day since we left England, it seems to have gone in a flash and the first two I found very depressing, but now I'm beginning to adjust myself and reconstruct the pattern. No letter from you I think, or did the last one arrive just after mine went?

I envy you cosily ensconced in your room reading seventeen books on King Offa (is he the Mercian man we took a brief glance at when we did Saxon England?. As a matter of fact I feel somewhat chary about exposing my small brain and doubtful grammar to one whom I'm always reading about in magazines described as the Cream of the Country's brains (you). I've just finished an article in the Illustrated Weekly about universities and there you are, creamier than ever, the luckiest, cleverest brightest-futured class in the country. I hope you feel like that, not poor and hard-working, I expect it hits you both ways. We are all terribly proud of you anyway and never utter a sentence without mentioning our son-at-Oxford! ... Daddy is just about to sell his gun, so there goes our last simple pleasure, and then the company wonders why all the young men are resigning when they see us in our state of poverty after twenty five years of hard work. Never mind, I wont depress you further, we will send the other fifteen pounds this month, in fact now, when do you start your vac? I'm glad you got "Cider with Rosie" as I shall be able to read it again, one of the few books I want to. I've just read "Don't Tell Alfred" by Nancy Mitford which is most amusing, an ideal antidote to King Offa. Granny sent it to me for Christmas...

The next letter from my mother is dated 6 February.

My dear Alan,
Thank you for a letter received a couple of days ago, as usual I've lost track of when I last wrote and what I said, have given up keeping a diary since I came back so hope I don't repeat myself too often. ....I was interested to hear of your studies, my idea of heaven would be to browse through old manuscripts picking out the pith and drawing conclusions, I wonder if anyone will have gone through those Levens Hall letters before we retire! Couldn't you spend part of your long vac grubbing about for evidence, or would that be too much of a busman's holiday? I haven't had time or opportunity to do any more excavating since I came back ... I will bring one of my pots home for dating this time. Who is your tutor, is he old or young, sympathetic or eccentric? I wish I could have an hour with him a week, I'm hysterically hurrying through Fisher trying to piece together European history so that we don't suddenly land in the middle of the Renaissance without any idea of what went before, but it's a formidable business and I have my doubts about Anne's passing it. ... I wish we could get some of those films you mention, but the chances are too remote to consider. I have read "Of mice and men" and thought it wonderful, one of the few books that I remember and have haunted me, but I haven't read any other of Steinbecks. I'm still reading my otter book and trying to spin it out, but I wish I had read it before I took on my otter as I would never have made the mistake of trying to take a full grown animal away from its owner, they simply die being far more affectionate and intelligent than dogs. .... The tempo is mounting as the Duke of Ed. Approaches... (Fiona) has just got a long letter from Anne Johnson saying Martin was forming a band, whether as amusement or a career I cant make out, but I don't think he's good enough to make a career of it is he? I must say I'm glad Fiona is out of that gang, she is much more sensible now ... I see there is an art school much advertised in Oxford, but I imagine the accommodation question is impossible isn't it? It would be nice if you could both be there cashing in on each other's friends, or would it be ghastly? I do hope you aren't finding yourself too short of money, the enclosed will tide you on a bit I trust, will it last till the end of the term (?) or not? I know you must be short, but I hope things will improve gradually, I'm sure they will, anyway your second and third years we should be able to help more. Daddy has just said hang onto it for a couple of days before you cash it if you can – but I daresay the bank can stand the strain otherwise.
Much love, don't get The Asian [?flu?] *Mummy*

The next letter has an Oxford postmark of 13 February.

Dear Family,

Many thanks for the letter – and the money, which I presume has arrived in the bank although by now I just don't ask if I have any money there – just in case I haven't! I feel rather guilty as I keep asking you for more when I know how difficult things are, but it seems to go amazingly quickly here – and I will have to spend some more soon – on a football shirt and trousers (I have been borrowing a friends all this term!). I hope and think I should be okay until the end of the term but then – the abyss opens! I will be going on to a "Work Camp" – which sounds pretty ominous –but is cheap (£2 – 5sh – 0) for a week and at a beautiful place – Lee Abbey (near Taunton I think). The idea is for one to work manually on the estate in the morning then have the rest of the day off free – getting one's vacation reading done one hopes! It is all run on a broadly Christian basis – something like V.P.S.[1] *I suppose. I am hoping to help at that (V.P.S.) at the end of the holidays for a week, so will only be home for 4 weeks. Sorry to keep pressing you but I might as well warn you 4 weeks in advance – as I will need a bit of money for the vac (for V.P.S. £5- 10s) etc. Now let us soar away from that bubbling, scum-covered lake, of gruesomeness (the topic of money in case you didn't guess!) into the realms of higher values and speculations!*

I don't wish to disillusion you about all this "cream of the cream" stuff as regards Oxford, but you just have to read my letters to dispel those illusions! Admittedly I am finding it the most stimulating and enjoyable period of my life and am thrilled with (almost!) every minute of it – but there is no doubt that the general level of conversation – if this is anything to go by – is not very high. There seem to be only two subjects talked about – as I think I am always telling you, Love & Religion. At the moment the former subject is very involved – or rather the petty affairs which all my friends are carrying on are involved. The Lakes really have nothing on the cross-complications, scandals and gossip here. The main trouble being that all the boys know the same sets of

[1] Varsity and Public School – Camps

girls and one can't have a girl in to tea without all one's friends coming in and making embarrassing comments etc!

For the last week I have been trying to work and read a good deal – but it is rather a losing battle against the continuous stream of haggard individuals who flop in demanding coffee, cigarettes and sympathy!! The chaos of coffee-cups, records and books was made worse by the fact that the hostel as a whole gave a party last night – with my room (being the biggest) the centre of it. Now this was especially unfortunate as I had been invited to another party that evening by a girl called Thérèse – and so could not attend ours.[1] *Apparently it went quite well however – partly I think because I suggested the idea of a strong "punch" at the beginning (with the "Macfarlane" recipe), it was a great success.*

One of the disappointments last week was our non-appearance on T.V. I told you about the fuss over the attacks on Lectures in the "Isis" I think. Well on Tuesday B.B.C. T.V for some odd reason sent their cameras etc to "telerecord" Worcester College having their sausage & mash lunch!! Having suffered the misfortune of being able for a change to see our revolting sausages under the bright arc-lamps, the film which it was rumoured would be on Friday evening wasn't shown.[2]

How was the Queen? I have been keeping an eye out for Jorhart or Nazira P.O in the papers! Terrific about Scotland wasn't it!? Look after yourselves. With all my best love, Alan

My mother wrote again on Monday 18 February.

My dear Alan,

I've kept this over to tell you the only Big News for years – the Duke's visit but alas nobody scratched anyone else's eyes out or tried to assassinate him or was sick when they were being presented, in fact it all went off dismally well. [a very amusing letter on life in Assam.] … Never mind I enjoy teaching Anne, we have come to the end of the Middle Ages and are making a vast chart with all the main events, statutes etc. marked in different coloured inks which is great fun and I hope useful. I find Fisher fascinating and feel very superior knowing who the Wends are but find it difficult to introduce them into normal conversation! If you ever see a good 2nd hand biography of Wolsey I would love it (don't spend more than a shilling on it) I feel he is the Key Figure of the Tudor age. Strangely enough we never did the Tudors that I remember and my knowledge of them is based on old films about Henry VIII throwing chicken bones over his shoulder. … We will send some money for your holidays, I hope you wont be too short, perhaps you could take a job for a week or two if you are, Martin still doesn't seem to be settled but David has worked himself into advertising I gather. I hope Granny and Granpa avoid flu which is taking its toll of the old but it always sounds worse than it is. Everyone sends love & promises to write & lots from me – Mummy.

I obviously sent out some reports on an international match between Scotland and perhaps Ireland towards the end of February. The letter refers to a football match 'last Saturday', which can be dated as 25 February. So this letter was almost certainly written on Tuesday 28 February. It is written on headed 'Worcester College, Oxford' notepaper.

Dear Family,

The enclosure of the football accounts has given me a chance to use our 'posh' notepaper. Unfortunately one cannot have both a crest and an address on the same sheet. Talking of these reports – terrific isn't it?!! If only they can do as well against England it would be wonderful. Even if they lose against them Scotland will have considerably more points than the "sassernacks". The Scotland-Ireland match won me a pint of beer from an Irish friend and I hope the next game does the same from another – Englishman.

I have been holding back from writing – partly through a combination of hard-work, laziness and waiting for your letter which I received yesterday – thank you very much. I'm surprised to hear of Fiona's hectic

---

[1] There are several letters from a Thérèse of St Clare's Hall, a sixth form College in north Oxford, referring to my lending her books while she was ill etc.., as well as short notes about the party. She was also mildly encouraging me in the pursuit of a girl called Heidi at St Clare's.

[2] *The incident over 'Isis' led to the founding of the Oxford Students Union: see* http://en.wikipedia.org/wiki/Oxford_University_Student_Union

gadding-about – I thought she went to India to calm down etc?! Stirred by my deep worry for her safety – staying up so late etc I was inspired subconsciously (while looking for another poem "The Owl & the Pussycat") to read a tragic tale which should perhaps be hung by Fiona's bed – as am about to spend considerable energy copying it down I hope she will profit from its example – perhaps you know it already?

I then copied out three verses of Edward Lear's poem 'The Cummerbund' first published in the 'Times of India', 1874, starting 'She sate upon her Dobie…

At the end I put a note to the effect

As you can see all the hard work I've been doing has turned my brain!

After a spot of flu (I was feeling miserable last Thursday – Saturday) I have decided with only a week (or less – exams start on Monday I had better get down to some work – therefore I did over 11 hrs on Monday) and aim to do over 8 hrs a day the rest of the week. The main difficulty is that it is revision – and of Latin (Bede) at that!

I think you have probably now reached the most exciting period of English History – Tudors & Stuarts – and I'm sure you will enjoy it. I will keep an eye out for a book on Wolsey and also for one on Thomas Cromwell – Henry VIII's financial genius – an obscure but intriguing and probably important figure. I think charts, maps etc are always a good idea and make the thing more alive. You are speeding on ahead of me – we have just reached M. Carta – and had to do an essay on Angevin kingship last week. Now that you have done the historical side of the Middle Ages – is the time to read Shakespeare on it – Dick II, III & the Henry's – I saw Richard II done by the Oxford University Dramatic Society yesterday – apart from the rather scratched record of the trumpet fanfares which whirred above our heads – it was glorious. Richard himself was most captivating although a bit "dainty" perhaps.

Last Saturday the Worcester football XI went over to play St Catherine's College Cambridge – I was still suffering from flu so didn't much enjoy the outing, especially as the game was played in a mud-pit in a howling rain-storm – & we lost it 3-1. But I did enjoy seeing "High Society" with all the stars Crosby, Sinatra, Armstrong etc in it – I presume you have had it out at the club? – if not it might be a good one to get. I leave the dogs, cabbages, cooks, Anne's work, Miranda, Daddy, the new thatch, Fiona's worries etc thankfully in yr hands and turn with a sigh to Bede. All my love to you all, Alan

The next of my mother's letter comments on a letter from me which is dated 1 March.

My dear Alan,

Thank you for your letter written on that lovely spring day among the crocuses, I remember the Worcester College gardens so well, but never thought you would be sitting there as part of the landscape so to speak. … Our twentieth wedding anniversary to-day, the girls are both going out to a bachelor's party so we shall celebrate it like Darby and Joan with a bottle of whisky we have saved since Christmas. … Talking of money, Daddy has sent some home and I will send you a cheque for £10 the day after to-morrow to start you off on your holidays, let us know exactly how long the vac lasts wont you, and how things are going in that line. I think your idea of teaching in the long vac is a good one, it'll give you an idea as to whether you would like that as a career. But will a prep school take you for five weeks? The Outer Hebrides sounds delicious too, see if you can find a broken down croft for us to buy as a retreat when the pace gets too hot at Field Head.

Three days later, on 4 March, there is a three page letter from my father, which clearly had enclosed a cheque. Most of it was about life in Assam and will be included elsewhere.

My dear Alan,

Mummy asked me to send you the enclosed as she has gone out for the day. I hope that it will tide you over for a little and I shall try and send some more during the month. What a business this finance all is and I am sorry that we can't, at the moment, make things easier for you. … I enjoy getting your letters immensely and love hearing all about your activities both scholastic and social. It must be a wonderful life and I wish that I could have managed to go. … Lots of love, Daddy

My mother wrote again on 17 March.

My dear Alan,

I think you will be home again by now, refreshed physically and mentally and ready to appreciate the daffodils which must be blooming Wordsworthily everywhere…. We were all interested in your Hungarian friend,[1] *as you say Oxford must be a hard place to hold a girl but I hope you'll manage to do so for a short while anyway as she sounds most unusual and interesting – a bit terrifying too with a brain like that, what is she reading? Its so hard to find anyone who measures up to ones impossible standards of beauty, brains, and nice nature and life must necessarily be a series of compromises, but just occasionally a figure appears to fit exactly. And alas disappears again rapidly in most cases but leaves you with the happy knowledge that there may be more like her or him.*

Your spiritual reawakening I can only be glad about for your sake, its something that seems beyond my range of experience now, perhaps because its an experience implicit in Christianity and slightly suspect in the Perennial Philosophy – not that I'm decrying it but having been won over by the concept of patient self discipline and self denial as the way to happiness, emotional "giving of the heart to Jesus" is just meaningless, though I can see that stripped of the luxuries of sacrifice and prayer the two could mean the same thing. Anyway if youth is not the time for messages and awakenings what is? If only the message could be conceived and delivered in a broadly human way instead of a narrow religious one. I'm not in the least embarrassed to discuss religion by the way, its one of my favourite topics, inexhaustibly interesting because there seems no final answer that fits the state of the world. To more mundane topics, I hope you passed your exams, what if you didn't? To more mundane still, I'm sending Granny a cheque by sea mail, she doesn't seem to have got my last letter. We'll have to send her something for your keep so hope the £15 can be spun out as far as possible, I know you'll do your best. Gather Martin has had a crash, poor Beryl, thank heavens our worries are only money ones! Much love to all from us all – Mummy

My birthday letter to my sister Fiona is date-stamped the following day, 24 March.

My dear Fish,

Many <u>very</u> happy returns for your birthday – goodness – to think that you'll be 17 and no longer just an innocent (?) teenager. I hope the next year is a wonderful one for you and that you grow in wisdom and bodily beauty and all that sort of thing. If you are at about the same stage of development as myself – and they always say that girls are about two years ahead of boys – you will be at the most exciting period of your life – with new horizons opening out before you and, I hope, the creative genius stirring within you. For the first time in my life I feel <u>almost</u> as if I could write some good poetry or prose – but of course I am too lazy to try!

You seem to have been leading a very gay life out there, but I am confident that you will not have neglected your studies & reading – perhaps! On the other hand if I had gone out to India the chance of meeting any nice & eligible girls would have been practically <u>nil</u>. I hope the ease with which you can pick and choose does not spoil you for when you come back to "the rat race" – actually if you can get to somewhere like Edinburgh, London or Oxford you will be very happy. I do hope you are <u>thinking</u> at least of coming to the Ruskin Art School (I think it is called) in Oxford – it would be very interesting to compare gossip etc and I know you would love it – though what dear Mama & Pappa would think of the idea I don't know!! I was very sorry to hear of your embarrassing situation & disappointment over the "convent" job – I do hope you can get another before the hot weather.

Fortunately, perhaps, I will only be up here [Lake District] for about 10 days, so will most of the gang but in case you haven't heard I will give you the slight bit of gossip I know. Mike Bod is still keen on Vivien I think – David M-F is down south near Oxford – Steve – have you heard from him? – is frequently in hospital with various diseases & moaning the absence of girls! Martin has got crazy over a girl called Caroline something from Sharlott Mason College – she is very musical & now teaching at Windermere Grammar – Martin seems to have forgotten all about Jacky – & the whole thing is wonderful. He has also formed a group like the Shadows – 2 electric guitars, drums & saxophone which he <u>says</u> is tremendous – I haven't heard it yet!

---

[1] The first mention of Julianna S who features prominently over the next few months.

Lastly myself – I am spending the vac rushing about – a week in Devon – a few days in Oxford & London then 10 days here & then back to Oxford via London & Iwerne. I am feeling wonderful for various reasons – among them that I passed my Latin Prelims somehow (could you tell Mummy?) & secondly I have met the most wonderful girl etc – a Hungarian called Julianna who I mentioned in my family letter. If things go on as they are now I may fall for her in a big way.

I hope your life will be equally rosy and that you meet "the man of your dreams" etc.

Could you tell the others I will be writing in 3 days – when I get an air-letter form?

With birthday wishes & love, Alan

The next letter from me is written from Field Head, and date stamped 27 March.

Dear Family,

Many thanks for your letter which was awaiting me when I arrived at Oxford – I trust Fiona will have got my birthday letter by the time this arrives – in fact her's should be a few days early. The last few weeks have gone in such a rush that I haven't quite sorted things out yet so will probably repeat my last letter a bit – please excuse me and put it down to the fact that "Smoke gets in my eyes" – if you see what I am hinting at!

Anyhow the rest of the week in Devon was wonderfully invigorating and by the end of the week though my hands were fairly blistered I was literally enjoying sledge-hammering! I rather fancied myself in my black jeans & red-checked "lumberjack" shirt! As I think I said the people were all very kind, thoughtful and happy and I came away with a lovely glow and a determination to live a more "worthwhile" life! Naturally in contact with the realities of life most of the sentimentalized ideas etc I had acquired were quickly knocked away. Perhaps it was unfortunate – at least some of my earnest friends would say so – that I went back on the Saturday to Oxford. I arrived about 6.0 without any definite place to sleep, and 2/7½ in my pocket (there is definitely a sense of exileration [sic] *in being completely in the hands of fate – the fascination of being a tramp I should think). Anyhow I fixed things up with the college so that I stayed 'till 4.0 on Monday – when I went in to London to see Robert & Angela. I spent nearly all the time with Julie discussing everything under the sun – and listening to her tremendous collection of records which includes Dylan Thomas "Under Milk Wood", T.S. Elliot's "The Wasteland" as well as a lot of music – we also visited a scruffy but rather amusing coffee bar called "The Muffin" and studied "humanity" – mostly in the shape of beatniks and smooth Italians.*

In London I spent the first evening out – as Robert & Angela had gone out to see Lord & Lady Pakenham for dinner (of course!). Anyhow I spent a very pleasant evening – I went to see my first film for at least four weeks! – shows how hard I had been working at Latin – boy am I glad about that!! – it was "From here to Eternity" and recommended by Robert. A very good American film about Pearl Harbour before the disaster – and though perhaps exaggerating the soldiers love for the army, still very touching – but not sheer sentimentality. Afterwards I wandered back, poking my nose in at two "dives" – firstly the "Café des Artistes" – supposed to be the beatest" place in London. I only penetrated to the first cellar, crowded with throbbing Juke-box music – pulsating in between the jostling people. I sat and had coffee and studied the fake mushrooms stuck on the roof – and the (probably) fake blond hair of both male and female beatniks, and their genuine look of complete boredom.

Then I went and had a cup of coffee in another place – I can't remember its name. I was told there were guitarists etc there but we had to join a club to see them – so I didn't bother – (It looked quite respectable in case you are getting worried!)

I travelled on Tuesday night _ after having been to the House of Commons where I watched a bit of an amusing debate, and had a snack with Robert. The journey up was uneventful & since then I have been trying to get up momentum in my work – and did actually achieve quite a bit yesterday. I really must get going next week.

I think I told you most of the "gang" news. Gr & Grandpa are very well & Granny – as she will no doubt tell you – got 1, 2 & 3 in the National. Very wild weather at the moment, spring only showing through with hesitancy.

Sorry to babble on so long about myself! I hope everything goes very well with you – look after yourselves & work hard!?

Lots & lots of love to you all, Alan

The next letter from my mother was dated 28 March.

My dear Alan,

We were delighted to hear from Granny that you had passed the beastly Latin, what a relief, does that mean that you are finished with it for good? I don't think we had a letter this week, as you were travelling, but I trust all went well and you're feeling really refreshed in every way. We envy you the flurries of snow… We started "Jane Eyre" yesterday which is pure pleasure, but I wish we had something more inspiring than "Twelfth Night" to do, I hate the puns and the taunting of Malvolio and all those dreadful old men. We are launched at last into the Tudors, I try to keep one king ahead and while we're doing Henry VII I'm mugging up the breach with Rome, I was in the middle of reading about the dreadful Borgia Popes when we had the Catholic Priest, Father James, a Spaniard to stay the night. We got involved in long (very good natured) arguments on the subject, fruitless of course, and then he sang for us… He speaks seven languages, plays three instruments, and spends his life in broken down buses going to visit little communities of catholics twenty or thirty strong – it seems a strange waste but he is happy and I suppose satisfied that his talents were not meant to be used. …. Please thank Granny for sending the book, and also the "Boyfriends" which Anne is thrilled with. Daddy wants to add a line to this so I'll leave him some room, so sorry to hear about Martin's do with Gran's car, not his fault which makes it worse. I do hope he'll start taking a career more seriously soon. [A short note in my father's hand…] Well done passing your Latin, like Mummy I haven't the faintest what that means but hope you haven't got any more of the beastly things to cope with. … We shall planning to come home again soon. Hope you have a decent hols, Lots of love from us all, Daddy

My mother's next letter is dated 6 April. It is posted to Field Head and redirected to 'V.P.S. Party, Clayesmore, Iwerne Minster, Dorset, and date stamped in Ambleside on 12 April.

My dear Alan,

Goodness knows where you will be now, or what doing, I still don't know in fact how long the vac is, I thought it was eight weeks but judging by your letter to Fiona it cant be as you only plan to have ten days at home. Perhaps you will be going back to Oxford early, I hope the money will last but this travelling is expensive unless you can hitch hike or go by bus, anyway I suppose Granny will have helped you out if you were short. I expect we'll be getting answers to all the questions any day and meanwhile will try to get something into your bank to tide you over till your next bit of grant arrives. I'm going to make enquires of the council to see if Fiona can get a grant for an Art School and perhaps if you meet anyone connected with the one at Oxford you could do a little enquiring about that too i.e. Is there any hostel or what not attached to it and how difficult is it to get into and are the students madder or badder than most?! … We listened to the Boat Race during the course of the evening, what a tragedy, I haven't read a full account of it yet.[1] *Your birthday letter was most welcome. Strange to think it was in my seventeenth year that I met Daddy, how quickly the old routine starts up again. How is the "old routine" going with you? Do send us a snap of Juliana if you can get one, I hope it flourishes but it must be a tooth and claw struggle in Oxford – good luck to you anyway … Our mental stimulation through reading "Jane Eyre" is our set book which is the big moment of the day and the whole family gathers round to listen, and I'm reading "The Leopard" to myself which is enchanting. I have at last got the Italian Wars sorted out and am waiting for Green (I've sent for a copy so don't bother) before plunging into the Reformation proper. According to John Lampett who is an honours graduate, the way to pass exams is to know one part of your syllabus really well and not attempt to finish it, so I'm going to get dug into the Tudors and European History and leave the Stuarts for the last couple of months. Where are you at now? Wish I was closer as I'm sure you could be invaluable! …. Ah well never mind, only five more years. … spring in Oxford will be wonderful too especially if you're in love will you be able to hire a dinner jacket for the balls says she prosaically?*

My next letter is addressed from Iwerne Minster on Sunday 16 April

Dear Family,

A letter was forwarded to me here at Iwerne – thank you very much for it (Mummy). I'm glad all is going well with the tea, 'mahliberry' (how does one spell that word?) that Fiona's birthday was quiet but pleasant – I expect the horses illness will be well into the past by now the tea-making well under way. Also it will be getting very hot. Although I would have willingly changed weather a month ago – now our positions are reversed as here

---

[1] Cambridge won by just over four lengths

it is perhaps the most glorious time of year with the lengthening days which, despite their frequent showers, in occasional periods of radiant blue give a hint of the summer – "The flowers that bloom in the spring tra-la, bring promise of sweet summer sun."!

Before I go on – if at times this letter wanders a bit, please ascribe it to the difficulty (self-imposed) of writing and trying to listen to Tchaikovsky's 4th Symphony simultaneously!

I think I last wrote from Oxford – was it? – Just after I had arrived from seeing Julie in London? I will assume so anyhow. In Oxford I had to write my holiday essay on "The Scottish Monarchy in C11 & C12", which is principally a discussion of how, why & when did the amazing "Norman Invasion" (a peaceful one) occur which altered the whole pattern of Scottish society from a non-feudal to feudal one. Perhaps an abstruse, but certainly a fascinating problem. I managed to complete it in about 17 pages of large foolscap – which should give my tutor a headache!

Apart from this work and reading a fascinating book by Naomi Mitchison called "The Corn King & the Spring Queen" or at least half of it, I didn't do anything particular in Oxford. The book – like most I read has had a considerable effect on me (I seem to be very easily influenced – & can change my whole mood by merely reading a poem, a double-edged characteristic) – it has suddenly opened to me the whole field of knowledge concerning the Greeks – high on my reading list at the moment, along with some books on the line of "The Lord of the Rings" and "The Crock of Gold" are Plato, Aeschylus etc – formidable sounding people but no doubt a fascinating labarynth in which I am about due (at my age & mental stage) to get lost in for a while. I want to read as much as I can next term, even if I have to get up early to do my work.

I am glad to hear that you are enjoying teaching Anne so much – as you rightly say it is probably you who are learning the most. I wonder if it would be any help if sometime I sent you out by sea-mail a few of my essays, or French exercises (completed) which I did during my 'O' level year? Just to hearten you by showing how illiterate one can be & yet be able to pass!

I came down to Iwerne (by bus as instructed!) on Tuesday. As far as finances are concerned I will be able to tide over until I get the next bit of my grant. I should be getting £60, therefore would you like me to pay – say £35 towards my "battels" which will arrive at the beginning of term? Then if & when I need more money during the term I will write for it – this will put off at least expenses for you.

I am still anxiously on the look-out for a job for the summer – tho' fear it is getting a bit late for finding a prep-school job & therefore I may have to [do] some more menial task – doubtless very good for me!

It has been a pleasant week here, though not entirely restful as I have along with other "Senior" campers had to serve & prepare meals, sweep, wash etc. My main & specialised job is mixing orange & lemon juice for the whole camp – so if I can ever find a job which requires the mixing of a hundred orange-juices I will be well away!

I am going back to Oxford on Tuesday & our 8-week summer term begins on Saturday.
Look after yourselves and be very happy in all you do – I am thinking of you a lot.
With lots of love to you all, Alan

The boys' camps, starting from even before I went to the Dragon, and then repeated almost every year at the Varsities and Public Schools Camps at Iwerne Minster, had a very considerable influence on my emotions and thoughts. Only once, however, is there a detailed account of what I was thinking and reading at these camps, and this occurred over this visit of a week or so in April 1961. Because of their influence, and the fact that experience was repeated and lay behind many of the sentiments I express in my letters and poetry, I shall include most of the contents of a small notebook which I have kept from this camp, prefaced by a photograph of me with other 'Senior Campers' and three of the 'Officers'.

Iwerne Varsities and Public Schools Camp – note the Bible in my hands (third from left)

Alan Macfarlane,

Worcester College.

Oxford.

On Prayer.

The Need.

"For what are men better than sheep or goats....
If, knowing God, they lift not hands of prayer
Both for themselves and those who call them friend."

"More things are wrought by prayer than this world
dreams of" – Tennyson.

What is prayer?

"Prayer is lifting up our hearts to God.
We praise and thank him; we speak and
listen to him; we confess our sins
and receive his forgiveness; we seek
to know his will; and we make
requests for others and for ourselves."
– The New Catechism.

Monday Morning.

i) Commendation into God's Hands, & Dedication of Day.
ii) Ask for holy Spirit "Come holy Ghost".
– continual presence.
iii) Lord's Prayer & prayer for all whom one knows
iv) Prayer for a) Strength, humility
b) Those one will meet.
c) Guidance.
d) Power to overcome sin.
v). Learn verse.
vi) Thanks for day.

"Monday."

i) Spirit of Quiet & Rest "Be still & know that I am God".

Adoration. ii) Ask for insight & guidance in bible. ("Open thou mine eyes....")

iii) READING.

iv) Choose i) One verse to meditate on. (perhaps write down)

v) Meditation. – example – promise etc. – Listen for God's word.

Confession. – – – – – – – – – – –

i) General Confession of sinfulness. "Father I have sinned before heaven & towards thee...."

ii) Specific sins. i) Body. – Lust.
ii) Mind –
iii) Spirit –

iii) Pray for thanksgiving.

Thanksgiving. – – – – – – – – – – –

i) For Home & background.
- parents.
- school.
- Oxford.
- opportunities.

Supplication.

i) For Family.

Mummy, Daddy, Fiona, Anne, Granny, Grandpa, Aunts Pat, Jean, Julia, Angela Uncles, Alec, Alan, Robert, Richard, Billy. – all cousins – Evroline etc. Great Grannies & Grandpas, Nicholas Felicity.

– pray that i) Kept in health & happiness & protection of God.
ii) Meet Thy holy self – Christ & come to know thee.

ii) For families everywhere – a) Unity b) Love, c) Knowledge of God.

"Tuesday."

Adoration
i) Spirit of Quiet & Rest. "Peace [illegible], my peace [illegible] wit you"
ii) Ask for insight & guidance in bible.
iii) READING. "a lantern unto my ft"
iv) Choose i) One verse to meditate o.
v) Meditation. let God speak - listen.

Confession..
i) General sinful State "I have sinned against thee in thought, word & deed"
ii) Specific Sin: Hypocrisy & Dishonesty. before others & before God.
iii) Prayer for forgiveness.

Thanks.
i) For FRIENDS.
a) At Home.
b) " [illegible].
c) Past friends.
d) College.
e) The Rest.

Supplication.
i) For friendship.
ii) For special friends in need.
iii) For [illegible]

"Wednesday"

Adoration.

i) Spirit of Quiet & Rest. "Let not your heart be troubled".
ii) For Insight & guidance in reading. "Speak Lord. for thy servant heareth . . . ."
iii) READING.
iv) Choose 1 vs to meditate on. (perhaps write down to learn)
v) Meditation – let God speak.

Confession. a) General Sinfulness. "I am no more worthy to be called thy son."

b) Specific Sin. – Lack of Charity
   a) In our relations with others.
   b) In our thoughts " ".
   c) " " " relations with God

c) Ask for forgiveness.

Thanks For a) Position (Oxford)
   b) For comforts.
   c) For intellect & opportunities in past.
   d) For all the times thou hast led me. (York; Iwerne; Retreat; Lee Abbey etc)
   e) For romantic relationships.

Supplication.

a) For present work & activities at Oxford.
b) For my future job.
c) For all those teaching or learning:
~~Borstal Camp~~ Borstal Camp.

"Thursday."

"A still small voice".

Adoration. i) Spirit of Quiet & Rest.
ii) Ask for Insight.
iii) Reading.
iv) Choose 1 vs to read (& copy down)
v) Meditate & listen
vi)

Confession. i) General Sinfulness.
ii) Lack of Faith & Hope.

Thanks i) For the Bible.
ii) For being brought to Christ in the past.
iii) For the inspiration of other Chris_
iv) (For the " of Christ.

Supplication_ i) For all Christians - especially
ii) [illegible], & are preachers & teachers
ii) For [illegible] Abbey, Retreats, [illegible].
iii) All those outside Ch.

esp. Julian); [illegible], Sue, Jane S, Michael & St. Paul.

"Friday"

Adoration. i) Spirit of Quiet & Rest "Be still & know that I am God"

ii) Ask for insight – "Show me thyself within thy word".

iii) READING.

iv) Choose 1 verse – meditate.

v) Meditate – example, promise – [illegible].

Confession.

i) General Confession of Sinfulness

ii) Specific Sin – Pride

in (a) Achievements.

(b) Spiritual (goodness)

(c) in pretended "virtues".

(d) of popularity etc.

Thanksgiving.

i) For HEALTH. – of mind & body.

ii) For SAFETY.

for work of doctors & nurses.

Supplication.

* i) Physically ill – disease. mental sickness.

– in any kind of pain – those hurt in accidents

ii) Those poor & underfed – underclothed

– esp. in the East, India etc.

"Saturday"

Adoration. i) Quiet & Rest: "A still small voice".
ii) Prayer for insight:- "Open thou mine eyes..."
iii) READING.
iv) Choose - a verse to meditate on.
v) Meditate. - ask for God's guidance & spirit

Confession. i) General Confession.
ii) Carnal Weakness.
a) Desire & lust.
ii) Gluttony.
iii) Self-feeding.
iv) Ask for forgiveness.

Thanks. a) For Christ's example & death.
b) For the physical beauty & wonder of the world.
c) For body & love

Supplication.
A. For World Affairs. i) Leaders. ii) Countries. iii) Relationships
B. For Peace.
C. For leaders of this country & those in responsibility -

"Sunday"

.1. Spirit of quiet "Be still & know that I am God".
(Adoration)

Adoration

ii) Ask for insights "Open thou mine eyes that I may behold - - -"

iii) READING.

iv) Choose 1 vs.

v) MEDITATE round it - letting God speak.

Confession

i) General Sinfulness. "I have sinned against thee in thought, word & deed"

ii) Specific Sins.

Hypocrisy.
Thoughtlessness.
Anger
Envy

iii) Repentance & ask for forgiveness

Thanks

i) For the blessings of the week.

ii) For thy Cross & Passion.

iii) For the Church

iv) For the saints.

Supplication

i) For thy Church & its leaders

ii) For the coming week. i) Dangers ii) Opportunities

iii) For all those one has met.

iv) For the opportunity to witness

"Holy Communion."

A. A service of remembrance - all agree. degrees.

Exodus 11, 12. - Passover.

1. Cor. 5 7-8. ; Luke 22, 7-20.

A command from Christ - vs 19.

A means of Grace.

Thank him afresh - - for his sacrifice with a prepared heart 1. Cor 11. 20-30

Doctrine of the Cross.

Propitiation. Rom 3;25. "Jesus.... to be a propitiation"

- a satisfaction of God's justice by a sacrifice.

1 John 2;2. "and He is the propitiation for our sins" Heb 9;22. "without shedding of blood is no remission."

Reconciliation.

Colossians 1 21;22. "through (His) death to (make) you holy and unblameable."

God has turned to face us.

God → us

Before Cross

After Cross. but we have to 2 Cor 5: 19.

Rom 5; 10, 11.

We need to receive the reconciliation. an offer which must be taken up.

- then we become AT ONE / MENT!

REDEMPTION. – the slave market. – i) Being a slave to Gal 3;13. (Laws of God)

ii) the price 1. Peter 1: 18,19.
"redeemed with the precious blood of Christ."

iii) the consequent freedom St Mk 10:45.
Eph. 1:7.

B.R. 14/4/61.

BIBLE.

Authority of the Bible.

2. Tim 3: 15,16. – What the bible says of itself.

(1) 2. Peter 1:20,21 = "moved by the Holy Ghost."
– (like a wind over a wood)

(2) J: confider [?] once in it.
Matth 5; 17 "to fulfil the law."
(give the "map" of the "O.T. content & meaning
St John 5:39. Christ linking himself with the O.T.
John 10:35
Sums it all up.

Bible like a portrait.

(3) i) figure – gospels – central.
ii) background – O.T. – context.
iii) clothes of – epistles etc.
figure – amplification.

(4) Remarkable prophecies Isaiah 53
(Written 800 yrs before Christ)

(5) Remarkable unity. Luke – doctor.
1700 yrs writing. Amos – farmer.
44 diff writers. Isaiah – Aristocrat
Peter – fisherman.

- ii. attitude of God to Sin. 21.

cf. { Gen 3:24. - Isaiah 59 : 1,2.
Rev ~~[illegible]~~. 21:27.

∴ ONE mind behind it.
(Christopher Wren - St Paul's)
(Conductor · Orchestra)

⑥ Way in which it lasts -

Mathew 5: 18.
1 Peter 1 : 25.
- (Jer 36: 20-21. first attempt to destroy the bible)

⑦ Power in world -
i) James 1:21 - make a difference
ii) Acts 20;32. able to save us & build us up.

2 Tim 3:,15. " - Able to make us wise unto salvation" help others.
" a dispenser of the bible."

16/4/61.

SERVICE (from life of Simon Peter) · J. Fletcher

i) Call to service :- Mark 1:17. "fishers of men"
- not merely a selfish enjoyment -

ii) Nature of Service
- Luke 5:10 " thou shalt catch men"

GREAT BIBLE WORDS.

i) **WORKS** Eph 2:8, 9. "By grace we are saved ... not by works"

- good works - the fruits (results) of faith.
  - spring from a true & lively faith.

2. Tim 1:9. - "saved .... not because of works ..."

Titus 3:5. "according to his mercy he saved us".

- Pleasing to God if we are Christians & evidence

" good works follow salvation.

"I cannot work my soul to save
For that my Lord hath done
But I will work like any slave
For love of God's dear son."

ii) **BELIEVE** * John 3:16. "For God so loved the world ...."

Act 5:14. "And believers were the more added to the Lord."

(a) You can believe about. ἐν
(b) You can believe on (into) εἰς
trust in.

|| metaphor
a frozen pond
- will you go onto it?
commit, trust.

* James 2:19. (+20)

"Faith without works is dead".

John 1:12. - a definition " sons of God ... believe on his Name".
receiving =

iii) **BLOOD**. 1 John 1:7. "The blood of J.C (death) cleanses from all sin".

Levit 17:11. Rev'n 1:5. "washed us .... from sins .... in his own blood".

- blood - means that poured out - a life laid down - instead of another - sacrifice

Verses for Conversion.

Admit yr need. Rom 3 v 23
(all have sinned)

Rom 6 v 23
(sin matters)

Believe. why we must Jn 3 vs 16.

Commit. Romans 12 vs 1 & 2.

strength. 2 Cor 12 vs 9

where joy is. Ps 16 vs 11

Ye neither go in yourselves, neither
suffer ye them that are entering to go in

SEE Corinthians B.

Ch 24 vs 42 "Watch therefore: for ye
know not what hour your Lord doth
come.

Ch 25 vs 40 Inasmuch as ye have done it
unto one of the least of these my brethren,
ye have done it unto me.

v 44 "When saw we thee an hungred, or
athirst, or a stranger, or naked, or sick, or in prison,
and did not minister unto thee?"

35.

Verses for Conversion.

Admit yr need. Rom 3 v 23
(all have sinned)

Rom 6 v 23
(sin matters)

Believe. why we must Jn 3 vs 16.

Commit. Romans 12 vs 1 & 2.

strength. 2 Cor 12 vs 9

where joy is. Ps 16 vs 11

Ye neither go in yourselves, neither suffer ye them that are entering to go in

SEE Corinthians B.

Ch 24 vs 42 "Watch therefore: for ye know not what hour your Lord doth come.

Ch 25 v40 Inasmuch as ye have done it unto one of the least of these my brethren, ye have done it unto me.

v44 "When saw we thee an hungred, or athirst, or a stranger, or naked, or sick, or in prison, and did not minister unto thee?"

Sexual Morality.

Romans 13: 13-14.

Romans 14: 13.

1 Cor 5.

1 Cor 6: 12: 13: 15 – 20.

1 Cor 7: 1-2; 9: 25 – 28: 36 – 37.

Gal 5: 16 – 26.

Eph 5: 5.

Col 3: 5.

39

Timing.

Morning Prayers: – 3-5 mins. before or after br'fast

Evening Prayers. 4 possible after Dinner. 5-10 mins.

1962 Morning Prayer – From book.
Mid day,
Thanks at meals.
Evening – Book & More & Reading
Compline.

Sunday – Communion & Read Bk – 1 hr

Sacrifice
Time – 3 hrs a week
Money – 5/- collection
& 1/4 of rest.
& Sunday afternoons.

The battels for this Hilary term have survived and are stamped by the National Provincial Limited, 6 Jun 1961. Some of the major items are: Inclusive charge for Board and Lodging £55.10.0, University and College Dues, £28.4.0, Tuition Fee £25.0. prepayment for T.T. 1961 £25.0.0.
I received £53.4.0 from the Local Authority and paid £25 of the total of £65.8.8 , so £40.8.8 was owing.

To supplement the financial background, I have the cheque book stubs from January to early March, as follows:

21 Jan – Latin Prelims £2
21 Jan – a friend for University Exams (to be paid back) £5
23 Jan – £2-10

8 Feb – £3
22 Feb – £3
1 March coach fare to Lee Abbey (R.Watson) £1-10
1 March Dragon dance £1-5[1]
I seem to have been drawing out very little cash for myself.

The last letter relating to the holidays was written by my mother on 22 April.

My dear Alan,
It seems a long time since we heard, but I expect your exertions in Iwerne have kept you busy and now you'll be back at Oxford, armed with some more of your grant I hope. Granny sent us a large bill so I hope with what she gave you and we sent you were all right, I presume so as we got no word, what about the last term's battels? Let us know what they are, and I'll have to drop a line to the bursar if there's going to be any delay in paying them. As you said in your last letter, the thought of taking a useless but well paid job is odious, but a continual shortage of money is almost more so – its hard to find a compromise! I should think the sort of job that would satisfy and yet keep body and soul and family together would be with one of the U.N. organizations – the British Council or something like that which would give an opportunity to travel as well. But I suppose that sort of job is very sought after. No harm in trying though. … Anne and I seem to be dawdling a bit with our work… Sometimes I feel very confident and at other times quite hopeless, anyway whether she passes the wretched exam or not I cant believe this year has been wasted. In history we seem to be taking a terrible long time sorting out the Rennaisance and the Italian Wars and haven't started Henry VIII yet, admirable as is Mr Fisher, he presupposes knowledge that I haven't got and I have to read each chapter at least three times before I can sort it out! We have nearly finished Jane Eyre and enjoyed it so much that I rather wish we hadn't got to go through it again dissecting and making character studies. … Sorry for such a boring letter, we live such completely different lives at the moment that its hard to find points of interest. I do hope you'll have a happy and successful term and your love life will go smoothly, Juliana sounds enchanting and most unusual, just my sort of person in fact but I wont be too enthusiastic in case its all a Thing of the Past by now.
With much love from us to you from us all, Mummy

Apart from the letters, there are a few remains of the term not concerned with academic work. There are cards for the Worcester College Football Club, where I was playing in at least one or two matches. There is a card for the Worcester College Boat club – where I took no part at all and do not remember watching. There are the services for the Chapel and the talks to the religious Woodroffe Society. There are programmes for 'The Man of Feeling' from the Wadham College Film Group, for March 2-4, and for 'Richard II' at the Playhouse, which I certainly attended. There is the Oxford Union Society Hilary Term programme, but I don't remember attending any meetings. There is a card for an 'At Home' on March 24 for St. Gregory and St Macrina House. This was in Park Town and it is not clear what it was – it states that 'The Companions of the House' are 'At Home', and congratulated me on my election to the Companions. But it now appears to be a guest house and then seems to have been a hostel of some kind. On the back is a note: Thursday 6.0 Sherry party, COSMOS. I may have gone to this U.N. meeting, since there is also a note: 'Dear Robert, Is S. African Boycott official Cosmos policy?' to which there is a reply in another ink: 'Not to my knowledge certainly'. There are also a number of rather abstract drawings on it.

One other thing which is worth noting is that there are several pages of poetry which I laboriously copied out. On 20 February there are ten verses of Keats 'La Belle Dame Sans Merci', a poem I would quote from a couple of months later when writing

[1] A dance at the Dragon School in north Oxford, where I had been a student.

about Julianna S. Undated, but probably from this same term is 'Ode on a Grecian urn' by the same author. I also copied out 'Duncton Hill' by Hilaire Belloc, in March.

Also from this term I believe is 'Rondel' by Swinburne, which I copied into a letter to Juliana S, as described elsewhere. On the same sheet is 'Beauty' by Dante Gabriel Rossetti (A Combination from Sappho). These two poems suggest the kind of pre-Raphaelite mood I was working myself up into.

And as the Spring approached, I copied out a poem by Laurie Lee which was one of my grandfather's favourites. I was reading 'Cider with Rosie' at this time, and the poem, which has remained a favourite, was 'April Rise'.

Other extract from this period were made at the religious retreat at Lee Abbey, briefly referred to in a letter to my mother. These are extracts from "By Searching" by Isobel Kuhn (the missionary to the tribes of Burma). I copied out passages on 'Culture', on Prayer (in response to challenge), on 'Spiritual dryness – the Doldrums' and 'Don't look shocked', and 'Frankness'.

Julie (Julianna): Spring 1961

Julie kept a small diary with sketches during the first couple of months of our time together. Here is one page, May 2nd, to show her hand and a drawing.

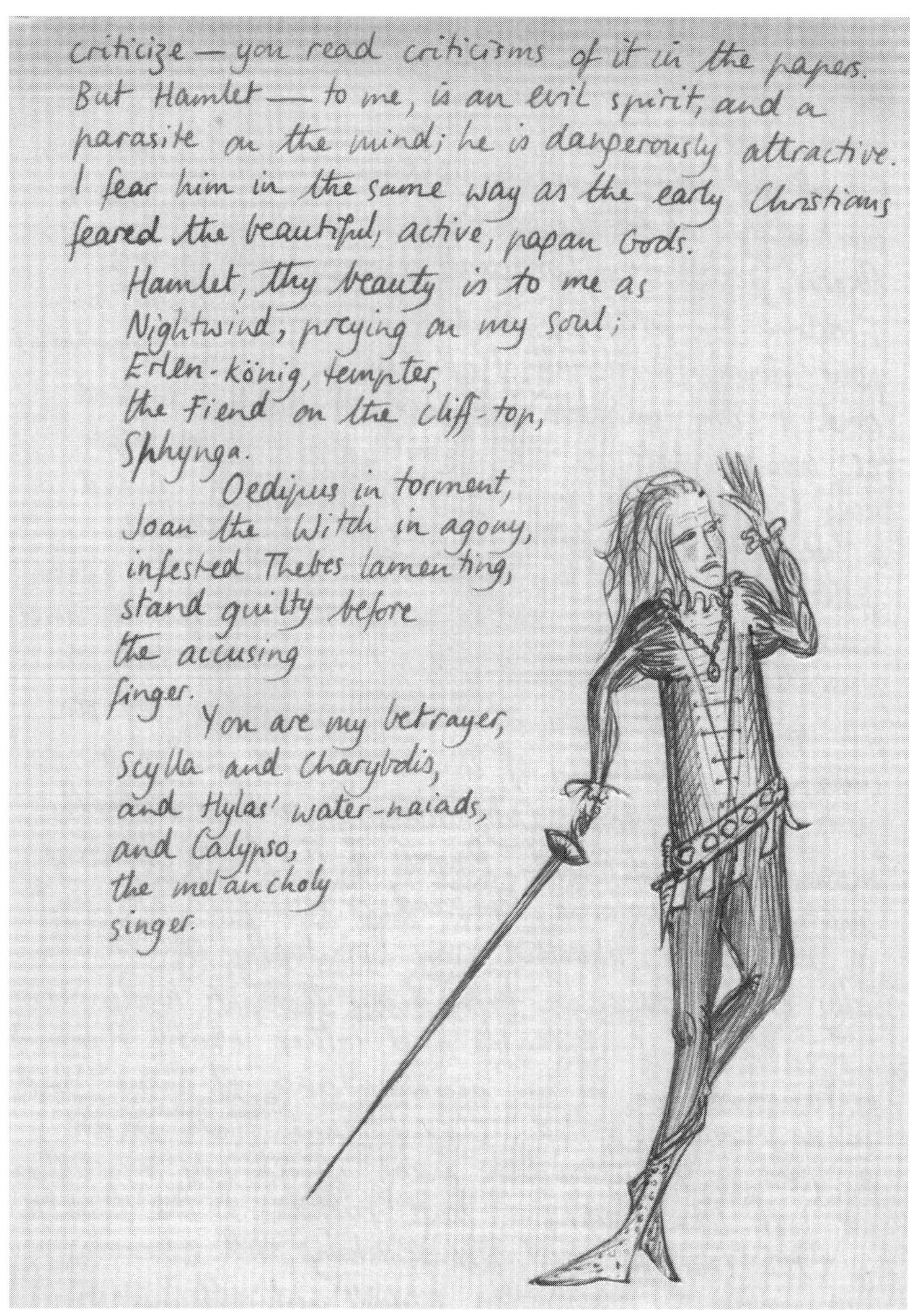

criticize — you read criticisms of it in the papers.
But Hamlet — to me, is an evil spirit, and a
parasite on the mind; he is dangerously attractive.
I fear him in the same way as the early Christians
feared the beautiful, active, pagan Gods.

Hamlet, thy beauty is to me as
Nightwind, preying on my soul;
Erlen-könig, tempter,
the Fiend on the cliff-top,
Sphynga.
Oedipus in torment,
Joan the Witch in agony,
infested Thebes lamenting,
stand guilty before
the accusing
finger.
You are my betrayer,
Scylla and Charybdis,
and Hylas' water-naiads,
and Calypso,
the melancholy
singer.

My relationship with Julie (a.k.a. 'Pusseybite') started in late February or early March 1961, when I was nineteen and a quarter, and she was seventeen and a quarter. We remained friends and in contact until the late 1970s, and have renewed contact again recently. Only the first six months, or so, as I recall was the relationship one of boyfriend and girlfriend; later it mellowed into a deep friendship and finally we both married, I became godfather to Julie's first son Titus, and then we drifted apart after writing frequently to each other for ten years.

The relationship was one of the most important in my life. My first real girlfriend and such an interesting and mature one at that. She introduced me to many worlds of which I had not really known, particularly, as a Hungarian, the world of continental culture including music. She was also interested in the magical world on the edge of ours and shared with me the process of trying to retain some of that magic. I think I shall deal with our relationship mainly chronologically. The period of intensity, the first six months, will be dealt with under those terms and vacations, and then I shall bring in the later letters when they were written.

Julie was a student at St Clare's. This is described on its current website as growing out of a scheme to establish links between British and European students after the Second World War. The original name was The Oxford English Centre for Foreign Students, which later became St. Clare's Hall, and then St. Clare's, Oxford. Since there were very few women's Colleges at Oxford at that time, it was important as a location for potential female friends for undergraduates.

The stage is set by a piece I wrote in April 1961, soon after I met Julie.

"Pusseybite"

"Fade far away, dissolve, and quite forget
What thou among the leaves hast never known,
The weariness, the fever and the fret
Here, where men sit and hear each other groan"

I was sitting idly swilling my feet in the lemon-grey-green water, gazing into the willow-mirroring depths. The tepid water which had so long swept past reed-trembling banks looped-back on itself into the small backwater – and rested. Under the heavily thatched sky the gnats danced and played with the swirling dace. It was a warm grey day in spring when "all the world sweats with bead of summer in its bud". I had escaped from myself all morning by working on my essay but now I was alone "in pensive mood". With the luxury of getting into the smooth cool water on a stinging summer day I let my mind drift off into other worlds, and gradually through the green twilight of roots and bubbles another time and another place opened out before me. It was as if, cleansed and refreshed, I had landed again in solid reality – as a water rat gliding down from the bank reaches the entrance which leads him to his cosy home.

The first time I met her was at Sally Oppenheim's. I had suggested when asked to tea by Sally that she should ask some friends – preferably beautiful ones – as well. Therefore it was with satisfaction that I noticed that there were four tea-cups on the heavily laden central table. Not that I didn't like Sally – she is a honey but – well I won't go into it. Anyhow the first to come in was Gabrielle who though rather too thickly-built was very sweet and had a very pretty face and smile and an engaging habit of just sticking the end of her tongue out and dimpling when she smiled. Then Julie came in. I let out, or rather kept in, a groan. This I remember distinctly – but <u>why</u> I can't really remember – except that in her tight black sweater and purple skirt and "old" hair style she looked rather slinky and sophisticated. She then sat down and perched, hands folded on the edge of a chair and gave her opinions in a rather mincing and affected voice. She was obviously intelligent, and as I heard some of her activities and plans (like that of having a "Road Offences" club to perpetrate as many offences as possible) I thought she was merely trying to be "angry" and so teased her gently. Perhaps the first moment when I felt anything more than interest was when she lay on her front on the floor and, kicking her heels in the air, drunk her tea from a saucer – just to show that she was "beat" in action as well as words – she seemed then somehow to be very childlike. We talked mostly about our sisters & brothers, and Julie raved about her brother Peter who she said she wanted to marry. Anyhow at the end I asked them all round to tea on Sunday.

In the intervening days, I occasionally thought of Julie and Gabrielle in between preparing for my Latin exam. I felt that Gabrielle would be much more my type – but rather to my annoyance it was Julie's rounded freckled face, with its child's mouth and slightly-upturned nose that kept floating into my vision.

The tea-party was rather hectic and generally a pretty ghastly affair and I didn't get much chance to speak to Julie. But strangely I found myself wanting to talk to her, and the pleasant American girl Kathy, with whom I was politely talking, noticed this and asked me (nicely) whether I wouldn't prefer to talk to the rest. I never analysed myself – nor did I have an inkling that something was dragging me towards her – in fact now I come to think of it I think it was magic.

Sally had kindly invited me to go and have tea again on Wednesday and something made me say as she went "same place, same time, same people?!" Anyhow all three were already there when I arrived. Was more at ease now and enjoyed their remarkably intelligent conversation very much, though Gabrielle and myself often smiled at each other when the other two strayed deep into the flowered fields of "Art". Even yet I was unaware of the net that was being drawn round me, a net so gently being tightened. I had earlier made some remark about wanting to see Julie's monstrous-sounding landlady so as we left together she said that I must go and have coffee sometime. Sacrificing time I had meant to spend on my essay I asked her to come and see a play or film that evening – she said she would like to.

Looking back, my mind seems to have been numbed or partly so. I found that there were no good films or plays on at the right time so wasn't quite sure what we should do – and was rather taken back when she suggested that we should just sit and talk. But the time sped away, as she sat demurely and we politely discussed art, religion etc. She almost immediately told me that I was intending to be a priest – Anglican – and then maintained for some time that this would be the ruin of me. I in turn tried to convert her to Christianity – a phrase [sic] through which she had passed at school and now regarded merely as an interesting and rather terrifying – if true – way of life.

It was perhaps on this evening that I first became aware of a sort of battle between our two values of life – and it is only now that I am beginning to realize that the battle is that of personalities – a battle which she is confident of winning and intellectually and even physically (using sensualism) could do no doubt. But the certainty which helps me as I pick myself up after each struggle with her is that she is merely fighting to break down my belief (perhaps unwillingly as Erif Der was used by her father to break down the power and Godhead of Tarrik)[1] – but I have a hold on the Truth, something positive rather than negative, something which has, on the pinnacle of history, fought the final battle with evil. Let me not try to pretend even to myself that I am "better" than Julie in any way – the only difference is that she stands on her own; like Prometheus she challenges the Gods with the force of her own reason, forgetting that that very reason is a part of God. She said to God "Not yet" and sought escape in the realms of Beauty, Literature, and Philosophy. "Across the margent of the world I fled, And troubled the gold gateways of the stars, smiting for shelter on their clanged bars; fretted to dulcet jars and silvern chatter the pale port o' the moon." I pray that one day she will know the truth of these words "Ah, fondest, blindest, weakest, I am He Whom thou seekest! Thou dravest love from thee, who dravest Me." – oh goodness I am suddenly getting very theological! One thing at least we share in common is the joy of being able to laugh at ourselves in our most serious and intense occupations and pleasures! Life is too serious not to be taken as a joke!

After having hypnotized her – or rather she pretended to be – we wandered back. The first few minutes I was bewildered – she told me she was a virgin – to which I wasn't quite

---

[1] Erif Der was the Scythian Spring Queen, and Tarrik the god-king who appear in Naomi Mitchison's *The Corn King and the Spring Queen* (1930).

sure what was the correct reply – should one say "Well done old girl! – dangerous times these – what?" Or "– bad luck – the spring is almost here so don't get too impatient" or some such sympathetic remark? In the end I asked her weakly why she had told me.

It took me some time to lose my shyness, and when I first linked arms I felt a terrible shivering going through me – (no doubt another part of her magic!), and now I was under her spell. It was a misty night – with the moon just glistening through; the cherry trees were in luscious blossom – the whole scene was almost too like a "musical's" love scene to be true. I could almost hear 'angel' choirs singing "Overhead the moon is shining, bright the blossom on the bough; nothing is heard but the song of a bird – filling all the air with singing." (Student Prince). We were both very happy however, and it is an evening I will treasure.

We wandered along the pavements, singing patches of songs "The Owl & the Pussycat" etc & repeated childish poems. It seemed suddenly as I found this girl, still a stranger in most ways, shared many of my loves that a little wicket gate had opened onto the "Secret Garden" of my inner life. Now no longer would I wander alone through the rose-laden paths of Poetry and Music, I had a companion " a limber elf" who could point out many of the hidden beauties of that mysterious world, and whom in turn would gaze in rapture at some of the beauties which before had been too secret to share. Suddenly Shakespeare's sonnet (perhaps Marlowe's) came to exciting life,

"Come – live with me, and be my love,
And we will all the pleasures prove
That hill and valleys, dales and fields,
And all the craggy mountains yields.

There will we sit upon the rocks,
And see the shepherds feed their flocks,
By shallow rivers, by whose falls
Melodious birds sing madrigals.

...

A belt of straw and ivy buds,
With coral clasps and amber studs;
And if these pleasures may thee move,
Then live with me, and be my love.

I still don't know whether any girl can fulfil my utter dreams – and whether any girl would want to. I don't know whether my whole emotionally charged picture of "love" is "a vision, or a waking dream," and if I will find that "fled is that music: – do I wake or sleep?" If I do – in the harsh stage-lights of this world – find that my beliefs grow "pale and spectre-thin and die" I will echo with sadness Caliban's heart-broken cry "when I waked, I cried to dream again, " and with Melancholy dwell – " His soul shall taste the sadness of her might, and be among her cloudy trophies hung." Oh goodness – I am sinking into my "anthropological" mood now!

At last it was time to say goodnight – and largely by her contriving I found myself in her arms with mine in hers too – and then I got a sudden shock. Hardly had our lips met then she was forcing my mouth open and "French-kissing" me. Staggered and slightly dismayed I broke it off. For some strange reason I have never got any special thrill out of this kind of kissing. It may be that it offends my religious scruples – it may be my youthful fear of something being touched by another's tongue (it used to be cups). Anyhow as I had her bike I went home – my mind clouded but whirling with the luscious delight of future anticipation and an evening of happiness – with an invitation to coffee the next day.

I was frightened when I rang the bell that in the daytime we would meet as stranger – and at first I was faintly uncomfortable. Her room was very pleasant – with a mass of Cocteauisms on the wall and she had a gramaphone and some wonderful records, among which I remember especially " Under Milk Wood" & "The Rite of Spring" and a very short snatch of the "Moonlight" which I heard. The whole afternoon (for I stayed till 4.10) merges into my mind into a glorious glow of a first initiation. We sat – me with my back against the bed and she leaning forward opposite me, with our arms around each other gazing into each other's eyes. "If thy mistress some rich anger shows, Emprison her soft hand, and let her rave, And feed deep, deep upon her peerless eyes."

I seem to be afraid of the animal side of love – the striving, barbarous cruel side of passion and as yet get sufficient pleasure out of merely gazing and playing with her face. She told me that I was gentler than her brother, and I expect wanted me to love her more fiercely, but I do not want to plunge straight in, but let each drop of the ambrosial juice swirl and roll over my tongue before I slowly swallow it – to immerse myself by inches into the warmth and delight of Love. As yet I was content to play like a butterfly with her.

"Kissing her hair I sat against her feet,
Wove and unwove it, wound and found it sweet;
Made fast her hands, drew down her eyes,
Deep as deep flowers and dreamy like dim skies;
With her own tresses bound and found her fair,
Kissing her hair."
(Rondel – Swinburne)

I felt she was a fairy – too insubstantial for earthy love till I had somehow found her real. The whole time I have felt that the whole affair was somehow like the poem "La Belle Dame Sans Merci" – this captures the feeling of being bewitched I had and now:

She took me to her elfin grot,
And there she gaz'd and sighed deep,
And there I shut her wild sad eyes –
And kiss'd to sleep.

Oh that I don't
"awake and find me here
On the cold hill side …
Alone and palely loitering.

Again I have wandered into the "forests dim" of Poetry – but if I don't find the track soon I will never get to the end of this!

One other incident I remember especially about that afternoon. Pussy (as I will now call her) went off to have a bath and came back smelling of fresh soap and lavender-water – she was radiant and warm-cold and threw her arms around me. Then we walked arms round each other and joyous, to the Ashmolean.

As I had an essay to write and then went down to Devon for a week I didn't see her for 8 days. During this time – happy at my work in Devon I only missed her occasionally. But I felt keenly that we were split by our different faiths – her's (I think) based on Beauty and Truth – mine on Christ. I felt, perhaps for the first time really in my life the urge to pray and lifted her to God in my prayers – now I can merely trust in His mighty power.

I arrived back for two days in Oxford – two days of bliss – in which I spent nearly all my time with her. It was now that I began to climb the slippery and dizzying paths of sensualism. I discovered the joys of lying with my head pillowed on her breast, my arms stroking her bare arms and back.

Pillow'd upon my fair love's ripening breast,
To feel for ever its soft fall and swell,
Awake for ever in a sweet unrest,

Still, still to hear tender-taken breath,
And so love ever – or else swoon to death.
(Keats – Last Sonnet)

I felt the pain of losing many easy inhibitions which had often sheltered me – I found myself doing things I had mentally condemned other people for and it hurt. But for a few golden hours I was no longer alone – I knew the peace, the rest of being completely myself with someone else. This was helped by a funny little trick we had. As I lay with my mouth often filled with her hair I often felt the urge to say something – but held it back because it sounded silly or too forward. But she would sense my reserves and prompt me to speak my mind – and I would do the same with her. But I don't know whether in her case latches were still undrawn and thoughts and schemes still blanketed. Since these moments of a limited intimacy I have faced many new problems – how much should man be dictated by sensuousness? Is God against physical Love – surely not, my anguished mind cries. How true for instance is the following?

"He that followeth nature goeth not far out of the way. The identification of sexual desire with sin is not only the most morbid and deleterious conception ever invented by our self-torturing brains, but is also a shocking blasphemy against the procreant urge that quickens the whole of our planetary existence. .... Jesus himself, on the few occasions when he gave his attention to such matters, dismissed them with a reserved utterance of magnanimous ambiguity. Is it not the jostling of old forest taboos with the personal morbidities of Paul of Tarsus ..."?

Phrases like the following echo, full of promise, through the long caves of my mind.
"Chastity without charity lies chained in hell. It is but an unlighted lamp. Sensuality is the measure of a man's virtues."
"Bon animal, bon homme" (French proverb)
"... to attack the passions at the root is to attack life at the root. The praxis of the church is inimical to life" (Nietzche)
"... sans passion il n'y a pas de vertu"(Stendhal)

Abstinence sows sand all over
The ruddy flesh and flaming hair,
But desire gratified
Plants fruits of life & beauty there.
(Blake)

(All the above from "Love & Death" – L. Powys)

Again I must extract myself from the tempting side-roads and again pursue my path – this time I hope to the end.

I remember various odd incidents out of those two days – coffees in the Muffin – the time I tripped over a table when leaning forward to kiss her good-morning. Or the black bathing suit which she liked on the travel-poster on the wall – and the little "den" down under the Muffin. And the last afternoon when we wasted precious minutes playing cards – precious minutes before I had to leave for two weeks.

Two weeks of memories – Of three letters – Of waiting for Monday.

I arrived in London two weeks later on a Monday morning and went to see her after lunch. I spent the rest of the day there with them. Vivi – a nice French girlfriend was staying – and together we drew murals and went to see two Italian films in the evening. The three days passed quickly, but they were days of half-awakened hopes and desires, for to save Vivi and others being uncomfortable we had to behave normally with each other. Only occasionally would our hands meet, or as I squatted & drew the mural she leant forward and her breasts touched my head. Sometimes we were alone and then we furtively kissed and parted. I left on the Wednesday evening in a deeply melancholic mood at the thought of two weeks without her and a considerable amount of work to do. But the first bitterness has passed and the future lies (glittering?) ahead.

I have not tried to describe her … the girl I whom I worship – "her beauty of mind and beauty of body" because I couldn't – and even the attempt would somehow be like trying to cage a rare bird. Perhaps Llewellyn P[owys] could have caught something of her magic as he did of Dittany – but I worship and am content.

"O lovely Pussy! O Pussy, my love,
What a beautiful Pussy you are,
You are
You are!
What a beautiful Pussy you are!"
("Owl & Pusseybite")

… slowly my mind whirls back up through the green depths. And I am back on the evening bank, where the last dappling of the dying sun striped the young green willow shoots. Stillness breathes gently and a water-rat slides, velvety, into the darkening water.

It is worth including here one other reaction to the encounter with Julie. The following is a poem which I am pretty sure I wrote. My hunch is based on the fact that several of the words have been crossed through and alternatives suggested. The fairly dreadful quality also suggests that though I attributed it to an 'Arnold Williams' (who Google cannot locate as a poet), it was mine all along.

I can date its composition quite precisely, for it is on a page with the following written at the top:

Books Used.
Essay : Henry II's judiciary and administration – G.O.Sayles – The medieval foundations of England.
I was reading Sayles and doing this essay in early March (about March 9th) 1961. So this, if it is indeed my composition, is one of my first surviving flights of poetry at Oxford.

So it was written exactly during the period in late February or early March when I met Julie. It looks as if it refers to my feelings of being flattened by her brilliance – something I obviously told my parents about and they comment on, as well as describing in the account of our meeting.

"On Domination and Inspiration"

The crushing cushion of a thousand plans
Smother in downy heaviness my restless thoughts
Which heave, pant, shudder, like expiring fish
On the dry sands of a lost individuality.

This mind was green with gentle thoughts
Which laughed with the sun-specked leaves
Of friendship – was full of glades of tiny flowers
Which, minute, unobserved deeds of kindness, blossomed.

This land is dry, is dead, and where once
The rainbow fountains played and stroked
The surface of deeply dreaming pools

A few crusted, brackish smears, sweat death.

Where is the wind? Where the fire?
Where the untamed strength of stallions
Uncurbed by hands which hold
With loose reins of iron?

A mind that was nurtured gently in
The protection of a thousand walls of glass
Now lies exposed, beaten flat by the storm
Scorched by the sun – will it rot – or bloom?

The first letter I have is one from Julie on 18 March, written to Penny, Julie's close friend and someone who would become my serious girlfriend in my last year at Oxford. Penny has returned this to me along with some other letters of Julie's from before and after to me. I will only abstract two short comments from them relating to myself.

6, Winchester Road 18.3.61

.... My brief affair with Pip has come to an end, to my parents' huge relief... At the moment I am going with a very nice Worcesterite called Alan Macfarlane. He went down at the usual time, but returned for this weekend, and we spent a lovely day together to-day (and will spend all to-morrow together too.) I must confess I was awfully pleased to see him, because tho' I don't love him, and probably never will, tho' he loves me, he is very good company, being full of a charming openness of nature and very reliable... My great friend Sally Oppenheim and I are gathering together the last fragments of Oxford manhood for a farewell party on Wednesday... The weather in Oxford has been simply wonderful this past week, and I go for long walks in the country every day. (With the aid of my bicycle.) My favourite route is through Marston fields ... afternoons are spent there, reading Childe Harold and Paradise among the celandines in the thick grass. It's a wonderful life.

The first letter to me is addressed from Julie's home, Denham, Beaumont Rd, London S.W.19 and dated 23 March 1961

My dear Alan,
Thank you for your brief. How kind of me it is to answer you so quickly – esp. because I've just had an extra hot bath and am feeling drowsy. An additional pleasure for you should be the manifestation of trust I have in you, which will be made evident as you peruse this missive, by the fact that the subject matter herein is of a nature so incriminating, that by sending this to you I am laying myself open to any amount of blackmailing, should you ever be so sadistic as to take advantage of it. However, fita voluntas tua.
Here is the briefest account of the developments since you were here.

There follows a two-page account of a prank which Sally and Julie had devised, whereby a number of guests were invited for tea with two people, presumably someone at St Clare's. There are also three small drawings. It ends...

I spent this morning trying to buy black genes. I mean jeans. Unfortunately I couldn't find a pair small enough. Robert taught me a lovely limerick. Do you know it?
There was a young man from St. John's,
Who tried to seduce a few swans.
When out came the porter
Who said 'Take my daughter:
The swans are reserved for the dons.'

Looking v. much forward to seeing you. I miss you too. Honest I do.
With lots of love from Pussybite
[with xxxx Ad nauseam?]

The next letter was written from London on 26 March and includes a number of rather nice drawings, including teddy bears, dogs, and two dolls and self-portrait of Julie.

My dear Alan,

Your anthology didn't have to be forwarded; I read it in between pulling Cocteaux off the walls, and stuffing Ushbati into my pockets… [talk of visit of brother to Oxford, haircut and various doings.]
This evening Vivi & I went for a long walk on the common in the moonlight. It was very beautiful – The heath was blackly barren, its vegetation undulating, slightly so that it seemed to mingle with the rippling black lakes on the horizon, the whole large open expanse forming a formidable and voracious living ocean. The sinister atmosphere was increased by the broken, blackened moon that looked like a leperous wart on the dark serenity of the sky, across which bats flitted; and occasionally owls were seen throwing their clumsy but charming bodies across the open spaces like bumble-bees or fat, nectar-drunk moths.

At the moment I am writing in bed and 'tis almost fairy hour'… By the way, Peter has bought tickets for 'The Lady from the Sea' for the Monday you arrive. Would you like to join us, or take the opportunity to see something at Cov. Gar., or something else? If you tell me in good time we can fix it….

Oh I'm shocking – I wanted to congratulate you on doing so well in your prelims & I quite forgot! Anyway, darling, I'm really delighted about it. Some time I will settle down to writing, and I'd love to attempt the sacred theme of Owly & Pusseybite; it's a good idea. If it is not worthy, I shall burn it in a sacred vessel as happens to most of the things I attempt.

Does 'From Here to Eternity' boast James Dean as its here – or is that 'East of Eden?' Anyway I'd love to have seen it, because I simply adore him after 'Rebel without a cause.'

Darling, this is such a dull letter & I've got absolutely no news at the moment…

I'm looking forward to seeing you on Monday next. Ring as soon as you get here. But you must write soon anyway. I loved your last letter, but next time don't cheat by anthologising. (Althou' it's rather clever & v. impressive, despite your forebodings.) (i.e. Stop it – I like it!) Have a happy & uninhibited fortnight if you can, & think of me a lot. With all my love. Je t'embrasse. Viele küsse. Con d'amore. Pusseybite
P.S. Enclosed are two photos taken at 1½ and 5 respectively. You can't have a recent one: I don't look so nice any more.[1]

The next letter is undated and from 'Denham'. From internal evidence it is written about 28 March, referring to the boat race on Saturday 1 April ahead and my visit to London on Monday 3 April. I shall only type out a little of a long letter written in the early hours of the morning.

My dearest Alan,
….
I was terribly glad to get your letter, and just laughed myself into fits over it. You managed to disguise that nothing had happened to you very well. Everything seems to have happened to me. What happened before Sunday has completely gone out of my mental recess. However Vivi & I spent our most boring afternoon ever at a tea-party given by an ancient school friend…. By the way, we haven't got any tickets for next Monday yet, but are going to see "Jacques" on Thursday. I hope you will still be here. Tuesday we went to tea with Nicky (Julie de la Mare) and later to 'The Witches of Salem… the 'Witches' was simply marvellous. …. This afternoon and evening were rather ludicrous, for in the space of a few hours Viv and I were forced to make the acquaintance of two extraordinary but grotesquely similar women at the Victoria & A. M., and Sadler's Wells respectively. Fat, foreign, middle-aged and didactic, both clad in black, they were, albeit unconsciously excellent parodies of one another, and at the same time, a living example to the young. The opera to-night was unworthy

[1] I have one of these photos still, though it looks a little between those two ages. On the back is written what presumably is Julie's full name – Anna-Petrova Eugenia Elisabeth Julianna S.

of the title, and had nothing more than a fancy dress parade to recommend itself to one's interest. ('The Cunning Little vixen') …
It's 4 now, and I expect morning will soon be gilding the sky, tho' that's not a subject I know very much about.
Why can't you say Fiat voluntas tua? It seems all right to me.
Looking forward to seeing you on Monday, very much.
With fondest love, Pusseybite Basia mille post centum, ad dementiendam xxxxxxoooxxxx
P.S. if you write immediately I shall get your letter before you arrive.[1]

The next letter was written a couple of days after my two-day visit to London, from Denham on 7 April. It is almost all about Julie's doings, so I shall just include a couple of descriptions to show the kind of cosmopolitan and quirky girl she was.

My dear Alan,
Thank you for your prompt letter. [There follows a picture and description of the mysterious lake on Wimbledon Common, which Julie tried to encourage her friends to visit late at night – but which they turned away from. The following day was spent painting, with a visit to the theatre in the evening.]
'Jacques' I found wonderful, despite the adverse criticism it has received, despite the fact that I understand it, as the critics evidently do not (for the most part) and find that there is very little there.… [There follows a recipe for luxurious cocoa]

I have finished 'Sword in Stone' & loved it. The end made me sad too. But – why bring Robin Hood into Arthurian legend? (Altho' I somehow find the constant quotations from Shaks. Permissible.)
[There follows a detailed description and drawing of clothes for a wedding.]
We'll discuss the poems & books when we're together – tho' you must neither place great confidence in my interpretation nor in my choice of pertinent books. … Good-bye darling, sorry this is such a short letter, but I really am too tired to write any more. I hope to see you all on Tuesday. With all fondest love from your Pusseybite. Kisses & Hugs.
Sunday Morning. I kept forgetting to post this… we wandered into the Soho underworld. Only two years ago I was secretly frightened to walk there even with my parents after the theatre. Now, however, I feel as safe there as in my own house. We met some interesting C.N.D. types at the Partisan with whom we discussed politics (they were socialists) and we spent the evening wandering round with them.… In case your pédé friend doesn't happen to know, the place where he'll meet the "Gayest" types is the "Glock" (i.e. the Gloucester Arms) which is wedged in the middle of that little passage leading from Gloucester Green to Elliston's. I believe the leading Chelsea meeting-place is Troubadour. Did you notice any "gay" types when you were there? …
By the way, calm your fears: Vivi liked you very much, as did all my family, and she was touched by the gift of Cleopatra. …. Love Love Love Love Love Pusseybite

The next letter was written from London on Sunday 16 April, and illustrated with three small drawings.

Dearest Alan,
Thanks for your letter. As you see, I sent you a t/gramme on Thursday; for having taken your intention of coming to London on Tues. as a fixture, I was somewhat worried at having heard nothing of you. You certainly sounded a bit depressed in your last letter. Perhaps the healthy homely Christian atmosphere was lacking in amusement? [a reference to the V.P.S. camp] I love the idea of your sweeping – it reminds me of the little Italian street-sweeper whom Axel Munthe saw among the blessed in heaven. (He's sweeping star-dust with a little broom made of the angel-feathers he's managed to find.) [small drawing of the same.]

How funny that you should begin studying Satanism just as I am giving it up! Yes – I had a final meeting with my witch-friend (under Peter's supervision) last Tuesday afternoon. Peter is so determined in his efforts to break me away from these people, that he has really left me no option but to promise I will have nothing more to do with Black Magic. No – now don't jump up & get prematurely excited about the mysterious way in which

---

[1] There are four rather delightful drawings; two of cats and two of cats in human clothes of an antique kind.

God works – this is not the first step in the answer to your prayer: in fact I am now more determined than ever not to allow myself to take the easy way of Christianity. With me it would merely be escapism.

Sally came to tea this afternoon. She helped me with the mural &, I regret to say, quite ruined Venus, & turned the beautiful low-breasted woman into a red-Indian. Apart from this unfortunate set-back it is going very well. … [accounts of various parties etc., learning words of dirty songs, dress for a party.]
I haven't done any work yet, except write a rather dull story which I am going to send to a few women's magazines in the hope that one of them will print it. ….
St Clare's have not yet said where I will be staying, but I am coming up next Sunday, & will let you know very soon. Write back immediately. You have my permission to indulge in amusing galanteries so long as you remain faithful in spirit! I shall expect to hear a minute-by-minute confession! Fondest love, darling. I am very much looking forward to seeing you, Pusseybite xxxxx

Thursday [20 April] London.

My Dear Alan,
Thanks for your letter. This is just going to be a short note, principally to tell you that my address is 378, Woodstock Road, where I shall have a single room, with three other girls in the house. Alan – you child – what precautions have you taken against my magic? Of course love potions spells exist (and their efficacy is highly dubitable) but do you, pray, see me getting up in the middle of night to collect stinging nettles from graveyards, or slitting the throats of unfortunate little mammals so as to drink the bloody brew? I have not looked up the scriptorial references, as you no doubt wished me to, nor do I intend to, but I will explain what I meant re. 'the easy way of Christianity' when we meet.

So glad you like 'Corn King…' it's one of the books that influenced my thought & actions for years. I'm bringing 'Dorian Gray' for you to read. It'll break your heart. I'm bringing some records back, too, tho' not Fischer-Dieskau, as they all belong to Peter. …. If you go to Blackwell's, could you get me the nicest copy of Gide's 'Les Nourritures Terrestres' in the French department, & put it on my account? (Under the name of Julianna S, St Clare's Hall.) You could take this letter, or they might doubt your authority, in which case I'd have to wait till Monday.

Jitters about next term? I've got enough to worry about re. my lodgings – my room – the girls there – whether I can use my gramophone – stay out all night – get on with my landlady – have boys in my room – so I must say I'm not in the least worried by the idea of seeing you (Which I shall expect to do on Saturday at 3.0 p.m. my room.
A bientôt!
Con multo amore etc
Julie & Pusseybite xxxxxxx

Academic Work: Spring 1961

This seems to have been the term when we consolidated our knowledge of the Anglo-Saxons and moved on to Edward I, in other words up to 1215. Then in the following vacation I started to cover the period 1216-1307, as well as writing a very long essay on Norman Scotland. There was also some revision of Bede, probably as a preparation for the Latin prelim exam which I was re-taking. I was also getting some intensive coaching in Latin with the later distinguished political philosopher and expert on Marx, David McLellan, then aged in his twenties. Fortunately, I finally passed.

This work on Anglo-Saxon England and the Normans and Angevins covers a period that has always really interested me since – in relation to the origins of modernity – so it will be good to see what I read and thought.

At the start of the term, I did some 'collections' or informal College exams. There is a set of essays entitled 'English I', with marks and comments, which I shall include. My answers covered six sides of paper.

The first essay I chose was:

4. 'By what means did the kings of the C7 and C8 maintain their authority over their kingdoms.' I wrote two pages and received the following mark and comment: 'B. Some good points. But this is a terrible jungle, full of muddles and opacities. The first paragraph alone is a ragbag of things which as they stand are half-truths.' The next essay, on 'Assess the part played by the monasteries in the establishment of English Christianity' received the same mark and was 'Very badly arranged'. The third essay, was 'During the century after the Conquest the feudal host was never the main source of the Crown's military strength.' After labouring for nearly three pages I was given a gamma plus – a terrible mark – with a note ' 'You've missed the point. See J. O. Prestwich, 'War and Finance in the Anglo-Norman State', T.R.H. 1954'. Fortunately my last essay, on '"The common counsel of the realm is something the king has reason to fear". Is this true of the C13?' was considered to be better, getting a mark of Beta plus 'Though again muddled.'

The final mark for the whole exam was Beta minus, with the comment 'You remember quite a lot, but half-remember more. You argue perceptively at times and with miserable disorder at others. If you can write more clearly and more calmly you will do much better than this.'

Looking at the essays, this was perhaps a little harsh; James Campbell was young, brilliant and keen and only about seven years older than I was. But it fortunately did not daunt me, and later in the term and year I managed to win the longed-for approval.

There is also a short essay on 'Feudalism' on 12 January. I had arrived back in Oxford on Tuesday 10 January, and this was written just before term began. Perhaps it was for my own purposes, as there is no mark on it. On the same day, perhaps again as preparation, I wrote 'A Survey of English History' (420-1066). This consists of six pages of writing, divided into six chapters. It looks like a synthesis of my vacation reading.

As for other teaching, there is evidence that I was going to a set of lectures by R.W. Southern on 'England and the Continent 650-1150'.

Essays during the term

Essay 1: I began plans for an essay on 'Discuss the view that most significant development in the Church in England between 664-900 (are those which) reflect the pressures put on it by the political needs of the kings.' I had begun to take notes and plan the essay on Friday 13 January and continued on the Saturday, Sunday and Monday, taking twelve pages of notes and finally writing an essay on Tuesday 17. Again there is no mark.

Essay 2: A week later, on 19 January, I made 12 pages of notes, and on the same day wrote a long (5 and a half pages of foolscap) essay on 'Discuss the nature of the power of the Mercian Kings.' There is no mark and no comments. This was one of the pieces of work I mentioned to my mother in a letter.

Essay 3: On Tuesday 24 January I started to take notes for an essay entitled 'Discuss the Value of A-S [Anglo-Saxon] Poetry to the Historian.' There are eight pages of notes from Dorothy Whitelock, an edition of Beowulf and other works, but no essay, though there is a detailed essay plan

Essay 4: On Monday 30 January I took extensive notes for a review of E. John's recent book, Land Tenure in Early England which had only been published the year before. I then wrote a five-page essay on this.

[NOTE This review, like most of those in magazines and papers, is designed as an aperatif, an invitation for those who have not read the book.]

30/1/61

Essay 4.

A. Macfarlane.

1

A review of John's "Land Tenure in Early England"

That a new co-ordination and analysis of important A-Saxon tenurial problems was urgently required has been shown by Professor John's latest book. In this collection of essays he propounds many stimulating and often novel interpretations. Many of the accepted views put forward by giants such as Chadwick, Stenton and Maitland are fiercely contended and the weight of the documentary evidence makes the challenge a serious one. In this complex, closely argued and scholarly book we have many precious veins of thought, though they may often be obscured by over-complicated phrasing. For the author using the new evidence of the Red Book of Worcester and studies in Vulgar Roman law, tightening the links between England and the late Empire, and hopes to give at least a more plausible explanation of the relations between king and subject in an age when there is so little direct evidence, and conjecture takes the place of fact.

Rising out of the mass of documents and arguments there emerge about seven main conclusions. John maintains firstly that "it does not seem possible to avoid the conclusion that English book-right borrowed its leading notions (as well as its form) from the Vulgar Roman law, and that the origin of book-right in England represents the insular equivalent of that early reception of Roman law from which Mr Levy has convincingly derived the early tenurial law of the barbarian kingdoms." This is in sharp contrast to the widely accepted view that there was a complete divorce between the Latin originated form of book-right and the Germanic origins of the law.

His next step is to support Maitland's theory that the fiscal and justiciary rights conveyed by book-right, are more aptly described as "superiority" than "landownership" as Chadwick and Aston have called it. The difference is in views not only in words. For 'superiority' implied that the tangible rights of book-land consisted of the "diversion of the products of taxation to a favoured subject"; Maitland's critics, however, had been forced to minimise the importance of the feorm. John agrees that the main difference between folk-land and book-land lies in the "intangible rights of free disposition and perpetual possession." But he will only go this far with the accepted view. In this next chapter he attacks the previous balance which swung towards the importance of free disposition, for it was based on a conception of early Germanic custom as having very strict rules of donation. This traditional view is summed up in the quoted extract from Vinogradoff "The folkland is the holding of an individual which is governed by the ancient folkright and therefore subject to restrictions which tend to preserve it as a family estate ....". Therefore, according to the accepted view, the aim of landowners in getting book-right was to "give the sitting tennent a power of choosing his heir - denied him under folk-right ... the "ius perpetuum" was a relatively unimportant concomitment.

John however argues first that literary and narrative evidence suggests that early English law

* did not know of any unrestricted (see p 48) donation ... and that book-right was intended to create for the Church at first, a perpetual and unrestricted tenure of land." In fact according to John "the evidence suggests that book-right took land into the family not out of it;" that book-right created "ius-perpetuum" and so revolutionized the tenurial system by strengthening the precarious hold of landowners on their property.

John then spends a chapter showing that Stevenson's theory, that the three burdens of bridging, repairing of fortifications and the "fyrd" which were definitely imposed by Offa's reign were there "ab initio" though not mentioned, is false. The final conclusion he comes to is that the first two of these burdens were imposed during Aethelbald's reign by about 750 AD and "fyrd" service probably in Offa's reign. It may be disputable but it is challenging.

Here the author ends his more general approach and turns to study a specific set of charters, their authenticity and the light they throw on the broader problems of A-S land tenure. Again challenging Stevenson he maintains that the "Altitonus" charter and the even more dubious "indiculum" ascribed to St Oswald are not completely spurious and can be used with care as evidence. The first conclusion he draws from their evidence is that "the hundred's well-known judicial and administrative functions must be set in a much more important military context than hitherto." Another conclusion is that "it seems hardly possible that any tenurial revolution, any original feudalism, can be put down to Norman influence." His interpretation attacks the commonly accepted theory of a serious break mainly by William's invasion between pre and post conquest England.

Finally the author in a brief attack on the "evidentiary" school maintains that Anglo-Saxon charters were not merely written witnesses to the transactions they record (as propounded by Galbraith and Hazeltine) but also "dispositive" instruments. And that their dispositive function was the primary one.

Essay 4. A review of John's "*Land Tenure in Early England*" A. Macfarlane.

His conclusions therefore are challenging, and will constitute a serious advance in Anglo-Saxn studies if they are based on convincing evidence and are the logical conclusions of this evidence. John realizes the impossibility of proving "up to the hilt his thesis" the strongest he can say of the one of theirs on The importance of the "ius perpetuum" as an intangible right - is that "it is a plausible thesis, that it is compatible with the scanty evidence, and that it illuminates some difficult places in Early English history. Because the evidence is scanty most of it may be dismissed as possibly untypical, but the arm of coincidence must be stretched far to make this possible. The thesis set forth here squares precisely with the charter formulas; it takes the charters to mean what they say; and it interprets them more completely than its rivals." There is not time or space to examine his reasoning and illustrations in detail, but we can decide in a general way, on each of his conclusions whether the author has put forward a serious case or not.

Professor John examines the early charters and shows fairly convincingly that "only in a limited sense do the charters employ stereotyped formulas - at least the early ones" in parts they mean what they say. From this he deduces that their common legal background was "the creation of a ius perpetuum" - but that is also the background to the vulgar law of the Empire. Two other connecting factors between vulgar Roman law and English book-right are the use of the word "facultas", a piece of jargon which was used even by Bede, and the right of manumission common to English book-right and the Vulgar law. With considerable references to charters this is the foundation of John's first theory - on the borrowing of legal notions from the vulgar law. It is a highly attractive case.

His main argument, and it seems to me a strong one, against the theory of Maitland that "In all probability the folk-law of this early period knows no such thing as testamentary power. Testamentary power can only be created by the words of a book" is that in Stenton's own words "royal charters which are earlier than the C10 rarely contain any provisions definitely governing the descent of an estate or the conditions of its tenure". Why should laymen take such pains to get book right if it did not record any interference with the traditional rules of inheritance - as long as this was their principal motive (as the scholars maintain) Another argument, that it was hereditary right or "ius perpetuum" that was given to the fraudulent abbots when they bought monasteries. He quickly mentions other ~~diffi~~ obstacles to the accepted view – no trace of endowment by magnates; (the silence of Bede except on royal enrichment), and the fact that it was taken for granted that all monasteries were family monasteries. Finally in the form of the charters he sees that the protection of the anathema is against later kings not against the family of the grantee. Therefore the aim of the donation is keep the land in the family to strengthen the precarious nature of the tenure against the king, not to escape from family restrictions. It is a strong argument, and certainly deserves to be answered (if it can be) by the advocates of the previous theory.

His chapter on the Imposition of Common burdens on the church is ingenious, plausible but precarious, for it needs ~~possibly~~ only one document before 749 mentioning a common burden to destroy the whole thesis. John easily dismisses Stevenson's general argument that "liability to military service and repair of fortresses are such primitive requirements ... that is unlikely that they were suddenly imposed" by a swift reference to the Frankish Empire where this is exactly what happened. John as a basis for his alternative hypothesis attempts with some success to prove the validity of CS 178 which Stevenson had dismissed as untrustworthy. He then shows that although by CS 178 (749) two of the burdens were specifically mentioned "fyrd" service was not, nor do Boniface or the Worcester charter mention it. His main argument against the "ab initio" imposition of "fyrd" service is Bede's letter to Egbert and an explicit statement of Bede Bk III ch 24 (III possessiunculis terrarum ... " denying "fyrd" service.

This re-examination of charters to decide their validity is one of John's main devices to support his contention. The extreme case of this is the Altitonantis and "indiculum" in relation to the Oswaldslow charters. Although John's use of these charters is brilliant it seems at times as if he is perhaps overstretching his conclusions. For example he spares no pains ~~to~~ trying to prove a general validity for the Altitonantis CS 1135 although he is forced, though, to admit that the anathema is "quite exceptional", the witness list has nothing "very seriously objectionable in it" ~~and~~ that is all probability of genuine the dating clause the foundation of the whole charter is "the earliest example of Annunciation dating in Charters by nearly a century;" – but he concludes by saying that the bulk of CS. 1135 may be used cautiously by the student.

Essay 4. A-Saxon.

A review of John's "*Land Tenure in Early England*". A. Macfarlane.

John's views then are based largely on minute charter examination and interpretation, and indeed it cannot be denied, as he himself maintains, that most of his theories seem to fit the stated meaning of the charters exceptionally well. His usual method of argument is to state the current view, show how this contradicts or leaves unexplained many features of the charters, and then puts forward an alternative view. This view though largely culled from charter sources also comes from narrative sources and poetry (especially in his highly attractive theory on the precarious nature of early tenure, with its classic example in the oration of Widsith). Sometimes for lack of evidence he uses a method which he calls "retrogressive method from the known to the unknown." His attacks on the mistakes of other historians vary from the penetrating "Sir Frank Stenton basing his view on his idea of book-right and partly inferring the nature of book-right from his view of early English society." to the almost vitriolic "Round was always better than most of us at not seeing awkward evidence, and he failed to notice ....."

The task of the reader is not made easier by the rather dry and involved style of writing, though it is perhaps well suited to the subject matter. It is probably petty to point out linguistical mistakes in such a work of scholarship, but a sentence such as "there are pointers to show what all this naval business was about" has an unpleasant ring to it, and the author's continual misuse of the word "suspicious" when he means "suspect" in the last few chapters is perhaps unfortunate.

The very smallness of these criticisms however will only serve to magnify the splendid contribution of John. He has presented a book which, although for the most part only providing highly plausible alternative interpretations incapable of real proof, will probably produce a revolution in A-Saxon studies. It is a brilliant, scholarly, minutely detailed and challenging work.

Campbell's comments. That's very good. - a fair and clear criticism - well done

Essay 5: I did another essay on the same topic, but covering a later period, for I have twelve pages of notes on the topic 'What difference did the Norman conquest make to the tenure of land by the nobility and king?' The essay I presumably wrote is missing. This is dated 1 February.

Essay 6: There is another essay on 'Discuss the relation between Church & State (900-1066)'. There are some pages of notes, and the essay plan is dated 8 February. There are no comments on this long, six-page, essay. This is undated, but must be around 8 February.

Essay 7: is undated, and was on 'What were the main threats to the Conqueror's rule in England and how effectively did he met them?' I have the essay plan, – but no date. It must have been about 15 February.

Essay 8

I have both extensive notes and a long essay (ten pages on smaller paper) on 'What light do the succession of Henry I and Stephen throw on the balance of political power in their period?' This seems to have gone down well as I have written in a comment, 'Good – that's admirable. You have sorted it out well.' I seem to be progressing. This must have been about 21 February

There may have then been a gap, perhaps for my Bede revision and preparation for the Latin prelims.

Essay 9: 'What were the strengths and the weaknesses of the royal administration and system of justice under Henry II?'

On Monday 8 March I started to take notes (10 careful pages, complete with diagram of the Exchequer) for an essay on one of the greatest of English kings, Henry II for Essay 9.

① 9/3/61.

ANGEVIN. "What were the strengths and the weakness of the royal administration
(1) and system of justice under Henry II ?"

Henry II came to the throne after an interim of anarchy. The country had learnt its lesson from weak government and it was ready for a strong rule, provided there was peace and efficiency. The wide extent of the Angevin Empire and hence the necessity of the king's prolonged absence also required the early restoring of a centralized and powerful administration and justice. The first step to this was the destruction of the independent and localized power held by many of the turbulent barons. The Coronation Charter, though very short, guaranteed peace and hereditary right, then Henry, having disbanded the mercenaries, resumed many of the royal demesnes, recklessly granted away by his predecessor. He suppressed most of the earldoms and destroyed the "adulterine castles", of which there were rumoured to be over 1,000. Three more measures of reform consolidated the king's power. The overhaul of military feudalism in 1166 (a new feudal assessment in which Henry raised the "servitium debitum" of those who had already enfeoffed too many knights) and also made sub-tenants do him homage as liege lords. By the Assize of Arms (1181) Henry reconstituted the fyrd and finally (leaving out for the moment the "Inquest of Sheriffs) within a few years the King succeeded in suppressing the overweening & localist justiciars, thus making possible the developement of the system of the itinerant justices.

Before Henry's reign jurisdiction lay largely in the hands of either the old shire courts or the new feudal & franchisal courts of the aristocracy: so despite the royal nomination of sheriffs, the inauguration of eyres, justice - especially criminal and possessory - was independent of the King. But the King's right as "preserver of the peace" to interfere in justice was indisputable. It is the great strength of Henry's justice that he presented a cheaper, safer, swifter, more equitable way of settling both civil and criminal cases. By the increased use of justices on eyre, the developement of the writ "praecipe" (which removed actions peremptorily and immediately to the royal courts) the King withdrew power from the local and baronial courts. In cases of possession the use of the jury decision in the Assizes of "Novel Disseisin, Mort D'Ancestor, Darrein Presentment & Utrum" was so preferable to the previous feudal methods that an increasing flow of business was attracted to the circuit justices and to the developing central court - at Westminster. Increasing business brought increasing fines and this in turn helped the administration.

Ultimately the test of the strength of the royal system of justice lay in its measure of centralization - and this was developing swiftly in Henry's reign. Although eyres had been held before 1166 the Great Assize of Clarendon gave this great impetus. By 1170 there was an almost complete circuit system in operation - although actually there was as yet a continual process of adjustment and change. (as demonstrated by the arrangements of 1176 (6 circs) & 1179 (4 circs). The real significance in relation to the strength of the royal justice is obvious. The justices were mostly from the court of exchequer, thus with their increasing duties - judicial and administrative - including a vital supervision over local govt officials - they helped to bind the local courts to the king's justice. Again Henry's almost complete success in 1170 in breaking the power of those noblemen who had acquired shrievalities was a source of immense strength both to the administrative and judicial power of the King. Instead of independent, over-powerful and unscrupulous barons there were in the localities a considerable number of officials appointed by the Crown and carefully supervised by it through the itinerant justices on the judicial side - and by an increasingly competent and inquisitive Exchequer on the administrative. Instead of a source of weakness the sheriffs, their work increased, but their independent power decreased were a source of strength.

It is easier to point to the strengths than the weaknesses of justice under Henry II. Nevertheless there were still gaps left for his successors to fill, though his success was enormous. A basic weakness in royal justice in the broadest sense was the absence of an effective police force. The volume of crime was enormous, and although we cannot blame Henry for their absence, it is undoubtedly true and noteworthy that the whole system of detection, arrest and even procedure was inadequate in this age of violence. For though Henry introduced more extensively the use of the jury - in the words of Bracton "no one may be convicted of a capital charge by testimony". Purgation, ordeal and combat were still used - but there was evidently a waning faith in these methods, witness the article in the Assize of Clarendon ordering accused men of very bad reputation - even if successful in the ordeal - to be banished from the country. It was only in 1215 that trial by ordeal was finally condemned.

A serious gap during Henry's reign in the royal system

ANGEVIN.

"What were the strengths and the weaknesses of the royal administration and system of justice under Henry II?"

was in the sphere of ultimate right of ownership. This was still determined by a slow, cumbersome and tedious process (see the case of Richard Anesty) - for a proprietary action was recognized as properly the province of the feudal court. The use of "essoins" such as illness or the Crusade, conflicting evidence etc might make a case drag on for months after a general Eyre. But this was merely a temporary weakness for later the efficient and speedy petty assize of "novel disseisin" replaced the "Grand Assize" as the method of determining ownership (as well as possession).

Many of the sources of strength in justice were also sources in administration. For instance the subordination of the sheriff to the control of the central government, so that he became the executive agent of Henry's will, the link between central and local government, and an obedient middle-class official who served writs, summoned juries, arrested culprits, executed judgements, and collected taxes rendered to the exchequer twice a year - made centralized administration possible. The similar way in which the itinerant justices strengthened the king's administration is also evident. So far however we have only dealt with the connections between the central administration and the localities, it was to a large extent the growth of the Exchequer, necessitated by the increased flow of business which gave strength to the king's administration.

The Exchequer, both a financial bureau and a court of law was the quarters of a staff of clerks engaged in writing writs. The whole of the "Dialogus" illustrates its importance, especially financially speaking, in the twice yearly collections of the accounts & revenue from sheriffs. Even in the king's absence the Justiciar as its head could issue writs under his name and seal, and take every kind of decision. The smooth working of the administration, apart from the scheming of John & unpopularity of William Longchamp in Richard's absence, is evidence of the strength of the system. Again the strength of the administration is apparent, but the weaknesses are less so.

On the whole they were minor and often inevitable ones. For instance the shortage of documents concerning how much was owed by various shrievalties, or by whom land was owned. The Red Book of the Exchequer says that "there was no sum of the county in any roll of Henry II or King Richard - till his 8th yr".

The Domesday Survey though invaluable was obviously often out of date. Another minor weakness was the lack of seperation between the exchequer and "curia regis" for though one was and administrative and one a judicial council they often had an almost identical personell. Again it might easily be maintained that the risings during Richard's absence - though encouraged by his sale of offices to the rich and powerful - shows that the sheriffs had not lost their independence completely. It is interesting to notice one way in which they had managed to retain too much authority, for the 1194 instructions forbids a sheriff to act as itinerant justice in his own county. In 1176 no fewer than 8 out 18 justices apt'd at Northampton in that year gained this double power.

Finally we must not forget a source of considerable weakness in both the justice and administration of the King; this lies in the few shires which retained considerable indepence from royal power, especially the county Palatinates of Chester and Durham. ①

There had been no deliberate attempt to eliminate feudal jurisdiction, though there had been to eliminate most baronial administration - but this does not mean that the King had no scheme behind his actions. He meant to hand on a strengthened and centralized kingdom to his son, and despite minor weaknesses and the baronial discontent which spasmodically flared up in reaction to these reforms Henry was extremely successful.

i) Possession
ii) Procedure under inditement - King got much more money.
- an indited man's chattels goes to King.
iii) Not sufficient account of the quantity of litigation.
- no account of development of C't of Common Pleas.
- justices more trained - Glanville.
- good favour needed to get a writ.
- use of pipe rolls
- how much money to King. - enormous amount of writs.
iv) Justices extortionate. - but they didn't buy the office.

① Palatinate of Chester. pamphlet of Barraclough

The notes for this essay are very neat and methodical. There are six foolscap pages of notes on G.O. Sayles 'The Medieval Foundations of England', chapter xxi, two pages of notes from chapter xii of A.L. Poole, From Domesday Book to Magna Carta' and two pages of note (with a large diagram) from the introduction and text of the 'Dialogus de Scarrio' edited by C. Johnson.

I also made a detailed "Chronological Table" (616-670) – in relation to my work on Bede and there were various other pieces of work on Bede. For example, on 22 February there was 'Bede – Revision'. I revised a whole lot of topics, such as the Easter Controversy, the Results of the Synod of Whitby, made plans for an essay on 'What does Bede tell us of Mercia – its achievements & organization in his Third Bk?' A couple of days before I was also making summaries of his third book. It may be that this was all in preparation of doing my Latin Prelims exam again. There are more than thirty pages of notes at this time.

Essay 10: This must have been right at the end of term. The essay was titled 'The first three Angevin kings neglected England for the sake of their continental possessions.' Discuss.' I have the ten-page (on small paper) essay, with some pages of notes and an essay plan. There is no comment.

We were clearly under some pressure, with ten essays in the eight weeks of term, three or four sets of lectures at least, Bede and Latin revision. But the comments suggest that I was enjoying the work and getting involved and gaining in confidence.

Work in the Easter Vacation

The most impressive piece of work is the Vacation Essay which I handed in at the end of the Spring Vacation (on the Normans in Scotland). I commented on it in one of my letters to my mother. The notes for the essay start with two detailed maps and then thirty-two pages of notes. The Essay plan is four pages long and notes that I hope to write parts A and B on Saturday and then parts B and C and the conclusion on the Monday.

I had mentioned to my mother that the essay was seventeen pages long, but in fact it is twenty, including a detailed genealogy of the descendants of Malcolm I. James Campbell has written in some quite detailed comments and suggestions throughout the text.

He was clearly interested in the subject and liked the essay. He wrote the following long comment on the essay in pencil, in a minuscule hand, as was his wont.

> 'Beta +++. A good and methodical essay. Your use of extracts from the sources is admirable. It is a pity that you did not have more time to investigate the church and the towns. They cannot properly be left on one side as distinct subjects. In Scotland, as in England in the 10c, the lavish endowment of royal monasteries was a means to as well as an expression of royal power. It was easier to introduce monastic tenants than it was to introduce laymen. David I, if we are to believe Knowles, was the greatest monastic founder of his day. In the case of towns economic development made it possible to create a strong support for royal power out of almost nothing. The development of the wool-trade was probably more important to the kings of Scotland in the 13c – 12c than it was even to the kings of England.'

As well as this long essay, I also did some quite extensive reading and note-taking during the holiday. There are some sheets headed HOLIDAY WORK Easter 1961. These start with 'Facts 1216-1307', which would prepare me for the following terms work. These were mainly taken from Powicke's work on English medieval history. I also took notes from other, less impressive, works such as Bryant's popular 'Makers of the Realms'. In all, some 20 pages of notes.

Summer Term 1961

My first letter from Oxford was written on Monday 24 [April]

Dear Family,

I've been in such a rush over the last week I can't remember whether I've had a letter from Mummy this week – but I definitely had one from Fiona when I arrived back from Iwerne – thank you very much "Fee". Before I forget I will try and find out soon about the "Ruskin" art school for Fiona – all I know about it, is that it is considered to be quite good, but one suspects that many of the students (mostly girls) come largely for the "Oxford" social life – naturally one can tell them by their "ultra-arty" clothes from a considerable distance!

I arrived back at Oxford on Tuesday after a very enjoyable and (spiritually) refreshing week and immediately had to start preparing for "beginning of term" exams. Unfortunately however my detailed calculations were thrown out by the tutor setting the exam on the day before that on which we expected it. I am slightly worried that I may have to do it <u>again</u>, for although I knew all the laws, treaties etc I had no idea of the sequence of events or the careers of individuals. It was a purely factual paper and <u>all</u> the 30 questions were compulsory, and so I was completely stumped by several – and in those like "name and date all the archbishops of Canterbury in the C13" – I just made up facetious remarks as answers – and I'm told this tutor doesn't like that! I went to see my new tutor (Karl Leyser in Magdalene – supposedly brilliant) this morning and he was most charming – and even offered me a sherry! (He is taking me for European History 1494-1648)

Julie came up to Oxford on Saturday and I have seen quite a bit of her since then. I am rather worried that I will fall really seriously for the girl, for although it would be lovely in some ways, its much too early for me to get <u>really</u> keen on a girl. But whatever happens it will be an absolutely glorious summer if things go well, as we share hundreds of mutual interests – and she is charming and lively company.

Our first venture out together however was not in some ways a great success – but the fact that we both treated it as very amusing is perhaps a good sign! We set out up towards "The Trout" – along the canal, with a picnic lunch. Naturally when we had gone about 2 miles it started raining lightly – so we ate our lunch on a bench under a tree – beside the main road! Then it started raining hard, and the cars splashed past and the people in them smiled in either a sympathetic or superior way – I must say it must have looked rather pathetic – us sitting huddled under a tree! I guessed at the time that someone I knew was bound to see us – and sure enough on Sunday morning the College <u>Chaplain</u> came up to me and said "You really did look pathetic sitting out by the level-crossing with your arm around that girl!! – it <u>almost</u> made me embarrassed

I am enclosing the college battels – but will pay £25 of them out of my Lancashire grant. Re this, I am feeling rather guilty about something I have done so will get it off my chest now. In a rash moment (actually I had thought about it longingly for a long time) I went and exchanged my guitar for a better one. I won't go into the tremendous difference it makes to the tunefulness of my renderings – (but I do feel much more ready to take it on the river than the other tinny one). The difficulty is that the difference was £11 – this is why I am only offering to pay £25 out of my grant. Of course I will pay it back to you when I sell the boat – or when I get a job – and you owed me about £6 I think. But I still feel guilty because I know how we are at a very difficult point. I do hope you will be able to manage the £40. I will be preparing myself for your rebukes meantime!

I hope everything is going well – and that you all prosper in your various occupations. What worlds there are between "Assam dust and rice" and the dripping chest-nut trees and steaming stones of a wet April day in Oxford!

Lots of love to you all, Alan

On 1 May my mother wrote:

My dear Alan,

The most beautiful morning, almost as beautiful as a May morning at home… Work continues, how I wish I could join you in your sessions with your new tutor, European history muddles me terribly, specially the religious wars, I only have Fisher who is wonderful but too difficult to read to Anne without constant pauses for elucidation. We seem to be spending an awful long time on the Henries but as it brings in the Renaissance and Reformation I suppose that fair enough. Anne is trying hard and improving so much in every other way that I don't worry too much, the problem is what to do with her next year, she has no definite ideas and ours only run along lines of economy!

Which reminds me, don't feel guilty about the guitar, we did owe you something and we don't want to be paid back. I will send the battels this month, will write to the Bursar my usual conciliatory letter, this should be the last time we're late as there'll be a good gap before we have to fork out again. I think the best thing for you would be to get a job on a farm for a month as soon as you leave Oxford, out in the open air with no mental work involved, it would give you just the change and rest you need and something in your pocket for the rest of the vac. I could write to the Langworthys if you like and see if they know of anything.

Lets hope that the summer lives up to your expectations, to be young and in love and at Oxford must be just about a perfect state of affairs, I shouldn't worry about taking things too seriously, you're certainly too young to think of marriage but surely just at the age to do nothing else? Anyway whatever happens (and one must leave these things in the hands of God surely?) it is one of the major pleasures of life to find someone who thinks and feels the same way as oneself, there are precious few, in my whole life I've only met half a dozen. I only wish you could have more to spend on Julie, not that she minds I'm sure but it would be nice, ah well at lest you're learning that money is not to be scoffed at, much as one would like to.

I envy you your reading of the Greeks, I've promised myself that for the long evenings of our retirement, while I'm out here I want to read local and Indian history and philosophy – when I've got time. That's silly, I know I could make time by getting up earlier, but when the girls go I don't intend to go to the club or waste time with people that don't interest me and shall spend a happy four years browsing. Its strange that all ones life one is plagued by a sense of ignorance and time passing and the faster it passes the more ignorant one becomes. … Fiona is turning into quite a reasonable person actually, I think you'll enjoy her company, for the first time ever!

The next letter is dated from Cherideo May 13.

My dear Alan,

So glad to get your letter describing a more successful outing with Julie, it sounded idyllic in fact and made me very homesick, last May was so beautiful though of course you missed it being in Norway but I shall never forget it. We cant really complain of it here, its still very cool and the flowering trees are coming out and transforming Nazira P.O. into a dream of beauty, all the birds are nesting and there are flashes of blues and golds as they fly about with food for their young and every open patch of ground is a lilac sea of water hyacinths. Oh to be a painter with the power of transforming and interpreting this riot of life and colour, I would rather be able to paint than anything else though I suppose of all the arts it would be the most frustrating as you could never interpret the moment exactly as it was, the tricks of light and shade and the feelings they evoked. …

I heard from Billy[1] *the other day and he says he might be able to fix you up with a job if you aren't already fixed, he likes his new school, perhaps he could get you in there. But I still feel a manual job in the open air would be more relaxing. I suppose this is the month for Balls and I hope you'll manage to afford at least one, Daddy and I went to one at Oriel College when we were there, but I only remember a very old tortoise with the college shield on its back, I think you have to be part of the place to enjoy that sort of thing (balls, not tortoises). I am on the point of writing to the Ruskin School of Art among others…*

The next letter is just over a week later, dated 22 May.

My dear Alan,
Thank you for a letter about some lovely May evenings, very homesick making. I remember those Oxford evenings so well and I always wished I was young and uncluttered to enjoy them properly (i.e. by the three of you aged 5, 3, and 1!) so its nice that you are having the chance. The trouble is that the combination of pleasant companionship and idyllic surroundings occurs so seldom in life that one is inclined to spend ones time looking nostalgically backwards …

We are still with Henry VIII and the Emp. Charles, I cant see us ever finishing our syllabus, we shall probably be working day and night for the last couple of months. I have just been lent "The Thirty Years War" by C.V. Wedgewood which looks interesting and is a subject on which I know less than nothing …

I think Fiona must have taken the poetry book I kept when I was in love as I cant find it – but I wasn't very original I'm afraid. There was Donne "Dear love for nothing less than thee", and "Being your slave what

---

[1] My mother's oldest brother.

can I do but tend" and Yeats "Had I the heavens embroidered cloths" and one called "Love is enough, though the world be waning" and one "Because we made a promise you and I" authors unknown, and a dreadful one "I do not love thee, no I do not love thee, And yet when thou art absent I am sad" which I seemed to like excessively! Oh and "Now that we two have been apart so long" which I don't think is very good poetry either but I still like. I'm sure you must have found all these. How quickly the wheel turns, it only seems the other day that I was writing them. Do you know that lovely one "Be thou at rest this night?", and "Autumn" by De La Mare which isn't strictly love but very mournful and haunting. I'll try and find my book, maybe its lurking in some corner.
Daddy and Anne champing round wanting their lunch, so no more. They send their love, we all want to know what Julie looks like!
Much love from us all – Mummy

I had been searching for a holiday job. Through a contact mentioned in the following letter, I finally got a job at a boys' (now a mixed) preparatory school, Copthorne School near Crawley in Sussex. I have the letter calling me to an interview dated 16 May.

TELEPHONE
COPTHORNE 311

COPTHORNE SCHOOL LTD.
DIRECTORS: MRS. M. WORKMAN
H. C. S. WORKMAN
P. J. H. WORKMAN (HEADMASTER)

COPTHORNE SCHOOL
SUSSEX

16th May, 1961.

Dear Mr Macfarlane,

Thank you so much for your letter of 12th May saying that you had heard from Richard Steele-Perkins.

I shall be very pleased to see you one afternoon in the near future for an interview, and would suggest next Sunday, 21st May as the first convenient day, or Monday, Tuesday, Wednesday following 22nd, 23rd 24th. I will leave the time entirely for you to say, and I would also suggest that if you are travelling by train that you come to Victoria and take a train on the Brighton line to Three Bridges, where you will find taxis waiting, and one will bring you to the school. I will gladly refund you all travelling expenses.

I hope one of those afternoons will be convenient, and I shall look forward very much to meeting you.

Yours Sincerely,

P. J. H. Workman.

PUT 0534.

Trains
10·25 - 12·18.

Return
4·45.
6·20. (fast)
6·35.
8·0 (fast)
9·25.
9·48.

One interesting letter which I had about this time was from the girl who had introduced me to Julie, Sally Oppenheim. Sally remained a close friend and the following long letter shows her delightful bantering tone. She refers to Anouilh so the letter was probably written in May when his 'Ring Round the Moon' was being performed in Worcester gardens. She also refers to my friend David Isaac and gives a rather whimsical picture of number 5, Beaumont Street. The letter tends to be in a continuous stream, so I have added some paragraph divisions.

For Alan, with lots of love and kisses

Dear Alan,

Please don't slay me for

i) Barging in like a hippopotamus and

ii) Using precious file paper.

Actually the whole operation of writing incriminating notes was thwart with danger. You see, you didn't have a biro or even a pencil, so I was stuck. It was rather a waste of time to come all this way and not even leave a note, and so nursing my aching heart at not seeing you. I had to crawl around all the rooms in No.5, looking for something to write with. Oh! The danger! I crept into all kinds of rooms, but no one & no pencil. Anyway I finally found myself inside the room opposite – gramophone playing full blast, but no one there. So I stole (Julianna would be very pleased with me!) this biro; but I don't like the colour at all. I like black biros. Actually the idea has just come to me that if I stick around, writing this touching little note, you might appear like Jove, in a clap of thunder, so I'll just go on creating this masterpiece ad lib.

Someone is creeping furtively around on tip-toe. Perhaps they're trying to steal a biro too. But too late! I have got the only apparent biro in the house. It really is <u>*most*</u> *odd! – all kinds of strange noises around the place. Ghostly wirelesses playing to nobody at all, and furtive footsteps on the stairs – help! Now someone's whistling – not quite so weird – people often do whistle – but they don't creep around the house – help! There they go again – into the room where I stole this biro – Any minute there will be screams of "Help! Murder! Thief!" someone's stolen my biro!" and then the police will come and find me with the incriminating evidence in my hand. But what an anti-climax! No screams, no frantic yells, just the tea-time score board in that awful B.B.C. drawl.*

Can I paint a mural on your wall? In fact if you don't come back by Midnight, I shall be forced to vent my thwarted passion on painting some glory just above your bed. Did you ever see "The Horses Mouth" – super film – full of crazy impassioned artists – and as one of these strange misunderstood creatures, I shall leave my mark in a turbulent, swirling smosh of blue biro. And then even Jove for all his claps of thunder won't be able to get it off, and Mrs Smith [the College hostel warden] will give questioning looks.

I am very pleased to see that you're reading Oscar Wilde's fairy stories. This shows bon gout – more than the creature who is playing that wretched score board all over the place; I <u>*hate*</u> *cricket, such a pointless way of knocking someone out with a cricket ball. It's such an innoffensive game. I like games where everyone goes quite bestial and hits everybody everywhere – that was how I used to play lacrosse in my youth – such a smosh there was after every game!*

Oooh! You are lucky to have such a long letter – even though it is on precious file paper. Anyway my letters are bound to be better than your essays.

Oh dear – more furtive footsteps in that room – I'm sure they must have discovered the theft by now. I feel very guilty, but still people shouldn't leave things around for temptable people like myself. Oh help! I was just going to apologise and own up etc when I saw HIM. A big man, with glasses, so fierce, so grim; he would have slayed me I know. So I didn't make a sacrifice of myself, I opened the door, looked, and ran – he ran downstairs, evidently more scared than even I was. Actually, people do so say that when a lion eats you, he is more scared than you are – Awful lot of nonsense don't you think – Why did he start to eat you in the first place?

I decided to complete my ebb of morality and I painted my nails all silver and grey with some stuff I found on your desk, called Silver Fizz. I thought that from its name it would make my nails look like champagne, but unfortunately not – they look rather funny instead.

Oh look Alan! A malteser! Better and better – I really am a very accomplished thief. That is obviously my metier in life. I shall go into partnership with Julianna, and we will become those female pirates in the seventeenth century, hurling knives, and wearing baggy trousers, and looking just a teeny bit strange. It might even be a bit hopeless, because one can't very well pirate a Queen Mary or something like that and I would feel just faintly ridiculous charging around the First Class deck in baggy trousers shouting and hurling a curved knife around. Actually they might think I was in fancy dress and take no notice; but even then I wouldn't be a very good pirate.

Whose are those paintings on the floor? I walked all over them by mistake, but they don't look very much different after all my trampling. I think I'm turning into a hippopotamus, because I do trample all over things and I eat leaves – Couldn't find any in your room. Pity.

I wonder what the time is – I shall just <u>*have*</u> *to go and steal a clock now. Which room shall I choose? Not the same one – that would be much too obvious. Thieves must be careful.*

[New sheet of foolscap paper.] *It took me at least ten minutes to decide to use this last sheet. I dittered and dottered, but being very unscrupulous I decided to use it; so if you are* <u>*livid*</u> *(and I don't blame you) remember, as you aim the gun, that I did at least think twice, even if I took the wrong decision. I can never spell that word, but can't find a dictionary – Ah! Another thing I can steal – when I've finished this house really will be in an uproar. But not to worry – I shall go seek a watch and a dictionary.*

Found the clock, but it was too big to take away – but the ignorant fellow had no dictionary. So I still can't spell that word. It's ten-past four and everybody is crashing about – not furtively any more however.

Actually, I really did have a very good excuse for coming to see you know – It took me ages and ages to think it up – but at last I hit on it. I've brought back David's scarf at last and I wondered if you would be terribly sweet and give it to him. There! Wasn't that a clever excuse? Sometimes I really am quite ingenious. You know, you don't have to read this, by now it's turning in to nonsense, and not even poetic nonsense at that. My adored brother [Nicholas Oppenheim] came to see me this afternoon, but only for about 5 minutes, so I was very sad after he'd gone. Have you lots of confessions to make? I haven't, I don't know if that's just my blameless life, or my lack of standards, either way however, I have a blissfully clean conscience. A few nights ago I lost £2 playing dice, and that was one reason why Nicholas came round, to give me a big row on the vices of Oxford. I don't know who told him, but still the ghastly secret is out, and my reputation ruined. "She's a loose woman" goes the cry, and all Oxford gives me black looks, as I creep along the gutter, cloaked in black velvet shame.

Oh dear, I fear that you are not coming back, and so my desperation is unleashed, and the hell hounds of despised love are rushing all over your room. This is too melancholic, but I won't paint the mural on your wall, I have far too kind a nature for that, but not to worry – I shall paint murals elsewhere.

I am working like a Dracula, and have just had a mock exam this morning for 3 hours. But still time skips & hops down the abyss of lost hours and I am left gazingly after his hooped back. The exams start in two weeks, kicks and merriment for all –

Universal bereavement I fear of genius if I fail.

Be frank – have you ever had such an equally long, or an equally interesting/boring letter in your life!? I really envy you – I shall have to write one myself to myself and then have the utter boredom of reading it. How boring can one get?

Sounds of people lurching upstairs, and staggering down again. Would it be inquisitive if I asked what went on here? I will not presume however, and with my usual discretion, I shall creep downstairs as furtively as any of them. Be with the people! Do as they do! Let's all creep furtively around and play sardines in poky corners. I love sardines, we must play one all over Oxford, and I should hide under a dean's bed and this his wife would catch me and presto! Fame in Oxford! Again I should be draped in shame and people would point and say "beware! She's a loose woman". Oh dear, such great miseries arise from such harmless everyday games. Voila – the circle of life – as vicious as an iron cleat' OW!! OW!! OW!!

Poor, poor Alan if you've staggered this far, my heartiest condolences – if ever I've seen a more clichéd letter or a more tepidly phrased one, I would sink in Worcester pond like a true Anouilh heroine. Voici Ondine!

Many apologies for my rudeness in making free in your room, and with your paper.

T'is a vile thing 'tis true, tis vile 'tis true –

I really am very presumptious I know.

Anyway – love you my snogget til I'm a cinder and ashes, and all corroded and burnt up – WOW! Sally

A week later, on 30 May, my mother wrote again.

My dear Alan,

I don't think we've had a letter this week, but we're not worried, this is the month of revelry for you and I hope you could take part in some of it and the weather has been kind. ...The girls and I will be coming home by boat in April [1962], in time for Anne and I to run round picking buttercups and collecting rabbits bones for our Biology, and finding someone who can talk French to her too I hope. As Daddy only gets three months leave there wont be much time except to settle down and pick ourselves up again but one thing I'm going to do is climb Coniston Old Man!

I was reading in the Spectator about some Diploma in Youth Work that Manchester University was offering, it means a year there after graduation but might be worthwhile, of course the kind of jobs you would get as a result would never be very highly paid but would be rewarding, and there would be scope to travel I'm sure. I haven't mentioned this to Daddy by the way, as I know he rather hankers for something plush in I.C.I. or Shell, but I'm sure the Rat Race is a deadly way of living and only leads to ulcers, and the recipe for a happy life is service to some cause you care about. You would think Daddy would have learnt the futility of Business and the deadly uncharitableness of the whole set up, he thinks is only applies to Tea but I'm sure its universal. Perhaps you still have the church in mind, anyway it is your mind and you must make it up for yourself! We were just saying the other day how things have changed in the last generation, even in our day parents decided on their sons careers – and then were most grieved if the results were poor. That much progress has been made –

and yet I suppose its just as easy for a boy to make mistake as his parents, and leaves him with no one to blame it on. Enough of this vapid philosophising, the trouble is there isn't a great deal of news...

A letter just arrived from you, most welcome. I'm glad you've got a job, it should be interesting and give you an idea as to whether you'd like to spend your life at it. How are the economics going to work out? Are you going to be able to manage till then, and will you be self supporting while you're there? Your holiday schedule sounds nice, the only thing that strikes me as unnecessary perhaps is the ten days in the Lakes and then all the way back to Devon before going to the Hebrides. I'm sure Billy would put you up for that time and save all that travelling, and Julie could maybe come up and stay later? I'm thinking of the expense of course, but perhaps Richard will be able to drive you to Iwerne. You must go and see the Marsdens while you're there, I had a card from them at Christmas and have been on the point of writing ever since.

You seem to be at the same stage of History as us, but we had to "do" Luther in a single lesson and all Fisher says about Zvingli's character is that he is the most attractive of all the reformers – perhaps you can tell us why? I must say I would prefer to linger over a single period than hurry along a syllabus, I got the official one from London University the other day and it said it was looking for knowledge of the broad outlines of history, not technical details – this means questions like "Discuss the Social progress made between ..." or "Comment on the religious situation during ..." which is far more difficult than simply to learn the acts of the Reformation Parliament! I am trying to make Anne <u>*see*</u> *History as a living performance, and when she's asked for "The problems that faced Charles V" to imagine herself in his place, with his background and upbringing, and think what her problem would be. Perhaps this is a little fanciful, but it is so much easier to remember facts that you understand. I'm deep in Neale's "Queen Elisabeth" at the moment which is a model of historical writing, you must have read it, it brings every character to sparkling life, without embroidering or distorting. If you ever find you don't want to keep any of your essays on Luther or anyone, we should love to have them as you have so many more books of reference. In English I'm battling against the essay writing taught in all the books, "Introductory para, two or more intermediate paras, concluding para" which leads to such deadly and stultifying writing, surely its much better to jump in with both feet, say what you've got to say, and stop. I think so.*

I have my book here[1] *– have you found a PUBLISHER?! Will send it off straight away.*

Could you please fill in the bits of this form re. Time & Fees in College & send it on to L.C.C. Preston – Percy Lord, B.Sc.

Lots & lots of love from all – Mummy

From time to time I would write reflective letters to Ian Campbell, my closest friend at Sedbergh School, who had returned to Canada. I kept carbon copies of these and will include them at relevant points. Here is part of a letter I wrote on 2nd June 1961.

OXFORD IN THE SUMMER

In the summer – of the old grey walls spread with sunlight like treacle, of the waving bursting green chestnut trees that line the roads, of the quiet green cloisters of Magdalene or New College – the lush cricket-watching grass – and of course the rivers. Winding up from the Thames runs a small tributary, the Cherwell. It is all that a punting river should be – lazy, warm, willow-banked, fish-peopled, scented and luxuriant. In this idyllic background of youth, beauty and spring I have felt the first, though feint [sic], *stirrings of love. Feelings which naturally infuse all else – the plays, the summer balls, the punting trips with an added glory. At the worst these eight weeks will provide some wonderful memories.*

It would be folly in a short space to try to capture the nature of Julie. There is no doubt that she is very intelligent indeed – she is or may easily be a genius – she was certainly a child prodigy. All my friends would endorse that she has a tremendously powerful and magnetic personality – a feature partly accentuated by her considerable participation in Satanism – a fascinating topic – do you believe in it? – or rather in its effectiveness? Not facially at first particularily beautiful – one would not stop in the street to look at her – yet she has lovely eyes and lips and a sweet nose. Also she has a very nice figure – 36-24-36 I think – nearly ideal – and I am just under her guidance beginning to break down the prudish fears I had of any physical admiration of a woman's body. Don't misunderstand me – but I am only just beginning to realise how wonderful are the smooth roundness of a woman's breasts etc. I trust I'm not conveying the impression that I have jumped from

[1] *The Children of Bird God Hill*, which was duly published.

chasteness into open debauchery – you can trust me I think But I have certainly learnt quite a bit from her. The wonderful thing is that from the very first we have been able to discuss everything absolutely openly. I have told her things which no one else on earth knows & vice versa. Loneliness, separation from others which seems to be the greatest unhappiness afflicting human life is thus being, for a time at least stopped.

We share most things (not all!) – money & expenses, letters, thoughts etc – it is wonderful. But soon the term will be over – what then?

I realise that I have let myself go a fair amount in this letter – don't take it all too seriously. I do hope you will treat me likewise.

Sadly there only seems to be only one letter from me to my parents during this term. This was postmarked in Oxford on 13 June.

Dear Mummy, Daddy and Anne,

Thank you very much for your letter. I'm sorry I haven't written for so long but events have been gathering speed before the end of term waterfall. I feel like a tiny coracle being relentlessly carried nearer to the brink of the Niagara falls – which is in about 5 days term [time]. Then I will go straight to Copthorne School – and try not to be too sad that this wonderful term is over!

Partly on your suggestion, partly because Julie's parents are rather unenthusiastic about the idea Julie will probably not be coming up to stay in the Lakes – instead I hope to see her in London. Also this morning I received a very aristocratic invitation as follows: – "Lady Oppenheim at home on Tuesday 11th July for her daughter Sarah-Jane (A friend of mine & Julie's) at the Follows Dining Room, The London Zoo (!), Dinner Dance 8.30 p.m – 1 a.m.'.[1] *It strikes me as rather an interesting idea – one has lovely pictures of offering champagne to a friendly polar bear or sharing a cheese straw with a conversational kangaroo!*

The big news or event of the last week was our party. This will need some explaining. I don't think I have ever mentioned the fact that Julie and I were having this party. This was (a) because I didn't want you to worry about the finances – (b) in case it was a drastic flop – then I just wouldn't have mentioned it. But as it was so successful – and such a tribute to Julie's genius – I will tell you about it.

We decided early in the term that it would be nice to have a party before Julie went down from Oxford. Therefore – having decided that the weather was too doubtful to risk having an "Owl & Pussycat" punt-party – we would hold it indoors. At last we found a nice room – moderately large (about 5 times the size of our drawing room at Field Head) and pleasantly furnished – it belonged to the Roman Catholic chaplaincy and so we hired it. Next we hired a 6-piece jazz-band (it turned out to be very good indeed) and was much appreciated.

Julie organised almost everything else – decorations, drink and most of all food. On the night there was a really wonderful spread of food – jellies, Russian salad, a ham, 8 chickens, fruit salad, ordinary salad, two dishes of tuna salad, tomato soup, ice cream, cakes, veal pie – just to mention a few of the less exotic dishes! There was so much that 70 people hardly ate half of it – and we took some of what was left up the river the next day for a picnic. I have been trying the finish the rest up since then!

Anyhow we invited about 65 of our best friends and after endless worries because it looked as if there would be too many girls etc the numbers were just right – and everyone who wanted one had a partner. We had candles stuck in bottles for lighting and there was a wonderfully gay and friendly atmosphere. Naturally there was a lot of work clearing-up etc – and things were made more complicated by the fact that various parts of the building were opened out as an extension of the Catholic chapel – so we had to creep around with plates of dirty crockery. Of course while we were washing up – during the service – one of us (Julie) had to knock over a case of glass bowls! Ah well happy memories! Anyhow it was certainly worth it – even if it will take me two or three weeks to pay back my debts to Richard from whom I borrowed a little money. The guests seemed to be thrilled. I feel a bit like someone trying to sell something! – but here is a typical thank-you letter.

Dear Alan,

Juliet and I both enjoyed your dance on Saturday immensely, and we would like to thank you and Julie very much indeed for such a wonderful evening. Quite the best party of the term and such a welcome change from the normal run of things. Yours, Anthony

---

[1] I still have the invitation; and also a cyclostyled half page set of instructions of how to get to the zoo. 'Transport to the Zoo will be provided by canal barge from Little Venice, Paddington, W.2. Guests should be at British Waterways Office at 8 p.m.' etc

–All very satisfying!

Julie really is wonderful – and if she wasn't quite so strong-willed and frighteningly brilliant would make a perfect wife.

Anyhow when I write again I will be teaching. All my best regards to anyone I know out in Sonari. I have written to Fiona.

Lots of love to you all, Alan

UNIVERSITY OF OXFORD

A. D. J. Macfarlane, Esq. of Worcester College

has permission from the Proctors for a Party of approx: sixty four persons

at Upper Newman Rooms *on* Saturday

the 10th *of* June, 1961 *at* 7.30 *p.m., on the*

~~*usual*~~ *conditions*, ~~*viz.: that the names of the Members of the party be sent to the Senior Proctor beforehand, and*~~ *that the party break up by* 11.45 *p.m.*

Senior Proctor

Date 8th June 1961.

A list of those we invited by Julie with annotations.

Julie Simon.

I seem to have 34 girls & 31 boys on my list. all of whom I mark thus: ƴ

At Home.

At the Newman Room Sat 10th J

Dancing 7.30–11.45

Dinner Jacket

Evening dress

R.S.V.P.

Roger Wirwood.

ƴ Dick Piggott ✓

ƴ Bas ✓

ƴ John Sykes ✓

ƴ " Cheddwick ✓

ƴ Chris Machin ✓

ƴ Mike Beeston ✓

ƴ Colin Jacobson ✓

ƴ Tony Ma[illegible] — Juliet Anderson

ƴ Tim Nowd

ƴ Chris F-Gibbon — Rose

ƴ Roger

ƴ Dick Smethehurst

John Munles

ƴ Piers — Hubert Rutherford 19, Collingham Road. Kensington London.

ƴ ([illegible])

ƴ Alastair Small

ƴ Phil Druce

ƴ Laur. Hart

ƴ James Stow

ƴ Paul Hyams

ƴ Nic Oppenheim. Christchurch

ƴ Oleg.. "

ƴ Mike Wynn-Jones

ƴ David Phillips

ƴ ~~James~~ S. M. Aupedlais

ƴ Peter Blunt Merton

ƴ Rev. Peter Goulder.

ƴ Chris Power. I have sent them one.

ƴ David Jackson. Was this tactful to Sally?

Chris Power.

~~John Sykes~~.

ƴ ~~Roger~~ Andrew St Johnstone.

ƴ David Isaac.

~~Peter Goodkin~~.

Reservere girls. Vivien? * Lucy? * Anna? * Sylvia. [illegible] Jayne Caldwell Sue Bryant *

ƴ Peter's friend

ƴ Sally Oppenheim ✓

ƴ Mary-Gene Gazitua ✓

ƴ Rachel Pakenham ✓

ƴ Nicky de la Mare ✓

ƴ Terry Baxter ✓

ƴ Sue Croome ✓

ƴ Sue Wardlaw — ill bed.

ƴ Kathy Moses

ƴ Penny Marcus ← S. Wimbledon Park Court *

ƴ Barbara Lessing ← 14, Hillsleigh Rd. London. Kensington W.8.

ƴ Elke Lehrer

ƴ Sian Coburn

ƴ Meral

Win Koopmann ƴ

Hilary Beasley

Anabelle Watkins ƴ ƴ

Viviane Yelland ƴ

Tessa Vintress * ƴ

Jenny Marten ƴ Wimbledon Park Road.

Jane Smith ƴ London. S.W.18.

Hope ƴ

Rosemary ƴ

Joanna Benson ƴ

Esther Pedlar St. Hilda's ƴ

Pussybite. ƴ ƴ Gabrielle

Juliet ƴ Marry? *

Rose. ƴ Fina? *

(Anna?) (28)

The list is written out twice, with various markings to show people who had accepted etc., with asterisks, and comments. I shall divide into girls and boys as they were written out on the first list, where Julie has written 'I seem to have 34 girls & 31 boys on my list', though I then added some more.

Almost all my friendship set are there established by the end of the first year – both male and female. Most of the male guests were from Worcester, whereas I presume most of the girls were from St. Clare's. I imagine it was the putting together of our two sets of friends which made this such a successful party.

The last letter from my mother was written on 13 June.

My dear Alan,

You will be in your Prep School by now, I didn't realise term ended so soon until I heard from Richard yesterday. I do hope it isn't too energetic, or rather that the energy is mostly physical and that the rest of the term the staff are congenial. I'm sorry you ran out of money, I was rather afraid you might be short but as you didn't mention it hoped for the best! How are things now in that line? Let us know if you are able to save anything out of your wages (what are they?!) and can cope with travelling expenses. Did the county give you anything towards them?

... I do think it's a good idea to get the wanderlust out of your system while you're young and without responsibilities, although then I suppose your judgement isn't very mature...

If you ever see an Everyman edition of Hakluyts voyages I would love it, Foyles seem a dotty crowd, every bill they send me is wrong and we are now having a long correspondence about a Mr G.C. Unwin who they think lives with me and who buys the same books and they ask me to please make him pay his bills which are duplicates of mine! So I've given up getting anything from them, actually have all I need now... Let us know your exact holiday plans and dates, I do hope it will be a lovely summer for you,

Much love from us all – Mummy

Other ephemera

I have the membership cards of the same clubs and organizations as the previous term. In relation to religion, there is the Worcester Chapel Services card, and Woodroffe Society.

There is the O.U. Travel Club and Vactic, Trinity Term card. Vactic was the student vacation travel information centre. I don't remember going to any of the talks.

There is the Oxford Union Society Trinity Term card. I don't remember going to any of the debates – but should have done so, as some were interesting, including that in 2nd week when the motion was 'That the abortion law in this country is inadequate and sadly in need of reform.' It was proposed by Mrs Lena Jeger.

The only other social engagement was with the Provost – an occasion for me to sport my terylene trousers at the end of term event:

> The Provost requests the pleasure of the company of Mr A.D.J. Macfarlane at a Garden Party on Thursday 15 June 1961, to meet Sir Oliver and Lady Franks, 4 p.m. to 6. p.m.

This would have been in the Provost's private garden, a lovely one. I don't recall it.

*

It was under the influence of Julie, it seems, that I began to write poetry, though I had written a little while at Sedbergh. I make due apologies for the fairly awful quality of many of the poems and reflections which will begin to infiltrate these pages, but in order to see inside my heart and mind they are a necessary part of the story.

One of them written around this time is as follows:

'On recovering from a fit of melancholic self-pity'

The heedless crowd elbowed past, laughing, jostling
In the wet, neon-reflecting street
And I felt a shudder and a retching
Convulsion at their happiness, their solidness.
Old-forgotten nursery tales came into my mind
"Why is everyone happy when I'm so sad –

When I can feel a mist around my eyes
And the

[mercifully this is unfinished!]

So ends some gleanings from my happiest term at Oxford.

Half of the Worcester students, Summer Term 1961, I am far left in second row

Academic Work: Summer Term 1961

Given the large amount of time I spent with Julie and friends this term, it is with interest that I turn to see whether I got much academic work done and how it was received.

There are four large sheets headed '1st Yr. History Collections – English History 400-1215.' Since this was the period we had completed at the end of the second term, I believe that this was the test paper which I did at the start of the summer term. I did an essay on 'Account for the "Reformation of the Tenth Century"', on which the mark was Beta minus with the comment, 'All right, but you don't go far into the subject'. The next essay was on 'What do you understand by "Anglo-Norman feudalism"?' for which I got a Beta plus with 'Good, up to a point'. Then there was 'Compare Anselm and Lanfranc', which was Beta Gama 'Very thin indeed' and finally 'What were the causes and effects of the growth of the universities in 12th century Europe?' for which I got a Beta. The total mark was Beta minus. Not very impressive.

In terms of lectures, I have a printed list for the term, part of which is below.

FACULTY OF MODERN HISTORY

Lecture List for Trinity Term 1961

Subject	*Lecturer*	*Time*	*Place*	*Course begins**
BRITISH HISTORY				
The Celtic Background of Early Anglo-Saxon History (*one lecture*)	Mrs. N. K. Chadwick (*O'Donnell Lecturer in Celtic Studies*)	F. 5 (19 May)	Schools	
Justice in Medieval England	Miss N. D. Hurnard	T. Th. 11	,,	
The Government of England 1066–1307	Mr. H. E. Bell	W. 11	New College	
Stephen's Reign (1135–54)	Mr. R. H. C. Davis	F. 10	Merton	
The English Church after the Conquest	Mrs. S. M. Wood	W. 12	Schools	
The English Church in the Thirteenth Century	Mr. W. A. Pantin	S.10	,,	
Towns, Trade, and Population in the Later Middle Ages	Miss B. Harvey	M. 10	,,	
The Hundred Years War and English Society	Mr. K. B. McFarlane	W. 11	Magdalen	
The English Church in the Fifteenth Century	Dr. V. H. H. Green	F. 10	Lincoln	
The Coming of the English Revolution 1529–1641	Mr. L. Stone	W. F. 10	Wadham	
The Reign of Charles II	Mr. P. G. M. Dickson	F. 12	St. Catherine's	
India 1707–1907 (*Selected Topics*)	Mr. C. C. Davies	T. 10	Indian Institute	
The Origins of Methodism	Dr. V. H. H. Green	F. 12	Lincoln	
Religion and Society in Nineteenth-century England	Mrs. J. M. Hart	T. 12	Schools	
The House of Lords in the Nineteenth Century	Mrs. C. R. Dick	M. 12	,,	
British Foreign Policy 1815–1914	Mr. A. E. Campbell	Th. 12	Keble	
British Social and Economic History from 1815 (*first four weeks*)	Mr. D. T. Healey	F. 11	Barnett House	
The British Conservative Party 1846–1914	Mr. A. E. Firth	W. 11	University	
Imperial Defence as a Factor in the Evolution of the Commonwealth 1850–1914	Mr. D. K. Fieldhouse	W. 10	Rhodes House	
Joseph Chamberlain: a Reappraisal	Mr. M. C. Hurst	Th. 10	St. John's	
British Constitutional History 1914–1953 (Le May Documents) (*About four lectures to conclude*)	Professor Beloff	Th. 10	All Souls	
The Evolution of the Commonwealth 1919–1961 (Keith, &c.)	Dr. A. F. Madden	M. 10	Rhodes House	
**GENERAL HISTORY				
The Councils of Ephesus and Chalcedon (I, *I*)	Mr. A. G. Mathew	M. 11	Blackfriars	
Religion and Society in the Age of St. Augustine (I, *I*)	Mr. P. R. L. Brown	T. 11	All Souls	
Introduction to the *Corpus Iuris Canonici* (II, III, *II, III, IV*)	Mr. E. W. Kemp	S. 10	Exeter	
Europe in the Tenth Century (II, III, *II, III, IV*)	Mr. A. D. M. Cox	Th. 11	University	
Germany 919–1056: Society, Economy, and Culture (III, *III, IV*)	Mr. K. J. Leyser ✓	Th. 12	Magdalen	
The Mediterranean World in the Twelfth Century in the Travels of Benjamin of Tudela (III, *IV, V*)	Dr. Roth	F. 11	History Faculty Library	
The Fourteenth Century Renaissance (IV, *V, VI*)	Mr. A. G. Mathew	T. 11	Balliol	
The Economic Development of Western Europe in the Later Middle Ages (IV, V, *V, VI, VII*) (*two lectures to conclude*)	Mr. P. S. Lewis	M. Th. 11	All Souls	
European History in the Fifteenth Century (IV, V, *VI, VII*)	Mr. C. A. J. Armstrong	W. 10	Hertford	
The Papacy in the Fifteenth Century (IV, V, *VI, VII*)	Miss M. E. Reeves	T. 10	Schools	
Cusanus (*four lectures*) (IV, V, *VI, VII*)	Professor Jacob ✓	T. 11	All Souls	
Renaissance Warfare: Social and Technical Aspects (*seminar*) (V, VI, *VI, VII, VIII*)	Mr. J. R. Hale ✓	F. 5	Jesus	
Problems in Spanish History (Fifteenth and Early Sixteenth Centuries) (IV, V, *VI, VII, VIII*)	Dr. J. R. L. Highfield ✓	Th. 12	Merton	
Cujus Regio, ejus religio 1555–1697 (VI, *VIII, IX, X*)	Dr. J. W. Stoye	Th. 10	Schools	
Maritime Aspects 1559–1648 (VI, *VIII, IX*)	Mr. E. H. F. Smith	F. 10	St. Peter's Hall	
European Peace Treaties 1559–1715 (VI, *VIII, IX, X*)	Professor Wernham	M. 12	Schools	
General Problems in European History in the First Half of the Seventeenth Century (VI, *VIII, IX*)	Mr. J. P. Cooper	M. 11	Trinity	
The Russian Empire and the West in the Eighteenth Century (VI, VII, *IX, X, XI*)	Dr. N. Zernov	Th. 10	Keble	
France and Europe 1789–1814 (VII, VIII, *XI, XII*)	Mr. C. H. Stuart	M. W. 10	Christ Church	
Problems of Church and State in Europe 1789–1815 (VII, VIII, *XI, XII*)	Mr. J. D. Walsh	W. 12	Jesus	

* Lectures begin on the first possible day after the beginning of Full Term (Sunday, 23 April), unless otherwise stated in this column.
** Figures in brackets in roman type refer to the numbers of the old prescribed periods; those in italic type to the present prescribed periods. (*See* Oxford University Gazette, No. 3022, p. 212.)

Monday 5.0.

"How do you explain the triumph of monarchical govt in Flor." (Medici Princip)
Ridolphi "Savonarola"
Hale "Machiavelli" – what was wrong with oligarchy
Roth "Last Florentine Republic" || Rubenstein – ("[illegible] Problems" Ren'e Studies" [illegible]) || Baron – "Crisis of Ren'e" –

English History

My first essay was on 'The first three Angevin Kings neglected England for the sake of their continental possessions'. Discuss.

Essay 1: I have a five page essay, with a detailed essay plan and a number of pages of notes. There is a page of notes on the supervision, but no note as to what James Campbell thought of it. The essay is dated May 1961.

Essay 2:The next essay was on 'The minority of Henry III settled the balance of power between the king & barons for the C13'.

Essay 3: 'Did the activities of the Papacy do more to help or hinder the cause of reform in the C13'? There is a five-page essay with the approving note in my hand, presumably Campbell's comment, 'Good – sensible'. There are three-quarters of a page of comments on the essay, and also a number of pages of notes and a detailed essay plan.

Essay 4: is given below

June 1967.

ENGLISH HISTORY (4)

(i) "Explain the main changes in Ecclesiastical Architecture 1150-1300"

Architecture like all other art forms expresses the spirit of an age. Thus to explain its progress we must investigate why the ideals aspirations and thoughts of a nation change. Being a somewhat complex problem I will content myself with studying firstly how the actual physical forms of ecclesiastical buildings changed in these years, and secondly how the spirit which undoubtedly infused unity and pattern into the new techniques was related to the changing spirit of the contemporary world. For it is obvious, though sometimes forgotten, that the technical innovations of pointed arch, ribbed vaulting and flying buttress did not make a new style, for style is not just an aggregate of features but an integral whole – using of the materials, new or old in a special manner for a specific purpose.

Likening the Gothic movement to a young sapling (which has just been constructed in an original form from various pieces of earlier woods) the age in which it was planted in 1140 at St Denys near Paris was one well suited to its essential qualities growth, freedom and internal strength. The dry hand of scholasticism was slowly lifting, feudalism in its old rigid form was beginning to yield before the growth of towns, the use of mercenary armies and the increase in a non-feudal national spirit. In the ecclesiastical world the dominance of the old-type monasteries was passing and the importance of bishops and secular clergy as well as the new Friars was growing apace. Most important of all, a more settled civilization allowed and encouraged the secularization of culture. But here it is important to remember several fundamental differences between England and France. The former did not share the latter's great cleavage between the regular and secular clergy and therefore felt the Cistercian influence of simplicity and restraint (to which was due in no small part the English abandonment of the chevet plan in favour of the square East end, as well as the moulded capital without foliage). Secondly the tradition of Norman church building strengthened the English love of simple wall and textured surface.

The greatest change Forced to put a date to it we would have to say that the Gothic style was introduced in about the 1150's. In fact the Abbey of St Denys, the choir of consecrated in 1144 heralded it in France while Canterbury Cathedral (1175) saw its introduction in England. Although some of its techniques such as ribbed vaulting at Durham and pointed arches in various places had appeared before. Short of space, I will deal with French and English early Gothic together at first then differentiate them. The general effect of the change was that the massive columns, earth-bound arches and thick walls of the Romanesque period changed rapidly into slender and tenuous piers; high, ribbed roofs; and lofty and window-filled walls. Certain structural problems had faced the Romanesque church builders, but the builders of the late C12 broke these fetters and so were free to create their new vision. The main problems had been connected with the difficulties of designing the ribs of rib vaulting merely with semi-circular arches, the danger of outward thrust from really lofty nave vaults and the awkward shapes presented by the ambulatories round the apses. The solution of these difficulties provided the medium for the new inspiration.

The application of the earlier-used pointed arch to the design of ribbed vaulting and in the ambulatory vault provided both structural safety and aesthetic attraction. While by the flying buttress the thrust of the vault was carried over the side aisles with struts formed of half arches to heavy masses built upon the outside of the side aisles. This was the essence of the technical change. But other changes took place too. Ecclesiastical ornamentation increasingly grew profuse and changed. The grotesque feeling and neurotic cruelty of the Romanesque work almost completely disappeared instead we see growing naturalism. After 1200 the crocket form with its uncurling vivid movements became common – a fresh and spring-like spirit was appearing. Likewise – modest though it was – plate tracery was beginning to be introduced – and it was to be only a step from here to the increasingly complex bar-tracery.

Canterbury Cathedral was undoubtedly largely influenced by France – but in Westminster Abbey (begun 1245) – although the high vault and some of the tracery details are French – the ornament and arch shapes are English. In the stage which is known as Early English (roughly from 1150-1280) the complete English church plan was developed – Salisbury typifies it with its great length, square East end, two transepts and its lack of height and width as compared to the French cathedrals. A study of Salisbury with its elementary tracery, simply moulded tracery without carving and clear abacus, and its use of slim black marble shafts – shows the main qualities of the Early English Period, simplicity yet richness (in the complexity of pier arch mouldings) length and charm –

ENGLISH HISTORY (4) ③ June 1981.

(ii)

"Explain the main changes in Ecclesiastical Architecture 1150-1[illegible]

its origins in technique but with a different approach and interpretation. The Gothic style in France emphasises spatial concentration - it urges us up and East. Salisbury with its square East end and double transepts is still the sum of added units, compartment joined to compartment. Rheims is vigorously pulled together, Lincoln comfortably pulled out - and this is corroborated by the West facades especially of Wells which is not even an attempt at the logical projection of the inside system (as it was in France). Pevsner interestingly sees this as representative of national characteristics which still prevail - the distrust of the consistent, logical, extreme and uncompromising. Unfelt in Norman architecture, rising national consciousness began to shape different paths for the two forms of Gothic. And here we find reflected in Architecture a tendency shown also when in 1258 the Provisions of Oxford became the first official document to be proclaimed in English as well as French or Latin, it also contained distinct anti-foreigner sentiments. The Crusades were not least important among the causes of an increasing consciousness of national differences. While Simon de Montfort's rebellion has often been considered as a manifestation of this spirit.

The Gothic movement arose from an intense desire to build simply and beautifully churches completely vaulted in stone with ribbed vaults, with nave, clerestory, windows and side aisles, and later with large areas for stained glass, its decorative details developed after the essential structural advance had been made - in the striving to find the loveliest and most appropriate ornament for such structural form. Gothic was developing in the age of St Francis, of the "dolce stil nuovo" and the French epics of chivalry, of St Louis and the Crusades in the age when men and epics such as Wolfram's "Parsifal" combined the ideals of chivalry and religion. An age of growing awareness of Brother Sun and Sister Earth, of the beauty around - not yet the beauty of the world, but of God's creation. So, as yet ornament in the churches though increasingly naturalistic, was subordinate, ministering to a greater cause, the glory of God. Pevsner describes how the Gothic style brought to the new motifs and the old a new purpose "to enliven inert masses of masonry, to quicken spatial action, to reduce a building to a seeming system of innervated lines of action". For instance it seems certain that the primary object of a Gothic vault was its appearance of immaterial lightness rather than any actual physical lightness.

Once the young tree had taken root, had grown tall and put forth young green shoots it is much easier to understand further developments. After the first technical mastery was obtained experimentation continued in the details - in the blending of the various elements and in the creation of more beautiful decoration.

In France as the Gothic style had arrived sooner so change came sooner. From about 1200 Early Gothic gave way to what is known as High Gothic - Chartres begun in 1194 being an example. By various changes, such as the replacement of sexpartite vaults by vaults, half as deep with only diagonal ribs and of exterior shafts which run soaring from floor to vault without a break - the upward and Eastward thrust was accelerated. Amiens, Rheims, Beauvais and Cologne, among others, achieved this tremendous balance between two dominant directions of tension. As in England there was an increasing amount of window-space and stained glass.

In England there was no marked change in the structural form of the Church - but from about 1250 there was an ever-increasing emphasis on various interior details - the whole period being called the "Decorated" style - and the first half of this period was called "geometric" from the fact that there was a consistent development of geometrical bar tracery. Every possible combination of simple geometrical curve was used - trefoil quatrefoil, sexfoil, curved triangles etc. At the same time the richness and complexity of mouldings and use of sculpture and ornament greatly increased (for instance on the West Front of Wells).

Then about the beginning of the 14c - for instance at Exeter Cathedral (1280-1367) reversed curves and flowing lines in tracery heralded another stage - the "curvilinear". Soon the geometric basis was forgotten and the tracery windows often simulate leaf, tree or branch forms (West Window York - 1338). Exeter exhibits all the tendencies - immense development of vaulting by the introduction of tiercerons, and a growing enrichment of carving throughout. Its forest of branching vaulting ribs, ranked colonettes of clustered piers etc combined to make an effect of warmth, richness, invitation & mystery. There was an accompanying lavishness in all types of Church furniture - such as tombs, chantries, screens, and choir stalls - and also a development of simple English stone spires.

Again these cathedrals and churches re-echo the thought and emotion of their century. The growing delight

ENGLISH HISTORY (4) ⑤ June 1961.

(iii) "Explain the main changes in Ecclesiastical Architecture" (1150 - 1300)

in detailed beauty, in richness of pattern, in the world around them as compared to the austerity and severity of earlier centuries. The C12 century and C13 architecture reflected the achievements of classic scholasticism - lofty and increasingly intricate. The encyclopaedic works of the the English Dominican Bartholomaeus Anglicus or the "Summa" of Aquinas were a combination of logic and intellect with belief and faith. ~~Truth was not what could be proved, but what conformed to an acce~~ And as in speculative theology with Duns Scotus and Occam, so in architecture there was a tendency towards a more and more complicated and even sophisticated elaboration of Truth. At the start structural necessities had provided nearly all the necessary decoration - now forms ~~were~~ becoming merely decorative.

The first wave of inspiration had been structural - the use and careful decorative development of ribbed vaults, the general use of the pointed ~~vault~~ arch, ~~the~~ and the flying buttress. Then coming on top of this and sweeping it on and up and mingling with it came the second wave - decoration. The development of tracery, the accentuation of structural features by ~~bands of~~ mouldings, carvings and crockets; the use of forms originally structural for ornamental purposes - buttresses, gables and arcades. And in carving and other decoration a general tendency towards naturalism. The change was ~~that~~ the same as one witnesses every year in the life of a tree - first the bare branches and trunk - then the first signs of spring - small uncurled leaves - then come the green shoots and there is a veil ~~of~~ or net of green spread ~~of~~ over the tree. By 1300 English Gothic had just passed this stage and would soon be clothed in its ~~rea~~ rich summer foliage.

Romanesque architecture related to music - (by fascination in mathematical relationship)

Other factors: i) What churches are used for.

- C13 architecture better for preaching.

Stained glass started in C11. - to fill church.

- Romanesque churches encrusted with carving.

Romanesque = Norman.

~~Albigensians.~~ Worsley.

The nine pages of notes for this include some detailed copies of drawings by me – unusual in my essays, illustrating the whole history of architecture up to Gothic. This is something of a departure for me dealing with aesthetics and art.

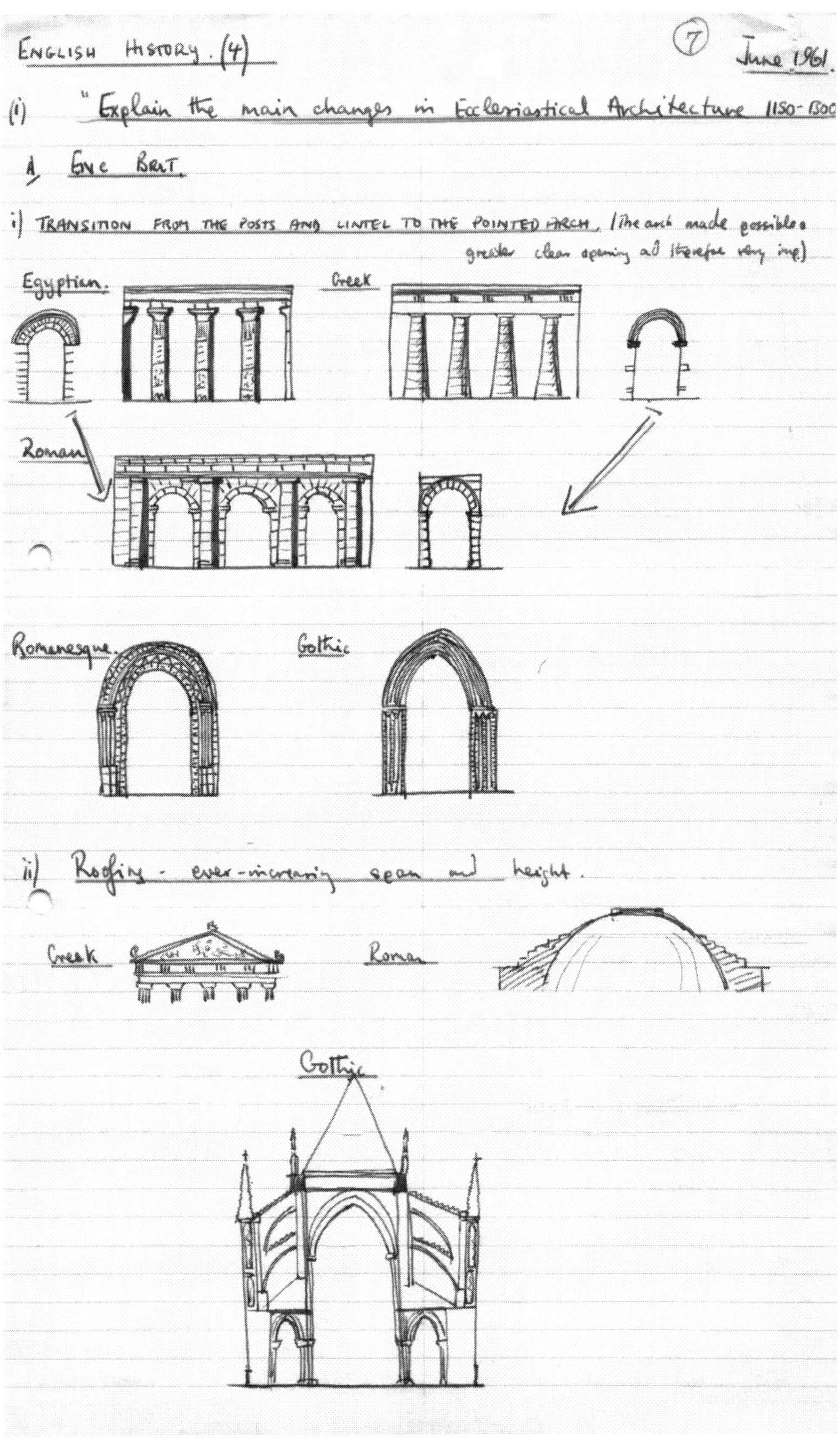
ENGLISH HISTORY. (4) ⑦ June 1961.

(i) "Explain the main changes in Ecclesiastical Architecture 1150-1300

A. Enc Brit.

i) TRANSITION FROM THE POSTS AND LINTEL TO THE POINTED ARCH. (The arch made possible greater clear opening and therefore very imp.)

ii) Roofing - ever-increasing span and height.

Essay 5: 'How inevitable was Edward's failure in Scotland?' There is an essay of four and a half pages with the high accolade from Campbell of 'Not bad at all' written at the end by me, and then half a page of notes on the essay. There are also essay plans and quite detailed pages of notes.

European History

There was a bibliographic sheet for 'European', which was for the essays for Karl Leyser. This gave the author, short title and the library call mark, and some ticks in red to show which sources I had read and found valuable. On average, I seem to have at least got as far as finding about eight or nine books and articles for each essay, and often ticked five or six of these.

What is encouraging is that this shows a wide range of reading for each essay, and not just essays based on the Encyclopedia Britannica, as I had long thought! I also copied out carefully all the History Finals exam questions that had been set over the last few years, and annotated them into themes. For example, in 1959 there were three questions on France, 1 on Turkey, 1 on art, 1 on education, 3 on the Netherlands etc. I similarly analysed 1949, 1960, 1953 and 1954.

The essays I did were as follows:

Essay 1. (April) 'How do you explain the triumph of monarchical government in Florence?' There is an essay of just over five pages with the comment 'Very good – but wrong period'. There are also three quarters of a page of detailed notes on the supervision. The eight and a half pages of detailed notes for the essay are from the Encyclopedia Britannica, and four other books. There is a detailed essay plan of two pages.

Essay 2 (May) ' Were the French invasions of Italy 1494-1529 profoundly at variance with the true interests and traditions of early C16 France?' This was six pages long, and I have written down Leyser's comment as 'Very well done'. There are also two pages of detailed notes on the supervision. I also have eight pages of detailed notes from various books, plus an essay plan.

Essay 3 (May). 'What tensions, crises and conflicts can you discern in Maximilien's Germany? ' The essay is just over four pages, with over a page and a half of detailed comments. There is no general remark recorded. I have over ten pages of notes for this, and a detailed essay plan.

Essay 4 'A Survey of the reign of Ferdinand and Isabella and its aftermath the revolt of the Communero suggests that they had not worked miracles and that the "New Monarch" was a myth". Discuss. The comment is. 'Good- a painstaking & careful effort', and there over half a page of detailed comments. I have the extensive notes for this essay. I read and noted from three books, some ten pages of notes, and there is a detailed essay plan.

Essay 5. (May) 'Did Luther betray his own message?' An essay of nearly six pages, but with no comments on it. I have eight pages of notes and a detailed essay plan.

Essay 6. (June). '"The limits of Turkish expansion also entailed the immediate decline of their Empire." Is this true of the time of Suleiman the Magnificent?' The essay is five pages long, with the comment 'Yes – well done'. There is almost a page of notes on comments by Leyser. I have eleven pages of notes for this essay, as well as a detailed plan – dated June 1961.

As this essay is one of my first attempts at a wider kind of history of a comparative kind, something I would relish later in life, I shall include the essay here.

EUROPEAN HISTORY [6] June 1961.

(1) ESSAY ON: "The limits of Turkish expansion also entailed the immediate decline of their Empire." Is this true of the time of Suleiman the Magnificent?

Introduction

The rise and fall of Empires nearly always seem to fit into a pattern. A time of youth and vigour, usually of cruelty and barbarism mellows, remains poised a varying time in a state of maturity, then crumbles - usually from within - to collapse, a mouldering carcass of corruption and weakness. If we compare the Ottoman and Roman Empires we find many similarities - especially in the cankering abuses which heralded their end. Each

cf with Roman Empire similarities

i) saw the decay of its rulers, felt the devastations of an
ii) overweening military caste, felt the strain of prolonged and far-flung wars against the German and Persian states. But it is dangerous to take the parallel too far for Rome was driven back by hordes more virile but less civilised than herself - while the very contrary was the case in Turkey, where practically - untouched by the swirling waters of the Renaissance, Reformation and Counter-Reformation - she lost her impetus and seemed to stagnate. This stagnation was a slow process, but it has been the general rule to trace the start of the decay to the reign of Suleiman the Magnificent, for one can derive a gloomy satisfaction from tracing the seeds of final decay in the most glorious epoch of a peoples history.

One Theory

And this interpretation has also been able to bring two strands together by showing that this was the very time when the Ottoman Empire reached the limit of practical expansion. It would be very satisfactory if we could prove that the remark of Mohammed II "Our Empire is the home of Islam; from father to son the lamp of our empire is kept burning with oil from the hearts of the infidel" is truer than even he realized. That the Turkish Empire fed on the loot, land and slave labour derived from her conquests. Without expansion she would not survive but must immediately decay - or so it may be maintained.

Growth → time of Suleiman

It can not be denied that the Ottoman empire for a long time expanding amazingly rapidly - was brought to a practical standstill in the reign of Suleiman. Having crossed from North West Anatolia to the Balkans Murad I in the 1360's was the real founder of the Ottoman Empire. Then the Sultans returned to Anatolia and Mahomet I (1403-1421) and Murad II finally subdued the Turkish Anatolian emirates. In 1453 Mahomet II took Constantinople and his successor Selim the Grim continued on the path of conquest by extending

Murad I (1360) (1st founder)
Mahomet I
Murad II
Selim

the Empire eastwards and southwards - pushing the border towards Persia and defeating the Mamelukes of Egypt. At first Suleiman was equally successful. In the North west he

Suleiman i) captured Belgrade and Rhodes in 1521 and then in a great ii) victory in the plain of Mohacs (1526) gained a considerable part of Hungaria including Buda. iii) On the Persian front he won and held Iraq and Erzerum, and most of Kurdistan and western Armenia. iv) Furthermore he opened up a new road of expansion by his development of naval power - and by the victory off Preresa gained the initiative in the Med, not lost until Lepanto.

Limit of Expansion on N.W. — But by about 1540 distance, enemy opposition and physical conditions had set a limit to his victories. A renewed war with Austria in 1549 - after the peace of 1547 - ended in no real change in the position in the treaty 13 years later. The border was hardening. Ferdinand was erecting a formidable barrier against the Ottomans by rebuilding Hungarian fortresses. The years of rapid conquest were gone; victories now cost much more and brought far less reward.

& S.E. — Likewise in the S.E the tactics of evasion of the Shah and the irremediable difficulties of remoteness, terrain and climate had brought profitable conquest almost to a standstill. A war to annex Georgia, Persian Armenia and Azerbaijan would be certain to involve vast expense. So on this frontier also the Ottomans had almost attained the furthest limit of valid and justifiable expansion. How far did this cause decay?

1) Differentiate symptoms & causes — It is extremely difficult to differentiate between the causes and symptoms of Ottoman decline. For instance was the slackening of military discipline and hence loss of efficiency a cause or result of their weakness? And even more important was the poor quality of many of the future Sultans only a cause of decay - was not it also an outward manifestation of inward corruption as well? Realising this difficulty I will not draw too sharp a line between the two.

(i) Decline - military standards & obedience — One major cause-cum-symptom was the decline in military standards and obedience. This first really manifested itself in 1525 when the Janissaries, restless at the three years of peace demanded a renewed campaign. Their tendency to an increase in their excessive power, especially under Suleiman's weak successors is shown at Selim's coronation when they forced the Sultan to let their children come into the ranks. It had been Suleiman who had opened the door by allowing them to marry.

their increase in power shown — (a) due to lack of conquest — no recruits — Their decline was undoubtedly largely due to the ceasing of conquest. Their privileged ranks were made up of specially trained men either captured in war or enrolled by the five-year slave tythe. It can easily be seen

European History [6] June 1961

(3) Essay on :- "The Limits of Turkish expansion also entailed the immediate decline of their Empire." Is this true of the time of Suleiman the Magnificent? H. Macfarlane.

how when the frontiers of the Empire were no longer being pushed forward the belt of surrounding territory which had furnished a continuous supply of captives for the enormous slave-trade of the Empire soon became depopulated by raids. Between about 1630–1650 the custom of pressing native Christian boys into the service of the Stilten in the "kullar" ceased.

Sipahi mutinous too

reasons

The Janissaries were not alone in finding the cessation of profitable conquest irksome. The sipahi also became rebellious – for instance in 1589 they compelled Amurath to reinstate the grand vizier Sinan. These feudal landowners were especially frustrated by the fact that although their numbers continued to increase by additions from among the slave class there was no longer great tracts of conquered lands out of which new timars could be conquered. This economic and social discontent is largely the explanation of their increased envy of the "kullar" or privileged class – which caused an all important disunity within the Empire.

no new "timars" for them.

Abuses & corruption in landholding

– result

Another feature of the decline was developing corruption and insecurity in regard to landholding, with such abuses as tax-farming and governmental sale of lands for gratuities, thus destroying the very basis of the feudal system of estates. The landholding system being of a tangled nature – a natural consequence of the amalgamation of widespread tribes who already had deeply embedded customs – meant that the administration became increasingly bureaucratic. Such a multiplication of relations acted powerfully towards decentralization, for the regulation of countless details could be attended to better from points near at hand – a dangerous tendency in an Empire so widespread and so recent. Suleiman made attempts to systematise the situation – and with some success. But he could not remove the causes of the complication. Instead by giving the right to obtain timali to the inferior classes he unknowingly set the precedent which, followed by the sandshaks and pachas with their slaves finally led to the central authority of disposing of timali as gratuities without regard to their military potential. The result was that in a few years a sanshak instead of providing 100 sipahis – pofter only provided fifteen or so.

decentralization

Suleiman unable to stop

inadvertently starts

result

Ranke maintains that it was necessary for Turkey to

Importance of Sultan

have a mighty and warlike chief for its animation, and continued campaigns and progressive conquests to give it movement and activity. Whether the second was essential it is difficult to measure, but the decline in the quality of the Sultans immediately after the reign of Suleiman undoubtedly contributed considerably to the decay of the Empire. Largely dependent for strong government and success in battle largely on the Sultan who was head of every institution in the land, the decay of the army and the conditions of land-tenure can be traced largely to the lack of this central control. Weak Sultans followed one another Selim II, Murad III, Ibrahim and Mahomed IV, while the effect a powerful Sultan could have is shown by the success of Mahomed Küpülü in re-establishing command of the Eastern Mediterranean, and after he died of his son Ahmed in temporarily reforming the administration of the Empire. Harmful practices such as the custom of killing all rival relatives when ascending the throne, or later of the "kafes" which weakened the Sultan by years of virtual imprisonment, so that he gave birth to weak sons, who in turn were confined and further deteriorated, contributed to this loss of quality. But at first this contribution to Ottoman decline seems not to have been caused by any real fault within the Empire but by mere misfortune.

the other weaknesses stemmed from

Küpülü family

at first mere misfortune

The Two Institutions

The Ottoman Empire was ruled by two seperate institutions - the (1) Ottoman Ruling Institution and the (2) Moslem Institution of the Ottoman Empire. The former (1) wielding the sword, the pen and the sceptre, was composed largely of Christian-born slaves while the latter (2) in charge of religion, learning and law consisted completely of the Mohammedans - in other words the Turks and largely the sipahis. The greatest danger to the whole Ottoman system lay in the rivalry of these two great institutions and in a tendency of the ruling Institution towards decentralization and division into its component parts. We have seen how the envy of sipahis was stirred up by social and economic stress resulting from the cessation of conquest. In the last years of Suleiman this envy manifested itself in the demand of large numbers of the troops recruited for the armies of Selim and Bayazid to be raised to the status of janissaries or members of the Kullar. The disequilibrium between the two was heightened by the drying-up of the supply of Christian slaves, the very foundation of the Ruling Institution. This meant that the Moslem Institution gained dominance, and while engulfing the other it absorbed much of the corruption and venality which had spread outwards from Constantinople, while itself imposing a stultifying rigidity and conservation on the hitherto progressive part of the State.

Greatest danger - rivalry

more acute

(2) engulfs (1) absorbs its poison

Rigidity

Despite the man-made canun law of Suleima fundamental changes remained almost impossible for it was

June 1961.

(3) Turkey (cont'd)

the Moslem law-interpreters, determined to preserve the Sacred Law who increasingly dominated the Sultan and passively obstructed change. Hence Turkey found herself, in

Results

i) such important matters as military weapons and tactics, being overtaken and left behind. Lybyer calls this the "real tragedy of the Turk" that - bound hand and foot by the scholastic Mohammedanism which reached perfection in about the 14 ... they could

ii) not amalgamate the subject Christian peoples, already confirmed in nationalism by the events of centuries. The deadening system

iii) stilled their active spirits, imprisoned their extraordinary adaptability, and held them at a stage of culture which ... was before long passed through and left by the progressive West. In fact the Turks holding an Empire long divided & in attempting to fuse it into one vigorous nation, harmonious in every part, and run through by patriotism managed to solve the administrative and governmental phase of it but not the religious and hence social and cultural unity.

(Margin: In fact only a half an Empire)

It is difficult not to be impressed by the large amount of evidence supporting the view of obstruction in expansion leading directly to decline. Instead of satisfying and occupying subjects with loot, slaves and lands foreign warfare - especially that against the Portuguese - and the Persian and Hungarian wars of Amurath's reign was a serious drain on Ottoman resources. Undoubtedly this caused many of the internal abuses which gradually weakened the Empire's power - the inactivity of the Janissaries, the jealousy or discontent of the sipahis. But we must also notice that the decline was not rapid. Lepanto did not see the end of Ottoman military power for she still held many of the ports off North Africa - Tunis and Algiers, Tripoli, Tunis. It was not until over a hundred years later at St Gothard (1664) and even more seriously at the defeat before Vienna in 1683 that the Ottomans began to be driven back. Under weak Sultans she might be disintegrating slowly, but it was by no means a strikingly immediate collapse. It seems that it was a foredoomed failure, for lacking complete internal unity she could not hope to remain for long balanced between advance and decline. Nations must either expand or contract, and the awakening of Catholic Europe prevented Westward expansion, and distance and conditions Eastward.

(Margin: Conclusion. War became a burden and caused many abuses. BUT DECLINE NOT SO RAPID AS MIGHT BE THOUGHT)

Yes - Well done.

I remember well that Karl Leyser was a rather shy man – who used to skate through from his inner room to the outer one where I was taught. He listened intently and then poured forth a set of comments. These were brilliant little mini-essays and I took them down as fast as I could. There is a page of comments on this essay, and they were split into four little sections. I shall give them in full as an example of how rich the supervision feedback system could be.

Were there signs in the first C16 that the Turks were already out-gunned & out-fixed on the Northern front? Mohacs was the defeat of a crumbling & divided power – and that even this disaster might have been avoided. The Siege of Vienna [illegible] – was it only the climate & conditions which turned them back. Wasn't the artillery & war-gear of the West better already? It was only through the Sultan's welcome to Western émigrés etc or Ruling Institution that progress went on. They gradually lost contact & went behind – not inventive. In the first half of the C16 they did not advance as fast as the West. The Spahis · light cavalry – their service only lasted from Spring – Autumn – they weren't up to the new German fighting methods.

Cf with Romans.
Concordia, pax, servilitas, rex lex, they did have certain ideas which they gave to their conquered lands. Nothing in the Turkish Empire of a binding and cementing nature (like the Church fellowship of the Byzantine Empire). The Ruling Institution was the inner fortress & the subjects – ~~the~~ every Sandshakbeg, Beglebeg became a minor Sultan – decentralisation. Turks as conquerors no policies – nothing to offer to their conquered pop'ns. In fact the Moslems wanted to keep the infidel infidel – because then he paid a head-tax. In fact the Turks aided the existing religious hierarchy of the Greek Church: never even wanted to keep a cultural unity. Having defeated the Mamelukes they restored them. The only pop'n became thoroughly absorbed were the like primitive warrior races in the mountains of Bosnia and Albania.

1525 Janissaries [illegible].
Shows the absolute necessity of successful war. For this reason limitation meant things were going wrong. The limits were inherent in the system because Spahi's could not be used every year. Sea-power they used the Barbary – almost an indep power.

– as they could not [illegible] more posts – sub-division of posts within the Empire.

BALKANS.
The Turks were popular in the small states outside the Empire. They meant a replacement of the chaos & oppression of minor principalities. At first a release from oppression.
But – then questionable in C16 whether the increase of military commitments & the oppression of sandshaks. The larger number of officials the larger the amount of corruption.
– [illegible]

ESSAY 7: (June) 'What signs of growing distress and opposition can you see behind the façade of absolute monarchy in France 1516-1559?' A shorter essay of 4 and a quarter pages, but with the comment. 'Very well done. That's interesting' –

It thus looks as if I did between ten and twelve essays in the term – and succeeded reasonably. In fact I wonder whether this was the term when I really began to move up a step in my historical understanding and self-confidence. And, if that is the case, whether it is related to the mature and varied social life I was leading, largely thanks to the relationship with Julie described in another chapter.

*

At the end of the term we would go up to the Senior Common Room at Worcester and there the tutors would read out to the assembled group, including the Provost, their report on our work. I have a sheet of paper on which, very soon after the event, I wrote down their comments.

Leyser
Mr Macfarlane is one of the most judicious & hard-working pupils I have taught. He does not skimp and all his remarks are based on good, sound sense. He has always put forward well arranged & balanced essays and shown modesty and historical sense. If there is one short-coming this is his lack of passion – if [he] had a streak of this almost of cruelty and of daring his essays would be excellent. Still I have enjoyed taking him very much.

Campbell
Well Provost. I would say the same – well-balanced, sane, careful, hard-working but lacking that burst of confidence or passion. He is almost too modest, too moderate, too good-tempered & equable. But if he continues to work hard he may well do very well.

Summer Vacation 1961

This was one of the two summer holidays I would spend as an undergraduate, and in many ways the most carefree, as there was still a long way to my final exams. Also the summer vacations were long – over three and a half months from mid-June to the end of September. How did I fill that time?

I spent about six weeks or two months teaching at Copthorne School, both to earn some money and to find out what teaching was like – as a possible career. I think I found it rather dull and frustrating and all that I can really remember is trying to inject some Christianity into the school – to the dismay of other teachers. I also remember wandering moodily over the rather lovely countryside hoping to find some beautiful maiden to court.

After Copthorne I went to the religious camp at Iwerne Minster for ten days – and perhaps started to find the Christian evangelical earnestness less attractive. The other major event was a hitch-hiking visit to the Outer Hebrides. I remember the rain, the small tent, the beautiful church at Rodel and camping above it, the Callanish stones, but not much detail.

These activities left very little time, I suspect, for the Lakes and my grandparents. The only notes in my grandparent's diaries were as follows:

Thursday 17 August 'Alan arrives'
Sunday 20 August 'Alan leaves for Scotland'
Wed 13 September 'Alan leaves for Bolton with Porter'
Wed 27 September 'Alan leaves for Oxford'

My mother's first letter of the holidays is dated June 27.

My dear Alan,

Your first letter from your prep school just arrived, I gather you're viewing it with mixed feelings, anyway its all Experience. I cant imagine anything worse than hundreds of small boys of that age, all bent on not learning anything, but I suppose there are one or two who make it all worth while. I'm sorry you ran out of money again, I'll send the £7 to Granny, but will you let us know exactly what the situation is, whether you are able to pay Richard back out of your wages and if you will have anything over? What are you now going to do between the end of your job and going to Iwerne? And when will that be? We'll send something at the end of July anyway, but would like to have an idea of your needs during the vac. Are you going to the Hebrides by car, train or hitch hiking? I'm sorry Julie wont be able to come after all, I gather her parents thought they were all asked, hope there was no offence taken?

... I am at the stage where I'm quite certain that we shant be able to finish any of our syllabuses, the pity of it is that we cant linger over things that interest us but have to keep pressing on with that awful Target looming in the mists. We've at last abandoned Henry VIIIth and are whipping through the next two reigns as I can foresee that Elizabeth is going to take an eternity. ... Copthorne sounds a lovely place, how did you hear of it? I read a letter of Richard's in the Spectator, about Billy Graham, I disagreed needless to say but it was a good effort getting it published. Have you been reading the Sunday Times articles on religion in the universities? Very interesting, I wonder how it has affected you, if at all? ... Hope you're not feeling too bad about Julie, is she coming to Oxford as an undergrad? Much love from us all – Mummy

The next letter from my mother is dated July 12th, but refers to an earlier, lost, letter of mine, so I shall place it here.

My dear Alan,

I've taken to answering your letters when I get one which I hope isn't leaving too big gaps, life is so absolutely timeless here in the hot weather that unless I keep strict diaries, which I don't, I find myself lost.

Anyway thank you for a letter we got yesterday, reading behind the lines I fear you aren't enjoying school life much, never mind it will be nearly over by now. We liked the snap of Julie, she looks most attractive, fancy being brilliant as well! Will she be trying to get back to Oxford? Re. the money, I suggest you pay Richard back half what you owe him and we'll pay him the other half, £6. This should leave you enough until we can get some of our pay home to you which we will at the end of the month, but it wont arrive till the first or second of August. Make sure that you aren't short for your London stay, I'm sure R. wont mind waiting a bit longer but I'd rather you didn't borrow from Granny if you can help it ... I wish you could get us a cheap edition of the "Lord of the Rings" is it in paper backs? The Cowans have been telling me about it for years but I've never read it. By the way do go and see the Marsdens when you're in Iwerne, I shall be writing to her to say you'll be along. And the Cowans on your way north, they'll be in their new house.

I wrote from Copthorne School on a Sunday 9 July.

Dear Mummy, Daddy and Anne,
Firstly let me thank Annie for her letter. I was very pleased (and surprised) to get it and almost more pleased to see how much Annie's letter-writing had improved both in thought and expression. It shows that Mummy's teaching is having a considerable effect. I am glad the pupil as well as the teacher seems to be enjoying the work and hope that the practice exams go well. No, I haven't been able to keep up with the hit-parade for a while – though I expect Martin will tell me it all when I get up to the Lakes! The latest "pop" record I have heard is a rock'n roll version of "Grieg's Piano Concerto" – awful isn't it! I am just <u>waiting</u> for David Whitfield to get hold of the Messiah – Hallelujah chorus – that really <u>will</u> be the end!

I don't know how far you have now managed to piece together my holiday plans – but here is a final statement. After leaving here on the 27th of July. I will stay in London for about a week to see Julie (by the way Julie's mother didn't dream of suggesting they should all go up – it was merely that she was attempting to be complimentary – and being Hungarian did not make her meaning clear) – and Julia (& Billy) have invited me to go down and stay at their delightful new house not far from here over August Bank Holiday – when R & Angela will also be going. If I can keep the children amused I will be a very welcome guest! After Iwerne (ending on the 18th) I will go up to the Lakes for a day (by bus <u>if</u> I can – it is much cheaper) and then on to the Hebrides – I am not sure how.

I am still enjoying myself very much here – though I don't have much to do <u>in</u> school. I spend most of my time either taking outdoor activities such as swimming & cricket or else on my own work – my Map of the "Lord of the Rings" – my history and my reading. I have just re-read "Wind in the Willows" and enjoyed it far more than I did first time. It really is delightfully written and some of it – such as "Piper at the Gates of Dawn" is very beautiful. I expect one phrase out of it will make all the humour and characters rush back into your minds. "I wonder" said Toad to himself, "I wonder if this kind of car <u>starts</u> easily."(!)

Yesterday was the big day of the school year – "Patres" (fathers) you can tell what sort of a school it is from that one Latinism!). But it wasn't wildly exciting. 150 parents, younger brothers and sisters in their company jaguars descended with boxes of strawberries, wirelesses and deck-chairs and swept their sons away to the nearest hotel for lunch. After this they returned and in between the showers sat bravely watching the Fathers v Boys cricket match with the West wind whistling past their "special" hats. I umpired for a while and then went and took swimming. The only two incidents of real interest for me were when one of the visiting younger brothers was pushed-in fully dressed into the swimming bath (he was rescued!) and when I met one parent – a Professor Swan – a white Russian who now lives in America and lectures on the B.B.C. He had met many of the great Russian composers and had actually lived in the same house as Rachmaninov!

Next week I should have more to write about as I am going up to the "deb" dance on Tuesday and, I hope, going on a choir outing on Thursday. Bye for now – look after yourselves and be very happy.
Lots of love to you all, Alan

The reference to 'Wind in the Willows' is reflected in a small blue notebook in which I made copies of things I was reading at this time. On 17 July I copied in various passages from the 'Wind in the Willows', including Mole's first impression of the river, toad on being knocked down by a car, the woodland pageantry, winter nakedness, Toad on seeing a car, Toad's prison, hot buttered toast. I then copied in various extracts from Victor Gollancz, 'From Darkness to Light', on serenity, rustic sayings and other things from Russian, Chinese and other authors. I remember finding the book highly stimulating. There were also poems by Leonard Clark, Wilfred Rowland Childe and Paul Verlaine. There was a passage by George Meredith in one of his poems, 'Golden Lie the Meadows', another poem on 'The Wood' by Leonard Clark, 'A fair' and 'A spring morning in London'.

Thomas Randolph on 'Married Love' – beauty in a woman, sums up part of my love-sick attitude.

> When essence meets with essence, and souls join
> In mutual knots, that's the true nuptial twine
> Such, lady, is my love, and such is true,
> All other love is to your sex, not you.

On Tuesday 11 July, I went up to London for the big debutante party at the London Zoo. I still vaguely recall that I did not enjoy it – and that is mentioned by my mother in a letter to me. I imagine I was too demanding, wanting demonstrative affection etc., which Julie did not provide. This is supported by the following two letters.

Probably aware that this was going to be a turning-point letter, this is the one letter to Julie of this year of which I have taken a carbon copy.

Wednesday [12 July] Copthorne School, Sussex

My dear Pusseybite,

I have just come back from a solitary walk. The paths were bespangled with rain drops and the rhodedendrons dripped noisily. It has been a wild wet day with lowering clouds and sweeping waves of rain but about 6 it began to clear and now it is calm, fresh and clean. The earth which has been cracking and burning during the long drought has almost been sucking in the moisture – the lush vegetation is visibly blossoming as the long draught trickles to its roots. My heart and mind are full of impressions of dripping clover, moisture studded dog roses and a tranquil sky. I feel myself soothed, grateful, uplifted, serene and happy. How quickly are wounds covered over.

Last night seems like an aching dream now but I suppose it must have been true. I hope you managed your journey back alright – Gabrielle very kindly drove me back as she was staying just nearby. I suppose you will have started your job by the time that this arrives – good hunting, and don't get picked up as a Russian spy – or anything else!

I do apologies for my behaviour darling, especially if it made you unhappy. I know there was a considerable measure of childish selfishness in my attitude – and you are quite right I haven't any particular claims over you. But in one final attempt to prevent a reoccurrence of last night I will make an attempt to explain my attitude to our relationship, and why I felt so miserable last night. I know I won't manage – because as yet I'm bad at introspection – but see if you can discern the general drift of my remarks!

As you will have realised I have for a long time been building up a perfect girlfriend – much as you have been doing with "Peri" [Julie's imagined son – Peregrine?]. As my parents have been abroad I have been unable to lavish much love on them – I only consider them as wonderful, kind, love-worthy but not loveable people. I have affection yes, but I'm not sure it is love. Hence I have been seeking someone with whom I could share every thought and action. Who would believe in and love those things I believed in and loved – when I found you I was sure I had found that person. At first, quite rightly I think, I saw religious differences as a hindrance, but your other merits over-weighed that – for instance your frankness, your sympathy, your interest in beauty, things spiritual and in the importance of remaining child-like in certain respects. Hence the time I spent with you during the end of the Easter Term and the Summer Term was perhaps the happiest of my life. If you had been a boy I like to think we would have been very close friends – and that the real basis of our relationships was not sexual. But to quote C.S. Lewis, 'when the two people who thus discover they are on the same secret road are of different sexes, the friendship will pass very easily into erotic love. Indeed, unless they are physically repulsive to each other it is almost certain to do so sooner or later.' With me, at least, it was sooner – and although you have always maintained that you have never been physically attracted to me, for a while at least you encouraged me.

So the term passed and during it I gathered many happy memories like globules of honey to sustain me through the barren weeks that lay ahead. Because I believed that once I had found another person who liked me for [what] I was – and knew all, one I had tasted this blessed release from loneliness, the haunting loneliness which arises from our own fear of being known, and from the outside worlds indifference and even hostility to our attempts at exposure (I have often felt that the reason why you provoked hostility from certain people was because you handed yourself over to them, partly stripped so to speak, and they resented this). I would be heart-broken when 'the vision splendid had faded into the light of common day'. Added to this was the fact that I wasn't sure whether I was in love with you or not.

Imagine then my surprise and joy at finding that apart from spells of sadness in the evenings I was not too unhappy down here away from you. I still cared for you enormously and thought of you a lot – but there was not that long deep ache which I have sometimes felt jab me – and I believe would be with me if I loved you with all my being. I still loved you with my mind but away from you my heart was not in shreds. I was, to tell the truth, a shade disappointed. Nevertheless I looked forward eagerly to your letters, and apart from my sorrow that it would be such a short time to the Dance on the 11th I felt that for four hours we would be able to share our hopes, our adventures and our memories. Sentimental rubbish – you may say. And you were right. Quite truly darling, I didn't come up to London for the Dance. I came up to see you. If there had been a choice of seeing you for an evening, or going to Sally's party, I would have unhesitatingly chosen the former. Your letters kept saying "we will discuss this when we meet as it will take up far too much space here" etc. Then came the evening.

There is no need to dwell on it. By all standards [carbon of a passage missing] … you spending about an hour altogether dancing and talking with Hubert. After all we will be able to talk together when I come up to London – and this was an evening when you should meet people. I saw all this – and also that as I was professedly not in love with you – and that you would be going abroad soon, there was no reason why you should have spent the whole evening with me. I went downstairs and wandered around arguing all this out in my mind, and then looking at myself in a mirror. I agreed that I couldn't see any reason why you shouldn't prefer to dance with Hubert for a while (I'm not trying to be self-pitying or nasty darling – this is exactly what I <u>did</u> think at the time. I have a habit of smiling ruefully at myself on the occasions when I look at myself and decide that I can quite understand why girls seem to tire of me). But sadly all these philosophic thoughts were immediately dispelled when I saw you dancing with your cheek laid on Hubert's.

The first blows had been struck earlier – firstly when you said that you were going to stay with Sally from the 1st August. (I think I had told you I had hoped to be in London 27th July to about Aug 6th, though now I will change my plan). Secondly when you seemed so abstracted – so almost indifferent. I know you weren't really, but I got the impression that you were hailing me as a friend who you met in the street, one's face lightens with joy – then one forgets and is absorbed again in the problems of crossing the road. You hardly said anything about anything – and I felt my foolish prattle was merely disturbing you. Worst of all, although I felt somehow I should treat you defererentially almost as a stranger – yet suddenly I was again overwhelmed by love – Eros – call it what you will. Perhaps it was the result of 3 weeks alone in the country – certainly I felt every minute I was with you precious.

These are some of the reasons why I was so dismayed when – having been so absorbed in yourself with me – you suddenly seemed to blossom with Hubert. I know I have no right to monopolise you, but it was just the disappointment when I realised that after so much happiness together you were just as happy dancing and talking to a boisterous and, which unjustly I thought as an outsider – as with myself.

This has been long, rambling probably revoltingly self-pitying – certainly very self absorbed. I hope you'll forgive it. I'm afraid you'll either have to accept it all as part of me or acknowledge that I have been deceiving you all along and am not worthy of you – which I have suspected anyhow!

To sum up – I want you as a friend – and by a friend I mean a person who will always help me – listen to me, share my dreams and my enthusiasms. If out of all the adventures, happy and sad, this could arise I would be overjoyed. I'm afraid the conditions I ask are probably too harsh and I don't suppose I have a right to ask them. They are that in my presence –until you are going steady with someone else – especially when I'm only seeing you for a short period – you should be prepared to spend most of your attention on me (as I certainly will do on you), unless of course you are with your family or with other girl friends. In return I will give you my friendship for what it is worth. Whatever you choose I will always pray for you, think of you and remember with great gratitude and happiness our time together.

The immediate problem is how to continue. I would still like to make the map for you (so if you could send the suggestions sometime?) and hope you will write up the account and send me some photos of yourself. A difficulty is that although I only really want friendship, and so do you, when I am with you I find myself wanting to kiss and fondle you. I can (and did) restrain myself but you might as well know how I feel. I don't suppose it will be a good idea for me to come up this Sunday. I wait to hear how you feel about everything before I finally decide – and also before I decide whether I ought (for your sake as well as mine) to see you again before you to go Italy. If I am only going to get worked up into a state of misery (and I really was very unhappy on Tuesday evening) every time I see you it wont be pleasant for either of us and its no solution saying its my fault. I know it is!

[Sentence illegible…]… by trying in a short piece to alter the nature of a relationship.

Darling, I hope this letter hasn't saddened or bored you. It hasn't really captured what I meant to say but if any of it is unkind please forgive me. I know deep down in me how wonderful you are! It just seems that on the surface I too am having difficulty in adapting myself to a changed relationship. …. clinging the rock of my old idyllic vision of… [illegible couple of lines…]

There is a three page 'Wardrobe List'. Here are some samples.

Wardrobe list

Formal Clothes.
3. You must have a new suit instead of your blue one, which is – frankly – awful. Get a formalish one if you can't afford two – there are many substitutes for the informal suit. Have one made in dark grey, really dark, I mean but completely plain. Never go in for fancy mixtures and patterns. A tall boy can carry them off, but they look clownish on boys of your height…. This should be the most important item in your wardrobe…. [sketch of length]
4. The trouble with your shoes is that they are too round at the toes. [drawing of three types of shoes – 'The third shape is correct'). Have you black shoes? You should have…..
5. You are too old to wear a duffle-coat. A cream raincoat (full length, belted) is quite respectable. Again, it must be simple - & make sure it fits perfectly!

Informal

1. *Corduroy [sic] is wonderful for jackets or trousers, especially in dark green or yellow ochre. If you don't dare to try this Bohemian artist look, don't try. Never wear anything you dislike. (But I like it.)*
2. *Wear crisp, fresh white shirts, not limp cream ones, not (on the whole) coloured, striped or patterned viyella or flannel…*
3. *Are your grey flannel trousers really good enough? Do they fit the requirements stated in A3?*
4. *Invest in one two jumpers (thin knit, v-neck, large size!) from M & S. your colours are oatmeal, sand, light mustard, apple green (Granny Smiths), lightest blue. Never anything strong & dark. Wear them with shirts but only with cravats, not ties! ….*
5. *If you don't dare to get a corduroy jacket, you should get another tweed to replace you present, over-worked one.*
6. *I suggest you get a new pair of jeans & throw your black ones away. Your new ones must be really tight & fairly high-cut. In the palest blue denim possible. Hunt for them till you find some that are really pale enough.*

If you get everything on this list the minimum cost would be between £60-£90. As this is obviously impossible just do your best without being extravagant, but remembering that you ought to have all these things by the time you are 25 and certainly before you are 30, and they are more important than a guitar or a radio or even a car, in my opinion, so be resolute, & good luck with your budgeting.
IF IN DOUBT – consult "The Julianna Dress Agency Ltd"

The next letter from my mother is dated July 23rd alluding to a letter that arrived for her birthday on 22nd July.

My dear Alan,

Your letter yesterday arrived very accurately on my birthday, and I'm sure your subconscious must have prompted it. Don't worry, I quite understand you have lots else on your mind at the moment. I do hope you made up your tiff with Julie, I'm sorry the dance wasn't as good as you'd hoped, I imagine all that high class entertaining is inclined to be dreary, I don't know how the wretched girls can get through a "season" of it. The animals sounded fun though. I think you will be with Billy and Julia now, or just about, so will send this there, I hope you have a fine week end and that the thought of facing the road and going to the sea is [not] *too fearful. Give them all my love.*

Life goes on its steamy way, I spent a very quiet birthday alone with Daddy as Anne has gone away. I envy you the Hebrides, what I couldn't do with just one misty shieling just now! You must write us long and mouth-watering descriptions and look round for a croft we can retire to when the crowds round Field Head become too oppressive. … I have now got to write a forward to a book about some Assamese gent of whom I know nothing. The author of the book assures me that he is on a par with Byron, Shelley, Wordsworth etc. He may be right, but dare I say so in my preface? It is the sort of book that nobody will read, poor author, he is a terribly earnest young man burning to discuss Byron, Keats, Spenser etc. but his English is quite beyond me and the only contribution I can make to the conversation is "Pardon?".

We are sending £20 at the end of the month. Let us know what you have managed to pay Richard. Please thank him for his birthday letter if you see him. Much love to Robert & A & all the Jameses, will be writing to former. Mummy

My next letter was a late birthday letter to my mother. As I tried to illustrate it, I will put in a scan of the letter to show the drawings.

Friday.

Copthorne School
SUSSEX.

My dearest Mummy,

Please forgive me for being late with your birthday letter - but I was thinking of you on the day and wishing you MANY HAPPY RETURNS - as I do now by letter! I hope you had a peaceful and relaxed day, as I know that is what you would consider the most enjoyable kind of birthday, rather than mad gaiety in the mid-day sun! As usual I am too spineless to organize a present - but I will get ~~th~~ you one ~~present~~ when you come back as I am doing with Fiona and Annie, perhaps a copy of "The Lord of the Rings"?

I do not feel sage enough to offer you any words of wisdom on this august occasion - (as you will have to do very soon on my 21st birthday) - which is not far off now.

(I have given her a dreadful head I'm afraid!) - have replaced it!

Instead - as I don't want this letter to be just another ordinary "newsy" letter I will try to do some illustrations

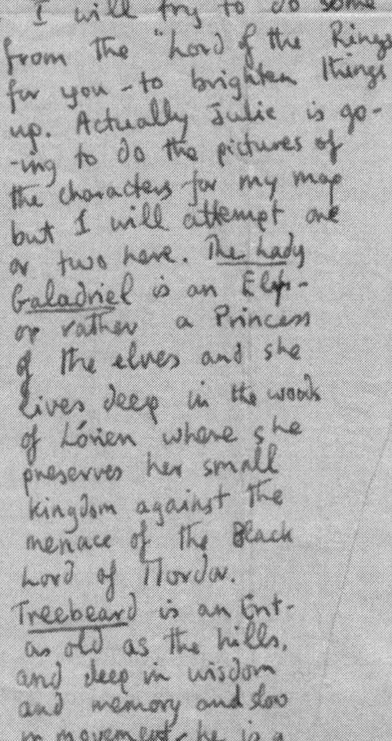

from the "Lord of the Rings" for you - to brighten things up. Actually Julie is going to do the pictures of the characters for my map but I will attempt one or two here. The Lady Galadriel is an Elf - or rather a Princess of the elves and she lives deep in the woods of Lórien where she preserves her small kingdom against the menace of the Black Lord of Mordor. Treebeard is an Ent - as old as the hills, and deep in wisdom and memory and slow in movement - he is a

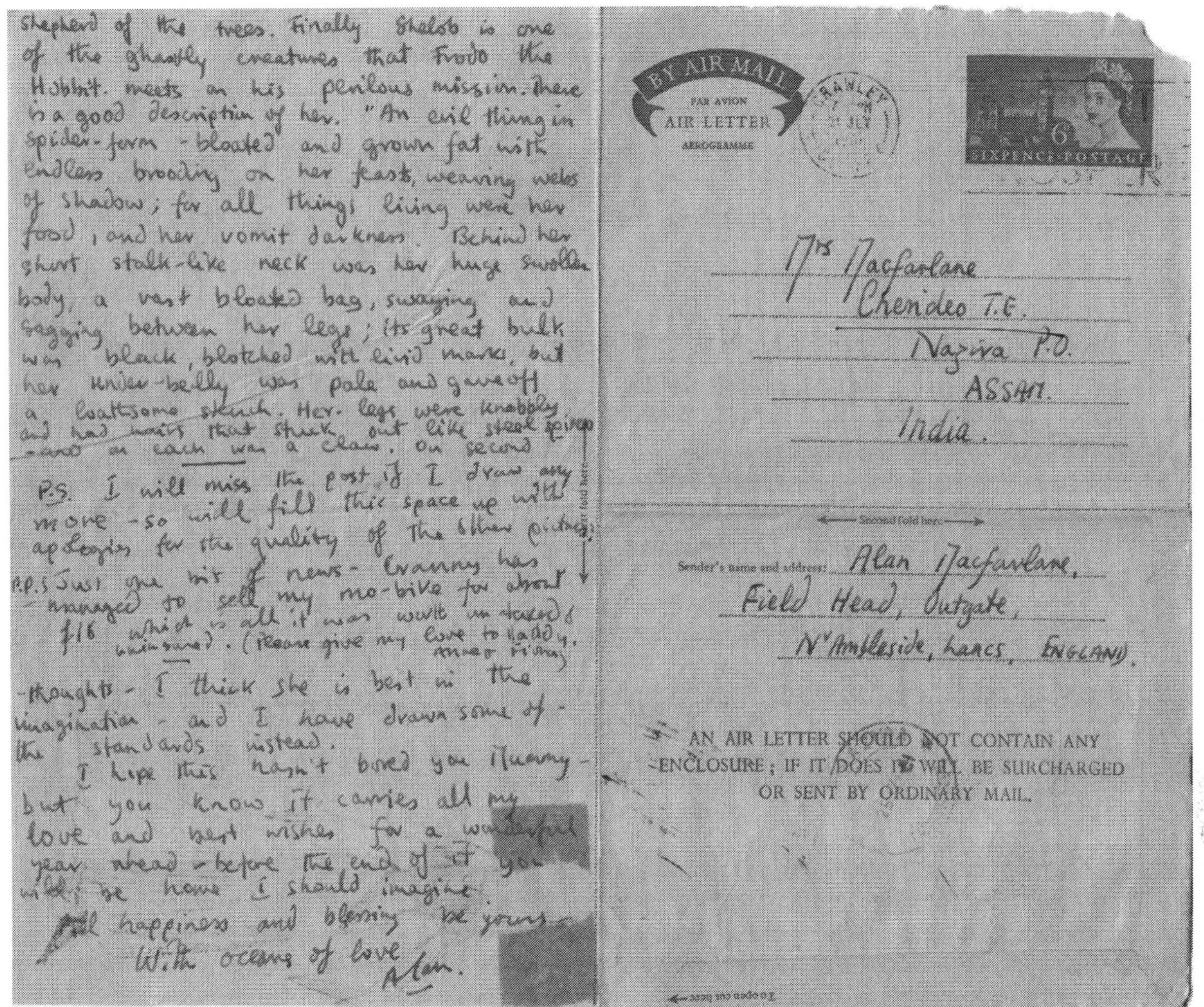

shepherd of the trees. Finally Shelob is one of the ghastly creatures that Frodo the Hobbit meets on his perilous mission. There is a good description of her. "An evil thing in spider-form - bloated and grown fat with endless brooding on her feasts, weaving webs of shadow; for all things living were her food, and her vomit darkness. Behind her short stalk-like neck was her huge swollen body, a vast bloated bag, swaying and sagging between her legs; its great bulk was black, blotched with livid marks, but her under-belly was pale and gave off a loathsome stench. Her legs were knobbly and had hairs that stuck out like steel spines - and on each was a claw. On second thoughts - I think she is best in the imagination - and I have drawn some of the standards instead.

I hope this hasn't bored you Mummy - but you know it carries all my love and best wishes for a wonderful year ahead - before the end of it you will be home I should imagine.

All happiness and blessing be yours -

With oceans of love

Alan.

P.S. I will miss the post if I draw any more - so will fill this space up with apologies for the quality of the other pictures.

P.P.S. Just one bit of news - Granny has managed to sell my mo-bike for about £16 which is all it was worth un-taxed & uninsured. (Please give my love to Daddy, Anne & Fiona)

BY AIR MAIL
PAR AVION
AIR LETTER
AEROGRAMME

SIXPENCE POSTAGE 6

Mrs Macfarlane,
Chenideo T.E.
Naziva P.O.
ASSAM.
India.

Second fold here

Sender's name and address: Alan Macfarlane,
Field Head, Outgate,
Nr Ambleside, Lancs, ENGLAND.

AN AIR LETTER SHOULD NOT CONTAIN ANY ENCLOSURE; IF IT DOES IT WILL BE SURCHARGED OR SENT BY ORDINARY MAIL.

A letter from me to my old school friend Ian Campbell is dated 1st August (1961) and addressed from Field Head, though, as it states, it was written in London. I fortunately kept a carbon copy of most of this handwritten letter.

My dear Ian,

"The time has come the walrus said to talk of many things, of ships and shoes and sealing wax and cabbages and kings." (I hope I haven't used this start on you before!). I don't think I have ever been more conscious of the barriers that separate us – not merely of distance but of every accident of surroundings. As I sit in my black sweater, brown and black trousers and pink (I ask you!) cravat, I can hear "the roar of London's traffic" outside for I am actually writing from my Uncle's flat in Old Brompton Rd. I have so much to write about but what does *it sound like read over your extra-vitamin breakfast cereal in the clean salt air of a blue and silver Vancouver morning? But I must try as you have been magnificently energetic in writing me two letters and promptly replying to David Philips. For all these things I thank you. I found your letters very interesting and will try to answer some of your questions.*

But before that congratulations –the first on your 2nd class mark at University which sounds impressive tho' I don't know exactly what it means. The second on finding (or being found?) by as wonderful a girl as Joyce – she sounds great – you're a lucky man. But I will be discussing that fascinating topic more exhaustively later. I will leave the three most important topics to the end: faith, future and friends (in the broadest sense).

I really would like to come over to Canada before I get settled down in some job, so I will start thinking about 1963 (perhaps a bad year for you?), 1964 or even 1965. I think it almost essential to get a wide view of life before one gets settled in any particular groove – but the danger is that one becomes a wanderer and even if that doesn't happens one's friends and family get worried that it will.

This in turn leads on to that looming chasm – or rather chasm of chasms – one's career. What does Joyce say in this matter? I am sure she will be too intelligent to mistake such frippery as money, fame or even material success as synonymous with pleasure and an end in themselves. I totally agree with a rustic saying which I read in a deeply spiritual book ("From Darkness to Light" – Victor Gollancz – do read it if you have the chance). "The crowd cares for gain, the honest man for fame, the good man values success, but the Wise Man his soul." I believe firmly that looking on the human and psychological level many highly-paid jobs are not conducive to happiness, while others, demanding sacrifice and dedication, often prove a far better choice. This is obvious – and it is also obvious that when one is responsible for a wife and children, money achieves considerable importance – however much one may hate the stuff. I am not against highly-paid jobs merely because they are highly paid tho' I feel this is dangerous spiritually in itself – there is an ocean of wisdom in the words "it is harder for a camel to pass thro' the eye of a needle…" etc – for it induces a materialistic outlook on life – a self-satisfaction and self-sufficiency which I am sure corrodes even the most upright soul. I hope this doesn't sound like sermonizing – but I'm working things out for myself in this letter too!

As yet I have only in front of me the frame as it were of the job that awaits me. I am not at all sure what will fill it – but I hope it will be a "vocation" not a "job" and I hope it will be one in which I am enabled to give happiness to others – partly from gratitude that I have been given such a wonderful childhood, schooling & family – partly because it is a commonly observed phenomenon that happiness can only be attained indirectly and is most often reached by those who give it to others.

Another statement which caught my eye in V. Gollancz's book was "The more a man gives up his heart to God, to his vocation and to men, forgetful of himself and of that which belongs to him the greater poise he will acquire, until he reaches peace, quiet, joy, the apanage of simple and humble souls" – which seems good sense to me. I am growingly convinced that unless one has some kind of spiritual basis for one's life one is wasting one's life – one is like an empty post van travelling difficult roads to arrive without any contents – like a nut with no kernel etc. This is a conviction which one feels deeply but cannot prove logically – for who has found the soul? Every action one does, every thought one thinks, every desire, hope, feeling affects this soul – and in turn the strength and nature of one's spiritual life should have an outward manifestation in one's actions.

I think you were very right in thinking that doing "good deeds" would never make one a Christian – just as wearing an old school tie and talking in an affected manner would never make a dweller of RGS [Royal Grammar School] into an Old Etonian. One must work from the centre I think – if one wishes to be a Christian for instance by accepting that Jesus Christ lived and then died for the remission of sins and now lives again – and that if we ask him, sincerely into our lives, he will come in as he has promised in Revelation 3:20.

You ask a very difficult question "would you say that by praying and reading the bible a person will want to help?" I should say on the whole yes – but the danger is to expect a sudden philanthropic enthusiasm. Of course part of Christianity – it is one of the two basic pillars of "the law & the prophets" – but if one has been unused to thinking of others it is a struggle to begin – as it is a struggle even to say one's prayers & read a portion of one's bible each night. But like all worthwhile things, the struggle I have – found at least – is worthwhile.

There are still, and always will be, many doubts, and difficulties troubling me, but I am certain that Christianity in its essence as a message of humility, love, faith and worship is as firm a rock on which to build one's life as any in this shifting world. I am not yet convinced that it is the only one – but it is the only one for me – but enough.

I wasn't quite sure what you meant by your remark in your first letter that we both shied away from each other when we became "too intimate spiritually" – I think I probably agree with you – but am not certain until I am confident of exactly what you mean. I am not really on the same spiritual wave-length as Julie – but it is better that we are both on one – even if they are different – than that one or both of us should not be interested in these things. I wonder if you agree with this? When essence meets with essence, and souls join

In mutual knots, that's the true nuptial twine.
Such, lady, is my love, and such is true:
All other love is to your sex, not you.[1]

Or do you prefer to keep spiritual life distinct and private? I have a feeling I have misunderstood your remark.

My relationship with Julie, having overcome various tumults since a heart-breaking parting at Oxford 5 weeks ago, has settled fortunately into one of mutual esteem and warm friendship – which is perhaps fortunate as she is going off to Perugia University we will write to each other frequently but probably both find ourselves

---

[1] From Thomas Randolph, 'Married Love'

other partners. I think apart from the wonderful memories I have of the summer – and way in which I have matured (or feel myself to have). I have a firm and lasting friendship with a truly (torn – unusual?) personality – for all of which I am very grateful. Undoubtedly there is a danger of being very badly hurt – or of becoming too absorbed in an affair – but I know you will agree that there is nothing like a sweet and intelligent girl for helping one to grow up. It really is wonderful to have someone to whom one can tell anything and with me also Simone de Beauvoir was replaced by a more personal authority on the mysteries of woman. Before I forget will you please give my sincerest good-wishes to Joyce as a friend of yours. I know she will be "dandy" (to use her own expression) and tell her that if she ever does want to come to England I would love to see her and could help her I expect finding accommodation etc – if she doesn't know many people over here. What a pity we're not all in Vancouver or the Lakes together – boy would we have a gay time!

I haven't heard much about the old school. Mark Sykes is coming to Oxford next term and I will try to gather some news from him. Dallas Brett has also at last got in. I hear the Luptonian was nearly banned by the H.M. for approving of the gold-fish incident (perhaps you didn't hear of it? – Some one finally put goldfish in those round light shades in the school-library before a master's meeting! A.L. Morgan was suspected. I suppose you will have heard of the tragedy re. George. I have only heard vague rumours via my uncle.

Thanks very much for the information on the Hebrides – I am looking forward very eagerly to my visit – especially after reading "Ring of Bright Water" by Gavin Maxwell, an enchanting book about the west[1]

The next letter from my mother is dated August 1. It was sent to Aunt Julia at West Burton, and forwarded from there to the V.P.S. Camp at Iwerne Minster.

My dear Alan,

I hope this will catch you on your royal progress and that you're enjoying it, I've lost track of the weather at home. I'll get it off my chest and tell you that its still hot here but we feel we have turned the corner and in eight weeks time it will all be over. …

When I'm on my own [in Shillong] I shall spend a lot of my time up there writing my History of Assam which no one will read. Our other History seems to have come to an impasse again, we have been teetering on the edge of Elizabeths reign for several weeks which I try to get it straight in my head and filling in time with revision and reading from your Michelet, I think I've now got it fairly sorted out, the French Wars of Religion are my pet hate but the syllabus insists that it wants the "broad outlines" and not technical detail so I doubt if battles and treaties are called for, except the last one. I am to take over club Librarian soon … If you hear of anything special in the way of books I can send for let me know.

I'm a bit worried about your finances, Daddy says he cant spare more than £15 this month which he has sent home, but this wont see you up to the Hebrides. By the time the next lot goes it will be too late. The only thing I can think of is for you to use your motor bike money and we will pay it back when we get our commission. I have no idea how much you got for your teaching and if you managed to put some by for your holiday, Granny says she put the money into Premium Bonds so you'd better ask her to get it out again quick! I'm sorry about this, I'm afraid this is how its going to be till you leave Oxford, think how nice its going to be for you when you start earning though.

Thank you very much for your nice birthday letter, I'm longing to read "The Lord of the Rings", I can't think how we managed to miss it. I'm reading "Buddenbrooks" by Thomas Mann at the moment, the first of his books I've read, a long long family story and fascinating for its picture of a completely alien way of life. Its nice discovering a new author and thinking of all the pleasure in store.

Give my love to Billy & Julia and thank B. for his birthday letter which I will answer soon. Go & see the Marsdens at Iwerne. I think their farm is called Broad Lea farm. Much love from us all – Mummy

There is then a letter from my Uncle Richard.

2 August 1961 forwarded to V.P.S. Camp, Iwerne Minster

Dear Alan,

Many thanks for the cheque. I hope the money was useful in tiding you over the crisis & I hope the other cheque arrives.

---

[1] Here the carbon runs out.

I don't know exactly where you are at the moment … I'm afraid we wont meet at Iwerne as I am going to 'B'.[1]*… When we do meet up I would like to hear how your teaching got on. Meanwhile, I hope all your holiday plans work out well. Love, Richard.*

The next letter from my mother is dated August 9, and sent to Iwerne.

My dear Alan,

Your last letter came from London, and I'm glad you were seeing Julie, sad that she's going away for such a long time. You didn't mention Angela and Robert, were they there? The black sweater sounds real beat – and so practical, never needing to be washed! … she [Granny] *said Fiona had done some very good drawings, I am overcome by the talents of my family and stuff them down everyone's throats eternally. I hope you got the money in time, you certainly did very well and we are most grateful.*

… I have been lent a new History book, lectures on European History given at Magdalen College which is the answer to all my questions and amusing reading too. If you ever have a bean I would love C.V. Wedgewood's "William the Silent" which is in Penguins I think, he is a character who fascinates me. Fiona sent me some pastels from Shillong so I plan to spend some of my holiday trying to sketch the rice planting which is in full swing just now and incredibly beautiful but the glimmering reflections of the rice in the water which in its turn reflects the clouds is almost impossible to catch. … I hope this will find you let me know if you see the Marsdens & if I got their address right.

There is then another letter from my mother.

Cherideo August 28th 1961 - to Field Head

My dear Alan,

Your letter from Glasgow station at midnight just arrived, I cant think of anywhere more depressing, I do hope you finally got yourself to Stornoway and were'nt too stiff and rheumaticky to be able to enjoy the shielings – I don't know what they are either but imagine them to be rough, craggy hills, always dripping, with bits of rock jutting out on which eagles perch. You must let me know if I'm right. I'm very sorry about the money, I said Daddy had sent it and thought you would realise that it had gone to the bank, it went at the beginning of the month, why didn't you just ask the bank you clot? I will send the next lot to Granny to pay her back and she will be able to pay half Iwerne too, and you could pay the other half out of the fifteen pounds in the bank. We hate keeping you so short, especially after all your hard work, but send every penny we can. I expect you will get the doings about your next grant so let us know what it is.

Enough of this depressing subject, and on to another one, the state of my veins. Granny will have told you they've been all clotted, they are much better and I'm allowed up at last, but have to take things very very slowly… No news at all ...] Do tell us more about Alan Barnes, what is he doing now and why was he expelled. Also about the rest of the gang as Fiona is always keen for scandal, she does hear occasionally but the first letter writing phase is over. …

"Tell me not now, it needs not saying, what tunes the enchantress plays In aftermaths of still Septembers.." or is it still?

Anyway, much love from us all to all of you, Mummy

My mother's next letter is to Field Head and dated September 8.

My dear Alan,

No gaudy picture postcard of a shieling (Daddy says he has told us hundreds of times that these are walled in sheep pens!) but your birthday present arrived a few days ago with some pictures of country like the Hebrides – a lovely book which we shall read and read, thank you very much indeed though you shouldn't have spent all that money. I love that poem of Kathleen Raines and would like to read some more, perhaps you have the Gollanz anthology and I shall be able to browse in it. I have taken over the library and locked it up firmly, already sense disapproval from the people who have been stacking their book-shelves ceiling high at our expense for years, anyway I shall only be doing it for six months and should have a good supply to hand over to my

---

[1] There were two groups of the Christian Camps, 'A' and 'B', at this time.

successor. The first lot of books I've ordered are on the way and I'm longing to dig in, "Tudor Tragedy" is one and "The Burnt out Case" and Alan Patons new book of short stories.

.... I'm beginning to lead a more normal life but have to go very slowly, yesterday I tottered slowly round the compound and the steps to the kitchen, and my leg throbbed and ached half the night – very irritating.... In fact the whole world picture is not at its gayest just now is it, we're always treated to crisises in September when morale is lowest but I suppose we shall have to get used to living with them for ever. Terry, our bright young assistant, is fond of telling me that it was my generation that were responsible for the last war, but I get my own back by asking him what he is doing about this one! ...

I wonder if you could get a Nature Note Book for her [Anne] *(with one drawing page per one lined) which perhaps Granny could send with the next lot of mags? Don't seem obtainable in India. Let us know the doings of the Gang, if its still going, what is Martin up to these days? Poor Beryl must be worried stiff about him as he doesn't seem to make any progress towards a training. When are you going back to coll? At the beginning of October I think, I expect you'll need one or two new garments, let us know how the money goes.*

The next letter is dated Sunday which was 10 September, and post-marked 12 (a day when my grandfather noted in his diary 'Porter arrives', the following day 'Alan leaves for Bolton with Porter').

Dear Family,

No letter since last Monday hardly surprising as I left a gap of 2 weeks also. Before I continue my account of the Hebrides I will settle once and I hope for the next 3 months at least – financial matters. My battels from Worcester come to a total of £80-0-7d. I will be getting £120 on 13th October. I owe Blackwell's about £10 (since a year ago) – I still have about £6 to spend from the £15 you sent me – but have got to buy several books and will have to get a few more clothes (especially games clothes). Therefore if you could send me £10 to tide me over until the beginning of term – or else, I could not pay back Richard the £7 I owe him (for Iwerne) 'till then and borrow the rest. (P.S. I don't think I will have to – actually). Would you like me to pay all the battels out of the £120 this time – or would you like to spread it out – and to pay some of it now – and then the £120 will go further – and perhaps break the brunt of the bill next February? – anyhow let me know. Well – I hope that's got rid of <u>that</u> for some time!

I think we had just left Stornoway in my last letter. We travelled across to Barvas where we spent the first night (see Map for all this account.) – it was a glorious day and I spent the afternoon in fishing high up on the moors in a little rushy loch – there were a fair amount of fish rising – and I missed several – but only landed 4 small ones – of which I kept two of about 2 for supper – the rather disappointing fishing was amply compensated by the unlooked-for sunshine shining on the sparkling loch and, in the distance, on the sea. Next day I caught a nice trout of over ½lb – my best fish – in a hill loch up above Carloway. Hoping to catch a bus on to Callernish that evening we were waiting on the outskirts of the village as dusk fell and a cold wind began to blow when a woman came out of the nearest house and having informed us that there were no more buses invited us indoors 'till her husband came back when he might drive us. So we sat in the cosy little living room and she brought us tea and a plateful of cakes each – and the four intelligent and friendly children recited Gaelic songs to us and tried to teach us the elements of the language. When the husband returned he gave us all the fish he had caught then at 11.45 at night he drove us through a storm the ten or more miles to Callanish – showed us the famous standing stones and spent ¼ hour or so looking for a good camping site! (Of course he wouldn't <u>dream</u> of taking any money!) For lack of space this is the only story I can tell you about the hospitality of the islanders – but they really were wonderful all down the isles – as was the scenery as we travelled down into Harris – where the 'Yorkshire-moors-like' scenery of Lewis gave way to much more mountainous, wild and rock strewn country with a fantastic rocky coastline. We were offered a lift from a "co-op" van so jolted our way down the West coast of Harris with the rain pelting down – we were dumped at an outlandish spot some 6½ miles from our destination (Rodel) – but despite torrential rain we managed to get two lifts most unexpectedly (a long story) and arrived at Rodel – only to find at the harbour that the boat for N. Uist – to which we hoped to go – couldn't put in to the rocky harbour as the sea was too rough. So we spent the next four days ('till the next boat) camped in a gully just by a little stream – it was a delightful spot and we cooked exclusively by wood-fire (there being one of the only two woods in Harris – a few rotting trees – nearby). We spent two of the nights anxiously waiting for the tent to collapse – for there were continued gales and our tent pole had bent badly on the first night – but somehow it held out.

On Wednesday we caught the boat to Lochmaddy and had a whole day's glorious travelling in bright sunshine down the coast by bus overland to Lochboisdale, and on that night to Barra – needless to say the scenery was inspiring and varied. We arrived at Barra at 12.30 at night and spent two glorious days exploring the coves and wonderful sands which I have already partly described. I arrived back at Oban on Saturday 11.30 a.m and after a night spent in the back of a bus and other more exciting adventures I arrived home at 12.0 next morning with ½d (I had had 6/8d when I started!)

Sorry for this compression – but I have kept a diary so will describe more fully when you're all here.

I have been so carried away that I haven't even enquired about Mummy's health – but I have been thinking of you a lot Mummy – I do hope you're better (doesn't that sound weak?) but once again you will know what I feel and mean.

I have been attempting to work very hard for the last week – partly successful – but obstructed by a M-Fé "Toga" party etc. Jummy[1] progressing. All my love to you all, Alan x

P.S. I have been trying to get "William the Silent" – but it is only in a 12/6 stiffback – so will wait 'till I can get it 2nd-hand – am sending something else meanwhile – hope you haven't been given this one already!

I wrote again a week later, in a letter dated Sunday September 17th, from Field Head

Dear Family,
Thank you very much for your letter Mummy – I was very happy to hear that you are improving and hope that by the time this reaches you will be almost if not completely better. Unless one has a considerable faith in something beyond this life it strikes me that this is a very miserable time to be living. Apart from all the tensions and crises etc I alone know 3 people who are very sick – largely thro' worry in two cases. Mr Doogan is in Liverpool hospital with a bad nervous breakdown – one side of his body is paralysed so I hear – Jummy (who has just gone down with Beryl) is of course still very ill and apparently Vivien's father has just had coronary thrombosis out in Nairobi – isn't it all miserable – the sooner I get back to the Outer Hebrides the better! Will you be coming back this year – or have you decided to wait until you have some money? In some ways waiting would fit in better with me as I would then be recovering from exams, but what about the girls?

I will be sending out the Nature Note bk soon – when I can get it – and also "Peter Abelard" which I absolutely adored and hope you like. I am reading voraciously – all the time when I'm not working or forced into society – and am becoming quite a recluse. I'm just starting Angus Wilson "Hemlock and After" and dip into "Love and Death" and the "Rubaiyat of Omar Khayam" at intervals – both highly intoxicating. I want to try and get some of Llewelyn Powys' books as I loved that one so much. Unfortunately I have to do a considerable amount of work at the moment – and am going up to Oxford on the 27th to really get down to it. In spite of this however I have lived a comparatively gay social life for the last week.

David Porter came up on Tuesday afternoon and we went down to Bolton on Wednesday evening and saw a Walt Disney film. The next day we went over to Southport to see Stuart Black and with another Old Luptonian, Tony Rink, had a very hilarious get-together. Stuart's house, as you may remember, is just near the Lister's – but fortunately for my peace of mind Gill is back at school! In the evening we went to Southport and joined with the local talent at a jazz club – most enjoyable.

I think you'll find that while Fiona has steadied up I've got wilder – tho' I suppose its only a phase of reaction or something. I think I sometimes rather frighten Gr & Grandpa at my suggestions that I should go and ask to be put in prison etc! At the Southport hop I amused myself by explaining to various nurses etc how I was an escaped convict from Brixton – while to another I proposed marriage (so far I have collected 5 different refusals!) – but after all I won't be under 21 awfully much longer will I?

I have spent this afternoon quietly enough chugging up and down Windermere with Anne Johnson and Mike Boddington. It seems the gang is breaking up a bit. Martin & David are going south (and it looks as if their parents may be possibly selling their houses too & moving – tho' it is only at the gossip stage as yet.)

By the way Mummy I asked you where your children's story script was – if you could send it home if it is out with you? – could you let me have it please as I would like to read it – and if [you] *don't mind perhaps adapt a little of it? I'll see. Look after yourselves & keep & get well.*
With all my best love to you all, Alan

---

[1] Neighbour Mr Buckmaster was ill

My mother's next letter is dated September 18.

Dear Alan,

A letter at last, but of course as I suspected the other one went astray, or perhaps they didn't have any Air Mail stamps in the Hebrides and it will turn up eventually. Anyway thank you very much for your very detailed one that did arrive, we were delighted to hear of your adventures and followed your progress on the map, it sounded lovely and we are quite determined to try and find a croft there to which we can retire when the pace at Field Head becomes too frantic – if only they don't start rocket stations and testing grounds as I believe they are doing on North Uist. We sit and talk for hours about our peat fire and the smell of bannocks cooking (probably burning!) and the waves and seagulls and seals and sunsets – how delicious it sounds just at the moment. Did you see any deserted barns or habitable buildings of any kind when you were there?

I'm sorry Granny spilt the beans about having sent "Ring of Bright Water" to Anne, actually don't tell Granny but A. has exchanged her copy for something else so it has all worked out fine. I would [like] *to keep an otter too if I lived there, but Daddy is Off animals and I suppose ther'd be the problem of what to do with it when one went away. Anyway its nice to dream about it all, and helps us through the dreary September days.*

... Now that I'm club librarian I've been having some really good light reading too, just finished Graham Greene's "The Burnt Out Case" which was very good although not up to his usual standard quite, but the Catholic Fathers reminded me very much of our lot out here. Also a sort of thriller "The Seven Lean Years" by Celia Fremlin which was excellent, Granny should put it on her library list. I'm now embarking on "The Tudor Tragedy"... Please don't worry about William the Silent, unless you happen to see the Penguin edition any time. I'm still only half way through the Thirty Years War and shall really have to get our skates on if we are going to leave the Tudors, such a pity one has to have this sense of hurry hurry hurry all the time and cant just browse and explore all the avenues and speculate, a pity one has to study for exams at all in fact in the sense of learning reams of facts. I was reading an article by an educationalist the other day in which he said he hoped the day would soon come when students would be allowed to take reference books into exams, so that they wouldn't have to waste so much of their time mugging up facts and would be able to be tested on their ability to sort and interpret. Very sensible I thought.

... While we're on the subject, I'm enclosing a cheque herewith which I hope will see you over till you can get hold of your grant. Did they give you the same as last time? It would appear so from my calculations, but not Daddy's so let us know. Could you pay £60 for your battels and we will pay the remaining £20, then you will have £60 to carry on with. The battels seem to have gone up considerably, is this to be a termly thing? The company are now paying quite a hefty sum towards the school fees of children up to the age of eighteen – they would, everyone else is gloating. Ah well, we shall stagger on, but I wish we didn't have to keep you short and I wish after all these years Daddy could have some relief form the continual hopeless task of dragging ends together.

... What happened to Jummy, did he have a relapse? And is the rumour true that the Manzi Fes are leaving. Much love to you all from all of us, my letters should be more cheerful soon! Mummy

At this time I wrote a reflection as I looked out of my bedroom window.

Thoughts on looking out of a window – Sept 24 1961 at a beautiful evening when the world is shadowed by many calamities & dangers (Berlin etc)[1]

Stillness – and the soft flush of evening
Dreams on the flower scented air
Voluptuously reeling – and stroking
The autumn leaves with golden pollen.
Gnats, bird song and grazing cows
Alone break the breathless waiting hush –

---

[1] The reference to Berlin is to the Berlin Crisis, which lasted from May to November 1961, and the start of the building of the Berlin Wall.

Waiting for Night to steal from the skies
To rise like heavenward dew and
Suddenly be here.

Single sounds come loudly across the waiting fields – starling swarms homing – the trot of horses hooves – the mowing machine – but then the blanket returns.

But that moment of waiting is almost over – in the smoke – wood–smoke still air where the white cat lingers on the last sunlit stone day is sucked, gently inevitably as the death of man into far off lands and warmth, beauty and vitality ebb into the coffin spangled with its myriad frozen gems.

So, as each daisy, each fading rose, distinct and separate, merges curls in on itself and dies to sight. As each soaring swallow-soul returns from its ecstatic flight to nest so the world never so beautiful, never so rich in promise and in need waits for night, for the beasts that skulk and swoop from the sky, to descend when mans mind grows dim.

But even as night comes – so comes day " and death is a sleep or a darkening between a day and a day'

There is final letter from my mother dated September 26 which alludes to events of the summer.

My dear Alan,

You'll be back at Oxford by now, plus the bottom half of your suit I hope, I had wanted to get a coat this winter, perhaps you'll be able to out of your grant? I hope the money we sent arrived all right and didn't bounce, there seems to have been some hitch about it leaving Calcutta but it should have been there in time. Thank you for a letter we got a few days ago, full of sad news about Mr Doogan, I wonder why he should have a breakdown, he struck me as being such a well adjusted person.

Its strange that you should find pain and misery an argument in favour of religion, I find it the biggest stumbling block to accepting a loving god, when I walk round Calcutta and see the suffering of people and animals, all undeserved, I find myself unable to accept it as the way a father would treat his children. One can only presume that he has somehow placed himself in a position when he cant help. I know one is not supposed to judge such things with a limited human brain, but what else is there to use? As for blaming the devil, that is just so ludicrous – ah well there is no time or space for more of this now. My mind is running along these lines as we have just had Father James the Catholic priest staying with us, for the first time he was tired and depressed, after a lifetimes work they are being chivvied and chased and undermined and he wouldn't be human I suppose if he didn't feel rather hopeless and resentful. ..

We're <u>coming home</u> next spring, still without any money but I cant keep the girls out any longer, Granny is very anxious for us to retire and buy the other half of the house, nothing would be nicer but we want to see you through Oxford first, we don't get a pension till Daddy is fifty so it would be longish gap to fill with doubtful jobs. When you are through I think we shall probably risk it, if things don't improve here anyway. Anne and I are going up to Shillong next Friday… I hope we shall be able to make a pilgrimage to see the house where you were born, how happy we were there, I can still remember the wood fires and the peaceful emptiness of it, war and all. Not a very good world to be born into as you say, but when has the world been good, the more history I read the more thankful I am I wasn't there.

Have just read "The Tudor Tragedy"…. Anyway I found it very interesting, the chapter on Henry VIII is the best description I've read anywhere of him, but the background to Tudor living was far from merry. How far are you now in your history? Miles ahead of us I expect. I wrote to the head of the correspondence college very crossly to complain of his model essays, said they were dull and pompous and not suitable as models and got a very nice letter back saying he was inclined to agree and would see about it. I suppose it was "the customer is always right" attitude, but it made me feel very influential! I've been reading Stendhal's "Scarlet and Black" but alas find it dull too, terrible admission, I simply cant get interested in any of the characters even though they are terribly well drawn, the first ten chapters are taken up describing how the tutor tries to pluck up courage to touch his employers hand, he's such a horrid little worm and she is limpid as a summer stream but not nearly as lively, in fact they're both bores. But it's a classic, so obviously its me that out of touch.

Yes I will send you my book but I don't think it will interest you much, its really just a vehicle for some Indian fairy stories I translated and not in itself much of a story. I paid £14 to get the wretched thing typed, so you wont lose it will you – not that I have any hopes of publication but I thought it might amuse my grandchildren as its based on the lives of Fiona and Anne when they were out here before.

Was most amused to hear of your junketings with David Porter, one of these days someone will accept a proposal and then you'll be sunk! I hope you aren't missing Julie too much, this should be the best year for you whatever the world situation and good years don't come all that often so make the most of it. Much love from us all – Mummy

I do not have much in the way of ephemera from this holidays. In relation to Copthorne school there is a cheque for £32-16-0, made out to A. Macfarlane Esq, on 24th July and signed by the Directors. This may have been my final salary, though why I still have the cheque, I am not sure. There are two English essays by boys with comments by me. There is also a cyclostyled quiz sheet, 'General Knowledge Summer, 1961'. It is less complex, witty and high level than the Dragon General Knowledge quizzes.

I clearly did a lot of work in the final month of my summer vacation. For example I have 6 detailed pages of notes on the French Wars of Religion. I also have eight pages of writing, a mixture of an essay and detailed notes, for the topic of 'Louis XIII & Richelieu', dated September 61. There are twenty-eight pages of notes on 'The Netherlands Independence to 1609', also done in September. Clearly I was very keen on the subject and working hard. I wrote an essay on the subject in the Winter Term.

Supplementing this were: About 20 pages of notes, dated 2nd and 3rd October, on *La Préponderance Espagnole* by Hauser. This was reading done before the formal term started. There are also ten pages of notes, including a map, on *Netherlands – Political History (1609-1713)*, dated September 1961. There are twelve pages of very detailed notes on Michael Roberts, *Gustavus Adolphus*, dated September. There is a five page essay – most of it in note form – on 'Mercantilism – Introductory Notes', dated September. There are there pages of essay on 'The Counter-Reformation' and two pages of a short essay on Calvinism.

The Journal of the Tour to the Hebrides

(with acknowledgement to Dr Johnson)

I have a small red notebook in which I kept notes of our Hebridean Tour of August 1961. It is headed, on the first page, 'Outer Hebrides 1961'.

The JOURNAL begins with a list of what I took with me.

Equipment List

Clothes
3 prs socks, 2 pr w[alking] shoes, 1 pr gymn-shoes, 2 handk'fs, 1 heavy vest, 1 light vest, 2 prs pants, 2 shirts, 1 tie, 2 jerseys, 1 pr longs
1 pr long shorts, 1 sou-wester, 1 mac (plastic), 1 pr rubber trousers, groundsheet, 1 towel
Etc
1 stove & pan, 1 bottle fuel, 1 torch, 1 lamp, matches, 1 map?, 1 compass, 1 tent (spare string & skewers – 5 lb 10 oz.), sleeping-bag (2lb 12oz), fishing equipment, money (£9, ticket to Glasgow), scissors, toilet equipment (roll: shaving), string, soap water bottle, mug, pencil, & notebook, rod, knife, midge cream, mending kit, food containers, meths
Food
Kendal mint cake, packet soup, eggs, salt, bread & butter, tea, sugar

16 lb 10 oz
Total weight – about 18 lb

Outer Hebrides August 20 – September 2nd

Sunday 20th

Set out from Lakes on Glasgow coach in drizzle. The fells ponderously misted, draping their wet skirts down to the roadside. A tedious journey arriving at Glasgow at 7.0 in the evening. Wandered around the lonely Sunday night streets, saw the "Gun-Runners" and a Brigitte B[ardot] frippery and then retired to Queen street waiting room for the night. Locked in I slept on the dusty cement floor – first experience of the ¾ automatic deflating pillow – consequently tousled and sleepy onto the 5.10 Mallaig train.

Monday 21st

Jerked and puffed thro' some splendid scenery – sadly it was misty & drizzling – but fine waterfalls and heathery outcrops – train very full. Arrived at Mallaig in the rain at 12.15 – nearly missed Alastair Small and Michael Davies[1] who were waiting for me. Already on the train I had heard my first Gaelic but on the boat many of the folk spoke it. As we approached Stornoway some of the men started to sing Gaelic songs – all very picturesque as we passed the trawling vessels and heard the gulls scream. Then having voyaged in drizzle most of the way the sun broke loose and we had our first view of Stornoway. Up till then we had spent most of the time in the lounge –partly watching the amusing side-play between a newly arriving lad from the Isle of Man and a young Stornoway lass – both were slightly taken aback I think.

[1] Both were friends at Worcester.

The Harbour – one of the biggest (the biggest above Glasgow on the West Coast) and also the safest – is set between two peninsulars – one grassy and low – one higher, richly wooded and crowned by a lighthouse, tower and pseudo castle. It has two main parts – with a broad road running along the front where several busses stand. The houses – like all those in the island – are thickly built and on the whole of varying shades of grey. But there are bright whites, ox-reds and green as well, and many variations in style– a regular hotch potch. There seem to be a large number of young people in Stornoway – especially girls – and it would doubtless be a very good place to find an attractive, cheerful, thrifty and hard-working wife – also there are a good supply of old "gaffers" – leaning against walls – "sometimes I sits and thinks, sometimes I jest sits" – the whole attitude is fairly summed up in one man's words "ah well – time doesn't matter here anyhow." Everything is relaxed – the shops will open for one at any time in the villages – one can go and have a meal in the Sailor's Hostel – even if not a sailor. It is an interesting tradition that many of the inhabitants come down and meet the mail boat in the evening.

Anyhow having procured some fish and chips we searched for a camping-site and had our first taste of highland hospitality when a farmer showed us to a comfortable place behind his house and I enjoyed the delights of my first ever "night-under-canvas".

I can't remember what we ate but the whispering of the wind past taut guy-ropes, the buzz of midges etc was a new delight.

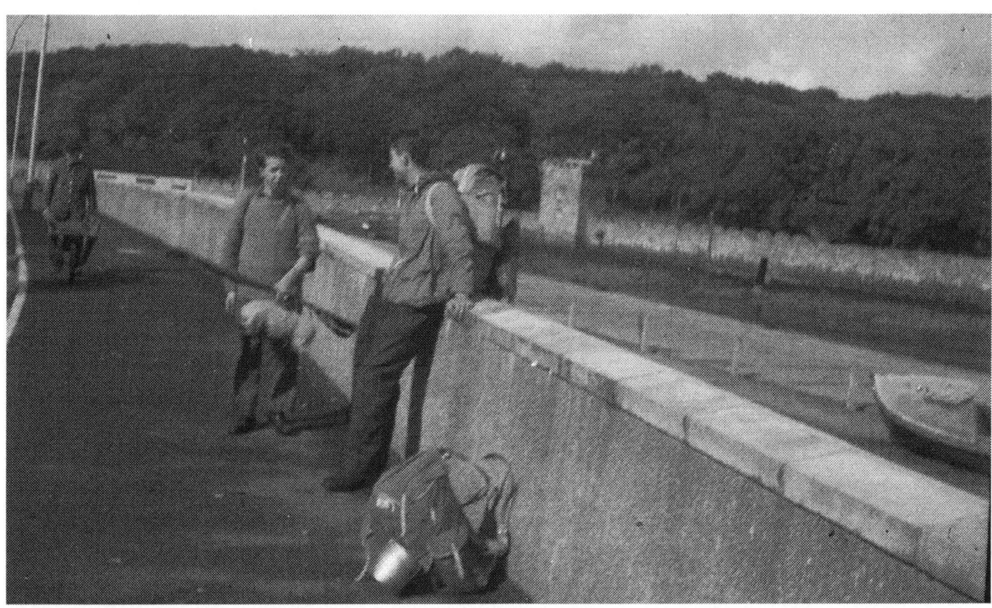

Mike Davies and I in Stornoway, taken by Alistair Small

<u>Tuesday 22nd</u>

We awoke to a fine sunny morning and after visiting Stornoway caught the bus for Barvis – our first experience of Island transport. The bus – unutterably old and rattly – was fascinating in itself. Blue – with a non-functioning dashboard it seemed to be a general delivery lorry also. At last it rattled off – full of Gaelic speaking inhabitants and with a veritable barricade of ruck-sacks, parcels etc at the front. I stood swaying in the middle trying to consume an apple-pie with one hand holding a rod with the other. We lurched up onto our first peat-moor; and the sun spangled the necklace of sapphire lochans that lay reed-rippling in every hollow along-side the narrow tar-mac road (these roads have passing-places every few hundred yards). North Lewis is fairly flat – and covered with peaty slopes & bogs. Everywhere one sees chocolate cake peat-cuttings and every croft has its pile of neatly-stacked peat outside. The houses are usually very small – 3 or 4 rooms and widely spaced in groups of from 2 to a dozen, most of them have a potato patch and a small field of corn or wheat and a few sheep and a cow perhaps also some chickens. On this and their wages from fishing – the great industry of the Isles (esp Stornoway) – and from spinning Harris Tweed they live their simple lives. Their drinking habits are difficult to tell – there are very few pubs – in fact Stornoway has the only two in Lewis while some villagers have to go some 90 miles there & back if they want a drappie. One suspects however that they keep their own store. At Barvas I got off the bus while Alastair & Michael went on to the tip of the Island (Butt of Lewis) where they were invited to tea by a Glasgow school-master. Meanwhile I tramped up into the low hills over a peat-bog and fished. I had many rises but only landed four 8¾, 8½, 7½, 7" – rather disappointing but it was a lovely evening and the loch was very beautiful – green reeds shimmering, blue water, grey rocks – and brown banks. We camped up beside a little stream in a little valley – lovely night – no trouble.

Wed 23rd

Fished again in the morning at Barvas – no luck. Another beautiful day – very fortunate – got the 3.0 bus into Calloway where I missed the others so went up to a nearby loch and caught a nice ½ lb (or over) trout – about 12". Again very beautiful – higher hills – every colour very exaggerated and of course that indescribable tang of freedom, heather and peat in the rain-clean air (naturally a very good apettite [sic] up here – the others found me and after they had looked at a broch [iron age stone structure] we met at about 8.0 – a very cold evening. We had just found there was no bus after all and it looked as if we were stranded for we had wanted to go on to Callernish. So I went up to a little house nearby and asked if they could drive us in – at a price – in their van. The man was out but Mrs Macaskell after seeing us standing out in the cold (I had begun to do some cabbage-hops to get the sympathy of someone) asked us in. It was a really delightful and hospitable family – Isabel was the mother's name and her children were Iain (10 – birthday 14th Feb), Mairi (11 – b 24th Dec; and twins Angus and Christine a very serious and serious-faced girl (8 – birthday 22nd June). Address Mrs I. Macaskell, Hillcrest, Carloway, Isle of Lewis. They gave us tea, scones and cakes, warmth, sympathy seemed full of beans and happiness – they all talked gaelic well and were very intelligent. When the husband came in, he gave us the fish he had caught and then took us in his van to Calernish – a nightmare drive in the back – cold, wet (it was now pouring) and bumpy with no lights, gripping odd fish, tent poles etc. We arrived at about midnight, saw the standing stones by moonlight and there he drove us around for a considerable time to find a camping-site. At last we found a flat patch and put our tents up in strong gusts of wind and rain. I went in the big tent as the pole of mine began to bend. A very windy night and we got to sleep at about 2.0!!

Thursday 23rd

We awoke to a gusty, cloud-quilted morning and found ourselves on very exposed ground – but with a marvellous view over a sea loch, low hills and the three circles of standing stones – the largest of which is famed and is the second largest in Britain – its shape is roughly with two barrows at A and B – the centre stone is 12 ft and the whole is enveloped in mystery – who made them and why – they stand lonely savage on a wild rocky coast. We then went down to the village store for supplies. These little corrugated iron shacks surprisingly frequent – are a feature of each village. They are seldom open but when one gets in they store a very wide variety of goods – but mostly non-perishable – fish, meat, eggs, vegetables and milk are difficult to get. One can only obtain them from the travelling co-op vans or the crofts – but the latter have to be avoided as they won't accept any payment.

We caught the 3.0 bus to Stornoway – for we had to go via there to Harris. It was a lovely drive – but not as wonderful as the one from Stornoway right down Lewis to Tarbert.

In Lewis it was a "Fash" day – ie one of the 2 communion days of the Scottish churches – therefore everything was shut (voluntarily) and all the people were strolling around the town. We had a delicious fish & chip tea in the British Sailors Mission (tho' we looked patently unlike sailors) and then caught the bus at 8.0 for Harris.

It was a beautiful evening – still so that the lochans were mirror-calms – and with the sun beginning to set in a yellow haze over the western heather slopes. At first it was the wild, free Lewis peat moors – inhabited only by gulls, sheep with their wool stained with red and blue marking dye, and cows – either black or white or the long-horned, red-brown and delightful (and inquisitive!) highland cattle. Also on our journeys we have seen quite a few black & white collies some of them friendly & in beautiful condition. The only birds I have seen were sea-gulls, some kind of kestrel or buzzard, wrens, curlews and black-hooded crows (and various ducks – swans & grebes). No pigs, goats, horses etc – and hardly a tree to be seen – in fact none.

As we went South the mountains grew larger until near the Harris border we could see the range including the highest in the Hebrides 2,600 odd ft straight up from sea-level – the sea in the shape of long loch Seaforth with its mountain island being on our left. Here it was that we saw one of the few remaining "black houses" in Britain – a house with no gable, chimney and made merely of 4 dry-stone walls and a thatch roof – the smoke comes out of the windows.

As we climbed over an 800 ft pass before reaching Tarbert the land around lay desolate thickly littered with great boulders and uninhabited – except for one lonely croft – a drear place in winter! We rattled down to Loch Tarbert in the dusk and camped on the West side of the Isthmus near the sea – it was very stony and midge-infested but we finally managed to get to sleep.

Friday 24th

A drenching rain beating on my tent when I awoke. I found a pool of water formed on one side about an inch deep – I have never felt less like getting up. But the other two were keen on getting to the Southern tip of Harris – Rodel – where there is a very interesting church – so I kept seeing dripping heads bobbing past the entrance of the tent. My extra sleep ideas were shattered when I learnt that we had been offered a lift to within 6 miles of Rodel by a co-op van – so I made a mad dash to pile my sopping equipment into my haversack & get dressed without touching the dripping sides of my little tent – then got the tent down in the beating rain wearing my non-too waterproof clothes – quite a mess!

The ride in the van was certainly thrill-packed! It was a terrible road & an old lorry so that we bumped and crashed along stopping every few seconds to pick up a fallen box or tin – but it was very kind of the driver to take three of us and our luggage in an already well stacked van as well as the lipstick-smeared but cheerful girl-assistant and her young cousin! We scraped past various obstacles such as a lorry that had gone off the road and several groups of cows and on the whole roughly 20 mile journey only sold about 2 packets of cigarettes and a packet of soup! We were finally dumped in the driving rain (against us) in the middle of nowhere – and were soon slogging, wet through along the road – unable to see more than three yards ahead. However we finally came to a tiny village and on enquiring if we could hire a van we were offered a lift in an ancient bus to Leverborough [1] – it appeared that a bus co[mpany] operated from this tiny village!

At Leverborough we got a lift – still in the rain from a calor-gas van and so arrived at Rodel – soaking wet and leaving a trail of kippers behind us! (we only recovered two) – having found the hotel exorbitantly expensive 25/- b & b we went up to the old church.

Made of large slabs of local stone and simple in design it was built in the 1520s & restored twice since. It is mainly interesting for its blending of Celtic & Norman influences in its narrow windows etc & the ornate Macleod tomb – it is bare & a national monument.

We then went down to the little rocky harbour with its two jetties and quota of local fishermen. It stopped raining & the sun shone but the stiff breeze prevailed and after an anxious period of waiting we were disappointed that the boat went by – and it was too

---

[1] Leverborough was an attempt – frustrated by local lack of co-operation – by Lord Leverhume to start a fishing port to supply "Mac" Fisheries.

rough for the ferry. We therefore set about looking for a place to camp. First we went up the mountain behind and pitched the tents on a high flat space. But fortunately we decided to move down into a little gully by the stream for there was a force 6 wind in the night!

Saturday 25th

Spent the day camping by same bush – hoping to get across to North Uist – but no luck. A tragedy in the morning – the top section of the tent pole bent – nothing really we can do about it.

We spent up to about 3.0 trying to get some paraffin (pink) for the primus and all walked into various local shops – but only managed to get meths. Hence we have been cooking on a camp fire since – extremely successful & fortunate as we are camped by one of the only two woods in Harris. We also constructed a wind-shield which was absolutely essential as there was a tremendous gale in the night.

It was indeed " a night to remember" for the whole tent shook and flapped and the rain lashed down outside and I had visions of the weakened pole collapsing and three bedraggled figures in pyjamas trying to move camp in the pouring dark. At about 10.0 there was a startling thump and we discovered the tent (the fly sheet) had slid down the pole a foot down to a ripped hole – we lay there petrified watching the pole bending ominously – but all was well and we awoke to our amazement to a serene, sunlit day.

Sunday 26th

A quiet day – the islanders whether "wee frees" (the "Free" church of Scotland), United Protestants (descendants of Calvinists) or merely C of S observe a very strict sabbath – they disapprove of any unnecessary movement.

The highlight of the day was the gaelic service we went to in Leverburgh. It lasted some 90 minutes – with a 45 [minute] sermon in gaelic (and seemingly considerably emotional). The congregation was large – the order of the service was quite unique and the only singing was unaccompanied – led by a chanter and a sort of haunting wailing (like the wind over the moors) of the psalms was in gaelic and taken by a thin character with a butterfly collar and drooping moustache.

The rest of the day seems to have been occupied in making food over our smoky fire. In the evening a lad came down from a neighbouring croft and gave us some milk – typical generosity.

Monday 27th

A less windy night – in the odd few spare minutes I am trying to read Jessie. L. Weston "From Ritual to Romance" – extremely good.

I heard some interesting facts about an enormous sailor-like man we had seen pottering about down at the harbour he spoke very well however and seemed to be suffering from some nervous complaint.

He is Oliver Cootes[1] from a fabulously wealthy Jewish family – his brother was governor of Kenya etc – and he was absolutely brilliant at Cambridge – but became unbalanced during his last exam – and is kept up here well out of the way by the family.

It was a blowy misty day and in the afternoon after walking over the neighbouring hills to Stroud I walked up the hill behind our camp. It commanded a magnificent view of the rocky surf-edged inlets and the many scattered islands. Behind rose higher mist-peaked hills and the sea and road crawled tiny at my feet. I spent some time watching two hawks – probably kestrels – swaying and pivoting on the wind – quite a windy night.

Tuesday 28th

After a semi-gale in the night we left our little stream at mid-day and went down to the harbour where we chatted to a gnarled sailor and watched the heavy swell crashing on the rocks and throwing spray thirty feet in the air.

---

[1] Walter Fleming Coutts was temporarily Governor of Kenya in 1959.

We caught the 2.30 bus and bumped and jolted along the East coast. A very rocky, seaweed-strewn shore – with many lochs, fresh & sea – and little crofts dotted in the hollows. The ground seemed surprisingly good – for in every flat patch there was barley & oats. The last stretch of 9 miles – sarcastically called "the Golden Rd" was unfinished – a rutted mud path.

We camped at the same place as earlier – but this time the wind was the nuisance – it changed in the night and I awoke at 12.0 to find all the fly-sheet pegs out – the wind had changed and was whipping straight down the loch at our tent & once again – after reciting the 23rd Psalm – we miraculously survived.

Postcard of St Clement's Church, Rodel, Harris. This is addressed to my grandparents. Tuesday, Rodil, Isle of Harris

Dear G & G, having a grand time out here – tho' we have missed one of our connections and have had to stay on Harris longer than we intended. But it is wonderful mountain scenery – very wild and colourful and well worthwhile camping in.

I hope to arrive home on Sunday or Monday. I trust you forwarded the money as it was urgent. Hope all goes well. Lots of love, Alan

Wednesday 29th

A long day's travelling – and impressions too condensed & multifarious to describe. We left Tarbert & the Lochmor at 1.20 in a strong South wind and sunshine – it was pleasantly rough. A gorgeous passage down the coves & cliffs of East Harris – with the brown above – a lace of white spray and the blue wrapping. So we rolled into Lochmaddy, capital of N. Uist at about 4.0 – a small village with only about two shops. We then got a MacBraynes bus and travelled down N. Uist, Benbecula & S. Uist to Lochboisdale capital of the last.

How can one hope to describe in a few lines the silver beaches & rich crofts of the West coast of N. Uist – of the flat, barren strip of Benbecula – and mountainous strong S. Uist? There were a thousand lovely lochs, many little thatched cottages & many beautiful hills all wrapped in a pastel remote dream-air of the "Western Isles" – it was a glorious drive.

We then took the Claymore at 11.30 for Barra – and arrived very sleepy past the floodlit castle in Castlebay at 12.30 ish. We made for the nearest patch of grass & camped.

Thursday 30th

We awoke to a glorious sunny morning – and found ourselves overlooking a long – land girt bay with an old castle standing on an island. The village of course is famous as the scene of "Whisky Galore" and "Rockets Galore" and we saw Compton Mackenzie's house which is now used as a seal factory.

We decided to spend one day walking to the North of the Island and one day back – and thus saw nearly the whole of it.

It is about 8 miles in length – not counting the Northern tip – rocky on the East coast but flatter and with glorious beaches on the West – and down the centre a range of mountains – the highest Ben Heaval about 1,500' high. Thus it contains features of all the other islands and combines them into one charming, unique, blend.

The islanders – tho' not very progressive are charming, hospitable & generous and preserve to a considerable extent their local habits & customs – e.g. they still speak Gaelic & have their own "caley's" parties – to which I imagine tourists are not particularly welcome.

The others went on ahead to a sandy beach on the North foreland where we were to meet while I tottered the 7 odd miles with my heavy pack – hoping fruitlessly for a lift – it was a pity about the pack & also later that I was prevented by my anxiety at not finding them for 3 hours from really enjoying to the full the glorious sea-coast. The bays were exquisite – the golden sand curved unbroken for miles & reflecting the sun in the shallow sea made it electric blue – while the long waves from the Atlantic thundered along the beaches. The last mile was along steep cliffs where the sea thundered and swirled on rocky pinnaces of covers. The isthmus – only about ¼ mile wide – with a beautiful beach on our side & the shell-beach (an aerodrome – clam field & source for shell factory) on the other. There are many small islands dotted along the shores – and S. Uist and Eriskay are visible from any hill.

Friday 1st

Our last day on the islands – and another memorable one – warm, dry and very still – but with haze. I walked around the North Headland for some while and could just see the mountains of S. Uist above the haze.

I spent a considerable amount of time looking around Oleagarry House then caught the bus along the East coast – very rocky & like Harris.

Spent the evening on the edge of the sea near Castlebay where we ate some delicious herrings that had been given to us (a fishing boat had put in near North Bay and deposited a cask full of fish free for the local inhabitants and when Alistair & Michael – on their way to climb Heaval – passed they were given 6 fish) – we ate them on the shores in the gathering dusk and then drank a last dram from the "Old Malt" whisky bottle which had been such a faithful companion, then hurled it far into the salty depths of the darkened water. We then made our way via the coffee bar to the harbour.

The fishing on the island consists of about 5 lochs – and costs 10/- per week or 15/- per f'night. Sea-fishing is supposedly good.

We lay in the waiting-room singing rounds & hymns till the boat came in & then had an absolutely glassy crossing – we have been miraculously lucky as it is a very stormy area.

Altogether a wonderful holiday and the foundation for many more I hope.

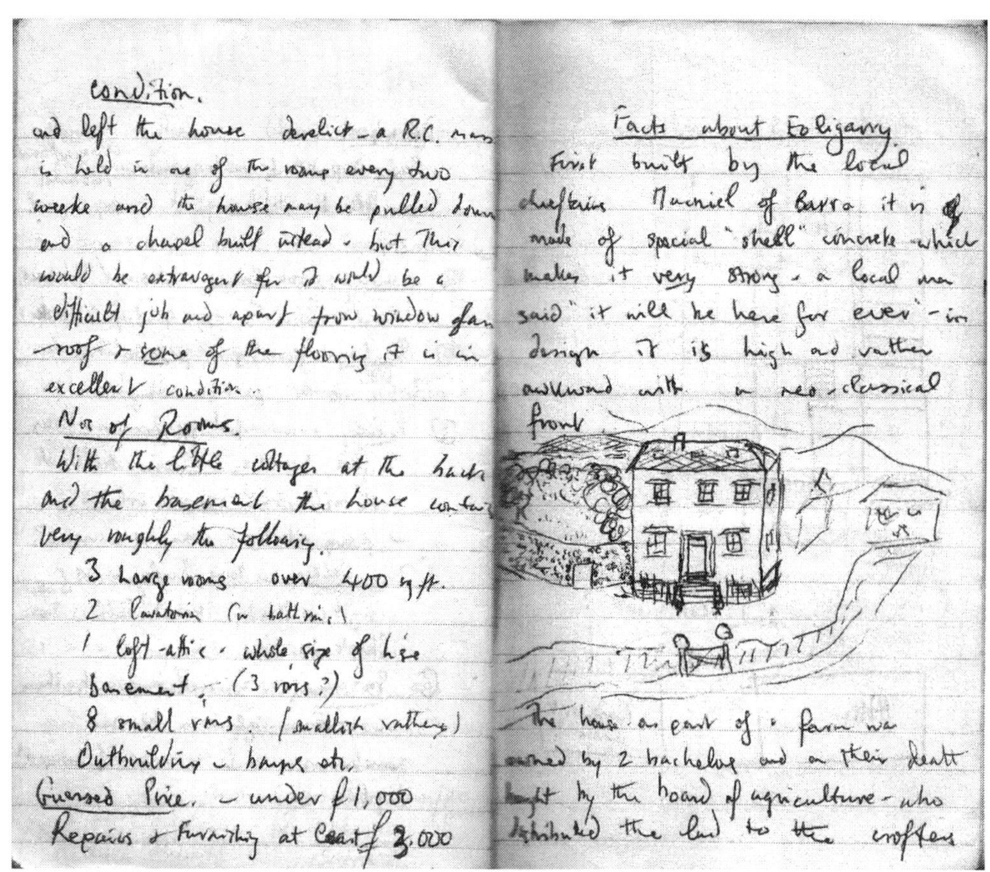

condition.
and left the house derelict – a R.C. mass is held in one of the rooms every two weeks and the house may be pulled down and a chapel built instead – but this would be extravagant for it would be a difficult job and apart from window frames – roof & some of the flooring it is in excellent condition.

No. of Rooms.
With the little cottages at the back and the basement the house contains very roughly the following.
3 Large rooms over 400 sq ft.
2 Lavatories (no bathrms.)
1 loft-attic – whole size of house
basement – (3 rooms?)
8 small rms. (smallish rather)
Outbuildings – barns etc.
Guessed Price. – under £1,000
Repairs & Furnishing at Cost £3,000

Facts about Eoligarry
First built by the local chieftain Macneil of Barra it is made of special "shell" concrete which makes it very strong – a local man said "it will be here for ever" – in design it is high and rather awkward with a neo-classical front

The house as part of a farm was owned by 2 bachelors and on their death bought by the board of agriculture – who distributed the land to the crofters

I was clearly interested in trying to persuade my parents to look at Eoligary House with a view to possibly setting up a hotel there. They did visit it, but felt it required too much work – they bought a croft on North Uist instead. The house fell down some 16 years later (1976) and nothing is left of it. It seems to have been owned by Compton McKenzie, whom I now learn was married to a distant relative. Here are some practical notes I made on the potentials.]

Jottings re enterprise opportunities - Harris.

Special Attractions:
Lochs – free breeding ground for fish.
Sea – unlimited supply of fish (& salmon & sea-trout)
Water – hydro-electric power
Sea-weed – fertilizer
Sand – destroys heather
Land – very cheap – low rate
- Labour – v. cheap but scarce

Climate – warm & wet – good for agriculture (veg grows very well if topsoil)
Market – not too good – enquire
Rowans – rowan jelly etc
- "worms" idea [About this time I was starting to get interested in worm farming]

<u>Disadvantages</u>

i) Distance from large markets & transport therefore either luxury goods <u>or</u> necessary local products.
ii) High winds – bad soil
iii) Lack of co-op from locals
iv) Capital

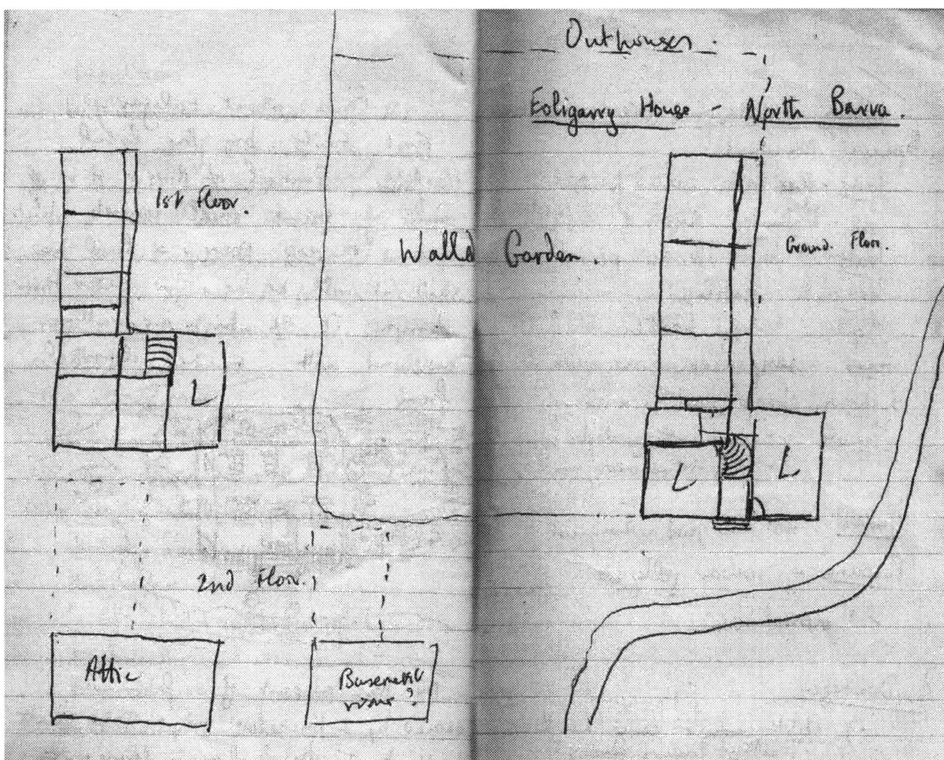

Facts about Eoligarry

First built by the local chieftains Macniel of Barra it is made of special "shell" concrete which makes it very strong – a local man said "it will be here for ever" – in design it is high and rather awkward with a neo-classical front

The house – was part of a farm owned by 2 bachelors and on their death bought by the board of agriculture – who distributed the land to the crofters and left the house derelict – a R.C. mass is held in one of the rooms every two weeks and the house may be pulled down and a chapel built instead – but this would be extravagant for it would be a difficult job and apart from window glass, roof and some of the flooring is in excellent condition.

Nos of Rooms.
With the little cottages at the back and the basement the house contains very roughly the following.
3 large rooms over 400 sq ft.
2 lavatories (or bathrooms)
1 loft attic – whole size of house
basement (3 rooms?)
8 small rms (smallish rather)
Outbuildings – barns etc.
Guessed Price – under £1,000
Repairs and Furnishing at least £3,000

Attractions.
Barra Airport ½ mile away – Glasgow £5 single (40 mins)
Barra Isle – beautiful, unspoilt scenery – great variety.

1. Fishing – Loch fishing – cheap (10/- week) – Sea Fishing – good, free (rocks)
2. Sailing – Boating – possibilities – many little islands to visit tho' perhaps dangerous?
3. Riding – wonderful opportunities – long flat beaches – grassy hills etc – 15 mile trek round island. – pony-trap & day excursions?
4. Walking – some lovely views & sights (a) Standing Stones (b) Seals (c) Water Shoot etc.
5. Swimming – unrivalled sea bathing in coves and glorious beaches – sometimes a mile or more of unspoilt golden sand

Domestic. Domestic labour cheap & good. In the walled garden with suitable manures etc one should be self-contained as far as veg goes – meat, locally grown (sheep & cows) very good & very cheap – also fish (sea) v. cheap & good – while sea-trout, salmon & trout could probably be induced to come – rabbit & chickens. Rabbits, chicken, fish – 3 kinds, beef, mutton, veg.

To conclude
It is a wonderful place and anyone who came here once would want to do so again – it seems a real investment.
Man i/c Revd. Macullum (R.C. priest), Northbay, Barra (owned by local Catholic church)

Second Year: 1961-62

Winter term and vacation 1961

Inside my room 11:4 , with windows onto the garden

Worcester College Calendar, Michaelmas 1961

JUNIOR COMMON ROOM

President: R. B. Sutcliffe

Secretary: D. M. Sachs

Food Member: L. Garey

Drinks Member: P. Hyams

Keeper of the Laundromat: D. I. Strachan

Chairman, J.C.R. Art Fund:

Commem Ball Organiser, 1961: T. M. Stockdale

Editor of Calendar: N. E. Davies

CHAPEL SERVICES

Holy Communion:
8.00 a.m. Sundays and Holy Days, and on other days as shown in the diary section of the calendar.

Mattins:
9.30 a.m. Sundays.
8.00 a.m. Weekdays except on Fridays.

Litany:
8.00 a.m. Fridays.

Evensong:
6.00 p.m. Sundays.
10.00 p.m. Thursdays.

Compline:
10.00 p.m. Mondays, Wednesdays, Fridays.

Intercessions:
10.00 p.m. Tuesdays.

Service of Preparation for Holy Communion:
10.00 p.m. Saturdays.

COLLEGE SPORTS CLUBS

Rugby Club	*Captain*: B. J. G. Sperryn *Secretary*: D. I. Strachan
The Boat Club	*Captain of Boats*: J. R. Houghton *Secretary*: J. D. Jackson
Cricket Club (1961)	*Captain*: P. J. Mackeown *Secretary*: B. J. G. Sperryn
Hockey Club	*Captain*: B. A. C. Marr *Secretary*: M. Bennett
Squash Club	*Captain*: M. Phillips *Secretary*: J. H. M. MacKinnon
Association Football Club	*Captain*: P. L. Druce *Secretary*: L. E. Hart
Cross Country Running	*Captain*: R. R. West
Fencing	*Captain*: D. Brindle-Wood-Williams

COLLEGE SOCIETIES

Thomas of Walsingham Society	*President*: J. V. Hagestadt
Debating Society	*President*: S. Stanley-Little *Vice-President*: N. Annesley *Secretary*: M. F. Whitemore
Chess Club	*Secretary*: G. C. Taylor
Woodroffe Society	*President*: N. E. Davies *Secretaries*: R. D. Martin, A. McE. Small
Wheare Society	*Secretary*: C. Jose
Buskins	*Secretary*: C. Jose
Worcester/Somerville Music Society	*Secretary*: E. J. Walters
Thorold Rogers Society	*President*: M. P. Maine
Odling Society	*Secretary*: R. D. Martin

LECTURES

	9 a.m.	10 a.m.	11 a.m.	12 noon	Evening
Monday					
Tuesday					
Wednesday					
Thursday					
Friday					
Saturday					

WEEK BEFORE TERM

WEDNESDAY **11 OCTOBER**

THURSDAY **12 OCTOBER**

FRIDAY **13 OCTOBER**

An appropriate day for College Collections

SATURDAY **14 OCTOBER**

Another appropriate day for collections (if you've managed to come up yet)

MICHAELMAS TERM

SUNDAY **15 OCTOBER**

Trinity 20

8.15 p.m. J.C.R. Meeting

9.00 p.m. Woodroffe Society — N. E. Davies, "Why believe?" (4:4)

MONDAY **16 OCTOBER**

1.30 p.m. Buskins Business Meeting in 10:1

8.15 p.m. Boat Club Freshmen's meeting in Nuffield 6

TUESDAY **17 OCTOBER**

A.F.C. 1st XI v. St. Catherine's (H)

WEDNESDAY **18 OCTOBER**

St. Luke. Holy Communion 8 a.m.

1st V v. Balliol (H)

Cross Country v. S.E.H., Keble, Univ.

Hockey 1st XI v. S.P.H. (H)

Checkers Heritage.

FIRST WEEK

19 OCTOBER **THURSDAY**

A.F.C. 2nd XI v. Pembroke (H)

20 OCTOBER **FRIDAY**

8.15 p.m. (10:1) Buskins play-reading: "Christopher Columbus" by MacNeice, to be produced by the Secretary

Talk by Graves 5.0 p.m.

Cross Country v. Exeter

2nd XV v. Merton (A)

21 OCTOBER **SATURDAY**

1st XV v. Caius, Cambridge (A)

ENTERTAINMENTS

Scala: Frederico Fellini's "Lights of Variety". Judy Holliday in "The Solid Gold Cadillac".

Playhouse: 16th-18th "Murder and Mozart" — music and poetry arranged by Neville Coghill. 19th-21st E.T.C. Minor, "Pantagleize", by Michel de Ghelderode.

New Theatre: Royal Ballet.

For information on films throughout the term, contact B. A. C. Marr.

C

MICHAELMAS TERM

SUNDAY — **22 OCTOBER**

Trinity 21

Preacher at Evensong: The Chaplain

MONDAY — **23 OCTOBER**

A.F.C. 1st XI v. S.E.H. (H)
2nd V v. Brasenose (H)
Hockey 1st XI v. Lincoln (A)

TUESDAY — **24 OCTOBER**

1st V v. New College (H)
A.F.C. 2nd XI v. Wadham (A)
Hockey 1st XI v. Trinity (A)

WEDNESDAY — **25 OCTOBER**

8.15 p.m. Buskins play-reading: "The Balcony" by Genet, to be produced by Harry Weiss
1st XV v. Balliol (A)
A.F.C. 1st XI v. King Alfred's, Wantage (H)
Cross Country v. Keble, Jesus, Pembroke

SECOND WEEK

26 OCTOBER — **THURSDAY**

Thomas of Walsingham Society: Andrew Bowden on "Cobham's 'Cubs'"
Wheare Society: 8.15 p.m. in 10:2
A.F.C. 2nd XI v. Pembroke (A)
2nd V v. Corpus Christi (H)
Hockey 1st XI v. Christchurch (H)

27 OCTOBER — **FRIDAY**

1st V v. Pembroke (H)
2nd XV v. Lincoln (A)

28 OCTOBER — **SATURDAY**

St. Simon and St. Jude. Holy Communion 8 a.m.
1st XV v. Moseley Nomads (H)
A.F.C. 1st XI v. College of Technology (A)
Hockey 1st XI v. Oriel (A)

ENTERTAINMENTS

Scala: Mylene Demongeot, "Notte Brava", with "Paths of Glory"
Playhouse: Aeschylus, "The Orestria" — Meadow Players
New Theatre: Royal Ballet

MICHAELMAS TERM

SUNDAY — **29 OCTOBER**

Trinity 22
8.15 p.m. Woodroffe Society (4:4) J. M. Hinton, Esq. on "Philosophy and the Christian Faith"

MONDAY — **30 OCTOBER**

A.F.C. 1st XI v. B.N.C. (A)
Hockey 1st XI v. New College (H)
8.15 p.m. in 4:4 The Chaplain — "Prayer" (I)
Debating Society: 8.00 p.m. in the President's rooms

TUESDAY — **31 OCTOBER**

1st V v. Lincoln (A)
2nd XV v. R.A.O.C. Didcot (H)

WEDNESDAY — **1 NOVEMBER**

All Saints Day. Holy Communion 8 a.m., Choral Evensong 6.30 p.m.
1st XV v. Magdalen (H)
O.U.B.C. Fours begin
Cross Country v. B.N.C., St. John's

THIRD WEEK

2 NOVEMBER — **THURSDAY**

A.F.C. 1st XI v. Hertford (H)
A.F.C. 2nd XI v. S.P.H. (A)
1st V v. Christ Church (H)
Hockey 1st XI v. C.C.C. (H)

3 NOVEMBER — **FRIDAY**

2nd XV v. Balliol (A)
2nd V v. Lincoln (H)

4 NOVEMBER — **SATURDAY**

1st XV Ampthill (A)
A.F.C. 1st XI v. Accidentals (H)
O.U.B.C. Fours end

ENTERTAINMENTS

Scala: Hitchcock's "The Lady Vanishes", and "La Main Chaude."
Playhouse: Aeschylus, "The Oresteia"—Meadow Players.

MICHAELMAS TERM

SUNDAY — **5 NOVEMBER**

Trinity 23 (Fawkes, Martyr)
Preacher at Evensong: The Rev. R. A. K. Runcie, M.C., Principal of Cuddesdon Theological College

Children

MONDAY — **6 NOVEMBER**

Hockey 1st XI v. St. John's (H)
A.F.C. 1st XI v. S.P.H. (H)
1st V v. Gladiators (H)
8.15 p.m. in 4:4. The Chaplain — "Prayer" (2)

TUESDAY — **7 NOVEMBER**

1st V v. Magdalen (A)
A.F.C. 2nd XI v. Exeter (A)

WEDNESDAY — **8 NOVEMBER**

1st XV v. Oriel (A)
2nd V v. S.E.H. (A)
O.U.B.C. Senior Pairs Begin
Cross Country v. Balliol
8.15 p.m. Buskins play-reading; play to be produced by a freshman

Tea 4.30 Valentine Appleby

Meeting 8.15 Public Rm.

FOURTH WEEK

9 NOVEMBER — **THURSDAY**

A.F.C. 1st XI v. Univ (A)
A.F.C. 2nd XI v. S.E.H. (H)
Hockey 1st XI v. Hertford (H)
8.15 p.m. in 10:2. Wheare Society
8.15 p.m. elsewhere. Thomas of Walsingham Society: Laurence Stone, Esq. on "Latest developments in the study of English History, 1485-1640"

Corporate Communion.

10 NOVEMBER — **FRIDAY**

2nd XV v. B.N.C. (H)
2nd V v. Magdalen (H)

11 NOVEMBER — **SATURDAY**

1st XV v. Emmanuel, Cambridge (A)
1st V v. Clare, Cambridge (A)
O.U.B.C. Senior Pairs end
Hockey 1st XI v. Clare, Cambridge (H)

ENTERTAINMENTS

Scala: H. G. Clouzot's "Les Diaboliques". Bergman: "Waiting Women".
Playhouse: 6th-8th: O.U.D.S. Minor — "The Devil's Disciple" by Shaw. 9th-11th: University Players — "Sergeant Musgrave's Dance" by John Arden.
New Theatre: Ian Carmichael in "Critic's Choice" by Ira Levin.

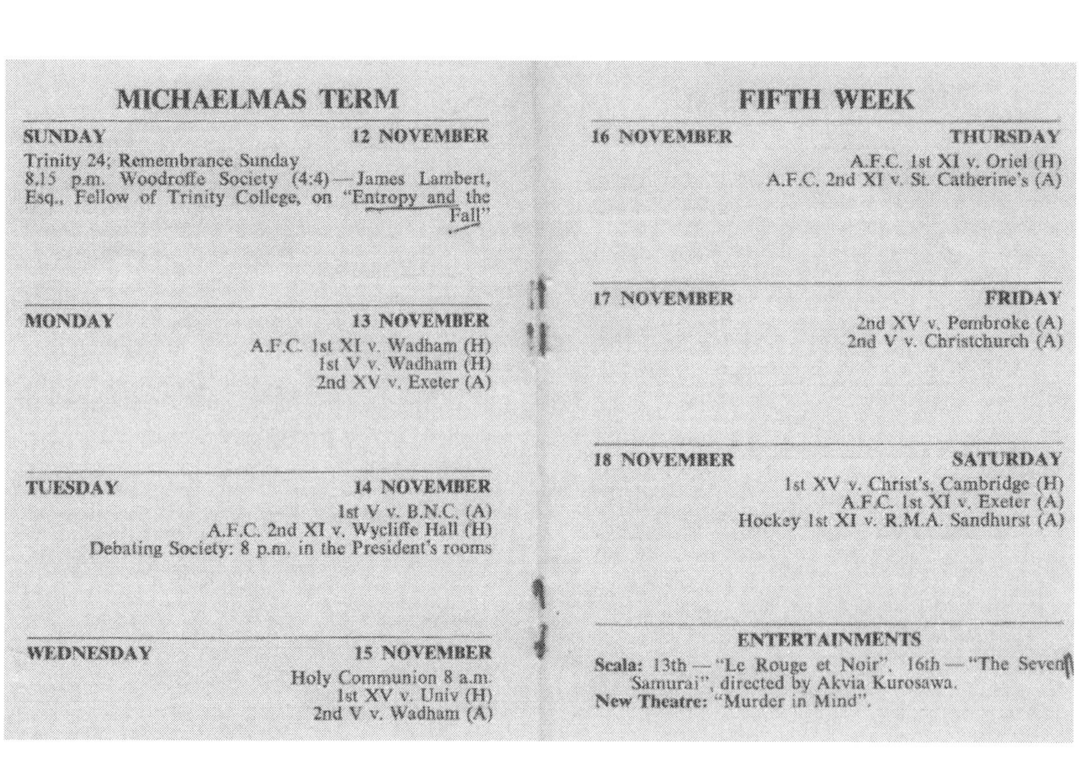

MICHAELMAS TERM

SUNDAY — **12 NOVEMBER**

Trinity 24; Remembrance Sunday
8.15 p.m. Woodroffe Society (4:4) — James Lambert, Esq., Fellow of Trinity College, on "Entropy and the Fall"

MONDAY — **13 NOVEMBER**

A.F.C. 1st XI v. Wadham (H)
1st V v. Wadham (H)
2nd XV v. Exeter (A)

TUESDAY — **14 NOVEMBER**

1st V v. B.N.C. (A)
A.F.C. 2nd XI v. Wycliffe Hall (H)
Debating Society: 8 p.m. in the President's rooms

WEDNESDAY — **15 NOVEMBER**

Holy Communion 8 a.m.
1st XV v. Univ (H)
2nd V v. Wadham (A)

FIFTH WEEK

16 NOVEMBER — **THURSDAY**

A.F.C. 1st XI v. Oriel (H)
A.F.C. 2nd XI v. St. Catherine's (A)

17 NOVEMBER — **FRIDAY**

2nd XV v. Pembroke (A)
2nd V v. Christchurch (A)

18 NOVEMBER — **SATURDAY**

1st XV v. Christ's, Cambridge (H)
A.F.C. 1st XI v. Exeter (A)
Hockey 1st XI v. R.M.A. Sandhurst (A)

ENTERTAINMENTS

Scala: 13th — "Le Rouge et Noir". 16th — "The Seven Samurai", directed by Akvia Kurosawa.
New Theatre: "Murder in Mind".

MICHAELMAS TERM

SUNDAY **19 NOVEMBER**
Trinity 25
Preacher at Evensong: The Rev. G.C. Triffith, S.S.J.E.

MONDAY **20 NOVEMBER**
A.F.C. 1st XI v. The Queen's (H)
2nd V v. Trinity (H)
8.15 p.m. in 4:4. The Chaplain — "Prayer" (3)

TUESDAY **21 NOVEMBER**
1st V v. S.E.H. (H)
A.F.C. 2nd XI v. Christchurch (H)
8.15 p.m. Buskins play-reading: play to be produced by Christopher Maclehose (volente decano)

WEDNESDAY **22 NOVEMBER**
Holy Communion, 8 a.m.
1st XV v. The Queen's (A)

SIXTH WEEK

23 NOVEMBER **THURSDAY**
A.F.C. 2nd XI v. The Queen's (H)
2nd V v. New College (A)
Hockey 1st XI v. Occasionals (H)
8.15 p.m. in 10:2 Wheare Society

24 NOVEMBER **FRIDAY**
1st V v. Trinity (A)
Hockey 1st XI v. Merton (H)

25 NOVEMBER **SATURDAY**
1st XV v. Bicester R.F.C. (H)
A.F.C. 1st XI v. St. Bartholomew's Hospital (A)

ENTERTAINMENTS
Scala: "Look Back in Anger".

MICHAELMAS TERM

SUNDAY **26 NOVEMBER**
Last after Trinity
Woodroffe Society
8.15 p.m. in the Public Room, New Building, Archbishop Lord Fisher of Lambeth will answer questions.

MONDAY **27 NOVEMBER**
A.F.C. 1st XI v. Balliol (H)
2nd V v. S.P.H. (H)
Hockey 1st XI v. S.E.H. (A)

TUESDAY **28 NOVEMBER**
1st V v. C.C.C. (H)
2nd XV v. S.P.H. (A)
A.F.C. 2nd XI v. Hertford (A)

WEDNESDAY **29 NOVEMBER**
1st XV v. Exeter (H)
Hockey 1st XI v. Ripon Hall (H)

SEVENTH WEEK

30 NOVEMBER **THURSDAY**
St. Andrew. Holy Communion, 8 a.m.
8.15 p.m. Thomas of Walsingham Society; speaker, Dr. Robin Jeffs
Christchurch Regatta begins
A.F.C. 1st XI v. Lincoln (H)

1 DECEMBER **FRIDAY**
2nd XV v. New College (H)

2 DECEMBER **SATURDAY**
1st XV v. Clare, Cambridge (H)
Christchurch Regatta ends
Hockey 1st XI v. Exeter (H)

ENTERTAINMENTS
Scala: "I Soliti Ignoti" and "Bullfight".
Playhouse: E.T.C. Major, "Peer Gynt".
New Theatre: The Old Vic.

MICHAELMAS TERM — **EIGHTH WEEK**

SUNDAY — **3 DECEMBER**
Advent Sunday
Preacher at Evensong: The Right Rev. C. M. Chavasse, formerly Bishop of Rochester
8.15 p.m. J.C.R. Meeting

MONDAY — **4 DECEMBER**
8.15 p.m. in 4:4. The Chaplain — "Prayer" (4)
A.F.C. 1st XI v. Pembroke (H)

TUESDAY — **5 DECEMBER**
8.00 p.m. The Debating Society meets in the President's rooms
A.F.C. 2nd XI v. Lincoln (A)

WEDNESDAY — **6 DECEMBER**
Holy Communion, 8 a.m.
1st XV v. Christchurch (A)
W.C.B.C. Open and Novice Sculls
Cross Country v. Oriel, Westminster

7 DECEMBER — **THURSDAY**
A.F.C. 1st XI v. Trinity (H)

8 DECEMBER — **FRIDAY**

9 DECEMBER — **SATURDAY**
Term ends

ENTERTAINMENTS
Scala: 4th — Chabrol's "Les Cousins". 7th — Alec Guinness and Peter Sellers in "The Lady Killers".
Playhouse: 4th—6th: Balliol Dramatic Club, "The Tinker". 7th—9th: O.U. German Club, "Der Zerbrochere Krug" by Kleist.

The first letter from my mother was at the start of term.

Cherideo 4 October

My dear Alan,

The eve of our departure for Shillong, this time to-morrow we shall have started on the eight hour drive to Gauhati, then a couple of hours up the hill and it will be cool – lets hope not too freezing though as I don't suppose a Government School will have many fires ... We heard from Granpa that you had got off to Oxford safely, you'll be well and truly dug in by now, you must try and get in some games this term as there wont be so many distractions perhaps. The Buckmasters weren't back when he wrote but they'll have to do something about rescuing Granny from the dacshunds, poor Jummy, life can't be any fun for him now and its amazing really that he is carrying on at all. Your descriptions of the autumn trees and skies made me feel quite ill at the thought of all we are missing, there'll be lots of other autumns of course but I shall be forty five before I see my next, I think I miss it more than anything else. We have some new terms coming out, everyone is to get leave every twenty one months so it will mean that one has to take it when-ever it falls, winter or summer, it doesn't really affect us much but people like the Rosses are naturally delighted. We are also supposed to be getting a raise in pay but are sceptical, they will probably give us just enough to put us into a higher tax bracket, its what usually happens!

My only letter for the term dated Sunday 8 October, from Worcester College.

Dear Family,

Thank you once again for your letter. I expect you will have been up to Shillong and arrived back by now – if you have managed to bring Fiona back with you – all my love to her especially. I hope Mummy and Anne enjoyed their holiday up there very much, and are now both completely cured. It is wonderful to think that in a few months you will all be home. I wonder if we will have changed much? I am expecting to see two very smart and sophisticated young ladies walk into Field Head – for that matter three! Now that I am growing slightly clothes-conscious I am also growing self-conscious about my looks – and can already see the first signs of baldness and a double-chin – imagine it! Ah well my philosophic outlook on life will tackle that problem when it comes. Talking of philosophy etc Mummy's last letter expressed all sorts of doubts about the "Problem of

Pain" – but I won't try to give my views as it would take much longer than this letter – also Fiona would possibly throw it down in disgust. It is really rather a problem writing to four different people in one letter!

I have been working very conscientiously at my European History. My period, from 1494, ends at 1648 so I will now be behind you. I spent last week immersed in the Dutch Revolt – William the Silent and all that – it is a fascinating, especially since there is a heated controversy between historians as to whether there was any real difference between the people of the N & S Neth's. Geyl has almost debunked the old view and seems to prove convincingly – to me at least – that there were many common features in the N & S and that it was merely strategic and military factors which caused the split and settled the border along the river-lines. I am getting really interested in my present work – but I feel that it is rather a waste just to work when I am up here – I can do that anywhere. How is Anne's work going? – if she ever does a good English essay or suchlike I would love to see it.

I'm sorry you didn't like "Rouge et Noir" – a friend of mine doing French actually agreed with you and said he thought Stendhal was overrated. I am also reading – or have just finished, another French classic – some short stories of Guy de Maupassant which are needless to say – brilliant, though at first some of them rather horrified me – he certainly believes in showing human nature in all its rottenness as well as its beauty!

As my gramaphone is being repaired and there is hardly any one up at the moment I have been living a very quiet life – but I managed to get out to two plays. The first was "St Teresa of Avila' with Sybil Thorndike – simple and touching. It was especially fascinating for me as St T. is one of the outstanding characters in the period of history I am studying. She also attracts me both as a poet and mystic – rather in the same way as St Francis does – in fact I find myself very magnetized by mysticism and R. Catholicism general[ly] – probably just a phase!

Then on Friday evening I went to see Shaw's "Heartbreak House" which was superbly acted and hilariously funny, but didn't really seem to emphasize the moral (which the programme said it contained) – no doubt my lack of sympathy or observation.

I had a letter from Julie a few days ago and she seems very happy in Perugia. Most of the time I don't miss her – but occasionally I grow rather sad when I think of the wonderful times we had together last term – but there are as many good fish in the sea etc!

I am glad you are sending the ms of the book – I hope it will reach me safe.

Look after yourselves, and get Fiona working at the shorthand typing!

All my love to you all, Alan

The next letter from my mother is on 17 October, again from Cherideo

My dear Alan,

Alas I never got off your letter in Shillong, I bought an Airgraph but then went all mean about buying a pen and ink, sorry! Two letters for me on my return, with the wonderful news of your grant, needless to say we were thrilled, it'll make all the difference. I'm sure you should take the credit, it's probably due to your tutor's report, anyway I hope it'll ease things for you, you'll be able to feel you can buy the odd clothes and records without carrying loads of guilt round afterwards. Granny wrote the same day with news of a large win, and we heard our pay was to be increased (haven't heard by how much yet) so altogether felt hilarious. Money doesn't matter of course, but how blissfully happy one feels to have some nevertheless. We thoroughly enjoyed our week in Shillong…

The next is on October 27

My dear Alan,

A letter to thank you for, and also "Peter Abelard", for which many thanks, which arrived at the beginning of the week and which I've been trying to make last by only reading two chapters at a time, but last night I simply had to finish it. Like you I adored it, it is exactly the sort of book I like best, the only thing is that I come out of it in a daze and feel discontented and let down that life is not like that nor is anyone as fascinating and lovable, it seems to recreate a life that one knew once, somewhere, perhaps only in dreams or imagination. I agree that the mystique of Catholicism is very persuasive (I never quite know what mystique means but it feels like the right word) it appeals to both intellect and emotion, at least it does once you have accepted the fundamental truths – which in my lucid moments I cant. I wonder what Granny would feel if you became a Catholic, she is all for introducing the inquisition in reverse! Me, I'd be more likely to turn Buddhist or even Hindu which I suppose would shock you equally – when will we learn tolerance, the whole of history is a miserable drama showing the lack of it.

We had the Durga Pooja here last week, the big festival of the year, sort of harvest festival cum primitive mother-earth propitiation ceremony. We went down one evening and walked round the lighted stalls and paid our respects to the image, a ten armed goddess treading on the neck of her husband who is unconcernedly killing a lion. Ridiculous? Wicked? Symbolic? But the expression of the coolies as they kneel in front of her and hold out their hands for a bit of sacred coconut is just exactly the same as you see on faces as they are offered communion. Anyway right or wrong I always enjoy the pooja, the smells of frying spices and incense and burning torches and burning rubber and the happiness of the coolies seems exciting, in spite of the foot of mud one has to plod through as it always coincides with the last burst of rain…

Have you read Roberts new book on the H. of Commons? I would like to get it, perhaps Granny will send it to me for Christmas, she usually buys up most of the first printing! Have you any particular wants? We cant get the feel of Christmas here but I suppose will pretend with the help of a bottle of something, how crude that sounds but Christmas in Assam is crude I fear...

Your birthday letter to Daddy will probably arrive to-day and he'll be delighted, being a Tuesday there isn't much we can do to celebrate but we shall talk about our croft in the Hebrides.

The next letter is dated 9 November.

My dear Alan,

I'm very sorry I didn't write last week but I spent it in bed with flu and such a blinding headache I couldn't open my eyes, I staggered up for the week end as we had Robert Shaw to stay, and for the last few days have been trying to carry on still feeling as if I had half a ton of cement behind my eyes – but now at last I feel a little better…. [Description of going to Anouillh's 'Ring Round the Moon' – by coincidence the one performed by Worcester and which I went to the previous summer.] *I've never seen anything of Anouillhs before but this seemed singularly pointless, perhaps first class acting would have made the difference, at least there were no horrid creaking pauses though… At the dance we met a new assistant with a Sedbergh tie, Roger Mayo by name of Powell house, a great streak of about six foot 2" who is a year senior to you and remembers you vaguely… You didn't say much about Anne Johnson, has she changed and what is she going to do with herself? ….*

I worry most about Anne's work… We've come to the end of Elizabeth at last and are about to embark on the Stuarts which should be more familiar ground as it came into our syllabus but that was a hundred years ago.

I'm glad your grant arrived at last, do you think you could pay all your battels out of it this time, and we will pay the next two lots, we are getting a raise in pay from January which should bring in another couple of hundred pounds a year if the tax people don't get hold of it. Have noted your remarks about Christmas, please don't think of sending anything to us, we can leave our present paying till we meet. Fiona has written which I hope will make up for this feeble effort, With all our love & thoughts, Mummy

The next letter from my mother is on Saturday 18 November

My dear Alan,

*You will be glad to hear that I shant be spending this letter moaning about my head or veins as both are quite better. I thought I was never going to throw off my flu, but simply sat in the sun and refused to be lured out to the club or anywhere else and it has quite gone. My leg doesn't bother me at all either so please don't waste any sympathy on that either … my mornings have been spent teaching and my afternoons retiring to the summer house with "The Thirty Years War" (yes still) and lying in a deck chair trying to keep my mind on Wallenstein and off the birds and butterflies. Anne writes notes or essays after lunch, and then we do some poetry or Twelfth Night while we drink tea, we are doing some quite pleasant poetry, Yeats, Walter de la Mare, Rupert Brooke, Manley Hopkins etc but I find it rather difficult to "teach" it, particularly to someone who hasn't much natural interest. … I cant remember saying she [*Fiona*] wanted to write, actually she has no leanings in that direction, you seem to have inherited the nack. At your age I knew I could do it if only I had the time, now I realise that what I had was a tiny little talent not the world shaking genius I thought. Now also I have no ambition at all, if I wrote it would be purely for money – which brings me to the confession that I still haven't sent off my book. I will do so I promise, so that you will get it when you get back to Oxford, if not* *sooner. The thing is, its too long and very boring, not at all what you expect I'm sure. I've just finished "The Disenchanted", a very amusing (and sad) story, supposed to be based on the life of Scott Fitzgerald, its in Penguins. There are so many books I want to order for the library but sex and crime are the order of the day among planters, I never bother to get any of them out as Terry's father sends him all the proof copies from Michael Joseph. Anne's only reading these days is recipes…*

Have you any serious thoughts on careers? A silly question as you obviously think and talk of it all the time, I read the letters in the Sunday Times from undergrads and was amused that they were all scornful about Good Jobs, ironical when their parents have sent them to university with that one end in view – but I think they're right (the undergrads)…

This time next week we shall be frantically pinning up the mandarins and I shall be reminded of Mrs Knappett's dining room, what years ago it seems. Much love from all of us, Mummy

The next letter is dated 29 November.

My Dear Alan,

I'm afraid this is overdue by three days, I thought I'd wait over the week end so that I could tell you about our exciting Spree, and when I went in to collect an airgraph form at the Nazira P.O. on Monday they hadn't any… All this and I've forgotten to thank you for the William Saroyan which arrived last week, Fiona snatched it first and loved it and now I'm reading it and find it enchanting, just the sort of book I would like to write, why cant I? Thank you very much for sending it (I was horrified to find out how much it cost to post) any paper backs you don't want are always welcome but please don't send them Air Mail. Anne and I are at last into the Thirty Years War and she is actually enjoying it, have been dreading it but by careful selection of the interesting passages it is coming to life.

I suppose your term is almost over now, I wonder if you'll find something to do in the vac. or have enough to occupy you with reading. I think you'll have to get yourself a dinner jacket this winter, out of the old grant. I'm afraid, I'll have to write endless letters for Christmas as I'm too late with cards as usual. We are going to do without presents this year, at least that's what we are all telling each other now but I know at the last moment there will be a panicky change of mind. We shall be leaving on December 17th, spending one night rhino watching at Kaziranga on the way, and returning on 27th…

Feel a bit guilty about work but I will take our poetry book with us and hope that the change will refresh us and put new life into the Functions of the Kidneys and Concessive Clauses. Where are you now in European History? Hope your courtly and cosy love life is going along well, perhaps the Christmas dances will throw up something more positive?! Let us know all the scandal and who likes who, that is if you aren't too out of touch by now.

Much love from us all, Mummy

The next letter from my mother is undated, but was probably a week later, in early December (my birthday is on 20th December).

My dear Alan,

No letter from you this week, I imagine because you are breaking up or coming down or whatever the expression is. Anyway I hope its successfully accomplished and you are back in your little room at Field Head with all the windows tight shut and the electric fire on which is how I always remember you.

Here I'm sitting on the verandah before breakfast and looking out on a glittering world of cobwebs and dew, with doves cooing and wood smoke in my nostrils, the best time of the day although at this time of year its hard to choose… [recounts a mother forbidding her son to marry a Khasi girl] I hope I shall never try to interfere with my children and will accept with a good grace whatever they have to offer in the way of wives or husbands of whatever creed or colour. This particular girl was intelligent sweet and beautiful which is as much as anyone could reasonably expect and the fact that she was a lovely shade of golden brown needn't have made any difference as far as we could see…

Alas my pleasure in the actual fishing has gone, when I see a fish on the end of a hook I feel only its pain and fear, so silly really. Our Manas trip is fairly well organized… I wish you could be with us, I shall always remember when you went off on your own on the elephant and I thought you hadn't got anything and then saw the huge monsters dangling by your legs…

This letter isn't a birthday one, but I shall be writing again for that in a couple of days. I hope it arrives in time you know we shall be thinking of you, it is the day we arrive at the Manas so we shall toast you by the light of the hurricane lantern with the wind from the gorge roaring past the bungalow and perhaps a tiger or two. I wonder if you would get a Christmas present for Granny and Granpa out of the enclosed, I thought a Gardeners Diary or Gift Token for Granpa and perhaps another Pyrex dish for Granny to match the one we gave her for her birthday, unless you know she wants something else specially. I'm afraid you're going to find yourself rather stuck without your motor bike but perhaps Martin will lend you his if he's still there. I wonder how he did in his exam. I must write to the Buckmasters, and will be writing to Granny to-morrow tell her. …. Sorry for a short letter but another will follow in a day or two. Much love

The next letter is dated 11 December from Cherideo

My dear Alan,

What with the Festive Season and all I'm not sure when to send this, but whenever it arrives it is a Birthday Letter and brings all our love and thoughts. I don't suppose you will do anything wildly exciting this year, but I know Granny will rattle up a super spread for you and perhaps you will climb a hill and think solemn thoughts about time and its passing. It seems quite unreal to me that you are twenty and I'm filled with thoughts too, nostalgic and sentimental ones mostly in which first teeth and pattering footsteps figure prominently. Sad thoughts some of them though, about how little we've really seen of you during your growing up, I've often wondered whether the advantages of a good education really make the long banishment of ones children worth while. What do you think? Perhaps though parents are not the best people to bring up their offspring, being too involved with them, childhood is a pretty dreadful time whatever you do with it, one never suffers in the same way again, if that's any comfort! We shall be arriving at the Manas on the 20th, I wish you could fly out and spend that fortnight with us…

I've just heard from Pat Cowan, I'm glad you are going to see them, it should be fun comparing notes with Nicola who is apparently enjoying Cambridge so much that she has to go to bed for several days at intervals to recover.[1] *…I will be writing again for Christmas, just before we leave, Daddy sends lots of birthday wishes of course, I'm afraid our present was a small one perforce but you know what we would like to give you. Have a happy day and think of us crossing the Brahmaputra and bumping down that long dusty road to the Manas, and we'll think of you all cosy and coddled. Much love from us all, Mummy*

*

My next letter is dated Sunday 7th December, from Field Head.

Dear Family,

I don't know if this will get to you before Christmas – I doubt it, but it brings all my love and good wishes in retrospect and also all "New Year" greetings. I hope my present, and my last letter have arrived, and of course that you had a <u>marvellous</u> time up the river – I'm longing to hear all about it. By the time your letter arrives I will be 20 – how strange! I don't feel it at all! No doubt you have often remarked that in a few months Fiona will be 18 – a significant age for Mummy!

There isn't very much news – which is perhaps just as well as the Christmas letter is by custom a special one meant to gather together 'fragrant memories from the past' and 'quiet hopes for the future'(!) But before I start getting <u>too</u> airy-fairy thank you very much Mummy <u>and</u> Anne for a letter this week. Mummy's was a shortish one (not the birthday one) and Anne's – as well as a most pleasant surprise, was extremely interesting (<u>and</u> well written) – I don't want to swell either teacher or pupil's head but I think that if I had been able to write as well as that at 16 I wouldn't have failed my English 'O' level! I don't know if I'll have time to write individual letters back to Anne and Fiona, but will excuse myself by saying that they have a share in these letters every week.

I hope that all of you are well – not only Mummy but also poor Daddy who is sweating away to keep us all alive (and also to help the tax man to grow even fatter it seems!). My love to each and all of you, especially at this time. I will be thinking of you often as you laze in the warm, orange-juice-thirst, sunlight while I am

[1] Nicola was the older daughter of my godmother, Pat Cowan.

crunching across the frozen and glittering fields by starlight, or sitting filled with Christmas-lunch & stupefied in front of the Queen "My dear people, my husband and I..."

The bit about the "frozen fields" is already true. After a week of warm rain it has turned bright and cold and the ground was crisp with a film of frost and patches of ice, when I went to church this morning. The trees were hard, bent, black against the morning sky – even the sheep looked cold, huddled together – I can't resist adding "The owl for all his feathers, was a-cold; the hare limp'd trembling through the frozen grass, and silent was the flock in woolly fold". (I think I was unconsciously parodying it anyhow!)

Now the news. Jummy is still very poorly. Beryl is still bearing up – but what a strain! I have tried to help and am reading "101 Dalmatians" still – but feel I can help Beryl most by mere sympathy. Martin is hardly ever in – and thumps on his drum endlessly when he is. We are on different wave-lengths and I find it difficult to talk to him – except about 'pop' music or girls. I haven't seen Steve – Simon isn't back yet. Anne 'J' came up yesterday but I haven't got in touch. Michael Bod' with his "Mephisophelian" beard looks well – and is lamenting the absence of girls (most of them – or rather two – having been driven to the Continent by him!). I will keep you informed on 'La Dolce Vita'. Gr[anny] & Gr[andpa] are well – still fairly T.V. mad, but Grandpa is also reading a good deal, and doing crossword puzzles etc – but I don't know why I'm telling you this – they can tell it all to you anyhow!

The pattern of my days is very restful. Up at 8.45. Work for 3 hours in the morning. Work for 1½ hrs in the afternoon, go for a one to two mile walk, and then return to crumpets and tea. After tea, I read to Jummy for an hour or so, and then read until supper (I have just finished 'The Secret Garden' (for the second time this year!) and 'Orthodoxy' by G.K. Chesterton – which I will send out (the latter) as it is marvellous) and after supper I either watch anything decent on T.V (i.e. a western, "Perry Mason" or a good comedian!), read, listen to my records or write letters. (By the way – talking about 'The Secret Garden' have you posted your type-script yet Mummy?) No doubt later on in the Vac things will get hectic, e.g. rushing about etc. R & A are coming over for Christmas lunch, and I am going back with them for a day or two – not to mention the Cowans – (perhaps Nicola will turn out to be a human version of the "ugly duckling"!?!)*

Now onto the general 'rhapsodizing'! If I could manage it I would wait a few days then I could study Mummy's birthday letter which will be almost certainly a brilliant example of this difficult art – but I must get this off.

I think it is probably better to look forward than back (tho I have nothing against the past, against those golden days when Daddy and I went fishing in the Shetlands, or when Mummy, the girls, and I first came to Field Head; when we played padder; fished in Black beck; went blackberry picking or sledging; fed the ponies; freed the sheep from the brambles; had the party at Mrs Knappets; went swimming in Esthwaite; went over to the sea; up the Duddon and so on and so on...! But there are yet more glorious days ahead.

This summer the house will be even more wonderful than ever. I might even be able to refrain from fighting with my <u>dear</u> sisters! There will be twice as many strawberries, plums, apples, pears etc; the fish will be twice as plump, and even if we are twice as broke as usual the weather will be twice as good as it has been this summer (with Daddy home). It will be marvellous – I only hope I don't have to work too hard!

Or again looking further ahead I see three young married couples and all their squealing brats trooping up to a little highland village. After the station-master has recovered from his astonishment he will lead the returned Macfarlanes to the little croft, nestling under the misty mountains. The long-haired cow will look up inquisitively & stop its drinking, and the chickens will come squawking towards the new arrivals. Behind them, one brushing lard out of her hair, the other wood-chippings, will arrive the A.P's [Aged Parents] arrayed in their tribal cloaks; gladly welcoming the three women, three men and six or seven "bairns" to their small but hospitable mansion!!

Ah well – it does one good to be carried away occasionally!

Finally all my very best love – look after yourselves & each other – and be seeing you soon, Alan

I wrote periodically to my Sedbergh school friend, Ian Campbell, and one of these is headed 'On Choosing a Career' The Two Questions. (from a letter written on 17th December, three days before my 20th birthday and written in the Lakes). Again I took a carbon copy, which is rather faint, but most of it legible.

i) *Having missed the broadening benefits of National Service I feel it would be both beneficial and enjoyable to spend two or three years after University doing something which would give me an experience which would be unattainable in my later life when I am in some 'groove'. (It would also give me longer before making a final decision and enable me to get a wider view of the various 'points of stress' where my service would be of most value. What should I do?)*

ii) *What final career should I follow? I must admit I have no intimation of the answer to either of them – but am slowly building up a few rules by which to measure any opportunity when it comes.*

In reference to the first questions – "what experience would be most beneficial and enjoyable before I settle down"? a few obvious alternatives suggest themselves.

i) *Travel. Either round the world (see later) or to some special place where I would meet different peoples and conditions, perhaps learn another language, certainly stretch my insular outlook.*

ii) *Teaching. This would be enjoyable and allow plenty of time to continue academic work and provide long holidays in which to travel etc. (I taught in the summer as I think I told you enjoyed it immensely.)*

iii) *Continuing the above two and going to somewhere like Sarawak (like Geoffrey), thus continuing enjoyment, stretching of the mind and benefit to others.*

iv) *Further study, if possible reading for a D.Phil (a 3 year thesis) or perhaps a Diploma of Education (a year) or even of something practical like Agriculture. You suggested something close to this when you mentioned getting a Master of Business Administration at Harvard – tho my further degree would probably be of less financial value.*

v) *A totally different job. Getting the job of a market-gardener, or a porter with the MacBraynes boat at Stornoway (I will return to the Hebrides later!) or an office boy or such like. Many of the jobs would be unpleasant (it would probably be best to change about fairly frequently) but one would be meeting completely different conditions and classes and would no doubt be toughened (tho' I am still as dreamy and idealistic after my work in the prostitute haunted (that's perhaps over-strong) Norwegian ship.)*

- *if you can think of any more alternatives for that time please let me know. I haven't really time to go into the merits of each of them but they should I think be weighed up with the following general rules in mind.*

    i) *What opportunity would there be to meet out-of-my-groove people (if you see what I mean!)*

    ii) *What basic problems would this bring me up against (sickness, poverty, ignorance etc)*

    iii) *How might it conceivably be of use – either in my future career (if I am able) in choosing it if I am not.*

    iv) *In what would its enjoyment lie (e.g. would the thrill of globe trotting counterbalance the homesickness, tiredness and mental strain which always accompany travelling (even when only abroad for 3 weeks!)*

Even as I write the above I feel increasingly inadequate to write out in precise ways the principles which ought [to] govern one in such a decision. But you will be sad to hear I am determined to continue my impossible task!

At the moment I feel very attracted to the idea of globe trotting. Of setting off gaily, my earthly possessions tied up in a handkerchief, 2/6 in my pocket, facing all danger and difficulty armed only with my resourcefulness and a British passport. And then writing a book about it afterwards! I would launch out till I came to Vancouver, make some money there (with your help) then we would together go to Asia (perhaps dropping in on Bob Pears in Australia or was it New Zealand?). Arriving in North India my father would give us work on the Tea plantation and in our spare time there would be fabulous mahseer fishing in the hills and we could dig up the lost treasures of the Ahom civilization (if we hadn't already found gold while prospecting in the Canadian Rockies & caught enough Salmon to make us wince when we saw a sardine tin). Then around to Europe, via Rome, Greece, Spain, wherever we wanted to see in Europe. And then after you had stayed with us for a while you could move on home to the loving arms of ? (that is assuming we hadn't shocked our middle class relations by taking our loved one's with us!!). Already I can see the tossing Waves, New York, the long grain fields of central America, the Rockies, the grizzly bears and then off again. The Orient, the swaying palm trees, the throb of Eastern music, the Glory that was Greece, the Grandeur that was Rome.

Suddenly I come back from my dreams. I smell supper downstairs. I think I can hear the sausages frizzling, the fire is very warm – is it worth it? Call me a stick in the mud – I haven't really decided yet.

Would it be enjoyable? Would one learn about Man and his problems (which for me after the first commandment (N.T.) is the central purpose of my life) – Would it be entirely selfish?

If you are at all interested in this subject please give me your ideas – as you can see mine are very muddled!

I had intended the above to be merely an introduction to a much profounder study of the principals on which one should choose a career! But I know you would much rather hear about my trip to the Hebrides.

[sadly I seem to have taken the carbon paper out here!]

The next letter from my mother is after the trip to the Manas, and is dated December 28.

My dear Alan,

Well we are back, sunburnt and rested and delighted to get two letters from you to greet us – your long Christmas letter was especially nice and made me feel ashamed of the feeble birthday effort I sent you. I was tired and taut, but a fortnight without lessons or servants has put me right and I hope this serene feeling wont disappear the minute I put my foot into Nazira club as it usually does! We loved your cards, and needless to say have been thinking of you all the time we've been away – most of Christmas day was spent saying "He'll just be getting up" or listening to the Queen or whatever. I'm glad Robert and Angela got over and hope you enjoyed your stay with them, and saw some younger faces – though I dare say its quite restful to be with older people after Oxford. I'm sorry to hear about Jummy, is he in pain or is it just weakness? I really must drop Beryl a line, its hard to believe that Martin could be so selfish and unhelpful.

I don't really know where to start, we meant to keep a Journal of our trip but were too lazy, couldn't even be bothered to read though I solemnly took "The Defeat of the Spanish Armada" out every day in the boat. ...[Car breaks down in Gauhati...] We spent quite a pleasant day in Gauhati as it happened because we found ourselves next door to the Museum and the Public Library, so were able to potter round the old Ahom shards (quite a lot of them lying outside on the ground smothered in weeds!) and the Library was really wonderful with every sort of book, I was deep in an enormous volume called "The Reformation" when it started to get dark and Anne dragged me home. .... I gather your Christmas day was icy too, I hope you will get a party or two but I fear will have out-grown the teen age gang. I shall be interested to hear about the Cowans, Felicity writes regularly to Anne and sounds a real character but too young for you I suppose?!

My love to all, I shall be writing soon. Enjoy yourself & don't work too hard – when do you go back?

Much love from us all, Mummy

Finally, there is a letter dated January 13 from Cherideo which relates to holiday events.

My dear Alan,

... First of all a very big thank you for the parcel of books which arrived a couple of days ago, I've always wanted to read Tolkien and know I shall love them – you and I have the same taste in books. Daddy is half way through the first one now, he started by being a bit sceptical but is now thoroughly involved with the hobbits and I'm longing for him to finish. I'll bring them home with me as it must have been a wrench for you to part with them – thank you again. Granny's parcels also arrived so we have a feast of reading in front of us. I'm re-reading "Montrose", I always enjoy Margaret Irwin though she always takes the obvious and rather exaggerated view of history. We have just finished the Civil War and with it our syllabus so are now going to do lots of brushing up, European history is our weakness though we like it best. Anything you can collect on the subject for our return will be very welcome, particularly on Charles V.....

I do hope you enjoyed your stay with the Cowans, we all look forward to hearing about the family and the new house. I wonder what sort of job Martin will make of the coffee bar, it could be a real money spinner with a gay décor, a band and some really good coffee and eats – tell him Fiona will redecorate it for him. But how typical of Gran to undermine Beryl's attempts to get him into something definite and worthwhile. I don't know if you will be back at Oxford by now, but if so all our usual wishes for a good and exciting term. I feel awful about my book, the thing is that though it is not worth a thing, it took so long to write and cost so much to type that I hate to entrust it to the Indian Post. I'll bring it with me (it will arrive almost as quickly that way anyway) I don't think it's the sort of thing you could be interested in anyway!

Much love from us all, Mummy

Academic Work – Winter Term 1961

Written in pencil on the back of a card is the following work planning note: it may have applied around now.

6 hrs work
9 hrs sleep

Breakfast 1 hr 8.30-9.30
Work 3 ½ – 1.0
Lunch 1 – 20
?Games 2-50
Work 5-6.30
Dinner 6.30 – 7.30
Work – 7.30 – 9.0
Record player etc 9 – 11.0

My holiday work hours are suggested by the following note on the back of an envelope where the front is a poem written on 10th December, there is a work plan which is as follows:
Work 9-0 – 1.0 (½ hrs break)
Walk 2.0 –3.0
Read 3.0 – 4.30
4.30 – 5.30 tea
Work 5.30 – 7.0 (Revision)
Spare – Read? Organise Etc.

At the start of the term there was a history collection – testing us on the knowledge of the previous term. It was clearly a great disappointment in many ways.

"History Collections" Winter 1961.

NOTE. Although I am not certain whether this collection is meant to be merely on what I covered last term I have been forced to write 3 out of the 4 essays on the period after 1559. For – as you will see from the list of last term's essays only questions nos 1, 6, 7 in the period before 1559 are at all relevant to these essays.
[There is a note in Harry Pitt's hand: 'I told him to choose the questions he wanted from Period V (II) & Period VI (I) in the 1957 Schools paper – *thought* that wd cover the new option – but I don't seem to have succeeded. HGP]

My short essays with comments were:
Period VI.
4. Assess the elements of strength and weakness in the Turkish system of government in the C16.
I got a Beta for this with the remark: 'What makes you think that there were no taxes: To begin with every Christian subject had to pay a poll and a Land Tax and Soliman had the remnants of Byzantine fiscal practice at his disposal too'

VI.1 2. How successful was the Counter-Reformation?

I got a Beta minus minus for this. 'This does not really carry much conviction, partly because you do not reflect about what success in a religious movement and institutions like the post-tridentine church means. Avoid reference to yourself. [I had used the phrase 'and to me it seems a highly successful one']

VI. II.7. 'To what extent may Francis I and Henry II be said to have been absolute sovereigns?'
Again a Beta minus minus. 'It is equally questionable whether the greatest office-holders, the nobles of the court and military grandees were any less powerful as patrons and virtual 'owners' of their places than the provincial purchasers of places.

6. 'But for the Duke of Alva the Revolt of the Netherlands could never have succeeded' – Discuss.

There is a detailed planning sheet
BIBLIOGRAPHY – Books Used European History. Winter 1961

This gives the name of the author and short title, the call mark in the Library, and some red ticks, between one and five, presumably depending on how I rated the books. From the ticks, it suggests that I read half a dozen items, on average, for each essay, a mixture of books and articles.

There was no mark on this, but just the comment. 'I am not familiar enough with latter day literature on this to say much but you must give up using the first person in writing the answers. [I had written 'I doubt it' and 'on the whole I would agree' – both circled in pen.]

The final mark was Beta minus minus, a lower 2:1 I suppose, or lower.

'This is a disappointing paper. You cannot expect to find your essays all over again in an examination-paper and a glance at that of 1957 suggested that you were unduly pessimistic about what you covered unless your reading was excessively confined and I had the impression that it was not. You must be a little bolder in your attack – on the Turks there were signs of it – to yourself Justice. It would be a pity if your careful and judicious work on weekly essays could not be minted into examination answers. KL [Karl Leyser]

If this paper was taken at the start of the Winter Term, as I suspect it was, then three out of the four essays had been done on the basis of vacation reading – with no essays or tuition. A minor consolation.

*

There is another set of collections on European history which is unfortunately undated. I suspect it may also be at the start of the Spring Term, but as it is retrospective examination on the previous term and vacation work I shall put it here.

The good news is that while there are no comments or individual marks, at the top there is written in 'Beta plus plus', a creditable mark.

The essays were on:
'What is the significance of the reign of Maximilian I in the history of the Empire!'

‘Why was the revolt of the Communeros unsuccessful?’

10. ‘”Neither his life nor his teachings support the view that Calvin was a prophet of modern capitalism”. Discuss.’

I shall include this particular short essay as it is on a theme that has continued to interest me for many years.

10. "Neither his life nor his teachings support the view that Calvin was a prophet of modern capitalism." Discuss.

As many people have pointed out, the main difficulty encountered in the "Protestantism and Capitalism" squabbles is that each writer has a different conception of 'Protestantism' & even more so of "Capitalism". For the purposes of this essay however the latter will be defined - as Tawney defined it - as 'a society based on the use of accumulated earnings (capital) for the furtherance of industry by private persons'.

Another danger, and there are many, is the tendency to associate capitalism with all that is worst in our way of life, materialism, industrial squalor even colonialism. Here again we must distinguish between the use of money to make further money, and the pursuit of money as an end in itself, as the final glory of life and its justification. The latter is obviously a heresy which even Calvin could not have conceived! So, the definition of "capital" is the crux of the matter. With some of the possible meanings Calvin plainly did preach pure "capitalism", for he maintained that money was not evil, was in fact something to be increased by all fair means (and here of course his definition of "fair" is much narrower than ours) and as a suitable worldly object for men, tho' of course subordinate and a means to spiritual ends. But in even going this far he was, unwittingly, opening the door an inch, to the flood of money-grubbing which would take his blessing and forget his sanctions. The Roman Church had always condemned usury in all its forms, tho' of course like all rules it was constantly broken. The stream of documents in the C14 and C15 & the invective of men like Land shows that there was pressure on the Church during these centuries to modify its views so that man might do business profitably and not sin every time they lent, borrowed, invested or speculated in the most harmless way. But the Church stayed rigid - it was a vehicle of God and laid down the rules of 'perfect life' - even if this was unattainable. Then came Protestantism.

Luther, & very like Wycliffe, was driven to a repudiation of Rome. Once the chain had been broken this human dynamo poured forth his ideas, weighted by his own alert and theologically trained mind. And in doing so he let loose that beast which has appeared of such different shapes and colourings to each man - individual interpretation of the scriptures, and the sanctity of individual opinion. Once this idea, tempered into a weapon of steel by Calvin's logical doctrine of Predestination, had been put into men's minds there was only one logical conclusion – each man must decide for himself what is right or wrong. Anyhow that decision is of little importance because whatever he does is merely a jig-saw piece already shaped, and constituting a part of a preconceived picture; either hell or heaven. It is these basic attitudes to religion which have shaped our thinking, not the individual pronouncements, or wordy controversies on certain specific points of dogma. But what would Calvin say if he saw our modern capitalistic society?

The expectation is that he would be aghast. A man who above all worshipped self-discipline, who in his life attempted to found a Church-ruled state, faced with our absolutely Erastian, money-by-any-means society, with God locked in a Sunday box – he would be horrified! But it would be an illogical horror, and Calvin was nothing if not logical. Firstly he himself proclaimed the inefficacy of works in a truly 'Pauline' spirit. So why does our rotten outward surface shock him; those predestined are still saved. As Luther gravely remarked "to externalise religion is to degrade it"; and Calvin should be, as a disciple of Luther, delighted that we had so successfully managed to prevent nearly all our Christian beliefs from coming to the surface and causing bothering obstacles to the pursuit of our worldly aims! Secondly if the pursuit of money is not harmful, and even good, where does one draw the line at the means of that pursuit? Where one's conscience draws it? But no doubt the more unscrupulous of our business-men have so trained their consciences that they hardly ever offended against them. No doubt Hitler was following the dictates of his conscience in exterminating the Jews!

But Calvin was no child. If he did not see clearly where his ideas would lead, he himself in his life and writings stressed the importance of conforming to the established rules of morality. For tho' this was in a sense illogical he was not blind to human weakness. It is those who have pulled down those props, while propagating his doctrines, who have

This is a passionate, but rather obvious and superficial essay, as it now seems to me.

The final essay was on '"Ruined by a persistent failure to know when to cut his losses." Do you accept this judgement on the foreign policy of Philip II?

*

To make the dating of these collections more difficult, there is another Collection Paper, headed 'European (I) Period VIII'.

There are three essays (I was asked to do four).

'How did Lutheranism reflect the personality of its founder?

'How do you explain the military success of Ottoman Turks under Suleiman?'

'Was there a Spanish "middle-class" at the death of Chas Vth?

There are no marks or comments on the paper itself, but there is a letter from my tutor Roger Howell, who supervised me in the Winter Term.

St John's College, Oxford
Dear Campbell,
This collection of Macfarlane's seems to me to be a good, sound, safe 2nd over all with occasional touches of something better and some indications of something worse.

Negatively, he doesn't always write an answer to the question but rather writes around the subject (especially in the essay on the Spanish middle classes where he introduces 17th c material into an essay that is supposed to deal temp Charles V. Also, he has only found time to do 3 questions which shows rather poor planning.

I am not entirely qualified to judge this paper since I have never taught the pre-1559 part of the paper, but that is my judgement for what it is worth.
Yours sincerely, Roger Howell

*

Essays etc. (This, I guess, was for Howell)

1. What were the causes of the Revolt of the Netherlands?

I have seven pages of notes for this essay, which were supplemented with extensive earlier notes I had done at the end of the previous vacation.
The essay is five pages long and there is a comment 'Really quite good', followed by one or two specific comments.

2. The wars of Religion – how much religion?

October 61.

Essay [2].

"The More we analyse the French Wars of Religion - the less we find of religion." - Discuss.

When Henry II died in 1559 he was succeeded by a minor. - This disaster and the minorities of the next reigns, coinciding with economic, social, political, dynastic and religious factors not to mention the return of many impoverished nobility from the recently ended Spanish wars gave the opportunity for all the discontent and tension to explode into the French Wars of Religion. In these wars motives are so mixed that it seems that none of the participants themselves were fully aware of the forces which threw France into turmoil. The confusion was worse confounded by sporadic outbursts, such as the peasant risings in Guyenne, which were only vaguely related to the central issues. All writers agree, I think, that superficially the struggle was one for power between Protestants and Catholics, embodied by the League and the Huguenots but they diverge widely on the motives which drove men to ally themselves to these causes or to side with the Politiques or Catherine de Medici. For while no one would dispute that the Calvinist organization was indispensable to the Huguenots' [illegible]ce, they interpret the causes of people being Huguenots or Leaguers in very different ways. How much, for example, was religion just a binding force, a useful channel for the mob to vent their anger at poverty and despair, the bourgeoisie their irritation at gov't restriction, the nobility their ambitions and particularism? - and how much was there of genuine religious feeling?

At one time the French Religious Wars - as their name suggests - were interpreted entirely as a theological, doctrinal and moral struggle. They were seen as the re-action of the intelligent part of the community to the undoubted abuses of the Catholic Church, the pluralism, the non-residence, worldliness and ignorance. This disgust, historians saw, inevitably led to rebellion against the crown, for since the Concordat of 1516 the monarchy had a vested interest in the status quo of the Church. Thus attack on the monarchy was then seen to use other forces which were also beginning to grow restive under the existing régime, especially the nobility; The wonderful coincidence between the ecclesiastical hierarchy of the Calvinist church and the pyramid-like feudal military system of the nobility helped to bind them closer - so they launched an attack, which in turn provoked a Catholic re-action headed by the Guise faction and the Wars began. Recent historians, as in their work, have been eager to find new causes for the wars, and their emphasis has been on the economic, social, dynastic and feudal interpretations. An example of such a conclusion is that of Salmon who in an article on "Henry of Navarre" maintains that the Crown was attacked by "a resurgence of feudal separatism, and a nascent constitutionalism in direct contrast - an attack in which the former was discredited by the interplay of personal ambitions and the interests of foreign powers - the latter by religious discord and legal involution." For him it all ends very neatly by these two forces destroying each other - leaving the Crown to emerge triumphant. Let us examine the various forces at work.

Economic historians have rightly stressed the financial dissatisfaction of the times. The price revolution which reached its peak in the years 1550-70 caused much hardship, especially among the peasants and lesser nobility and Koenigsberger maintains in relation to Hainault that this would account" for the growing discontent among the nobility in 1560's" aggravated by demobilization. A brief survey of the monarchy's position shows the grim position. In 1559 - two years after the first state bankruptcy - there was a debt of 40 m, a - more than 3½ years taxation. After the cessation of war the position grew worse not better and in 1580 there was another bankruptcy in France; & in 1586 the king was forced to pay 50% on loans. The practical results are only too obvious - among them is the stifling burden of taxation, especially on the small cultivator, the ruination of many of the growing "rentier" class, the poverty of the lesser nobility and the non-payment by the crown of the increasingly voluble bureaucracy. This must undoubtedly have prompted some of those who joined the Reformed movement thinking they would find there a justification of usury, a weapon against the king or a possibility of loot.

Economic discontent merged into social upheavals. The merchant class were attracted to the new religion with its essentially bourgeois and oligarchic organization of elders and deacons, which gave them justification for making money, and they could use it as a weapon against the oppressive and disorderly monarchy which injured their material interests. Poverty, hardship and degradation must have encouraged many of the mass of lower clergy and wandering friars who became the militia of Calvinism. We cannot dispute that outward manifestations of religious fanaticism were insolubly mixed with social and political discontent as in Normandy. There purely social motives worked in Dauphiné where the lower classes were devoted to reform but when the religious became merged in a social conflict of people against the gentry - a conflict which the Venetian ambassador believed to be more social than religious and likely to spread over France.

As economic merges into social so social does into political and dynastic. This aspect has always been realized - for the ambitions of Charles of Lorraine and of Condé; of the Politiques and of Henry II were patently not primarily religious, social or economic, again Catherine's seemingly complete lack of principle or even grasp of the importance of such things to others was shared by Henry III and led both of them to political murders which overlooked the existence of sincere religious feeling. There is abundant proof that Bourbons and Guises harnessed the passion of religious controversy to further their ends. The conspiracy of Amboise is a clear example - once it was believed to be a religious revolt - used by Condé - but now

The More we analyse the French Wars of Religion the less we find of religion – Discuss

it appears clear that though many Huguenots responded it was political not religious its purpose being to replace the Guise by the Bourbons – its membership not being exclusively Protestant and its activities being flatly opposed by Calvin and most responsible ministers – again the massacre of Vassy and the subsequent war were largely political – indeed in 1560 the Florentine ambassadors, one of whom had prophesied that civil war between Guise and Montmorency would break out, thought that dynastic struggle was its deepest cause – religion its cover.

Then again the avowed intention of the Politiques who would apparently "rather the kingdom at peace without God, than at war with him" and whose very reason for existence was the desire to resist the influence of Rome, to advocate state supremacy over the Church and elevate the monarchy, shows the importance of political factors – As does the League of 1584 which, when it had become national, aimed at the extinction of the House of Bourbon in favour of the Guise not merely from religious motives but because it was bound to Guise ambitions. Though we can see the strength of this argument its insufficiency as a sole explanation is easily shown – for instance by the behaviour of Coligny who became a Huguenot from conviction, or by the general behaviour of the members of the Montmorency family whose conduct showed that creed was stronger than family or that parts joined different sides.

Another interpretation is that of "the feudal reaction, the conservative revolution, the particularist and medieval revolt of centrifugal forces especially in the nobility. It is an argument which has been applied to the Netherlands revolt by Geyl and there is undoubtedly some force in it. For instance the Catholic League of the nobility in 1576 had essentially conservative aims – Henry III and his successors were to be preserved in their authority without change, the provinces were to have their ancient rights restored to them, there were constant demands for the calling of the States General and particularism was asserted under Damville and Condé to a highly dangerous degree for the unity of France. Another aspect of this centrifugal tendency was the calling in of foreign powers England, Spain and Poland for instance against the Crown. But an examination of the demands of the Estates of Orleans, the Deputation of Pontoise or the Manifesto of Condé embodying as they do the aims of the Huguenots while showing a general re-action against the pressure of the monarchy by feudal claims such as the increase of municipal liberties and baronial jurisdiction have the articles inserted by the

3rd Estate of a distinctly anti-feudal nature. Thus we can see no precise coincidence between Huguenotism and feudalism.

So we have examined, very briefly indeed, a few interpretations which rival the religious one - but the importance of each shows that one alone cannot wholly explain the wars. Even all of them together fail to give an absolutely satisfactory picture - and the study of a few selected events will show that religion was a powerful force - more so than has perhaps been realised of late. The insufficiency of the previous theories is shown for instance in the fact that they fail to explain fully why the educated classes, especially those at Universities, and Lawyers joined the Huguenots. Or again Neale's statement that the nobility were largely converted with, along with their wives, but while the women were moved by "a revulsion against the moral & religious laxity of Francis I's reign" and so were converted - their husbands were prompted merely from a hope of materialistic gain or political advantage, this seems to be somewhat harsh!

We have seen that the Amboise conspiracy and first religious war were largely political - with religious overtones. But it is more difficult to decide which motive predominated in the "Meaux" plot and the following wars. Undoubtedly the suspicion of Huguenots that Catherine was hatching a Spanish alliance, a fear which increased when Alva started his repressions in the Netherlands was a reality. In the interval of the Peace of Longjumeau unofficial killings went on and probably many Protestants after the death of Condé at Jarnac and defeat of Moncontour, felt they were fighting for their existence.

The next great landmark is the Massacre of St Bartholomew. Out of the mass of opinions on the motives for this and the character of Catherine the general view has arisen that although the possibility of such a carnage had long been in mind as a desperate measure its final execution was not premeditated, but the despairing act of a woman obsessed by fear. So we cannot ascribe it primarily to religious motives - though in Paris its execution was directed by the Catholic authorities and it utilized religious frenzy to the full. Its results however are extremely important in trying to gauge the amount of true religious enthusiasm - for we now see the movement, apparently shorn of all its attraction as a political force, with no scope for the ambitious, no redress for the malcontent, yet held together by its discipline & fervour.

Soon however it was joined by the Politiques which finally led to the peace of Monsieur - but not before it was shown that Catholics and Protestants could unite against a common enemy.

It might be as well at this point to explain why, in answering this question, I have omitted mention of constitutional theories. The

"The More we analyse the French Wars of Religion - the less we find of religion"

reason is simple - as Armstrong points out - justification of their rebellions came as a result not a cause of those rebellions. Such documents as Bodin's "Respublique", the Franco-Gallia or the "Vindicae" were never used as documents to initially excite opposition or support of the Crown - therefore in a way they are misleading if used to indicate the motives which fired the wars. Another reason, shown by the fact that during the years 1572-3 when the Huguenot movement was undoubtedly at its most purely religious after the Massacre, the pamphlets were still largely concerned with secular or imperial concerns, is that the writers came largely from the lawyer class and should therefore only be used to study their attitude.

The years 1576 which saw the formation of a proper Catholic League heralded eight years of confused fighting - a time of "petty, anarchic, detail" as Neale calls it when court faction was again to the fore and religious zeal after the first burst of Catholic horror at the Peace of Monsieur seems to have been at a low ebb. But with the death of Alençon religion again played an important part in reviving the League which joined Guise ambition to Catholic hatred in an attempt to exclude the Bourbons. One interesting point to notice here is the importance of Catholicism in deciding Paris in favour of Guise and also in the resistance of that essential city to Henry IV. When Henry at last entered Paris he recognised the power of Catholicism by expelling the Jesuits in 1594 for being "corrupters of youth & disturbers of public order".

It would need a book to deal with any one of the causes touched on in this essay - but if it has given a glimpse of the confusion of motives which all inter-acted and re-acted to cause the war it will have partially succeeded. Before I end I would like to stress the importance of religion - not as directly causing the wars but as a live and meaningful force in France. Historical writers so often dismiss it as a vapid cover for more materialistic designs partly because by nature its influence is immeasurable - statistics are more easily compiled concerning food production than devotional feeling - partly because for many nowadays belief has either ceased to exist or is merely an intellectual assent - not a way of life - a motive for existence which it could be and was for many in the C16. Grant recognises this when he says that "the driving force of the Huguenot movement was the passionate belief ..... of Calvinism". The same may be said of some of those who fought for Rome.

I clearly took this essay very seriously and there are nearly twenty pages of foolscap notes in preparation for this essay, taken in October. This was a continuation of work I had been preparing in the vacation. The essay, written in October, was five pages long. The only general comment at the end is 'very complex'.

3. What were the mistakes of Philip II?

I have the essay, which was almost six pages of foolscap. There are a few comments from Roger Howell at the bottom, but no general comment.
I have nearly 24 pages of notes for this essay, based on a number of books and replete with a number of graphs and statistics. I clearly worked very hard on this. Here are also brief notes on a revision class on this.

4. What was the achievement of Gustavus Adolphus?

There are ten pages of notes for this essay, dated November 61. There is a note to see my very extensive notes before the term began from Roberts 'Gustavus Adolphus'. There are also a few notes on 'Sweden: Revision Class'. The essay itself was five pages long, with a few comments at the bottom from the tutor but no general assessment.

5. Give a summary of the main lines of argument re Economic interpretation of C16
There are twelve and a half pages of notes for Essay 9, November 1961, on 'Neither the causes nor the effects of the Price Revolution were as simple as historians have assumed.' There was also a detailed two page essay plan. I have just the first two pages of an essay on this subject, dated November.

6. Was Wallerstein more than a mere adventurer?
I have over twenty pages of detailed notes for this essay, complete with maps etc. And also a detailed essay plan. (And, interestingly, two and a half pages of typed notes by my mother on the Thirty years War.)
The essay itself was five pages long, with a few comments by the tutor, but again no assessment.

I have more than twenty pages of detailed notes for 'Essay 6', November 1961 on 'What constitutes the statesmanship of Richelieu?' The essay itself is six pages long.

I have sixteen pages of essay notes and an essay plan, dated November, for an essay on 'Were the basic problems of Dutch politics the same after 1609?' I have this essay, which is noted as Essay 9, November. It is nearly seven pages long, but there are no comments on it at all. There is also a page of notes on a revision class on the Netherlands.

I also have lecture notes on lectures 2 and 3 of Prestwich on Henry IV [I am not sure which term]

I also have ten pages of notes for an essay number 8, November 1961, on Turkey (1560-1960)
There are also lecture notes on lecture 1 of Stoye on "The Ottoman Empire" (1566-1739) – though which term this was, I am not certain.

There are also nearly ten pages of detailed notes on a set of four lectures by John Cooper on 'Introduction to problems of European Economy 1590-1650'. I remember these well, in Trinity College. I greatly enjoyed them and found the new world of French demography and economic history – my first exposure to the Annales School and the new Cambridge history, extremely stimulating.

To be frank, none of the above essays particularly attract me much now – they are almost all to do with politics and international relations and represent the kind of history which I had done at school and which, later, I would try to escape from.

Ephemera

It is noticeable that the amount of 'ephemera' for this term is more than all of the previous year – another indication perhaps that this was about the time, in my new room in College, that I stepped up my preservation of papers with a view to, one day, working on them.

There were the religious cards: the term card for the Oxford University Church of England Council, the Worcester College Chapel card, and the Oxford Inter-Collegiate Christian Union card, and a card for St Aldate's.

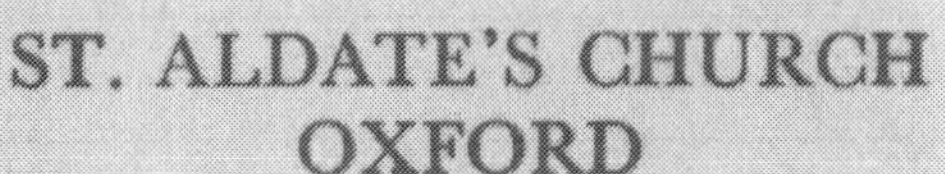

ST. ALDATE'S CHURCH
OXFORD

(ST. OLD'S)

MICHAELMAS TERM, 1961

ASSOCIATED CLERGY

The Reverend KEITH DE BERRY, Rector and Chaplain to the Oxford Pastorate, St. Aldate's Rectory, Pembroke Street. Tel. 42056.

The Reverend RICHARD WATSON, Chaplain to Wadham College and the Oxford Pastorate, 23 Leckford Road. Tel. 57512.

The Reverend MICHAEL CHANTRY, St. Aldate's Church and Chaplain to Hertford College and the Pastorate, Holy Trinity House, Littlegate Street. Tel. 42359.

Organist and Choirmaster:
Mr. John Long, M.A., B.Mus., F.R.C.O.

SPECIAL EVENTS

SUNDAY, OCTOBER 22nd at 11 a.m.
DEDICATION OF NEW EXTENSION AND VESTRIES
by the LORD BISHOP OF OXFORD
in the presence of His Worship the Mayor, Aldermen and Councillors of the City of Oxford.
Preacher: THE ARCHBISHOP OF UGANDA

SATURDAY, OCT. 21st (Rectory Room)
7.30 p.m. OVERSEAS SOCIAL to meet and hear the ARCHBISHOP OF UGANDA.

SUNDAY, OCT. 29th (Rectory Room)
THE BISHOP OF COVENTRY will speak. Tea at 4 p.m.
CHRISTIAN RESPONSIBILITY RENEWAL CAMPAIGN BEGINS.

MONDAY, OCT. 30th (Town Hall) 7.30 p.m.
CHURCH MISSIONARY SOCIETY RALLY.

MONDAY, NOV. 13th
7 for 7.30 p.m. PARISH DINNER (Town Hall).

TUESDAY, NOV. 28th (Rectory Room)
8.15 p.m. MISSIONARY FELLOWSHIPS MEETING. Speaker: The Rev. Dewi Morgan.

SUNDAY, DEC. 3rd
6.30 p.m. ANGLO-AMERICAN SERVICE.

WEDNESDAY, DEC. 6th
7.30 a.m. PASTORATE TERM-END COMMUNION.

FRIDAY, DEC. 8th
4.30 and 9 p.m. REPRESENTATIVES' MEETINGS.

SATURDAY, DEC. 9th to TUESDAY, DEC. 12th
CHRISTIAN ADVANCE WEEK-END CONFERENCE at Sunbury Court. Leaders: The Rev. Douglas Webster (C.M.S.) and the Rev. Richard Marsh (Warden, Scargill).

Entertainments: I seem to have been a frequent visitor to the Oxford Playhouse. For September there is the London Ballet, Sleeping Beauty, which I do not remember, yet there is a ticket stub for the evening performance on Saturday Sept 30. The Saturday performance was Giselle (Act 2), Eaters of Darkness and Light Fantastic.
In October there are programmes for 'Heartbreak House' by Bernard Shaw (which I mention going to in a letter to my mother) and 'The Oresteia of Aeschylus'. I underlined the Aeschylus in my College diary. There is also a programme for 'Murder and Mozart' ('An Evening of Dramatic Poetry and Chamber Music arranged by Nevill Coghill'). I remember this vividly as an electrifying occasion when I really first fell in love with Mozart. In November there is 'The Caretaker' by Harold Pinter.
For the New Theatre I have three programmes. One was for 'Teresa of Avila' with Sybil Thorndike in the first week of October. I describe this briefly in a letter to my parents; another for 'Swan Lake' by the Royal Ballet on Monday October 23 and

finally for 'The Merchant of Venice', which was performed in the week commencing 27 November.

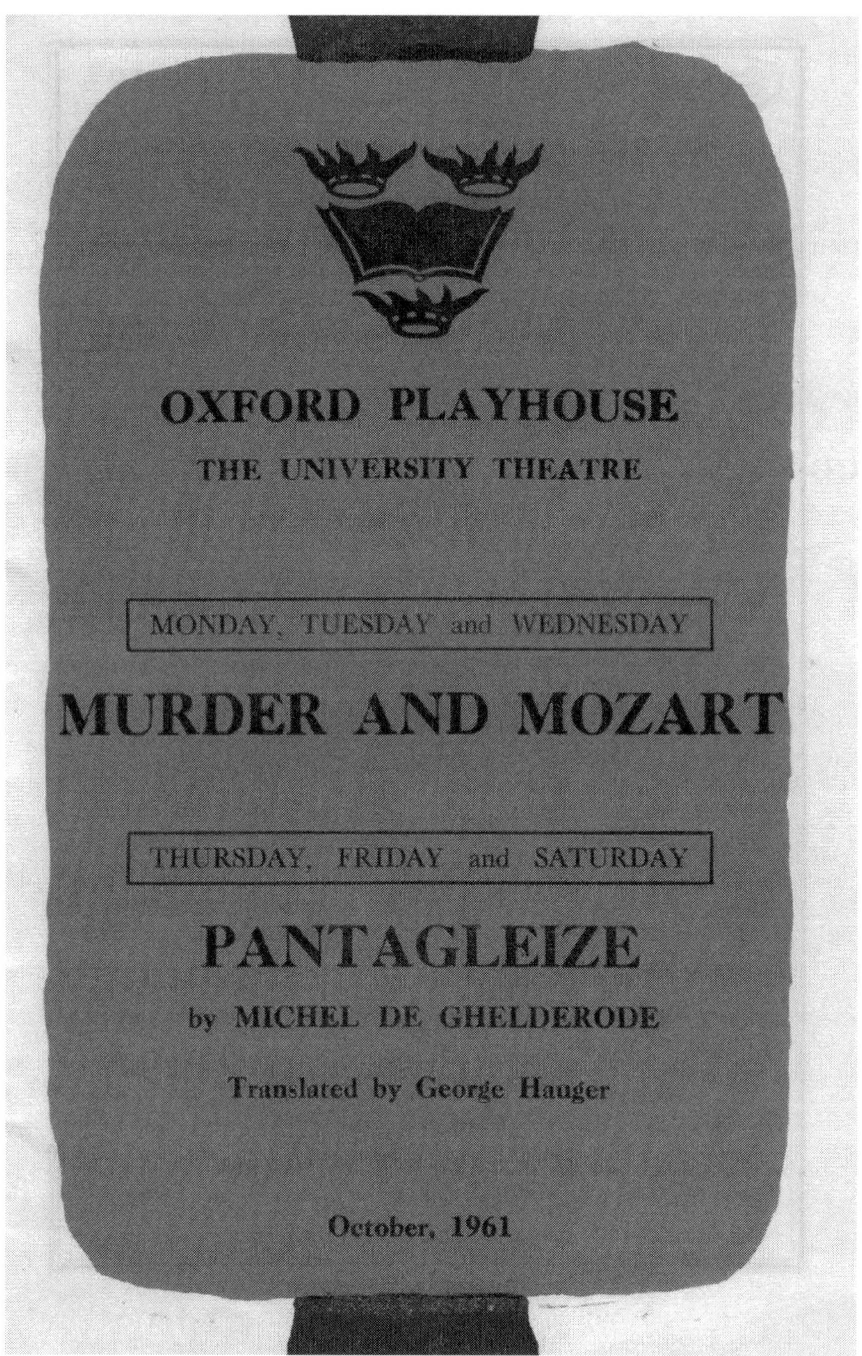
OXFORD PLAYHOUSE

THE UNIVERSITY THEATRE

MONDAY, TUESDAY and WEDNESDAY

MURDER AND MOZART

THURSDAY, FRIDAY and SATURDAY

PANTAGLEIZE

by MICHEL DE GHELDERODE

Translated by George Hauger

October, 1961

Other entertainment: I have the programme for a concert of the Balliol College Musical Society on Sunday 22nd October, with music by Haydn, Brahms and others. All were string quartets.

BALLIOL COLLEGE MUSICAL SOCIETY

1260TH CONCERT: SUNDAY, OCTOBER 22ND, 1961

At **9.0** p.m. (Doors open at 8.45 p.m.)

QUARTET IN F MINOR, Op. 20, No. 5 - *Haydn* (1732–1809)

Allegro moderato
Minuetto
Adagio
Fuga a due soggetti

QUARTET No. 6 - - - - *Villa-Lobos* (1887–1959)

Poco animato
Allegretto
Andante quasi adagio
Allegro vivace

QUARTET IN A MINOR, Op. 51, No. 2 - *Brahms* (1833–97)

Allegro non troppo
Andante moderato
Quasi minuetto, moderato
Allegro non assai

WANG STRING QUARTET

Alfredo Wang (*Violin*) Gordon Mutter (*Viola*)
Stanley Popperwell (*Violin*) George Isaac (*Cello*)

NEXT CONCERT: Sunday, November 5th, at 9.0 p.m. Recital by Bruno Hoffmann (*Glass Harp*).

Social and other: I have the Oxford Union Society card for the term. One has a pencil tick against it – 3rd Debate. 2nd November. "That this House deplores the Americanization of British culture."
Mr Christopher Hollis. Hon. William Douglas-Home.

1st Debate. 19th October.

"That this House has no confidence in Her Majesty's Government."

MR. MICHAEL STEWART, M.P. MR. DENZIL FREETH, M.P.

2nd Debate. 26th October.

"That in the opinion of this House this country should unilaterally renounce any policy based on Nuclear Weapons."

MR. EMRYS HUGHES, M.P. MR. CONSTANTINE FITZGIBBON.

3rd Debate. 2nd November.

"That this House deplores the Americanization of British culture."

MR. CHRISTOPHER HOLLIS. HON. WILLIAM DOUGLAS-HOME.

4th Debate. 9th November.

"That this House welcomes the Government's decision to seek entry to the European Economic Community."

MR. ANTHONY GREENWOOD, M.P. SIR EDWARD BOYLE, BT., M.P.

Speakers' Classes will be held on Wednesdays at 2.0 p.m. during 2nd—5th weeks inclusive of term.

5th Debate. 16th November.

"That in the opinion of this House the reunification of Germany should not be the object of Western policy."

MR. SEFTON DELMER, O.B.E. BARON RÜDIGER VON PACHELBEL.

6th Debate. 23rd November.

"That in the opinion of this House the machinery of Mass Publicity should be demolished."

MR. JOHN WAIN MR. FRANCIS WILLIAMS, C.B.E.

7th Debate. 30th November. PRESIDENTIAL.

"That in the opinion of this House moderation is not a reliable principle for politics."

MR. R. H. S. CROSSMAN, O.B.E., M.P.

8th Debate. 7th December. FAREWELL.

"That this House prefers Saturday night to Sunday morning."

There will also be an additional Freshmen's Debate on Tuesday, November 21st.

I also have my 'Vade Mecum' for the term, cost ninepence. This lists all the events and clubs and other opportunities in great detail. I have not marked anything in this magazine, but in a prosaic way on the back have written 'Basil, coffee/biscuits/ chocolate, write Pat, Books – post

*

Around this time I was clearly trying to systematize my intellectual efforts. There is a set of sheets which is just headed 'December 1961'. It may well have been written as some kind of assessment, or New Year's Resolution.

WORK & READING – random thoughts.

1. Purpose of work & reading.
   a) Enjoyment
   b) Train brain – For exams
      More generally
   c) Knowledge.

The last of these will arise out of the former and the first will be a by-product of the middle one, therefore it is the middle which needs organising.

2. THE TRAINING OF THE MIND.
   i) The Basis – knowledge, facts, – MEMORY
   ii) The Assembly of facts & knowledge in response
      - Patterns – ideas already meditated on
      - Construction of argument. Logic & analysis.
   iii) Expression – "style"
      (a) Word power & vocabulary
      (b) Construction of the sentence

(c) Construction of the paragraph
(d) Construction of the essay
(e) Illustration, metaphor & simile
(f) Comparison

Suggested reading.

FOR EXPRESSION. Macaulay; Hazlitt; Tawney, Problem of Style; The Art of Writing; and any good writers.

FOR CONSTRUCTION OF ARGUMENT.
Descartes: " A discourse on method."; Aristotle

Basis – knowledge, Facts.
(a) The acquiring & noting of facts. – Selection
(b) Memory.

There are then several pages where I have copied in the headings under ii) and iii) above – ie. assembly and expression, leaving plenty of space to add in thoughts and references – which, alas, I never did!

Julie's letters from Italy : Winter Term 1961

Julie and I had stopped being a definite 'couple' in August/September 1961, but remained close friends for some years. This enabled a warm and open relationship where Julie could act as an advisor and confidante. We were keen to collect materials together as a memory of our relationship.

The first is dated 25 September 1961 from Perugia.

Dearest Alikins,

Here is the first of those much-discussed missives. I hardly know where to begin. Perhaps I'll be completely illogical and start with a description of my room. [At the end of the long, illustrated, letter]. I have brought all my diary notes and your tickets and programmes, and I shall compile them into a volume as soon as I find a suitable one.

Do write soon and tell me about your Hyper-Borean expedition.

With fondest love, Pusseybite

The next letter is dated 12 October.

Dearest Alikins,

I received your Oxford letter this afternoon, and Countess Pecchiolli forwarded the other one a little while ago. I'm glad you had such a fruitful and congenial time in the Hebrides. Yet gladder that you have found my wonderful and adored recording of Winterreise. Don't buy Shöne Müllerin – get the second part of Winterreise. I find it transcendentally lovely. My favourite song is Manche Tränen, which I sang at midnight to the scandalised Florentines, wrapped in a great black-watch robe of mohair like Lucia de Lammermoor, coming over the Ponte Vecchio after a particularily inspiring concert in the forecourt of the Pitti Palace. …

It amuses me that you persist in imagining the life I lead must be sordid and sinful! Quite on the contrary, mon cher, I have never before lived in such complete, utter and <u>blameless</u> indulgence! …

Now, read 'The Woman of Rome' by all means: it's an excellent book and I, personally, like it very much; but <u>not</u>, I repeat, <u>not</u> as a background to my life! The life of a pre-war, starving, orphaned, child-prostitute is all very pretty and edifying, – but has nothing in common with mine. Also, my sweet, don't feel fidgety about my acquaintances. I am <u>not</u> in love with any of them. I don't intend to be, and I shall make no ties with anyone here that I shan't break on leaving.

Thank you for your poem about Oxford. (May I whisper? I think it's very funny.) The Celestial Oxford, i.e. the one I put in my pocket and carried away with me is wonderful. However it's the only Oxford that I consider real (in the sense of valid) and since I know its no easier to get to than Heaven itself, I try not to feel too homesick about it. (I am, all the same. I'm homesick for Hyde Park too; the Hyde Park of Peter Pan. It sets my heart alight with flutterings of ill-ease, and makes me feel the way WW [William Wordsworth] felt when he thought of the mighty waters rolling evermore on that distant shore. Luckily I brought with me some beautiful photographs of Oxford and London by Gordon Fraser. I shall stick them in your album before I send it to you (some months hence!)

I'm so pleased some of your friends still remember me in Oxford. I should like you to tell me nice things like that often. (No: don't. Because if you told me things that weren't true and I didn't know the difference, I shouldn't enjoy the true things properly either, for thinking they weren't genuine. Do give everyone my love, especially Alastair and John C.

You don't mention my driving: do you disapprove? Just imagine, I shall drive down to Oxford all by myself right at the beginning of next term and take you to Woodstock or Dorchester or Abingdon! …

However you could certainly write to Jo Benson who's staying at 122 Iffley Rod with Gabrielle. Tell Sally she's a naughty girl not to write to me…. Write soon, and tell me of your amours & amourettes. I shall be ready with advice & encouragement. Fondest love, Pusseybite.

P.S. Is the name of that friend of Lewis's & Tolkiens' who writes on Angelology, Charles Williams? Who else was in their group. What did they call themselves? What about the <u>MAP</u>?

[There is an unfinished picture attached – 'My bedroom view']

My bedroom view — finish it yourself if you want to I got bored. (All roovers are pink.)

Perugia 25 October

Dearest,

I cannot tell you how sorry I was to hear of Bas's accident from you, and from John, whose letter I also got this morning…

The little work which I grace, in my last letter to you, with the appellation of "novel", is intended for children, of no definite age-group; possibly nine upwards. It is unusual but I am not sure if it will appeal to anybody. By unusual I don't mean fay or whimsy – just heretical. That's to say, it breaks all the accepted rules of modern story writing. There is no adventure – hardly any plot even – instead of being the drably middle-class "Oh jolly bang on" children of the Enid Blyton tradition, or even the shy, ugly but captivating creations of Sutcliffe or Trease, these are robust, over-intelligent, over-privileged children, with charm, personality and individuality.

…

Thank you for your informative research on Charles Williams. I wonder what you mean by saying his novels have cathartic value? Normally I imagine the c.v. of a novel lies in that the characters act as their readers would wish to, but cannot. As C.W's subject is angelology, perhaps you mean that people who like me would love to be angels, feel that they are, when they read them?!

By the way I received a card from Florence signed PAUL. As Paul h[yams] is the only one I know, I imagine it must have been form him… Would you also save me the energy of writing to David I[saac] (tho' I know I ought to) by giving him my best wishes and all the news you care to impart. I shall try to write to John to-day…

…. Pam and I bought a gramaphone – rather like yours. …

I think it is impossible to withhold from you something that is going to tax your credulity to the full. I have been practising Catholicism for the past month, going to mass and benediction each day, and having studied the catechism. Father Michael [Hollings] has sent me a Missal and I have a rosary. My first communion will not be before my return, on the wish of my parents… How much your prayers helped me is a question open to doubt; let us give you the benefit of it. I hope so much that you will not be bitter about my choosing a branch of Christianity opposed to your own, and that you wish me well. …

So, darling. A long letter, and one which I hope has not left a bad taste in your mouth. I think I have told you all my news.... Then I shall return with him to England, somewhere early in January. After that – I don't really know.
Give my love to all your friends. What are Jo and Gabriel doing? Hugs and kisses, Julie

My reaction to Julie's conversion is written a Worcester College crested card dated October 29th 1961.

<u>After hearing of the conversion of a dear friend (J) to Catholicism.</u>

In the outer regions of space thunderous forces crack and thunder, might meets force – right faces evil and the dream of man is disturbed by strange rumours of a cosmic strife. [Too much reading of C.S. Lewis and Charles Williams!] But men awake and see all round the unchanged changing world riplingly reflecting every myriad shade of human passion and endeavour – warming it slightly as a calm lake reflects the splendours of a giant tree taking the leaves all of so close a shade – yet each distinct, and by the slightest ripple blending them into a calm whole.

So men awake – and know not that another leaf has fallen – one slipping leaf in the bird song air has glided to its long home where it will turn into a gossamer spiders-web before losing itself in the thick rich soil. But that leaf has dimmed the powers of hell – if only by one atom – and it has filled my heart with a gratitude, a warmth such as burns from an autumn tree that preens in the golden sun.

The battle will go on – force will oppose force, but on that strange duck-board the Church, that floats in the pond of life another being – ridiculed as a foolish duck has clamoured from the waters of desire – those clinging waters so warm but which will cool, and clog and freeze as night comes and capture all who stay too long in a skin of ice. While those who painfully clamber forth into the naked air will find it cold at first – cold and lonely, wet & greasy to foot – opening up above into an unfamiliar world of immensity. But when the sun sinks through the crust of protection which has barnacled onto the bird – then will the sensitive soul feel her lord.

O lord who madest the bubble of the dabbled water
O lord who made the liquid splash of ducks on summer afternoons
O lord who made the rustle of autumn leaves
O lord who made the leaning of willows
O lord who make the drifting of smoke
O lord who made the spreading of ripples
O lord who made the grey of old walls
O lord who made the velvet sheen of the duck's head
O lord who made the dream of golden leaves in the sun
I praise thee.

The next letter is dated 4th November, from Perugia

Dearest,

Thanks so much for your letter. Will you forgive me if I write you a short news-letter in note form this time, as I want to get it off quickly, knowing you'll want to hear les nouvelles, but not really having time to write properly?

a.<u>Catholicism</u>. a. <u>Yours</u>. Good, darling, but do be awfully certain of yourself, won't you. I think Catholicism – or rather Proselytization – is becoming something of our generation. I've met countless contemporaries who have wanted to change over, tho' one thing & another, I'm the only person of my immediate acquaintance to have gone thro' with it. I think you'd be much better of[f] as C[atholic]. It's a religion capable of appreciation on so many levels of perception & intellect. At the same time it will prevent you from getting too mixed-up. Whereas introspection – i.e playing with fire – is an important part of C. thought, by following exactly the rather dogmatic, but excellent precepts laid down in the Catechism you will shift the weight of decision and responsibilities, and will never again be in doubt about what course of action you should follow. <u>If</u> you can

escape doing things that by C. standards are considered sins, there is no doubt that you will be better than any of your contemporaries.
b. Mine. It for me is just a tantalizing carrot-on-a-cord dangled 1000 light years away from my reality. Your 'infuriated devil' is not getting much of a fight from me – in fact I know I'm in greater danger than ever before. Daily communion, and confession two or three times a week is my only means of not getting too deeply involved in sin. Even so, I'm just making & breaking promises all day. You see almost every action of my daily life in the past would have been termed a sin, and one cannot break habits of a lifetime in a month. What makes my danger worse is that I am considered a saint, and no one want to believe how evil I am. Still, I suppose there's always hope. My baptism was wonderful. It took about two hours, and the little chapel was quite full of guests… [description] …
j. I see a question in yr. letter referring to point g. – monendo. Answer: the beauty & joy of using one's imagination resourcefully, by the example of the rather literary children in the story.
k. Nice to have seen Oresteia. I like Agamemnon best, perhaps because I studied it the most. I don't like the Furies, but Ingrid said she did, only the day before your letter came… Glad you had a nice time with Jo. Give her my love, and ask her if any of the photos came out well. (I should like a few prints if you can possibly wangle any, but put you on your honour not to keep any of me unless I came out nicely.)
l. I dread leaving Freedom, tho' naturally I'm longing to see all of you again. Of course it will really be leaving one life for another, rather than freedom for captivity, because I shall be pretty independent when I get back…
m. Judy's very sweet but I don't know whether you'd get on with each other for very long. Ask Gabrielle. (And give her my love.) …
o. It's Guy Fawkes to-morrow! Burn a sparkler for me!
p. What's a 70 m'for bomb? [I had presumably written 70 m'ton[egaton] What happened to the people they dropped it on?
q. Sure you want to write a summary of your views? Don't bore yourself my sweet.
s. Might go to Rome next week with Pam for a few days. Shall I stay there? – Perhaps it will be more amusing than Perugia.
Write soon – Fondest love, Pusseybite.

The next letter is undated, but probably about the middle of November and from Rome [of which there is sketch]

Darling,

I'm not going to write you a proper letter now, 'cos there's so much I have to do. I know it was all notes last time, too, sorry darling. Write you a proper one next time. This is chiefly to re-direct your next letter. Wish you luck with Margaret, she sounds sweet, & just right for you. Got some advice, my sweet – stop analysing yourself! And above all, stop thinking of rational excuses for everything you do! Really, I think you're no better than a kitten that's got itself tangled up with the wool its been playing with. Listen, I suggest you see a confessor for some really intimate advice. Personally I think you ought to have some strictly non-emotional sex experiences with the right type of girl – and for goodness sake don't get married for another 5 years! I say this because I'm afraid your frustrated sex feelings plus your quite unnecessary guilt complex will lead you to a pre-mature & unfortunate marriage. Don't let yourself think, with the rest of our generation, that marriage is anything you can dance in and out of – consider it as something that will definately [sic] bind you for your lifetime. It's dreadful that men think less about whether they should marry or not, than girls do about whether or not they should surrender their virginity….
What month are you? (I've been amusing myself with Astrology learnt from Pam.) …
Re Christmas presents, darling, I don't mind, but please nothing expensive. Have you any special wishes? Something specially Italian, perhaps? Fondest love, Pusseybite

P.S. 'Roman Tales' won't help you (tho' do read Moravia – he's very good.) However, he writes about Via Marqulta in 'La Noia' ('Boredom').

The next letter is also from Rome, and dated 30 November.

My dearest Alikins,

You say "please write v. quickly" so, with my coat & scarf already on to post other letters, I am pausing to answer you immediately. What a serious letter, my sweet, but not boring at all! Why do you always imagine your letters to be boring?

I'll come to the main point first – sex. Margaret seems a sweet girl, and I certainly don't suggest you spoil a nice relationship by being inconsiderately forward – not to speak of lustful – with her. Treat her with respect, as you treated me, and save her for better things. No, I meant quite another kind of girl, and since I am really quite incompetent to give you advice of this kind, I do beg that you talk very frankly with your chaplain about it, as soon as possible. Now, does that sound very muddled?

I know I set you off on the introspective train, but I am very glad you have stopped the tick-machine now; you had quite long enough with it. I've always been introspective, but Peter broke the habit by getting really determined, and even confiscating or destroying new books I had just bought, if he didn't approve of them. … Oh, can you give me Paul's address for a Christmas Card? Who else do you think I should send one to? … I suppose David Isaac had better have one since I never wrote from Perugia… Fondest love, Pusseybite

The next letter is also from Rome on Wednesday 13 December.

Dearest Alikins,

Thank you for your letter. As usual, I am answering by return of post…. I'm glad you found such relief in your confession, tho' rather sorry to think how soon your fervour will melt, like ours, and your sessions there – once bursting with faith will become social occasions. Perhaps your layer of naiëvity will protect you. I hope so.
…
I think, mon ami, that you no longer love me. Don't jump up, or bite your tongue. I know this is a horrid question to ask, but I hope you will, as an old friend, bear with me and regard this ommission [sic] of tact indulgently. Perhaps I am wrong & the tone of your letter is due merely to an infiltration of the bitterness you experienced in Oxford. I am so sorry you are suffering from it. I felt it continuously, & in a terrible degree at school, but not since, I am thankful to say. Then, it lay in the fact that the grace I had was not generated by outward good things such as love, right-mindedness, security and well-being but from within: from my natural intelligence, ambition, and complacency. This is a kind of sickness and naturally prevented me from reaping any benefit from my actions. This can be explained by psychology or religion. I am sure your difficulty stems from other sources. I hope your anonymous but respected granny (to whom , greetings) will nurse you back to happiness, & help arm you for the struggles of next term. Please write soon, to Lech [Austria]… I wish you a wonderful & happy Christmas, my sweet. Enjoy yourself and radiate some cheerfulness to me! Thank you in advance for your present. Fondest love, Pusseybite xxxx

The last letter I include here is one dated 12 January 1962, from Julie's London home.

My dear Alikins,

Thank you so much for your letter (received in Lech), and also for your presents. I specially liked the miniatures book, and the Shan bird. (I hope your granny didn't mind.) Sorry not to have written before.

The Lech holiday was delightful and I met several really nice people. I have been back nearly a week now, but both Peter and I had terrible colds …

Having read my letter thro' at this juncture, and not wanting to give you a false impression I shall repeat one of your own much-loved phrases to you with earnest emphasis: "Don't take my words too seriously." …

Hope my letter hasn't bored you awfully, duckie, or upset you by the undertone of selfish discontent. Looking forward to your news & views – personal & Oxonian. Please post me a copy of Vade mecum as soon as poss. Am taking my driving test in Feb. May drive to Oxford even before then, however. Will give you due warning! All love, Pusseybite.

Spring Term 1962

Sadly all my letters in 1962, except for two to my father in the summer and one to both parents in December, have been lost. The fact that my mother was home for half the year would, in any case, have diminished the flow. Therefore, in terms of letters I shall have to relay my life as reflected in numerous letters from my mother through the year, which fortunately I kept as an almost complete run.
My grandmother's letters to me over my Oxford years seem to have been largely lost. Just during the first half of 1962, and particularly in February and March, there are half a dozen letters. I shall include parts of these as they give some impression of the Lake District background and the character of my grandmother, who still influenced me deeply. And since we were now just good friends and there are not so many of them, I shall include the extracts from Julie here as well.

It was a busy term. There is a small filing card (the five by three-inch card which was to become such a central feature of my life from now on) which is headed (in true Benjamin Franklin fashion):

'A "full" day at Oxford. Thursday 8/3/62'

1. Up at 8.0
2. Work (writing essay) 8.45 – 11.50
3. Tute [tutorial] with Lady Clay 12.0 – 1.15
4. Help at Oxfam 1.20 – 2.40
5. Work (reading Berlin) 3.0 – 4.0
6. Meeting of society 4.15-5.30 (Canterbury Rd)
7. To another society at Keeble – which is over 5.30-6.0
8. 6.0 – 6.30 find people to take evensong
9. 6.30 – 7.20 go to blood doning
10. 7.20-8.15 Have supper (fish & chips), return to Worcester, attempt 4 times to ring up Julie
11. 8.15 –10.0 Go to Walsingham So' – talk by Hilton on Marxism.
12. 10.0 – 20. Send a telegram to Julie
13. 10.30 – 11.20 Read Edwin Muir's poems.
14. 11.20 – 12.0 have a bath
15. 12.20 to bed

What is extraordinary about this to me, apart from the multi-level and busy activity, is how much I have forgotten – almost all of it – the work at Oxfam (this term, though I do remember doing so at some point), the blood giving, the talk by Hilton, the sending of telegrams etc. If only there had been more of these micro-diaries.

Ephemera for the Spring Term

A few hints of what I was filling my time with outside work, and in the absence of a serious girlfriend, is shown by the 'ephemera' which have survived, another large bundle, suggesting I was systematically collecting these things. This includes:

Social and recreational: Oxford Playhouse Guild (Undergraduate and Student Scheme), which enabled me to purchase tickets at Undergraduate rates. On the back is written, London Opera (2/-)

A programme for the Oxford Playhouse for 'Alice's Adventures in wonderland', January 1962.

A programme for 'In Camera' by Jean-Paul Sartre, preceded by 'A Social Success' by Max Beerbohm, at the Oxford Playhouse in February 1962.

The Oxford Mozart Singers and Orchestra had a Mozart and Brahms programme at the Town Hall, Saturday February 3rd at 8 p.m. (I have the ticket for the Gallery, price 5/-)

Unusually, I have a reaction to this concert, which can be seen under 'Private Writings'.

A programme for 'Tosca' at the New Theatre for Friday, March 2nd.

The Oxford Union Society Hilary Term card.

There is one 'At Home' card, for Saturday March 10th at 8pm. from Hope Stallybrass (a name I remember, but in what connection I am not sure), who was at Brasenose College.

Vocational: I have the Hilary Term 'Cosmos' (U.N.) card, where again I was a college representative.

There is also a Registration Card for the Dulverton Youth Scheme (whose address was Reading), with my name on it.

I have a card for Amnesty for Hilary 1962, where one meeting is noted, Mr Peter Benenson, founder of Amnesty. My friend Tim Garland was the Worcester representative.

Religious: This was probably the height of my religious fervour and this is reflected in perhaps the largest collection of cards:

The Hilary Term for OICCU (Oxford Inter-collegiate Christian union). I have marked the back with an added name of a college representative, my friend Alistair Campbell.

There is Worcester College Group Bible Studies group, part of OICCU, with eight meetings.

THE AIM

To present the claims of the Lord Jesus Christ to members of the University, to unite those who desire to serve Him, and to promote the work of Home and Foreign Missions.

THE BASIS OF MEMBERSHIP

I desire in joining this Union to declare my faith in Jesus Christ as my Saviour, my Lord and my God.

" CHRIST AND UNIVERSITY LIFE "

Three Addresses
by the Rev. M. A. P. Wood, D.S.C., M.A.

October 21, 22, 23—
St. Ebbe's Church, 8.15 p.m.

MID-WEEK TALKS

Oct. 24 **" Christ and My University Life "**
Rev. M. A. P. Wood, D.S.C., M.A.

Nov. 2 **" Living the Christian Life "**
Rev. P. S. Dawes, B.A.

The North Gate Hall,
5.00 p.m. Tea at 4.30 p.m.

SUNDAY EVENING SERMONS

Oct. 15 **The Freshers' Sermon**
The Rev. J. R. W. Stott, M.A.
Wesley Memorial Church, 8.30 p.m
(By kind permission of the Minister)

Oct. 22 **" Christ and University Life "**
The Rev. M. A. P. Wood, D.S.C., M.A.
St. Ebbe's Church, 8.15 p.m.
(By kind permission of the Rector)

Oct. 29 **" Christ and Intellectual Barriers "**
The Rev. E. M. B. Green, M.A.

Nov. 5 **" Christ, our Eternal Life "**
The Rev. H. J. Parks, M.A.

Nov. 12 **" Christ, the Good Shepherd "**
The Rev. J. Stafford Wright, M.A.

Nov. 19 **" Christ, our Judge "**
Professor D. J. Wiseman, O.B.E., M.A.

Nov. 26 **" Christ, our Crucified Saviour "**
Leith Samuel, Esq., B.A.

Dec. 3 **" Christ, the Risen Lord "**
The Rev. J. McKechnie, M.A.

St. Martin's and All Saints' Church,
8.15 p.m.
(By kind permission of the Rector)

ALL MEMBERS OF THE UNIVERSITY ARE WELCOME

I have the term card for the Oxford University Church of England council
The term card for Worcester College Chapel

The term card for St Aldate's Church suggests I was still attending this evangelical church, but I don't remember attending any of the meetings, though the Sunday sermon by Keith de Berry on 'An Answer to Psychological Tensions' might have been attractive!

Sport: I have the term card for the Worcester College A.F.C. (football). I was playing a lot of matches for the First XI, on average two a week, including an away match against Emmanuel, Cambridge on 27 January.

Date		Opponents	Ground	Result
		FIRST XI		
JANUARY				
Monday	22	St. Peter's	Home	
Saturday	27	Emmanuel, Cambridge ...	Away	
Monday	29	Balliol	Away	
FEBRUARY				
Thursday	1	Corpus Christi	Away	
Monday	5	Queen's	Away	
Saturday	10	Old Bradfieldians	Home	
Monday	12	Magdalen	Away	
Saturday	17	Salesian College	Home	
Monday	19	St. Catherine's	Away	
Thursday	22	Wadham	Home	
Monday	26	City Police	Home	
MARCH				
Thursday	1	Pembroke	Home	
Monday	5	St. Edmund Hall	Away	
Thursday	8	Merton	Away	
Saturday	10	New College	Away	
Tuesday	13	Brasenose	Home	
		SECOND XI		
JANUARY				
Tuesday	23	Wycliffe Hall	Away	
Tuesday	30	Balliol	Home	
FEBRUARY				
Tuesday	6	St. Peter's	Home	
Tuesday	13	Pembroke	Away	
Tuesday	20	Ruskin College	Home	
Tuesday	27	St. Catherine's	Away	
MARCH				
Thursday	8	Brasenose	Away	
Monday	12	Queen's	Away	

I am top right, with longer hair. Paul Hyams on my right.

*

The first of my grandmother's letters for my Oxford period is dated January 17th, from Field Head.

Dearest Alan,

Thank you very much for your letter & I enclose herewith your Premium Bond covering £20 & I think a good typewriter is a good investment – I will send you my typing manual (if I can find it!) & so you can learn the right & touch type way –

The library has just been[1] *& I have the "Frontier Doctor" life story of sir Henry Holland whom we knew so well in Quetta & a book by Richard Church "Calm October" – I am a greater admirer of his. – Your trunk was collected same morning as you left & I do <u>hope</u> it have [sic] arrived by now. – I am so sorry about your cold – trust it won't prove to be the prevailing 'flu – Jummie appears to be having a good day & a Mrs Higson & friend were over there when I went to collect Beryls books. Beryl went in to see Gran: yesterday afternoon as she has been put into a flat so Grandpa sat with Jummie – Peebles is one of the worst flood spots in Scotland & the T.V. pictures of it were quite frightening so I hope the Cowan's house is high up. – Derwent water has overflowed & joined up with ? so Borrowdale is just one immense lake. – We have had torrential rain & gales but it is quiet to-day & I must go down & see Mr Haslam – I'll post this as I go. – Where is your 2nd pair of black shoes? I did not take them to be mended & can't find them anywhere. – The Mortons & Mrs Knappett are coming to tea on Sunday so that the Mortons can give her brochures etc on the Dolomites where they go & she wants to go to.*

Take care of yourself –

Lots of love from us both,

---

[1] This was the mobile library service, which toured even the more remote lanes and came to our house in the Lake district every few weeks.

Your loving Granny.

The first letter from my mother is dated January 22nd, from Assam

My dear Alan,

Your letter from Oxford just arrived, and I am sorry to hear about your beastly cold which you've probably forgotten you ever had now. We were all very interested in the Cowans, I knew Felicity was going to be a winner but I'm glad Nicola is attractive too as I always felt a bit sorry for her. We'll cope with the battels but if there is any delay I'll write to the Bursar, he was very nice about it last time and I've had years of practice in letters to Bursars! I was delighted to hear that you were thinking in terms of the U.N. as I had been for a long time, it would seem to combine a worthwhile with an interesting existence and though you wouldn't think so to hear us talk the money part really is the least important – the trouble with our job is that it is neither rewarding financially nor spiritually and I'm sure business is equally futile in all its aspects. But you'll probably change your mind again several times, Anne's essay in her last test was "on Choosing a Career" and my advice to her was to say that it didn't matter much what career you chose because your capacity for pleasure and interest could be satisfied outside or inside it, rarely both. Needless to say, she didn't believe me. She is sitting beside me now writing notes on "The Hound of Heaven", I wish I knew more about Francis Thompson. … Hope this torn form will arrive – Much love from us all – Mummy

In relation to the stalling on battels, there is a typed letter from my mother in the College archives which may relate to this year.

Cherideo T.E.
Nazira P.O.
Assam,
India, Jan 30th

Dear Sir,
My son, A.D.J. Macfarlane has written to say that £60 of his battels remains to be paid and I am writing to apologise for the delay in sending this. My husband will get the money home just as soon as he is able to collect it, towards the end of this month I hope, if not at the beginning of March. I trust this will be all right.
Yours sincerely, [sig.] Iris Macfarlane Mrs D.K. Macfarlane

The next letter from my mother is dated January 29th.

My dear Alan,

Thank you for a rather short letter. But I know how difficult it is when we are living such different lives and we do appreciate the fact that you bother to write regularly at all when you must spend most of your waking hours scratching away with the old Parker (have you still got it?) February is such a dead month anyway that one feels mentally as numb and leafless as the rest of the world looks. This is where I should toss off a few lines of "The Waste Land" but the only bit of T.S. Elliot I ever remember is the bit about wearing the bottoms of his trousers rolled which never seems appropriate somehow. Then there is E. St. V. Millay with her "My sky is full of small birds flying south" which I feel more appropriate than your winter. Do you know her poetry? I think you would like it, it has a certain virility in spite of her depressing name. I have just finished reading Laurens Van Der Posts new book "The Heart of the Hunter" a very touching account of the Bushmen, their legends etc., beautiful descriptive writing which I press on Anne constantly as a model. I loved it but both Fiona and I came out in a daze, read it and see if you can grasp the bit about the "first spirit". …

Tom Darby has resigned (did I tell you?) I wish we could too in some ways though there is still so much I want to see and learn about the east. It would be lovely if your job with the U.N. (you notice I have got you fixed) brought you out here for a year or two. The Camb. Undergrad is doing some Village Welfare work after he has finished with his Tibetan Refugees, and I'm sure the U.N. must have similar schemes. We could meet on leaves and visit exciting places and you could Broaden Your Outlook i.e. come round to my way of thinking on religion and philosophy! Come to think of it, from your point of you [sic] this probably sounds a very dreary programme. …

Haven't heard about our passages, shall probably get 24 hours notice but only have a few rags to pack. The girls plan to get hugely lucrative jobs as soon as they can, I still haven't heard about Fiona's grant (if any) so cant decide where she will be for her art, Oxford would be fine but where on earth would she live? Everything will suddenly click into place I expect, I remember these periods of indecision and blankness before. Must write to Granny now, I don't mind your hair long if its clean and well brushed but long, scruffy hair is horrible and I shall nag you about it unceasingly! Much love, Mummy

From my grandmother on Feb 1st Field Head, Outgate, Nr Ambleside, Westmorland

Dearest Alan –

Thank you for your very welcome letter and I'm glad you saw Geoffrey B & Vignoles[1] but now I'm not so sure as Cambridge has a small-pox suspect – can you remember when you were vaccinated last? – Yesterday it blew & rained without stopping but to-day is sunny & scintillating [sic] & our first aconites & snowdrops are coming up. The sight of them always turns my heart over – Richard will be up from April 16th so we will not be so earth bound & might get around to see some beauty spots – Old Haslam has been removed to the Old Folks Home in Ambleside & giving them as much trouble as possible! Last time I went in to Jummy he was quite gay & better than I had seen him for sometime. We have given permission Shuttleworth has dug a pathway through their shrubbery into our car space so that Jummie's chair can be wheeled at a good gradient until we have a car Beryl will drive her car in & make it easy for J: to be put in. She is panting for her uncle's estate to be wound up & so let her buy an estate car & give room for him & chair etc. – I have finished my annual marmalade chore – 70 lbs – & changed to a Scotch (Dundee) recipe which I like very much & hope the family will do so too – I am going in for my Bridge to-day & will take Haslam a few flowers. – It must be the first time in his life he has been made to do something against his will & he was in a real frenzy last time I saw him here.

Angela has engaged a French girl au pair & she goes there to-day – Robert said Lucy took to her at once which was a hopeful sign – It is such a serene household that the girl should be happy as long as she is also helpful – the forms for Annes G.C.E. exam are all coming to me & as the Candidate has to sign herself & returned before March 1 I am having to send them out to her & hoping there will not be any delays in their return.

Lots of love from us both –
Your loving Granny.
G.P. is going to sit with Jummy this afternoon

On the back I have written what look like notes about holiday arrangements. 'March 17 (Sat) – 24th (Sat [April] home – 17 days. Camp April 11-19 [presumably religious camp], Come up [back to Oxford] April 27.

The next letter from my mother is a week later, dated February 6th.

My dear Alan,

Well the planets don't seem to have conjoined to any purpose, and the world goes on for good or ill, I must say there have been several occasions during the last few days when we've thought that now would be the moment – but on the whole this particular bit of the world is hard to leave now…

Your last letter has just arrived, we were interested to hear about Geoffrey, we had just been talking about him and wondering if he was back from the East. Is he going to do mission work? What news of Ian Campbell? Fiona has had letters from Lois and Jill Sinnot and Piggy lately and everything sounds just the same except that Lois is in London learning to type, Jill still seems to be waiting to marry Mike but I'm glad Mr Doogan is better…

I have embarked on the Lord of the Rings now that Daddy has finished the first volume and am absolutely immersed, I get the feeling all the time that it's a country I know and half remember, whether from fairy tales or dreams or what I don't know. I have always had the sneaking feeling that the Little People are still around and

---

[1] Geoffrey Bromley and Charles Vignoles were both Old Sedberghian friends.

sometimes catch sight of one out of the corner of one eye, intimations of immortality or just genetic heritage? Whatever it is, I find Frodo and Co quite fascinating and will be blissfully happy in their company for several weeks. I wish I had read them to you when you were small, but they weren't there were they? I got Roberts book this week too, but have only dipped into it...

We still haven't heard about our passages but the descriptions of English weather we get don't make us want to hurry back just at the moment...

I'm glad you did well in your exams [college collections], *we take it for granted that you always will but you must be glad that the exam period of your life is coming to an end, you've had more than your fair share over the past few years. Didn't you say Tolkien was in Oxford. Couldn't you go and see him. I would love to know what is "behind" his books, what exactly is the power of the Ring for instance. ...*

There are the three letters I have from my time at Oxford from my grandfather. The first is date-stamped 8 February from the Lake District. As it is so unusual to have a letter from my grandfather, I shall include all of them as some indication of our relationship.

February 8th Field Head

Dearest Alan,

I am very delighted with your present [obviously a birthday present – a Dictionary of Quotations] which is going to give me a lot of pleasure in addition to being a great help with Crosswords. I have been dipping into its store of jewels & find the book most engrossing. You must never worry about my birthday – I certainly never remembered my grandfathers!

Letters from your mother & Fiona yesterday – How exciting their arrival will be! I'm glad you enjoyed the concert so much.

Martin has been taken to Court, for causing a nuisance to a neighbour from noise of his juke-box! Jane is here for few days. They asked to be remembered to you.

I have sown my sweet pea seeds & do hope they will be a success.

Yes, from the papers we read that the undergrads had behaved very badly to Macmillan – Moral – never believe half one reads or hears.

I see that 4000 workers on the Jaguar car have stopped work because the management wont dismiss 2 men who didn't join the general strike on Monday – this sort of thing makes one ashamed of ones countrymen. I wonder what Tawney would have thought.

I hope you are making headway with the typewriter. I'm glad your visit to Cambridge was such a success.
Much love, Grandpa

The first of Julie's letters I have from this period is dated 9th Feb. It is written from her home in London.

Dearest Alikins,

Many thanks for ?? and your note. Far from being depressed, the reason for my prolonged silence was the hope that I could write to tell you I was going to spend a few days in Oxford. However, I failed my driving test...

What are your entanglements, my dear? Do you mean in connection with Margaret and does this mean you are suffering from Troubadour-malady? (A form of castration-complex if you follow it back to Madonna-worship, worship of matriarchal deities etc. then to primaeval man.) Or is it with a new girl? Do tell me all about it if you wish to, and be assured that you have a sympathetic reader! My love to you, and to all who ever remember me. Pusseybite

The next letter from my mother is on February 14th.

My dear Alan,
An interesting letter yesterday, full of exciting doings that made us very envious, the thought of doing something really civilised again like going to a play or even a film less than ten years old is delicious. The odd thing is that when we are at home we never go, or have any desire to go, anywhere! We still don't know when or how we are

getting home, the company is being very unhelpful about cheap passages but presumably something will happen, it would be nice for Fiona to take part in some of your May celebrations, one dance anyway, she could stay with Uncle Ernest perhaps. Or Robert…

She [Anne] and I are now drifting back through our work, trying to take a Broad View –I am collecting information and writing theses on subjects like "The Rise and Fall of Spain" and "The French-Hapsburg Quarrel" which seem obvious choices for questions. At present I'm working on "The Church through the Ages" which will keep me happy till we sail…

We were sorry to hear to-day that old Haslam had died but it was the best thing, sad that he had to be moved at the end. Martin seems to be getting into trouble (much to Grannys glee!) but Ambleside does seem to be a little stuffy…

I really must write a Telly play about our rousing revels but I suppose they are no worse than those of any other small closed community…

If you ever see old "O" level exam papers being sold, could you get a few, History & English particularly. Much love from us all, Mummy

The next is from my grandmother, dated Feb17th.

Field Head, Outgate, Nr. Ambleside, Westmorland

Dearest Alan,

I have left this letter later in the week than I meant – I saw a letter from you to Beryl but she has been too harassed to tell me anything about it, Jane went on Thurs: – Martin drove her & kids (from Liverpool) back home & Jummie has had 2 hard days since. We've also had a taste of the hurricane, it was quite frightening but our sturdy little cottage just sat tight without budging while our T.V. aerials writhed crazily aloft – I don't know how they stayed in tact – Last Sunday & Monday we had torrents of rain as well & the Brathay rose over the bridge & several roads were flooded and now trees are down. I've never known such wild weather but poor old Sheffield etc have been tragically hit – I went to Mr Haslam's funeral on Monday – only Nellie Jobson (his family's old housekeeper) Mrs Barr & I went – I hear Mr Brownson is very keen to buy the cottage – it would be nice if he came here as there is a girl of your age group to cheer things up.

I have the weekly Bridge 4 here on Monday & unfortunately I could not get a single person so the Brewsters are coming which will make 5 –
Must hurry for postman –
Hope you flourish.
Lots & lots of love from us both, Granny
Have you got to "Shall a Lad slash a fag" yet in typing!

Julie wrote from the Hotel Wittebrug in 'S-Gravenhage, Room 70, 19.2.62

Alikins, old dear,

I do hope your party went terrifically well. So sorry I couldn't make it. And now you're all in a swirl of commems, lucky Oxonians that you are! Did you change your mind about going? … [various news] Do write to me if you can – the sooner the better! All love – Pusseybite

The next from my grandfather was from Field Head on February 20

Dearest Alan,

Congrats on your football win. It was wise of you to have a Tetanus injection.

Your programme for the next vac sounds a very good one. I shall be interested to hear about your visit to the Borstal camp.

I thought the great gale would tear down our T.V. aerial but it survived – The hounds of spring are indeed breaking winters traces [Swinburne] – I am sorry for Hamburg & the midland cities.

Mrs Barr reports having seen primroses out & there is certainly a feel of 'blessing in the air' I enjoyed reading that work by Saroyan you gave me & I treasure the book of quotations. I have never discussed religion with you as I am rather a doubting Thomas and find miracles such as the virgin birth and the resurrection a stumbling block but I do believe theres a divinity that shapes our ends – though it is hard to see his manner of working when one looks at the present state of the world.

Grannie is having a lot of bridge & had a bridge do here yesterday.

I hope Oxford will win the boat race with its Italian boat & lets hope the river wont be rough. I see that women are to be admitted to the Oxford Union.

Good luck to the work!

Much love, Grandpa

On 21 February my mother wrote:

My dear Alan,

A nice letter from you just received, and I'm answering in rather a sleepy mood – partly the weather which is sleepy in itself, heavy with rain that wont fall, and partly because of a late night last night and the night before and before that… In the evening we joined with a gang of the lads and sang round a camp fire for an hour or two, it's a funny thing how much happier both Daddy and I feel with the young than with our own generation who all seem stuffy and duly and bogged down with trivialities.

I don't think the "immortal longings" you describe will fade, but whether you will be able to trap them is another thing. I have often thought along those lines, and have recently been milling over an idea connected with legends of India (brought on by Lord of the Rings I expect) and of trying to collect and interpret them in some way that will clear my own mind and bring out some shining Truth that runs through and yet transcends them. I don't suppose I ever will, because the feeling one gets from beauty is impossible to described or account for – not only beauty – I feel my scalp prickle and tears come to my eyes when I read about the death of Sir Thomas More or one of Queen Elizabeths speeches. The closest anyone seems to have come to describing it is Moment of Truth but that is so overworked a phrase, Zen Buddhism has some good shots and Wordsworth doesn't do badly – anyway you should be thankful that you feel it at all because a surprising amount of people don't. When we were reading Francis Thompson I tried to describe the feeling to Anne and she just couldnt grasp what I was talking about.

I think your ideas of teaching for a year or two are good, what about the Peace Corps which I see is looking for volunteers? You could collect lots of material for writing – as you see my scheming is all directed to getting you out here for a year or two! …

We still don't know about our passage, I'd better stop saying this and tell you when we do know, when exactly is your vac? I fear we shall miss it anyway, what a pity, I'm sure you could have helped us a lot. ….

The next is five days later, 22nd February, from Julie, back again in London.

Dearest Alikins,

I am coming to Oxford next Saturday (the 2nd March)! I do hope you haven't made any plans. Needless to say, I can't come by myself till I pass my test, so I shall be driving down with Chris Mungall, of whom (I think) you know. The plans – always subject to your own – are to drive up, arriving before lunch, and returning in the evening. If you like the idea, we'll hazard the weather and I'll bring a pique-nique. What would be really delightful would be if you could call on Gabrielle and Jo (don't leave it too late I beg you) to persuade them to join us, and if they can, invite Paul, whom I'd in any case like to see, to complete a party of six. … That doesn't leave us very much time for each other, but if you'd like to, I'd be delighted for you to accompany me to these interviews in place of Chris, if you aren't afraid of my driving (there's no risk involved in such small journeys, tho' they are, of course, illegal.) The only problem is to find someone to amuse Chris while we're away…. If you'd invite John Chid or Alastair or anyone else whom I like, and who'd like to see me, to keep him company, that'd be nice as I'd have a chance to see them too. Otherwise I think ther'd be no time for extra visits. …

I do hope I haven't shoved too much responsibility on your hard-worked shoulder, mon ami! Or that I haven't upset any plans. Play havoc with mine if you find a better system for doing everything. And do 'phone me with reversed charges if you have a last-minute query. Till then, adieu, adieu de tout Coeur! Love, Pusseybite

Next are two telegrams, one is dated 27 February to me at Worcester. 'Visit Postponed I Shall Write Love = Julie'. The second is 8 March to me at Worcester. 'Please ring at earliest convenience love = Julie'

My grandmother wrote again on Feb 28th from Field Head

Dearest Alan,

Real winter back with us & I am so sorry for the poor ewes as lambs are due – there are 2 in the back fields & as they belong to the Barrs they will have to be extra strong to survive. The snow disappeared from the fields yesterday & the "thin" wind dropped so I hope things will be easier for me to-day as I am going in to Kendal for lunch & Bridge – Do hope you are keeping fit. – Beryl & I went to see "Gigi" on Saturday & the Shuttleworths sat in with Jummy as I think he is too unfit for Grandpa to cope alone. J: was better yesterday – he swings up & down & was very down after Jane left. Mrs Bolton is going down to Angela for the first week after the baby is born & then I will go down for a week or little more if she is not fit enough to cope – Marie-Luce, the French girl, is a great success & does the shopping & looks after Lucy & is very willing but cant organise or be expected to do the cooking. I note your dates & we look forward very much to having you with us again in roughly a months time – We have got our own T.V. back & it is grand after the indifferent loaned one – we now wait for the bill! – We simply loved Gigi – it really is perfect in every detail. Mr Haslam has left his cottage as a Trust in memory of his wife plus his money to be a holiday home for clergy & families. So all the covetous eyes must turn away. I hope his money will be sufficient to put it right. I go in each Thurs: for snack at M's coffee bar & it is very peaceful & I wonder if the Juke box will be allowed to start up.

Take care of yourself,
Lots of love from us both,
Your loving Granny

The following week, my mother wrote on March 1st, her wedding anniversary.

My dear Alan,

Auspicious day – we are spending it like any other except that Daddy is remarking gloomily at intervals that I'd never have married him if I'd Known, and the cook made a special pudding for lunch which didn't quite work out. Daddy sent for Ogden Nash's Collected Poems for me which were out of stock, and went in to get a bottle of sherry and found it was Rs 47 so didn't get it naturally and this has made him still gloomier. Myself I consider we are very lucky, after twenty one years we have good health, three nice children and still love each other, and I don't think one could ask much more. No money of course but half a house in the most beautiful place in the world which is worth a million to me…

Are there any hostels in Oxford where Fiona could stay if she went there?…

I wonder how your love life is going now? I think one must expect to be hurt quite a lot where relations with the other sex are concerned, but it is worth it and all adds up to the business of living. The dread of getting "involved" with another person leads to a sterile and empty existence, though there are degrees of involvement I must admit. But there are so many degrees of loving too, and nobody can really give advice. Fiona is reading the Bhagavad Gita at the moment and keeps hurling questions like "Mummy what is the Ultimate Reality?" at me when I'm seeing the cook…

We have now heard that a passage is more or less definitely booked for us on the "Canton" leaving on May 8th and arriving on Granny's birthday. This is a bit later than I'd wanted but it will mean Daddy will only have about six weeks on his own and it will be less expensive… When is your vac, and when do you want that £10? Is it for the vac? As usual I'm afraid you will be short, what about taking a job for a couple of weeks, to earn some cash – something purely physical which could rest you at the same time? Watsons Café for instance? Or Martins?

There follows a short note in my father's handwriting.

… Feel much happier now that passages have been booked and something definite happening at last. Have been reading all your letters with great interest but am terrified with all the knowledge you have accumulated! I am hoping that being a simple chap (me) we shall, still, have something in common. Looking forward to seeing you very much, very soon, Lots of love, Daddy (What an effort!)

On March 7th my grandmother wrote again from Field Head

Dearest Alan,

Thank you very much for your very interesting letter & you are lucky to have seen those 2 Operas & so enjoyed them.

The blizzards have departed but we are now enduring very sharp frosts & the poor sheep must be very hungry as the grass is just dried dead straw. Beryl had some in her garden yesterday! – they must have skipped over by our garden gate & as B: has now opened up a path from our car park into their garden – the sheep must have gone up there. They had a wonderful meal off her lawn until we got Stanley Barr & "Prince" who cornered them & dropped them one by one into the field below. Beryl thanks you very much for your letter & so glad you contacted Janet. – Dusty & Jane have bought a second hand "Consul" & are coming up for the week end of 16th – driving up by night & down the same way – I hope it is a success. – Martin is going down with them so as to see a girl friend in London – Hazel I believe this one is – & come back by sleeper. The 3 women coming out to play Bridge here on Monday had had great adventures as the wheel of the car had come off & bowled away across the road. – They had only banged their heads & had had to get a taxi to come & rescue them & so were ¾ hour late – ... Robert had to go to Germany on 12th with Sub: Committee of Estimates so I hope everything is safely over before then. – I also hope I shall be back by 25th but anyway you & Grandpa can manage for a day or two. – Please bring back both suit cases of mine as we will need the them for our wanderings. – We are looking very much to having you with us again. –

Much love, as always, & many blessings, Granny

The next letter from my mother is dated March 8th. (It is not an airmail form, as a cheque was enclosed.)

My dear Alan,

I hope this will catch you before you leave Oxford, have just got your dates and you go down? – earlier than I thought. I hope to enclose a cheque in this, but will be getting an exact statement of the situation in your next letter probably. It'll be easier for you when I'm home and can send you driblets, but I'm afraid you'll never really have enough till you are earning your own! We have at last got our passages, on the "Canton" which leaves Bombay on May 8th and arrives on 26th. This is later than I'd hoped, and leaves very little time to get acclimatised but Daddy is delighted as he will only have about six weeks on his own. I'm afraid we shall miss your May Balls too, but you were probably not going to indulge in many, they must be expensive luxuries. Perhaps you will be able to come to London to meet us, I'm waiting to find out when exactly Anne's exam is, if it's the beginning of June we shall probably stay down till its over. I want to take her to see "Luther" and "Twelfth Night" if I can, but cant plan anything…

I would be grateful if you could send out those exam questions if you have copied them, History chiefly, specially European, and English Language…

Your descriptions of spring were homesick-making, it will be over when we arrive, and I shant see another for four years, how sad how sad… I have nearly finished "The Ring" but I'm trying to make it last as I don't want to come to the end, I feel sometimes it is almost more real than my real life.

Much love & a happy vac – Mummy

The last of the letters from my Grandfather is dated 13 March.

Dearest Alan,

That Mozart recital must have been a great treat. I am looking forward to hearing again some of your records. Not long now before you are back here. Icy winds are still blowing – hounds of spring on winters traces – and not much sign of life in the garden except the birds which are singing madly in full throated ease. [quotes from Swinburne and Keats]

Tomorrow we go down to the village to vote for Sandys in a Lancs County Council bye-election. We have received a notice to be present, if we are interested, in an appeal by Boddington against certain restrictions put on his use of land in connection with his caravans. I understand it is to do with water supply from a stream which, if used, might curtail the supply of water to certain farmers in the locality. A.J.P. Taylor has been giving some talks on T.V. on the twenties which are interesting. He isn't a very engaging personality & his talks are better read (in the Listener) than heard. Does your history syllabus include current affairs?

I often browse through the Dictionary of Quotations. It makes me feel good to come upon Shakespeares shout of joy

Full many a glorious morning have I seen
Flatter the mountain tops with sovereign eye
Kissing with golden face the meadows green
Guilding pale streams with heavenly alchemy.

And to read that when a woman asked Samuel Johnson why in his dictionary he defined a pastern as a horses knee he replied – "Ignorance, my dear lady, sheer ignorance"!

Time for lunch – a nice bright day but the wind from Greenlands icy mountains cuts like a knife!

Much love, Grandpa

My love of poetry must have been sharpened by a grand-father who in a short letter managed to include shorter and longer references to three poems and a hymn.

Academic Work : Spring Term 1962

Unfortunately most of the work is undated. But from the few dated pieces, it looks as if the work was concentrated in two areas.

English History with James Campbell

Essay 1
On 24 January I started to take notes for an essay on 'To what extent is it true to say that we see in Edward II's reign not only a political but also a social and economic crisis?'
There is an essay of seven and a half pages. Campbell's reported comment is 'Good… careful, judicious, in fact excellent.' There is a half-page of notes on comments made by Campbell. There are about 20 pages of notes for this essay dated on 24th. There is also a Revision Class on 'English II (a) with Campbell. It is mainly an outline of the Origins of the 100 Years War.

Essay 2
The second essay was on 'What does the Peasant's Revolt reveal about the nature of English society and English government?' There are over twenty pages of notes for this essay, curiously also dated 24 and 25 January.

Essay 3
"Discuss the views of Postan on the English economy in the later middle ages."
There are over 26 pages of notes for this, and an essay plan. There is a seven page essay on this – with no comment or remarks.

Essay 4
'Does the study of the English Episcopate in the C14 & C15 do anything to bear out the statement that "the later medieval church in England was in process of decay"?'
There is a five page essay – with no notes on it.
Eight pages of notes in hand and some typed notes.

Essay 5
'What light do the 'Paston Letters' throw upon the social history of C15 England?
There is an essay of seven pages, with no notes or comments.
There are about 30 pages of notes and then the essay, which, looking at it again, is rather disappointing and superficial, despite being on social history which I was becoming particularly interested in.

①

What light do the 'Paston Letters' throw upon the social history of C15 England?

Fifteenth century England might be called 'Britain's answer' to America's 'wild west'. Superficially likenesses include the sheriff with his 'posse' (comitatus), attempting to keep control over a population which was for the most part armed – with knives and bows instead of revolvers –; the blood feuds carried on bitterly, (such as that between Lord Bonville & the Earl of Devonshire) against a background of violence and mob justice when a man could be suddenly pulled off his horse and killed (as Sir Humphrey Stafford's son was murdered) – when, according to Bennett "Men took the law into their own hands, and avenged their imagined wrongs to the very utmost," and we see the overawing of juries and sheriffs by local 'big' men, the importance of outlaws and the dramatic seizing of prisoners from jails. The precarious position of law was not the only result of that rawness in the one case rising from the westward migration, in the other from the unsettling of traditional patterns by social, economic & political change; a deeper similarity can be seen in the attitude to land; there was land-hunger, a land-rush. In both, new families were seeking to cut out for themselves a ranch or estates, and they were prepared to use almost every means to this end, legal or otherwise. The Paston letters might be with profit compared to letters of a pioneering family in the American West. Nor does the analogy necessarily end here – both families send their sons to 'college' one at Oxford or Cambridge, one 'back East' to prepare them for the struggle to consolidate and expand family properties. Both families use marriage as a useful piece in their game of estate-expansion. Both read a little and have a venerated collection of books. Perhaps – if the American settlers are Puritans or Quakers, both are religious and regard the local chapel or church as the centre of their village or town. Perhaps the most interesting thing such an analogy might show is the importance of law and respect for law to the two communities. And the main object of this essay is to discuss how far the Paston letters show a breakdown in law in the C15.

Bennett takes the extreme view that "Laws were in vain. Statutes against the hire of retainers with a distinctive livery and against the maintenance of quarrels were of little avail. The times were troubled and confused; and in the midst of all this internal anarchy the weak and innocent masses of people suffered as best they could." Later he goes on "most men of position, and consequently their hordes of followers, laughed at the law, because they knew they could generally overcome it .... Many preferred to rely on strength and cunning rather than on legal proceedings ... the law was another pawn in the game, whose pieces were trickery, force and oppression." Margaret Hastings, quite rightly, sees this as an overstatement, or rather as only a view of the more superficial side of law. But she willingly admits that there was to some extent an administrative breakdown; "Many lawys and lytylle ryght; / Many actes of parlement, / And few kept wyth tru entente" / as a political song put it - or more ~~poetically~~ picturesquely "The lawe is lyke unto a Welshma's hose, / To eche mannes legge ~~that~~ shapen is mete." (Hardynge's chronicle).

The political chaos of the century, aggravating social tensions caused by ~~the~~ the death throes of feudalism, were bound to affect, ~~to~~ some degree, the common law. How much were the repercussions felt by the Norfolk family of Paston?

The ~~Paston~~ Pastons had risen largely through the skill of William Paston in building up family properties round the village of Paston and protecting them by his knowledge and reputation for law. The necessity for vigilance and study of the law was duly impressed on his son John, and the failure in both these qualities in his son Sir John led ~~later~~ to a considerable contraction of the family lands. The Pastons protected their possessions by every means within their power, by the law (their letters are full of lawsuits) by the influence of patrons - especially of Sir John ~~Bardolf~~ Fastolf - by favourable marriages - for instance of John Paston to Margaret Mautby the daughter of the neighbouring squire - and by placing their children in the houses of great landowners or the nobility. This last measure is ~~seen~~ demonstrated when John Paston sent ~~his~~ one son, (later Sir John) to the King's court, and the other son, also John, to the Duke of Suffolk's court.

Mention has been made vaguely that ~~they~~ protected themselves "by the law" - what, then, was the 'law' and how powerful was it? Can we, like Postan's of the judicial field, ~~brighten~~ challenge the traditional view of the C15 which saw it as an age of corrupt justices, bribed juries and ineffective royal courts?

For families like the Paston's the most important organs of justice were the local courts, directed by the sheriffs and justices of the peace, ~~the court of common~~ plea and the Court of Chancery, primarily of use ~~aimed~~ for those who were prevented by poverty or the power of some neighbour

②

PASTON LETTERS.

from receiving justice. An example of when this latter court would be of vital use was the oppression in Westmorland. R.L. Storey in his "Disorders in Lancastrian Westmorland" shows how several magnates such as Sir Henry Threlkeld and William Thornburgh, among men who had sat in Parl't as knights of the shire – prevented impartial justice being done in that county. It was often the same in Norfolk, for instance when the Paston's enemy Justice Yelverton was visiting, or when Daniell was sheriff in 1446-7.

Litigation, it is true, flourished. Bennet states the obvious when explaining this as "due to the changing fashion of the times by which men held lands by lease, instead of by feudal service; and also to the "scrambling & unquiet times," which only left the law courts as a last resort to the oppressed." But there were defects both in the system of law and in the men who administered and used it, which made it far less of a final and satisfactory expedient than it might appear.

Apart from the lack of dynamic energy at the top, which resulted from the disturbed political situation the main inherent weaknesses in the system itself were that it was terribly slow in summoning, effectively, the defendant in a case; that the payment of officers by fee rather than entirely by salary made the cost of law suits prohibitive; that the ambiguous nature of the jury – regarded as both witnesses and a group of judges of evidence, made provisions for cases where justice went astray inadequate, and that the dependence on the sheriff for the execution of court decisions was not wholly effective, largely because he was appointed annually. But it was not these weaknesses in the system which were the root of the trouble. Miss Hastings, speaking of Henry VII's reign says "he did not reform any of the defects of C15 administration. What was needed was better enforcement and a changed spirit among the lords spiritual and temporal" and thus touches on the two main springs of inefficient justice, corruption and the weakness of the monarchy. The examination of the former brings us at last to a realm which is largely illuminated by the Paston correspondence, for they lay bare the bribery, pressures and bribery which must have been prevalent throughout England.

Such contradictory views have been taken of this subject that it is worth quoting two examples before studying the facts. Holdsworth maintains that "it is "no exaggeration to say that by the middle of the C15, the rules of the common law were either perverted in their application or so neglected that they ceased to protect adequately life and property." On the other hand Denton states that few things are "more striking than to follow the calm dignity of the law and its official administration as judges passed from county to county, and to note the observance of most of the legal forms of courts of justice, even in the midst of the strife and noise of angry partisans." Not absolutely contradictory, yet nearly so.

The presiding judge, a cornerstone of law, was not always unbiased. There were none of the scandals of the same magnitude as those of Edward I's reign, but the example of Justice Yelverton's conduct, and the views held of him by Paston and his supporters reveal his partiality, and there is no reason for thinking this case exceptional. Again in 1451 Paston and his friends had requested the king for an "Oyer and Terminer" commission, but on this was sent Justice Prisot whose friendship with Tuddenham and Heydon (those chiefly complained of) was notorious. He showed open partiality, even moving the court from hostile Norwich to Walsingham which was more favourable to Tuddenham and Heydon.

The above incident leads on to another way in which justice was corrupted. This was by the pressure put on juries and even sheriffs to perjure themselves for fear of a powerful noble or even of the king's anger. The classic example is the attempt of John Paston to indict Lord Moleynes and his supporters for attacking and pillaging Gresham. Before a trial could be held, the Sheriff received a letter from the king, ordering him to see that such a panel was formed as would acquit Moleyne. Apparently this happened fairly frequently as Paston remarked, no doubt as a bitter joke, that such letters could be bought for 6/8 each. On this occasion extra pressure was brought to bear by the Duke of Norfolk & Moleynes, while in the case mentioned earlier of the Commission of "Oyer & Terminer" being moved to Walsingham, Tuddenham made sure of his acquittal by appearing with a great force of retainers to intimidate any opposition. A reported conversation between Steward the Chief Constable and Edmund Paston emphasizes the pressures brought to bear on those administering justice. The distraught constable asked what he should do for in the assize between Paston and another man, Paston's opponent was backed by Sir Thos' Tuddenham. Edmund advises him to give true justice "and then he needs never to dread him of no attaint &"- but it was not always as easy to do this.

(3).

Essay (6). PASTON LETTERS.

Often, when force could not be applied directly, bribery was used. John Paston was once informed that certain men had no other livelihood than by taking bribes, it was a measure taken by the comparatively scrupulous like Sir John Fastolf, as well as the Tuddenhams and Heydon's of the world. Sir John rewarded the sheriff for a grand jury panel favourable to himself - after directing John Paston to "Labour to the Sheriff for the return of such panels as will speak for me." The widespread perjury of juries can be seen by the lengthy cross-examinations and investigations during the hearing of Fastolf's will, all of which seek to prove that the witnesses are, or are not, guilty of taking bribes or of giving false evidence. Often the sheriff could be persuaded to favour a certain side; "And they report" (Clement Paston writes to John Paston) "that they have a sheriff to their mind who will make execution, or else return that you have wasted deceased's goods, so that they will have a writ to take you." So important was the support of the Sheriff that Heydon says "rather than he should fail of a shire this year comying for his entent he wole spende £1,000 to procure a favourable sheriff. Add to the above the frequent royal pardons, for instance in 1452 and 1472, and we can see the forces, which according to Bennett "continuously undermined medieval justice." Margaret Hasting's conclusion is that while there is enough new evidence to justify a new trial of the hitherto gloomy picture of C15 justice - yet "there is no escaping the fact that the top layer of C15 society was in a state of confusion and disorder, and that reforms were necessary when Henry VII seized the throne..."

Many incidents in the Paston letters reveal the wildness of the times. Several times Margaret Paston warns her husband or son to be careful whose company he keeps - she believes that "they (Paston's enemies) care not what they do to be revenged and to thwart you, so as to have their own will in Sir John Fastolf's lands." In 1472 Margaret complains sadly that those who have snatched Caister castle "took out of Mautby close 16 sheep ... menaced and shot at my farmer. I dare not send men to gather the rents." Another time John Paston is told to "ride as fast as you can for your own safety." The attacks on manors such as Gresham and Drayton, and the siege of Caister all illustrate a disrespect for the law. On a superficial level the causes seem simple enough. Bennett attributes it to the breakdown of feudalism - the rise of a middle class of an urban population and a large number of landless labourers - combined with the emergence of sheep-farming as the most profitable agricultural venture - but he mistakenly assumes that this led to "men becoming more & more

Bunk!

cf. McFarlane bastard feudalism

"superfluous" which, leading to bands of vagrants roaming the country, was the direct link with lawlessness. Undoubtedly larger factious landowners were able to find ample support from the vagrants who sheltered under their wing, but this was not the deepest social cause of the restlessness. Also Bennett is half right when he says that the political upheavals allowed much of the lawlessness - as he puts it "all the anarchy was able to flourish ... because there was no sufficient strong power to stamp it out." But all attempts to see a direct link between years of greatest political disruption and an increase in local lawlessness have almost completely failed.

Bennett is putting an extreme case when he says "vagrants realized that under the livery of a great lord he was practically immune from ordinary justice, and he knew that, so long as he fought when ordered, and gave his master no trouble, few questions were likely to be asked as to how he spent his leisure." But there is considerable support for this in the Paston correspondence. Gangs of lawless outcasts, usually under the protection of the "wicked three" - Daniell, Tuddenham and Heydon ravaged almost unmolested. When one of their number was indicted the rest would come down with so overwhelming a force that the jury would be overawed. Examples of such open lawlessness were the threats of Walter Aslak against William Paston, the seizing and imprisonment of Hugh Wilton by William Tailboys, the exploits of Charles' Nowell's gang "who would issue out at their pleasure, sometimes six, sometimes twelve, sometimes thirty or more, armed jacked & salleted, with bows, arrows, spears & bills, and override the country and oppress the people and do many horrible and abominable deeds (such as attempting to kill two servants of the Bishop of Norwich as they knelt at Mass on Mid-lent Sunday). After the 1st battle of St Albans lawlessness probably increased, as there were "great gatherings of people and hiring of harness. It being well understood that they be not to the King ward, but rather the contrary, and for to rob". Margaret was "in daily fear" in abiding on the estates, and well might she be for her husband, within a month was savagely attacked in the midst of a crowded shire house by one of the Sheriff's men. Many other examples could be cited. Nor are the Paston letters alone in pointing to this disorder. "The evidence of the coram rege rolls" as Professor Jacob states "shows what a great deal of disorder pervaded the country not merely in a "tempus turbationis" but at times normally regarded as peaceful."

(8)

PASTON LETTERS.

There are too really fundamental problems which emerge from this mass of evidence. The first is was the disorder worse than it had been in the C14 - and if so - as it presumably must partly at least have been a result of political inadequacy can we see each year of political disruption reflected in a growth of lawlessness. No definite answer can be given to either. It is certain that the C14 had had its troubles too - and complaints of abuses had been profuse well before the C15. In fact the judicial scandals of Edward I's reign and the similar, tho' milder scandals in the mid C14 led Professor Holdsworth to conclude that there was a rise in the standards of professional honour. I would probably agree with Miss Hastings "that the breakdown, however serious began towards the end of the reign of Edward III, and that the later Plantagenets should share in the opprobrium hovering over the Lancastrian and Yorkist.

What evidence then is there for a connection between the drastic upheavals, particularly those of 1450-1 1459-61, 1471-2 and 1483? In a short study of these years and the amount of letters in each of them dealing with disturbances I have been unable to find any appreciable increase in lawlessness, with two notable and perhaps significant exceptions. The dramatic attack on (i) Margaret Paston in her house in Gresham by Lord Moleynes retainers, numbering some 1,000 men all fully armed and bringing siege equipment took place in 1450 - a time of unrest and just before Cade's rebellion when the government was weakened by foreign failure. The other (ii) outstanding attack on Paston property also happened in a year of disruption 1469. Then it was that the Duke of Norfolk sent a small army of some 3,000 men to seize Caister castle. It is questionable whether he would have done this if the defeat of the king's forces by the Earl of Warwick had not provided the opportunity.

~~Justices~~ Judges become very rich.

Political Theory

It was during this term that I started to work in an area which has come to mean a lot to me later in my life – namely political theory. Of course I had made some ventures in this field both at Sedbergh and in my first year, when considering Tocqueville etc., but this was the first serious immersion.

We were to study three texts in detail: Aristotle's *Politics*, Hobbes' *Leviathan* and Rousseau's *Social Contract.* We also did some work on nineteenth century political thought.

It appears that I had started to work on this already, for on a sheet headed 'Vacation Work – Winter 1961-2', there were 6 items. The first three were the three texts by Aristotle, Rousseau and Hobbes. On the back are copied out a number of questions on political science, and I also have a number of published exam papers. These took the form whereby we had to complete four answers, the first being to comment briefly on passages from the set authors.

There are Collections, presumably at the start of the term, which were marked by James Campbell. There are comments on four extracts from these authors. For the first, on Aristotle, I had the rare distinction of getting an alpha beta, then on Hobbes a Beta plus, and on a second Hobbes a B?+ and finally on Rousseau a Beta. The overall mark was Beta plus plus. These were good marks, especially from Campbell.

For an essay on "The Law of Nature and the Civill Law contain each other and are of equal extent". How does Hobbes arrive at this position? I got a Beta plus with the comment 'Too much an essay on H in general. He goes into more detail on this problem than you describe e.g. the case of ??? (unreadable)

The next essay was 'What exactly does Rousseau mean by "La volonté générale est toujours droite"? For this I got a Beta with the comment 'R's theory has much more to it than you allow'.

Finally, there was another essay on 'To Hobbes education is chiefly important as a political nuisance.' Discuss. This was a Beta minus. 'Again, you oversimplify too much.'

The total mark for the paper was Beta+??+ - an upper 2:1 I suppose

There is a detailed essay plan and a 9 page essay on 'Discuss the strengths & weaknesses of Aristotle's 'Politics'. There is no comment or mark on this.

In the first week of term, 24th January, I wrote answers on various 'Aristotle gobbets', about ten detailed pages. There are no marks or comments.

There is the first sign of the use of a typewriter to take notes. I took extensive typed notes from Sabine, *A History of Political Theory* (12 pages of notes) and half a page from Bertrand Russell on Aristotle, and two and a half pages from Barker, 'Aristotle's Politics'.

There are notes on lecture 3 by Prest on Aristotle. (There are also notes taken a year later on one lecture (lecture 6) by Isaiah Berlin on a series entitled 'The romantic Revolution in Political Thought', given on 8th February 1963.)

A month after the first set of gobbets on Aristotle, I did a number of gobbets on Hobbes, on 22 February. There are nine pages on this – but no comment or mark.

There is then an essay (Political Science ii) undated:

'When and where, according to Hobbes, should the subject obey?' This is five and a half pages long – with no comment or mark.

⊙. (13) POLITICAL SCIENCE (ii)

When and where, according to Hobbes, should the subject obey?

Hobbes is notorious for his contradictions, and it is a consequence of this that his interpreters take such differing views of his 'real' meaning. Some have seen him as an authoritarian and an absolutist, the prophet of Marxism; others like Oakeshott as the supreme individualist, the forefather of the 19 liberals. Plamenatz sees him as a lone peak "he finds no room for any essential part of either of the two more important European moral philosophies" while Oakeshott calls him "in purpose tho' not in doctrine, an ally of Plato, Augustine and Aquinas" and traces back the lineage of his "Will & Artifice" tradition into the ancient world through the later scholastic nominalists and Augustine. Let us consider then how these interpreters have approached the complex problem of political obligation.

Sabine takes the view that enlightened self-interest is the touchstone of obedience. "Strictly speaking" he maintains "Hobbes is saying merely that in order to co-operate men must do what they dislike to do, on pain of consequences which they dislike still more. In no other sense is there logically any obligation whatever in his system." The sovereign is only justified by power; "if resistance is successful and the sovereign loses his power, he 'ipso facto' ceases to be sovereign & his subjects cease to be subjects" - This is shown when Hobbes admits that an outside enemy defeats the Sovereign the covenant is dissolved. Sabine puts this even more clearly when he says 'Since all human behaviour is motivated by individual self-interest, society must be regarded as a means to this end. ..... the power of the state and the authority of the laws are justified only because they contribute to the security of individual human beings, and there is no rational ground for authority except the anticipation that these will yield a larger individual advantage than their opposites.' In fact morals and conscience are identical with self-interest and one is, according to Sabine's interpretation, only obliged to obey as long as one considers the alternative worse. The alternative, according to Hobbes, is anarchy and only the threat of death, chains or imprisonment are worse than this, hence one is obliged to do anything which a Sovereign with power commands except undergo imprisonment and death when one can resist. But Sabine, interpreting more broadly, would suggest that each man can balance the benefits to be derived from obeying or not obeying and that, if one did not have such a mania for security as Hobbes, or unreasoning dread of the supposed brutish "state of nature" which loomed over him, one could often decide, and be justified in deciding, not to obey.

Oakshott attacks this "self interest" theory thus. "The error that lies in attributing to him a theory of political obligation in terms of self-interest; ... is an error, not because such a theory cannot be extracted from his writings, but because it gives them a simple formality which nobody supposes them to possess." Oakshott then suggests another theory. He divides obligation into three kinds, physical, rational and moral. 'Superior power (causing fear) ... puts a man into bonds and therefore obliges him. Further a man may be prevented from willing a certain action because he perceives that its probable consequences are damaging to himself .... In this sense, men are said to be 'obliged' to will the mutual covenant; it is a course of action 'dictated' by fear and reasoning." "But", Oakshott continues "the sort of obligatoriness that is attributed here to the rational perception of consequences, is of course, nothing to do with these perceptions being natural or rational laws ... they oblige merely 'in foro interno'." These then are physical and rational obligation, and are the kind of obligation Sabine speaks of. But now Oakshott goes a stage further and brings in 'moral' obligation. 'This", he says "is the effect of authority. The sole cause of moral obligation is the will of the Sovereign authority ... I am morally bound to obey the will of this Sovereign ... Because I have authorized this Sovereign .... and am bound by my own act.' 'Moral obligation is (in fact) being bound by the law (will) of the authorized Sovereign; there is no other law independent of this law, and no other moral obligation independent of this obligation." Certain implications of this are stressed by Oakshott: 'The covenant does not itself create a moral obligation ..... on the other hand, this and any other covenant may become morally obligatory if and when the Sovereign authority commands its observation; ... moral obligation is not based upon self-interest ... self-interest is a rational, not a moral obligation; ... it does not spring from the superior power of the Sovereign authority. Right is never identical with power, and the Sovereign that had no Right (that is, no authorization*) could bind only physically, not morally)" This argument's weakness is shown by the case of a victorious invader who becomes Sovereign without any special authorization, but whose new subjects are obliged, according to Hobbes, just as much as they were to their old more 'authorized' Sovereign.

* - what does this mean?

Warrender, tho' rather abstruse and not entirely convincing, agrees that Oakshott's introduction of a completely seperate 'moral' obligation is not justified by the text. He says of Oakshott's rational type of obligation ... "we have not been able to find evidence in Hobbes' doctrine of a type of obligation which meets the formula required and which can be distinguished from moral obligation as he conceived it." In the place of O's three kinds of obligations ... we have discovered only two basic kinds,

(15)

HOBBES (ii)

physical obligation, which controls involuntary actions, and moral obligation which controls voluntary actions." I would dispute the use of the word 'moral' here, unless we consider rationally pursued self-interest a 'moral' concept. Warrender points out another weakness in Oakshott's interpretation, and it seems also in Hobbes! "To the question 'Why am I morally bound to obey the will of the Sovereign?' Hobbes answers 'Because I have authorized him,' but as to why the subject should be morally obliged to obey the command of a sovereign authorized by him, has to be regarded as an unanswerable question or as a dogma." The political covenant itself does not make any conduct morally obligatory, but it becomes morally obligatory if and when the sovereign commands its observance. On this view Warrender points out "little can be said to the citizen who sees a prospect of a successful rebellion, for the only reason, if any, that can be given as to why it is morally wrong for him to withdraw his obedience to a will that he has authorized, is that the sovereign has commanded such obedience; and this would not appear to be a sufficient reason." From this Warrender goes on to argue the necessity of moral obligation in the state of nature - "in foro interno."

Leo Strauss returns to the Sabine view that Hobbes equates morality with the desire for preservation. Hence "what man does from fear of death, ... alone is fundamentally just ... Hobbes' last word is the identification of conscience with the fear of death which permits a systematic differentiation between justice and injustice, between moral and immoral motives." This appears to be true to Hobbes, but also an absurd conception and Strauss's next remark "that this makes possible the distinction between the attitude of the unjust man who obeys the laws of the State for fear of punishment ie without inner conviction & the attitude of the just man, who for fear of death, and therefore from inner conviction ... obeys the laws of the State" seems to me an example of Hobbes' obsessive fear, a fear which at the end overcame him at death and covered his mind, with fear of hell's tortures, leading to a doctrine of fear as the basis of all morality which was carried to absurd lengths. Our minds react against this obsession which painted such a lurid picture of the alternative to obedience and we echo Bertrand Russell's view that "A State may ... be so bad that temporary anarchy seems preferable to its continuance, ..."

Out of this tangle at least one fact has emerged, there was an inner conflict within Hobbes. He had what Berlin calls a "negative" view of liberty, which meant that he agreed that some portion of human existence must remain independent of the sphere of social control if man's central nature or essence was not to be 'degraded' or denied, but he had to reconcile this with an all-powerful Sovereign. In fact he faced the problem of trying to set up two all-powerful Sovereigns, the public one and the ultimate right of the individual to order his life so that he would exist and be able to seek felicity. A man cannot, as he so rightly says, have two masters, hence his ultimate failure for by a logical extension of the powers of both Sovereigns there will be an ultimate clash; a man will be forced either to disobey his Sovereign or his own innermost nature. He may indeed be forced to kill that Sovereign, rather than be killed. It is in this way that Hobbes is ultimately an individualist.

But what does he actually say on the duty of obedience? "Covenants entred into by fear, in the condition of meer Nature, are obligatory." Why? Presumably because it is in the interest of a person not to break the law, for then he would return to that barbarous state. For one should constantly consider "that the estate of Man can never be without some incommodity or other; and that the greatest, that in any forme of Gov't can possibly happen to the people in generall, is scarce sensible in respect of the miseries, and horrible calamities, that accompany a Civill Warre, ..." This is in fact the self-interest argument. And it is repeated when Hobbes says "because preservation of life being the end, for which one man becomes subject to another, every man is supposed to promise obedience to him, in whose power it is to save, or destroy him." This was strengthened in Hobbes eyes because, without any empirical basis, he maintained that the good of the Sovereign and subject were identical. "For the good of the Sovereign and People, cannot be seperated. It is a weak Sovereign, that has weak Subjects; and a weak People whose Sovereign wanteth Power to rule them at his will." Ideally perhaps, but in practice this is, obviously, not always true.

cf. Rousseau

At times Hobbes lays down a harsh absolutism. "There can happen no breach of Covenant on the part of the Sovereign; and consequently none of his Subjects, by any pretence of forfeiture, can be freed from his Subjection." And "because every Subject is by this Instution (of the Sov'n) Author of all the Actions, and Judgements of the Sov'n instituted; it followes, that whatsoever he doth, it can be of no injury to any of his Subjects ...." He concludes that "it appeareth ... both from Reason and Scripture, that the Sovereign Power, ... is as great, as possibly men can be imagined to make it." In practice this means, obviously, that men should obey in every detail, for ultimately it will be to their own benefit. In fact obedience should apparently be unlimited for "though of so unlimited a Power, men may fancy many evill consequences, yet the consequences of the want of it which is perpetuall warre... are much worse." "Unto thine own self be true" is turned into a moral measuring tape, ~~and~~ when "self" means the basic desire and right to live. Nearly always this prompts us to obey the Sovereign, but there is, as has been pointed out, an inner citadel which cannot be assaulted. ~~The fi~~

The first and ultimate natural right "is the Liberty each man hath, to use his own power, as he will himselfe, for the preservation of his own Nature; that is to say, of his own Life; and consequently of doing anything which in his own Judgement & Reason, he shall conceive to be the aptest means thereunto." The Covenant is artificial, set up by man for his own good "for no man giveth, but with intention of Good to himself", hence if the Sovereign is threatening his inner self by chains, imprisonment or death he has a right, and a duty to his essential self to resist, hence "a covenant not to defend my selfe from force, by force, is always voyd." "for man by nature chooseth the lesser evil." In the case of such a threat not the subject, but the Sovereign, by betraying the purpose of his institution, dissolves the Covenant. This is a point Hobbes emphasizes. The Sovereign, tho' under no Covenant, is there for a certain purpose, if one likes on certain conditions, which if unfulfilled dissolve the Covenant. "The Obligation of Subjects to the Sovereign, is understood to last as long, and no longer, than the power lasteth, by which he is able to protect them. For the right men have by Nature to protect themselves, when none else can protect them, can by no Covenant be relinquished... the end of Obedience is protection." It is interesting to note here an echo back to the Aristotelian conception that life is not ~~to~~ enough, that the State continues for the existence of good life, for Hobbes goes on to say that the Sovereign Power is instituted for the procuration of the Safety of the people and safety means not a bare preservation "but also all other contentments of life."

~~In a sense~~ then we can say, then that a subjects duty of obedience is dictated by fear of the consequences of non-obedience, either immediate punishment or a reversion to the horrible state of nature. Again the subject can measure it by whether the State is fulfilling the purpose for which it was created. Here it is worth-while noting a comment of Strauss's: "The introduction of the new "resolutive-compositive" method of analysis into political philosophy presupposes the previous narrowing-down of the political problem, i.e. the elimination of the fundamental question as to the aim of the State. .... the new political science (of Hobbes) from the outset renounces all discussion of the fundamental, the most urgent question. "What is the purpose of the State?" The aim of the State is for him as a matter of course peace, i.e. peace at any price. The underlying presupposition is that (violent) death is the first and supreme evil." Unlike Aristotle, Hobbes failed to speculate, or rather assumed that he had, the final answer as, to the purpose of life. If we reject this basis, the view that life's purpose is to continue its existence and search for that elusive quality 'felicity', we reject the whole 'Leviathan'. If we accept this we can travel with him down the two roads of supreme individuality and supreme absolutism till they meet headlong.

I clearly took a lot of notes for the Hobbes essay – there are seventeen typed pages from various authors, including Sabine. There are also lecture notes from Keith Thomas's lectures, during the following next term.

As for Rousseau, my work was equally thorough. There are five pages of Gobbets, with some specific comments, but no general comment or mark. There are also over 20 pages of detailed notes from various authorities on Rousseau, and detailed notes on Isaiah Berlin's article on 'Two Concepts of Liberty'.

At some point I went beyond these set texts. There a number of notes on various authors in relation to an essay on 'To what extent was Marx the disciple of Hegel'. There are seven typed foolscap pages of notes from Wilson's 'To the Finland Station' which I particularly remember finding very exciting.

Finally, there were three sets of notes and an essay on 'How far were the teachings of the Utilitarians modified by J.S. Mill? There is the four page essay.

How far were the teachings of the Utilitarians altered by J.S. Mill?

Early Utilitarianism was largely an 'ad hoc' philosophy, a set of rules and principles laid down to fit the gravest needs of the time. Thus Ricardo's widely divergent views on the necessity for economic legislation can only be coordinated when applied to the practical problem of tariff on corn. As the younger Mill said, their theories and their practical ideas were dictated more by a love of efficiency than of liberty, what they wanted from their basic psychology and philosophy were scythes to cut away the legalistic, economic and political anachronisms and evils of their times. The psychological basis for their theories was worked out by James Mill long after Bentham had been using the felicific calculus for practical improvements - and we can say that it was John Stuart Mill who first attempted to give a philosophical explanation of the "greatest happiness" principle. While their preoccupation with the practical rather than the theoretical contributed enormously to contemporary improvement it did mean that as conditions changed during the century and new needs replaced the old their solution became increasingly unsatisfactory. It was John Stuart Mill's task, largely unconscious though it was, to break down the rigidity of the old system & to point a hesitant finger towards a far more complex and uncoordinated jumble of theories in politics, economics, psychology and justice. As the younger himself said "If I am asked what system of political philosophy I substituted for that which I had abandoned I answer no system - only a conviction that the true system was something much more complex than I had previously any idea of"

The basis, in theory, of Utilitarianism, was the felicific calculus. That a man is motivated by pain and pleasure and that these can be roughly measured. From this springs their morality - all actions are good which tend to happiness - their idea of government - government is a necessary evil which by allotting rewards and punishments coordinates & harmonises the interests of its subjects - their views of justice and of economics. And it was at that very root of the older utilitarianism that J.S. Mill struck. As Sabine points out, the undermining of the hedonistic calculus did not necessitate the overthrow of the 'greatest happiness' principle, for Mill stuck closely to that theory on ethical grounds while he rejected hedonism. The classic statement of the earlier hedonism is Bentham's remark 'Nature has placed mankind under the governance of two sovereign masters pain & pleasure

It is for them alone to point out what we ought to do, as well as determine what we shall do. On the one hand the standard of right & wrong, on the other, the chain of causes & effects, are fastened to their throne." Happiness is the end of life, it is the basis of morality, and it is measurable and only differing in quantity between different people – or as Bentham says "Quantity of pleasure being equal, pushpin is as good as poetry". It was here that J.S.Mill struck, and his admission that there was a qualitative as well as a quantitative difference in pleasure was the start of a comprehensive, tho' fragmented, refutation of the Benthamite arguments. His statement that its "better to be Socrates dissatisfied than a fool satisfied" is an expression of a conception of "moral character which is consonant with his own personal idealism" but thoroughly at variance with hedonism. In fact Mill was abandoning egoism and assumed, having won his freedom that social welfare is a matter of concern to all men of good-will, and regarded freedom, integrity, self-respect & personal distinction as intrinsic goods apart from their contribution to happiness." "The central moral idea in Mill's ethics" concludes Sabine "like Kant's, was really respect for human beings, the sense that they must be treated with a due regard for the dignity that a moral being deserves & without which moral responsibility is impossible" – this is far from a moral theory in terms only of a calculation of pleasures & pains.

The rejection of the basic hedonistic premiss had occurred early in J.S.Mill's life. After a breakdown in 1826 he had written "Those only are happy who have their minds fixed on some object other than their own happiness; on the happiness of others, on the improvement of mankind, followed not as a means, but as itself an ideal end. Aiming thus at something else, they find happiness by the way". His specific rejection of hedonism comes in his "Utilitarianism" when he tells us that if one of two pleasures is, "by those who are completely acquainted with both, placed so far above the other that they prefer it, even though knowing it to be attended with a greater amount of discontent, & would not resign it for any quantity of the other pleasure which their nature is capable of, we are justified in ascribing to the preferred enjoyment a superiority in quality, so far outweighing quantity as to render it, in comparison, of small account." Later he says "It is of importance not only what men do, but also what manner of men they are that do it" and no amount of juggling, though he does attempt this, will reconcile this with Bentham's pure amalgamation of virtue & the pursuit of happiness

(2) (16)

As has been said, the rejection of the felicific calculus did not necessitate the rejection of the "greatest happiness" principle. It merely allowed altruism in the pursuit of that 'greatest happiness' and gave man's actions some inherent morality beyond mere necessity. Man was no longer virtuous instinctively, but with the absorption of Kantian ideas through Coleridge, by exercising a self-imposed discipline.

The increasing need for discipline of some sort was apparent as J.S. Mill reached maturity. The 'laissez-faire' economics of Ricardo, the free-hand given to government by Bentham, countered on the other hand by a strict individualism which saw all government as evil and while allowing unlimited interference in theory recommended the minimum in practice – all these were breaking down before the changes during the C19. J.S. Mill saw that Utilitarianism would have to reconciled to a form of collectivism and some form of economic control was demanded to prevent inhumanity. On the reverse side he saw an increasing threat to the individual. He did not share his father's confidence in the power of reason and hence of education & he saw that democracy was not as simple to operate & as unbiased as the earlier Utilitarians had imagined. "When society is itself the tyrant" he warned "it practices a tyranny more formidable than many kinds of political oppression since ... it leaves fewer means of escape, penetrating more deeply into the details of life, enslaving the soul itself." The two of the great weaknesses of early utilitarianism, given the industrial & demographic changes of the C19 were "that as a social philosophy it had no conception of a social good, and its egoistic individualism made it look with suspicion on the validity of any such conception, when the total welfare of the community was becoming a principle object of concern, and as a political philosophy its theory of government was wholly negative, at a time when it was becoming inevitable that government should assume a larger responsibility for the general welfare"

J.S. Mill had broken its egoism – but how else did he adapt Utilitarianism to changing conditions?

Firstly he abandoned economic laissez faire ... but here he merely accepted the need for social legislation, probably on humanitarian grounds, with no clear theory of

J.N.H. 1962 Rabb (European History)

its justifiable limits. The trouble was that he never really analysed the relationship between freedom & responsibility. At times he retained the traditional view derived from Bentham that any compulsion or even any social influence is an abridgement of liberty. Yet he never supposed, as ~~the~~ his forbears had, that there could be any important freedom without law, and when he identified liberty with civilization he did not imagine that there could be civilization without society. He was making a tentative movement towards the idea, later expounded by Green, that the function of a liberal state in a free society is not negative but positive. That legislation may be a means of creating, increasing & equalizing opportunity & liberalism can impose no arbitrary limits upon it – though of course he laid supreme emphasis on the rights of personal liberty. He no longer thought government an absolute evil, for it was not merely, as it had been for the earlier Utilitarians, an instrument of coercion. With a more organic view of society, with a new-found realization of the psychological nature of society & the dependence of political upon social institutions he defended government not because it was efficient, but because, as with Rousseau, it could give man something he did not have before. The real argument for political freedom, he thought, is that it produces & gives scope to a high type of moral character. He thus opened up a whole new relationship between society & the individual.

His main contributions to political science were on the negative side a destruction of an unwieldy & rigid over-simplified ~~scheme~~ system – & on the positive a new & ethical respect for human beings; an acceptance of political & social freedom as itself a good, not because it contributed to an ulterior end but because freedom is the proper condition of a responsible human being; the conviction that liberty is not only an individual ~~but~~ good but also a social good, that to silence an opinion by force both does violence to the person who holds it & also robs society of the advantage it might have had from a free investigation & criticism of the opinion, and finally that the function of a liberal state is not negative but positive. Love of liberty is the connecting thread beneath his apparent contradictions – contradictions which are summed up by Dower when he says "J.S. Mill was an empirical philosopher who became almost an idealist, a Utilitarian who undermined the creed, a determinist who yearned to believe in freedom of the will, a hedonist who taught self-sacrifice, an individualist who became a kind of Socialist, a democrat who distrusted democracy, a rationalist who embraced a limited 'Theism.'" Here we see the transition between early & late Utilitarianism

Towards the end of the term, I started to work with Lady Clay on Tudor and Stuart history. I note that I went for a 'tute' with Lady Clay on 8th March, which is when we probably first met and she set me my first essay, which was titled 'Why was the opposition to Henry VIII's Reformation so exiguous?' The essay is dated 15 March. I have the essay of five and a half pages, with half a page of comments which I wrote after the supervision. There is no general comment or mark.

Lady Clay, the widow of Sir Henry Clay and daughter of A.L. Smith, sometime Master of Balliol College, was already in her seventies by the time I met her. She had been married first before the First World War and had over the years known many of the great Oxford historians and others. She was related to the Mitchisons and Mitfords and her son-in-law was the politician Peter Shore. I greatly enjoyed her company and after I returned to oxford to do a D.Phil. I would visit her in her flat in 121A Woodstock Road most weeks and she would fill me in on the oral history of Oxford. She was one of the teachers who were employed by Worcester College to fill in their teaching.

Probably the next essay, which I remember particularly enjoying, was also done this term. It was 'Discuss the strengths and weaknesses of the Elizabethan Church settlement and the changes in the meaning of Puritanism 1558-1640'. Again, there is no comment, but some notes I made on the supervision. I shall deal with the main part of the teaching for this paper under the summer term, when I recall that it took place.

*

This term was when I really became increasingly engaged with my work and was steadily spending an average of six or seven hours a day on it. I was also typing a good deal of my material, having bought a typewriter and learnt to touch-type. I was also increasingly filing my materials in various ways – including on small five by three cards – and also borrowing the extensive notes of Brian Harrison and starting to type out sections of them. It was also Brian who introduced me to the use of card indexes.

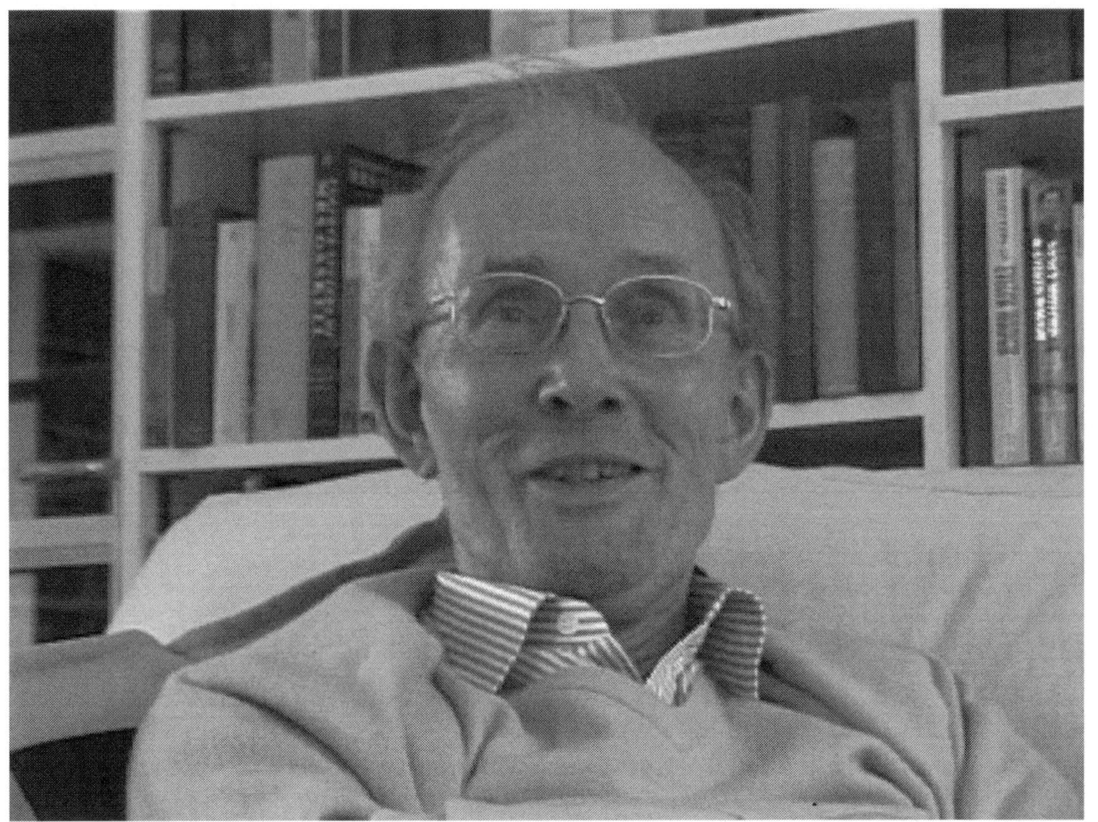

Sir Brian Harrison, fifty years later

Private Writing : Spring Term 1962

This was the term when I spent most effort on trying to write poetry and prose alongside my academic work.

<u>"Poetry and Painting" – a few reflections.</u>

I am increasingly convinced that an analogy between learning to paint and to write is highly fruitful. Firstly it exposes the temerity of those who launch straight into writing without a study of its principles and techniques. Painters, like musicians, spend laborious hours merely on the mechanical side of their art before they attempt to convey their vision to others. A violin must be thoroughly mastered before it can be used to interpret ideas, mood or feeling. How then can many of the modern 'beat' poets hope to convey their, no doubt burning and flashing thoughts, when they have never studied their materials? So much for the need. How is the study to be pursued?

The painters brush is the writers pen: his colours are the poet's images metaphors, similes and evocative words which give rich life to the skeleton of the argument: his shapes and form, the form (i.e. sonnet, stanza etc) rhythm and the relation between different parts of sentence and of the whole work. More minutely – light and shade, depth and dimension, movement and poise all have their equivalent in the written word.

From this we can deduce the sheer divisions of technique. We can also note that painters study the works of other great artists and that they learn to perfect their technique by methodical practice. If he is weak in his drawing of 'hands' he will spend considerable time drawing and re-drawing them. It is from the heights of mastered technique that the painter sets out to explore his own individual path, not from the valley-bottom of inexperience. One of the greatest innovators in Poetic diction, Wordsworth, studied Milton and Shakespeare and even copied their style before he shook himself free.

Apart from the merely practical benefits of such an analogy there are rich aesthetic and intellectual rewards. By a more penetrating search into the principles of one branch of art we shed light onto the others which hitherto had remained dark. For example a study of the technique and ideals of the English Romantic poets throws considerable light on their contemporary musicians. The main intellectual result is a heightened critical faculty: the main aesthetic one a keener appreciation of all forms of beauty, not merely of that portrayed in the works of man, "but of life and nature" – of man and in the world around.

> "As imagination bodies forth
> The forms of things unknown, the poet's pen
> Turns them to shapes and gives to airy nothing
> A local habitation and a name" W.S.

<u>View from Worcester Library Oxford 21/1/62</u>[1]

A sea-gull catching a flash of silver on its back high above the winter trees on an absolutely clear, sunny morning
Drone of aero-planes, clatter of builders with their drills.
The grey bellies of heavier clouds: the complete whiteness of windrift, wiped, whisked clouds.
Setting sun thro' black winter trees. Sky clear – except for wispy clouds. Dense mass of black trees – with hardly any green stain left on right. Ridge of roof on left. Sun setting thro' the net of a tree. Where the sun is – none of the smaller branches can be seen for the

[1] This must have been written in the Old Library, which has magnificent views over the court and grounds, not the working library at the top of the stairs.

golden glow – only the great twisted, nobbly trunk & main branches forking up & then breaking forth into a finer and finer mesh of small twigs wriggling like little black eels into the sky.
Ones eye is magnetized as it dies, pure yellow with not a touch of red. Even the main trunk is being eaten into by the gold fire.

– and now only lit up by the after-glow every branch rides clear in the yellow sky – and for the first time we notice the wind rocking the branches.

There is a small three by five inch index card titled 'Reflections' and dated 23rd January 1961[2]

Much of the unhappiness at Oxford arises from a conflict between the undergraduates and the world around. Those who send them here, relatives and even scholarship committees, have accepted the standards of the world – materialism, bigotry, contentment with the second best – in fact compromised. Youth from its idealism, from its intuitive perception of what is 2nd-rate, and from its enthusiasm resists the efforts (often unwilling) of the tutors to push on them the tighter harness of more work, more competitive exams and the general 'get-ahead' atmosphere. Much of the resentment against accepted standards is unconscious, a deep exasperation and disillusionment which often stifles any creativity in the more sensitive, and results in escapism (films, women, drink, talk) and a general façade of detached cynicism in which everything genuine, beautiful or fervent, every religious, political or intellectual effort is greeted by an elaborate yawn or a string of nick-names.

What is to be done? The basis probably of the problem is that it is not attacked deeply enough – no attempt is given to provide a constructive plan, or a sound basis of ideals – new, all-engaging ideals – at the start of a boy's career here. He drifts.

One other observation (on a card) is headed 'Impressions on a wet (Sunday) in Oxford, Jan '62. This was probably the following Sunday, 28th January.

A cold, rain-gusting morning when the drops scud down the Sunday-morning-bare, streets, slide under cars and then leak out again. When the water oozes up thro' the worn shoes of the tramp and his thread-bare coat clings limply to the shivering body; when the water forms little dams of sodden paper in the gutters and when the dirt, grit and sand on the pavements is patterned by miniature tidal-waves. When cars, corrugated iron and the old grey, weather-beaten cloister drip dank, slimy water: When the happy raise their faces and let the clean kiss of the wind brush away their tear-stained cheeks: when the sad and weary vainly try to thrust away the weight of the burdening rain which slides down thro' the grey air, somehow side-steps their umbrellas and finds its home on their spine; when young couples huddle under umbrellas; when the old huddle in doorways waiting for shining red busses. When life is wary and wet and wonderful and wet.

I was clearly experimenting in form and observation, with a view to serious writing – putting into practice the notes on poetry and painting quoted above (at the end of the Winter vacation).

On meeting a pretty girl (Eldyth) – Matter and Mirage. 30/1/62

You – who with the careless grace of
Silken, eye-veiling hair, with direct grey eyes
Calm, motherly hands; whose smiles and pursed
Lips can capture, can break a heart – and
Will you too, pick me up to play with
Me with your looks? And will I fall and
Grovel in your careless service – and hurl

The glories, the pleasant pain of an
Unattained vision, the energy and the desire
For an all-consuming fire which will burn and
Fuse my soul into a new & docile
Shape? Will I in one swift moment forget,
And let fade the sublime, the ecstatic vision,
And satisfy in a more real, yet poorer
And meaner way the wishes of my heart?
I do not love her, I see her now
A pretty girl, bright & gay. Will I one
Day lie sleepless; see her beauty in the
Stars and in the mists, echo her name
And chime forth her charms? What, and
How will it transform? Is she the shape
That will fit the dream – or will it die?

On an index card dated 2nd February [Friday] I have written:

PAIN: On a little girl in hospital (aged about 5)

I had been sitting playing my guitar to the other children when I was asked to come to play to a little girl over in a cot by herself. As I approached, all I could see were the bed clothes humped up – then I saw they were kept up by a mettle-grid to keep them off the living flesh which lay beneath.

The great shock was the girls face. It was not ravaged by spasms; it was not deformed or prematurely aged and wrinkled like another little girl I had seen; it was beautiful and fresh. But this made the clouding in the large, enquiring eyes the more terrible. Every feature was perfect, the hair in a fringe of brown over a smooth, unwrinkled brow – the mouth soft and made to smile – and yet no smile would come: for across her waist was a great brown, scabby scar.

She was a child who should have played in the courts of the sun – who should have danced after the Lamb of God across the "pastures green" and here she was – silent, uncomprehending why she suffered and twisted on a rack – was she bitter. Why…?

Two days later I went to Christ Church cathedral for a service and wrote (in green ink on the usual cards) the following:

Thoughts – Temporality. 4/2/62 (on the next card to the above, headed 'Thoughts – In a mood of melancholy-joy')

"this unintelligible world"? Perhaps.

It was certainly lightened when I went to 'Sung Eucharist' in Christchurch this morning. There the drifting notes of the trebles, intangible, pure as moonbeams relaxed me 'till – like Wordsworth I was in "that serene and blessed mood … when laid rest by the power of harmony" – but by a strange occurrence the product of this mood (Wordsworth "we see into the life of things") preceded the calm – or rather preceded Christchurch. For as I left the College to go there I felt deep in me the temporality of the towers and houses. I saw them as a shadow, a shifting scum on the surface of the world, which would dissolve like Shakespeare's "temples, palaces etc" – and even the earth hard, spinning its "diurnal course, with rocks & stones and trees" seemed a thing of mist. Only the spirit, that is the Platonic essence, the immortal being in man seemed real, and through the streets I felt the presence of gigantic forces beautiful or "terrible as an army with banners" prowling or singing beneath the cold grey winters sky and acting thro' the mechanical, stilted, puffed up little animals who strut, and cry and laugh away their twisted lives, chained.

On the same day I went to a concert, which included Brahms' 'Requiem'. I wrote the following short reaction to the experience.

Brahms Requiem Concert

During this the highest and the lowest emotions battled within me – it was an epitome of the struggle between spirit and flesh, between the sordid cesspool of lust and the pure untrammelled yearnings of my spirit. In the balcony there was a person trailing his hand over the side – all I could see was the hand clawing, or waving time over the white stucco scrolls and figures that insidious as ivy formed a cancerous growth on the clean lines of every part of the building. The hand wandered aimless, convulsively clutching at knob or leaf when the music grew tense to the sawing of stretched violins, then relaxing and moving on in the deep lament of the soprano. So my mind was searching, to be suddenly made rigid by the triumphant climax of a thunderous march and then emancipated from the rigidifying shock of the music it moved on, searching for?

St Augustine said "You are restless until you find your rest in him" – is this the deepest spring of the hard, damned-up feeling inside me; the tension and the "weary weight of all this ...[the rest is missing]

On Sunday 11th February there is another card:

WINDY NIGHT – Sunday, Oxford
Windy winter's night – chalk faces of the women waiting furtively under gas lights – their coats blown hard against their bodies. Paper & leaves blown in the gutters & dust & grit into the eyes & hair. The smell of chips on the air – the flapping of macs. The huddled group of bandsmen playing in the shelter of a building watched by one or two curious pedestrians.

The sound of the wind. The moon racing behind slight cloud. Two lovers huddled together in a shadow. The hard lights, hard shadows, hard lines & harsh wind blowing the people like leaves. Only the soft colours of a stain-glass church window and the sound of voices singing inside add any warmth to the drab vacuum – along which hollow, masked & taut figures twitter, scurrying & swooping, like the dirt & filthy, used scraps of paper.

On Friday 16th February I wrote on a small index card.

Thoughts on the nuisance of straying thoughts when studying Hobbes.
Ideas burrowing about in the brain like busy moles – poking their noses up inquisitively when I am trying to work, and throwing up heaps of earth to break the clean symmetry of my labours. They are not maggots, turning putrid in my mind, for I feed them and nurse them with images, ideas & poetry – but must they intrude when not wanted? Can one never pen them in; will they always lead me down 'White-rabbit' holes to warm caverns where nestle their offspring, naked and brown as the earth they eat, or further deep into the delved earth where lie hidden-caves of enchantment, lit by the pulsing heat of the earth's fire-core. Here where I stand in awe and look around at a dazzling world of stalactites and glittering lakes, fashioned by the skilful hands of dwarfs and beautiful with the encrusting of precious stones. Must my mind hearken to the slow music of the great river that runs through these caverns [Coleridge] when it must be clear of distraction as it toils up the wounding flint-road of dusty Hobbes?

The same day, 16 February, there is another card.

OUR MOODS: A hypothesis.

They may be likened to tides. Freud has based everything on sex. If this is so one can say that our frustration, ebbing and flowing in man as well as women, dictates all our other moods – our depressive self-analysis, our appreciation of sensual pleasure, even our religious enthusiasm. Can those periods known as 'spiritual deserts' be a re-action to the state of the tide – a tide which seems moved by some great power like a moon – but power which we have not traced. When the tide is on the turn and is just creeping over the furthest sandbanks we are most happy. Later it begins to eddy faster, filling every channel, swinging in pincer movements round every "pregnant bank" and immersing it, carrying all before it until it batters on the rocks of our personality, till the air is fully of the shrill wine, hurtling spray, and we are dizzy with longing, – this is the time when poetry, fanaticism, elation, art, can be skimmed from the surface. The time when the patient poet, like the angler, feels the deep tug, and then the steady run of an idea and knows that he must battle to bring it to land. The time of frenzy, of supreme joy lasts but a while. The tide oozes out – leaving a high-water mark of self-disgust, of brackish slime over everything. The joy is gone – instead the stale-salt tang, the dead fish and the rotting jelly-fish greet the wanderer on the long sands. Now is the time of melancholy when life stretches long, level, bare, crossed by meaningless footprints. Is this an explanation?

On a card dated 16/2/61 Winter Sunset

A foreboding sunset. Great masses of purple cloud rent in places by a savage wind & showing through delicate pinks, greens & golds. As seen through the naked black winter branches. The pink is like the pink of the 'rock' one buys at seaside results. The bluey-green like the sea on shallow white sand with sun shining. The gold has a touch of red – blood-gold – and the whole is melting and moving, slipping and changing rapidly under a lowering sky. A pageant of funeral pomp for the dying sun. All the colours, blend & fuse – but light blue is streaked by light pink: it is as if one hand dipped a water colour brush into various colours and let them run together.
At times, there are only small gaps of light through the dark mass, then it opens like a flapping tent door and a mass of evening blue & pink is seen.

I seem to have cheered up a little the next day for on 17th February there is a rough and fair copy (on cards) of a poem.

In the Style of an Elizabethan Love lyrick

Shall I compare thee to the sun's first ray
That lights the woods and hills so green?
Shall I compare thee to the break of day
That gently smiles e'er it is seen?
Shall I compare thee to the sunset sky
Slow ling'ring in the golden west?
Shall I compare thee to the soft wind's sigh
That strokes the blackbirds summer nest?
Shall I compare thee to the dewdrenched flowers
That sparkle in the dancing dawn?
Shall I compare thee to a springtime shower
That weeps upon the grassy lawn?
In all of these, thou hast a part

And all of them a part in thee;
And yet my love, my dear, true, heart
Thou art the Queen of all I see.

I cannot remember whether the above was addressed to anyone in particular, but it may have been to the same girl as another written the following day, Sunday 18th February.

In the style (?) of Elizabethans: To Joanna

The dark, drear, night is turned to dappled day;
The hard, flint, road is lined with mosses soft.
My heart wept blindly, seeking its single way
But thou found me, and bore me up aloft.
The cold bright world is filled with warmth from thee;
The false, taut, faces break with fresh-grown smiles;
As, deepdown, moves the everlasting sea –
So moves my heart, when laid to rest by thee.
My lone, bleak, castle stands in mountains grey;
As one, lone, house amidst the forests gloom;
But close, safe, secret, moves they spirit gay
A light, warm, love, to fill my inmost room.

Following the theme of being distracted from Hobbes of a week earlier, on 22nd February I wrote the following.

On looking out of a window in v. early spring.[1]

Smells of a spring day – the burning of last years wood,
The fresh earth breaking under the furrow, the crisp
Smell of a clean year; purified and purged by
Winter – stirs me with strange longings. A cold
Wind plays with the gaunt trees, but the sticky
Buds swell, and blindly break forth almost visibly.
Winter tires to hold spring down, but between
His fingers little flowers and shoots press up.
Listen – you can hear the sap rising, you can hear
The gush of life – the whirling, thrusting force tearing
Through the bowels of the earth, while the afternoon
Sun smiles nervously before it is pushed roughly
Away by clouds and tucked in its bed by evening.
Try and watch the Spring and it stops, like a
Child creeping up in 'Blind Man's Buff'. Yet one
Knows that it is coming inevitably closer and one
Expects at any moment that it will pounce
On one with a shout of child-like glee and
Hug you in triumph. Take a last look at
The patterns, the naked clean limbs of the
Trees, catching the sky in nets of twigs. Take a
Last look at the brown earth, like an open
Wound. Soon the sweet succulence of summer will

[1] Composed when supposed to be working on Hobbes.

Have donned her green and gold dress. This
Restlessness moves in the blood – a strange yearning
Which lifts my spirit out into the sun-patched
Lawn, where the ducks whisper anxiously, conscious
Of the approach of an enormous force, of a
Power which will lift and hurl them into a
Second of ecstasy, a second when every moment,
And meaning of their summer dabbling, of their
Search for food in slimy shallows – of their
Mud and water, grass and bread-crumb, life
Is swept into a whirl-wind meaning – gathering
All into a second of infinity.

The Ducks know, yet bound and manacled by stronger bounds than iron – by self-respect, environment and perhaps a little, by love, we watch through the window and turn away and sigh. And continue our work, so that we may gain more self-respect, and a more-shackling environment, and stare through an even thicker pane of glass at the meaningless, useless, purposeless, satisfaction of futility and fruitfulness!

On 4th March 1962, I wrote what is perhaps a rough poem. I shall use the original version, but if there are significant changes in the fair copy, these are added in square brackets.

It is headed with a phrase from Wordsworth "The World is too much with us "[getting and begetting we lay waste our powers…]"

Well, what of it? What if the world and all its loveliness
All that poets have wrung in ecstasy from the jealous hours
If all the precious secrets – sounds, smells, loves and jests
Of the sick sad world will end?
Well, what if Shakespeare
Spoke in vain of unaltered love, if every triumph
[If Milton dreamt blindly, and Wordsworth wandered lost]
Of the human mind, every work of genius is the chance
Compilation of atoms? Can it matter that our brief lives
Beat blindly, as purposeless as a struggling moth against a light?
What if men go mad, hanging over the immeasurable void
What if cancer bites the bones and the leper festers
Unattended? Who cares if men sit gloating on their little
Hoardes while babies die in hunger, or the sick beggar
Grovels in some Eastern street for a coin from an American
Visitor? Take hence your simpering charities – for the world
Is dying. God is dead man's life is sucked from him.
But still he goes on, empty, but feeling bloated on his
Emptiness – as a starved child's belly distends with
Nothingness. And who has killed the purpose of the world?
Is it Science – can knowledge beat the brains of its
Maker? Can the One True Light be dimmed by a dusty
Mirror of itself? Then is it philosophy? Has men's minds,
Restored by the warmth that spread from Italy, grown
Alive and thrown off the coat, the cloak of religion
That kept it warm when the world was cold when Rome
Was Gone? You say what of it? You wonder dimly why
The 'suicide–rate' goes up. You murmur depreciatingly
When you hear of immorality – and sigh over another strike.

You cannot understand why mental illness afflicts our youth
Like some great second visitation of the Black Death
You cannot understand the rebelliousness of youth – or its
Apathy. You do not see why our favourite reading is "Mad".
I would sing you a song of beauties gifts;
I could joy with you at the glories of love;
I could escape into the fairy world of the Television and the Radio.
But instead I escape, I retreat into a reality of music & poetry.
For only great artists seem to know that there was an
Absolute – they alone seemed to touch the ground – to
Feel the solidness of the absolute beneath the shifting, yielding
Structure of life. So I escape, I retreat to light a candle
From them, to warm my soul at their heart before
My shivering, naked, baby spirit is frozen in the uncertain
Winds & bitter cynicism. The kind hypocrisy & gentle
Unconcern of a world of dead souls, of men who every day
Watch others die, suffer & live faithless, purposeless lives & do
Nothing – who condition themselves to cease to care.
And why should we care if it all means nothing?
If destruction, the incarceration of – not five hundred
Screaming factory workers, – not five thousand tormented
[five hundred Bradford workers...]
Passengers on some great blazing ships, – not some
Five million shrunken, silent Jews, but five thousand
Million in a screaming, blazing world, is hanging over us
And we muddle on?
[Millions on a blazing world along with every work
Of wonder & beauty they had found there
Or created; this is hanging over us – I Youth's
Bitterness, & the fear in the corner of its eye
Surprising? Ours is a blighted generation. The
Buds are withered by frost before they burst.]

No need to panic you say. No need to get emotional,
Man has always muddled through. Quite sane, much the best
Attitude I agree. But can you be surprised at the waste
Of spirit – at the moral drainage? Can you now understand
The pale faces of youth? "What would you do if
You only had 3 days to live" – they ask one at
Examinations. Ask the world what it does. Especially
Our philosophers lead the way, they place
Stakes for us in the pit of death. The Oracle
Of the age speaks...]
As man's mind has carefully been taking away
All the feather cushions, at the other side of the
Jump. The Oracle speaks "I believe when I die I shall be dust" – can we be surprised when the
Masses, listen to the Voice of the Philosopher and
Join their chorus – then set forth in the desperate
Unhappy pursuit of happiness. Don't get worked
Up you say – you are young, when you grow up...
When you see the world as it really is. Oh I know
I will compromise and then I will turn and be
Unable to understand my children – for they thank the
Lord, are born with soul's whether we have let them

Die or not, or fight to nourish them. Oh Lord
Help is in that fight – for the world does not
Even realize that there is a fight.
[For, blessed be God, they are born with soul's
Whether we wish to save them from this agony
Or not: And each one of them has to fight
For himself to nourish & save his
Spirit. And in that fight they must
Turn to something outside this
World, something forgotten by the dead world,
Something perceived as the heart of reality
By the great artists of all times; for
If they turn into themselves or out to
The world, they will die!]

The following day I tried to avoid the miseries by way of escapism. I have another two small filing cards dated 5th March.

<u>The Hebrides. Written in longing.</u>

To where shall we flee? Can you escape still?
Then come with me; skim, swallow-soul to the enchanted lands
The haunted isles of the North where solitude sings.
Smell the rich brown peat in the summer heat,
Smell the salted rocks, the sea-weed sands,
The straying smoke and the sting of spray.
Reach with me into the heart of that wild land
And bring back peace. The peace of
A lone kestrel circling high – taut winged in the wind
Above a mountain peak; the quiet of
An inland moor, where blue lochs
Lie unripplingly still on summer days
Blue as amethysts, frilled with velvet-green weeds
In a setting of purple heather; the stillness
Of a summer's evening on the long
Trembling sands, under the clear, burning-bright, air;
The deep calm on the face of an old man
Watching the gulls, as he fills his pipe, seated
On a little harbour-wall. When your soul screams, and
The world screams insanely in return, turn
Your face to that veiled land, lift the veil
To reveal her trembling beauty –dream
Of the wild, sweet, moors, the pounding seas on
A stormy day – the screech of gulls
The sadness of a curlew – and the ribbon
Road winding, single, through the misty and
Musical miles of the faery Isles.

As with some of my spring writing in the Lakes, I wrote about the frustration of waiting for spring to take firm hold and lead into summer, as in this last piece under Hilary term. On 5th March I wrote on a couple of cards.

<u>Spring & Winter – Impatience at seeing snow.</u>

Out of a leaden sky, snow drifts down through the contorted trees. It thinly spreads on grass & branches – but melts on the paths. Quick gusts of wind catch & stream it along the side of the old buildings; it is tipped by a side-wind and grazes to a halt; a second's rest before it vanishes. Why now when the shoots spring forth, eager for summer, do you still flood down onto this Sunday-still world? When, oh, when will the wild rush of spring leap clear from the pool of nature like an iridescent trout? The battle was nearly won – spring with its green banners rampant, and insignia of white on green marched proudly in the distance. The dim drums of desire sounded from the depths of the earth and echoed restless in our hearts – as the wild goose, tamed for a time by man – hears the call of the south and longs to be free. So, chained, Spring bleeds white to escape winter's vice – she is stretched taught on a rack of ice – but her spirit will not break. The inevitable urge of resurrection – the irresistible longing for fruition – for escape from the winter womb drags and strains at the loosening fetters. March – mad with the fever of youth – lifts the trumpet to his lips – soon it will sound and the great tournament, the ordered pageantry of Spring and Summer – the music of a thousand blended voices – the harmony of a thousand crusted colours on a field of cloth of green will rise, passionate as a love on a lute, glorious in green and gold, forgetful of the brown, the white and the black which like some dark, perilous chapel saw the birth of a summer of light. How can this beauty be? And how can it not be? When, when will you come?

A week after I wrote another poem, dated 12/3/62

<u>After meeting Judy twice.</u>

Calmness fills my restless heart,
Its loneliness is gone,
The winter, frosted, bare and numb
Has changed to delicate Spring
Not the passionate wholeness of Tristan's love
Not the burning ardour of Abelard
But the first delicate tip
Of a flower which pushes up
And one day may blossom rich & precious
The soul's sad sobbing for its lonely self,
The craving for a beauteous maid,
Are over, and the joy and calm
Before love starts are here.
As a waterfall seems poised before cascading,
As the sun pauses a second before rising,
As a bird flutters delicately before landing,
As a bee hovers before entering the succulent flower,
So poised, hesitant, clear yet confused,
I wait ready to dive into the enveloping
Waters of love.

It was during this term that I decided to write a few poems in the style of Dylan Thomas. Although I like his poetry, I felt that the enthusiasm of one of my friends was too extreme and I suggested that if I wrote some poems in his style, my friend would not be able to differentiate these from a selection of his other poems. I examined some of his poetry and isolated some of his favourite words and images, and compiled them into a free-flowing set of poems.

The resulting poems are, to a certain extent, deliberately meaningless. Yet I think they are worth putting in not only as an example of an exercise I undertook (voluntarily), but because despite their derivative nature, they give glimpses of my thought and observations – admittedly in a very indirect way.

One poem consists in two versions: I shall take the corrected version.

<u>"And I heard the dead blood working…"</u>

And I heard the dead blood working in the womb,
Spinning through the seconds of time's iron entrails;
Ribbing the red ghosts of the sea with sinews
Of itching salt. Thorny fires twisted my thighs,
Lighting the roots of my secret dreams and
Flaying to a fever the spindrift sun's gloating eye.

Sea-drift slime oiled the world's sap,
Driving love and grafting it to forked time.
Death shrouded, my flesh sucked the skinless worm,
The maggot and the slug that twists in the hair-bone;
Spinning ever nearer the apple-green veins of Christ
Into a cloudy glory of the skies.
[the last two lines a tribute to Marlowe? 'See where Christ's blood streams across the firmament'?]

Men-mad, I struggled in the twisted gut of my loins;
Hatching demons from marrow-mould and windily
Waving a word-wand over my actions. But time
Teemed in the grass of my brain, echoing
Over the rich vinelands of the thirsty stars
Fusing the fire of the skull into black blood.

<u>"Here in this spring…"</u>

Here in this spring, stars float along the void;
Here in this ornamental winter
Down pelts the naked weather;
This summer buries a spring bird.

Symbols are selected from the years'
Slow rounding of four seasons' coasts,
In autumn teach three seasons' fires
And four birds' notes.

I should tell summer from the trees, the worms
Tell, if at all, the winter's storms
Or the funeral of the sun;
I should learn spring by the cuckooing,
And the slug should teach me destruction.

A worm tells summer better than the clock,
The slug's a living calendar of days;
What shall it tell me if a timeless insect
Says the world wears away?

Lilting house grass was green

Lilting house, grass was green, the windfall light,
The happy yard, golden, foxes barked clear and cold,
The sabbath rang slowly.

Fire green as grass.
As I rode to sleep the owls were bearing the farm away,
Walking warm, house high hay,
Green & golden
Lamb white
Swallow thronged
The childless land
Sang in my chains like the sea.
The mustard-seed sun
Switchback sea

A square of sky sags over
The golden ball spins out of the skies
The scythe-sided thorn.

Another version was:

I slept windowless, strongly soldered to the
Tender world, and woke 'neath a patchwork quilt
Under a square of sky that sags over, and
Clutches the golden ball that spins out of the skies.
Rank, worm-warm earth, drank my breath
And snuggled close against me, through seed
And root I felt the inmost fire, fanning a
Windfall light which dies to the clear-veined
Moon. Foxes bark clear over the
Lilting, house-high hay and the owl is abroad.
Shadows slide into place slyly – the night is near
The night for the itch of love, flowers forth.

I was amused to find that my friend was quite unable to detect which were the poems by Dylan Thomas, and which by myself.

I also tried to write a poem in the style of T.S.Eliot. I was reading 'The Four Quartets', which I tended to read every year for some years. My favourite, which I read at that time, was 'The Four Quartets', and I started this exercise by copying out several snatches from that work, for example:

'Present, past & future,
Footfalls echo
Memory. Dust – rose-leaves
Dry the pool, dry concrete, brown edged. Drift of the stars
A time for the wind to break the loosened pane
Figures dauncing, which showeth concorde
Earth feet, loam feet.
Living, dead'

My poem was:

When patterns dissolve in timelessness
Perhaps time will dissolve timelessness.
And our fleshless faith will reel
'Neath the region of the summer stars –
Where the dust settles on the hollow moon.
Bone of man & beast likewise melt
In the mirage of a dry, sandy, pool
Signifying nothing. The vibrant air is
Filled with patterns on a leafy afternoon
When figures dance on the dappled bank
But grey in the winter's grip the wind
Fuses into an unbroken breaking sameness.
So time will dissolve and quite melt
Through the running river of a thousand
Timeless sighs.

*

A rather curious episode during this term was my determination to launch out into an Arthurian fable. The scheme behind this is fortunately spelt out, so I can see roughly what I was trying to do.

I am including the two attempts not because of any literary merit they show – for there is probably very little indeed – but because they do give flashes into my state of mind. It is clear that this was a time of a serious tussle between my idealism and my growing sexual and other frustrations. Not totally inappropriately I tried to express this through writing in the Romantic Love form beloved of the troubadour literature. The influence of my favourite writers is clearly present. For what it is worth, here are the two attempts, clearly influenced by Tolkien, C.S. Lewis, Tennyson and others.

The first was outlined on a set of small filing cards, headed 'The Pilgrimage' and on the last as 'The Quest'. They were dated 23rd January, which was the first Sunday of the Spring term.

<u>The Pilgrimage – or the search for beauty.</u>

A long work, part prose, part verse, which would narrate and illustrate the supposed journey of a young knight in search of the grail: the grail a symbol of beauty and truth; a visible manifestation of eternity.

His travels would take him through many lands – each of them, created, physical illustrations of a poet's dreams. E.g. a bare, simple land with lofty mountains, deep chasms, lakes & hamlets – Wordsworth, or deep, lush woods and ripening corn fields would shelter Keats, and so on. The first years journey would take one through the English Romantics who would one by one give their supposed views on poetry, art, beauty, truth, happiness, God etc.

By means of passages of poetry (using the same rhythms & vocabulary as the original) it would be attempted [sic] to catch the spirit of each and provide an unmistakable background (no names given) to the conversation held with each.

For the sake of variety the hero may on the way meet dangers – dragons, goblins etc who will be personifications of earthly temptations & vices. The spirit of adventure & sheer creative inventiveness will be maintained by the lack of any but the very broadest of patterns for the work. i.e. he does not, as the author does not, know where he is going! He merely knows what he is searching for – essence – the essence of beauty which Keats was certain was truth. His mission will probably never succeed [sic], but he may bring back a few crumpled leaves, a few fleeting glimpses of the mystery; of the "sense sublime of something far more deeply interfused…"

The aims are.

i) to make a study of poetry more interesting (and more critical)

ii) to increase creative output & stimulate the imagination

iii) For enjoyment's sake

iv) To have a record, a clarified vision, of my ideas on the more important problems of life, injected by the accumulated wisdom of poets. Like Shelley's cloud – the whole will probably largely be a projection of my own corrupt views into the mouths of others – but if Wordsworth was right in maintaining that "the shades of the prison-house close around the growing boy" I only have a few more years before "the light that never was on land or sea" ..."fades into the light of common day..." Perhaps I may capture one fleeting vision which will be lost if I wait until I am hardened and encrusted by 2nd-hand opinions & compromise.

I also explained the underlying purpose of the piece to my second serious girlfriend, Penny, in the long letter I wrote to her on my 21st birthday on December 20th December, as follows.

Did I tell you I wrote a story about one of Arthur's knights searching for the grail – symbolising my search for beauty and certainty, for someone to love and an ultimate good to believe in? Just before the end Sir Tristan had to fight a monster, obscene and lecherous, which represented my struggle for purity and innocence despite sexuality.

*

The first version of this work is a fragment, the first six lines typed and the rest in hand. I am not certain when the next attempt was made. It is dedicated to Judy, who I was going out with from towards the end of the Spring Term.

THE ADVENTURE OF TRISTAN & THE HOLY GRAIL

"Ay, in the very temple of delight
Veiled Melancholy keeps her sovereign shrine."

One evening, as the shadows slid round Camelot, a young squire rode in over the drawbridge. Tristan was his name & noble was he, fair of face, clean & strong. Like the blue river were his eyes, & his hair was as gold as the rich corn in the meadows. But pale was that face, & pain lay deep in his eyes. Sorrow was chiselled in his high forehead, & his strong shoulders seemed bowed by some unseen weight. As the shadows were lengthening had he come, & like one of those very shadows did he seem; mysterious & veiled by sadness. Many wondered at his coming, but not for long, for there were many other things to occupy their minds. Among these was the weather.

None of the oldest peasants, ruminating over their frothing tankards in the long evenings, could remember a summer like it. After a sweet & early spring, summer had embraced Camelot like a full-bodied, warm-breasted, lover. The country had never been so beautiful, it seemed, as, day after day, the treacled warmth cascaded down into the rich meadows; & under the prolonged sunlight the villagers turned brown like ripening berries. In the early mornings the many towers gleamed above the dew-trembling meadows & the cows chewed wetly through the beaded grass: but as each day or on man & animal alike sought shelter. The cattle would stand chest-deep in the river, & the ladies of the court took venison pasties out into the deep-flowered woods. There under a canopy of green lichens, they spread dazzling white cloths on the mossy stones & watched the birds & lizards hunt in the cool foliage. Many would have been the sparkling tournaments, gay with penants & the clash of knightly arms; many the hunts through the echoing woods after the noble stag. It would have been as summer rich in wine in joy, & in romance if it had not been for the shadow that lay over the once happy land. In the midst of the beauty of Camelot there was desolation; a maggot moved in the rose. The sound of weeping was heard in the long stone corridors & through the scented gardens the pale maidens wandered downcast. And why this mourning?

Only a week before Tristan's arrival the Holy Grail had been seen, & now the great fellowship of the Round Table was dispersed in eager search for that wondrous sight.

There is no need to tell at length of that bitter-sweet hour; of its joy & of its agony. My reader will know of the Grail – of how, when Lucifer was cast out of Heaven, one stone of great beauty was detached from the marvellous crown which sixty thousand angels tended [him]. Of how this stone fell upon earth, & from it a vessel of great beauty was carved, which came, after many ages, into the hands of Joseph of Arimathea. He offered it unto the Saviour, who blessed & used it at the Last Supper, & whose blood flowed into it from the spear wound on the Cross. After many further adventures this holy vessel at last came to the kingdom of Logres where Arthur ruled.

On that fatal summer evening all lay hushed in the dying light which faded from the dreaming woods & meadows. Suddenly a mighty flash, as of lightning, lit the tapestried halls where the knights were dining. As they glanced at each other wondering, a great sweetness flowed into the hall: sweeter it was than musk-roses & more fragrant than honeysuckle. Then around the dreaming castle an enormous silence began to move, velvet-footed. The very jackdaws were hushed, sensing the presence of some mighty spirit, & in the midst of the silence one sweet, infinitely small yet ravishing & overpowering harmony drifted like a hawk through the gleaming halls & over the twilight fields – piercing the knights with indescribable joy mixed with sadness. As its echoes died, leaving the silence more profound, there came a rushing wind & for a second the Holy Cup, burning with blinding light even tho' veiled in white samite, hung before the stunned knights. And on it they saw fiery letters forming the words "Only the pure in heart shall see God; follow me, he who will."

Many had gone. Gawain & Gareth, Lancelot & Kay (Arthur's childhood companion), Girfleet the Swift & Taliessen the humble, Gareth, Geraint & Parsifal the Pure. Amidst the wailing of women they had vowed to seek the Holy One, to pierce to the innermost heart of the mystery & to become one with the beauty, to see the cup unveiled & perhaps, if it was His will, to cease in that moment of exstatic vision.

So in a bridal morning in April, when the thrushes sung from the dew-diamond hedges, the knights set forth. Bright & gay were their hearts & bright & gay their plumes & penants fluttered – emerald, ruby & white – in the spring sun. Light were their hearts, youth & hope shone from their eyes. But Guinevere from her tower, & Merlin brooding along where the reeds whispered, knew that many would never return, & their hearts were sad.

Far & wide the knights travelled, deep in the witch-filled woods they sought, & high in the haunted mountains. They dared the slimy seas, & sailed to forlorn lands; & many were their heroic deeds, & many their adventures. Tales are told elsewhere of how many fought & conquered, & others fought & fell. Of how only a few, after perilous trials & bitter sufferings, had glimpses of the Grail. Of how the mighty Lancelot became mad & wandered like a beast in the woods, & of how only one was successful. How after voyaging through Logres & Lyonesse & Cornwall, through many fair cities & many black forests, he at last came to the Grail castle. How he spent a night of vigil in the Chapel Perilous & then pierced the mystery. But here we will tell of the sorrow which befell Tristan, Tristan whose name means 'sadness'.

In the midst of all the sorrow Arthur had still noticed the unhappiness of the young squire. So, one evening, as the king brooded at the head of the half-deserted table, on an impulse he sent for him.

"Why so sad, my son?" he inquired. "Surely, as a stranger, you do not feel our loss so deeply?" After a pause the youth replied.

"Oh king, this is the reason of my sadness. When I was a child I played in the woods & by the babbling streams; I watched the kingfisher scatter jewels on the river, & I heard the nightingale sing. I was full of joy but also of peace. Dizzy with happiness I ran through the mossy glades & plunged in the chrystal pools overhung with leafy ferns. I lay like a lizard on warm rocks & felt the sun drying the beaded moisture off my back. I ran through dripping woods & felt the wet kiss of the rain on my lifted face. I worshiped sun & rain, wind & water with a fierce devotion. And I clasped all these pleasures to my heart, hoping by that embrace to hold them for ever. But one day as I played in the autumn wood I heard a distant voice calling me & for the first time I knew myself to be alone, & I knew that I desired another. In that moment I found my clutching hands empty, for the joys & passions, the haunting sights & smells of my youth, had slipped through my hands like chrystal drops. Since then I have searched for my other self, for that voice heard like far-off piping through the leaves. In the depths & in the heights have I searched & I have found only … emptiness. Restless I have walked the night's starry path; eager I have opened many a curtained door into secret gardens only to find … nothing. Through heat & cold, night & day, hills & dales I have searched unceasingly & I have found … nobody. O king, where is that voice & where my heart's ease?"

At this the king looked even sadder & his voice was gentle as he replied. "Tristan art thou called, & rightly, for thy lot is sadness; your way is the path of suffering & of seeking the unattainable. It is the path of the Grail. Alone & afraid you must go to seek this mystery through peril & temptation & you will only attain to it in the very Valley of the Shadow of Death & in the jaws of Hell – if you attain at all. Failure means death-in-life, & success …? But who can foretell the holy mysteries of God?"

"If you choose this path you must prepare yourself, for only the pure & undefiled can approach the Holy Cup. But first, if it is your will to hazard this, I will make you knight & equip you as I may."

To this Tristan replied "Through many lands have I wandered & my spirit is wary, yet, if this alone will quench my soul's thirst then let me go in the faith of the Lord."

So Tristan was knighted amidst pomp & pageantry. He spent a long night in vigil in the tiny chapel in the rock depths of Camelot & afterwards kissing the king's sword & vowed his constancy in the quest. Then the king gave the young knight fair & gleaming armour; a sword, bright & bitter-edged; a shield bearing as its crest a white dove; a helm, a breastplate of silver, a spear & a plume of purest white with one strand of blood-red. Lastly he was mounted on a white steed, which bore him long & faithfully, until it was torn down under him by wolves in the wastes of northern Seffaridim.

Thus equipped the last of the holy knights set out in pursuit of the Grail. Clothed in purity & filled with desire, he went forth one morning in the early autumn & was soon lost to sight in the blazing woods. But as he cantered through the fields of ripe corn the peasants, bare-shouldered & brown gathering up the harvest, stopped their work for a moment & gazed with awe, for not even at the passing of Gawain had they seen a nobler or more resolute figure.

Many lands & adventures did the youth see, & his golden hair became flecked with silver. He fought the bear-man Ogran in the Valley of Skulls, & triumphed over the Witch of Arédor by his purity. He lay bound in the castle of Slob the Giant for over a year before he escaped & revenged the giant's treachery. Black & terrible were the monsters he met, & beautiful & fair the maidens. Yet did his sword & spirit prevail. As summers changed to bleak winters & the promise of each spring reached fulfilment in successive autumns Tristan wandered further & further from peaceful Camelot until one day it chanced that he came into the wild land of Sefferadim. This was a remote peninsula, reaching out into the Western sea, & onto it the mighty ocean rolled incessantly with hollow thunder. Bleak was it, & strange tales were told of this faery land of the utmost North by peasants sitting round the hearth in the far off regions of the South. Here in this desolate but hauntingly beautiful land of broken rock & heather, of long sands & steep cliffs where the sea & sky swept the winds over the moaning wilderness lost his faithful companion Phreseus, his white mare, & it was here that he fulfilled his quest.

After the death of Phreseus Tristan stumbled on wearily on foot, until he found himself on a long beach on the sea's edge. It was late afternoon & the long rays of the sun lit the sands so that they shimmered pure gold. For a while he trudged on, so great was his desire & the pain within him, but at last, exhausted, he stood leaning on his sword, one tiny figure in the immense calm of sea, sand & sky. And as he stood he felt the peace of the elements invade his restless heart. He watched the panting wavelets kissing the sliding sand & murmuring secrets in the ear of the land. For a moment his heart lifted in adoration to his God as the sun sank into a pool of its own golden blood. Then, in that moment of exaltation, when sun & sea were mixing in a froth of greens & golds & the moon was lifting herself from the darkening cliff behind him he heard a voice of one singing far down the sands.

As she came closer he saw that it was a tall lady, dressed in flowing robes of dark green which set off her swan-white neck & her black hair which flowed to her waist. Her eyes were dark coals & as she came closer & he could look into them he felt himself ravished, bewitched by her proud beauty. Then his pure spirit went out to her & he stretched out his hands to hers. But in that moment a terrible change came over her. Her beautiful eyes, once clear & bright, bulged & grew dull. No longer was she tall but grown squat & venomous like a toad. To his bewildered eyes she looked like some bloated spider, with viper's tongue & leprous skin. Hissing, beady eyes filled with hate, it crouched before him. But, for Tristan, even worse than the monster itself was the strange weakness & nausea which swept over him; for his fear & hatred were mixed with a terrible desire to embrace this foul creature, to obey its obscene wishes. He was torn within & he felt the sickness rising within him. His spirit stumbled, & faltered as some tiny candle flickers & nearly dies in a great hall when a cold wind suddenly blows: but in that moment of utter weakness he felt a presence within him & the desire passed from before his eyes like some murky vapour. Only just in time, for in that moment the monster sprang forward with surprising agility, like some great tarantula spring on its prey. In his danger he felt his ancient sword in his hand & as the beast rushed, bigger than a great bear, he lunged deep into its overtowering belly. The knight felt the blade go deep into the flabby unprotected flesh, saw green, puss-like liquid bubble out round his hand, & heard the monster give its death-scream filled with hate & horrible awareness of its end; then the beast collapsed on him & he fainted amidst the folds of its sagging & putrifying flesh.

When he awoke the weight was gone. He could see the moon high above him & a multitude of stars like frosty gems in Night's crown. Most blessed of all night's gifts was the fresh, salt breeze, which he sucked deep into his lungs to clear them of the foul reek of the monster. Deep in his side lay the bruises left by the monsters' fall. But they & even the tender beauties of the night were all forgotten by the young knight as he lay recovering; for above him stood another maid who regarded him gravely for a moment & then pillowed his head on her lap. Far greater did her beauty seem to Tristan than the bewitching loveliness of the first maid. She was fair & dressed all in white & she wore a girdle of beaten gold. As she stroked his bruised head she sung soft & sweet lullaybes. She seemed to be surrounded by some mystic radiance & her song was filled with a more passionate pleading than the melody of the nightingale. Of beauties too glorious & too sad for the eyes of men did she sing; of sea-girt isles lying in the blue chrystal of southern seas; of the island-valley of Avalon & of the mysterious Castle of the Holy Grail; of the plains of Heaven & of the mystery of god. And as she sang Tristan found rest & his loneliness vanished. His soul flew out to meet hers & fled deep into the depths of her wild eyes & there, with holy awe, he found mystery & ineffable love, understanding, bubbling mirth, & joy: but she wore, as a cloak, sadness. Before she left him, she kissed his hand once, & his spirit faltered in its ecstasy, so that he lay for a while in a stupor. When he awoke he saw that she was already far down the sands from him. With wonder he saw her get into a white ship accompanied by seven ladies in black. As it sailed off over the summer sea she turned once & saluted him, a gesture full of promise, as well as of the sorrow of parting. And he was alone upon the bleak sea-shore.

No wonder then if there suddenly fell upon him a terrible melancholy. No wonder that he felt as if his soul had been scooped out of him & hurled far out to see & was even now drowning. Amidst his blinding tears the world, the glitter of the stars & the crimson dawn rising in the East all turned grey. For one second he ceased to hope, he closed his mind, lost his God & wept like a child. No further could he go. Bitter & alone he lay above the incoming tide. Then, even as he lay, singing echoed over the water. He stirred, & lifted his head wearily, as the voice of his beloved calling him died away, hope surged back. At that moment he saw at the water's edge a tiny, battered, coracle. Hardly knowing what he was doing, he walked to it & pushed off. An off-shore wind caught the little craft & bore it out into the immensity of the ocean. Gathering speed it move out into the blackness. Beyond Tristan lay the dawn.

The reference to Judy concerns a brief affair I had with a girl at the end of the Spring Term and start of the summer. She was part of the circle of girls, Julie, Gabrielle and then Penny, who dominated my life in Oxford during these three years. A couple of the very few photos I have of this period include her with some of my friends on a hill above Oxford.

Myself, Judy, Paul Hyams and John Munks .

Spring Holidays 1962

The first letter from my mother is on March 18th, and handwritten.

My dear Alan,

Anne has been using the typewriter for making lists of French verbs and it has ground to a standstill in protest – hence this illegible scrawl. Late too, I keep sending for Airgraph Forms and finding Nazira P.O. has run out! … The daffodils must be dancing for you, how wonderful, I shant see them for years except (wait for it!) with my "inward eye". I wonder if any of the Gang will be up for Easter, let us know about them & Martin's Café & everything. Please thank Granpa for a letter, we're waiting for news of Angela. I'm glad you saw Julie again, did she fail her "A" levels or is she just waiting for a place…

I will send another £5 in my next letter, is this all you are going to need for the vac? i.e. have you any grant left at all? Daddy has sold his gun & is going to sell the car – just in case you think we aren't trying!

On March 20th my grandmother wrote from Field Head. It was written to me addressed as: Alan Macfarlane Esqr, Lee Abbey, Lynton, N. Devon.

Dearest Alan,

Angela had a daughter yesterday evening & I presume she will be called Emma Rose as that had been the choice if a girl. I'm sorry it wasn't a boy this time but it will be a pair to Lucy – Mrs Bolton is down but I will go down next week & I only hope you & Grandpa will be able to manage for a week on your own! – I hope you are having a serene & restful spell & will be able to find your way back without too many snags. – Yesterday was our first day of warmth & we walked down to Hawkshead calling in on Haslam's place as we went & its pathetic to see the fencing down on both sides & the sheep have been wandering in & out. – Dusty has bought a second hand "Consul" & he brought up Jane & 2 kids for 2 days & its cheered Jummie & Beryl up, tho' the latter said she could not have stood up to a longer spell. – Don't forget Fiona's birthday on 1st for a letter – they are due on May 26th & the first part of the voyage is bound to be terribly hot – Sarah is going to have her tonsils & adenoids out which is sorely needed – If you went straight to London early Saturday there is an afternoon train on Saturday but you might attach yourself to the train which comes from Exeter straight to Crewe & there change but you are an experienced traveller & will surface O.K. Your shoes have come to light – under the girls bed! Just shows how often I sweep under – I was down at 5.45 A.M. this morning & should get through a lot of letters. –
Much love & so looking forward to having you home,
Your loving Granny

Lee Abbey was described in a brochure as follows.

PLEASE READ THIS AS SOON AS POSSIBLE AFTER YOUR ARRIVAL

INFORMATION FOR LEE ABBEY GUESTS

YOU ARE VERY WELCOME TO LEE ABBEY and we hope that your time here will be a most happy one.

"We" are the members of the Community. There are upwards of fifty of us, working in the house, the offices and the garden, on the farm and on the estate. We are here to serve you in every way we can. You will recognise us by our red labels. Please ask anyone of us if there is anything you need to know.

We shall be grateful if you, also, will wear your label all the time you are here. If you have not already found it please look for it on the window sill in the Entrance Hall, and, if you cannot find it there, ask the Community member on Office duty. The wearing of our labels is such a great help in introducing ourselves and getting to know one another that it is worth the little trouble involved in remembering to keep them on even in the later days of the house party.

THE INFORMATION INSIDE IS IMPORTANT. Will you please read it as soon as you can.

The house stands on the site of the old grange farm of the Manor of Lintona mentioned in Exon Domesday as the property of Ailward Tochesone. It passed into the hands of the Cistercians at Ford Abbey and later became the property of the Wichehalse family who took up residence here in 1628 to escape the Plague. It was then known as Ley and remained in this family till in the early part of the XIX Century it was bought by Mr. Charles Bailey, who was responsible for rebuilding much of the house and adding the Octagonal Lounge, the Towers, etc.

After two generations the property was sold to become an Hotel and during the last war was used to house a Boys' Preparatory School.

In 1945 a body of Christian men and women banded together to purchase and develop the property which was dedicated to its present use in June 1946 by the Bishop of Exeter.

The house with its 260 acres of woods, pastures, cliffs and shore, are yours to enjoy.

The next letter from my mother, dated March 28th, is again not on an airletter form, with a cheque enclosed.

My dear Alan,

Herewith another little dribble, hope you haven't had to borrow too much, perhaps Richard will be able to give you a lift down South? ... A nice long letter from you, and the exam papers, for which thank you very much… We were interested in your new girl, who sounds sweet, I hope she will still be when you get back, it must be jungle warfare with all those men about …

If you could find accommodation for her [Fiona], it would be nice if she could go back for a day or two after we arrive, she could then visit the Ruskin School of Art and see what the chances are of getting in. She might get a job in Oxford and go to evening classes instead, she rather regrets now that she didn't do her "A" levels, perhaps I should have insisted, its so difficult to know.

Our love to everyone, delighted about Angela. Much love, Mummy

The next letter is on an airform and the postmark is 9th April

My dear Alan,

Still typewriterless, so shant be able to say anything on this. … Your birthday letter to Fiona arrived the day before, we gave her a rather lovely Indian stole… Julia has asked us all to stay a few days after we arrive, but I've said only F will, then she can come over to Oxford & visit the Ruskin School of Art, she now feels she would also like to take a course in something else as well, Philosophy perhaps – can one go to evening classes in various subjects? …

We will send some more money this month, will juggle with the battels & hope to give you enough for a new pair of shoes! I know its not easy but as long as we don't let it get us down too much we shall all appreciate money so much more when we have some! Will try to bring my typewriter home for you & perhaps you'll sell some of your writing? Love to Granny & Granpa, delighted to hear about Emma, will be writing to them in a day or two. Boat Race today. Much love, Mummy

The next letter is from Julie on 9th April 1962

My dear Alikins,

Is your life as boring as mine? I think not. How shocking – I can't do a day's honest work without wishing I'd never begun it! … [House warming for brother Peter's house] As the invitations won't be ready till the 15th April, that means there'll only be 18 days warning! Isn't that dreadful! What makes it worse is that I suppose Ill have to send the things to people's houses instead of Oxford (where applicable) added trouble. Can you help me by giving me some of the addresses? Paul's and David's I have; but could I have those of John, Alastair … and who … bother – I've not got my list here, and I can't remember. Oh, I know, I wanted to ask you about Digby. He seemed nice. Is he? I think I'd like to invite him although I don't know him – but I can't remember his surname. Can you help me there? O – I remember – Eric's on the list, too. Is there any one whom you'd like to bring, or feel ought to be asked? …

Goodness – how awful of me! I quite forgot that your dear family must be home by now. Oh, Alikins, how happy you must be – I do hope you are! And of course you may bring your sister to our party if you'd like to – how shocking to have forgotten! ... When are you coming to London? Have you continued our Journal? Please write <u>very</u> soon. Much love. Julie.

The next letter from my mother is undated, but must have been written in mid April, and is on Assam Company headed notepaper. It was sent thus as there was a cheque enclosed.

My dear Alan,

Another small contribution, which I hope will cover a pair of shoes! Could you, out of your grant, pay the £20 of last terms battels and £65 of this and leave yourself with £15 and I will give you a cheque for the remaining battels as soon as I arrive – Daddy will have got the money for the car by then. I will be able to send you driblets of money when I'm there which will make it easier. Perhaps they'll increase your grant still further for your last year!

It is another three weeks till we leave, and a certain amount of sewing on of buttons is taking place and Daddy is flapping madly about our passports but by and large we don't really feel as if we're coming. …

I don't seem to be able to find your letter in which you gave your dates but fancy you will have left Field Head by now and be at camp. I hope your idyll with Judy will continue through the summer term, but I suppose in Oxford one must constantly steel oneself against disappointments in that line? I'm reading the most amusing book at the moment "Promise at Dawn" by Romain Gary, you'd enjoy it. I wonder what the new musical "Camelot" is like, I cant help feeling they're treading on sacred ground, but T.H. White seems quite satisfied so I suppose we shouldn't grumble. … Sorry for this very uninspired effort… but I don't suppose Letters from Mum play a very vital part in your life just at the moment! Much love, have a wonderful term – Mummy

The last letter of the holidays from my mother was that dated by postmark in India as 15 April.

My dear Alan,

… I think you must be back at Oxford by now, and I hope found Things the same as when you left?! Write to us at Aden and Port Said and let us know if you can whether you have found some accommodation for Fiona, for two nights say, it wont be worth her coming for less and if you cant find her a bed she will come straight back with us and leave the visit to Julia till later. She wants to get a job fairly quickly to earn a bit of money so that she wont have to be working all summer…

Our programme is to leave here on May 5th, spend the night in Dum Dum Airport and fly to Bombay on the 6th. We'll have the 7th in Bombay which will be hot…

You should start keeping a note book in which you jot down all the odd people and events (like the diary that girl leant you) that might work into a story or novel, I often wish I'd done that as I've met some extraordinary characters in my travels and remember so few of them. I'll hand them on to you in future, I should never have the energy to type all those thousands of words again.

I'm glad about your typewriter by the way, this is a heavy creature and I wasn't much looking forward to taking it home though Anne does all her work on it and says she can't work any other way now. About Fiona, she will probably be going to Julia for two or three days from 27th so would want a bed for 30th and 31st approx. perhaps one of your girl friends could find her a place in a hostel. I feel so out of touch and really haven't the least idea of the chances of her getting to Art school or even a clear picture of what she will do when she does get there. Much love – only a month till we see you – wonderful! Mummy

The last letter from Julie during this period is dated Easter Night, and from London. This would make it April 22nd, the week-end before I returned to Oxford for the summer term.

My dear,

Many thanks for your letter with all your news and Digby's (not Timothy!) address. Before I forget, I should like you not only to give Eric an invitation, but to exhort him to accept, as I really like him very much, and would be disappointed not to see him. I think you said his name was Percepied [Pearse], but as I'm not sure about this, perhaps you would write his name on the card for me! If it doesn't arrive with this letter it's bound to arrive soon after, so please don't forget.

I hope you have had a nice Easter. Mine has been blissy….

I am happier in Catholicism than ever. My views are now diametrically opposed to what they were hitherto. Quantum mutate est ab illo! It is only by an effort of memory that I can recall the revulsion I once felt for religion in general, R.C. in particular. It is these memories that make me keep my rosary in my pocket when I pray in public places; or force me to pray silently, although by so doing I cannot gain indulgences; or force me to mitigate the genuflections & signs of the cross I would otherwise make, when in company. It is bad to be frightened of what people are thinking; but this I cannot help. …

Oh, I am most interested to know what changed the chances of Judy as a girl friend from a possibility to a probability during the vacation? Advice and tips. Judy is a thoroughly virtuous girl – not naïve, but fantastically pure, with a prudish mind but un-prudish reactions! She is also v. devout, and told me that she has only ever missed mass once! On the other hand it is only fair to point out that she is a snob. Also she is inclined to be petulant and moody if things aren't done her way. (This is chiefly on Gabrielle's evidence. G. spent a week at Judy's house, & said it nearly ruined their friendship because J. was thoroughly Bolshie (sic!) the whole time.) Of course all this is thoroughly confidential. I hope you won't think it bitchy of me to say these things. I really love Judy, and am only pointing them out because I am sure you'd be happier to know the worst, esp. when it's not very bad! My only advice is that you should dress impeccably (remember your shoes!!!) when you're with her – try to be fashionable if you can afford it – and treat her with unrelaxed respect. I think you will succeed best with her if you treat your friendship as a good and respectable Victorian beginning a conventional courtship.

Perhaps you could afford to take her to the theatre and out for dinner afterwards. Try borrowing a ticket to one of the exclusive dining clubs (Vade Mecum). Judy will be delighted by the sophistication and savoir-faire which you will be able to display! [then a good deal about Julie's room, with pictures etc]

Write when you can,

Affectionately, Pusseybite

Private writing in the Spring Holidays 1962

There are a number of descriptions of my life in the Lakes over this holiday.

On 28th March, Field Head.

An evening in March.

The calm evening moves in cloudy mass triumphant
Across the skies – its white pillars & grey columns
A long colonnade behind which the sun has sunk.
Birds slacken & drowse, the clank of milk cans,
Low of cattle & silence alone disturb the
Evening air. The rush of earlier winds &
Flurries of sleet are gone & only the bumpy,
Rough-grass fields are spongy and trickling down
To the brimming streams tell of their passing.
What is the mood?
Expectancy? What do you await? The night –
Cold & final, huddling the birds down in their
Wet nests & sucking prowling creatures from
Their lairs? Or spring, which has
So long lain pent, an over-swelling pregnancy
Which lies unnaturally still in thy womb?
Is there a tenseness of taut strings, as taut
As that couched cat ready to spring? Or
Do you lie down to rest relaxed by the
Fire and do the birds sing over a peaceful death?
For day you die!

Winter was clearly reluctant to loose its grip and two days later I wrote.

Field Head. 30/3/62

At the end of March: Written on a snowy evening

The march winds bend the bare tees & hurl their burden of hardened sleet at the frozen ground. Grey earth and frost-burnt grass are lightly strewn with white under a blank grey sky which sags to shroud the mountains. Who is out in this cold wet grey evening? Does somewhere a cowering tramp huddle under a hedge & pull his bare coat about him and feel in his pockets for his damp bread? Does the tired miner battle home on his bicycle, lunch bang-lung & grimy face bent to the whipping wind? Do sheep feel the bitter rebuke of merciless spring thro' thick wool & do over-eager shoots & buds, pushing too soon into the raw world wish themselves back in the deep warm earth – is all this happening as I sit by a fire & read & sip my tea?

As April progressed, the weather softened and I noted the changes.

Cloud effects. Field Head. 5/4/62

A grey mass of evening – fluffy cloud – with a touch of blue – stale & heavy with rain – but just the top edge which rears up & folds back is gilded by the already sunken sun & is warm with a touch of pink in the gold. Underneath the gold patch the cloud is less cold & seems to balloon out filled with a touch of gold liquid which seeps down to leaven the grey mass. Now another envious mass of grey froth has surged across & the golden gleam is lost.

There is also poem dated 5th April 1962.

To Judy, in her absence.

"Give me my Scallop shell of quiet"

"Give me the long rest which comes when passion's done;
The tranquillity of evening, after a storm has passed,
When the beaten fields smile in the dying sun,
And cottages, cows & sheep steam as they drowse.
Give me a single flower, complete & delicately shaped;
Or a single gossamer cobweb at the dawn –
Which Morning has kissed, & each precious strand draped
With clear, single, diamond drops.
Give me calm evening, serene & deep,
As it is smoothed away gently by night's hand,
Which caresses the quiet dales, soothing them to dreamless sleep.
Give me an old willow by a silent pool.

After the frenzied shaking of the world,
My love's hands are soft and furled.
In fairyland her spirit dwells
And her lips are delicate as those dells.
Calm are her eyes, smiling,
So that the storm in my heart murmurs cease.

In the midst of conflict her peace lies;
In the heart of coarseness a gleam of dew,
A gossamer thread that holds the world.
Rest, peace, calm are you.

[There are numerous crossings out and substitutions. The above seems the best version of this mediocre poem.]

Pinned to the above is another poem presumably written around the same time, of which there are numerous workings.

Give me a calm evening with sunset splendour,
The gentle night slipping like moonlight, delicate
Into this quiet dale, sheltered, still as a dream of peace.
Give me a single bloom, delicate as a single gossamer spider thread,
Touched imperceptibly with the kiss of night
Give me the rest after furious passion spent
The stillness of a summer moon hung in a summer night,
Give me this gentle peace & I will dream of thee.
Thou my love, tho' I know you not, move in stillness,
In calm does your young spirit move.
In the deep depths of fairyland do you slide,
And in this world you seem caught
An alien element, like a trembling insect

In dulling amber.
Amidst noise & rush I will turn to thee
For thou art evening, thou art the still sea
Thou art the still gossamer thread that
Holds the world on its axis, and in
Thee will I sink to rest.
Take not away thy peace.

Youth & Age: A reflection on a Spring Evening 12/4/62

As evening approaches on this fresh spring day the garden is greenly warm, savouring slowly the last rays of sunlight. It is very delicately beautiful, as delicate as the little haze of blue smoke that drifts from some smouldering rubbish. The hills are still in snow, and the trees barely brown, their little buds invisible from a distance; but spring is humming in the air and the excited birds flutter & court. Spring is here, and soon the voluptuous pantings of summer will fill the air with buzzing warmth like fur-warmed, bumble-bee, creature that she is. But what of those whose summer is past – and who can only wait for – Death? Is there then no restless longing to be young again, no fears that – Ah but who does not fear that fear?

I saw my grandparents walking in the spring garden. My grandmother, short and smothered in a blue shawl ambled round benevolently watching things growing, smiling at the single daffodil. My grandfather in cap & brown jersey poked slowly at a pile of burning leaves – last year alive. I do not know what they were thinking, whether they mused on youth, or were content to be – but I do know that my heart went out to them and I was sad. Sorry that soon we would have to part for a while, and they would take the long journey alone, while I picked my way onward down the flinty road.

Summer Term 1962

Half of Worcester students and staff, I am third from the left in third row

There are a lot of meetings cards and other ephemera for this term, which suggest I was very busy.

Religious:

Curiously I have a card for St Columba's Presbyterian Church and University Chaplaincy, the first such card. Associated with it was the Iona Society. Perhaps my trip to the Hebrides the former summer and Alastair Small my close friends interest in Iona made me interested? I don't remember attending meetings.
There was the usual Worcester College Chapel card and that for St Aldate's Church.
There were again cards for the Oxford University Church of England Council, and the Worcester college Group (of OICU) Bible Studies card, where we (did I go?) solemnly went through II Timothy and Titus.

On the social responsibility side:

There was again an Amnesty card, and one for COSMOS though I was no longer a representative.

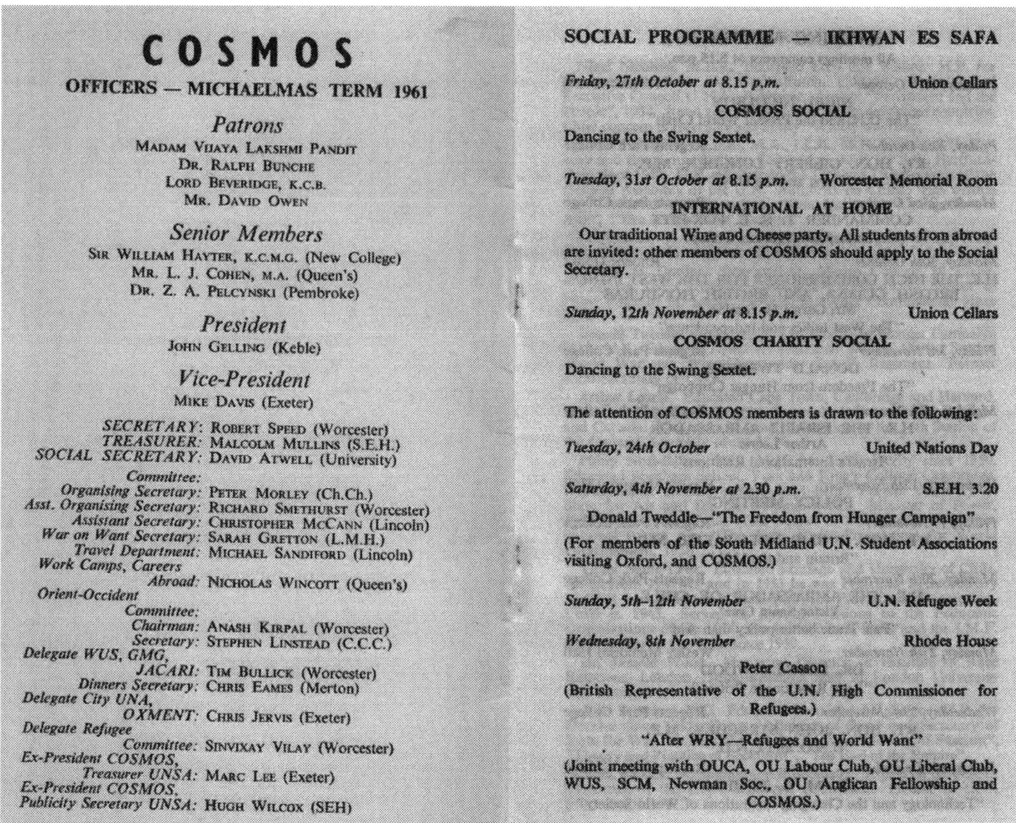

COSMOS

OFFICERS — MICHAELMAS TERM 1961

Patrons

Madam Vijaya Lakshmi Pandit
Dr. Ralph Bunche
Lord Beveridge, K.C.B.
Mr. David Owen

Senior Members

Sir William Hayter, K.C.M.G. (New College)
Mr. L. J. Cohen, M.A. (Queen's)
Dr. Z. A. Pelcynski (Pembroke)

President

John Gelling (Keble)

Vice-President

Mike Davis (Exeter)

SECRETARY: Robert Speed (Worcester)
TREASURER: Malcolm Mullins (S.E.H.)
SOCIAL SECRETARY: David Atwell (University)
Committee:
Organising Secretary: Peter Morley (Ch.Ch.)
Asst. Organising Secretary: Richard Smethurst (Worcester)
Assistant Secretary: Christopher McCann (Lincoln)
War on Want Secretary: Sarah Gretton (L.M.H.)
Travel Department: Michael Sandiford (Lincoln)
Work Camps, Careers Abroad: Nicholas Wincott (Queen's)
Orient-Occident Committee:
Chairman: Anash Kirpal (Worcester)
Secretary: Stephen Linstead (C.C.C.)
Delegate WUS, GMG, JACARI: Tim Bullick (Worcester)
Dinners Secretary: Chris Eames (Merton)
Delegate City UNA, OXMENT: Chris Jervis (Exeter)
Delegate Refugee Committee: Sinvixay Vilay (Worcester)
Ex-President COSMOS, Treasurer UNSA: Marc Lee (Exeter)
Ex-President COSMOS, Publicity Secretary UNSA: Hugh Wilcox (SEH)

SOCIAL PROGRAMME — IKHWAN ES SAFA

Friday, 27th October at 8.15 p.m. Union Cellars

COSMOS SOCIAL

Dancing to the Swing Sextet.

Tuesday, 31st October at 8.15 p.m. Worcester Memorial Room

INTERNATIONAL AT HOME

Our traditional Wine and Cheese party. All students from abroad are invited: other members of COSMOS should apply to the Social Secretary.

Sunday, 12th November at 8.15 p.m. Union Cellars

COSMOS CHARITY SOCIAL

Dancing to the Swing Sextet.

The attention of COSMOS members is drawn to the following:

Tuesday, 24th October United Nations Day

Saturday, 4th November at 2.30 p.m. S.E.H. 3.20

Donald Tweddle—"The Freedom from Hunger Campaign"

(For members of the South Midland U.N. Student Associations visiting Oxford, and COSMOS.)

Sunday, 5th–12th November U.N. Refugee Week

Wednesday, 8th November Rhodes House

Peter Casson

(British Representative of the U.N. High Commissioner for Refugees.)

"After WRY—Refugees and World Want"

(Joint meeting with OUCA, OU Labour Club, OU Liberal Club, WUS, SCM, Newman Soc., OU Anglican Fellowship and COSMOS.)

What were new was a complimentary ticket for four 'Freedom from Hunger Lectures', organized by the U.N. in collaboration with Oxfam.

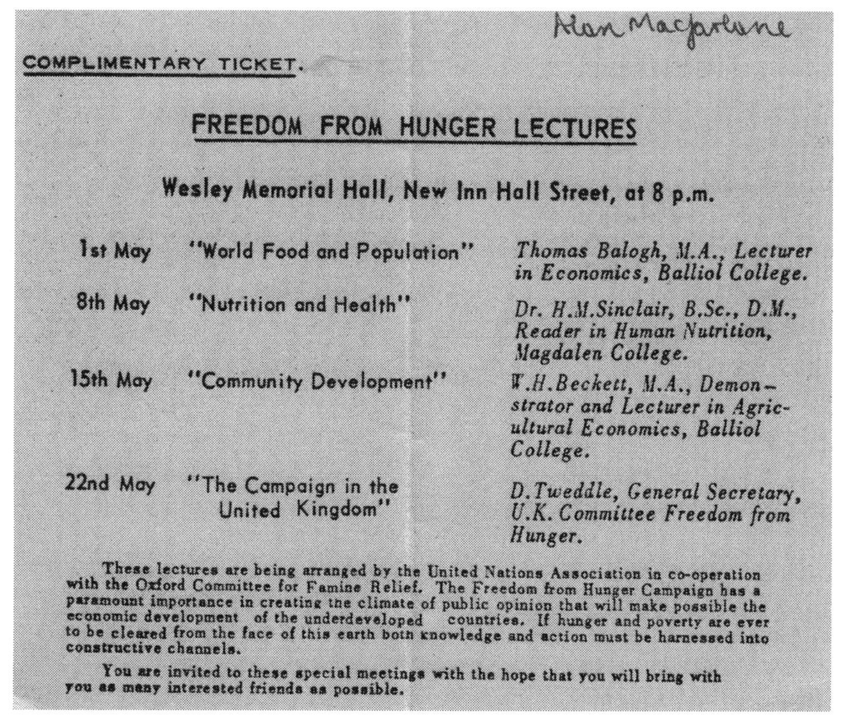

Alan Macfarlane

COMPLIMENTARY TICKET.

FREEDOM FROM HUNGER LECTURES

Wesley Memorial Hall, New Inn Hall Street, at 8 p.m.

1st May	"World Food and Population"	*Thomas Balogh, M.A., Lecturer in Economics, Balliol College.*
8th May	"Nutrition and Health"	*Dr. H.M.Sinclair, B.Sc., D.M., Reader in Human Nutrition, Magdalen College.*
15th May	"Community Development"	*W.H.Beckett, M.A., Demonstrator and Lecturer in Agricultural Economics, Balliol College.*
22nd May	"The Campaign in the United Kingdom"	*D.Tweddle, General Secretary, U.K. Committee Freedom from Hunger.*

These lectures are being arranged by the United Nations Association in co-operation with the Oxford Committee for Famine Relief. The Freedom from Hunger Campaign has a paramount importance in creating the climate of public opinion that will make possible the economic development of the underdeveloped countries. If hunger and poverty are ever to be cleared from the face of this earth both knowledge and action must be harnessed into constructive channels.

You are invited to these special meetings with the hope that you will bring with you as many interested friends as possible.

All the meetings were in Worcester, and one of my friends, Euan Porter, was the College Representative and organizing secretary, so it was probably through him that I joined. I also have the Oxford Union Society programme for the term.

Social and entertainment

I have a programme for Terence Rattigan's 'Ross', performed at the New Theatre, and the ticket counterfoil suggests that I went on 1st May. At the Oxford Playhouse, I have the programme for 'The Genius and the Goddess' by Aldous Huxley and 'Beth Wendel', performed in April. I also have an undated programme for 'The Seagull' by the Trinity Players, to be performed in Trinity Gardens.

Particularly important was my connection with the Worcester College theatre group, the Buskins. This summer they performed 'A Penny for a Song' by John Whiting in the College Gardens, and I have a ticket for 31st May at 4/- . I also have the very splendid programme, which shows that a number of my friends were involved and that the designer and director was my friend Mark Cullingham.

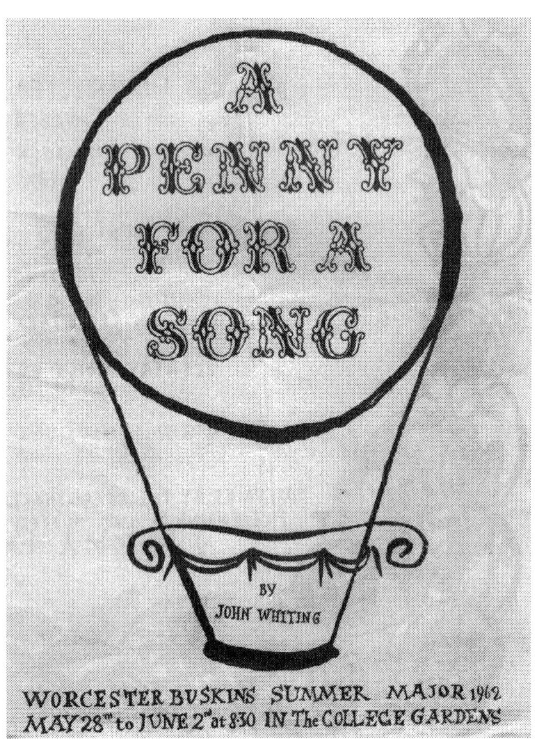

Inside the programme is a sheet of paper which brings back a flood of memories. Mark Cullingham had asked whether I could arrange a barbecue where I would burn some of the old bits of stage scenery and raise money for the Buskins. I agreed, thinking that I could fit it into a few hours of my busy schedule. But I remember that finding all the cooking utensils, and then cleaning the soot off afterwards in the small sink next to my room became a nightmare and took many hours. I resolved never to do anything like that again! But I think the actual BBQ was a success. Here is how I described it.

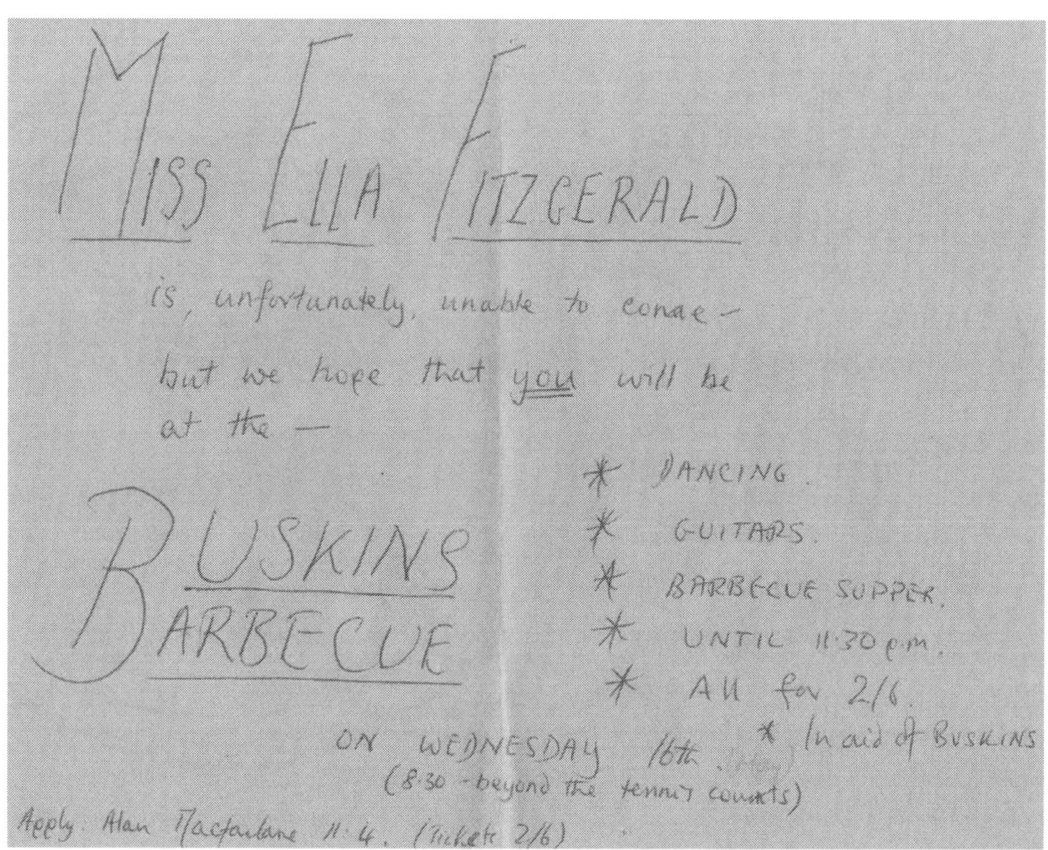

MISS ELLA FITZGERALD
is, unfortunately, unable to come -
but we hope that you will be
at the -
BUSKINS BARBECUE
* DANCING.
* GUITARS.
* BARBECUE SUPPER.
* UNTIL 11.30 p.m.
* All for 2/6.
* In aid of BUSKINS
ON WEDNESDAY 16th.
(8.30 - beyond the tennis courts)
Apply Alan Macfarlane 11.4. (Tickets 2/6)

Other entertainments were: The Worcester college Punt Club card, and a Poetry and Jazz evening in Oxford Town Hall on Saturday, 5th May.

OXFORD TOWN HALL

Saturday, 5th May at 7.30 p.m.

An evening of

POETRY
& JAZZ

Readings by

DANNIE ABSE
LAURIE LEE
Mrs. PASTERNAK SLATER
CHRISTOPHER LOGUE
ADRIAN MITCHELL
JEREMY ROBSON

with

SPIKE MILLIGAN

and the

MICHAEL GARRICK TRIO

6d. **ORGANISED BY JEREMY ROBSON**

Finally, and cryptically, there are:

A City of Oxford bus ticket, upon which is written 'He who starts with the leg ends with the boot' and a number of rather awful biro sketches on cards, of people, and faces and hands, and one of an implausible Dragonish worm, dated 3rd May 1962, and a Picasso-like eye drawn on 5th May. As this was the time I was thinking of writing a book about Oxford, I think, perhaps these were potential illustrations!

Letters in the Summer Term 1962

Sadly there are few letters between my mother and myself in this term. None of mine have remained, and my mother started on her home journey in mid-May, so the letters after that are less frequent and long.

The only letter from Assam was written on May 2nd.

My dear Alan,

Anne is grinding out her last notes on the typewriter (I'm leaving my Fisher [typewriter] *behind, he's too heavy to take) so will pen my last epistle from Nazira P.O. Cant believe we only have two more days here, piles of rubbish are collecting in corners and a lot of mending taking place but so far we haven't tried to fit anything into a suitcase – wailing & gnashing of teeth will ensue when we do as half of it will have to be flung out. … We were in hysterics over Davids party and its aftermath, I must say he might have warned you all to wear old clothes.* [This was a spoof party on an island on Windermere, where we were all stranded. We took revenge by arranging another spoof party at David's house.] *Granny is obviously revelling in the lurid telephone calls, rude postcards etc that have followed! You'll have almost forgotten it by now, back in the old Oxford rut, don't forget to let us know if you can find a bed for Fiona – hope you'll be able to come & meet us, I'll let you know arrival times. We shall presumably go to R & A's for a few hours anyway, & take the night train north. I'll write again from Aden & Port Said and try to collect plots for short stories – always a mass of them on board. You must expect a mass of rejection slips, too, couldn't have more than me, it's the time I've wasted on writing that gets me down but hope will keep springing eternal. … Much love – only 3 weeks! Mummy*

The next letter from my mother is an airletter with the heading P.O. Orient Lines, S.S. Canton. Indian Ocean May 12th

My dear Alan,

I feel like a travel poster, lounging on deck with a glittering sea in front & white clad figures gliding about with iced drinks on trays – lovely & luxurious for a short while though it would pall after too long. I feel we've been travelling for months though we set off a week to-day. We spent a night & day at Dum Dum Air Port & took the evening Viscount across to Bombay … Anne & I find it very hard to concentrate on Charles I but are making a brave effort to work for 2 hours a day. … Hope all goes well with you. Much love, Mummy

One of only two letters which I wrote and which have survived for the summer term was written to my father.

Sunday 13th May Worcester College, Oxford

Dear Daddy,

Here is the next unexciting instalment of my life in Oxford – I'm afraid once again it is a carbon copy. I sent the original off to catch the girls at Port Said. I hope things are going well & time is not going too slowly. For me, of course, it is passing much too fast.

Since I wrote the stuff below only one thing of interest has happened to me – and you will hear all the details in my next (combined) letter to you & the girls – but anyhow it was a visit to London yesterday evening to a party held by Julie which was great fun – more details later.

Oxford is doing very badly at cricket. Three Worcester men are on the team including Dryborough (capt) they have had about 1500 runs knocked off them for only 4 wickets!

Not much to write about since my last letter three days ago. The spring has become deeper & today especially has been very beautiful, thick with sunlight and growth, scented with cherry and apple blossom, the boughs laden with bird song. All the Banbury & Woodstock roads are flanked with blossoming trees or vivid green chestnuts and lace-curtain silver birches – it is too glorious to describe. Sadly, I am still over-busy and only catch gulps of the freshness and richness in between working & rushing around on apparently urgent, but I suspect footlingly unimportant, business – committee meetings, organising this barbecue etc. On Saturday, as I think I may have told you, I am going up to London (probably via Cambridge where I may drop in on Nicola Cowan) for some kind of party which Julie is holding. It will give me a chance of seeing Emma I hope [recently born]. I expect Granny will have told you of Robert's success & that his book on Parl't is selling 1,000 copies a month – marvellous. It makes me even more keen to write – quite irrationally I feel, if he can do it why not us…?

Yesterday evening I went to a "Heritage" (guitar-club) session down by the Cherwell. We sat round a camp-fire as it grew dark and played and sung as the river noises grew louder and the trees seemed to crowd nearer. With the wood-smoke, stars, moon etc it was all very idyllic. I met someone there who is at the Ruskin and asked her about entrance etc. She said that there were a considerable number of people leaving this year so there should be a fair amount of space. Apparently one needs no academic qualifications – just turn up with a few paintings. I will find out more from the officials & let you know about it all.

Today began beautifully, but almost immediately everything changed – there was a serious accident just outside the college – one could start philosophising about the insecurity of life etc – but I won't! [not in carbon] Will write again soon – until then all my love, Alan

The first letter from Julie is dated [Sunday] 17th May, from her London home.

Alikins my dear,

Ta ever so for V.M.[1] *and yr letter. I'm glad you enjoyed Saturday. I'm not clear about how or why Judy rejected you, but I commiserate. Anyway, I agree that Penny is a better idea. She is certainly very sweet; Sal who met her for the first time too, also thought her very nice. Penny's address is 5, Wimbledon Park Court, Wimbledon Park Road, W.W. 15. (Her surname is M, and she lives alone in a flat with her English mother; her American father having died when she was 7.) I know Penny will be thrilled to have you write to her, and tho' she's doing A levels this summer, I'd like to point out (perhaps unnecessarily) that if you'd like to invite her to your commem I shall be delighted for you both. I'd hate you to feel you'd be being mean – after all we can be great friends without behaving like an engaged couple. Sally sends you her love … All love, Pusseybite*

The next letter from my mother is on ordinary notepaper, with a crest and headed Canton 18 May

My dear Alan,

Another letter from you at Suez – kind boy – we loved getting it. We reached there last night & are now half way up the canal and due at Port Said this evening… We get to London on the morning of the 26th, but I don't know how long we shall be disembarking – so if you can meet us come to Roberts flat where we shall eventually fetch up. Fiona now feels she will have no clothes & would rather leave Oxford till later… Anyway give Robert a telephone number where I can reach you at about tea time on 26th if or any reason you cant get to London. I must talk to you at least.

The next letter from Julie is dated 6th June. Again from London

Alikins!

Just received your letter & stiffy[2] *for which many thanks. I'm awfully sorry I can't come, but when I tell you I shall hardly have three weeks at home 'tween now & October you'll not reproach me! After to-morrow, am doing "visits" (School Open day, etc.) with Peter, while my parents do the Lake District, and returning next Wednesday, we leave for Bath that Friday, and tho' I could manage your party that Sunday by stopping at Oxford after Bath, I really must get back home to get my things together for the Hague, whither I'm leaving the next days. …I'd be in London for most of July, and hope to see you then, otherwise I'm afraid it's no-see till next term! … I'm sure you'll enjoy the weekend with Penny, & do hope the party's a success; love to Dick, David, Peter & everyone – and you! Pusseybite*

---

1 *Vade Mecum* magazine

2 A stiff invitation card.

The next letter is undated, written on a Saturday from London, but appears to be in early June. In fact, my mother arrived in London about 14th June.

My dear Alan,

Got your financial statement yesterday but the family removed the letter! Anyway herewith – as usual haven't a great deal of cash available but will manage till Daddy comes. Anne & I have been a bit extravagant – had our hair done, went to see "South Pacific" & are going to "West Side Story" on Monday – but I feel she deserves it after two years of heat & hard work.... [Anne is taking her exams]. ... I want to see the Francis Bacon exhibition at the Tate & Granny wants me to go & see Olive & Wilhemina Stirling & other obscure relatives – but Bacon will win. Emma's Christening was fun, Mr Boggis, Mr Morgan & Mr Baine Smith were there and all asking about you. I am a godmother, & after all the promises I made in church Mrs Baine Smith said in a piercing voice as we were coming out "Tell me, are you still a Buddhist?"

Hope to see you, but if it's a nuisance ring up. I think the best thing would be to leave all your bits & pieces at Oxford for Daddy to pick up. Hope the party goes well, am sending the sickly shirt in case you want it.
Much love, Mummy

My second letter to my father is on Sunday [17th June] from Worcester College

Dear Daddy,

Just a scribbled note to cheer you up if your [sic] are feeling lonely. I can't remember when I last wrote, I expect it was one of those joint letters, anyhow I don't think I have written since the girls arrived. I met them in London, at the station, and we went back to Robert's. Mummy has probably given you her impressions of the strange monster, long-hair etc, she met – i.e. me! Anyhow it was lovely seeing them – tho' Anne made me feel very small! They were very brown, but needless to say, very worn out by the journey and just sat resting (& Fiona moping over her Engineer!) 'till they went off to the Lakes. I hope to see Mummy & Anne next week when they come down to London. I have only another six days and then I will be going up North. Goodness, how I am longing for those mountains & streams, the coolness (it has been very stuffy in Oxford recently) & the quietness after the rush of this place. (I expect you echo these thoughts!)

Actually it has been a very happy term – perhaps my last term as a 'real' undergraduate – as I will be out of college all next year & having to work hard. Indeed, having seen the list of books I am mean to read next vac' it looks as if, sadly, I will be up to my ears in work next holidays. But I am determined to do lots of fishing, walking, fruit-eating etc as well. I don't know what the financial situation is – and I expect Scotland is out of the question but I am determined to catch some sea-trout whether it is in the Duddon or the Western Isles. I will get the tackle ready before you come.

I have been spending my time in a mixture of very hard work and occasional relaxations. If I name just the relaxations it will sound as if I do nothing but enjoy myself – which is true – but I also do a lot of work (about 8 hrs a day if possible.) Last week I went to three parties (one – on Saturday – given by me & three other friends) – to a Swedish film & a Russian play in Trinity gardens – while on Monday I stayed up to 3.0 a.m. working!

Well, see you before long. I hope all goes well 'till then.
Much love, Alan Macfarlane

My mother wrote again on 20th June to my father.
My darling,
The eve of the exam and Angela and Robert due to return in a couple of hours so the picnic is over. ... Alan rang up last night, I'm not going to Oxford after all, travelling is so expensive, he has got a lift up as far as Manchester so I said to leave his heavy trunk and bits and pieces and you would collect them. I can see you leaping out of your seat with horror, but Oxford is not out of your way darling, You don't have to come into London at all, ... I will send a little map in my next letter. [I think this must have been when my father left the car with hand-brake off in front of Worcester, and was prosecuted, or at least cautioned, by the police.]... Alan is going into digs next term so has to clear all his rubbish out of his rooms, and it'll save an awful lot of money if you can bring it up, otherwise he'd have to go by train. Please don't get het up about it. Alan is going to work in a Borstal home for a week or so in July but I hope he'll cut his hair or he'll be taken for one of the inmates...
By the time you get this there'll be only two weeks to go about!
... Hugs, Totty

The next letter was probably a day or so later, from 174 Old Brompton Road. It must have been written on about 21st June.

My dear Alan,

Further to our rather hectic conversation on the phone! Leave your trunk & bits & pieces at Oxford, it'll be just as easy for Daddy to pick them up there – just take what you need for a couple of weeks.

I'm sorry we didn't get to Oxford, but expect you had quite enough on your plate this last week without bothering about escorting your family round…. Anne's exam starts to-morrow, she seems fairly calm… All news when we meet, hope the money will last you but send an S.O.S. if not. Much love, Mummy

*

Once or twice a year I would write to my best Sedbergh School friend Ian Campbell in Canada to give him a full account of what I was up to. I tended to keep a carbon copy. Here is one of the letters, written on Tuesday June 19th from Worcester College.

Dear Ian,

Many thanks for your long letter. Sorry to have been so long in replying, but you know how it is – piles of work etc.

Firstly – your news. I agree, you must know J. pretty well by now. I am interested to hear that you still hold to your idea of not getting married until you are over 25, even tho' you and J. are obviously as much 'in love' as most people are when they get married. I have come round to your way of thinking, and have abandoned my romantic ideas about getting [married] as soon as possible, in favour of the hope that I will have seen quite a bit of 'life' before I settle down. I can't speak with any authority on the problem of how far one should go with a girl one really knows well – as I have, as yet, never been out with any girl for more than about 4 months. I am fairly sure of two things however. On the one hand I agree with Blake that: –

"Abstinence sows sand all over
The ruddy limbs & flaming hair,
But Desire Gratified
Plants fruits of life & beauty there."

I agree that the prudish fear & condemnation of sex, that the absurd and overweighted emphasis given to sexual 'crimes' has & is overdone. I am convinced that the love of Peter Abelard for Heloise (a very good book if you have not read it – "Peter Abelard" by Helen Waddell) which was unbounded, was not evil. But somehow I have to try to reconcile, as a Christian, the beauty & desirability of free love with the teaching, not only of Paul but Jesus himself. I think that perhaps the reconciliation can be made if one puts love-making in its context. If one really loves the girl & will soon marry her – & if one does not become so obsessed in the physical side as to forget all else, then I think perhaps that if one wants intercourse it is not wrong. One cannot lay down rules, but if one remembers (a) To love God first (b) To love your neighbour as yourself – i.e. to think about the girl as much as the satisfaction of your own desire and to be, above all, terribly careful not to hurt her. But I hesitate to think how I would act given your situation. I think perhaps my Sedbergh upbringing might keep[ing] me on the straight & narrow!

Please give Pat my love & congrats on marriage. A few years ago I might have been shocked but that is impossible in the Oxford atmosphere – which though not, in practice, particularily corrupt, spends its time talking in a casual manner about every perversion etc there is. I will give you a sketch of the slight advance in my love life later in the letter.

I was particularily interested in your remarks about what you intended to do after university – for they curiously run along a practically identical groove to my recent ideas on the subject. I have been thinking for some time of where in the world is the most desperate need, where it would be best to throw my puny weight, and also where my talents could most usefully be employed, where I could fully develop any potential I have. On a <u>*material level*</u> *the most urgent needs seem to me to be –*

(a) The population problem – (hence food etc)
(b) Medical problems

(c) Peace & the prevention of nuclear war
(d) Racialism & other intolerance.

On the spiritual level there are certain ideological battles which need to be fought.
(a) the threat to personality & the individual. i) from mass media & the pressure of industrialisation ii) from outside & hostile ideologies – principally communism & totalitarianism
(b) the threat to spiritual values by i) Materialism (i.e. the everyday pressure of 'normal' life) ii) Apathy.

As you can see, I have not really worked out these ideas very well. But if possible I would like to stand in helping in both battles – the physical v hunger, disease, intolerance etc & the intellectual & spiritual v the pressure of the forces of the world. I am not sure yet how to work this out in detail, but I am certain to some extent that while the second involves largely the preservation of integrity & belief in the personal living of a life of faith, hope & charity – the first needs as its weapons every device offered by modern science. First one must analyse one's motives for wanting to help others & consider whether one's practical activity will be of real & lasting value. (Sorry to write in this lecture-room style – I have been writing too many essays) – I find it useful in this context to remember that many people have pointed out the danger of "philanthropy" or "do-gooding" as it is scornfully called in Oxford. For instance many have pointed out that unless one is very careful one only stirs up more unhappiness by trying to change things. (I am starting this letter again here after a few weeks interval in which I have left Oxford & am now at home so it will be rather disjointed I'm afraid!)*

I think I must learn something practical – at the moment my knowledge is dangerously divorced from the physical necessities of the world. I do know that I want to avoid a job in a city if possible & also one which involves money-making, but apart from that I'm pretty foggy. I suppose that the talents which I should use are the ability to write, and a certain measure of proficiency in the art of making friends.

My life's work is obviously connected with what I do after University. I am working very hard (my exams & the end of my time in Oxford) are next July. If I can get a good degree I would like to do post-graduate research, perhaps in something more practical, tho' I have left it a bit late I fear for a scientific education. Perhaps I could do a course in agriculture? Anyhow I am determined to have at least a year between leaving University & doing further academic work, and in that year do something down to earth – to purge me of my bunged-up ideas.

Perhaps I shall teach abroad, perhaps work in a factory, perhaps come over to Canada? I am still dreaming of going round the world – partly for enjoyment, partly to give me a further clue as to what I should do, and perhaps to provide material for my writing – (I am increasingly attracted to writing). You go down a year after I do don't you? Will you be doing anything straight away? Write to me fully about your ideas for a career as it may help to sort out my muddled mind.

I have just bought a cheap tape-recorder on which I intend to tape a lot of classical music (I have got to the Mozart-Bach stage) and also perhaps some of my work. I had better warn you that I have become a slave to 'organization'. I have filing cabinets, letter trays, index systems etc galore & work out my time to the last minute. But I hope to be able to throw it all over when I have a degree.

My love life is stagnant – but pleasant enough. I am now just 'good friends' with Julie, the Hungarian girl. Instead I am writing seriously (she lives in London so I have no real chance of doing more) to another girl – Penny. I met her at a party in London for some 20 minutes last term & she came down to Oxford to see me for a couple of days at her half-term. She has exams this term – she is 18 and leaves school this term. Surprisingly sophisticated for a schoolgirl she is pretty – has a nice figure (she tells me she has perfect measurements) and is both intelligent & sensitive & shares most of my likes and dislikes (which is perhaps not such a good thing!) – music, poetry, children's stories on one hand – cruelty, intolerance, apathy on the other. I am hoping she will come up to the Lakes to stay for a few days sometime this vacation.

The family is home – tho' so far I have only seen them for a fleeting moment on their arrival, at the moment my mother is in London with Anne (the younger sister) who is taking her G.C.E. Fiona has sobered down a little, matured, grown more thoughtful & looks like turning into a first-class artist (painter) – she is hoping to go to the Manchester art college in September. My father will be arriving back in the third week in July. I am spending most of the vacation doing academic work at home – but hope to get a job for 2 weeks & am camping with some Borstal boys for 2 weeks in Wensleydale.

Write when you can Ian – and forgive me for being so long (& so boring!). I will write again soon I hope.
All my best wishes to the family,
Yours, Alan

Penny - Summer Term 1962

It is worth pointing out that I am faced with a dilemma when surveying the letters which Penny and I exchanged between May 1962 and the end of the summer term 1963 (there are only one or two letters the following vacation, though we continued to write to each other into the late 1970s). Originally I fully transcribed her letters to me, and these were already lengthy, averaging about two letters a week over those eighteen months. Then Penny discovered and sent to me my letters to her, another 92, often very long, letters. When I typed out the full set, the word-count stood at over 100,000 – a book of 250 pages. To include all this would distort the account of Oxford. Important as the relationship was, to allocate between a quarter and a third of the text to these letters would be unsatisfactory – and probably unreadable. There is also the consideration of privacy which necessitates some delicacy in the handling of intimate letters between two young people.

Taking these two considerations into account, what I have done is to include almost all of my letters, for they indicate better than anything else my social, intellectual and emotional life in the last year of my time at Oxford. But with Penny's letters to me in the middle and last year, I have pruned them drastically. During the first term, as we got to know each other, I have included a fair amount. During the summer vacation I have only included a few which seem to show aspects of my character which would otherwise be unrevealed, or to show something of the reflection of my letters to her. For the two terms, the Winter and Spring, when the letters are most voluminous, I have only included a couple of Penny's letters in each term.

*

Penny had originally been invited to the summer party in June 1961 which Julie and I had organized. But she did not come. So I first met her at Julie's party on Saturday 12th May 1962 in London.

Julie urged me to write to her, but in fact Penny anticipated this, writing to me three days after the party. The fact that Penny was doing history meant that we had much in common.

May 15th [Tuesday] 5, Wimbledon Park Court, Wimbledon Park Road, London S.W.19

Dear Alan,

Would you consider me very impudent if I asked you to send me a copy of Trevor Roper's pamphlet 'The Gentry'? I was told ages ago to read either Tawny [sic] or Trevor Roper on the 'Rise of the Country Gents.' But neglected to do so. I was reminded of it again today, and spent the afternoon desperately ringing up the booksellers' only to be told it would take about three to four weeks to obtain. Since I know that they are more accessible in Oxford, and since you send on Saturday that you had Trevor Roper's Gentry, could you obtain another one for me from your source. I will, of course, be less negligent in sending you a P.O.

Did the others tell you how, having gone to a nightclub from Peter's we were raided by the police within 3 minutes of arrival? Very exciting, with, apparently, a big 'write up' in Monday's Daily Express – (cracks like 'Trying desperately to be Bohemian' prevailed throughout the column). A policewoman was most suspicious about Julie's splendid mohair rug, she was wearing, and poked and pawed it for the hidden marihuana. Unfortunately Julie and I were unable to supply a contribution to the upkeep of British legal bodies or to use up taxes by a short repose in prison. I think Julie was amused by the contrast of the incident to her party.

My paper reminds me to conclude – a charming phrase tho' written by one of Jane Austen's most unpleasant characters – Lucy Steele. I could, of course, continue in the same spirit.
I am, Sir, your obedient servant, but since women have been emancipated, the wording is inappropriate. Love Penny

I wrote back on Sunday [May 20th] from Worcester College

Dear Penny,

Thank you very much for your letter. I enjoyed meeting you on Saturday and was sorry I had to leave early.

You will find this pamphlet much more helpful than any single book – there are such violent conflicts of opinion on the subject that one would get a very warped view if one merely read T-Roper or Tawney by himself. I suggest that, if, as I suspect, you have not time to read the whole of the pamphlet you read the articles by T-Roper, Tawney, Hexter (p.48) & Christopher Hill at the end of the book. From these you will gather that Tawney & T-R were arguing about different "gentry" and that they tended to over-emphasize economic and class interests as causes of the Civil War. It is all very fascinating, but probably too detailed for you to use in exams. I hope it is some help (it is a present in token of an enjoyable evening, Julie's party). (I was duly impressed by your copious references to Jane Austen!) I hope you like poetry and music… [the next part of the letter is written in a curious way, a bit like one of George Herbert's letters, in the shape of an hour glass].

I was right about you being introspective was I not? I wasn't before I came up here but I have turned inwards – esp' since I met Julie. Life is good at the moment, but it goes up and down very quickly. Someone in Worcester tried to commit suicide on the evening of Julie's dance – I can see what he was getting at too. Please write & tell me your telephone nos if you have time in the next few days, as I hope to come up to London to meet my parents back from India next Saturday & I would like to see you if I have any time to spare. But plans are not organised yet. Anyhow all the best with your preparations for exams – don't get too depressed about it & if you want advice on memory-training etc write to me. See you.

Love, Alan

The next letter from Penny is dated Monday [probably May 21st], and gives no address but a telephone number PUTney 0876

O homo nobilitate et celeritate praedite,

Thank you very much for the pamphlet(s) book of. What delightful presents you send for such unexpected reasons. Only a girl would call a historical pamphlet 'delightful', but everyone is so sophisticated and complex in history, and never acts for the reason stated. I can perhaps exclude Thomas Cromwell, who while being a reader of Machiavelli had none of the Machiavelian attributes, and who was determined professedly to make his king ruler of a national sovereign state, and the richest man in Europe. Henry should not have executed him for the sake of a smelly German woman and a French alliance. All this you know, but I do like to tell people about characters and things that I am fond of.

…

Yes I love poetry, music, painting and often people and life – except that which exists immediately around Wimbledon Park Road. Also bananas, navy blue cars, navy blue anything – exc. sailors, grey anything, even skies. Observer, Sunday Times Colour supplement (of the whole paper I only read that "little coloured thing" which Ivy Compton Burnet throws straight into her waste paper basket) books. But not only their content but also the covers and paper of well made books, flowers, English countryside, wind, dogs, cats, women with personalities and an ignorance of pornography, church architecture, and windows, altar pieces, candles, Anglican and RC vestments – but hate incense (esp. in RC church near Radcliffe), good sermons, and litanies, coca-cola, milk, hot chocolate, black coffee & sugar (w. or w.out cream), caviar cream cheese, Russian black bread, South Kensington, & Chelsea & Knightsbridge and Park Lane (still hoping that P. Lane will return to a two-way street and that Clore will pull down his hotel, and that …. No I don't like it now – it has changed too much) V & A Museum, London parks, hades restaurant, 'Amnesty' movement – do you belong to it? – if not ask for inform from Brigid Marsh – L.M.H. are you interested in working for individuals wrongly imprisoned for their political beliefs), copper, Gustavus Adolphus, Strafford (am being forced against my will to read C.V. W's revaluation), Sir Philip Sydney, Dutch Art, South America – Peru & Aztecs – clocks Berenson,

Sir Arthur Evans – Palmer is jealous, has marital troubles (know this for cert.) therefore has warped ideas on relation of philogy [sic] to architecture, and formulates theories then fits facts – anti-capital punishment – am tending towards labour party fr. staunch Conservatism because find Tories have not undertaken enough internal reforms, but think Gaitskell ought to be economics don – also hate the labour hoi-poloi movement. Antique furniture and glass, large brick fire-places, trees, Autumn (before cold)…

I wrote back on Wednesday 23rd May Worcester College, Oxford

Penelope,

Thank you for your bubbling letter – it sustained me through a very trying day when I had to do 11 hours work. This will only be a note, as I hope to see you in London.

Hill is not really a Marxist – and anyhow as long as one knows where a man is supposedly biased it is O.K. It is a man like Rousseau, who masquerades as a libertarian but is really a prophet of Hitler and Stalin, who is dangerous.

I will think up some dislikes – but they will all be too moralistic for words. I hate – Apathy & indifference towards suffering, cruelty and selfishness; most cities, esp' Northern industrial ones (except in the evening at the time which Beaudelaire describes so marvellously in "l'harmonie du soir"); Hobbes, Rousseau and most political theorists; hearty people with over-bearing manners and "fruity" laughs; prunes, beetroot, marmalade & all kinds of fat; sexual hypocrisy; capital punishment; racial & other kinds of intolerance (yes, I am a member of Amnesty); the thought of an "office" existence; hospitals (or rather what they symbolise); mass media – esp newspapers & T.V. – this arises more from fear & guilt conscience because I never read the former – (I see we clash here?); Enid Blyton; innocent women who don't know what they are doing; money & all its degrading accompaniments, which is made worse by its obscene but irresistible attraction; war and any form of killing from otter-hunting upwards; bourgeois morality; educational & social inequality; most kinds of dogs except sheepdogs & some bigger dogs; pettiness of mind & officiousness.

As you can see, I am not really a rebel & find it hard to find things to hate. There are far more things that I love. On the whole (this isn't (but does) meant to sound patronising) I approve of your list of likes.

You don't <u>write</u>, I suppose, do you? I would love to be able to – and can't make up my mind whether to attempt to i) Seek to find God ii) Strive to make the world a happier place, in a practical way for others iii) Write.

I think we share many characteristics – which is a bad start to any relationship! – but I'm glad you're hypersensitive – tho it will make you very unhappy ("He who lives a thousand lives, must die a thousand deaths" (Ballad of Reading gaol. Wilde. Read it if you have not already re capital punishment.) Would you agree however that happiness is <u>not</u> the aim of life (If not, what is?)

The problem of the enervating results of introspection will have to be postponed for now.

I hope revision goes apace. If you have time let a few of your suppressed energies in another letter.

I hope to see you.

Love, Alan

P.S. I enjoyed the quotation from J.A. [Jane Austen] very much

Another letter, full of crossings out etc. is dated May 27th. London.

Dear Alan,

I'm depressed. After riding on the waves of idealism and of hope that the level of education and culture of the masses <u>could be</u> raised by papers like the Mirror and Sketch, I came down w. a bump today when I heard that even where culture is offered, it is spurned, and that the masses just don't read papers in those countries where the standard of newspaper reporting is high. But everyone/ thing is so apathetic in England – no political, religious or social awareness exists, and won't exist either. If, however, we had a healthy 'conscious' people, we would be envolved [sic] in anarchy and ultimately would no longer be free of political prisoners.

…

Having never been to N. England, I cannot share your sensibility for it at night. Is it really as Baudelaire [sic] describes in 'Harmonie du Soir'. If so, my life has been vacant of such beauty for a long time. I would

have thought, fr. Descriptions I have read of industrial towns, B's 'Le Crépuscule du Noir' offers a closer resemblance.

Tell me about Yorkshire – I have decided I want to go riding on the moors, cantering for miles and miles, with the wind whistling past my ears. I desire this form of freedom very much.

Love, Penelope.

Monday evening [May 28th] Worcester College

Dearest Penelope,

I'm so sorry I didn't have time to see you when I was up in London – no, that is not strictly true. I was pretty short of time as my parents were longer than I expected, but the real reason was that I was afraid.

Afraid, partly that you wouldn't be as nice as I remembered you, on one hand, and afraid on the other that seeing you again would make me miss you all the more – and divert me from the concentration on my work which is necessary at the moment. This last consideration also struck me about your pining your heart away (I know I flatter myself!) about someone might be disastrous for your exams.

The moment I got back to Oxford I regretted it, of course.

I am rather miserable at this moment (full of self-pity!) as I have a bad cold, sore-throat etc, so would love a letter from you.

I suppose you couldn't get away for a day, & come down for the day on Saturday? I know this is giving a lie to my previous remarks but still ...! We have a lovely play on in the College gardens & if you could manage it it would be marvellous – I could probably find a place for you to be put up for the night if you liked.

Anyhow all the best in everything.

Love, Alan

Two days later, on May 30th Penny wrote again:

Dear Alan,

What a fortunate boy you are to receive a letter from me on two successive days:

'And the Lorde was with Joseph, and he was a luckie fellow' Tyndale's trans'n of Genesis.

But I doubt if my last letter would raise you from your chilly depths. Perhaps this one will, together with some aspros, which I am not enclosing.

After yesterday's gloom because of the masses, my spirits have revived. Summer has come, and I am surrounded by green: trees, bushes, grass. I am idyllicly [sic] happy. Of course I am as nice as ever. I don't really change, even tho I have many different moods. You probably saw quite half a dozen at Julie's. I can move quickly fr. Deep despondency to happiness – I attribute this to hyper sensitivism – While still gaining the most out of both.

Alan, I terribly sorry [sic] but I can't come down and see Midsummer Night's Dream. I know that the production is very good, and with the view from your room onto the lake, I would be in my element. But I have a great deal of history to revise, and a number of Latin set books, and however much outside forces urge me to go, I would not be coming with a clear conscience.

If, on the other hand, you would like to invite me up for the weekend – June 9th & 10th I would come willingly since I have half term then and the break would be good. The forces are chiding me again however I am resolute. You aren't offended are you. Think how I would be happy if I were there and also that I could raise your spirits the next weekend – that is, if you invite me.

Love Penny

I then wrote:

Penelope,

It is a lovely day. I am sitting down by the lake and there are birds and ducks of all kinds splashing and hunting for grubs and crumbs, and the wind is stirring the white candels [sic] on the chestnut trees and the long fronds of the willow, and the daisy-milk lawn is splashed with copper shadows and the sparrows were wading waste-deep through the grass and the wind is heavy with grass and silky warmth and the trees and the lake shiver with light which bubbles and bursts – and all is soft as cat's fur and as warm. And yet I cannot enter into it all; I feel a barrier, a veil between me and all this flower-full rich, velvet-green beauty. A shadow slides over my eyes and there is a hollow drumming which clouds my hearing. But enough of that – it is probably because I have a cold still! The world is really very wonderful.

Thank you for your two letters – the one depressed, the other elated.

To deal with the second first. Please do come down. It has been our play this week ("A penny for a Song") and "Midsummer Night's Dream" is on the 9th so if it is nice we could go. Would you like me to try and find you a girl's room where you could stay the night? If you write back promptly I will let you know if I can manage it – I think it would be possible. Also let me know when you will be arriving – (I think bus would be the best way down – it is far cheaper) – and I will meet you – come as early as you can. If it is as lovely as it is today we could go punting etc.

You will probably have forgotten most of the theories etc you put forward in your earlier letter re the 'masses', God, helping our neighbours etc. It would take me hours to outline my ideas on this – and every day they are changing. All I know is that if one has lost faith & hope, once one has let go of one's ideals, everything else will crash down – purposelessness, frustration & a meaningless existence will be all that is left.

Hoping to see you. Love, Alan

Another undated letter from Penny on June 4th suggesting what she would like to see in Oxford, is omitted, to which I replied on Wednesday, June 6th.

Dear Penelope,

Thank you for your letter. I also have made a mistake over the play – M.N. Dream is on next week I'm afraid – hope you're not too disappointed. There are several other college productions if we want to go (they're not formal dress). I will see about lodgings for you.

I will attempt to take you 'round the list of list of places you mention – most of which I have never visited; but I am not sure long historical discussions are very likely – I will be more interested to discuss literature, if you are doing English.

For the last three evenings I have been out for walks round the neighbouring countryside. Each time I have gone out with a friend in a car and wandered down lanes hedged with may & through fields of buttercups down to willow-banked streams. Each time we found little medieval churches standing in lush overgrown, elder-shrouded yards, full of dim light and the smell of evening grass and wood-smoke. Each time, also we found little, thatched & beamed village pubs. It was rustic England at its most picturesque – and all three walks were heaven.

I am absorbed in Marxism at the moment & all my hopes and ideals of changing the world are aflame once more. I am more determined than ever not to sink back and let the injustice & hatred, the misery and callousness of the world go on apace while I pursue my sheltered existence in some secure little job. But more of this anon.

Well, I will see you to discuss things. Look after yourself till then

Best love, Alan

After the visit, on Sunday 10th June, Penny wrote a medium length letter to thank me, from which I shall quote just the start.

Dear Alan,

Having written a long air-mail letter, I am now too lazy to stir myself from bed to change the paper. Thus you must be content with a piece of your Spicer's typing paper.

Thank you for a very pleasant weekend. I thoroughly enjoyed myself, but this is, perhaps, already known to you. The journey home was tolerable: Shortly after we left Oxford, we came to a wood of slender birch-trees, and through the pale green leaves – I could see the red sun setting into a valley, of thick white mist. It was very beautiful and mysterious. As I foretold London was depressing, after the splendour of some Oxford architecture…

I wrote on the same day, from Oxford, in pencil. This was the first time I added a poem, something which became a normal event. I have included some or parts of some of these poems since they often said in poetry what we could not express in normal words and are hence indicative.

Dear Penelope,

It is late and I must get to bed, but I want you to get this on Monday – even tho' it is only a scratched line – and a fragment of poetry (which might remind you of something?!)

It was wonderful seeing you. I hope you enjoyed your visit – although I know you did. Perhaps you have revised your opinion of me, now you know me for an inhibited, frustrated, often petty-minded individual?

Everything is too close at hand, and I am too tired (and rather sad too) to write a proper letter explaining my sometimes odd & occasionally, I suspect, thoughtless behaviour. I will attempt to explain it later, and also how much I like/love you.

This however is merely to wish you all my best wishes in your revision and to tell you that I am thinking of you – and hope you are of me. When I hear from you I will write a longer letter.

Meanwhile, all my love to you poppet & don't work too hard.

Con amore,   Alan xxxxxxx

P.S. My respects to your mother.

RONDEL (Swinburne)

"Kissing her hair I sat against her feet,
Wove and unwove it, wound and found it sweet;
Made fast her hands, drew down her eyes,
Deep as deep flowers and dreamy like dim skies;
With her own tresses bound and found her fair,
Kissing her hair."

I wrote again on Tuesday 12th June

Penelope,

Thank you for your letter – disconcerting as the quotation from Catallus is! My present mood about you you will find in the enclosed poem. It is from "Love & Death", and, as far as I know, is anon. I wish I had the energy to write something original about you, but am feeling rather exhausted having done over 18 hrs work in the last two days.

I will try to send you a snippet of my favourite poetry each day, perhaps with a comment on it if I am moved to it. This may bore you – if it will tell me. It is meant to cheer you up while you are under the strain of exams. If you ever have time to write I would love to hear from you. Also, if you have a photo of yourself I would like to have a copy.

Your letter was, as I expected, "second thoughts." It either means that (a) you don't want to become too involved until you know that I am involved too (b) that, as I have sometimes feared, you were not infatuated with me but with "The Oxford Undergraduate" or the "Poetry Lover" or the "Ex-boyfriend of Julie" or rather a mixture of all three. I don't blame you in either case – and am sometimes worried myself whether I am infatuated (love is a dangerous word) with a very attractive and sensitive girl (but not with "Penelope M").

But I didn't mean to bring up this subject – I don't want you to worry about our relationship while you are doing your exams. I hope your revision is going well – and you are not suffering from certain distracting thoughts which prevented me from working properly on Monday!

"Now what is love, I pray thee tell?
...It is a sunshine mixed with rain."

Am thinking to you. David & Bas send their love. It won't swell your head to tell you they both liked you very much – you must know it already.

Much love – Alan

FROM "LOVE & DEATH'

I have loved the beauty of your talking,
All the words you said

Nested in my mind like blackbirds singing
Treasured in the head,
I remember all, I have remembered
Every word you said.

I wrote again the next day, Wednesday 13 June

Penelope,

Thank you for the picture of Edward & the more cheering poetry. I have just been to "A Virgin Spring" by Bergman – which was fantastic, terrifyingly beautiful, sad and sorrowing, with an intensity of quivering agony like Beaudelaire's evening violin – and yet it ended in calm assurance. It has left me slight dazed.

Since then I have been discussing religion. The less discussed & the more practiced the better I know, but it is always an absorbing subject. I hope all goes well and you still remember me.

Much love, Alan

Enclosed is:

Keats: from Melancholy

But when the melancholy fit shall fall,
Sudden from heaven like a weeping cloud; …
That fosters the droop-headed flowers all,
And hides the green hill in an April shroud;
Then glut thy sorrow on a morning rose,
Or on the rainbow of the salt sea-wave,
Or on the wealth of globed peonies,
Or if thy mistress some rich anger shows,
Emprison her soft hand, and let her rave,
And feed, deep, deep upon her peerless eyes.

This has long been one of my favourite poems, full as it is of sensuous anguish, of the aching beauty of sorrow. (Don't tell me – I know I'm a masochist!)

And I wrote again the following day, Thursday 14th June

Penelope,

Your letter was sweet and I do appreciate your writing in the midst of hard work – I enjoy hearing from you very much.

I have just been to Chekov's 'Seagull' so am once again feeling 'mixed-up'. Today I have been dreaming dreams of immortality & greatness, of beauty and of the life everlasting. I am more convinced than ever that without passionate idealism life can only be "weary, flat, stale & unprofitable". Hence I have included an exquisite image from Shelley – who, with his almost unbearably hot desire & passion for the white platonic ideal especially appeals to me in my present mood.

I hope all goes well – I think of you often, and wonder if you think of me? David & Eric send their love.

Look after yourself poppet. Love, Alan

P.S. Bas has just come & sends his love (!) also.

Enclosed:

Shelley: from 'Adonais'

The One remains, the many change & pass;
Heaven's light forever shines, Earth's shadows fly;

Life, like a dome of many-coloured glass,
Stains the white radiance of Eternity,
Until Death tramples it to fragments – Die,
If thou wouldst be with that which thou dost seek!
Follow, where all is fled! Rome's azure sky,
Flowers, ruins, statues, music, words are weak
The glory they transfer with fitting truth to speak.

The fact that I wrote again the next day. Friday 15th June, as well probably partly reflects my desire to give Penny support during her exams.

Penelope,

It is very hot and bright. The cottages are baking in the sun, and even in the mossy coolness of my room I can feel the heat pulsing past my window. It is because of this that I have chosen 'The Bait' which you probably know already. The first verse, with its delicacy & its idealization ('silver' & 'gold') epitomizes the idyllic countryside of the Elizabethans, while the last verse, mixes with the lyrical a core of metaphysical wit.

On days like today I dream of deep-embedded streams in the Yorkshire hills, of the trout moving in the shallows, and of the "flinty kind-cold" feel of the water as I wade up the rushing stream. I dream of deep pools where I used to swim among the salmon, every pebble suspended in the emerald surge of the river. I dream of the flower-scented, lushly thick, woods of Keats' poems, and of a time when I used to wander in just such woods and hear the cuckoo and the wood-pigeon; when, through a gap in the branches, one could see the yellow glare of the corn fields, bitter and bright in the sun. I dream of the scent of mown grass and of the sea, of river-smells and the creaking of rowlocks, and I hear the murmur of bees, and the slight, soft surge of water creaming under the bow of a sailing-boat.

Consequently I don't get as much work done as I ought!

I hope everything is going well; this will be my last letter until Monday so all the best in everything. You know I think of you often.

Look after yourself Penny – and don't worry too much. When we have the beauties I have been attempting to describe, exams are not everything.

Much love, Alan

P.S. I hope this isn't too dull. This weather enervates me.

Enclosed:

<u>The Bait – John Donne</u>

Come live with me, and be my love,
And we will some new pleasures prove
Of golden sands, and chrystal brooks,
With silken lines, and silver hooks.

There will the river whispering run
Warm'd by thy eyes, more than the sun.
And there the enamoured fish will stay,
Begging themselves they may betray.

Penny wrote in reply to this spate of letters. I shall quote just half of this longer letter.

London – Saturday [16 June]

Alan,

You are a sweetie to write so often ('sweetie' bears no reflection on your virility). I have almost cut myself off from the present and from people, so I need to have outside forces breaking in for a short time each day. Your choice of poetry, however, counteracts the effect for I am transported into a reverie about nature, – wind, sky, clouds, and the sun, a shining copper sphere. Tomorrow I shall spend the day with my Aunt, who lives in Surrey. Her lawn slopes quite steeply, and owing to chalky soil it is virtually impossible to grow flowers. But lying back on the grass one is rocked to sleep in a bower as the tall silver-birch trees sway gently in the wind. And the Siegfried Idyll is whispered by the breezes.

I am pleased you are going to be immortal and great. What is 'mixed-up' about that? Obviously a biography will be written about you; thus you must decide now in what field you will be great, and direct your every action and thought to that end. It will make the task much easier for the Whig Historians. How delightful to be a full-blooded Whig Historian, to be able to set out the past only in a pattern for the present. Of course, I realise that one of the purposes of studying history is to understand the present by seeing the movements and trends in the past. It is foolish to distort facts, however, by going to extremes. Gilchrist, one of Blake's biographers, claimed that his subject was prophetic because Blake, taking an instant dislike to a somewhat bumptious engraver, had send [sic]; that fellow will live to be hung', and 10 yrs later he was hung for fraud.

The state of mind roused by 'Virgin Spring' is comparable only to the way Camus' 'L'Etranger' affected me. After both I wandered around stunned, bewildered, and more than somewhat dazed. 'Virgin Spring' is, I believe, the most poetic film I have seen; it has lyrical qualities as the two girls ride thro' the forests, and great intensity as the father thrashes/ chastises (?) himself in preparation for the slaughter; and sorrow as he falls away from his principles by killing the child.

…

I hope your party was successful – what a pity Julie and I weren't there to make marzipan sweets. Julie allowed me to eat most of the ones I made for yr last party, in consolation for not being there. Send my love to the others. Much love, Penelope

Enclosed was a poem.

<u>Cupid and Campaspe (John Lyly)</u>

Cupid and my Campaspe play'd
At cards for kisses; Cupid paid:
He stakes his quiver, bow & arrows,
His mother's dovers, & team of Sparrows; …
Loses them too; then down he throws
The coral of his lip, the rose
Growing on's cheek (but none knows how);
With these, the crystal of his brow
And then the dimple on his chin;
All these did my Campaspe win.
At last he set her both his eyes:
She won, and Cupid blind did rise.
O Love, has she done this to thee?
What shall, alas, become of me?

I wrote again from Worcester on Sunday 17th June.

Penelope,

How can I cheer you up? By telling you how fond I am of you? You know that already. Anyhow I hope you like this little book – probably you have it already. The quotations I have enclosed are a mixture of 'good advice' and a well-known gem from Tennyson which goes with my present mood – one of absolute laziness. It is useless asking how revision etc have gone, but if you ever have time I would like to hear how the papers are. I am certain that you will find the exams fairly easy as I know that you are more mature (intellectually) that I was when I took S's & are very hard-working. Anyhow I hope all goes well.

I will talk about myself as you must be sick of talking about your work. (Is this an excuse for getting on to my favourite subject?) I have been leading a comparatively gay social life in the second half of the week. I went to that party on the barge on Friday. It was fun, and very beautiful on the river at sunset, slowly being drawn up by the old cart-horse. I met several nice people (sex undefined!) and some of them came back for coffee afterwards. Then on Saturday was my party. It was, as all parties are, slow in warming up, but all the people I have met seemed to enjoy it very much. I acted the host etc & danced with all the fair (& not so fair) damsels and was asked to another three parties on the strength of it.

One of them was the same night so I went along at about 11.30. It was in [a] private flat, mostly coloured men & pretty, lush, Greek & French women. I was shunned by a French lesbian but was approached by a homosexual (who wanted me to have a "naughty two hours" with him) as I was about to climb into college at about 1.30. We had a chat for a while. So, it was a pleasant evening.

But, all the same, I wish you were down here! Still, I hope I'll see you soon. Look after yourself Penelope and do as well as you can.

<u>Much</u> love, Alan xxxx

Enclosed a sheet with:

"I will not cease from Mental Fight,
Nor shall my sword sleep in my hand.." BLAKE

" .... Know, not for knowing's sake,
But to become a star to men for ever';' BROWNING

"And though I ....understand all mysteries, and all knowledge; and though I have all faith ... and have not charity, I am nothing." ST PAUL

"Ask, and it shall be given you; seek, and ye shall find; knock, and it shall be opened unto you." JESUS

I kept up the spate of letters, writing again on Monday 18th.

Penelope,

Thank you for your long letter. I'm glad you sound quite cheerful. I expect that once the exams have started things will be O.K. When do your papers finish & when does your term end?

I rounded off my period of debauchery by going to another party last night – it was quite fun but nothing phenomenal happened. I am now longing to be home again and to wander around the mountains and explore all the secret streams and hidden lakes – "far from th(is) madding crowd." Even Oxford can become tedious in its intensity. My mother is in London with my sister (younger) who is taking her G.C.E. 'O' levels –they are staying at my Uncle's flat in the Old Brompton Rd – and they are hoping to go to the Francis Bacon exhibition (which you obviously enjoyed so much.) I will probably be going straight up North (getting a lift from a friend to Liverpool) on Saturday – but am not absolutely certain yet. We will fix up plans for next vac' etc when you are no longer involved in work.

I knew that delightful poem on Cupid you sent me – and also love it very much. Today's appointed piece is more a warning to myself than to you. It is Elliot in his preaching mood – which I rather like (I'm not sure he is saying anything very profound in actual fact).

Look after yourself poppet, and all the best in today's exams.

Much love, Alan

Enclosed:

T.S. Eliot; East Coker.

.... There is, it seems to us,
At best, only a limited value
In the knowledge derived from experience.

The knowledge imposes a pattern, and falsifies,
For the pattern is new in every moment
And every moment is a new and shocking
Valuation of all we have been.
....
Do not let me hear
Of the wisdom of old men, but rather of their folly,
Their fear of fear and frenzy, their fear of possession,
Of belonging to another, or to others, or to God.
The only wisdom we can hope to acquire
Is the wisdom of humility: humility is endless.

I wrote once again the following day on Tuesday 19th June.

Penelope,

How goes it? Well, I trust. My poem for today is a partial reply to John Lily's "Cupid & Capaspe". I have my favourite Wagner on the gramaphone & consequently feel more bunged up with serious thought & idealism than usual – but I think something light & amusing like this will be less demanding on you during your period of strain.

Nothing whatsoever has happened to me since I last wrote. I got up at 6.0 this morning to write a long & quite good essay on the C18 Church which my Tutor seemed to enjoy. I have an enormous reading list for the summer vacation – and my family will be justifiably worried when I shut myself up for some 8 or 9 hours a day!

It is the second to last night of "Midsummer Nights Dream" tonight – I really must make an effort and go to it.

A miserable letter today I'm afraid, poppet!

Anyhow...

All best wishes & love, Alan

George Peele: the Hunting of Cupid.

What thing is love? For sure love is a thing.
It is a prick, it is a sting,
It is a pretty, pretty thing;
It is a fire, it is a coal,
Whose flame creeps in at every hole;
And as my wit doth best devise,
Love's dwelling is in ladies' eyes,
From whence do glance love's piercing darts,
That makes such holes into our hearts...

This was the last week of term, and two days before leaving Oxford I wrote once more, on Thursday 21st June.

Penelope,

I am very sorry I missed my daily letter yesterday, especially as I had a long letter (& a photo) from you that morning – for which many thanks. The main reason was that in the excitement of getting a tape-recorder (which I bought yesterday morning) and of taping various of my friends records onto it, I left writing until too late.

I hope all continues to go well. You sound quite happy so far & I expect you are enjoying things now. The General paper was interesting, tho' I agree the science section was very difficult.

I rang up my mother yesterday & as a result have decided definitely to go straight up North on Saturday as my father will pick up my luggage at Oxford. This means I won't be able to see you – alas!

If you feel it would be worth your trekking up to the Lakes for a few days we would love to have you – and I'm sure you would like it. Just give the word & we can work out some dates.

All the best, poppet.

Much love, Alan Macfarlane

Tennyson

Now sleeps the crimson petal, now the white;
Nor waves the cypress in the palace walk;
Nor winks the gold fin in the porphyry font:
The fire-fly wakens: waken thou with me.
....
Now folds the lily all her sweetness up,
And slips into the bosom of the lake:
So fold thyself, my dearest, thou, and slip
Into my bosom & be lost in me.

I was now packing and preparing to go north, so on Saturday 23rd June – on the back of an invitation card, in pencil – I wrote a small message.

Dear Penny,

Am in a great rush packing so have asked someone to take this down to the late post – he is waiting. So all my love Poppet & best wishes – Will write a long letter for Monday. Much love, Alan

Now that the relationship has been established through quoting parts of both sides of the correspondence, I shall give a much smaller selection of Penny's letters to me over the next twelve months, for the reasons explained above.

Academic Work - Summer Term 1962

The two main topics I studied in the summer term were English history and political philosophy. Both had been started the term before, and I had covered the early Tudors with Lady Clay, and the set texts of Aristotle, Hobbes and Rousseau with James Campbell and Harry Pitt.

That summer was one where I came back to the period which has always intrigued me most, the Elizabethan and the seventeenth century. I had loved this at Sedbergh, and Lady Clay, though elderly, was an enthusiastic and delightful teacher, and later a friend. It was also the time that my excitement with political philosophy grew, not just because we moved beyond the set texts to the invigorating work of J.S. Mill and Karl Marx, but also because I went to some excellent lectures by my future D.Phil. supervisor Keith Thomas. I have very long lecture notes on his six lectures on Aristotle, Hobbes and Rousseau, and can see that I was very absorbed in them.

In relation to Marx, I have a fragment of independent testimony to the effect of reading his work, and particularly about him in Wilson's 'To the Finland Station', in a piece I wrote titled: 27/5/62 'On reading Marx', which is to be found in the section on private writing. There is also a comment on his effect on me in a letter to Penny.

In relation to Tudor and Stuart history, I had done one or two essays at the end of the Spring term I moved on to my third (the essays are undated) on 'Were James I's financial problems different in kind from Elizabeth's?' and fourth 'Why not the Puritan Revolution?'

I then moved on to the period after 1660 up to the middle of the eighteenth century, taught by Peter Dickson and Harry Pitt. All I can be sure of are the topics which I wrote extensive essays on – which I still have – along with hundreds of pages of mostly typed notes. There are no dates, but these are the subjects I covered.

'What issues were involved in the Exclusion Crisis & why did the Exclusionists fail?

'How did the economic changes of William III's reign consolidate the Revolution?'

'How did politics work after 1714?'

'Was the C18 Established Church performing its proper functions & was Methodism a judgement on it?' This was a particularly long essay – probably about four or five thousand words (three typed and four hand written foolscap pages). I do note in a letter to Penny that I wrote this essay on 19th June and that my tutor liked it.

Thus I did six essays on English history and two on political science.

*

In relation to political philosophy, we moved on from the set texts to the Utilitarians and to Marxism. On Marxism I did an essay on 'To what extent was Marx the discipline of Hegel?' I also worked further on J.S. Mill.

*

The following is a sample essay for the English history paper. I remember that Lady Clay was particularly interested in puritanism, as I was. I was also very intrigued by all the debates about the causes of the English civil war and was going to lectures by Christopher Hill and Lawrence Stone and perhaps Trevor-Roper on these themes. This is the fourth essay, so was probably written in early May 1962.

Essay 4. (1).

Why not the Puritan Revolution?

"And all the sober men that I was acquainted with who were against the parliament, were wont to say, 'The King hath the better cause, but the parliament hath the better men'...; in this remark Baxter poses the two unanswered problems which face the student of the English Civil War:- what kind of men were the leaders of the opposition to Charles government? and what were their motives? We have neither the sufficient facts nor the omniscience to give a satisfactory answer to either, but can merely point to the tremendous complexity of a revolution which threw up men as varying as Prynne and Cromwell, Laud and Richard Baxter, Prince Rupert and Hobbes. Its causes were multifarious - social, economic, religious, constitutional, personal, political and legal, and the immediate sparks which set it off included the Irish rebellion, the withdrawal of the Scottish army and the attempt on the five members. If we seek to lay too heavy a burden on any one interpretation it cracks under the strain - as Tawney's and T-Roper's theories have disintegrated. Even a man like Cromwell was not moved by a single burning ideal - who is to say whether he represents Puritan zeal or is the symbol of the depressed "mere" gentry, or the opposer of an unconstitutional government? Personal advantage and public ideals cannot be torn asunder - it was an age when there was a close organic link between the religious and social, the economic and the political aspects of a man's life. To isolate one aspect is to make the men of the C17 unintelligible puppets. The best we can do is to piece together the various deposits left by each new wave of theory and, drawing a truth from each, build up a vital picture of that tumultuous age.

Contemporaries were widely opposed on the causes of the war. Clarendon saw it as a conspiracy of men like St John, Hampden, Pym and others who moulded the others to their view. "... without doubt" he says "the major part of that body consisted of men who had no mind to break the peace of the kingdom, or to make any considerable alteration in the government of church or state: and therefore all inventions were set on foot from the beginning to corrupt them ....." This view has recently been enlarged by Allen in his "Drift to War" when he stresses the ignorance of the mass of members as to what they were doing - "Not seeing where it was going, it blundered into a position which only revolution could maintain." Clarendon does not inquire into the motives of the plotters - tho' Allen suggests that personal fear of a reaction in the king's favour would both lead to their conviction of treason and destruction of what they genuinely believed to be invaluable work - "it is very unlikely" Allen declares "that the action of the leaders from this time onwards were motivated by desire for personal gain or personal power."

Lucy Hutchinson stresses the religious aspect - with the king "were all the corrupted, tottering bishops, & others of the proud, profane clergy of the land, who by their insolencies, grown odious to the people, bent their strong endeavours to disaffect the prince to his honest, godly subjects..." Here is the source of the stream which finds its embodiment in Haller - who we will examine later.

"Truly, I think if the king had had money, he might have soldiers enough in England. For there were very few of the common people that cared much for either of the causes, but would have taken any side for pay or plunder." Thus, cynically, does Hobbes start his dialogue "Behemoth" which outlines how the innocent people were seduced into unnecessary rebellion by Presbyterians, Papists, Independents, Anabaptists and other sectaries, ... a great number of the better sort .. as that in their youth (had) read the books written by famous men of the ancient Grecian or Roman commonwealths .... the

Essay 4. (cont'd) ②.

city of London and other great towns of trade..... there were a very great number that had either wasted their fortunes, or thought them too mean for the good parts they thought were in themselves; and more there were, that had able bodies, but saw no means how honestly to get their bread.; Lastly the people were so ignorant of their duty ..... the core of the rebellion ... are the Universities." Hobbes' placing of all religious factions on the side of the seducers and his too heavy stress on the Universities weaken his argument - but it is surprisingly acute observation all the same. He recognises many strands which led to war, religious, economic - in the cities (tho' he was wrong in diagnosing the motives as 'having in admiration the prosperity of the Low Countries after they had revolted from their monarch') - intellectual ferment in the cities which included a love of what they believed to be liberty - ie ideological reasons - and social causes - the declining classes of T-Roper and rising men who desired more power than they already had - as well as the ~~labourers~~ unemployed. And he stresses the indecision of the common people.

Wasted?

Lastly Richard Baxter throws out ideas which have lately been taken up with vehemence. On the side of parliament were "... the smaller part (as some thought) of the gentry in most of the counties, and the greatest part of the tradesmen + freeholders + the middle sort of men, ..." He stresses the constitutional motives "Though it must be confessed that the public safety and liberty wrought very much with most, + especially with the nobility and gentry who adhered to the parliament, yet" he continues "was it principally the differences about religious matter that filled up the parliament's armies and put the resolution and valour into their soldiers". So the stress here is on social, constitutional and especial religious factors in forming the two sides. If it does nothing else - a study of contemporary views should warn us to beware from seeking too simple and single a view of the origins of the War. They may have been confused themselves but they almost all lay stress on more than one constributary cause. Unless we suggest that religion and ideology, that concern for the constitution and for law are merely a cloak for economic and social pressures we will have to admit that it was more than a social and economic struggle.

Tawney and Trevor-Roper's views need no detailed stating - nor do they need to be refuted here. It is our job to find out what has been left when the inaccuracies and exaggerations of the two theses have been purged by men like Hill + Hexter. Trevor-Roper's value is that he has thrown light on several indisputable threads in 17 life - the decline of some of the gentry and the significance of control of the state, of offices and pensions, and the reality of a struggle between Court and Country parties. But his attempt to equate social and religious groupings and to use the "ins" and "outs" & the declining "mere" gentry as an explanation of the war have been shown to be untenable. Not only is his thesis untenable, but it is also, as Hexter points out, irrelevant. "The rise of the gentry is not a hypothesis to be verified; it is a simple fact, a fact that requires explanation."... Tawney sought the solution to this problem in economic factors... for Trevor-Roper the problem does not exist ... he divides effective activity, before the outbreak of the Civil War, between Royalist aristocrats who are "in" and Presbyterian aristocrats who are "out" leaving the mere gentry in a posture of ineffectual intransigence .. This is turning our back on the problem."

Tawney does attempt to explain the reasons for the emergence of the gentry as leaders of opposition to the King, but his statistics and his conclusions have been attacked and almost annihilated. Hexter's conclusion on this hypothesis is that "it is an interesting theory, that the evidence is in large part... ..misleading, ambiguous, irrelevant, or merely erroneous." Hill concludes ~~that~~ on T-Roper and Pennington that "The Civil War was fought about issues of principle which raised large numbers of men to heroic activity and sacrifice..... ~~Tho~~ by their exclusive concentration on interests, whether economic, geographical, or those of patronage, the impression is given.....that all politics is a dirty game,... that principles are merely rationalizations" When a Marxist and leading economic historian concludes that "my whole argument has been that we should not think merely in economic terms... no explanation of the English Revolution will do which starts by assuming that the people who made it were knaves or fools, puppets or automata." ~~It~~ is it is indeed clear that the reaction has set in - that the historian must cast out his net again. Hill's view is echoed by Hexter who finds a new liberty in the failure of T-Roper and Tawney to pin man down as a selfish, grubby egoist." Both Tawney and Trevor-Roper" he concludes ~~his article on "Storm over the Gentry"~~ "have failed to show that the C17 revolution in Britain was due primarily to shifts in the personnel of the landowning classes and their estates... the outcome of the Storm over the gentry" licenses one to turn part of one's attention.. ... to what one very great scholar calls "Liberty and Reformation in the Puritan Revolution."

Before we leave the wreck ~~let us~~ we must be certain to salvage much that is valuable and fundamentally true in the economic & social interpretation. There were serious social and economic pressures both in country and court. There was strife and competition. ~~But~~ Some men were almost wholly moved by such forces consciously or unconsciously - even the noblest were influenced by them. But it is impossible to accept such a theory as a total explanation.

Having destroyed, having burnt down the tangled and exaggerated growth with the fire of Zagorin and Habakkuk, of Aylmer, Hexter and Hill how are we to reconstruct? Perhaps the best way is to tackle the problem indirectly by a discussion of certain important contributions to the study of the long-term and immediate causes of the Civil War.

Allen's "Drift to War" chapter in his study of English political thought contains several provocative thoughts. The problem he sets out to solve is why did the demands of the House of Commons change so astonishingly between August 1641 and February 1642 when "the House would seem to have drifted or been driven into a position in which it felt compelled to make claims that, a few months earlier, it had not dreamt of making." He dismisses the matter of the root and branch controversy as merely a cover for something much deeper. "The House" he says "was divided only on the question whether it were better to abolish episcopacy altogether or to retain it as an instrument of secular government... It appears very unlikely that any one would have fought for the sake of governing the Church in one way rather than another." Even in October, he points out, a Bill not merely excluding bishops from the House of Lords, but disabling all persons in orders to hold temporal office under the Crown, was passed by the Commons with little opposition. Allen's view is considerably strengthened when we remember Richard Baxter's comment: "... not that the matter of bishops or no bishops was the main thing (for thousands that wished for good bishops were on the Earl's side) though many called it "bellum episcopale"..."

Allen admits inability to tell how far ahead Pym and the leaders of Parliament planned – the

④

Essay 4

early in 1642 Pym "may actually have aimed at establishing a constitution which would make of the king little more than a figurehead, and practically place sovereignty in the House of Commons representing the landowning & wealthy classes. But the mass, he stresses, were led on by "fear, illusion & passion." Allen lays emphasis on the retirement of the Scot's army as a direct cause of the fear of reaction which led Parliament on Aug 17th to usurp what was indubitably a right of the Crown only, by issuing orders to secure the military stores at Hull...; Like Wedgewood he lays tremendous ~~emphasis~~ stress on the Irish rebellion as a contributory cause and admits that "it may well be true, as Dr Montagu has suggested, that the Irish rebellion made Civil war in England unavoidable, by forcing the majority in the House to endeavour to take complete control of all armed forces." We have noticed Allen's point concerning the personal fears of the leaders which leads him to conclude that "It seems probable that, by the end of November, little doubt existed in the minds of the leaders of the House that, for their own safety and for that of their cause, it was necessary to take control of all armed forces..." From this account we can see that constitutional & military considerations finally sparked off the war.

Miss Judson brings a welcome return to the undoubtedly fundamental constitutional crisis. Her main emphasis is on the astounding strength of the Divine Right theory, as a doctrine if not always as a reality. Coke's statements on this subject are especially illuminating – in 1621 he ~~said~~ argued in favour of the king's possessing the power to commit persons on grounds of state without the reason being given and said in 1622 of the king "trust in him is all the confidence wee have under God, hee is God's lieutenant." and a year earlier he had said

"I will not meddle with the King's prerogative, which is twofold: i) absolute, to make war, coin money, etc: 2) or in things that concern meum et tuum (property) and this may be disputed of in C't of parl't". Even in the 1628 Parliament, Sherland, one of the most zealous supporters of the parliaments' cause, said "The king may make warr, may make peace, call parliaments, and dissolve them - these are of the highest nature, for there the king is the lex loquens." The enormous time spent in constitutional disputes, the opposition to various illegal practices during the personal rule were not just cover for economic necessity. The Elizabethan ideal of a balanced government as expressed by James Morice late in Elizabeth's reign in the words "We agayne the Subjects of this Kingdome, are bore and brought upp in due obedience, but farre from Servitude + bondage, subject to lawful auctoritie + commandement, but freed from licentious will + tyrannie; enjoyinge by lymetts of lawe and Justice our liefs, lands, goods, and liberties in great peace and securitie ..." was breaking down. Many factors were leading to a change in relationship between subjects and King, and hence to a conflict between the royal prerogative and personal rights a conflict exacerbated by the incapacity of the Stuarts and mirrored in the writings of Hobbes.

→ D. H. Willson in his ~~interesting~~ article "The Privy councillors in the House of Commons" throws light on what was both a cause and a result of the constitutional crisis - the decline of the council and the loss of royal control over parliament. He traces James weaknesses and increasing instability - by 1621 Tillieres writes "His mind uses its powers only for a short time, but in the long run he is cowardly." This degeneration is reflected in the council - bullied and scolded, forced to share opprobrium for actions it did not support, increasingly the King

5.

Essay 4.

posted with mere administrators, and left outside the most private of James plans it no longer provided Parliament with the indirect leadership which had been so invaluable in Elizabeth's reign. As early as 1612 the Spanish ambassadors noted that James "maketh little or noe account at all of his Councillors and scarcely communicateth with them anything of importance." By 1626 the Venetian ambassador wrote that "there is no longer any council, as Buckingham alone with three or four of his creatures for show constitute it". Buckingham and Charles, in fact, were not looking for advisers in the council, but for men who would do as they were told." This cavalier attitude was not confined to the smaller men. Miss Wedgewood in "The King's Peace" points out that "Charles was as much inclined to pass over their (Laud + Strafford) as he was that of lesser men. He supported the Archbishop in his plans for the Church, but in most other spheres he resented his interference ... he went clean against his advice for instance in the favour he showed to Roman Catholics ..." Charles, Wedgewood thinks, undermined what would have otherwise been a realisable vision of authoritarian government; "The king wanted the thing done without the strenuous effort of doing it; he deflected the energy and discouraged the efforts of his two best ministers ...."

We have roamed far, let us return to the view of probably the majority of contemporaries - that it was a "bellum episcopale." The fierceness of anti-episcopacy can well be seen in Milton's Lycidas - published two years before the Long Parliament -

"Enow of such as, for their bellies' sake,
Creep, and intrude, and climb into the fold!
Of other care than they little reckoning make

Than how to scramble at the shearer's feast.
And shove away the worthy bidden guest.
. . . .

Besides what the grim wolf with privy paw
Daily devours apace, and nothing said."

Years of bottled up spiritual fervour, years of fear as the Counter-Reformation swept across Europe, the sublimation of many unconscious desires for freedom intellectual and moral can hardly be dismissed as an insignificant cause of the Revolution. Laud laboured for beauty, authority, learning and good taste. "all the things that England most needed short of the one thing that half of England most passionately desired, namely freedom for the individual to work out his own salvation in his own way. Man is not a wholly spiritual being & to represent the revolution as nothing but a religious upheaval would be false; but it is equally faulty to forget the burning ardour, the high ideals which moved men like Cromwell and Milton, Vane and Williams. Not all men were Miltons, but neither were they all Hobbses.

Recent Historians: Pearzke — Economic Interp'n of History.

Who are the 5 members who the King tried to get hold of them.

Private Writing - Summer Term 1962

I returned to Oxford at the end of the spring vacation in April. The term must have started about 26th of April. I was clearly in a mood when I wanted to start to assess myself and the place I was in. I was aware of being half way through my time at Oxford. So I sat down and drafted out various thoughts and poems.

Worcester Gardens 27/4/62 Spring

Spring has broken like a dropped egg & lies, quivering like the golden yoke, expectant, warm, before its time. Oh that I could burrow my hand down into its warm fur & feel its warm body deep in the bristling earth. Sun-soaked trees repose, trying to fight the itch & the unseemly skittishness of spring – which disturbs their grave maturity. Early butterflies let the trickling warmth ooze into their still-silk-wet wings. Fountains of bird song bubble liquid melody, & birds plume & search eagerly. Old ladies relax and stretch on the grass and brown skinned girls look crisply enticing in the first white blouses. White-cloud figures wander, vague as daffodils & the wind blows milkily over the creamy-with-daisys grass.

All is ádance, bubble-bursting, streaked, crisp, curling, radiant & pulsing.

Meditations. A spring room in Worcester (11:4), listening to Dvorak. 29/4/62

Soft pink evening brushes the trees and Dvorak trembles through the spring-like '4th'. Life is suddenly very peaceful. The rushing, mad trees, the twisted objects of our hurried gaze smoothed out, and like Wordsworth on his lake "all is still as a summer sea." Suddenly everything is very precious. It all wears that terrible beauty which clothes even the weary hands of the dying man. Every tiny bud, every solid branch & trunk in this beautiful park, the softness of my slippers, the open window, my tiny room with its hand-painted reproductions of Toulouse Lautrec, its bare electric fire, its uncomfortable chairs and the rush of greenery in the two flower pots with the sweet-smelling white narcissus – and Julie's heroes mug. All these, the music, the evening gardens, the little room whose untidy, uncomfort is especially dear, all these I love, and would hold. But I am forced on, and the moment of true vision will be jealously snatched from me.

On May Day, Tuesday May 1st I wrote down some further thoughts. They were the first ones to be typed out, as follows.

On Purity. Thoughts. 1/5/62

Adulteration weakens metals, it corrodes, it mars symmetry & fosters imperfection. Purity, purity of thought, of deed, of impulse & of spirit are the key of successful living – & by 'successful' is not meant prosperous, famous, integrated or even happy living, for all these may indeed be by-products (purity includes the steady pursuit of a given object & this will almost certainly result in the achievement of that aim in this world of flabby purposes where people are uncertain & perhaps more than usually ready to follow anyone with conviction & energy etc) but success or failure in life, if life has any meaning at all & that of course is the premise for even embarking on this subject, is at a far deeper level than that (or of course it may be that it is at a more shallow level) it is a matter of relationships; with others, with ourselves & ultimately with god through these agencies for we & others are only reflections of God "whatsoever ye do (or do not do) unto the least of these ye do unto me". But on purity; once agreed on moral standards & on the fact that every action & every thought we have will change & perhaps completely destroy our essence (Hell) it is of consequence of utmost importance both what we aim at & how we progress towards that aim.

Newspapers are	50% good	30% indifferent	20% actively evil
Television -		as above	
Poetry	80%		20%
Music	90%		10%
Religion (Organised)	40%	40%	40%
Religion (Private)	80%	20%	
Conversations	20%	60%	20% (Gossip)
Work	80%	10% (exams)	10% (false moral judgement)
Societies	10%	80%	10% (cliqueshness & pomposity)

Vicarious experience is dangerous for it becomes a drug, sapping our desire for the real thing, insulating us from real experience, esp' suffering to others & the sympathy we would feel.

Poetry is one of the most, if not the most, concentrated form[s] of language, it has a life of its own as has all language & is the strongest drill for a certain kind of inquirer after truth & the vehicle for expressing that uncertain beauty & sadness which trails like a mist on the limits of man's mind where it merges with eternity.

If we wd be either grt, famous, powerful, whether it is in business or in philanthropy one must cultivate will-power & its accomplice energy & learn to channel it by a drastically dedicated (ascetic) self-discipline & by strict organ'n. If one is to succeed in this way one must "Know thyself" by reason, probe, analyse, expose, re-arrange oneself. To be strong in this way one must know one's gt weaknesses. It means a turning in on oneself; a systematic spiritual, mental, & even physical organ'n of one's natural resources which can be stimulated & improved to an amazing extent. Memory, charm, capacity for distinguishing the essential, the technique of putting one's inspiration across, & of course the ability to work hard & long. All these are necessary & it all presupposes a tremendous desire & a conviction that the end is worth while.

But if one merely wishes to be holy, kind & good none of this rigorous training is enough. The spiritual journey & arming necessary is far more complex & arduous, but it is gradual & the struggle for perfection is the simplest of all the incomprehensibles.

The following day I just have a scrap, showing I was brooding.

<u>Evening – 2/5/62</u>

Why has evening this magic power? Perhaps it is because it is at the end of the day – the silence of death, the soul-sleep after the day. It is partly the smell – when the huffy stuffiness of day – swirling currents of warmth & smell of dust and movement & hate and bustle and warm grass and dusty feet – all these cool and coagulate, crystallise into perfect form.

*

The following day I clearly sat down to start to plan a book, or collection of essays, on life as an undergraduate in Oxford. This is rather extraordinary to me now. Not only had I forgotten all about this, but it foreshadows in a curious way what I am doing now – some 50 years later. And it helps to explain why, about this time, I was keeping all sorts of ephemera, making notes on my thoughts and reactions etc. Little did I know that many years later I would write a book on Cambridge, and my mind would return to those Oxford undergraduate days to complete the task which I rapidly sketched in here.

The first page was written on [Thursday] 3 May 1962 and is a plan.

Oxford – 1962

A study in poetry and prose of the mood of a changing city.

People
- i) the types of undergraduates & dons & towns people
- ii) Individuals & relationships
- iii) Problems
- iv) Situations: plays; parties, punts etc.

City
- i) The Seasons
- ii) The times of day.
- iii) The different parts of the city: parks etc – certain buildings etc.
- iv) The atmosphere.

Comparison – what others have said of it
Scholar Gypsy – Arnold – find out who has been there – Gollancz etc.

Assessment

*

A second page, undated, probably was written on the same day.

OXFORD – Planning.

Writers of contributions (In each case there was 'Person' and 'Subjects' – the latter has not been filled in. All had question marks against them.
D. Isaac, D. Roberts, P.R. Hyams, Judy Hudson [my girlfriend at that time], Margaret Cresswell [my late girlfriend], Susan Pleat [a potential girlfriend from whom I have a letter], Robert Mules [I do not remember], Julie S, Mr Campbell [my tutor].

Subjects
Physical beauty – Seasons, places. Sex. Religion. Work. Class. Societies. Perversions. Gossip. Sport. Sets. Parties. Individuals. Special problems. Special rewards. Theories & Solutions.

Sources for comparison & ideas.
1. Degenerate Oxford
2. Scholar Gypsy & Oxford – Arnold
3. Gollancz. "Timothy" & in anthologies (poems)
4. Gerard Manley Hopkins
5. G.K. Chesterton – Oxford (Essays)
6. Zuleika Dobson. Beerbohm.

I started on the task on the same day.

The first salient characteristic is the great dichotomy between the dreaming, unchanging city and the throbbing, bustling layer of new traffic, modern office-blocks & thronged streets. One can feel the soft grey stone of the old worn walls & towers as bones to the city, over which a new skin has been stretched. This contrast between serenity & bustle, between calm order & hectic modernism is reflected on the human level by the friction between the accepted, the traditional, the regular teaching & doctrines of scholastics & the rough, sceptical, bitter restlessness which moves like a series of small storm clouds over the surface of Oxford life – shutting out for periods the enjoyment, the calm & the warmth of this beautiful city. So, broadly, we have two major themes – the background of Oxford, its natural beauty, its changing opportunities, its gifts & its demands – and on the other hand we have the response of types of people – and on the other hand we have the response of types of people & individuals to the environment, a response which is to a considerable extent conditioned by extra-university factors such as changing conceptions etc in society. So, Oxford is a peculiar blend of beauty and ugliness, of change & permanence, of deep-set strength and surface fissures, of joy & sadness, of satisfaction and disillusion, of idealism & scepticism. It is, despite its famous traditionalism & conservatism, perhaps one of the most accurate barometers of English society – and can be studied with profit as both an indictment of certain aspects of the modern ethic and the failure of a materialist society to provide purpose – and also as a study of youth's restlessness. Further, it would be both interesting & profitable as an insight of how an actual undergraduate – eminent neither for wit nor intelligence, feels about the university. And its value as a serious study will be enhanced if a survey of various other views of the University are given – a sort of "Oxford then & Now".

(The penultimate sentence is exactly what I have thought and written some 50 years later – that this account of Oxford as an undergraduate has some merit from the fact that I was so middling an undergraduate.)

The following day, a Friday [May 4], I went out on a punt and meditated further. There is no evidence of who was with me.

Chewing apple-turnover, I lie on a punt. A medium breeze laps the water against the boat and waves the half-bare willow under which the punt is moored. It is still early spring & the young shoots & half-grown reeds & short grass has not lost its flashing green to the lustrousness of summer. There are other punts on the river, and undergraduates – self-conscious in their attempt to forget their supposed dignity, clumsily pole themselves up to the Victoria Arms. About half the punts have mixed occupants – and even these the men & girls self-consciously remain apart – and one feels that some at least of it is for "kudos". There are a surprising number of punts with just girls – probably pretending they are happy without men.

Up here the sky seems much wider, for the horizon is not piled up with buildings as in Oxford – and one can gain a brief exit – one can pierce out through the suffocating fabric of university life. But even here among the swooping swifts, with only the distant train hoot, the far off cry of children & murmur of far-off voices to remind one of the city – or just now a bell ringing. Here where one looks up into a tangle of branches – their outlines still clear because it is Spring, where the hollowed-out but massive bulk of the willow trunk – like some great worn-out brush with only the end bristles left – [small sketch] – here where the smell is all of watery things, of ducks feathers, of lush cress and reeds seeping & growing & squelching up from the mud, and filled with watery greenness like cucumbers. Here where the water finds secret caverns & holes under the bank where it plays with old tree roots, here where the rippling water ripples into rippling reeds up to a snowy-skie [sic], even here in the freshness & vegetating country full of animal freedom & growing things the old stale smell of Oxford blows its choking breath. Even here the undergraduates are bowed, even here one sees them reading for exams – for they cannot forget that soon they must return. But for these few hours they are partly free to be purposefully idle – to let their restlessness [sic] minds vegetate – to have no more problems than how to avoid the next punt – no more worry than not falling in. they can revel in doing something absolutely useless – in the most inefficient manner possible. For a time they can swim with those ducks who go as they like – busy but unquestioning.

The following day, Saturday 5th May, I wrote the following

OXFORD II

Work

Supposedly intelligent, the average undergraduate tends to become very lazy – & his laziness is often in proportion to his intelligence. `Much of the attitude to work is a pose – for it is considered to be bad form – a sign that one is wasting one's precious time – if one admits to working hard. "Oh, he's got nothing else to do except work" – is the usual way such types are dismissed. Oxford is very anxious to dismiss state's of mind which it cannot understand or is afraid of – it sneeringly condemns the O.I.C.C.U. as "spiritual scalp-hunters" or laughs to scorn the "do-gooders". This is partly a result of what one might call the "demand-fixation".

The average boy of 19 who comes up to University has a modicum of philanthropy, religion & public spirit in him; he also has wide interests many of which he wishes to pursue. From the moment that he looks in his pigeon-hole or walks into the Freshman's Fair he is subjected to intensive propaganda from the hundreds of clubs and societies & dozens of sects & religious denominations who are often genuinely concerned either for the work they are pushing – or for the welfare of the freshmen – but this all has the effect of making him feel that he is being "Got-at". Bewildered at first, he will later come to the conclusion that the only way to sort his way through the maze of conflicting calls is to throw them all over. But he still retains some genuine concern for spiritual values or for others but stifles this by the most effective method he knows – laughter (scornful).

Academical [sic] is, frankly, merely a necessary base for 90% of the undergraduates. This is because they neither have sufficient interest in the inherent subject-matter nor a sufficiently strong ambition to do well in exams or in individual essays which might have forced them into taking interest. Distractions, of course, play a considerable part in detracting for apart, and one perhaps mainly responsible for the lack of interest for time is so valuable and so much fresh experience must be crowded into a brief period that work is not considered first priority. But perhaps deeper than this lies disillusion. This is on two levels. There is the reaction against the idea of a degree as a means to a "safe & cushy job" – and there is the effect of living in a disillusioned age – when, symbolized by the existentialists – man's last few idols have been smashed – reason & education. Why bother to learn? It makes one no more happy. There is no longer absolute of any kind. One only launches out into the void. The vital premises of education have been taken away – and dimly the normal undergraduate realises this.

The "religious guys" whom everyone scorns & who are in many ways extraordinarily naïve, & often, sadly, sanctimonious & hypocritical, yet they are one of the few groups of people who care & do attempt to do something ("Refugee groups" – "Hospital" – "Work Parties") they do have a positive programme – and it is probably their quiet confidence that they have the answer which exasperates the restless, wandering, undergraduates more than anything. They have had it "too dam easy", "why should they have the answer & not me?" etc etc

Sexual frustration & growing pains cause much of the unhappiness.

Feeling of failure (having had too much asked of them) & especially a feeling of failure if one is unhappy (for if one is unhappy – where will one be happy?) – main contributions to suicide.

No contract between dons & undergraduates. Completely left to themselves (tho' still children, since national service stopped.)

*

The project of a book of essays on Oxford does not seem to have moved on, perhaps partly because a week or so later on 12th May I met my second serious girlfriend, Penny. So from then on we return to observations and poems.

27/5/62 On reading Marx. [A Sunday – I was in London to meet my mother and sisters who had just returned from India]

Black day over London: rain sluicing over the drab tenements and brick & weedy gardens. I am poised high up – looking out not only over this mighty black heart whose throbs of anguish are felt in every land, whose black blood is drawn into every vein of the world; but as I read 'To the Finland Station' I look down into the involved, saturnine heart of Marx, resilient, blindly beating itself on the door of knowledge, watering the modern world with its tortured sweat, agonised grinding of its massive heart. In the black heart of each of these there is hidden some gleam of the divine light – but how can I search alone amids [sic] the morass of lost ideology and materialism, when I feel every tearing doubt that Marx felt (and which London wears) straining within me?

"Seek not knowledge for its own
Sake but to be a star to men for ever." Says Browning.

We must turn in, in, more & more on ourselves, analyse & strive to understand, but the illumination we seek comes not from ourselves but from grasping on to God & holding him & letting him hold us. Once we have worked in and grasped the core of our being the current will flow outwards through us to light the world – to light over the blackness of Marx & London. To burn the blackness off with the fire of love.

Worcester Summer Evening (& memories) 8/6/62

Evening sunlight throws long gold-green fingers across the lawn, caressing the scented air and squeezing it as if the heaviness of grass-scents and of a day of sun & flowers had made the air into something thicker than air – into a translucent treacle.

Summer is still young so that the lanes are hung with may and there is no overgrowth – nor was the day intolerably warm where the red geranium flamed along the old dusty quads & the air went to sleep in little 'pump' quad.

I have been for three walks on three perfect evenings. What shall I pick out – the buttercup fields where the sweet clover crunches in the cow's mouth. The lanes with the high-piled grass and walls of snow and occasional miracle of cherry blossom. The blueness of quivering distant woods – seeming to stir and re-shape themselves into a blue fantasy of perfection like some reflection on the lake. The birdsong, bubbling & frothing setting the currents of the sweet, honey-suckle sweet, evening astir to shake the seed from the dandelion. The tiny flowers that lie deep in the forest of the grass, like dreams in the dark of sleep. The rivers & streams which curl through the meadows & woods, with their burden of rushes and lush overhanging willows, with the clouds of gnats waltzing above the swirl of the fish and the white reflection of the swan.

Then there were the little churches, lost amidst a heavy-smelling profussion [sic] of nettles, grave-stones appearing like battered rocks out of the sea of overwhelming growth,

& overhanging them dank cypresses & yews. Inside the churches it was dark and stone cool, moss cool, with light slanting in from the evening sun to light up some old wooden pew or stone pillar with gold & leave the hangings and tablets, the beamed roof & silent altar in retiring gloom. Peace and sadness breed in the quietness of these lonely churches to fall on the visitor like the heavy smoke-smell of their shaded grave-yards.

Alan, Penny and a friend on a punt on the Cherwell, photo by Erik Pearse 9th June

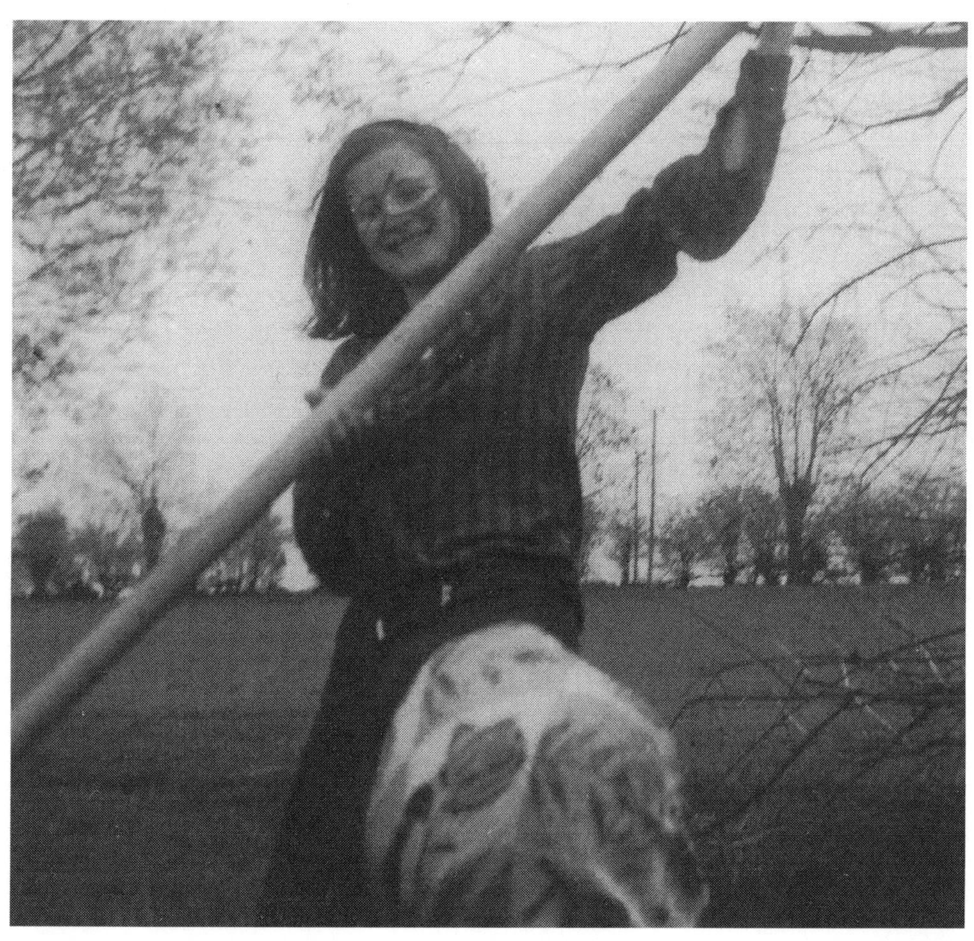

Thought 15/6/62

All aspiration, ambition, hatred and love are an outlet of energy – a current from man to God, from the finite to the infinite, from the relative to the absolute, which is often perverted (misdirected) & results in all the cruelties, bestialities & horror of life.

*

A series of poems about Oxford, written May-June.

Candle time and the burning of summer fires;
Now the evening closes its wet lids of dripping leaves
And a few last tears roll down its evening cheeks.
Oxford lies sulky, sent indoors before her time
By the rain, her young desires suppressed
And a peevish silence hangs like a bad breath
In the air. In numerous rooms smoke,
Desire, sour coffee and rancied thoughts mix
Into a brown swill of discontent. Youth is
Everywhere discontented, even here it strives
Giddily for the stars – but here earlier than
Elsewhere it grasps them & finds they crackle
Up in the hands & puff into dirty smoke – like
A dry poisonous puff-ball. Enthusiastically
They search on, eagerly opening the doors into
Other hearts – but the doors are slammed in
Their faces and they turn back on themselves
And for the first time enter their own chambers.
Here they find many strange & obscene objects
Relics of youth grown bitter with knowledge –
The fresh innocence has faded and they appear
As they are empty and sterile symbols of
Frustration & self-assertion. As one ascends the
Creaking stairs of the years, year after littered
Year is filled with empty boxes of selfishness.
And then comes that insistent instant the
Present and all the streaming gold which
Pours blindingly beautiful across the future.
Here too the analysing mind pulls down all
The romance & innocence – every action &
Every thought becomes greasily covered
With the excrement of pseudo-psychological
Self-knowledge. Self-revulsion accompanies
The bitterness of a hollow place where
One's god's used to be. One can no longer worship
Superhuman beings, one cannot worship others – one
Cannot worship oneself. Giddily, all bearings & landmarks
Lost one turns inwards & then outwards – tires
To lose one's thoughts in the thoughts of
Others, in films, plays, games, coffee parties – afraid
Of being left alone with oneself – afraid to meet
Oneself head on – afraid of the rotting corpse
That lies within – afraid of the skull & of

The unquenchable stench of decay. One searches
Desperately, battering, twisting, turning in
An ecstasy of horror to try to escape.
Sympathetic friends scream warnings – but
"How can you know when you do not feel".

Out of this orgy of self-pity, of self-
Analysis, of self-absorption only a conscious
Effort, the desire to go on can rescue
One. The moment we stop we will sink,
Like a man on water skiis. And where are
We going and what are our supports? Our
Supports are our will and our faith. Our
Faith that somehow, beyond all the
Torments – and through the agony of this
World's sweating passion – lies the Saviour.
If we hold on to him, if we fight & seek
Him – if we burn always with longing for
Him we will drag on & slowly will slip
Into our lives, as the colour slips
Into a morning sky and melts through the
Streets & over the torn and ragged world,
A growing faith – a love of others and
A forgetfulness of ourselves. Love, which is
The elimination of self in favour of another,
Is the path to heaven from the hell of madness.

Oxford: Contrasts

Morning

(i) I could not sleep, for all around
The world was waking.
Dappled sunlight streamed along the
Branches cascading into my room,
Wallflower scent drifted up the old stone
And waves of bird-song were breaking.
The air sparkled like the lake beneath the trees
Both mirroring the skies morning brightness.
Birds pulled plump worms from the wet ground
And a glimmering trance held the city in a
Web of flame.

(ii) the hiss of rain, the dripping of leaves,
The vicious smack of branches on the window
Told him that another day was come.
Tired still from sleeplessness, empty of hope,
He buried his head in the pillow
To drown the insistent whine & bumping
Of the traffic squelching past his grated window.

(iii)
The city was quiet now, especially in the old cobbled parts
Where the gas lamps shone in crooked corners.
And the cat walked alone. Where silence
Brooded, occasionally letting slip a whirling leaf
Between its fingers, or encouraging some
Hurrying figure to rustle past – so that her
Silence would return with increased force.
Old mouldering walls, impregnated with mosses & lichens
Seemed to whisper of days gone by,
And shadows moved as silent as the old grey
Monks who used to flit through the streets.
The scent of mown grass, and warm stone,
Of lush meadows & juicy water-plants
Mixed with wood-smokes & cooking suppers
Sidled down the crooked streets. Mystery
Beckoned to magic, Oxford had put on its
Old pointed cap & was weaving a spell
Dissolving the hard, tense city of
The day into a melting, sliding dream
Where the memories & the echoes of
A thousand happy lives, the creeping
Ghosts of the long years gathered to
Stare at the passer-by, and to catch his footsteps
And fill him with delight & fear.

On a separate sheet of paper, clearly written about the same time, are further fragments of a more general kind. There is another version of this poem, headed 'Inspiration: Penny a red-dress: Need for giving: Poem. "Emotion recollected in tranquillity"'. This dates it to the summer of 1962

(i)

From the winepress of my heart
Is the red blood pressed;
With an anguish of delight,
Is beautie's birth dressed.
And as the slow blood drips.
It splashes in a bowl;
Which I bring as an offering,
From the labour of my soul.

(ii)

When the world's wide-eyed wonder,
Creeps in on our gaze –
As the flooding, dew-splashed sunlight
Breaks out of the haze –
Then from the black waters
Of the drowning, drugging night,
Crawls the tired swimmer,
Into the warm and friendly light.

(iii)

Like a lonely coast at evening
Where the slow surf breaks
Long on the echoing rocks
In a shock of silver flakes
An evening life lies
A wild young land
Immemorably old with heather
And the purple of the sand.
And on each beach and inlet
The tide sweeps in and out
Bringing in the salt-splashing
Of electric-silver trout;
Swaying, as in longing
The tendrils of long weeds
Where the shrimp finds its shelter
And water-vermin breeds.
It is a sheltered fastness,
A sad and sinful land,
Where old crimes smoulder
And blood is on the sand,
Where an uneasy silence broods,
And restless winds sigh,
Waiting till the earth and rocks
Are drowned in the sky.
But beating on this barren coast,
The sea scours the grime,
Cleansing the smeared sand's sin
With the grinding power of time.
And each tide rolls with it,
A gift of shining things,
Old battered corks and boxes,
Shoes, lobster pots, and rings.
And when I squish along
The margin of the tide,
Prodding, pushing, peering,
Pulling junk aside –
Amongst the rotting corpses
Of a thousand salt-stale fishes
Of a thousand broken subjects,
Of a thousand broken wishes,

Hidden in the salty jungle
Of the slime-infested brine
There lie scattered memories
Of a far-off youthful time.
Worn-smooth by the working
Of the grinding chiselling sea,
A half-dead memories,
Will reluctantly let free.
Beaten into hardness,
Smoothed into form
We will pick them up wondering,
Feeling them still warm
For the seed we throw – like manna

On the labouring pregnant sea
Is brought back in beauty,
Purged by time & misery.

Three other fragments, undated, are clearly written at different times from the paper and script, but probably during this time.

Richness & warmth, colour and
Life – and outside the black
Cold, dead night. Here the
Sound of breaking of bodies,
The muddled impressions and
Reasoned minds, things
Understood and not felt –
But outside the still
Blackness, the stars above the
Mountains and no wind
Just the cats and furry
Killers who tear open
The screaming wounds and
Smash the light
Moves through my brain to you
And for a second there is
A blaze of warmth before
The eyes close in and the
Old woods march on
And the grass waves
Surge over our heads
And new generations sleep
And stir uneasily in their
Love.

Another strange poem:

Used-chewing-gum skies bellied rain
And the roads sluiced brown rives.
The mind sags likewise and only a
Gleam of former beauties tell of the
Times amidst hay, in the wing of an ecstatic tune
Or the drift of a trout towards the fly,
Through this dirt & damp, the grease of cold panes
And the clinging of straw to sodden clothes
It may be that some warmth, some
Delighting sunbeam plays on distant sound.
It could be that eyes enchant in some
Intoxicated dance-floor, and bodies
Hold each other's warmth in some deep
Bed of softest linen. Surely the waters
Still slap their blued sand & furry creatures
Snuggle into the earth? Surely the
Long flow of notes stream across the
Air in some theatre and all this land
Of broken impulses & broken promises,
Of half will & half wish, where all is gay

And sugar-sweet & lonely-dull
Where no sharp image remains
Will cease.

Then there is the following, headed:
Alan Macfarlane, Worcester College

A candle making gold hair stand
Against the dark – imprisoning your eyes
In the warmth of the melting wax,
An apples roundness body, yet unknown
And unknowing – an impression of synthesis.
All this means something, is real
In its unreality. Each object is related
And signifies a haven from the coldness
And singleness of the night. Notes
Rising and falling in a drift of time
Moving faster to the tail of the day's pool,
Bringing back images that were disjointed
And hardly understood, and with them a moment's
Peace. Of the leaves beneath the feet,
Wet and broken by concrete wetness,
Turning into the old stone of the buildings
Like wood to coal; of the sky amove
With circling ducks upon the lake
Of the sudden realization of joy in another's eyes
In the street, where moves the machine
Belt of men in their leaden dance
Of laughter in the solemnity of the great
God's house – where the serious stare
Of shadows behind sunlight, of reflections of
The lake in the trees in all their
Lamentations and loss of autumn,
Sucking back their drift to themselves.

Summer Vacation 1962

There are not enough letters to and from my parents or grandparents to justify a separate chapter devoted to letters. My parents were on leave during this summer and hence there is only one letter, written by my mother to my father before he arrived in England, which has survived. So I shall divide this chapter into three sections.

Firstly there will be the ephemera and the few letters from friends (other than Penny) that I have for the summer. Then an account of the period at a Borstal camp. Finally I shall include a couple of descriptions I wrote at the time.

Most important was that this was a summer spent with my parents. My mother had arrived back in late May and my father in late June so we all spent the summer together at Field Head. It is difficult to disentangle the memories of that summer, and in the absence of letters between us or diaries, there are only a few flashes of events from what remains.

One was a wedding on Friday, August 17th, at Saint Peter's Episcopal Church, Peebles, of Nicola, the daughter of my godmother Pat Cowan. I remember nothing of this. Nor do I know whether I went to the Christian Public School Boys Camp at Over Stowey in Somerset, for which I have two brochures.

There is one letter from my mother which seems to be written around the 20th of June, just before my father arrived.

Field Head – no date. Hawkshead 307[telephone number]

My darling,
I hope this will get you before you leave – no Air Letter in Hawkshead P.O.! I still don't know your flight number, time or even day of arrival but presume you've told me. John Lampett isn't now coming till after you get here – so I'm afraid nobody will be there to meet you darling but I'll send the A.A. map & a few pounds to the Air India Bureau, but hang onto all the money you can so you wont be stuck if anything goes wrong. Could you please pick up Alan's cases at Oxford, he'll let the man at Worcester Coll. know you're coming, you can skirt London and it shouldn't take you out of your way.

Home at last, after a hectic 2 days with Julia & Billy. ... We came back by bus & after one day together M & D left this morning & we've had a gigantic tidy up. The top landing is impassable...

Anne finished her exams quite cheerfully & now we're forgetting the whole thing till the results come in. It's the most peculiar feeling not having work to do, nice but a bit sad too. Alan and Fiona are very cheerful, they've gone off to a "social" with a Swedish girl Fiona has palled up with, Alan's hair slightly less frightful. He goes off to his Borstal Camp on Saturday for 2 weeks but after that will be home for good...

Have a good trip and hurry home my darling, the Aga is waiting to be riddled, lawns cut, walls painted – and I'm waiting too – All love till then, Totty

The next letter is to me from Julie on 12th July:

Dearest Alikins,

Many thanks for your letter. .... Penny was here for dinner a couple of nights ago. I wish I'd thought of giving her these things to take to you, but I didn't – so I've posted them myself as I shan't have time to see her before I leave. Terribly sorry about the delay....Lots of love to you. Hope you & Penny get great mutual pleasure from her stay with you. Love again, Pusseybite.

There is another letter from Julie dated 17th August.

Dearest Alikins,

Many thanks for your letter which I received in Rome. Our holiday was a great success in all respects, and none in particular. I am so glad all has worked out so smoothly re. Penny and wish you happiness with all my heart. I know she enjoyed her stay with you very much, so I have no doubt that you enjoyed her company too. … If you come to London, don't neglect me – I have news of the first importance that I daren't commit to paper, but am longing to impart to you! Love as always. Julie

My most intense relationships were with my girlfriends. But I also had many friendships with men, and particularly with half a dozen of my closer friends at Worcester College. Because we were together all through the term and did not feel it was worth writing much, if anything, to each other during the vacations, there is little trace of these friendships and what we discussed. The few letters I do have show a tone of bantering and teasing and exchange of ideas which went on almost every day over meals, on walks, in the evenings.

Borstal Camp Thoughts: 1962

I went twice on the Worcester-Borstal camp expeditions, once as an undergraduate, once, later, as a graduate. These camps had vague religious overtones – both the Chaplain of Worcester (Rev. Alec Graham) and the Catholic Chaplain (Father Michael Hollings) attended, and it may have been through attendance at Chapel that I became enrolled. In many ways, it has remained a formative experience in my life. The following is the account I wrote about the first of the two experiences, aged twenty.

We first camped for a week or so on the Yorkshire moors, at Spennithorne near Masham, then went with our Borstal opposite numbers to their camp. This Borstal was at Hewel Grange, near Bromsgrove, a Borstal from 1946 to 1991, when it became a Grade D Prison.

BORSTAL 22nd July

<u>Situation</u> – old family mansions – parks, avenues, tapestries, statues; then army camp & arms dump – bullets etc easily accessible in nearby lake (game of firing them in polish tins) [Described as 'the poshest prison in England' by a paper]

<u>Background of boys</u>
Usually for theft (cars or warehouses) second or third conviction. Many of them through boredom or broken homes had done this – gangs. Many from Liverpool. Exceptions – from good backgrounds – rebels. Occasionally for armed robbery – or G.B.H. (Grievous bodily harm).

<u>The Borstal</u>

Sentences between 6 months – 2 yrs. Usual term about 11 months – but up to 19. No definite term imposed at the beginning – merely put up grade 1 – 2 – 3; "leavers" according to opinion of "screws" & the governor. (Thus prejudice – on the part say of the matron – could double a boy's time). Their pay approximately 2/9; 4/3 & 6/3 according to grade. Allowed to buy tobacco, sweets & sugar – that is all. No food to be sent in. No fences etc (an "open" borstal)

Food – starchy, no sugar – bromides (?) – meat slab, gravy, potatoes(!), peas

BORSTAL 1962 (Typed out for three quarters of a page, and then handwritten.]

In a clearing in the wood a group of young men sat & lay, resting from scything nettles. A bowl, once filled with strawberries contributed by the older man who sat at one edge of the rough circle, lay emptied on the cut grass. A listener would have overheard a heated, but highly intelligent, discussion varying subjects, but principally on the merits & vices of the English penal system. The younger men criticising, the older man made a limited defence of the existing legal position – though he too added his criticisms. A closer look at the clothes of the group reveals that they are all dressed alike – in striped shirt, overalls & black denim jacket with a number sowed on it; they are in fact Borstal boys.

Once we realise this we will probably notice the strange absence of any "chip", of any disgruntled hatred of the society which condemned them. There are few rebels. They accept their condemnation as a just reward for their folly in getting caught. When they stole or fought they accepted the risk & the possible consequences added that flavour of excitement, lacking in the dull monotony of their ordinary life, which perhaps was one of the reasons for their crime. Their criticisms, often strikingly perceptive, are aimed at the injustices & pointlessness of the present system. And their objections are fired partly by the knowledge that the odds are practically at evens that they will be back in Borstal or prison within a year of finishing their present sentence – the average of re-sentencing is 45%. In ten or more months of boredom & frustration they will neither have learnt to hate the Borstal enough, or learnt to love the values of our society, of the outside world enough to be kept out. What then are the main criticisms of the boys themselves – and how pertinent are they?

Above all they attack a system which leaves entire control of how long they are to be in Borstal to a board of very fallible human beings. A boy is committed for a '6 to 24' sentence, that is for any period between 6 & 24 months. After a spell in prison he arrives at the Borstal as a 'Grade I' boy – meaning he gets paid about 1/9 per week – for tobacco, sweets or sugar, stamps etc. He will remain in this position as long as "the staff" think fit. Housemaster, under the Governor, have a preponderant say in deciding who gets their grades & moves up. If a boy gets on the wrong side of any authorities – be it "screw" or his matron they can prevent his promotion. There have been cases of 'favourites' being whisked through, while other boys, perhaps being less intelligent or even good-looking are made to serve up to 5 or 6 months in each grade.

Even if the housemasters & others are conscientious & honest to an extreme they will be unable to avoid offending a few boys. There are always some who grumble – probably rightly – that mere personal prejudice or dislike has told against them. Even on the favoured, the strain of not knowing whether one will be out by Christmas or only by next summer leads to an unnecessary & damaging tension & hostility. Even if the abuses under such a system are not as flaring as the boys make out, their bitterness & unending complaints, their accumulated resentment is a product of the system – a system which, as they point could well be changed.

The aim would be to eradicate as much of the human "error" in deciding the length of their stay as possible. This would mean the sentence, taking into account the nature of the crime etc, being more stereotyped – say sentencing a boy for 8-9 months. In case of really good behaviour he would get out in 8 – if bad, in 9 or, perhaps 10.

The disadvantages of such a system would be twofold, firstly there would be less coercive power in the hands of the prison officials – no longer could they hang a threat over each action of their charges – and in an "open" borstal where there are no physical punishments this would be quite a problem – for it is not difficult to prevent boys trying to escape – but it is almost impossible to make them keep tidy, work or refrain from pillow-fighting. Without the "cane" or "lines", the housemaster's task is far more difficult than his equivalent in the public school. This would undoubtedly prove a difficult problem. But is one which must be faced.

Secondly a certain flexibility would be lost. There are obviously cases where a judge, sentencing merely on one case could be wrong – and those who come into frequent contact with the subject could decide better, knowing both him & the nature of the treatment he is getting, how long he should have. For instance there was one case of [a] boy, convicted of armed robbery and later attempting to escape – on paper a serious case. In fact a short acquaintance showed him to have been merely temporarily mal-adjusted and in fact to be intelligent & sensitive – a writer & poet who after a brief aberration was prepared to take a balanced view of life & society. With the present elasticity he would probably benefit – it abolishes rigidity & lets errors through the net faster than a more automatic system. Both these objections have to be weighed carefully. But to my mind lessened dissatisfaction, lessened injustice, lessened responsibility over a boy's life in the hands of borstal officials, lessened strain & anxiety in the borstal would outweigh the disadvantages.

Two other abuses could be briefly mentioned – one of them is the food. This brings up the whole problem of what a Borstal attempts to do – is it punitive, retributive or merely a training ground? For it depends on which view is taken as to what they will eat. The food question at the moment seems to have provoked an escapist answer. An outline of the diet will show what I mean. Breakfast consists of skilly (a sort of porridge surprisingly edible) – tho' without milk or sugar & made out of Canadian Pig Food (Grade A1) Then comes mashed potatoes, broad beans & carrots, a square of meat (a sort of lump of mince) and gravy. All is fairly wholesome. So is the lunch; which is mashed potatoes, broad beans & carrots, a square of meat & gravy. Supper too consists of meat, the same veg & gravy, followed by some kind of stodgy pudding. At each meal there is unsugared tea. At first sight & taste the food is surprisingly good – as wholesome as many a meal at a public school. But day after day – month after month – for 12 months – with fish on Friday alone to change the monotony. No sugar – for energy is the last thing these boys must have – just bulk stodge to keep them going – but they mustn't have frustrated energy. Is there Bromide (?) in the tea? I don't know. It seemed probable from looking around at the surprising absence of sexual energy & frustration – and I was told authoritatively that there was – but I have no proof. But even without Bromide it is obvious what are the aim of the dieticians – keep cost to the minimum – keep (Carbohydrates? Calories?) scarce – so that they will be kept in a torpid, unexcitable, state & will be less likely to cause trouble. As for when they get back to their meat steaks – well!

*

It is curious that I wrote so little about Summer in the Lakes this, or any other, year. There are descriptions in letters and particularly in accounts of Penny's visit that summer. But for one reason or another, perhaps already sated with the beauty of an Oxford summer, I was not moved to sufficient intensity to write about the summer, except in a couple of excerpts.

<u>A summer evening. From my window.</u>

The last rays of gold pour over the Black crags pines and spill onto the row of red-sand firs beside the road. The garden is already in shadow where the midges play but the evening is alight with the lingering rays on Laterbarrow – red with autumn bracken against an ether – palest greeny blue sky. Black and white cows chew in the marshy field below the cottage and the church bells chime distantly across the fields. The stallion grazes in the hilly field to the right with the pine-clad sloaps rising to a low horizon. The evening is dreaming to a close. The tall pine stands grimly behind the B's [Buckmaster's] roses – and the light has ebbed from the nearest trees, from the field where the chestnut mare flicks its tale – one cloud hangs over the monument on Laterbarow.

The following piece is curious. At first I thought it described a walk with Penny. But Penny did not come up to the Lakes for another ten days or so. So it is a walk with an imagined girl, it seems, or else the dating is wrong. It shows the impossibility of separating off pure nature description from wider thoughts and emotions.

A Walk. 12th August 62

Wind, stretching the clouds over the mountains & streaking the sky with gold-grey. Beside me, linked in my arm, bending, as she walked, like the trees in the wind – a girl. Her clothes and make-up silver and white as the moon-to-be, her body softly covered like the cloud-covered mountains. Her hair like the streaming waterfalls, leaping from the rocks and hurled in spray to the pounding rocks. Eyes like the grey lake in its valley bed, old and yet flickering and changing its light.

The track through the pine-forest was wet – hemmed by pines which rushed past, trumpeting in the night – marching in dark legions across the hills. Wood-chippings and groaning firs spiced the wind, and the air vibrated with the brushing together of pine-needles and the hidden streams. Beside the track foxgloves hung their purple bells and a green luminous gloom radiated from the heart of the trees. It seemed as if the forest was breathing in thick, fast pants as each gush of wind shook the hills into agony. Great bells seemed to toll and their echoes swept from the black mountain.

She was like the earth, firm, yet yielding, open, yet mysterious. A daughter of the wild, filled with frightening desires, unconscious, unthinking. Her mind, sleepy and languorous like some dozing, well-fed, python, curled itself around the rock of desire. She seemed to be part of the moving forest – one with the urgency and the timeliness, the unrelenting purpose of wind and mountain. She did not need to think of the beauty of the evening – she breathed it in through her skin, sultry and saturated with sensuousness she seemed to tower as the mountain, the archetype of desire and fruitfulness. Thought would break the organic link between her and the wild scene. Her emotions soldered her to the travails of the world, the torment of wind and sky, of water and rock giving birth to this earth.

And what was I by her side? I with my repressed desire – my petty intellectualism. Holding myself in check – half afraid of my own impotence if I let myself go. Yet even my repression, even the stifled pleasure in participation of her rank body which lay, to be explored, swelling and curving as inexorably as the mountains, or the salt-sweetness of her lips, lax, yet firm by her gums, and warm flesh of her back – all these let me share and somehow reach through sense into insight. My mind had already tried to isolate and chrystallise elements of the evening's beauty I had attempted to cast a spell over each detail, to force my way into fairyland. Holding her hard I had pointed to a little stream that ran out of the dark channel of trees to gurgle under a stone-wall parapet under the track. As it glinted over pebbles I had forced myself into a smaller size – had seen the beck grow into a river, seen again the mighty sweep of Indian rivers and imagined that here monster salmon ran, and that on the bend where the stream ran into the forest a little house was carved where a hobbit dwelt and that deeper in the shade elves sang and dragons prowled. But beside me still, even in my straining dreams, I felt and knew her, I felt her unbelieving, earthy mind pulling me back, her arms round my neck forcing my lips closer to hers, forcing away all imagining and driving me beyond thought. But even as I sunk, the oblivion of sense brought balm, and the stale cabinet of my soul and mind were cleaned by a fresh breath.

As the night spread its fingers on the woods, its shadows slinking like wolves from the trees, my body and mind were no longer alone and ashen. A glow had been transmitted from the warm, drowsy, cats-fur warm, clinging girl beside me and the scrupulously guarded fire which I had allowed to burn within me had already purged and cleared some of the filth that blocked the imagination's pathway to truth.

During the last ten days of September 1962 I tried to capture a season which had been immortally described by many poets.

A walk – up near the Tarns. 21/9/62

Smells – bracken – juniper – moss & the wind off the hills.
The colours nearly all green – with old grey walls breaking them – even in the walls patches of green-stain moss – and at one's feet little, secret yellow & gold flowers. The tarn sparkling in the sun & the leaves just turning to gold as the bracken is browning. The grass, or whispy hay makes a thin film of white on the clearing.

Here the wild blackberry twines and rocks & thistles spout from the ground

Old juniper trees have branches & trunks of grey-blue and the curve of the mountains is deep, deep black blue. The only sound the fitful wind and occasional bubbles of bird song. Rowan trees heavy with red fruit and the whirr of the cricket. Freshness amidst fullness, autumn with a touch of spring – no coarse overblown lushness – but hard beauty in the firm lines of rock and tree & mountain.

And over all the mighty clouds sweep, blending all into a unity of pattern & stillness, dream & reality – huge power & tiny flower.

This description was being written alongside thoughts about writing something more theoretical on creativity, continuing my piece in the preceding February on our moods.

Artistic Melancholy & Madness – a study 8/9/62

1. Artists as most sensitive & most articulate, best source of study for the psychological stresses which cause depression & madness. Distinguish periodic, nervous, depression (e.g. Keats 'Melancholy' from full-blown depression e.g. Cowper)
2. It would a) Throw an interesting side light onto the particular mental & spiritual tensions of an age, which were usually below the surface (e.g. Victorianism – the depression of M. Arnold & Tennyson as Established religion is attacked or Nietzchke [sic] – the C19 fading of the absolute & ideal b) throw light on reasons for depression & madness – from a scientific point of view thus, perhaps, helping those dealing with depression etc. c) Investigate a recurring important theme in literature & a frequent source of artistic energy etc
3. Throw light on the materialism v spiritual, the science vs imagination struggle & show various mind's reactions to the growing scepticism of modernity.
4. Among those central to this study would be Johnson, Cowper, Tennyson, Nietzchke, & many of those mentioned in 'The Romantic Agony – Praz & of course Burton's 'Anatomy of Melancholy'.

A little later I wrote further around these themes:

21/9/62 [Friday] Purpose of poetry.

In the C19 it was to preserve the wonder of God's universe against the dreary scientific light: to build a new faith on a union of heart and Nature.

It was both a form of introspection and a reaffirmation of outward truths. In the C20 this wonder is needed all the more & all the more difficult to preserve. No longer can we escape from Science, like Tennyson we must study, amalgamate & accept it (see Wordsworth Preface) but transmute it into something above the commonplace. Poetry must be allowed to work; but it can also be used to explore the realities beneath human nature & to examine what is left of beauty & truth in the materialist world. A synthesis of heart & brain.

As I read further into nineteenth century thought, and prepared for a term when I would come to terms with Victorian doubters such as George Eliot and Tennyson and Arnold, I wrote on the central topic of the loss of absolutes with the loss of religious certainty.

The destruction of the 'absolute'. (between 21 and 26 Sept. 1962)

Up to C18 an absolute; even in C18 religion attacked as absolutely wrong & systems of ethics held to be absolute. The C19 study of sociology & psychology etc (evolution), took away such a conception & gave everything a relative value. Religion was not attacked but explained as a mental product.

This empirical, scientific approach led by sensationalists etc. It discredited the ideal & the spiritual except as manifestations of psychological phenomena – Marx & Feuerbach turned Hegel upside down – man the centre of the universe. As a result nothing could be said to be the 'truth' or 'beautiful'.

Anti-platonic – anti-poetic.

The world sterilized & cleansed.

This was necessary for progress & for a time it was supported by the Liberals, unaware that they were cutting their own throats – for how were they any more 'right' than anyone else? Protest of many sensitive souls – e.g. Wordsworth, Coleridge, Carlyle, Tennyson etc. v this 'relativism'. It led to an outbreak of neurosis & left the Catholic Church as the only maintainer of absolutism.

Finally, right at the end of the vacation, I very hurriedly sketched out the idea of a book on my home environment.

Study of Lake District – proposed work 27/9/62

1) As an intellectual & spiritual influence on many C19 writers from Wordsworth on (see Willey etc)
2) Its value today – what it should aim to be
3) Its history and the nature of its inhabitants (see Macaulay ch III; 'Hawkshead' etc).
4) A study of the varying meaning of 'nature' to each generation.

i.e. Past, Present, Future – value of the Lakes as a source of inspiration, happiness and life.

Penny – Summer Vacation 1962

In the summer term, as we began our relationship, I have given fairly full excerpts from both Penny's and my letters. Now I shall, on the whole, concentrate on my own letters, with just a few of Penny's, although, in fact, she wrote much less to me (partly because she was doing exams for part of the time) than I did to her. I have indicated what poems and prose we sent to each other, but have omitted the bulk of the pieces we copied out.

[Monday 25 June] *Field Head*

Penny,

As you can see from the address I have arrived home. I'm sorry for my slackness over the last few days but you can imagine that at the end of one's second year with 2 years junk to pack up one tends to get pretty rushed.

How are things? I hope all goes well & you are not getting too tired – Sheer exhaustion is the worst of enemies in exams. I am pretty worn out & intend to relax and regain strength amid these wonderful mountains. Our garden is lush with nearly-ready fruit – strawberries, raspberries, apples, gooseberries & pears and the smell of fresh green hedges & fields streams in at my window. It is wonderful to be home.

I got a lift up in a mini-minor to Manchester on Saturday & spent the night with a friend in Bolton. We went to a tennis club dance and I spent 2 hours watching a swirling mass of teds & their molls getting drunk – no, it wasn't as bad as that, but I didn't particularly enjoy it – perhaps because I was too tired to go & pick up one of the dolled-up women.

On Sunday I recorded the Franck 'Variations' & also my friend & I played & recorded some songs. I arrived up here in the evening. Only my elder sister – who is working temporarily in a grocer's before going to art school – is at home – (apart from my grand-parents).

Well, a deadly letter I'm afraid – it is still early in the day but I have to write now to catch the single post. Write (to the above address) when you can & look after yourself sweetie.

Much love, Alan

Enclosed:

The hunched camels of the night
Trouble the bright
And silver waters of the moon.
(Francis Thompson)

Monday 25th June Field Head

Penny,

Sorry about this typing paper – I have no other. I have just had a bath and am feeling drowsy. In the background are the Frank(c?) 'Variations' which I taped on Sunday – I like them more & more. Only about ten hours since I last wrote to you & I have been working, listening to music, or reading most of the time since then so not much to report. It has poured with rain, but there is a special magic about a garden on a rainy day – as I found when I slipped out for a few minutes this evening. The leaves tremble under the weight of each drop, and one notices their oil-skin gloss when the water gathers to globules and rolls off them. The flowers smell even sweeter, great blue irises and wild roses, with drops of rain in their nectar cups, and one drinks as well as smells their scent. The rain seems to be impregnated with the smell of the pine-forests on the hills from which it comes, and it murmurs and splashes like a contented child on the farm-house roof.

I have been reading T.S. Eliot's essay on Tennyson so today's poem is another piece of that poet's work (T's) which I must confess I had not seen before. Elliot sees Tennyson as the saddest poet in the English language – a rebel who had to conform, a religious man lost in doubt, a marvellous technician whose masterpiece was "In Memoriam" – an interesting view.

I hope all goes well as usual & that this letter will not make you day-dream too much. All my best wishes to your mother. Be happy poppet.
Much love, Alan

Enclosed:

Tennyson: In Memoriam

Dark house by which once more I stand
Here in the long unlovely street,
Doors, where my heart was used to beat
So quickly, waiting for a hand ...

Wednesday [27th June] Field Head

Penelope,
I haven't heard from you for what seems a long while – I hope all goes well. You must be nearly at the end of your exams (& your tether!). Write & tell me how things are when you can.
I went fishing yesterday. It took me considerable effort to get over the unpleasantness of impaling the rubber-slimy worms. But I quietened my conscience by putting all the plump trout I caught back into the beck. It is a lovely little stream – just like Tennyson's brook which "comes from haunts of coot & hern" – it goes through a mysterious gorge at one point on its tumultuous course & here it is overhung by mouldering trees & the air is thick with the watery smell of moss & dripping stones. Here, in secret pools, where froth eddies, I drop the worm and watch for the glint of a taking trout in the dark water.
I am just about to embark on "Alice Through the Looking Glass" today so here is one of my favourite passages from it. I find children's stories marvellously restful – a marvellous escape from the entanglements of Cromwell's foreign policy!
Write when you can poppet & decide to come up and see me for a week if you can.
Good luck in today's exams,
Much love, Alan

Enclosed:

But four young oysters hurried up,
All eager for the treat: ...

I have an original letter, undated, from Field Head. It is clear from the following letter, which I did send, that this is the depressed letter which I did not send. But it is revealing, so I include it.

Friday [29th June] Field Head

Penelope,
Thank you for your letter – tho' I nearly tore it up when I got it. – why? Largely because I have been indulging in one of my periodic moods of depression today. I know it is a luxury I should not allow myself – Juli quite rightly told me off for my self-pity. But don't you give me a lecture on the subject as it was mainly your lecturing tone – e.g. in your corrections of my spelling & remarks about the construction of 'National's' – that made me want to consign your letter (& you?) to Purgatory for a while. Sorry about this outburst. I think I am working too hard & with no company here (except my sister) I am boiling & frothing over with ideas with no-one to vent them on and & consequently feel depressed.
I am attempting to be as escapist as possible – I listen to Mozart etc; I read fairy stories – (have just finished "Alice" & am starting on a fairy book called "Tony Too"); I refuse to listen to the depressing news or watch it on T.V. But it does not seem to help. The glories of the evening, or the exquisite melodies of Mozart

only stir me for a while – and then I am torn back into my wrestling mind. I am fighting a losing battle against selfishness (as you will note from the tone of this letter!) against materialistic disbelief, against sexual frustration & consequent self-disgust.

Actually things aren't as bad as I make out & I am merely using this letter as an outlet & by Monday morning my mother will be back & I'll probably be happy as a thrush – (or as Toad when he got into his new car!). Also I am indulging in a childish attempt to crave sympathy & affection – yes I know it. But then I'm still a child (tho' I must not get into a 'Peter Pan' complex.)

My poetry today is from the best known piece of escapist literature in our language – perhaps this is why it has long been almost my favourite poem?

I hope all goes well Penny. Don't take this seriously, just do well in your exams & be happy. Am thinking of you. Presumably you don't want to come up to see me?

Love, Alan

P.S. I liked the Sitwell poem very much.

Enclosed:

"The same that oft-times hath
Charm'd magic casements, opening on the foam
Of perilous seas, in faery lands forlorn."

Monday [2nd July] Field Head

Penelope,

Sorry I haven't written for a while – I did write a whole letter on Friday evening, but it was so depressed & depressing that I decided not to send it next morning. Thank you for your letter – I especially liked the Sitwell poem. [The poem, which I have, though not the letter, is from Façade – 'Lily O'Grady, Silly and shady….and dust forbids the bird to sing.']

*Things are much better at the moment as my mother is home & several of my friends have arrived up North. My grandparents set off for a 2 months stay in the South this morning so it [is] just the family in the house. I have only just realised what a wonderful person my mother is (I hear you whispering Od*p*s!) – but it really is marvellous to have her back. Down to work again today – how is it going with you sweetie? Last few exams to come I suppose.*

Will you be able to come up for a few days do you think?

Much love, Alan

P.S. The poem is an early one by my mother – in a sort of E.B. Browning style. As she says, it is terribly sloppy & she has written some much better stuff since – but you might as well see her at her worst.

Enclosed:

Prayer for my daughter

Time, be kind. Do not deny
Heartache from her destiny,
But in all this world of hate
Keep her dreams inviolate…

Tuesday [3rd July] Field Head

Penelope,

Life seeps on. I am "soft-sift as sand in an hour-glass". How are things with you? Going well, I hope, pet.

I won't moan too much if I can help it – but I have had a pretty miserable day. Depression caused largely by a complete inability to concentrate added to frustration, both sexual and artistic. I <u>want</u> to write and ideas bubble up inside but after doing my quota of work I don't have the energy. Still two weeks holiday in

Yorkshire will get rid of this intellectual and spiritual staleness I hope. I feel better this evening after a walk and listening to some Handel on a tape.

My 'passage', which you will surely recognise, symbolises my renewed good spirits. The whole of the 'Song of Songs' is lovely and I will probably give you some more out of Isaiah later: Solomon's song has a freshness and innocency, a naïve delight in natural imagery which I find very attractive. Kathleen Ferrier is now singing "He was despised" so I will end.

Be happy Penny; & look after your mother.

Much love, Alan

Enclosed:

The voice of my beloved! Behold he cometh leaping upon the mountains skipping upon the hills…

Dear Alan,

I am sorry I have not replied to your invitation before. I started a letter on Sunday …. Of course I would love to come and see you, the Lake District, the rubber-slimy worms, your boat and the other various attractions. Unfortunately, however, I can't make it before late July or early August. I have to go back to school after the exams to hear my head mistress talk on 'Marriage and Morals' for leavers (wouldn't want to miss this) and to find out about work for next term… Alan, your mother's poem was delightful. My mama and I enjoyed it very much. I look forward, if I may, to seeing more of her poetry. …Joan Anglund predominates in our home at the moment. … Send my best regards to your mother. Love to you, Oedipus. – better than Orestes. In this age it is essential that one should appreciate one's parents since the family is one of the only units of society left.

Saturday [8th July] Field Head

Penelope,

Thank you for your P.C. I have cheered up already – and am off to Wensleydale today. I am looking forward to it very much & am going to cut myself off from all intellectualism. I am just going to exist for a change. This will mean that I don't suppose I will write any letters – so expect them when & if they come.

I spent yesterday sailing, rowing & cleaning my dinghy. I am hoping to sell it if possible – so that I can buy some more tapes for my recorder – I hate having to rub something off when I want to record something new. I have got some lovely singing – Bach & Handel Cantatas sung by Fischer-Diskau.

I am writing on this paper to please you. Actually I have found I prefer writing on that typing paper – it is roomy & lets me expand and flourish.

Strawberries & raspberries are ripening. Wild roses swarm in the hedgerows, and wild strawberries peep from the undergrowth. Summer leans over the hills in luxuriant ease, and the young thrushes rejoice in the soft wind.

(End of lyrical interlude!)

Look after yourself Penny and be happy. I hope to be refreshed when I write again.

Best wishes to your mother.

Much love, Alan

Enclosed:

Exam Paper

1. Outline (i) Henry VIII (ii) Stout Cortez.
2. Who had what written on whose what?

Spennithorne. Monday [9th July] Post-card

Penelope,

Just a note before the Borstal boys arrive, when I will be too busy to write.

This is a lovely place – Wensleydale – in the midst of the dales. I am a bit worried as to how I will get on with the lads but still …

Your term must be nearly over – I hope you enjoy(ed) Coventry. Sorry (I can't fit in poetry here). Look after yourself Penny & love to your mamma. Much love, Alan

Sunday [29th July] Field Head

Penny,

Thank you for your letter. I have been putting off writing to you until today because it is my one peaceful & slack time – I am, believe it or not, working (academic) hard the rest of the week & feel very tired. I feel equally tired & dispirited this evening (especially as I have just knocked a bottle of ink over a Persian carpet about 2 minutes ago.) But enough of my moans for now.

How are things with you? When are you coming up? Any date until 17 Aug or <u>after</u> 23 Aug will be fine. You just name it. That is if you feel it is still worth-while. Tell me how you feel. Frankly, sometimes I want to see you very much – other times, well, I wonder if we know each other well enough to undergo the (supposedly) gruelling test of living in the same house. Anyhow say what you feel. As usual I can't make my mind up – and am feeling generally mixed up.

The Borstal camp was fascinating & I could write you a long account of it. Of the mixture of obscenity & prudery, of the dishonesty & the complete frankness, of the cruelty & the kindness, of the curiosity & intelligence which make up the 'Borstal' character. Of the fascinating conversation, of the utter boredom & purposelessness of the Borstal and the heartbreaking surroundings from which many of them come. There is ample material there for a dozen novels and a hundred 'letters to the Times'. Often the boys were very sensitive – eg one has written a novel & a book of poetry (v.g) & is only 16. It was a searing experience. But home now among the long hills & chrystal lakes "far from the madding crowd's ignoble strife" from the knife-fights & gutters of Liverpool & the starch & staleness of the Borstal it is only too easy to forget. But even here among the glories of earth & sky it is only too easy to be miserable as I often am – why, I don't know. Somehow in everything – in my work, in my faith, in my happiness I feel like a train trying to go up too steep a hill – crawling painfully with much puffing, its wheels slipping & spinning on the metalled tracks. But enough of that. I always weep on your shoulder &, quite rightly, give you the impression that I am utterly self-absorbed.

I'm afraid the sale of my boat is out of my hands as my mother had put an advertisement in the paper before I got back. But it <u>may</u> not be sold for quite a time. I went out on the lake today in a motor-boat – it continually broke down, but it was a lovely day so it didn't matter.

We seem to have spent the last few evenings having sing-songs into our tape-recorder. We almost have a house-party here – two sisters and girlfriends of each of my sisters & my parents – 7 in all. Do come & join us if you feel like it. Get a bus from Victoria coach station to Windermere & give me a ring or P.C. (Telephone Hawkshead 307) when you are coming & we will meet you.

It is very late so mustFthere is also p finish. Hope exam exhaustion – if you have any – is worn off. Love to your mother,

Much love, Alan

Enclosed:

> Fair fa' your honest, sousie [jolly] face,
> Great Chieftain o' the Puddin-race! …
> (To a Haggis: R. Burns)

In an undated letter, on Wednesday, which I have dated as 1 August Penny wrote:

Alan,

Please don't be depressed. I am sure all this work is bad if it produces such an effect on you. Besides you are doing an injustice to History, for its study results in enlightenment & enchantment, but rarely depression, unless you are all-aware of the present. I share in your sadness about the Persian carpet. It forces me to remember the antiques, that I accidentally broke when I was younger – I dread that my daughter may follow in my footsteps.

Having written that I would like to come on the 12th, I want now to defer that date to the 25th, since Mama is possibly going away then for a few days, the later day would anyway be more convenient for me. Is it OK for you. Don't think I am running away. As when you eat shrimp salad, I too tend to postpone my pleasures. I should agree with your feelings about us living in the same house, were the occasion to arise. But surely it won't. You will go to stay at a hotel in Ambleside (no fair virgin should stay alone amongst stranger) and you may call on me at 11o'clock in the morning and at 3 in the afternoon. Sometimes, I shall seek your mother's permission to invite you to lunch, and, of course, you will take tea with your family and myself during the course of your visit in the afternoon. You may delight me by playing on the lute and the harpsichord I believe that our relationship will fare well on this basis. Love to your mama. Much love P.

I then wrote back to her on Bank Holiday, Monday [August 6th]

Penny,

Thanks for your letter. The 25th will be fine – better in fact than the earlier date. We are going up to Scotland, partly for the wedding of a second cousin[1] *(who is 19 and in her 1st yr at Cambridge) and partly to go on up to the Outer Hebrides where, on the island of Barra, there is an old family mansion, alone amidst miles of golden sands and 'faery seas', which I am trying to persuade my family to buy. If they do, I will go up there, probably, in the vac's, to work & to start 'doing it up' before they retire. This trip is taking place from the 17th-23rd (meanwhile the married couple may spend their honeymoon here) so we will be back just in time. I am looking forward to it very much. I won't start apologising for this place, for you will see for yourself the wilderness we live in.*

We had a party on Friday. It was to be 'beat' – red-lights, candles etc. It was in the kitchen & the whole thing planned etc (& guests invited) within two days. As far as I could see all went well – tho' we had 1 stone-drunk & another tiddly all evening and switching off the electricity at intervals, scribbling on the walls etc. I decided to let my hair down & "twisted the night away" & spent the rest of my time with a very young, but far from innocent, girl. Having read a certain amount of Lawrence (D.H.) recently this was an attempt to put into practice one of his ideas – ie. that one's relationship with a woman should occasionally be purely physical – that if one starts analysing, thinking or trying to discover 'spiritual kinship' with the girl one will corrupt & debase the relationship. Even if it is pure sex, it is pure. At the time it worked, but my all sorts of dangerous thoughts are running through my head, so come well prepared with arguments v free love!

Yesterday I went sailing. The boat isn't sold yet – you may be lucky still. It was very rough, but very beautiful. Hemingway would have loved the thrill of hard ropes straining and sunlight and storm beat into a fury down the narrow valley. Several times gusts made me lean right out and spray swept over the front. The hills, streaked with sunlight, full in their summer green, merged their tops in the clouds, and the waves glittered and dulled with the changing lights – sun & cloud, wind and mountains marched together triumphant, shaping sky and earth in ever-changing patterns, and battling with each other in a million-year struggle.

I have recorded some lovely music, Schubert, a Mozart opera, Brahms etc. To earn some money to buy another tape, I have been working for a day in the local coffee bar. For a short time it is a fascinating insight into the deadness of life, the spiritual vacuum, in which a cross-section of modern youth lives in. They spend hours sitting amidst the cigarette ends, drinking salty and weak coffee, tapping listlessly. It is hardly surprising that when they come into contact with the only pleasure which has not lost all its content – sexual – most of them have to get married hurriedly. I am convinced that the greatest threat to our society is boredom. It is boredom that fills our borstals and bingo halls … Still, enough of my prophetic strain for now!

Look after yourself poppet,
Much love, Alan

Penelope,[2]

Weep with me. Tragedy in the family. My little dinghy has committed suicide. Perhaps she knew she was going to be sold, anyhow she disappeared during the recent storms & rain and I suspect lies mouldering among the monsters that prowl in the lakes' depths. I will search, but …

For your letter, thanks. You are right about my being occupied by Clio – but it is more a case of rape than seduction, for I am finding Cromwell's speeches very stodgy and am having considerable difficulty in keeping going. I am reading some interesting books, however (about 5 of them simultaneously (!)), 'Erbert's "Essays", Einstein's "Relativity", Yeats' 'Poems', Goethe's 'Faust' & Edmund Wilson "Axel's Tower" [sic] (literary criticisms re 'fin de siècle' writers) – a real meal for a "culture vulture" like me! Bring some books up with you (tho' we have a fair amount) as it is bound to rain when you are here.

---

[1] In fact not a cousin, but my godmother's daughter, Nicola Cowan.
[2] Written about 15th August

About your visit (as this may be my last letter proper before you come up – we are going up to Scotland in a couple of days to the wedding etc). Come when you like. Go when you like. Expect shambles. Expect nothing – or whatever you like. If you let me know when you arrive we will meet you in the car. I hope you won't mind sharing a room with my sisters which you may have to do. Read plenty of Wordsworth before you come & then forget him & never mention him when you're here!

I've just been watching a film on a great Italian oil tycoon & this has once more sparked off thoughts on how best to employ one's life – to be a creative artist, to be a saint, or to be a philanthropist seems to be the most rewarding occupations. Each of them consists of giving & are rewarded by suffering. Each leads to persecution & each consists of a narrow path which can easily be lost and results in sterility, bigotry & even madness if one wanders. Perhaps its already too late to decide which of these one is going to be by the time one is of an age to think of such things. The only question is to decide in which field to apply one's abilities, artistic, saintly or otherwise. It is important to decide what will be one's final aim, for it is undivided will which accomplishes & succeeds.

What do you think is the greatest problem in the world today? I can't make up my mind whether to concentrate (outwardly at least) on the material or spiritual struggle. I.e. should one help, in boy's club, church or otherwise to fight v spiritual apathy, intolerance etc – or, being more practical, help to alleviate poverty, sickness, ignorance etc? The former, I am sure, is ultimately the more important problem, but the second is the more apparent & one can be more certain that one's answers to the problems are the right one's. What do you think you'd do if you were a boy?

Hope this hasn't bored you.

Much love, sweetie, & love to your mother. Alan

*

At this point we went to Scotland, from 17th to 23rd August. We drove up to the Outer Hebrides and crossed to the island of Barra and visited Eoligarry House, which I thought my parents might like to try to buy and convert into a home for their retirement. I had visited the house in my first summer vacation. However my father immediately realized that it was in too dilapidated a state by this time to be a possibility.

*

When we returned, Penny made the first of her two visits to stay with us in the Lake District. After the visit, I started to write up an account of the visit, which is unfinished, but quite revealing. From evidence in a letter a year later, it seems that we started off quite early with a row, but after that things were sweet.

As well as the written-up account of Penny's visit I have a sheet which gives the days and one or two notes. I shall interpolate these into the text in italics.

Alan's account: 25 – Sep 3rd 1962

[Saturday August 25 to Monday Sept 3rd]

"Two drifters off to see the world
With such a deal of world to see …
Both searching for the same rainbow's end."
('Moon River')

To recapture the eternal joy of a moment, embodying the sudden flame of ecstasy in enduring form is the artist's burden. He must impose a pattern on isolated incidents, weaving each golden strand into a web of magic without distorting or falsifying, without letting surplus emotion stretch or break the original experience. Of all the subjects which he treats, love, the most subjective, is the most uncontrollable – and in proportion as it is transiently beautiful, as it wears a glow "that never was on land or sea", as it reaches to the bitter stars, so it escapes from the coarse net of language, a beautiful shadow that flees ever deeper into the forests of doubt. Like some wild beast it must be approached gently, it must be watched in its every movement and a thousand pictures of it taken of which, only a very few may be true glimpses.

Saturday 25th August: Arrive: rain. Car – nervous – scarf: I have a cold; drinks party: "what a peach" – she sprawls on floor – comes to my room – sits on bed

The train slid in from the pouring rain, and it seemed a long while before I saw her face amidst the crowd. Naturally we were confused for a moment. I noted that she seemed very white and her voice more affected than I remembered it. We drove back amidst nervous conversation, while the massed clouds over the hills were occasionally speared by sun-shafts which struck green sparks from the dripping fields & woods. We apologised for bringing Penny into the middle of a sherry party and then were home – amidst the forced jollity of it all. Penny acted as self-confidently as ever – and lay full-length on the floor while Anne Hogg sat & devoured cheese straws. As it was breaking up I was pleased when Beryl whispered to me – "she's a peach". At supper it was first apparent that Penny would get on very well with the rest of the family. Not only did she have much to talk about with Mummy – which I had foreseen – but she also seemed to grow increasingly fond of the rest of the family. Apart from discussions, most of the meals were taken up in gentle teasing – for instance Fiona would tease Penny that her tummy stuck out – or I would be made fun of for not changing my clothes over-often. When teased Penny would sometimes blush slightly & this added colour and her wide smile which dimpled her cheeks and lit her grey eyes would make her especially beautiful.

Sometimes, with her longish hair kept down by a band and her serious, large, eyes she would remind me of Alice, rather self-absorbed, rather mystified by the world, seeing the world as a strange wonderland, and finding beauty and happiness in odd corners – in a little flower she would pick and carry, or in the feel of warm tarmac under her bare feet. Although much of her eccentricity was self-conscious in a sense – yet there really is something strange and wild about her, something which is all the more mysterious when found in a city child. Against she is very like Keats' "La Belle Dame sans Merci".

> "Full beautiful, a faery's child;
> her hair was long, her foot was light
> And her eyes were wild"
>
> – but without the cruelty of "La Belle Dame".

Among her enchantments were a fascinating mixture of naivité & sophistication, of wisdom & folly, of innocence and experience. Behind a façade of complete confidence, of independence and self-assurance there trembled a shy dreamer – whose dreams lay very close to the surface, so that she could be very easily hurt, so that she was scarcely able to bear her own weight but needed to be held and protected. But enough of describing – who would attempt to describe the rose flush in the East on a vaporous morning – or the sliding of sun-beams on a stream, or the miracle of a cobweb clustered with drew drops – or the scent of a rose sweeter than the summer seas, and as transient as a snowflake.

She is no saint either – even the rose has thorns, pride, arrogance, waywardness and others. But without these there would be no dark backcloth, no cold grey rock of human failing from which she could grow in beauty. As someone once said 'to understand is to forgive'.

- - -

On Saturday evening we spent the first of our evenings together in my room, listening to music, occasionally reading, but mostly talking and making love. During the week we learnt some of the sensual delights, but the danger of an over-emphasis on physical pleasure in relation to spiritual and mental self-revelation gradually passed. I do not regret anything, except perhaps my selfishness in demanding too much & too quickly from a girl as innocent & unspoilt as Penny, and will always delight in the memory of her sweet body, her warm lips and soft hair resting against me.

> "... drew down her eyes,
> Deep as deep flowers & dreamy like dim skies;
> With her own tresses bound & found her fair,
> Kissing her hair." (Swinburne: Rondel)

At times, after the heat of passion as well as during it, we came near to Shelley's dream

> "And we will talk, until thought's melody
> Become too sweet for utterance, and it die
> In words, to live again in looks, which dart
> With thrilling tone into the voiceless heart,
> Harmonizing silence without a sound.
> ......
> The fountains of our deepest life, shall be
> Confused in Passion's golden purity,
> As mountain-springs under the morning sun.
> We shall become the same, we shall be one
> Spirit within two frames..'

But with all our passion and harmony we fluttered uncertainly apart like two birds. For neither wished to become too deeply involved while exams, distance & a certain unsureness of each other marred a total union. And we drifted in a happy dream through the week.

Sunday 26th . Walked up to Tarns

On Sunday we walked round the Tarns. It was a dull evening but they were lovely all the same and being together was 'very heaven'. I helped you over stepping stones & retrieved your shoe when it got caught deep in the mud. You, especially, were touched by the grandeur and wildness of the scene, by the dark pines set against the hard, bracken and rock and the many-inletted tarn.

> In the words of the bard:
>
> "Gently did my soul
> Put off her veil, and, self-transmuted, stood
> Naked as in the presence of her God.
> As on I walked, a comfort seem'd to touch
> A heart that had not been disconsolate,
> Strength came where weakness was not known to be,
> At least not felt; and restoration came,
> Like an intruder, knocking at the door
> Of unacknowledged weariness."
> (Wordsworth: Prelude IV. l.127)

We stopped for a while to sit on a stone wall, and you walked much of the way barefoot.

Monday – blank
Tuesday – Went to Kendal in morning. Went to Brathay party.
Wednesday – Drove to Windermere & Latterbarrow
Thursday – Walked down to Hawkshead
Friday – Went to dam stream – then to Steve's studio. Steve came over in the Evening – singing.
Saturday – Went to Manby's studio. Anne's results come.
Sunday – Went to Church. Went to Duddon – Hardknott. Walked to top of Juniper hill.
Monday – Penny left on 9.26 train.

*

Monday evening [3rd September] Field Head

P.P.P.S. Sending this book is another excuse for writing.

Dearest Elf-child,

I am purposely going to limit this letter, partly because I am in the mood to gush and I know I musn't, partly because we agreed not to write too often. I am excusing this however by the fact that the first week of being apart will be the most difficult, and after that we will not be so dependent on letters. This is to cheer you up if you are still feeling miserable by Wednesday morning.

Thank you for phoning me, darling. I am sorry I was so abrupt – I warned you about me on the phone. Actually I don't know why we rang off so quickly, I didn't really mean to say goodbye & was stunned when I found we had said it. Hearing your voice made me even sadder and I have spent the rest of the day trying not to pine – goodness I am "soggy"! This evening I have started an account of your visit here, with incidental comments, which you may see sometime if you like.

It really was lovely having you here, poppet, and I hope you enjoyed it as much as I did. And now we have to get back to the grind, back to the loneliness and drudgery – still its' not as miserable as all that! Only when you are gone, however, do I fully realise how fond I am of you. If you ever grow melancholy or dispirited remember I am praying for & thinking of you – but I must stop before I get too sentimental.

Please give my love to your mother & believe, that I am, Penelope, your most humble, loving and obedient servant,

Alan (Macfarlane) xxxxxxxxxx ad infinitum

P.S. I will write properly later. Work hard & be happy.
P.P.S. The family all send their love.

Penny then wrote a couple of days later, calling me for the first time by a name taken from Tolkien:

Wednesday Morn. London [5th September]

Dearest Mr Tumnus,

Thank you for your very sweet letter. I wrote last night with the enclosed, but am now rearranging my sentiments since you answered most of my questions.

I hesitate to send you my lock of hair, for, in that it is silk-soft, fleeting, and ever-inclined to escape, it does not represent my affections towards you. Don't regard it as a basil-pot.

[I have the lock of hair and a small bracelet]

London is making her claims on me, and already I am susceptible. Even a week's holiday makes me realise that I must escape from the people, the dust, the artificiality, and the false standards on which life is based. I value London only for her museums, art galleries, walks and all that does not people. [sic]

My stay was wonderful, tho' my behaviour was objectionable. Yr father's remark seemed to epitomise all that I did. (Please insert another word for 'epitomise'. My mind has fallen blank.) The telephone call was foolish, but I was so nervous that I could have talked for ages on trivialities or said scarcely a word as I did.

There are so many things that I intended to say, but they have sifted away like sand.
Love to you, darling
I remain your Elf-child
(now my memory is returning)

P.S. We throw open our flat to you. Come when you like, and expect primitive conditions, tho' we may have progressed from that stage by the time of your visit.

P.P.S. Tell Fiona that I am making enquiries about 'Digs' in Manchester, but that I am as yet unable to contract the 'required' youth.

P.S. Love to all your family.

P.P.S. Will you pick some Juniper for me, and also send me the Commentary on 'The Last Sonnet'

I wrote again

9/9/62 Field Head Sunday Evening

P.S. I am sending the lipstick separately & juniper.
P.P.S. I have thrown away my old jeans (reluctantly!) and am off to buy a new pair!

Fairest elf-child, greetings,

Thank you for your letter and for the strands of silk once woven into your hair: "weave, weave the sunlight in her hair" (I know this line is not at all relevant but it has been floating through my thoughts for the last few weeks and I thought that if I gave it a roost on this page it would stop its restless pipings & flutterings).

I can understand your feelings about London – I find it harsh and gritty after the hills, and my poem, one of Blake's most brutally successful, adds to this feeling. But I needn't give you *a lecture on the need to see beauty and courage in the people who throng round. Despite their 'ignoble strife' there must be many 'beautifies of mind & body' among the 8 million odd inhabitants.*

I'm not quite sure what you mean by saying "my behaviour was objectionable" – and this isn't helped by the fact that I can't remember my father's remark that 'epitomises' it. I found your behaviour literally enchanting (after the first row). I still miss you very much, do you miss me at all, poppet?

I enclose all sorts of bits & pieces. Firstly my present to you – as a slight reminder of a wonderful time together. Remember not to start it now. And speaking of presents, thank you very much indeed darling for the cheese-dish – as my mother will have said, no doubt, it was very naughty of you to spend so much money, but they were all delighted with it. And thanks for the lock from your sylvan head (?) – have you read 'The Rape of the Lock'?

Also I enclose – your lipstick (I hope) – the comment on Keats' 'Last Sonnet' – and some Juniper, procured after a stormy and rainy voyage at nightfall to Juniper Hill. I felt very "gallant", like some medieval knight errant on a quest for his lady, and every sheep became a dragon & every grass mound an unscalable mountain & each trickling stream a bitter & uncrossable mountain torrent at the bottom of perilous cliffs!

Nothing much has happened. Felicity has been staying a week – she is at times very pretty and occasionally my sensuality is aroused, but even if she wasn't cold my deep feelings for you, darling, would stop me getting involved. This evening we had a few friends 'round, including Steve, & sung some more songs onto the tape.

I have had a mass of ideas about books I would like to write – one on children's stories for instance, another on the reasons for and kinds of, artistic melancholy & madness. (As will your handkerchiefs which I will send anon). [Some of these book plans are elsewhere.]

All the family send their love, and my fondest love to you Penelope and also to you mother.
I remain, as ever, affectionately
Mr Tumnus xxxxxx oooooo

[The letter is loose, with no envelope, and Blake has disappeared.]

There is another letter from Penny, dated by me as 11th September, thanking me for 'Fellowship of the Ring'. I will omit this.

I then wrote on Tuesday Evening [18th September]

Dearest Elf-child,

How are you, oh fairest one? May the light of ecstasy burn round you and the passion of joy surge in your heart. In other words – I hope you're happy! Thank you for your letter and also for the gift of the handkerchiefs – I will always think of you when I use them. Also, please thank you dear mamma very much for taking trouble in trying to help with Fiona. As my mother will have told you, we adopted the system suggested by your mother's friend and consequently managed to find a very cosy place for F.

My journey down to Bolton and wanderings round industrial Manchester roused my soul to a new anguish at the misery of the inhabitants. I don't know whether the grime, the smell, and the drab ugliness of the crammed houses is worse than the stunted, miserable people who inhabit them. But even the new blocks of multi-flats, which are supposedly the answer, are depressing in the extreme. "Money the minion ..." is the philosophy of 99% of the inhabitants – and even the supposedly cultured & intelligent family I was staying with were obsessed with it and were "Philistines". I hope all this does not sound too priggish and bitter – but my rigorous feeding on the 'classics' in art & the influence of the Lakes scenery has turned me into a perfectionist of sorts. Although I try not to condemn any particular individual, and tho' I realise that I myself am far more bestial than most of those I saw in Manchester, yet I refuse to admit that millions of people are <u>*meant*</u> *to live in those foul dung-heaps.*

To them they may not be dung-heaps, and I would admit that there is, at times, a strange beauty about cities. But how can the artificiality and drabness of their lives produce anything other than a life of meaningless materialism? I know that I am open to a thousand arguments in saying this – but I am convinced that unless something is done, and soon, that rare species, "the soul", will become extinct. No, I don't really think this, because I am also convinced "that all things work together for good"; but something must be done to counteract the spiritual deadness, the physical misery & ugliness and the intellectual hypocrisy & error that exists in the blackened wilderness of industrial Britain all the same.

But what is to be done? It is hard enough to escape the contagion of materialism oneself. My abhorrence of money is only a perverted form of materialism. As a start I intend to study the industrial revolution in detail, for it is in the age of its aftermath that we are living. The Church must obviously play a major part in the change – and itself must change, for judged by results it is painfully far from any real contact with the mass of people. Education, again, is another weapon in the crusade. Scientific discovery, as long as it is seen as a means & not an end, is another weapon – but the great and underlying principle is religion – for it is only from a love of God – a worship of something outside himself – will man a worshipping creature, be saved from worshipping himself (incarnate in false idols). But how is one to instil into man a moral awareness, an increase of spiritual perception, an increase in wonder, and a belief in the absolute? One cannot <u>*persuade*</u> *men to be religious by rational argument, tho' one can direct them to effective outlets of their religious spirits. One can, I suppose, in the end, only pray & try to set an example, and try to help those who are already searching. For only those who are still searching will find: "Seek and ye shall find, ask and it shall be given to you, knock and it will be opened..." (I know I have misquoted).*

What do you think of the above remarks – or do they not interest you? The great, personal, battle is to remain spiritually aware, to continue to feel spiritual truths deeply and not to become submerged by the weight of sense-impressions, or the subtle materialist propaganda of the world. But enough for now.

I enclose a poem of my mothers – which always makes me feel guilty that I have not made more of my precious-earned liberty. But I am very happy, that is considering the amount of work I have to do and the fact that you are so far away, my poppet.

It was reading Wordsworth's Prelude Bks I & II which, reminding me of the contrast of the joys of my upbringing to that of a normal city boy, started me off on my rave, so I have included a passage which will, I hope, illustrate my meaning.

Please write soon if you can, my darling, and be very happy. I am thinking of you often.

Your loving – Mr Tumnus

Enclosed are two pieces:

[Wordsworth]

....

Yet were I grossly destitute of all
Those human sentiments that make this earth
So dear, ...

I also enclosed a poem of my mother's

<u>*To my son; in war. April 1943*</u>

Finally, a few days before I returned to Oxford for my last year, I wrote on Sunday [30 September]

P.S. I enclose a cutting; what are your views on this subject; fierce?
P.P.S. My love to your dear mamma.
P.P.P.S. A few grains of Juniper for you to crush and smell. [They are still in the envelope!]

Dearest Elf-child,
I miss you very much, especially on Sunday evenings when, for unknown reasons, I always feel more lonely than usual. Thank you for your long letter – and tho' naturally, I would qualify much that you said I agree with a large part of your analysis of the causes and cures of the spiritual and cultural abyss in which we are living. I especially agree when you point out our presumption in judging others – but, tho' it cannot be justified, one has to if one is going to attempt to exert a beneficial influence on the world. But before I enter onto a discussion on that & various subjects a few 'more lowly' topics.

Don't work <u>too</u> hard – allow sometime for social life. As far as university entrance is concerned, they won't take you just because you know a few more facts than another girl – but because you strike them as a girl of culture, general intelligence and with outside hobbies & interests. So let yourself go a bit – but <u>don't</u> fall madly in love with some decadent but handsome artist as someone (who shall be nameless!) would be very hurt and turn more embittered than he already is (which is not very much as yet he tells me) .

I enclose the essay questions; not very exciting I'm afraid. Also another poem on Autumn which you might like. Your Jas Thomson was sombrely beautiful in a precise, classical, way. The picture evoked is as delicately but strongly made as an Adam chair and is full of the melancholy wistfulness, the abstract, yet detailed, view of nature, and the orocular latinisms of Gray, in fact an C18 poem. Mine is much simpler, more transient and ephemeral, but sadder.

I am going down to Oxford on about the 9th and the term begins on the 13th. Will you be taking any exams in Oxford do you suppose? Please write, if you can find a moment in between parties etc (do you detect a note of envy? I hope not!) before I go down. I have collected some wild-flowers for you but having pressed and stuck them on paper I have discovered they would break in the post so I will send them with my European file, or show them to you later…

There are many points in your letter I would like to take up – but here are a few at random. You say at one point "I am content for men to be atheists as long as they do not take Mammon for their God." It is one of my convictions that men <u>cannot</u> be atheists. As I said last week – 'man is a worshipping creature' – and this means that if he loses his traditional, heavenly, Gods he will erect another in its place – himself, sex, his party, his job or a multitude of Gods, car, family, music, books etc. This I have already said.
This theory can be applied with interesting consequences to recent history. In the C18 in England religion and science were in alliance – epitomized in Pope's epigram on Newton. Nature in all its beauty and symmetry was held to prove God's existence. All objects, all thoughts, all people were bound by a spiritual chain. There was an absolute good and an absolute beauty. This life was not all there was. Every action and thought of man had an absolute, not merely a relative, value. It was either right or wrong. One's whole life was set in a frame, a link in a chain leading to a perfect end.

An artist could believe in the immortality of his work; a Christian in the eternal and universal relevance of his beliefs and ethics. But during the later C18, C19 and C20 science and religion clashed. The bible was shown to be largely erroneous & conflicting, the creation a legend, the New Testament often mistaken. Psychology showed that man was ruled by dark Gods he had never suspected and that an internal explanation could be given for his beliefs and ideals, that man could have created God in his own image, not the other way round. Marx applied this when he turned Hegel upside down and said that all beliefs, thoughts etc were an ideological tree which sprouted from material and physical conditions, that we were shaped by our environment. Sociology, particularily the "Golden Bough" showed that the great religions were largely the products of certain needs of human nature – the desire for an explanation of physical phenomena such as stars, sun, storms etc, the desire for protection, the fertility cults etc – and that if one religion was admitted to have 'truth' they must all have it. This led to the greater study of comparative religion which seemed to enforce sociology's conclusions, showing for instance God dying for men in many legends and lands. It seemed, as every star or microbe was measured, that God was being squeezed into a smaller and smaller area.

For a time various walls were put up against the murder of God. Men escaped into Nature. Nature had been made a proof of God in the C18 – in the C19 Wordsworth became the first priest of 'natural religion' – God moved in the mountains, as "wisdom and spirit of the Universe". Many, Tennyson, Arnold, Mark Rutherford etc found their refuge for a while there. Anyone, they said, could see the 'glory that never was on land or sea' among the mighty shapes and mists of Helvelyn, or in the willow-dreaming vicarage of Tennyson's youth.

Others, like Shelley or Carlisle, blazed forth in prophetic vision, singing of the invisible world and scorning that around them. But inexorably the 'clouds of glory' were 'fading into the light of common day'. Despite the desperate attempts of Arnold to build a religion of 'sweetness and light', or of the saintly Newman waving his wand of medieval mystery over twilight Oxford, the intellectual foundations of not only established, but all religion, shook.

Meanwhile another deadly attack, that described by Tawney and touched on in your letter, was sapping the vitality of that wonder and joy which is the root of religion – the industrial revolution. On one side it made money the new God – on the other it enslaved, bored, degraded and stunted thousands, grinding them between boredom and over-working. And now where are we?

The masses are not interested. The middle-class (of which in fact the 'masses' are a part now) are half-heartedly hypocritical. There is no upper class. The intellectuals 'wander in mazes lost'. For from an intellectual point of view they are both most responsible and the most hard-hit. They have been left in a vacuum. "You have killed God" screamed Nietschke – and went mad. And the whole world is going mad – for it is looking into a mirror and sees .... Either nothing, or itself. For there is now <u>no</u> absolute. Abstractly this means that anything one may do has no <u>real</u> value. If one writes an "immortal" poem – it will be dust soon. If one fights against disease and poverty all one's life and dies trying to save a leper one is no better or worse than a hypocritical, sensual, bullying, cowardly pimp. Value is only relative. Pain, suffering etc etc have no meaning at all. There is no purpose in living, or in dying. Here is the agonized cry of one in the wilderness –

> *"And he, shall he,*
> *Man, her (nature's) last work, who seem'd so fair,*
> *Such splendid purpose in his eyes,*
> *Who roll'd the psalm to wintry skies*
> *Who built him fanes [temples] of fruitless prayer,*
> *...*
> *Who loved, who suffer'd countless ills,*
> *Who battled for the True, the Just,*
> *Be blown about the desert dust,*
> *Or seal'd within the iron hills?*
> *No more? ....Oh life as futile, then, as frail."*
> *(In Memoriam)*

And if all absolute's except our fleeting life are gone then only one philosophy, one ethics, is left for each of us – a headlong pursuit of material happiness for this alone is real. Life and suffering have no meaning, pleasure is the one God. It is hardly surprising that one of the most popular poems of the late C19 – the age of God's death agony – counselled this advice.

> *"Come, fill the Cup, and in the Fire of Spring*
> *The Winter Garment of Repentance fling:*
> *The Bird of Time has but a little way*
> *To fly – and lo! The Bird is on the Wing*

I am certain that this vacuum, this disease (I hope) is what prowls through the unconscious of our generation (I know a vacuum can't prowl!) and sends the sensitive mad, the weak into a dazed pursuit of pleasure and the crafty after power. But perhaps, and I hope, I am wrong.

Well, it's late and I will have to leave other subjects. I think of you often, my sweet, and wish I could see you but meanwhile you have all the love and prayers of yours,
Mr Tumnus xxxx

Enclosed:

Autumn.

There is a wind where the rose was;
Cold rain where sweet grass was; …
(Walter de la Mare)

Third Year: 1962-3

Winter Term 1962

Third year: 21 Worcester Place. My room was at the top left. Many years later.

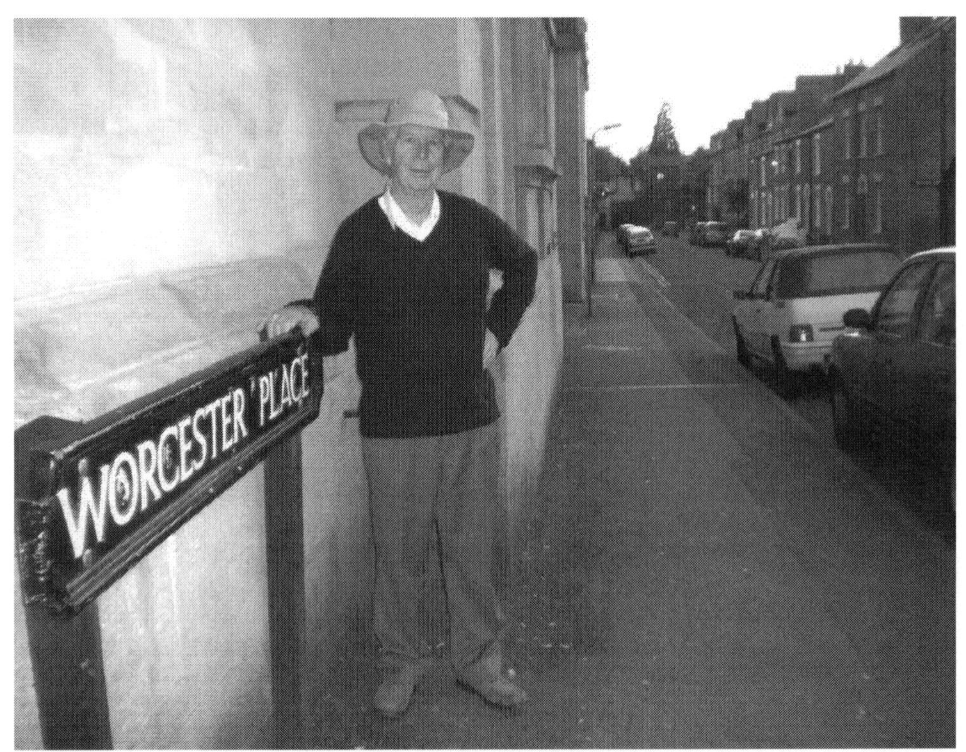

Ephemera for the Winter Term

In this third year I moved out of College into digs and started to keep scraps of paper with the cost of various foods and other items. This was probably largely prompted by the fact that, for the first time. I was not eating as often in College and having to cook for myself. The fact that almost all are dated suggests that I was trying to preserve them either as a record or as an account. Since they give a rather different small insight into my humble life in digs, I shall insert them here.

Firstly there is a sheet headed

Stores – Winter '62 Oct. 10

Cornflakes 2 pkt; Salt 1 pkt; Sardines 2 tins; Coffee 1 large (Maxwell Hse), 1 small (Nescafe); Soup 2 tins (large) Heinz, 1 tin conc' Oxtail, 3 pkts knorr. [The oxtail soup is odd, as I thought I was a vegetarian at this time]; Baked beans 1 large tin; Tea 1 pkt; Sugar 2 ½ lbs; cheese 1 lb (4/-); Tomatoes ½ lb; Apples ½ lb; Carrots 2 lb [1/4d]; Onions 2 lb [1/6]; Eggs ½ doz [1/9]; Potatoes 5 lb [2/3]; Milk (1 pt a day); Bread 1 small [10d]; Butter ½ lb; Marge; Bisc's 1 pk choc [1/7 ½], 1 ginger nuts; Beverage(!), 1 drinking choc & 1 milo; Ryvita 1 pkt; Beer 6x ½ Guinness [1/3 ½ each without bottle] ; Wine 1 sherry (16/-) & ½ wine (4/-); Ribena 1 btle (2/3); Dextrasol. [On a separate bill on the same date are some of the items above with their prices. I have combined these in the above list, where available, in square brackets.]

This seems to have been my initial stock, which was replenished from time to time as follows.

18th October.
Ryvita 1s 2d; Biscuits (plain) 1s 3d; Chocolate 1/7 ½; Bournvita 3/-; ½ lb Marge 10 ½

26th October
Cheese, 2 guinness, Marge – 6/10 ½ ; Vegamin; Paper h'chiefs; Asprin; Friar's balsam; Vitamin C tab; Cod liver oil; Beecham's powder. [Clearly I had a bad cold, which my mother alludes to in a letter.] There is also written at the bottom in a red crayon 'Refugees'. There are two sums of money in pencil at the bottom 5/- and £1/5/10 – which items they refer to is not certain.]

28 October. 1 pkt ryvita 1s 2d; 2 fish & chips 1/9; 1 Guinness 1/3 ½; ¼ lb cheese 11d.

29 October
4 ½ guinness; 1 lb sugar; 1 pkt soup – 7/8 ½d

8/11/62
Ankle Support [suggesting I was still playing football]; Butter ½ lb; Ryvita 1 pkt; Sardines 2 tins' Sugar 2 lbs; 3 x ½ beer: total 10/10 ½d

13/11/62 Bournvita, crumpets etc 5/-

14/11/62 2 lbs carrots; 2 lbs onions; 2 lbs apples – 6/4. Stamps 2/6

[Note: my Guinness regime had clearly started – and there is no meat and not much protein – Ryvita was an important part of my diet]

24/11 Books 4/10; Pills etc 12/-; 4 beer; ½ lb butter; Ryvita; 1 pkt choc bisc's; 10 senior service 2/3 [I am sure I did not smoke – must have been for friends]; 1 bournvita 3/-; Brook Bond tea 1/9

28/11/62
Butter; Crumpets x 2; Cake 2/6; Biscuits 1 choc; Beer 4; Shrimp paste 1/6 – 13/11 ½

Probably overlapping with the above, is another list of about the same date.
Cheque (ticked); Crumpets; Cake; Air-mail forms, Stamps etc 4/- ; Ordinance survey maps x2; History Maps; ; Shampoo; Box file; Coldrex 3/- ; Sugar; Ball; Ryvita; Eggs, Sardines; Beer; Typing paper 10/-; File 16/8; Maps 24/- & 9/-;

[Note, stationary was expensive…]

As regards going out for meals, I kept a note of the following:

16/10/62 3/4 dinner, 2/6 play
18/10/62 Film (paid for Eric) 4/6
27/10/62 2 meals 9/-
7/11/62 Supper & Lunch – Tuesday 6/-
12/11/62 1 meal 8/6
13/11/62 2 meals (lunch and supper) 6/-
18/11.62 Lunch 3/6
25/11/62 2 meals 7/-
[Going out for meals was quite expensive. Otherwise I seem to have lived simply. What is not certain here is how much I ate in College, which was only five minutes away.]

(Undated)
Dick – 4/3d (drinks)
War on want 4/-
Graph paper 1/-

One other indication of my costs is to be found in my cheque stubs, which indicated the following for this period (the bare sums are for cash for myself).

10 Oct £6
15 Oct £6
26 Oct £3
27 Oct Battels £6
28 Oct Dr Bruno Faust £7-7-0
28 Oct Gamages tapes £5-12-6
29 Oct £5
29 Oct Winter Ball £2-2-0

29 Oct Father Borelli £1
30 Oct Digs (Miss Norridge) £21-5-0 [rent]

2 Nov £5
9 Nov For Refugees (J. Munks) £2-12-6
13 Nov Blackwell's £2-2-0
14 Nov £5
23 Nov Paperback Book Shop £2-6-0
26 Nov £5
30 Nov £5

7 Dec £5
14 Dec £7
(three stubs without any details)

Looking at the other ephemera for this term, several changes are striking.
Firstly, the religious cards are absent. Where are all the OICCU and other cards of previous terms? It will be interesting to see what happens in the following two terms.
Secondly, the amount of entertainment is much reduced – probably reflecting my intense concentration on work in my last year.
There is hardly any indication of sport, except for a note from a 'Hugh' to the effect:

Dear Alan,
Rugger v Hewell Dec 8th. What position would you like? Full back booked!'

This was a match against the Borstal boys whom we had visited in the summer. I do not remember playing.
There are only two play programmes: one for 'Misalliance' by Bernard Shaw at the Playhouse for October and the other for a ballet on Saturday November 24th – 'La Fille Mal Gardée'. There is also the film programme for the Scala cinema though I don't remember going to any film in particular.
There is also a programme for a concert in Worcester College Chapel on Sunday December 9th, which has a religious and Christmas carol feel about it.
There is also a card for the Oxford Union, though I have no recollection of going to any of them.
There is my International Student Identity Card for 1962–3, and also a card for the Heritage Society, the student folk club, whose card is as follows:

PROGRAMME

Song Sessions—8 p.m., at the Chequers Inn, every Tuesday (except first week).

—

Guest Artists:

Saturday, 20th October—
GERRY LOUGHRAN (Blues).

Saturday, 27th October—
RORY McEWAN (Star of the Edinburgh Festival and B.B.C's "Tonight").
(Scottish and American Songs.)

~~Saturday~~ Friday, ~~1st December~~— 30 Nov
JIM BASSET (English Songs).

—

Other Guests will include:
A. L. LLOYD (Traditional English Songs).

—

Please see Posters for further details

Copies of "Sing," "Spin" and other such publications may be obtained through the President or Secretary.

For the visits of outside artists, members will be asked to contribute an extra 1/- per head towards the artist's fees.

—

This card should be brought to ALL meetings

One other event is the Worcester College Christmas Dance on Friday 7 December. I have the Double ticket. It was the dance to which I took Penny. (On the back are noted a number of religious notes, perhaps to hymn numbers such as 'In my heart. Jesus, Jesus').

Letters

During the Winter term and the Christmas holidays, before Penny visited the Lake District again at the start of January, there are 24 letters from me and 19 from Penny. In terms of length, mine are a somewhat longer on average in this period – Penny was doing University entrance preparations and exams. In terms of words, my letters constitute perhaps two thirds of the total of more than twenty-five thousand words in our correspondence for this period.

With Penny's letters I have included most of the longer ones, but again tended to include only the parts which either discuss matters or reflect something about our relationship.

*

The first letter from Penny I have dated as 5th October, although it only states Friday Morning.

I regret the length of this letter – I am up to my eyes in work at the moment, and will not have time to pour out my wrath against the present Abortion Laws before you go back to Oxford. These laws together with those on Homos, and also the Penal system have incensed me for a long time.

Tell your friend, shall we call him Septuagint – never to become embittered on my account. I may be outwardly wayward, but inwardly … Send all my very best love to your Mamma & Pappa, before they go back to India. Tell them I hope they are able to smuggle in some Toilet Rolls.

The next letter from Penny is on Wednesday [October 10th]

Is Oxford very beautiful now? I envy your being there in Autumn, but I must postpone my visit to that 'fair towered city' in the descending season of the year to next year. The descriptions of girlfriend of mine only increased my longing. Of course, I would love to come up and see you BUT …

How are you, honey? Are your ankle & bleeding nose better? I hope you've had your hair cut, and have sat in the bath for 2 hrs wearing your jeans to shrink them. I'll make you a spivy Ted-boy yet. Then you can infiltrate into Liverpool gangs, and establish a cell from which you shall infuse morality into today's youth. But I'm not so sure that it wouldn't be better to go as you are. If you bring yourself down to their level you will be corrupted yourself.

This is just the problem that is facing the Church today – how to be on a level to which people can approach, without lowering its spiritual standards, and consequently failing to influence. Anyway don't become corrupted – I haven't either authority or spirit to purify vice.

We have been moving furniture into the flat, recently, and it has all been fun… [description of] … Life is difficult for girls trying university. We are all wishing that we had been left alone and not educated up to this standard. The educational authorities have "tampered" with our intelligence – I would have been quite happy to leave school at 15, unaware of my latent potentiality, but fully aware of my potency, have worked in a factory, and then married a green grocer. I think a Green grocer could have been very Romantic. We could have toured the streets in his horse & cart, and I could have rung a bell, for everyone to hear. Now this pleasure is denied to me. Think of the limitless hours of the 'Telly' & the 'mass media'.

As you can see from the article I enclose, there are <u>at least</u> 40,000 abortions every year. This number reveals, amongst other things, how widely practised abortion is, & that any law to revise the present situation would not be revolutionary. As K. Whitehorn says 'we <u>do</u> accept abortion in this country, legal or not'. Yet because it is illegal, 40,000 risk mutilating themselves for life, because they are unable to have it done openly & properly in hospital, and in spite of the fact that they will not be prosecuted. … [several more pages to this effect].

Once the act is passed, however, one must continue to perfect contraceptives. It reveals irresponsibility in throwing aside the means of prevent conception, because one could resort to abortion.

One fear has always haunted me: as the risks of bearing children are gradually eliminated, today's youth who already are experienced, enough, will make intercourse a general practice, as a conclusion to petting, but being quite unaware of its essential meaning. It is well known that in primitive societies the emphasis on sex hinders the development of the intellect. The anaesthia of sex, drink, and today tobacco, is a means of alleviating one's miseries. Unfortunately it is negative, in that one abandons rather than eliminates troubles. There are surely so many better & more productive ways of solving the problem. Nearly all our letters have ended up worrying about the Masses. Ugh!

I apologise if the past couple of pages have seemed Woman's-Ownish – but at 12.30 am my mind and style aren't ticking in the normal way. Also I have not stated properly what would be the causes to the Act.

Alan, if you could send me your address, I will send your file direct to there, instead of to the College, where it may get mislaid in transit. Do you think that you could send me your obituary of Tawney from which to take notes. Apparently we are very likely to have a question on either Trevelyan or Tawney, since both have died within the year. I have innumerable articles about Trev., but only 'Tawney's 'Religion & the Rise' & 'The Acquisitive Society'.

Is your Landlady nice? I hope she is looking after you well.

Sunday Evening [14th October] Worcester College

I hope you are happy and well and your work goes satisfactorily. Thank you for your long letter – I will answer some of the points you mention first. Don't bother about my digs' address – I am only a few yards from college and come in every morning [presumably for breakfast] *so will be able to collect my file from there – Would you still like me to send my European History file? And if you w'd, would it be too late if I sent it in 2 weeks time? In answer to your plea for me to shrink my jeans – I already have bought a new pair which are <u>very</u>*

tight. (I couldn't get into them at first!) so you should like them – but my hair continues to grow. My digs and landlady are both delightful – tho' the latter almost over kind. No doubt you will see them both before I go. I am very sad you won't be able to come down this term – perhaps it is for the best, for though I, and therefore you, (for I expect I will be working longer hours) could both manage 2 days off it might have longer-term, unbalancing, effects.

I was very interested in both the article & your remarks on abortion. After exams I might go into it. But somehow I feel, from everything I have read so far, it is all too simple, too black & white; there must be some fairly strong (non-spiritual) arguments against it, or else reforms would have been achieved long since. As you point out, if one can have easy, painless, abortions and practically fullproof contraception we will be one step nearer the 'Brave New World' society where the animal pleasure of sex is totally divorced from all spiritual and mental considerations. It is true that fear (of the consequences) is not a sound basis for morality, and it would be ludicrous to argue for the retention of V.D on the grounds that it discouraged prostitution; but I am certain the problem is not as simple as many reformers see it. This does not mean, of course, that I would oppose reforms – for I hate and despise the present bestial laws as much as anyone – but the reform of the law would have to be done with full realization of the possible consequences. (Just to get my own back on your pointing out my various mistakes – I was interested in a certain word in the following phrase "the man is obligated to marry her" – aren't I petty!)

I enclose all I have on Tawney – I'm afraid it won't be much use.

I will refrain from launching another tirade against the masses (at least in this letter). Instead I will indulge in another of my favourite topics – myself! Bear with me, sweetie, for if you don't no-one will.

Tomorrow I start work in earnest – up to 60 hours a week, so I will be pretty exhausted. I feel as if I am just about to dive under a large ice-block and don't know when or where I will come up again. I have reached the C19 in English history which is fascinating, especially the industrial, religious and intellectual side. I have just finished Florence Nightingale by Cecil Woodham Smith – an absolutely fantastic person. I will send you my copy if you have time to read it.

I went for a long walk across the parks to Old Marston Church this afternoon. It was unbelievably beautiful, tranquil – the chrystal [sic] *essence of all the warmth and colour of the summer smoothed by the breezes of spring. Autumn is very late here, and many of the trees have not begun to turn yet – the willow-waterfalls still veil the river and the silver-birches quiver their million tiny leaves in the breeze – but the river was covered with sere leaves and boys were searching for conquers [sic] amidst rustling piles of chestnut leaves*

> *'Margarèt are you grieving*
> *Over Goldengrove unleaving?*
> *Leave, like the things of man, you*
> *With your fresh thoughts care for, can you?*
> ...
> *It is Margaret you mourn for.'*
> *(Hopkins)*

And the holly trees were aflame. And all above and around streams of bird song frothed like little waves on the inverted ocean of the sky. The Church was cool, grey, tiny and ancient, and we examined a C15 chalice (the oldest in use in England) – but everything merges into something else and now I am in the college chapel in the evening and the candles glow on the crucifix and the glory flares upwards borne on the ecstasies of 'Jesu, Joy of man's desireing' which is sung by the choir. And then again this merges off into last night when I returned through the enchanted night from a film and my heart was filled with praise, and then suddenly wrenched down into lust.

I hope this doesn't sound merely melodramatic or self-pitying, but am being torn apart. Half of me sees the world in a haze of glory – the other half aches at the cruelty and misery which lies all around; half of me again, also, is disembodied spirit, seeking God – while half is ravening beast lusting and prying. Penelope, I hope this isn't putting too much of a burden on you telling you all this – I don't want sympathy particularly as I will probably be fine by tomorrow – it is just that on occasions my sexuality reached a crisis and comes into bitter conflict with my ideals and the outcome is – self-disgust (and some poetry as well – of which I send a specimen which may give you a rough idea of what I am trying to explain.)

You talk of sex, tobacco & drink being anaesthia, and hoping that a better solution can be found. But where? As you know I am shut off from refuge in all of them – except in a perverted form. There is, I know in my deepest self, only one other escape – that epitomised in my other passage of poetry – which I quote at length because it is so delightfully written. I hope you love the Psalms.

Look after yourself my sweet one, I think of you often. Don't overwork or get depressed – and don't take the above too seriously.

Enclosed: Psalm 91

1. He that dwelleth in the secret place of the most High shall abide under the shadow of the Almighty…

My next letter is on Thursday evening [25th October] Worcester College

Just a short note I'm afraid – and on business.

a) Could you send my history file as soon as possible (& write also) – and if you have sent it and it has gone astray let me know.

b) Would you like to come to the Christmas Ball – December 7th (Friday) evening? I should imagine your exams will be over by then – and perhaps they would let you away at 5.0ish on Friday & you could spend the week-end down here. Anyhow, even if you can't come it's nice being asked! But I hope you can manage it. Please let me have an answer by Wednesday as ticket priority closes then.

I am just getting another of my miserable colds – but otherwise work etc go quite well. I have a nice poem of Swinburne's to send you, but do not have it on me.

Would you like me to send my European History file?

The first letter from my mother after her return to India is dated Thursday 25th October, from Assam. This was five days after the Chinese launched their attack in the disputed area of North East India, where the war continued until 20th November, when the Chinese withdrew.

My dear Alan,

I'm sitting on the verandah sipping fresh orange juice with the sun blazing down, lawn mower rattling, ferns rustling in a soft breeze and the bathroom being painted – so you can see am feeling less miserable and frustrated than the last time I wrote. This in spite of the fact that the Chinese are breathing down our necks and the Russians are steaming towards Cuba. Living permanently on the edge of a crisis certainly makes one live more awarely, looking ones last on all things lovely literally every hour. I don't know what the Chinese are up to but you needn't worry about us, as we can always slip up into the Naga hills and be in Burma in a few days. We haven't had a word from you since we left, but I think the mails are probably being confused by the state of emergency and likely to be held up.

You will have heard about the fiasco to the Kendal fraternity, [my sister Anne and Felicity] I was very fed up about it but on second thoughts decided that perhaps they were too young after all to cope with living on their own. I don't know what Anne is up to now, Fiona has made contact with Rupert and Alan Barnes, don't know that I'm thrilled about the latter but she is too busy with work and coffee bars to have much time for gadding anyway.

Life here has settled down into a very busy nothingness, I'm quite unwound and potter round in a tranquil daze doing a million unimportant things like fleaing dogs, digging, shouting at malis, Shorthand and drawing…. I'm going to start working a bit in the school and hospital next week… I'm going to write to Robert Shaw for his books on the Moguls too to make a study of them but whether I shall write anything about them I don't know. I find it such a relief not writing, and want to hand my enthusiasm and ambitions on to you. Perhaps that's just the effect of all this sleepy sunshine, an interesting subject for a book or thesis would be the effect of climate on religion and philosophy, though I'm sure it must have been done already. ….

I often think of you in your room, eating your calories (I hope) and living in the past. I hope the work is going well & not too many depressing moods bothering you – also that Penny is passing her exams, can't quite remember when they are. Hope the grant comes through too, let us know. Much love from us both, Mummy

The one letter from Penny which I shall include here was written on Saturday October 27th.

Thank you for your business letter. I shall deal immediately with the matters raised (There's some jargon back for you).

I would love to come on December 7th [Worcester College Winter Dance]. What a sweet idea. I shall have finished my exams by November 29th and would be spending the next week preparing for interviews which will or will not come. It will be ideal to escape to Alan's arms after my long Lesbian affair with Clio.

I am very sorry about not sending off your history-file. I have been meaning to for ages, but I never finally got around to it. I have sent it off separately from this letter since you wanted to know about the ball as soon as possible… The file has been exceptionally useful – I have modified my views about Pym, though I am not less sympathetic towards Charles. … I recognised a joy and exuberance in your essay on the Growth of Puritanism. It is very easy to find essays which you have enjoyed writing. Also I found useful your essay on the "Opposition to the Henrician Reformation".

Remembering your remark that you were tackling your work as if you were diving beneath a block of ice, how are you faring in the crystal caverns of the icy deep? Are you finding Truth amongst the blue still waters, or have you abandoned the envigorating [sic] air of pleasure for the murky depths of work? I hope you will not drown or lose your soul to someone else like the "Young Fisherman'. I would hate to see you floating with your long hair streaming behind you, beneath the surface of the water, unable to rise, and too far away for anyone to save you.

A new Cromwellian museum has just opened….

I went with Janet to the American Embassy, the day after the American blockade of Cuba. It was very inspiring, for I have never been amongst so many people – there were in fact about 4,000 – who were actively protesting against the dangers to world peace. Unfortunately after a while the sentiments of the crowd became diverse, and many were yelling insults at the Americans, which was not the aim of the C.N.D. meeting. [Description of events.]… *I have decided some time in the indefinite future, of the relationship between religion and art.* [Discussion of ideas on this in some detail several pages] … *As for historical studies, I would like to research into the relationship between the new Industrial capitalists of C17 and the government. … This long epistle is to make up for the letters which I have written but not sent. During this week I have been wretchedly unhappy, and "J'ai senti passer sur moi le vent delaile (??) de l'imbécilité." I planned innumerable ways of escaping from all my work and my present existence; I was even going to dash up to Oxford to see you. Finally, however, Mummy took me along to my Doctor, who gave much advice on tackling my academic work, and how to deal with essays; and … He was marvellous, tho' I do not know if the tablets he has given me are quite so effective.*

But this letter, too, full of a great deal of nonsense – a reaction to academic work – and perhaps just a little sense must suffice you for quite a time. Cambridge exams start in about 2 weeks time, and once they are over, I shall write to tell you about them. Pray hard for me, Tumnus. I feel very despondent at times.

Thank you for giving me access to the Macfarlane poetry anthology. Your poem brilliantly unified sentiment and poetic imagery. Descriptions like:

'silver dawn …
Powdering old buildings with rose & gold,
Wiping the shadows from her face,
And filling each heart w[ith] peace'

Or
'I saw this sad torn city
….stand crowned
Amidst its velvet fields as night
Drifted like the river mist'

[These are from a poem I wrote on October 12th]

are exquisitely evocative. 'Love and lust walk hand and [sic] hand' in every man; no-one can separate earthly from spiritual pleasures or desires, and I feel it is wrong to suppress one in order to further the other. Both have meaning; yet I believe if a man has neither wanted to, nor been able to participate in sexual intercourse, he can come into very communion with God, since all his interests are focused to this end. Yet I suppose that I should remember people like St Augustine. But St Augustine did not suppress his sexual desires (how dreadful this sounds – but he was quite a rake) so much as was satiated by it. He was a genius and having reached a situation from which he could not progress, he turned naturally to a source of unlimited love, which is never sufficient. That of god. I think frustration, because one has suppressed a desire unwillingly, is more destructive and negative, than a thorough participation, even up to "saturation-point". There is often, at least, some way out of the latter, if it applies to earthly pleasures. Sometimes it results in boredom, but this is usually because the participant lacks in imagination and intellect.

Now must part – Love to you, dearest heart. I miss you very much. I hope you recover from your cold, and do not drown in your work. Please don't send me any more business letters, unless they contain such interesting business as today's did

My next letter to Penny was on Friday [2nd November]

Thank you sweetie for your long letter, the file, and your second letter. I'm so sorry about your cold – I fully sympathise as I have just got over one (it came on last Thursday, but I took heaps of tablets – Vitamin C, Veganin, Coldrex, etc & gargled with T.C.P & used Friar's Balsam & within 24 hrs all the worst symptoms had disappeared – which is very unusual for me – so I suggest you get the above if you do not have them already.) I hope this C. Robin poem excerpt may cheer you up a little & also this book – which is a get well present (on second thoughts I will send the book separately as I want this letter to get to you on Saturday.) I also include a few notes on Rousseau – he is indeed a fascinating man, torn apart by sex and idealism etc. I am longing to read his 'Confessions'! The essay, as you will see, is a flippant introduction to a study of him – but no-one really understands him.

You ask for news of my activities – fairly dull I'm afraid. On Sunday however I went for a long walk up to Islip – which is a little old riverside village. The autumn, red-clay, countryside looked just like a Constable painting – very serene and filled with a golden richness & purity. The whole scene was charged with the last liquidfulness of Autumn – full of inexpressible sadness and beauty, every leaf and blade of grass very precious in its last moments. And now it is grey and thundery and the streets run gutters of soggy leaves and winter drizzle.

Over the last few days an extraordinary number of coincidences have all occurred forcing me towards an increased awareness of my vocation – which as I have known for long is in some social work – but now I think it may be concerned with the population problem. Among other factors has been my contact with two great social workers (one of whom I went to hear on Monday) – they are Father Pire & Father Borrelli. Do you know anything of either of them? The second, who I heard speaking, was a fantastic person (he spent a year living in the gutters of Naples – literally) – shining with purity, charity and joy. But I must not get too involved in such dreams – a good degree is the first step to whatever I want to do…

As for the outside world it goes from crisis to crisis – I only hear of it indirectly and such a mirror of real tensions I saw last night in a film "Advise & Consent" – the 'lid off the American Senate' – very good indeed.

I am very tired so will close now – but will write again with the book.

Enclosed: A typed version of A.A. Milne's 'Sneezles'

My next letter to Penny was written on a Sunday [4th November] Worcester

Are you very miserable, ma chérie? I hope not – tho' all this work tends to make one depressed – I was very mopy last night, but, fortunately, had a friend on whose shoulder I could pour it out.

I am just about to go off on a long walk over Shotover hill & will come back exhilarated and happy I expect. It is a lovely day and the city of dreaming spires amid its royal sash of autumn woods and mist-wrapped rivers should look very lovely. I may even sink to the depths (as my cynical friends would put it) and write some poetry.

Last night I started my exploration into the underworld of Oxford. As a preparation I bought some fish & chips and ate them from the newspaper as I walked along the streets – a performance which always gives me a glow, as if I was doing something naughty and unconventional (!) then I dived down the drabbest, dirtiest side-steet and found a very slovenly looking pub. But to my disappointment it was very snug and middle-class inside with old ladies sipping their beers and a few old gaffers chatting over the bar. All my visions of malevolent teddy-boys, sleek homosexuals etc were shattered. But perhaps more luck next week-end (!) I am convinced that such a survey will both give me a deeper insight into the varied life outside the ivory castle of university life, and, perhaps, I may be able to help even one lonely or maladjusted person. But I'm not sure my approach is right.

Swinburne this time – it is an exquisite picture of trackless nothingness, a vaporous emptiness conjured up by the use of vague, indistinct, terms – as T.S. Elliot has said of Swinburne "the diffuseness is essential ... it is one of his glories .... What he gives is not images & ideas – and music, it is one thing with a curious mixture of suggestions of all three ... in Swinburne there is no pure *beauty – no pure beauty of sound, or of image, or of ideas ... in Swinburne the meaning and the sound are one ... he uses the most general word, because his emotion is never particular, never in direct line of vision, never focused; it is emotion, not by intensification, but by expansion ... it is, in fact, the word that gives him the thrill, not the object ... his poetry is not merely "music" it is effective because it appears to be a tremendous statement, like statements made in our dreams ..."*

As you will find, the 'Lord of the Rings' has much of this dream-like quality and the same haunting rhythm.

Enclosed:

Studies in Song: By the North Sea Swinburne (an extract)

Penny wrote to me on Monday [5th November]

What a delightful book. The illustrations are exquisite... If this book is a token of your affections, then I esteem them highly. This is only another way of saying 'Je t'aime beaucoup'. Aimer is more mysterious than its rather mundane English equivalent, which, as you say, because of its frequent usage, is almost devoid of true significance. How sentimental I become sometimes!

I suppose I have written this unwittingly to prepare you for 'un petit contretemps'. For, however much I would like to see you on Saturday, I realise that your presence would disturb me emotionally, and I am sure I would not be able to recover by Tuesday. Even now I think of you too often for practical purposes. I wish I was a 'hard-hearted woman' who did not suffer the joys and agonies of emotions... Please honey, don't even ring me up. I am at the moment in such a vague mood that anything or anyone may easily distract me. What a goose I am. ... Thank you for your essay on Rousseau. It was interesting, though too detailed for my specific needs. Sabine is my bible. Whenever I choose to open it.

I am glad you have found your vocation. I sometimes feel guilty that I am less socially conscious than you and some of my other friends; for I want to buy a large house in Bucks or preferably in Cambridgeshire, far away from the bonds of modern civilisation, yet near enough to live a civilised existence. .... I think I see myself as a female Trevelyan... Unfortunately I do not have sufficient money to live independently, and yet I know few men who would be willing to support this type of woman. ... My present sympathies lie with Raleigh, who, according to T-Roper, was one of the first victims of the rivalry between the court & country parties... Thus I shall send you some of his poetry ... Now I must creep back to Eliz's glorious presence. Perhaps I shall meet you there. If you are looking for the sordid and wretched life of Oxford, we can go and visit, when I come up in December, a undergraduate at Trinity; he is philanthropic and seems to spend his time comforting unhappy people. ...

Will you really come up post-haste if I summon you. What a spontaneous relationship ours is. So long as the one does not suddenly stop being fond of the Other, it is quite idyllic.

My next letter to Penny was on a Sunday [11th November] Worcester

How are you poussiquette? Not too oppressed or nervous I hope. Don't worry I know you'll do very well and despite the attempts of our bureaucratic society there are still a few sacred places among the morning stars, places where the feet of the golden morning tread the mountains of peace, which can be attained by other methods than competitive examination! All the very best Penelope sweetie, but I will feel the same towards you however you get on, needless to say.

Thanks for your long letter. You say somewhere that you 'sometimes feel guilty' that you do not seem to be as 'socially sensitive' as me or some of your other friends. In fact I think this shows that you are healthier and more mature than us. As you will see from my Lawrence extract there is a tremendous danger in abstract 'philanthropy'. It is often a result of externalising an inner conflict, attempting to sort out the world when one has failed to sort out oneself – one must always remember the advice of Descartes "Conquer yourself rather than the world". But I'm afraid my inner schism is too deeply seated for me to overcome it – so I think I will land up in some social work. If I had enough strength and conviction I'd become a monk – for to drag a woman, however willing, through the brambles and barbed-wire I am hoping (in my masochistic way!) to go through in my fight against evil – would be selfish and cruel. Instead I will marry and my ideals will die away & I will become a fairly good teacher in a secondary school or something! But enough of that.

I have enclosed some Elizabethan melodies. I love Raleigh's 'Pilgrim', and as you say it is an important transition link between Elizabethan & Metaphysical poetry. I am beginning to have a fairly good idea of the inner conflict and the tense resolution of paradox and opposites which composes the attraction of Metaphysical poetry to our age which once again is making a desperate attempt to fit science and religion into one pattern.

But what are the especial characteristics of Elizabethan poetry? Perhaps you know something on the subject – I know little. But would hazard that its two dominant and most characteristic are its sincerity and its humour. When an Elizabethan was writing of anything love, God or anything else <u>*the whole*</u> *of his mind could believe in that thing – love might be " a prick… a sting" but it was something more than sex, something more than enlightened self-interest – it was an absolute, an ideal and this confidence allowed them to be flippant, obscene or mocking. For one only dares to make fun of something in which one has unshakeable confidence. Nowadays if we talk of the 'importance of love' it must be in an entirely serious tone without that shimmering air of mockery and slight fantasy which lights up the delicate swiftness of their lyrics. "Vicisti Scienti.. (I'm not sure of the ending!) "and the world has grown grey at thy touch". I am very much in sympathy with the arch romantic rebels Wordsworth & Lawrence at the moment who are trying to re-introduce life and spontaneity into this mechanical universe.*

Sorry for rambling – but I suppose I'm tired. Once again my sweetie good luck & don't worry. How long do the exams go on? – as I might send you some verses to keep you sane if it goes on long.

Enclosed (Anonymous)

Sleep, wayward thoughts and rest you with my love:
Let not my Love be with my love displeased…

My next letter to Penny is on a Monday [12th November]

Thank you for your note. This is all I can find directly on the subjects you mention – an essay by Lawrence on Democracy (probably pretty muddling) & two extracts from my political philosophy notes. The passage by Berlin is very good & worth thinking about as the distinction between the freedom to <u>*do*</u> *& the freedom* <u>*from*</u> *is fundamental. Anyhow poppet don't worry too much about such subjects. I knew nothing about socialism etc when I took my entrance & still know very little!*

Bitterly cold here at the moment but watery sunlight dribbling onto the crackling gold trees. Today is my 12 hrs work day so must rush. Be happy precious & think of me occasionally, neither too little or too much.

> *"Now it is autumn and the falling fruit*
> *and the long journey towards oblivion*
> …
> *And it is time to go, to bid farewell …*
> *[Lawrence: Ship of Death)*

Penny wrote again on Sunday [18th November].

Thank you for all your sweet letters – elles me portorient [?] si beaucoup de plaisir. Now the Cambridge ordeal is over and others still to come – in a week's time. .. The papers were interesting – I would send them to you, except that I need to go over them with my subject-mistresses. [description of papers – a long account]…

Enough of my long-winded moan. Alan, dearest, please do not be depressed about your work. Is there anything I can do to help you? Next term, having left school, I shall come up and see you a great deal. Isn't Angus a jovial youth? You must go to some parties, and to some lectures, for although you think they are a waste of time, some are wonderfully 'envigorating' and it would be good for you to get away from your books. At some time will you take Janet and I to the churches <u>*outside*</u> *Oxford? The older the better. Together, we shall lead you a dance. 'Oxford beware' of the Misses Gaster & M. Shall I come and mother you? I think you need it. Send me the telephone no. of your lodgings, then I can ring you at some time.*

I was distressed that you described the Oxford as sludgy. Janet and I had a romantic concept of snow feathering the towers and spires, and J was coming up especially to see the snow (and her boy-friend). [Description of snow, films etc.] …

Will you come down to London, after your term is over? You could stay with us, except the flat is just not large enough, but Robert would put you up wouldn't he? It would love to see you for a couple of days before Christmas.

I am sending you a poem by Lodge on 'Fair Rosalind'; the metaphors are exquisite, though conveying the traditional sentiments…. [Poem enclosed, along with several others copied out].

My next letter to Penny is on Sunday 18th November.

… The last week seems to have been one despairing effort a) to keep warm in this bleak, snowy weather b) to keep up to my prescribed work-syllabus. I have my termly essay for my Special Subject – O. Cromwell's economic and financial problems and policy' & this is so absorbing a topic – raising such questions as – why did Cromwell fail? (if he did) was the 'Revolution' the victory of a new bourgeoisie and the repression of the working classes etc – that I have had to read about 30 books on it apart from 1,000 odd page of set texts (last vac') as a result much compression will be needed to settle all this into a 40 min essay for Tuesday.

Simultaneously I am writing an essay on Peel which encompasses the years 1820-1846 and includes such huge topics as Radicalism, Chartism, the Anti-Corn Law League, the structure of the Conservative Party, the character of Peel etc. I have already, in four days, covered over 50 sides of typed notes and am now deeply involved in one of my pet subjects C19 reformers. After reading 'Florence Nightingale' by Woodham Smith I have become fascinated in what <u>makes</u> a reformer and what are the common features which such characters as Schweitzer, Wilberforce, Nightingale, Danilo Dolci, Cobden, Chadwick etc share.

Quite simply, using the Hegelian dialectic – that is thesis, antithesis and synthesis, or diagrammatically:
Thesis –> Antithesis –> Synthesis
(applied by Marx and meaning to him – thesis, capitalist society; antithesis, the revolt of the workers; synthesis – communism) – anyhow using this dialectic the thesis of such great figures was an emotional urge to action, often sexual, as in the cases of Ghandi, St Augustine and, perhaps, St Francis – this was in turn checked by an antithesis, their powerful will, which turned their energies in the direction of social reform, increasing the energy by damming & channelling it – like some great dam used for hydro electric power. The synthesis is obvious.

Now this is obviously oversimplified – and this is always the danger of using a systematization like the dialectic. For one thing it does not answer the problem – why should their energies be turned to helping others? As Lawrence points out in the quote I sent you last week often it is for selfish & base motives, tho' this may not, as far as these aided are concerned, detract from the value of their work. But why are some people sensitive to suffering & others not? Are we all sensitive at heart, tho' some of us shut ourselves up, compromise, refuse to give ourselves and thus become dead, perhaps through fear, perhaps through other motives? Or are we all basically self-seeking and such sympathy, in the best sense (Greek 'feel with') of the word, is a conscious effort; for a while at least. How difficult it all is – but I won't go on for you will not want to hear me drivel before you go to your exams (also this is a one-track subject of mine)

How much longer do they last my poppet? Also you have never told me what you are intending to do after the end of this term (also when does it end?) will you be staying on, or getting a job or even going abroad?

I enclose a sentimental but austerely beautiful de la Mare which is especially appealing in this 'sodden towards sundown' month. Oh for the soft summer again! – but winter has its clean, functional grandness and I am longing to see my mountains again with their patches of rock and snow and dead bracken, their stunted thorn-trees, old stone walls wet with winter mist and the becks in brown spate and everywhere the clear, wet bog-scented smell of damp heather. (Goodness!)

P.S. I am sickening even myself with all this idealistic tripe – so what you must feel I don't know!

Enclosed: Walter de la Mare, The Scarecrow

The next letter to Penny is on Tuesday Nov. 20th. Worcester College

Two letters to thank you for – you are a poppet. They came just at the right time – giving me added vigour in my wearying struggle with Cromwell's financial and commercial policy. And now it is all over, and, like you after your Cambridge exams, I feel elated tho' I have another essay for Thursday morning. The actual reading of the essay was rather an anti-climax for with the aid of numerous plans and graphs I showed how all the traditional theories of Ashley and others were nonsense. And after having stormed for ¾ hr I found that my tutor and the rest of the class were not prepared to put up any resistance at all and did not bother to defend the conventional views at all. I felt I had bulldozed a shadow. Still it was fun writing it and making 'Trevor-Roper like' criticisms of the accepted authorities.

Penelope it is very sweet of you to worry about me. I love you all the more for it. We seem to spend our time comforting each other, and one of us is always ending up "try to be happier my dearest". The trouble is that we are both essentially very serious minded and grave people and take each other's moans too seriously. I am sorry if my letters have been miserable lately – this is largely because I have been getting rather tired recently (approaching end of term) and this tends to make me selfish – and yours is the shoulder I naturally turn to. All the longings and sorrows (if any) of my soul poured onto you – for here my relations with my friends are necessarily very fragmentary. Anyhow please don't worry. I am essentially happy and have frequent moments of ecstasy which more than compensate for periods of gloom.

Such a moment of joyous wonder occurred, for instance, this evening when I was walking back from my 'tute'. My heart was relieved anyhow and then I looked up, letting the soap-sud snowflakes fall like sweet cold kisses on my face. For a few seconds the whole world was lifted up in beauty. The glistening patterns of the naked trees against the sky, the slender Church spire probing up into the cotton-wool clouds, the lights flickering off the puddles and the wisps of snow on the walls shimmered and danced forming patterns and dreams; in my mind I could hear the medieval bells tolling and the crackling of Christmas fires. Oh, I can't convey the wonder of it my sweetie, but the clanging joy and peace, the dark and light blended into a hymn of beauty.

All this sounds trite because I am too lazy to analyse my vision and to carefully select words to fit it – but such moments happen quite often. But there are dark threads also in the pattern – and I am glad it is not always a selfish sorrow I feel. For instance when returning from a bus three days ago I was accosted by a woman who was obviously drunk. She had just been jeered at by a group of 'teds' and I happened to catch her eye. There was enough sorrow in her face, in the hollow eyes, the flabby broken lips, the grimy, lined cheeks to fill a Dostoievsky novel. And I couldn't do anything for her. She wanted drink and I was too afraid and too selfishly prudish to help her.

I know self-condemnation won't help. "But you know what I mean". But as I said, on the whole, I am happy so don't worry. I partly wrote mournfully because I wanted you to write to me and give me reassurance – because I miss you. I wonder – do you think we are building up our fondness too much in our letters? Really we hardly know each other, yet we seem very alike, perhaps dangerously alike. We really are "two dreamers" – my friends all think me terribly sentimental as far as I can make out!

Now some practical plans. When does your Oxford exam end/begin? When does your term end? I would love to come to London and hope that you will come up to 'Field Head'; the Lakes are austerely beautiful in the winter. But we can plan things when you come up. Needless to say I will have to work somewhat next vac', but had planned to take a week off somewhere.

Thank you for all the poetry – some new, some I already like. Isn't it wonderful we both like this 'sloppy stuff'? I hope we will neither 'grow out of it' (if that is possible). I esp like Dowland setting.

I have been reading chunks of Blake (how well do you know him?) recently. I find him very challenging when I am feeling complacent – as I once wrote "he is that most terrifying of all men a realistic idealist" – his honesty and perception is shattering and his clear spiritual vision allows him to see all the sordid hypocricies of this world against a blazing backcloth of golden truth. His 'Proverbs of Hell' are a storehouse of wisdom – (and a good fund for debate subjects etc incidentally!) and a battle programme for any teenage rebel – listen to a few –

> *"Prisons are built with stones of Law, Brothels with bricks of Religion."*
> *"He who desires but acts not, breeds pestilence".*
> *"Drive your cart and your plow over the bones of the dead".*
> *"Sooner murder an infant in its cradle than nurse unacted desires"*
> *"Prudence is a rich ugly old maid courted by Incapacity"*

–then again there are prophetic intuitions.

"One thought fills immensity"
"Exuberance is Beauty"
"A fool sees not the same tree that a wise man sees"
"The cut worm forgives the plow"
"The nakedness of woman is the work of God."

That is enough be meditating on for now I expect!

There is another undated letter to Penny, probably on 21st November.

I am enclosing two newspaper articles on Chinese invasions of Assam, which I am sure you would want to see. I hope your parents are alright. [I refer to these articles in a letter to my mother]. *How dreadful for them to lose their home and all their belongings in India. If you hear from them soon, will you tell them how very sorry I am.*

At the moment I am reading Edith Sitwell's 'The Queen and the Hive' on Eliz. I….. [just a para of description]

My next letter is on Thursday [22nd November]

I am writing on this civilized paper because I am in Eric's room, supposedly listening to classical music and comforting him with my presence for the loss of a friend in an accident. He is working at the moment and I am letting Beethoven float round me.

Thank you Penelope for sending the newspaper cuttings – it looks as if the worst is past. For a while I was half-expecting to get a telegramme [sic] *saying my mother was back in England.*

How are you sweetie? Not too worried about the Oxford exams I hope. Have you heard any result from Cambridge yet? Presumably in answering your questions you start by spending 10 minutes planning roughly four questions – and writing out the times by which each question must be finished. The former means that your brain is working subconsciously while you are answering the earlier questions and it will also throw up a [blank] & facts which emerge in answering these questions can often be used in modified form later. It obviously requires self-discipline not to rush straight into scribbling frantically when you see everyone else doing it, but it is worth it. You must, obviously, make an organized effort to finish the number of questions set – and if you limit yourself strictly by writing down the time at which each question must be finished & dropping the question at that time you should manage.

At the moment I don't feel like doing any work for a little while as I wrote another essay this morning – getting up at 6.0 to do it. But now for my final essay I have been set the absorbing topic 'Victorianism' which includes a study of Victorian literature (including reading 'Middlemarch' which my tutor thinks the best novel in English literature) Victorian art & architecture & Victorian morality & religion – fascinating. But at the moment all I want to do is get to sleep. Thus I will end this very short letter by saying that I will write much more fully on Sunday when I should have recovered.

During my tutorial today I discussed my future with my tutor & he approved in principle with my reading a B.Litt. or D.Phil. if I got a good enough degree. If, as I don't really expect, I found myself able to do so I would like to take a year off in between doing something more practical. This would mean that I would be 25 before I finished my final degree – and you would have left university – what a thought! 'Procrastination is the thief of time' and 'idealism' is likewise.

The next letter from Penny is dated by me as 22nd November, London Thursday

Thank you for your letter. I am glad all goes well with you. I am passing through one of my dreamy vacuous states (I adored being called 'a dream rabbit') at the moment which is somewhat unfortunate for my history revision. … I enjoy, like you, I am sure, being sentimental and dreamy; as for your friends accusing you of sentimentality, Basil, certainly, is not living in reality, and David surely has an 'Achilles heel'. I shall come and find it, if he denies its existence. Beastly child I am breaking down the walls and barriers people set up to protect themselves. I did not, however, destroy yours. <u>You</u> did that for me, when one evening you revealed all your good and bad traits to me (There are no bad ones).

My Oxford exams start, indeed, on Monday and end by Thursday. We break up on the 20th December. For about a week or two, after the exams I shall be involved in further work, and (god help me) interviews: I should love to come up to field Head sometime. Perhaps after Christmas? But we can arrange that later. I went to an interesting lecture today on the Commonwealth.... You will have to endure a lot of culture while you are in London.

Do let me know how your parents are. I assume you had heard of the invasion of Assam, before I sent you the cuttings.

P.P.S. We are related to the Courtaulds, but in such way that both sides hush the matter up. I regret, therefore, I cannot offer you the Chairmanship. Perhaps Robert may find you a place in Parliament. ....

The letter to Penny in this first part of the winter period was written on Sunday [25th November] Worcester College, Oxford

P.P.S. In my selfish prattling I nearly forgot to tell you. My mother has been flown to Calcutta, but I don't know as yet if she will be coming on home.

This should arrive <u>just</u> before you start your Oxford exams. All my best wishes, love & prayers are with you, as you know; do well as you can my sweetest and enjoy it if you can. You should be getting quite blasé about exams by now – one can't go on getting worked up about these things time after time. A friend (girl) of mine here is also taking them – she has been at Oxford 3 years already (at St Clare's) and was a great friend of Julie's – she's not <u>too</u> worried about the exams as her aim is to <u>fail</u> (she quite rightly believes that 6 yrs at Oxford would be <u>too</u> much of a good thing).

Thank you for all your letters my poppet – though they only make me long more to see you. I can see it is going to be very difficult to draw a 'happy mean' between my work and seeing you as both are vital.

I went for a walk this afternoon through Wytham Woods – North of Oxford. It was misty and the further trees looked like elfin figures, slim and immense in the distance. Nearly all the trees were leafless and their splaying branches and the silver lichen moss made patterns of interweaving grey against the darker trunks. I walked down long cathedral avenues with massive beech and chestnut collumns [sic] supporting the grey dome, their tracery woodwork hung with silver rain drops. I could feel the strength of their roots beneath the ground pushing the heavy wood upwards and then letting the branches bend under their weight. The ground was rich with quilted leaves, forming a coat on the thick loamy clay-soil which clung to my shoes. The wood sung and chattered with birds, the quarrelling of starlings, the liquid siftings of thrushes and the frequent whirr of woodpidgeons, and the squelch of my footsteps drowned the moments of intense quiet when suddenly everything stopped and all the trees seemed to be listening to my intruding clumping. The 'earth-smell' was in the air, and the damp smell of a thousand mouldering leaves and wet moss. For a while I was absolutely at peace. Has this conveyed anything? As Elliot says, writing is a constant struggle with obstinate words and always the right expressions 'eel' their way through one's fingers.

I am just about to embark on 'Victorianism' (after another 3 days on Cromwell) and already my mind has been filling with preconceptions which will distort my findings. I am convinced that the only binding element in 'Victorianism' was fear. What else binds Arnold and Swinburne, Newman and Kingsley, Carlyle and Peel, Victoria and Browning and of course Tennyson & Geo Elliot, with their seriousness, their strict morality (even Swinburne & that post Victorian D.H. Lawrence had this), their energy & love of work, and their ornateness? It was a fear of chaos – the spiritual chaos which was left by the findings of science (which turned man into an evolved animal) and the material chaos produced by the industrial revolution. The constant stress on morality and hard work and the anguished search for God, by men like Newman and women like Elliot was the response. But more of that when I have read something about the period.

I have just, since writing the above, been to a talk on the University Christian Mission which is being held in the 4th week of next term & being led by Trevor Huddleston. Our college representative is chaplain of Christ Church Cambs & got a Theology 1st at Worcester 2 years ago. He gave a marvellous talk, well larded with quotations one of which I enclose. His sensitiveness and honesty shone forth and he had a charity which took one's breath away. I hope you will be able to come down during the mission next term (3rd week Feb) & meet him.

P.P.S. [on a card]

I have just received your two letters this morning so enclose the Cromwell essay. (Thank you very much for letters). I'm sorry it is so messy – I was allowing myself the luxury of scribbling since I thought no one would see it. As you see it deals almost exclusively with Cromwell's financial problems & how this affected his foreign policy & may be too detailed for your purposes. I hope you can understand the graphs (don't worry about the navy as this is an aside)

On reading through my letter of last night I winced several times at its lush sentimentality. Please don't take it too seriously.

I am just on the point of starting "Middlemarch" & my next letters will probably be full of it.

Enclosed: [copied out neatly on two cards]

Aldous Huxley: 'Human Potentialities'.
(Symposium at San Francisco. pp. 60-3)

'I would like to begin with a question, a very simple & seemingly absurd question: What are people for?...

The following day I made a note in relation to my reading of the time.

Knowledge – thoughts while reading Coleridge (Basil Willey) 23/11/62

True knowledge is to know a fact emotionally – to "feel it in the blood" and to let it change one's personality. Our receptivity is largely in proportion to a) our experiential maturity & b) our previous 'knowledge'. Thus experience – which is outside events modifying our character (the most obvious channels for such action are extremes such as suffering & love) has a direct relation to our ability to understand abstract ideas. The ability of ideas in themselves to modify and increase our experience is much less powerful. Thus over-long academic study is wasteful for until we have matured our personalities much of our study cannot be absorbed.

Like a sponge however – once the initial dryness has been overcome the absorbing power increases more rabidly [sic – rapidly] – till saturation point is reached.

Another, undated, letter from Penny is written about this time, probably on the 25th, in similar style, paper etc.

Dated Sunday Evening, London.

I am anxious for your sake. Although I sometimes sink into the depths of despondency, yet I am never there for long. But I feel your work has depressed you for rather a long time. Yet other than by writing to you often, and seeing you occasionally, and loving you always, I can offer no practical help. I would say that you must not work so hard or worry so much, but you evidently have to study for a First. So long as you never reach the state, at which would decide that your work serves no need. But I know that I need not fear for you on that account. Why am I so useless? And why can I not offer any good advice. Anyway I shall see you in a few weeks time – each comforting the other by his or her presence, for I am sure that my present jovial spirit will not last till then.

I have been reading Elizn Love Poetry, this afternoon and evening. Although their 'sincerity' in love is framed in such joyous or heart-rending language, I began to yearn for the subtle cynicism of the Jacobean poets…. [further comments and quotes] …

Have you read 'Pepita' by Vita Sackville-West? It the fascinating account of Vita S-W's grandmother, who is a Spanish dancer and who lives with [sic] in France…

P.S. Thanks for your Sunday Letter. Of course I like to receive your letters and they are never boring, as some of mine must be. …

P.P.s. Read Hill on Crom's 'Foreign Policy', v. controversial – damn Hill – he upset all my ideas about success/failure of Crom's F.P. – not good, just before an exam.

Thinking about this fifty years later it all seems true. It explains why my academic achievements at Oxford, despite very hard work, were limited – I was immature and had experienced few of the things, particularly political life, about which I was expected to write.

*

We need now to go back a little way to a series of letters from my mother which need to be read together. The first is dated Nov. 17th and is from Assam.

My dear Alan,

News from the front! A very peaceful front here with only the barking of the dogs to disturb it and the scent of brushes in the drain as the malis clean them. The real front must be a nightmare, so cold and hilly with Chinese peering down and flourishing arms that the Indian troops have none of, or perhaps they have now. ... We have only started to feel a slight pinch in that things like eggs and chickens are getting hard to buy and expensive...

I have been given the all clear to start my family planning campaign so am putting out some propaganda and hope the candidates come rolling in...

I do hope Penny is getting on all right with her exams, I was wondering if you would like to make your Christmas Ball into your birthday treat, perhaps Fiona and Rupert come for it and we could pay for the tickets? There isn't anyone really very exciting in the Lake District to make a party with, but you might want to have Penny to yourself or have made other arrangements. If you do think it's a good idea get the tickets and let me know what they cost...

I was wondering if you couldn't write to Victor Gollanz and see if he could find you something useful to do within the scope of your talents which are obviously literary or does that sound a dotty idea? I wish we could have another talk, already I'm beginning to feel out of touch with you & your work, these silly little forms are useless. My reading is still "The Golden Bough" its surprising how little I do too, its always a mystery to me where time goes out here...

Hope your food problems are solved, I constantly wonder what the 3 of you are eating, Leek soup I suppose?! Much love, Mummy

My mother wrote again four days later, as the political situation worsened.

Cherideo Nov. 21st [It is date stamped 23rd November and addressed ARRIVED IN CALCUTTA]

My dear Alan,

I don't know whether this letter will get to you but I'm hoping it may just. I'm afraid this is It and there is no holding the Chinese now, it is all terribly tragic and senseless, the casualties on both sides are phenomenal and one is riven with pity for poor Assam and what it is going to mean in terms of starving children. I think that by the time this gets to you (if it does) we shall be out, probably in which case I'll send you a wire from Calcutta or Singapore or wherever we land up. In any event don't worry because even wires will probably not arrive. I have a suitcase packed but of course we may not even be able to take that much, in which case have some woolly vests ready for me! It is very peculiar sitting on a peaceful sunny verandah eating breakfast and listening to the news telling one about oneself, it all seems quite unreal...

We got a letter from you and Anne this week, but nothing from Fiona... Don't forget to go to the Board for money if you need it as you will during the holidays, if I go to Calcutta I shall be able to send you some from there...

Don't let any of this divert you from your work which is the only important thing and your worrying about us wont make an atom of difference except to yourself. I want to write to the girls now, so will stop, love to Penny, do hope the exam is safely over. I expect we shall be seeing you all for Christmas, that would be a lovely thought. When does your term end? Much love from us both – Mummy

The following letter is handwritten from c/o Kilburn, Calcutta, and probably written at the end of November.

My dear Alan,
I hope my series of wires and letters have got through to you & you weren't too worried about us. It all happened so suddenly that we had no time to do anything but throw a few unlikely needs into a case and set off. We (the women & children) had planned to go to Calcutta by road, but when we got to Jorhat we were told that 2 R.A.F. planes were coming to pick us up. The disorganisation was utterly British, we were all penned into one building for 24 hours waiting for the planes which were variously described as Brittanias, Constellations, Dakotas, & helicopters & turned out to be Hastings – it was lucky the Chinese decided to call a halt as otherwise we should have been nicely trapped! It was a very painful business having to leave our husbands & possessions) the latter didn't bother me a bit actually) but we hope that some way will be found out of the muddle & we'll be able to go back.... I don't want to leave India until Daddy does so shall try & get a job here if I find we're not allowed back within a couple of weeks. ... I've sent £75 for December, I shall have it put into your account & will let you know more about the money side in another letter. Much love, keep working –Mummy

There is a second letter from my mother to my grandmother, written from Calcutta, probably on 27th November:

Dear Mummy,
What a debacle! It all seems like a bad dream and the air of unreality helped us through a rather grisly experience. .... [description of events] ...I shall stay in Calcutta for a month, by then we should have a clearer idea of the situation. £75 is coming home at the beginning of December which I will have transferred to Alans account & he'll have to organise the holiday expenses. I'm afraid it'll have to be an austerity Christmas without presents or parties, but I know they'll understand, I don't want to have to cancel Anne's course if I can help it but at the moment can't say what the arrangements are for paying husbands, £75 a month is the maximum we are ever allowed to send under the new rules so shall have to see how much A. is going to cost. Much love to you both, Iris.

*

My next letter to Penny was on Tuesday evening [27th November] from the Bodleian Library, Oxford

Just to take up one point which you made. Can you guess what? I will speak more of this before I see you. But re. this question – i.e. our physical relationship a few thoughts cross my mind. There is no need for me to stress the difficulties for both of us. You already know something of the measure of my sensuality & you can imagine that I'm not any the better for living my present eremitical life. Therefore, my sweetest, you will have to help me and use your greatest tact, for as you know, I have little self-confidence & if you withdraw too much or in the wrong way I will be hurt & go into another huff. But, darling, as you know I still attempt to live up to certain ideals as a Christian and apart from this if all my protestations of affection are not vain I will restrain myself if that is what you want. I don't regret last holidays – except that I would have gone much slower if I'd known how unspoilt you really were – and I know that we were still quite a way from intercourse, <u>but</u> I agree that if we are going to see each other fairly often for a longish period we will have to keep a beastly but necessary check on ourselves – despite what all my heroes like Blake, Lawrence, Freud etc say on the evils of suppressed desire! To conclude, my poppet, if you help me (and I help you) we must try not burn <u>too</u> fiercely. But enough of that serious topic.

Today I include a strange mixture of quotes – firstly a wonderful prayer of St Francis, simple, comprehensive and ardent. Secondly a piece of Dryden's Satire which I have just read (again) in Wedgewood's 'Poetry & Politics under the Stuarts'. I'm afraid one has to be bitter about something to write satire – but otherwise I would love to be a great satirist; as Knox said, it is the strongest weapon against ignorance, bigotry, pomposity, intolerance etc. Laughter is the one weapon which even dictators fear.

Enclosed:

Prayer of St Francis.
Lord, make me an instrument of Thy Peace. Where there is hatred, let me sow love; …

Dryden: puts into the mouth of the dying poet Flechnoe, bequeathing to Shadwell his supremacy over the realms of nonsense, the following lines:

> "Shadwell alone my perfect image bears,
> Mature in dullness from his tender years; …

The same day Penny wrote to me. Tuesday [27th November].

It was marvellous talking to you yesterday. I thought you said that you were incapable of holding telephone calls – you seemed to be fairly confident. I am sorry if I seemed depressed – it was a little frustrating to speak to you, without seeing you. However, do you think I could [come] *up this weekend? I would not disturb you, if I came on Friday afternoon, because I could go on a Grand European Tour of all my friends. In the evening you could take me around to see your acquaintances. Saturday I could spend in the Ashmolean, while you worked – I spend hours by myself in museums. In the evening, you might take me to this party at which you are singing. On Sunday, we could 'do' churches, or 'the walks' which you have praised so much. You see, I have planned it all. However, do say if it would be inconvenient. I think the plan would be better than your coming up just for Friday evening. I don't like treats in small doses. Could you also find me somewhere to stay? Would you write back as soon as possible to confirm it, even if you have not found anywhere – just to assure my mother in writing that I have a bed for the night – and not yours either. Sorry about the deceitful practices, but if you wait until you have actually found a bed, I might not have written confirmation until Friday at least. If this all seems rather short notice, can you afford to ring me again on Wednesday night, at about the same time. I promise I won't talk for long. BUT if you prefer I don't come up, don't hesitate to let me know.*

I feel much more confident about the special History paper today. … Apparently some of the questions were set by Mrs Prestwich whom you 'dismembered' in your essay on Cromwell. [further discussion of work] *… Love to you, my dearest heart. After my exams my mind is completely vacuous, so I can offer you no profound thoughts, if they were ever intellectual. However I shall write out a poem for you to consider.*

[Poem enclosed: Song 'That women are but men's shaddows']

I wrote again the next day [28th], on Wednesday evening, to wish Penny happy birthday.

You know you have my love and thoughts especially today. I hope you manage to have a wonderful day despite exams. Do you feel any older? I never do.

… As you will have gathered from the above I would love you to come down on Friday. I have, as you asked in your letter, found you some digs for Friday & Saturday night & though I will, as you have realised, have to do some work, it will be easy to follow your 'programme'. Please give me details of when you arrive etc – tho' I expect if I meet you when you arrive I won't be very anxious to go on working while you do a tour of your other Oxford boy-friends! There is a Brecht play on on Friday evening which we could go to if you like – tho' it would perhaps be a pity to spend our short time together in this way.

Since I last wrote I have done nothing of interest – except having a tea-party – all my friends – or rather some of them – this afternoon. When you arrive you will probably hardly recognize the gaunt, haggard, stooping figure who comes to meet you!? In the last three days I have done over 33 hrs work and as you may gather from this letter's vagueness it is beginning to tell. You will have to mother me, as you suggested, & calm my 'fevered brow', rocking me gently to sleep etc.

Could you bring a needle & thread with you as my jeans, being so tight, are growingly indecent and need mending? (I will then find out how unpractical you are.) …

Enclosed:
The Oblation. Swinburne.

Ask nothing more of me, sweet;
All I can give you I give....

There is a cyclostyled letter dated 28th November 1962 from The Assam Company, Limited, London.

Dear Mr Macfarlane,
All the men are remaining in Assam: all the women and children of the Managerial Staff, both European and Indian have been evacuated to Calcutta.
Here in Calcutta the company's Agents Messrs. Kilburn & Co. Ltd., have made excellent arrangements and the women and children are well housed and well looked after... The General Manager's wife is with them and has the brood under wing. ...
To sum up, everything seems to be under control and let us hope that nationally the same is true.
I have offered to go out immediately the Agents and General Manager think I can get to Assam and be of any use,
P Remnant, Chairman

The next letter after Penny's visit was written at five past four, on Sunday 2nd December.

Having had that conversation about when I should write it seems strange writing now, as you are still on the bus. No doubt we are both thinking of each other and generally looking moony! I hope the 'poetry and jazz' was enjoyable & that you managed to sleep well last night. It seems so useless writing – so artificial after two days together – so I won't write much at the moment. Anyhow I am still in rather a daze as you will see from the state of my writing. I will have to purge myself with this 'Victorianism' essay & I will use it as a distraction by pretending that I am writing it for you (I will type out & dedicate it to you if it is any good) & I will thus distract my energies. And how will you fare my poppy? Don't think about me too much – I'm not worth it apart from anything else...

Enclosed:

I was walking along the street ... I was stopped by a decrepit old beggar.
Bloodshot, tearful eyes, blue lips, course rags, festering wounds ...
(Turganev (quoted "Year of Grace"))

Song.

When, Dearest, I but think on thee,
Methinks all things that lovely be
Are present, and my soul delighted:
...
(Owen Felltham (1661))

I wrote again the next day, Monday 3rd,

"Out of the night that covers me, black as the pit, from pole to pole'... I write to you. (The "night" is my work in which I am drowning all my loneliness etc). This is just to give you one more re-assurance of my ....? Already, it will only be three days until we see each other (when you receive this). Come up when you like on Friday for although I will have to do some work & go to my "collection", I am sure the organisers of the Dance would appreciate your assistance. What colour will your dress be sweetheart? – so I can be gallant and pluck forth a rose ((or something) for you to wear.

My study of 'Victorianism' is more & more exciting. The enclosed poem – or rather a portion – you will know already. With one's normal conception of 'Victorianism' it is difficult to see how such ideas could have been so popular. I suppose people liked the escape into a rich, colourful, hedonistic world, where the grey and grimy industrial towns, the repressive morality, the stark faces of threatening new classes, the earnestness of the temperance movement etc could be forgotten. Every hidden desire of the Victorians could herein be realised vicariously – with no commitments. They revelled in the joy of playing with fire, of being naughty. It is an adolescent paradise in which they could shed Pilgrim's heavy pack of 'responsibility' and 'seriousness' amidst the languors and raptures of the lotus east where the lily dreams in the pool and the nightingale lets its liquid siftings fall' in the dim, spicy woods.

Enclosed:
'Omar'

Come, fill the Cup, and in the fire of Spring
Your Winter-garment of Repentance fling.
The Bird of time has but a little way
To flutter – and the Bird is on the Wing.
...

That same day I wrote to my parents [Monday 3rd December], from Worcester College. [It is addressed to Cherideo, and stamped Sibsagar 10th December]

Dear Mummy and Daddy,

I don't know how this will find you, if it reaches you at all. There is nothing I can really say about how sorry I am about this disaster. words don't mean much, and if I laid it on too thick I would be lying because I have been so immersed in my work that I have not had much time to worry about the outside world – which is perhaps a good thing. Anyhow you know that apart or together you always have my love and prayers and I know that whatever Mummy decides to do will be right ie staying out in India. As I never read newspapers I didn't hear about the disaster until a day or two after it happened, when Penny sent me some cuttings (which shows my ostrich 'head in the sand' state). By now, from the gradual news that drifts into my snug room, I gather things are improving. I got a carbon letter from Remnant or whoever is the 'Head'; it was sickening, full of patronising clichés about the General Manager's wife "having the brood under her wing" in Calcutta and saying how zealous he was to rush out to Assam if there was anything for him to do, with an odd aside dismissing Nehru as "intransigent" etc. Ugh! By the way I have had two letters from Mummy so the mail is getting through this way. The flight sounds typically 'British" & unprepared. How are you Daddy, perhaps this will reach you by yourself at Cherideo? If so, all my especial affection, while Mummy is away.

As for my own doings, two things seem to fill the whole horizon – my work & Penny. I am enjoying both immensely (if that doesn't sound odd??). At the moment I am writing an essay on a fascinating subject 'Victorianism' which means reading all my favourite writers like Tennyson, Hopkins etc. While I am talking of work – I asked my tutor casually if he thought it worth my while provisionally applying for a 'State Studentship' (that is a scholarship which should make me self-sufficient if I wanted to do some further study before I left University). He seemed to think it a good idea though of course it would depend on my degree. I don't think there is much possibility of getting good enough marks – but if I did I might spend a year abroad – and then come back & read a B.Litt (2 yrs) or D.Phil (3 yrs). This would mean I would be 24 or 25 before I finished – but pretty highly qualified & more certain of what I want to do. Do you think it a bad idea? Anyhow I don't expect the problem will come up.

Penny has been up for a couple of days this weekend & is coming up on the 7th for the dance. I have also invited her up to the Lakes (Granny suggested this!) for a few days after new year. As you may guess from this she is weaving a strong net round me & I will be ensnared before long – but we would neither want to get married for 5 years – so have plenty to [sic] time to cool our heads. We went for an idyllic walk through the frost-fields of Port-Meadow to the Perch & then on to the wishing-well at Binsey Church. Her exams are over – but she is not too optimistic re. the results.

My fondest love to you both, look after yourself; Penny sends her love also, Alan

Penny wrote on Monday [3rd December].

It was wonderful seeing you over the weekend. I had wanted to see you for such a long time, but when the occasion arose, it passed too quickly. Yet it seems strange that in four days time I shall be seeing you again.

You must plan some pleasant walks for this weekend. Despite my moans about my feet and toes, I found the scenery idyllically beautiful. It was fascinating to watch the amber leaves drifting down onto the road. Of course, I have told you how much I like autumnal colours and smells and I was secretly miserable that I might not experience Autumn in Oxford where it is said to be beautiful. ~~Although I missed the~~

Thank you for the books – I was thrilled to receive 'Le Petit Prince' – and I am looking forward to start reading 'Lords of the Ring' in a week's time. Dearest heart, you have given me some delightful books. Will you take me to your Children's Book Shop. I am fascinated to see it. There are few if any bookshops in London selling only children's books. I'll bring the Listener's and Times Lit Supp's extra supplements on children's books, which contain some articles on the material for and the presentation of such books. … [more on children's books].

I spent the coach journey studying the drawings of 'Le Petit Prince'. But it was so cold in the coach, that I fell asleep dreaming sweetly of xxxxx. [Account of a performance of jazz and poetry, including Christopher Logue and Adrian Mitchell.] … I am sorry, dearest heart if I was grumbling yesterday afternoon about the clothes I possess. I am not really interested in clothes, though I am concerned about colour combination. … In fact, all my money goes on books … If I need any clothes my mother buys them for me. … I had a wonderful weekend and thank you for that and all my presents. I am looking forward to seeing you. I shall try to find some Victoriana for you at the V & A. Please, sweetheart, dedicate your essay to me. I should be complimented by your action. Don't however, both to type it out especially for me – I can read it when I come down.

PS Alan, darling, I am not trying to stultify your social conscience. That remark was unfair on your part. I am merely trying to direct your interest to S. America. Ho Ho.

The next day she wrote again: December 4th London [Tuesday]

Thank you for your letter, in order to write which you emerged from your black pit. It cannot, however, be too black, because you write later 'My study of 'Victorianism' is more & more exciting'. I am glad you are enjoying it, and to further your interest I have bought a couple of booklets on 'Victorian Paintings' and on 'William Morris'. I shall bring them with me on Friday

I shall try to catch the same coach on Friday, as I did before. It may, however, because of this accursed fog – it is horribly thick and oppressive, and there is also a bitter frost (what a combination) – be cancelled, or delayed. Thus if I have not arrived by 2.00, do not bother to meet succeeding coaches, since I may well come instead by a later coach or by train. If this happens I shall come straight to your room. … At the moment I am listening on the wireless to B. Britten's Variation and Fugue on a theme of Purcell….

I shall, I am afraid, be unable to hinder the organisers of the dance, or rearrange it according to my tastes. I wrote to Jane at LMH, inviting myself to tea on Friday. Also a friend arranged for me to see her sister, who is studying History at LMH. It will be useful to know about the History Tutor before I am interviewed by her (My God, I hope I am – if only as a justification for all the work I have been doing this week).

Alan, honey, I picked up John Fielden's files today. I rang up on Monday evening, and suggested that since he lived in Islington, and since I was not sure if I could meet him at lunchtime, we met in the evening. Poor fellow stuttered out that he was married – it was amusing… He gave me a long explanation about the arrangement of his files – he certainly worked very hard, and suggested you went to some lectures by Habbuk (?), since they are not usually published later in printed form. He has apparently disproved Nef's thesis that there was a serious Industrial Revolution between 1540 and 1640. Because I told him that Hill believes that further study should be made into the relationship between the Crown and Industrialists during the seventeenth, John has selected some essays which he says show his own thesis. So Alan, darling, I am sure [you] *won't mind me reading some of his essays over the weekend. …* [further talk of essays]

Now I must return to my own black pit – it will be nice to share yours on Friday. I won't write again before then, Sweetie, since the post is thoroughly disorganised, and even this letter might not reach you till Friday.

I wrote again to Penny on Wednesday [5th December] from Worcester.

I will see you tomorrow! Strange – I thought these four days would never pass, but the agonies and delights of giving birth to my shapeless essay has distracted my thoughts. How are you sweetheart? Happy, I hope, and – oh, all this writing seems so trite after reading the Arnold poem which I quote. You must know it already, but its melancholy beauty, arising from Arnold's spiritual loneliness seems to capture that emptiness and sadness which filled the latter half of the C19th. Beneath the brash optimism, the vulgarity and the belief in progress; men were staring into the void and going sick with fear. The great minds of the later Victorian age were pessimists – George Eliot, Tennyson, Arnold, Darwin. And we still live in their shadow. As you will realise when you see my essay, I have externalised much of my own doubt into it, and for me as for Arnold the last stanza (of the poem) is especially true.

Whatever you may think of my religion – and I cannot hope or attempt to deceive you – I need your spiritual support as you need mine (?) Sweetheart I must believe, but what? Don't try and answer this, but be aware that I am searching, and have not found. You can help by turning me away from myself to you, but also realise that I am reaching for the stars. Much of my obsessions are self-pitying etc, but I still believe that something in me seeks – (whatever you like – Truth, God, Permanence).

And you my darling? Do you also search? I think so. Sorry to be so grave – its this essay. Let me know when you are coming on Friday – tho' I have a lot to do till 7.0. I have found, as you asked, somewhere for you to stay.

Enclosed:

Dover Beach

The sea of faith
Was once, too, at the full, and round earth's shore
Lay like the folds of a bright girdle furl'd.

There is then an undated letter from my mother, obviously written around the end of the first week of December, from Calcutta:

Will be home as soon as this – arriving next week!

My dear Alan,
Daddy forwarded your letter, & it was very comforting thinking of you sitting by your fire writing essays on Cromwell with the snow falling & the tape recorder turning. My life seems to have suddenly up-ended but as long as the three of you can carry on with yours uninterrupted I shant mind too much. Calcutta is a terribly depressing place.... [account of suffering etc] [what will happen etc?] I've decided that if nothing definite happens, I shall come home by boat, in January... [description of life] ... Tomorrow I shall go to the Park St Cemetery which is very interesting...

I feel so sad your birthday & Christmas should pass like this, but I'll get you a proper present & we'll celebrate properly when this nightmare is over. How is the grant going? Much love, & to Penny – Mummy

An undated letter, c. 10th December, from Calcutta:

My dear Alan,

What a strange way to be writing you a birthday letter, sitting by myself by the open window of a strangers house in Calcutta with the delicious evening Indian smells of wood-smoke & spice drifting in – and a sadness in my heart that I shant after all be with you to celebrate. We had news to-day that we're to be allowed back, and I'm going up to-morrow. I know you'll understand that that is where I must be, apart from Daddy needing me, this crisis has made me realise how attached I am to this hopeless, tragic, ridiculous country and how much I regretted leaving at a time like this.

You know, though, that our thoughts will be with you, I wish we could have given you a more memorable present, maybe the book wont even arrive in time. I shall get you something really nice on my way home next year, so that'll give you a year to think about it. If you are pleased with us as parents I can assure you it is nothing to our pleasure in you, it seems the most fortunate thing on earth to have children one really truly enjoys, as people quite apart from family. This last couple of weeks have shown me (what I knew to be true with my mind, but sometimes lost sight of) that nothing in life in the way of material possessions matters at all – that one is rich without them, as rich as we are with all that we haven't got. Horrible generalisations, much to be despised by Oxbridge – but I feel full of emotion & thankfulness to-night that Assam is to be spared the horrors that we thought were inevitable as we sped out of it. I have been praying consciously for the first time for years (to the God of the Gurkhas & Sikhs & Chinese too) but can't say whether this has helped…

I decided after all to put £50 into Fiona's account for the holidays as hers is in Ambleside, I leave it to you how to deal with it but as money is so hard to get home these days I know you'll go slow on expensive Christmas presents! Anne is staying in Edinburgh she says, wisely I think though Granny will be hurt.

I hope you'll manage to celebrate your birthday somehow. We shall be drinking your health and planning your future – wrongly I daresay.

With very much love and birthday blessings – Mummy

Penny came down for the Christmas dance on Friday 7th and I wrote again on Sunday 9th after she left.

As instructed – I write. I don't really need to say how marvellous it was seeing you (we will run out of superlatives soon!) – if possible, even more wonderful than the weekend before. My quotations from Keats, tho' not to be taken too seriously reflect my present mood. Did you have an easy journey back to London poppet? As I write you should just be getting home. I am thinking of you (see Keats!) – but will have to make a strong effort to get down to work tomorrow.

When I arrived back here, feeling fairly miserable, I found A/Angus/Alastair packing and John Munks in with him so I joined them for a while and played my guitar. But now I am alone again. John & Alistair go down tomorrow – Ralph & Mark (the one who helped design the dance & sat on the sofa with us) will alone be left up. Still, this horrible vacuum situated somewhere near my stomach & not caused by hunger (or normal hunger anyhow!) should fade somewhat tomorrow, in the 'light of common day'.

I don't feel like writing anything more – except that I miss you and hope to see you soon. Sorry for such a feeble letter, but you'll understand I know.

Keats

With every morn their love grew tenderer,
With every eve deeper and tenderer still; …
(Isabelle)

Then glut thy sorrow on a morning rose,
Or on the rainbow of the salt sea-wave, …
(From Ode on 'Melancholy')

Awaiting me in the Porter's Lodge at Worcester the next day was a 'Telephone Message for Mr Macfarlane 10-12-62 from Miss M'

'Will you send on notes on what men thought had been happ[en]ing have been more often the cause of change of whats happened. Please send by tomorrow.'

I wrote in reply to this message the same day.

In answer to your command I write – but if you really wanted help on the question about people's thoughts I'm afraid I have little to offer. Looking up that passage which I thought might be of value I find it almost completely irrelevant – but it is interesting so you will find it overleaf. If it is of any value here are some random thoughts on the subject. (if I remember rightly you took the years leading up to the Civil War).

(1) Oxford historians don't like historical theories. Break it down; apply it to a specific period and admit that there were many exceptions – that such a statement can be reversed (e.g. economic, subconscious movements, determining events) – so that it only has a limited value as an explanation. The truth in it is

- (a) *The Revolution, to a certain extent, arose out of misunderstanding and fear & tho' this had a real basis, doubtless, as Hill says in "Economic Problems..." "to the heightened Puritan imagination it seemed as if all over Europe the Counter-Reformation was winning back not only souls but land."*
- *here we have the crux of the matter. In a society in which society was an indivisible compound, in which religion, politics, economic factors etc were inseperable any attempts at change or reform in one sphere could be interpreted as an attack on some interest. E.G. James I wanted peace with Spain on economic & other grounds – but he was fiercely attacked by Puritans for betraying Prot'm. Often the Puritan & other fears had some justification – e.g. when they suspected Laud of attempting to subvert property rights by reclaiming impropriated tithes – but such fears were nearly always exaggerated. E.g. ship-money* <u>*was*</u> *spent on the fleet, and not just on the king. Again any attempts of Jas at toleration – e.g. in 1603 to R.Cs – was suspect. More & more men read sinister meanings into all the Crown's activities – and this made the crucial financial and administrative reforms impossible without a revolution. Upon a basis of fact – the genuine attempt to reshape the Crown's power even if it meant using prerogative courts, extra-parliamentary taxes etc under Charles – the opposition to the Stuarts built a superstructure of myths & fears.*
- *But I'm not sure the above is at all helpful as you will know it all already – and I don't feel very bright. Anyhow the General Paper isn't terribly important. The quote from G.M. Young is "... the real, central theme of History is not what happened, but what people felt about it when it was happening: in Philip Sidney's phrase, "the affects, the whisperings, the motions of the people"; in Maitland's, "men's common thoughts of common things"; in mine, "the conversation of the people who counted"...*

<u>Eliot: 4 Quartets</u>

Whisper of running streams, and winter lightning.
The wild thyme unseen and the wild strawberry...

Unusually, there is a letter from my father at this time – from Cherideo on 13th December.

My dear Alan,

I owe you for two letters and of course its your birthday, 21st. All the very best and I only wish we could be with you as well we might have been! This last three weeks have been of chaos, anguish, partings and reunions. All I know now is that Mummy is back in Cherideo, and we refuse to part again, even if all the Chinese descend on us. You will have had news in detail from Mummy, she had some wonderful tales, some amusing and some sad. I have kept her letters and will show them to you one day. I spent two days in Calcutta with Mummy the idea being that she was off to the U.K., so I thought I might as well see her off from Calcutta. This fortunately proved a waste of money as the ban for the return of European ladies was lifted, literally just hours before the Assam Co lot were due to go. Incidentally Mummy was one of the first to return to Assam and she is only Memsahib [wife of the Manager] *for miles round. Apart from this life has been quite normal...*

Typical of Remnant to write that piffle to you all... Glad you have been seeing Penny lately, she's a very nice girl and you are lucky.

Please give her my regards next time you see her or you write to her...

Lots of love, Daddy

There is a typed letter from my mother to all three of us the following day.

Cherideo December 14th

Darlings,

This is a Christmas letter for Fiona and Alan, I presume Anne is sticking to her plan and spending it up north. I just can't get the faintest feeling of the festive season what with all this coming and going, but it will be a very happy one for me, even though I'm sad I shant be with you after all. I have done nothing about presents except that I want you three to have five pounds each to spend on clothes or tapes and not on toothpaste! If this arrives in time would you get Granny and Granpa something out of my money too, I don't know what, gloves or slippers perhaps. Could you send the money to Anne please?

I hope you will have a very happy day darlings, not too concentrated round the Aga and the Telly, and will get a few presents. When you go to church you can say a big prayer of thanks from us, it seems miraculous that I'm sitting on my verandah again looking out onto the Naga hills with the lovely familiar shapes of the trees and shadows and the background of birds that I never thought I would see again. …[account of return etc.] … Give my love to Beryl, I'll be writing to her in a day or two, I gather Tansy [pet dog] now lives with us, I didn't think Granny would be able to hold out against her for long.

God bless you both, have a very happy time and I hope Pennys, Ruperts etc will be able to pop in and see you at intervals. All our love, Mummy

.

The next letter from Penny is dated Sunday afternoon [16th December]

It was marvellous seeing you during the last few days. I needed people and things to distract me from worrying about the LMH interview. The visit has been like a tonic, for I certainly feel better than when I came down on Thursday.

I hope you caught your train safely and did not leave anything vital behind. Let me know if you have, & perhaps we can pick it up on the way to Westmorland (You're being organised, man!)

The morning air in Oxford was pure and fresh, and I would have longed to have gone for a long walk. Perhaps next time I'm in Oxford, we could walk over to Binsey Church to attend the 11 o'clock service there, and afterwards go to the Trout (?) or even to the other pub by the river, for lunch. A capital idea!

My journey home passed off without event – it usually does unfortunately. I was enthralled by "A Little Princess" [sic]. *I have decided to adopt it as my bible, from which I might learn to emulate Sara's ways. Sara is the paragon of virtue, charity, and dignity, yet she is never priggish or smug. A delightful child. … Such are the complexities and intricacies of a woman's mind. Oh dear, I'm not a woman!! You told me, dearest, to remind you continually that I am still a nineteen year old schoolgirl.*

The poem by Herbert comes from 'Altar and Pew' which you have given me…
It reveals Herbert's strong belief in God's power, strength and eternity, despite all it's spiritual conflicts.

Tumnus, will you send my best wishes to your grandparents, and thank them very much for inviting me up in January.

[appended George Herbert's 'The Altar']

*

I seem to have left Oxford for the Lake District on the morning of 16th, leaving Penny in Oxford. There is a letter date stamped 17th December, Monday and headed Martin's Coffee Bar, Ambleside, (on my way home from London).

P.S. The errors of this letter are explained by my tiredness.

It is only a few hours since I left you amidst the sunshine of Oxford but the gulf which there seems to be between us in time/distance is represented by the changed surroundings I am in. Instead of the sunlight and grace of Oxford, when even Gloucester Green seemed purified and clean, I am sitting in this stale coffee-bar, with half-empty coffee cups and soggy cigarettes and the smell of cheap perfume. But I don't feel too bad – tho' I miss you poppet. It was marvellous seeing you, as ever, and despite 'violets' etc I hope you enjoyed it. I will see you in two weeks today!

I had a long talk with a young assistant lecturer I met on the train. He is editing a C15 text for a D.Phil and is an assistant tutor at Merton – mediaeval philology. He was able to give me some valuable information about postgraduate research etc. he also knows Tolkein a little and we had a fascinating conversation about literature, Lawrence, education, prisons, the Grail legend etc. Strangely (?) he was a heavy smoker & drinker & tells me Tolkein drinks large quantities of gin. If only I do well enough in my finals I will certainly do research – but perhaps this is the road to ruin (i.e. death of my 'philanthropic' urge) & a wise providence may supply me with a poor second or third so that I have to do something practical (the last idea can be used as an excuse anyhow!)

– but I am still in a fair muddle over the whole thing. This tutor was – according to himself – a 'militant atheist' – but we avoided any argument. But I got a lift back from Kendal with an ex-Indian army colonel, who started slanging Nehru in the most abusive terms, liberally laced with swear-words (despite the girl in the car) and I found it difficult not to get annoyed. I got the lift through meeting – quite by accident – an old girlfriend on the train. [Vivien]

I went out with her for about 2 weeks 2 years ago – then she went off with a friend. This is the first time she has been back for 2 years – and I am afraid she will find it rather quiet, as she loves being gay. I have already told her about you – you must meet her when you come up. She is rather over-blown (like a rose) but very sweet – and must be a good singer as she is going to Vienna to study.

Have you started Tolkein? I was talking to this Merton man about York University & he thought it was well-worth going to – apparently it is going to be run on Oxbridge lines.

Look after yourself my darling – I am very fond of you – and even wrote a poem to you on the train today.
[Probably the poem 'I stood naked before the fire of God…]

The next letter from Penny is just dated Monday Evening, probably 17th December.

By the time you will have received this letter, you will be submerged beneath the iceblock of work. Don't exhaust yourself too much, and go out for several long walks, otherwise your going home will hardly be worthwhile.

Is Westmorland looking beautiful? Is there snow? Is frost dusted among the leaves and grasses? Do write back and tell me about it, but don't use the words "dribble", "flabby" or "you know what…."

I slouched into school today, and was slightly relieved to find out that one of my friends who took the English exams at Newnham & St Hilda's had also not had an interview at either. She deserved to get in, much more than I did, for she is much more competent and reliable than I am. [more about entrance etc] …

The passage from 'Dialogues of Mortality' is the introduction to Rose Macaulay's Towers of Trebizond, in which she describes her spiritual conflict, her attempt to enter the Anglican Church. … [further elaboration and quotation of a paragraph about Trebizond…]

I am not sure that the Anglican church does in fact exercise 'a strange wild power'. Rather one of calm and tranquillity, surrounded by a silver or a rose-gold light. Oh dear, again a romantic vision of Christ's abode.

Now, dearest, now, I must finish. All my love to you, and please don't get too tired. I am feeling quite happy (!!!) now – and have found lots of CULTURE to indulge in. Annaily sends all her love – Penny-Poppy.
[A page of quotation from 'Dialogues of Morality' is included]

The next letter from Penny is dated 18th (crossed out) 20th [December 1962] from London.

Thank you very much for my Christmas present. Of course, I opened it – you could not expect me to restrain myself for FOUR days. I have been longing to read "The Human comedy" and of course Possum's Book of Cats is quite delightful. You are a sweetie. We also liked your card – I had not seen this particular Botticelli before – it is rather beautiful.

I am afraid this is going to be a rather gushy letter – though utterly sincere. I am enthralled by Tolkien, and I have just finished 'Fellowship of the Ring'. It's superb – I have been unable to get away from Tolkien during the last few days, except to go to necessary engagements. To think that I might not have read it, had it not been for meeting you, for I had been told so often during the last few years to read 'Lord of the Rings' that I inwardly rebelled and loathed the book. It was not until I had actually started reading it that I willingly wanted to do so. And now beasts, fierce animals or even wild men, like ADJM could not drag me away from 'Lord of the Ring', though I am sure ADJM would favour my alliance with Tolkien.

I went to a marvellous party last night. …

Alan, darling – can you tell me your uncle's arrangements for taking Fiona & me up on the 1st Jan. A friend who lives just round the corner from Robert at 95 Drayton Gardens wants me to spend New Year's Eve and the night with her. Frightfully "Les"!!! . Is Fiona staying with Robert? If she is, I could drop round there to meet her first thing on the morning of Jan 1st. [other discussion of possible arrangements for meeting] … Now Tumnus, have a marvellous Christmas and don't work. Send all my love to your family, and especially, dearest heart, to you – I am sorry for such an untidy letter,

The following was an unusually long letter, written on my 21st birthday as a kind of summing up of many aspects of my life and trying to chart out the future relationship with Penny. Its importance to me as a letter is shown also by the fact that I unusually kept a carbon copy of it, the only such copy of my correspondence with Penny.

Thank you for your letter – I hope this is not delayed too much by the Xmas post: if it isn't and arrives before the 25th, once more my love and best wishes.

My sweetie, forgive me if this is a serious or tedious letter. I have long planned to celebrate my 21st birthday by writing down some stray thoughts – an attempt to clear my mind before entering the battle of integrity v compromise, the absolute v the relative, life and death even. (for the explanation of these abstractions see later). Although I have been thinking about certain fundamental problems over the last few days, and especially today, while listening to the '4 Quartets', I have left the writing-down until, literally, the 11th hour and thought you might not mind a vision of my naked soul, my hopes and fears, 'at this still point of my turning life'. Doesn't all this sound grand? Anyhow, here goes.

I have been reading D.H. Lawrence's letters for the last few days (introduction by Aldous Huxley) and found in them an emotional and intellectual release and source of energy. Lawrence is so honest, so patently struggling to clear away the artificialities that cover life, and seems to face and partially resolve many of my own deepest problems. Much of my letter will be about the two crucial problems of my relationship to others – esp. re. marriage, and my relationship to God, esp re. my vocation in life. So I will start with a quotation – which Lawrence claims to be his central message – in a letter to T.D.D he wrote –

"One must learn to love, and go through a good deal of suffering to get to it, like any knight of the grail, and the journey is always towards the other soul, not away from it. Do you think love is an accomplished thing, the day it is recognized? It isn't. To love, you have to learn to understand the other, more than she understands herself, and to submit to her understanding of you … You musn't think that your desire or your fundamental need is to make a good career, or to fill your life with activity, or even to provide for your family materially. It isn't. Your most vital necessity in this life is that you shall love your wife completely and implicitly and in entire nakedness of body and spirit. Then you will have peace & inner security, no matter how many things go wrong. And this peace and security will leave you free to act & to produce your own work, a 'real independent workman'."

Do you think Donne and Lawrence would have liked each other?

"like any knight of the grail" – I like the image. Did I tell you I wrote a story about one of Arthur's knights searching for the grail – symbolising my search for beauty and certainty, for someone to love and an ultimate good to believe in? Just before the end Sir Tristan had to fight a monster, obscene and lecherous, which represented my struggle for purity and innocence despite sexuality. And now the story has come true. For we must both face the fact that action must be taken concerning our physical relationship. We are both too young to know if we are in love or merely infatuated. We both retain something innocent and uncorrupt; and we both know that physical love is not wicked or anything like that. I enjoy your wonderful body, and I hope you enjoy being loved. But over the last few days I have become increasingly aware that I am betraying both of us in allowing myself to indulge in the runaway delights of the body. For me it is alright. I find organic release, but for you, my darling, there is no consummation, only an increasing frustration. Is this true? I have been talking to Beryl [Buckmaster, next-door-neighbour] on the subject – she had a 5 yr engagement – and from the way she talks I gather that petting without intercourse made her frigid before marriage. As she put it, 'I grew accustomed to frustration'. Therefore sweetheart you will have to help me and together we will have to come to terms with this problem. On a long walk while you are up here we will have to sort things out – it would be impossible on paper. Please write back about this subject if you have any particular views on the matter.

Lawrence and a change of scenery has awoken my sense of perspective and relaxed my over-tired nerves. I was growing worried that my creative faculties seemed to have become achingly paralysed – but even before I arrived, on the train, I had written two poems and I have been thinking more clearly all the time. My exams no longer seem at all important. No 'swotting' will get me anywhere. The examiners are presumably acute enough to see through to my real intelligence and integrity and thus no use wasting my real intelligence and integrity and thus no use wasting long hours. I will still work – but spend more time on general reading, and not worry. I say all the above to persuade myself; for I am caught in my own soft-spun web of fear and organization. But I haven't worked much since I came up here.

All my twitterings on the edge of the past seems dustily irrelevant when I walk up to Juniper hill and watch the clouds and mountains mixing and swirling in the brooding winter winds. The bracken was red and sodden after the rain – with the yellow stalks showing through. The juniper bushes wipe gleaming sky-drops onto my sleeve as I walk up the hill and the soft mosses squelch and trickle at my every foot-step. From the hill-top I can see the clouds hanging in the valleys like smoke, or swirling past rocky crags. The tarn just below me is calm and reflects the bare trees and the sky. Above the huge bulk of Coniston the cloud breaks for a moment to let the sun pour down and against the brightness a swarm of sea-gulls swoop and screech. A warm wet wind, fern and moss smelling blows softly, and the world is clean and bare. God seems very close, as close as the single sea-gull which strays on taut wings above my head – swinging in a sweet curve down the streaming sunlight, its warm heart beating and its friendly eyes closely watching. My soul feels solemn and the whole days urge – to pray – seems more important than ever.

My darling, if my search for a God of love seems self-deluding, if it seems escapist, if it seems irrelevant, if it seems fruitless – it may be all these. But I must search, for without God my light is darkness and I cannot live in darkness. Unless I can find meaning and purpose, fixed principles and eternal truths, my whole life will be utterly valueless. Without God my love for you would be lust, my sensitivity to suffering, enlightened self-interest, my desire for beauty and joy, mere hedonism. Sweetheart, please help me. Help me out of my selfishness, seriousness etc, and I will try to help you. Above all we must be increasingly sensitive to each other's moods and feelings, increasingly tolerant of each other's weaknesses and conscious of our own. So easy to preach about – but, oh, how sanctimonious it sounds, and how difficult to practice.

I have, with my relaxing from 'workitis', gone through a slight reaction v my 'philanthropy' urge of last term. I still want to help those enduring terrible misery but have swung back more to a consciousness of the importance lying in what we are rather than what we do "the only wisdom is the wisdom of humility, humility is endless". To be spontaneously kind and humble. To love God and man deeply and almost thoughtlessly would be both a terrible and wonderful experience. For me and perhaps you there is merely the constant losing of the way, and then the rediscovery of the almost over-grown path. Fear is always around us – at this time, remembering Eliot once more 'in our beginning is our end', I am more than usually conscious of death "dark, dark, dark, we all go into the dark" – and what light will we have to guide us? "Yea, tho' I walk through the valley of the shadow of death I will fear no evil…" I quite by chance, came on a wonderful verse from Isaiah this morning. "Fear thou not for I am with thee, be not dismayed for I am thy God, I will help thee, I will comfort thee, I will uphold thee with the right hand of my righteousness."

And I would like to be a writer – a novelist or poet – and go to live by the Mediterranean. Lawrence's letter make me yearn for the warmth and richness and colour of the Grecian isles. Probably my temperament is cold and stubborn and Northern – but for the moment "oh for a beaker full of the warm South … with beaded bubble winking at the brim…"

It is late. I had meant to write much more. But enough. Don't take any of the above too seriously; tho' I think most of it roughly corresponds to my present mood.

If Fiona comes down, (to return to earth with a jolt) on the 28th. Could she stay for a few nights? I will understand if it is too much of a bother. I will write & confirm it (or not) when I hear from you.

A twenty-first birthday card painted by my friend Jane Buckmaster

The last letter to Penny which I am including here was written on Christmas Day, 1962, a Tuesday.

P.S. Excuse the (slushy?) tone of this letter.

Oh most beautiful daughter of the evening, greetings. May your eyes for ever shine with the mysteries of the northern skies, bright and pure and gentle as the moorland breezes. May your limbs forever run free as the

mountain streams etc. Gosh, what a start! But I mean it. I am feeling very sentimental, for obvious seasonal reasons and missing you especially much. I hope you are well, my poppet, and have had a wonderful Christmas – this will probably arrive long after the day. I sent you a telegram this evening – was it clear? If you <u>*can*</u> *manage Drayton Gardens it would be very convenient as Richard is staying at 174 Old Brompton Road, for the night of the 31st & if you could give the bell a ring at 9 a.m. it will be most convenient. If arrangements have been changed and you are at home with luggage etc you could ring him up after 10 p.m. Monday and tell him how to get to your place. I hope somehow you will make contact. Oh, sweetie, it will be marvellous seeing you on Tuesday: having stopped working I am now afflicted with an increasing awareness of suffering and by graver religious doubts…*

Jummie, next door, is almost blind and covered in terrible, petrefying [sic], bed-sores … but enough for now. It is Christmas day and it has been a wonderful one, with much to be thankful for.

Thank you very much Poppy for the chinese poetry, as you can see I have selected two pieces to include with my letter. As you say all the poetry is like their painting – delicate and in a minor scale. Over much of it there is a brooding sadness and transcience [sic]. It is obviously produced by a country that has known much suffering, where death and starvation was always very close and the small things therefore seemed infinitely precious. When one is tired of the vulgarity and profuseness of much western & especially Victorian poetry it is refreshing to turn to them – like turning from a large overblown 'Wagnerian' orchestra to Elizabethan lute music. I don't suppose I would have got round to reading it without your active help – thank you again.

I had many lovely presents – with a definite preponderance of book tokens (over £7 worth!) and money with which to buy tapes (about £10) also a suitcase and brief case (from Richard). I would like to rush out to spend all these presents, but I suppose it would be best to wait till Oxford.

Can you skate poppet? Although it will probably have thawed by the time you come up, today there was skating on Tarn Hows. We have some skates here, but rather odd sizes. The tarns, as you can imagine, are very beautiful. I went up for a walk there with Richard. There was a clear sunset, blushing the frosted mountains and sliding down the partly frozen lake, making each gaunt tree stand out in perfect detail. This morning when I got up for early communion it was even more lovely. The whole sky was rose and pink, and over the sleeping valley there was one bright star. There were no others in the sky – how easily it could have been Bethlehem. There was slight mist over the lake – but every field was adazzle with frost and seemed very close. The bare brown trees and criss-crossed fields were just like one of those Dutch 'skating' paintings. And tonight it has snowed so it may be even more lovely. I do hope it is as transcendently beautiful when you are up – but bring <u>*plenty*</u> *of socks as I don't want you moaning about your toes. I'm longing to see you solemnly plodding along in wellingtons (!) – but if it is this cold you will be unable to wear them. Is it very bitter in London?*
I have had several letters from my parents – including one from my father (very unusual) in which he sends his special best wishes to you & tells me how lucky I am knowing you, extraordinary how even the most level-headed can be deceived!? Did I tell you I wrote another semi-love poem, but very incoherent? [Perhaps the poem 'When will I see the flaming Xmas stars…]

If you can also manage to bring up the 2nd volume of the 'Lord' as Fiona wants to read it… When do you have to go down? We might be able to get a lift with my uncle on the 10th if you don't have to leave to go before and <u>*if*</u> *I manage to get enough work done while you are here…*

Mark will be up in a few days – but perhaps he may delay in this weather.

Enclosed:

<u>Chang Hua. Yearnings. V.</u>

My eyes stray beyond the four corners of the wilderness;
At ease I tarry alone…

<u>Wang Yen-Hung Brief partings, III</u>

I clutch at his war-coat, and our tear-stained cheeks touch:
The sails must needs be set for the urgent evening breeze.
Who says 'For a brief parting grieve not?'
This poor life of mine, how many brief partings can it endure?

Penny then wrote again on Thursday 27th December, between Christmas and her visit to our family in the Lakes at the start of 1963.

It is snowing!! Last night the snow-petals were falling like the blossom from may-trees in spring, but today they are dancing before the wind, as if they were autumn-leaves.... [further description] Is beauty eternal? Having viewed something wondrous, must we content ourselves for not seeing it again, by knowing that other forms of beauty exist elsewhere, to be found and contemplated? [further reflections on beauty etc.] ... Enough of this obstruse waffle. I don't think that the above reflects my mood. I am now feeling fatted and contented, and slightly drowsy. I am tired of turkey, and all other Christmas fare. We went to a series of lunch and dinner parties between Sunday and Wednesday at which only turkey seems to have been served. I think I enjoyed the trout best of all, which I had as part of Tuesday's lunch. FOOD IS A BORE. Despite all the Fxxd, I enjoyed myself very much, I hope you did too. I felt frustrated on Tuesday morning [Christmas day] because I was unable to find a small country church to which I could go. I have not been to a Christmas service and sung 'Hark the Herald' for ages. Aesthetically it is such a wonderful time of the year. Would you like to be a chaplain or a dean?

I am going to see you in five days time – whoopee. Don't work too hard, while I am up, though I shall probably bring dozens of book[s] with me. I hope you are looking after the third volume of Lord of the Rings for me, for the first two tomes are already very precious to me. I take one of them with me, wherever I go. I even read it yesterday, while waiting for a bus at sunset in the falling snow. ...

Darling Alan, it was marvellous talking to you just now – I hung up the telephone receiver and continued the letter. I am sorry that I had to hang up – it was mean of me to practise telephone economy on you, but this new system, STD (?) [Subscriber Trunk Dialling] *is SO expensive that, even though they are not on it, local calls are ruinous. I rang up Annaily this afternoon, and the call must have cost about 5/-. I am sorry if I was curt with Fiona, and your Grannie – I was a little bewildered by getting thro' to you so quickly, and then talking to so many voices in so few minutes. Please apologise to them, and send my love to your grandparents, and to Fiona and Anne, and whoever else may be in the Macfarlane abode. ... [More about Annailly -] She wants us to go to have a meal with them when we come down from Westmorland (You'll have to come to London). She probably also coming down to Oxford with Stefan late in January for a couple of days, when there will be another grand rendez-vous....*

I have been concocting plans for what I do when I leave school at the end of Jan. They are quite involved and I hope they will be resolved. Their resolutions depends partly upon you – Aren't I mysterious?!?

Now I must end my chatter. 'Hold thy tongue woman, and let us ....."

Attached are two verses from 'The Seasons' – Winter – by James Thomson

The Parks

Winter 1962-3

The river carries its ~~th~~ leaves, brown & yellow
Underneath its weeping veils of willows
And the warm air pours, thick with bird-song
Around me. Each leaf is separate & precious
Now, for they will go so ~~far~~ soon. One
Can see each of them tremble in the golden
Sunlight - The trees just turning,
Mostly yellow, with tinges of fiery red.
Their firm shapes just beginning
To show through. The holly trees
Are ~~the~~ half turned and seem to be
Burnt brown around their patches
Of flaming berries. I can hear a
Distant bell for it is Sunday. There
Are boys searching for conkers amidst
The crackling leaves & throwing up
Sticks to knock them down. The dace
Rise for midges amidst the leaves.
Young couples wander linked, stopping
To gaze deep into the river or turning
And kissing each other lightly for
Sheer joy of this blue, calm, warm
Autumn day. Undergraduates walk,
Thinking of the term ahead and old
Men sun themselves like frail butterflies
Before the winter falls. The season gathers
To a last, fresh, glory before the
Winter comes.

Another poem was clearly written near the start of my last year at Oxford and is dated 12th October 1962 [I sent this poem to Penny in a letter on 14th October, asking her to return it. She did so, having first copied it out and left a copy with the letter.]

Today I dreamt the world was mine,
That stars and moon and silver sands lay in my palms,
That glory streamed golden through my fingers
And the people of the earth sang for joy.
Deep sorrow's poisoned roots sprung into softest leaf
And autumn no longer scarred a darkening land.
I dreamt that through a thousand dusty streets
A silver dawn crept on sandalled feet
Powdering the old buildings with rose and gold
Wiping the shadows from her face
And filling each heart with peace.
I saw the stars draw close and the aching years
Grow small, I saw each bitter parting moving
Back into the joy of meeting and each
Willowed river winding back to its source.
I saw this sad, torn, city
Throw off its noisome cloak and stand crowned
Amidst its velvet fields as night
Drifted like the river mists.
I saw each separate, lonely, light
Where imprisoned souls yearned for comfort
Merge into the blaze of glory
That swept amidst the tangled fears
And hatreds that grew like thornèd briars
Choking and tearing at the weak hand of love.
But I saw lust walking the night in men's eyes
I felt their bodies twist and quiver
In agony of anticipation – their mouths dry,
Their hands moist, their bellies taught-wrenched
And their prey – the women – sleek-hipped
Sinuous, as cool and hot as dark forests
As easy and heavy as cats, asleep, in the noon.
And yet, inside, tortured by a thousand fears.
And I saw all this and my heart was torn.
For misery and joy, lust and love
Walked together, peace and desire
Mingled and melted in the shadows
And I knew not where to turn
But through it all I saw the thread
Of a total importance, I saw that
All was real and of utmost value
But that in the depths and heights
The battle was lost and won,
The conflict and the agony over,
The joy and grief finally joined
In one blended harmony of praise
That sustained every leaf, every minutest atom
In its resolved order and pitched man
Into the unfathomable mystery & love of God.
I saw all this and could not understand.

Psychology of a tortoise – etc 17/10/62 [I had moved into digs in Worcester Place, next to the College, which were in between private houses.]

> Possessive complex of a woman next door who spends hours watching, talking to and moving a tortoise. Follows its every foot step – occasionally intervening to put it in another place – clearly bored. Spends other times attempting to find weak spots in the wall – when she finds one gingerly pushes loose bricks into other garden.
> Subject for story. An apple tree – with many ripe fruit – but hanging over two gardens divided by a wall – in a small back to back lower-middle class area where house divided by 75 yds of garden – and where lonely figures can be seen in lighted rooms in the evenings.

On 26 October 1962 I wrote the following.

Oxford: an autumn night.

Autumn wrings its wet leaves over Oxford
And the traffic grinds thro' wet streets
Which blaze the myriad lights of the heavy city.
In the clogged air there is a smell of marsh mist
And the heavy lumbering of river-muddy cattle,
Old dripping walls slant off into tolling darkness
Where depths of sodden woods slap the lifeless ground.
A mood is here – a medieval sleep, which turns
And tosses in fitful wakening, trying to force
The new life and bustle and light into the centre
Of the town – watching it from the shadows
With high-towered scorn and from beneath suspicious
Doorways. Sad gloom of witchcraft inks the heavy
Stone with dark watered blood, drawing flickering
Fingers along the streets to draw the wounds
Away from the light into lightless tunnels where
It may sleep. Vacantly the empty, brightly chittering
Shops speak to the streets, and the crowd
Vacantly answers it. But below and behind
The whispering curse of the city can be heard,
A muttering call to the lingerer who
Chances to look for a moment down a side-walk
Who is fluttered like a leaf down some echoing
Cobble-clattering street, to lose the noise and lights
For the witching silence which is loud with
Silent bells and prayer. Here the swelling
River with its night smells of mole-like wet
Seems to run close in damp of reeds and weeds
And the strong buildings become rounded pebbles
In the stream of years. An infrequent light
Adds deeper gloom, a bubble of light toes on
The heavy waves of shadows, a flickering
Sightless eye in an enchanted dark. Old,
Wet and slimy as some deep mud-floored prison
The streets lie stretching out into the shelving
Hills and the clouds move fast, uncovering
For a moment a dripping moon, beneath
The unleaving trees, which scatter their bat-shapes

To the rotting paths. All is old and black,
Crowding out the sprinkled drops of central lights
Like oil crushes out water – and leaving the
Night to its ancient, tossing sleep.

This was accompanied by with some rather curious drawings. I include them not because of any inherent merit, but as fodder for future psychologists perhaps.

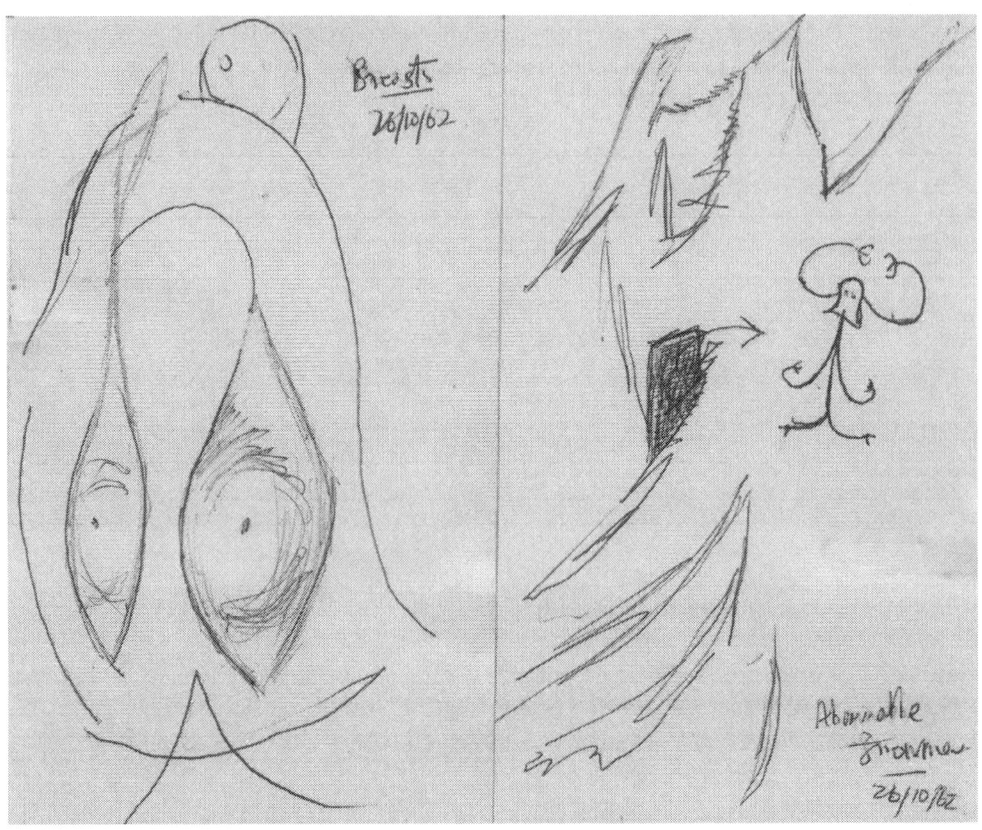

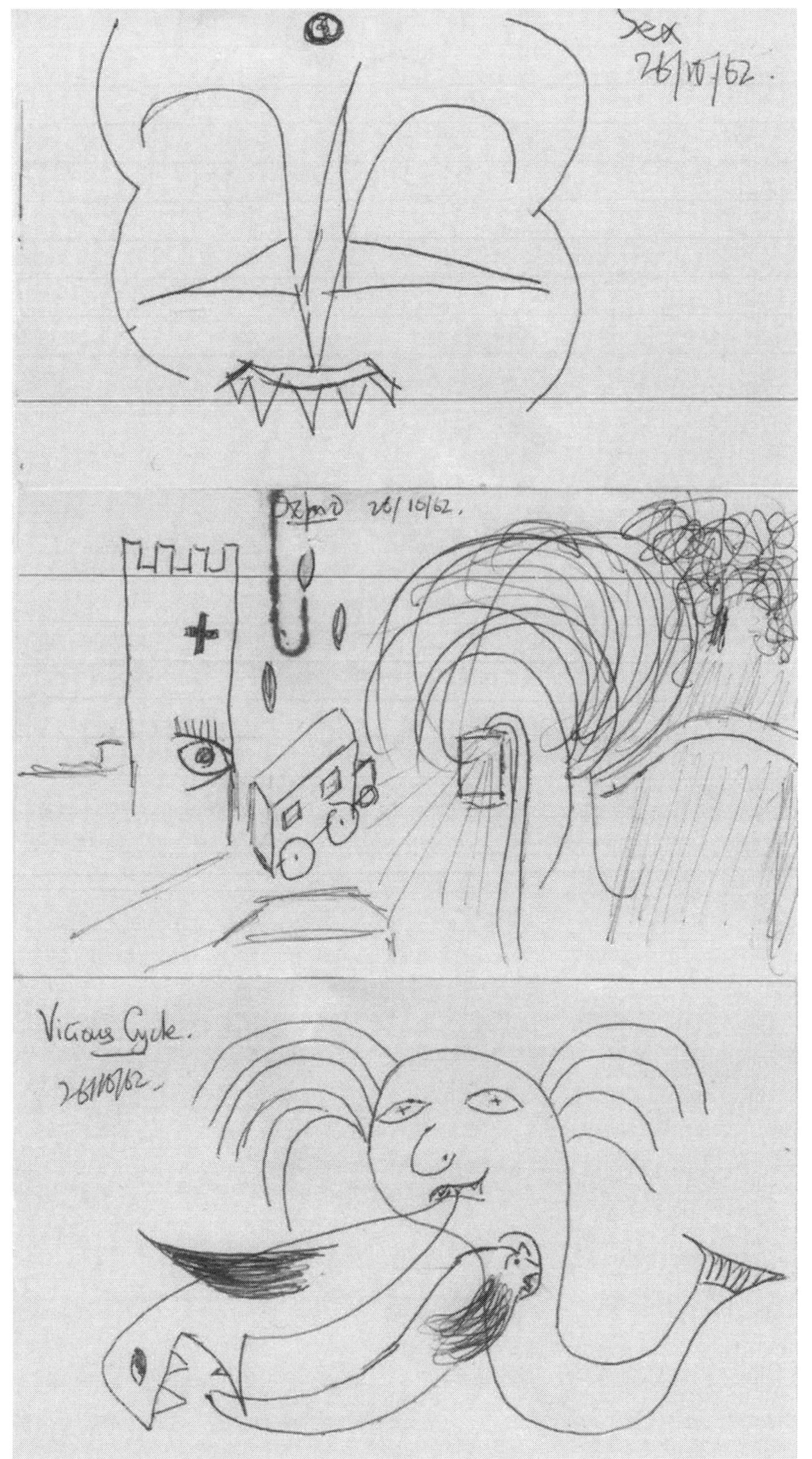
Sex
26/10/62.
Oxford 26/10/62.
Vicious Cycle.
26/10/62.

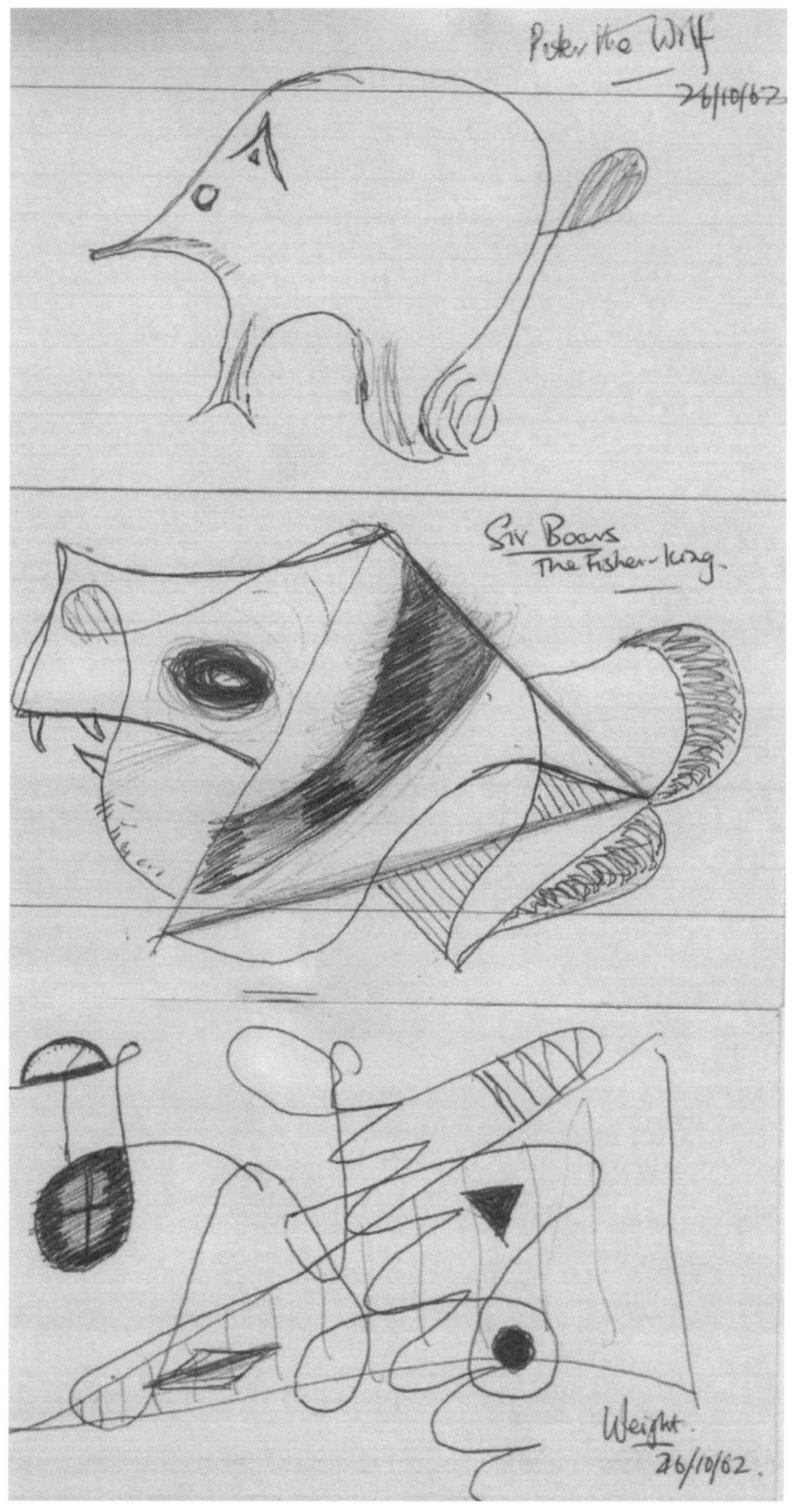
Peter the Wolf
26/10/62
Sir Boars
The Fisher-king.
Weight.
26/10/62.

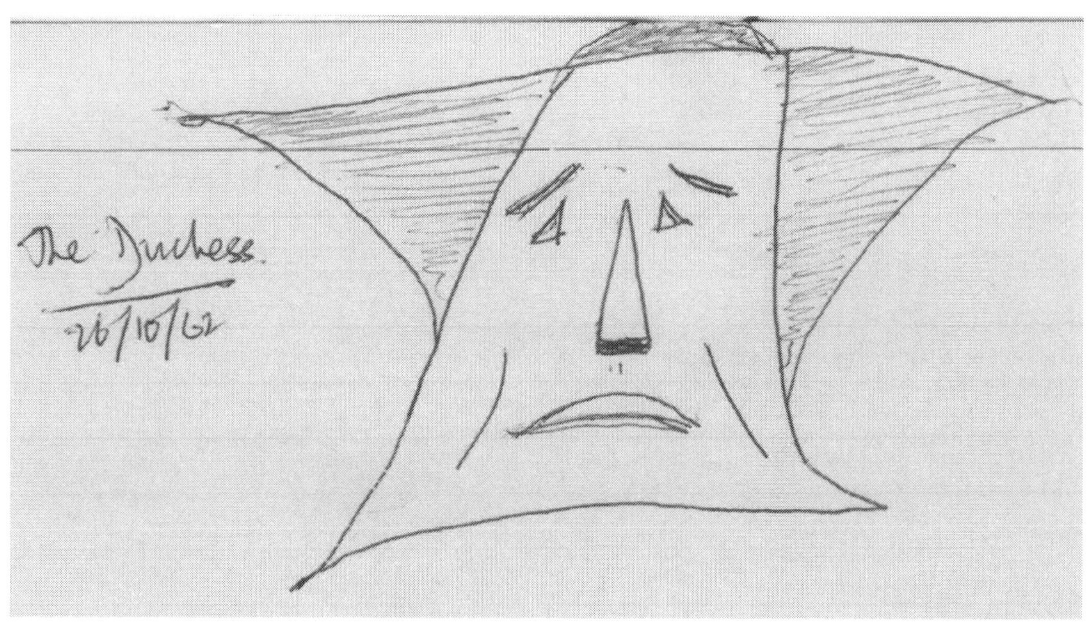

Another shorter poem is dated 4/11/62 is headed:

<u>A few impressions: autumn walk & hospital</u>

In the light of a child, as its face flares to smile,
In the drift of the leaves on the lake of the trees,

[seven lines heavily crossed through and the above connected to the rest with an arrow and 'expanded' written in]

What wouldst thou have me write?
Of the long autumn avenues where the leaves
Crunched like thick snow under my feet,
Where down the hills a row of poplars looked
Like some grey-green church ruin,
Where I discovered a large-black beetle
Making its cumbersome way, ungainly, over the
Mountain-jungle of the leaves? Shall I
Tell thee of the rain in my face
And the bird-song in my ears the
Drifting smoke of the willow-veils and the
Fur-green mould on the grey tree trunk?
Or of the bleak, angular, man-made concrete
Hospital with its humming nerves of pain
And arteries of agony, its septic smell
And its nightmare of jangling sorrow – and
In its wards a thousand frightened, uncomprehending
Humans – one of them a little girl – like Alice –
Long hair, serious eyes, solemn and unafraid,
Mischievous and timid – not knowing why the rack
And the beating, sawing, rubbing, clashing, jangling
World, poised between the beauty of
The natural world, and the pulped agony
Of the artificial keeps its reeling course.

Another poem was written on 18th December 1962

<u>'Sunlight & cloud'</u>

Written in Martin's coffee bar, Ambleside.

In the cloud-reflecting-window barred
Thunder sunlight a man moves on
The hillside & the rock rhythms of
The juke-box move into significance with
A sliding of sea-gull wings and cigarette
Smoke. The strong-barriers of the mind
Slide into an ecstasy of unity and
The world's insistent voices of experience
Brighten to a blur, like conversation.
The breath of joy blurs the mirror
And for a moment we turn out from
Ourselves and feel every chair move
And every growing twig against the
Mountain sky. Slow drifts the clouds
And for a time slows to a barely
Perceptible ticking, the heart is
Poured into the bucket of beauty
And in its naked streaming rush
It feels every steaming coffee-cup
And the weak Christmas tree lights
Dull in the sunlight catch fire
And burn a pattern thro'
And then it is gone

There is another poem dated 14/12/62 and headed 'Warrington'

Lights burst, surfacing on the sticky
Blue evening. Over the houses the
Smell of carols slides like tea-leaves
Round a cup; dreams, saunter
Into coffee-bars, rubbing nylon lips
Against the swinging doors and
Leaving lipstick.
Coffee-cups and the drift of
Scent and smoke. Nostrils of
The night breathes out used air
Through the factory chimneys – but
Warm through the blackness
Love springs with the lights –
Breaking into a spangling glory –
Beating the brackish water back
To the sleepless eyes in the
Alleys.
[there are several short pieces of music drawn in on this]

There is another piece of writing clearly written about the same time, in the same style on the same paper. Possibly the same day.

I stood naked before the fire of God,
And Truth commended with her
What is your love? And I hung my head –
For the years and the seas & times,
That moved thro' the depths of me,
The rhythms and tunes and rhymes
That swayed my thoughts and dreams
Were strong and bitter
And my life was weak and wild
And knew my self as a man,
But loved my love like a child.
And the world spun strange
That my eyes could not see,
How to know me from you,
Or to know if I loved only Thee,
And the ecstasy and the vision
That the wind I thought would bring
Hard the drift of far-off seasons,
But the salt brought its sting.
The iron entered the dove
And the fire burnt the rose,
And I saw my love wept
And I did not know my love.
If the tender night is gone,
What of the brittle day?
Where will shadows hide?
Where can the darkness play?
Where the sunlight in the garden,
Which lifted the swallow-rose
Against its setting of softness
Which the lichened wall-moss throws.
If you and I together
Are to explore the starry deep,
We must weave a world together,
Whose secrets, once gravely keep,
Out over the bitter conflicts
This sharpened field of thorns,
We must lay a heart-wrung carpet,
Soften than bare-foot lawns.

On my birthday, 20th December, I wrote.

The last lights linger – squeezing incredible gradations of colour, from the red blush of the sun through emblazoned gold, chrystal emerald, like the squeezed essence of young green corn, or the incredible green of some bird of paradise – then deepening, enriched to the rich amethyst of ripe (plums). Every feathery wand of bracken, every rock, every twig on every tree is outlined, and a halo of light seems to stream along the heights. As we turn from this peacock fan and gaze at the dark heights of the East a new miracle arises. Majestic the moon, full and gold, maker of madness, magnet for man, eye of the Gods, sails clear of the harbouring hills, and stately galleon of the night rides clear. Along the lengths of the level lake it glimmers, like a sash of honour on the ice. Through the pines, it watches – casting spells of ancient magic on the worshipping trees and kneeling hills. It walks in silence, and all is still, so still that the drop of a fragment

of ice in the far copse rustles right down the lake. (Skating) down the glistening lake like a phantom skater and breaking on the ear – numb and aching with the coldness of loneliness.
It is freezing the sap of the trees – ice forms on one's boots. And one can feel the Light echoing away into the darkness and leaving … night.

'To Xmas(?)/ (God?) (Penny?) 22.12.62

When will I see the flaming Xmas
Stars, singing thro' the soft night,
Echoing down the frosty fields?
And shimmering out over the ice-lakes – like
Stones groaning over the ice? Broken, brittle,
Reeds freeze in the solid mud and the
Crusted sheep trail sprays of thorns.
Every tingling spray of every branch is
Shot through with cold, the birds are drugged
With it in the trees. One aches
To think of the thin fish in their black holes
In the snow-water streams. And through the
Bitter purity and cleanness, the agony
Of unity, is born our Saviour. In this
Intense sadness, in the suffering of the
World, where homeless & clotheless children
Crouch over railings in Naples – clutching at the
Breath of soup, their stomachs torn by hunger.
Or men lie raving of this world's hate –
Their eyes blind with pain – their brains screaming
With the skinless lashes – the World's Saviour is born.
The dream and warmth is born indeed, through the
Dirtiness and squalor, the impurity of human hatred
A pure voice is heard 'Come unto me" – and the
World turns away, carrying a lightless lantern
Out into its desert dark.
The jollity and glory of Xmas is spun
Through with the richer black thread of suffering
Mocking the cheeriness – standing pale-faced.

[The reference to Naples arises from the fact that I had read a book about Father Borrelli's work there, had heard him talk, and was for some time a subscriber – I have the Xmas cards – to his charity.]

On the 23rd December, I wrote another reflective piece.

Christmas (an essay in self-mocking!)

"There were shepherds abiding in the fields…" in such prosaic words begins the account of the most momentous event in the history of the world. And why so outstanding? There is a desperate need in these days when all sincere convictions and emotions are hidden by a layer of sickly-sweet sentimentality and mean materialism by a gross and unhealthy growth which is partly induced by those who use all feelings, however, pure, to bring about our downfall, partly growing out of the insecurity and desperate searching of a rudderless world. What is that simple message? Why has it lost its force? What does it mean to us now? How can we recapture our sense of mystery, our child-like innocence, the awe and joy which moved deep in us when with child-face lifted we heard carols chime, or saw a lighted crib?

The first and self-evident fact is that Christmas can only mean something personal, something beyond an excuse for "jollity" when set in a wider context. In other words if it is celebrated as the birthday of a sort of "pre-Gandhi", or "pseudo-Plato" or even the "greatest philosopher" who ever lived – not as the birth of the Saviour of the World, the God who arose glorious from the tentacles of death and now lives for ever, it is not "special" – it has no great meaning for us now. The problem of letting Christianity strike down all the barriers which the World, the Devil & the Flesh erect against Christ I leave to others. What however should we seek to give and take from Christmas as Christmas?

"Joy, kindness, happiness, presents, – thus would run an enlightened answer. What else however? Thoughtfulness, unselfishness in fact 'Charity' in the sense St. Paul used it… "Charity suffereth long, is meek, is not puffed up … believeth all, beareth all, hopeth all, endureth all…. " Of all times Christmas is the time for making a special effort in this direction. For not only are there more opportunities than any other times of the year – but it is in many ways far more difficult to practice when the rush & hurl of festivities make one live more in the present, more spontaneously than usual. Prayer, care and watchfulness are needed Love for "our neighbours" is of necessity a sacrifice – and if offered with a broken and contrite spirit it is the best offering we can lay at the feet of the young babe in his manger. The details of such an effort are unpredictable. All we can do is ask for strength continually and keep our eyes and hearts open.

But a "charitable heart" is not the only gift pleasing to God. Praise and thanksgiving are acceptable in his sight. A sacrifice of time & thought, both in preparing & attending communion and services – the more splendid the more difficult – are the least we can offer Once again it is a unique opportunity both in its problems and in the many possibilities.

Finally it is a suitable time at which to recollect the events of the last year. An occasion in which we must tinge the spontaneous joys & blessing with a deeper consideration of past gifts and past sadness, of past triumphs and past failings. A time of clearing accounts, before we make out the books for the New Year. Out of the overstuffed drawers, out of the bricker-brack, from the w.p.b. [waste paper basket] of time we can save a few scraps and we can set the targets for the next year.

And in all this we must never forget to remember the shadow of God and of the cross brooding over the crib. Of the hound of the Heavens watching (and laughing!) with us.

The two following pieces were written on 1st January. That evening Penny would arrive for ten days, driven up by my Uncle Richard. Perhaps these poems are connected to that imminent event in some way.

Self-pity

To feel the sickness rising within one – to know the cruelty
Of self-pity, the desire to hurt the loved one so that she will be kind,
To feel no joy when Spring comes, to feel emptiness when
The longed-for hour comes, to feel the inner loneliness,
The stretching snap of all communication, is to feel the
Nothingness of death. The sour taste is soon gone – but the
Shadow is always behind the sun and one day will
Drown it. The uncertainty moves deep in one and one
Cries out for the land, and thorns are on the branch.
The eager hope dies in your eyes, and all the
While you despise your own meanness, your own
Intense ache crushes all that is fresh, all the wonder
And joy and you know that another thread of
Darkness has bound the light that was in you

And you rise again torn and weaker, trying to forget
Knowing you have betrayed...
This was the agony of self-pity on the cross.

Snow & Sunset

It had snowed and there was a sunset. The sky was
Clear blue, the ridge of hills on my left were dark, except
The farthest end which rose to a peak of golden
Bracken, very richly red with the glory of the sun, and
Yet dark against the far-off mountains; this was rough, as
Dry and broken as withered bracken, rocky and pine-plumed
And throwing into relief the sweep of the pink mountains –
Where the snow was like milk stained with the sun's
Blood, sliding in a broad flood over the breasts and
Shoulders of the firm rock. Nearer, the fields were swelling
Green and dark, the hedges black and the birds sleeping,
But the light lingered on the snow and seemed to
Fill the sky with morning, electrifying it
To a deeper blue, luminous and glittering with unfallen
Silver. My mind moves – up over the dark ridge on my
Left, through the stone-walled lanes, across the frosted fields
Through the first and down to the lake.
Here the sun's last blood is caught, very pale and
Orange in this iced chalice among the hills. For
A few seconds the Grail is here – burning with light
Deeper than the imagining of man – burning and smoking
Among the surrounding pines, streaming along the ice,
Warm with wonder and reflection, and then the
Sun sinks and the sky is blue and the moon
Rides pure over the black mountains and the
World is dark with sorrow at its loss.

Academic Work: Winter Term 1962

From various accounts and notes of this term, from Penny's letters and scraps of my own, it is clear that I was working very intensely – about 8 hours a day – and this and the following terms were the most hard-working of my time in Oxford. I was coming towards my finals and really wanted to do well, but was only of mediocre ability.

My Collections, or start of term exams, were still showing poor results. For example a set which I probably did at the end of this term, or perhaps at the start, were marked by Harry Pitt. My first essay was an answer to the question 'Did the Restoration Church Settlement attempt too little or too much?' was given a Beta gamma. 'You haven't the knowledge in sufficient detail for a good answer – see Ogg on the steps of the settlement & most important Whiteman's article in the THRS 5th series, vol. V. The next was: 'James II's policy was a revised version of the programme his brother had attempted after 1670'. For this I got a Beta Beta Alpha. 'Nicely turned essay – but thin on foreign policy'. The next: 'Was the religious life of England 1660-1714 on a higher level than the ecclesiastical history of the period would lead us to expect?' this was apparently dreadful – gamma minus minus. 'You know very little about the Church before 1714. The big Sykes book is little help. Look at his later books & read Ogg 'Charles II' vols. You don't even mention the Cambridge Platonists. The next essay was: 'How far is it possible to explain the financing of industrial expansion in the C18?' for which I got a Beta. – 'more difficult than you think. Your essay shows no connection between the new wealth & better credit facilities & industry. … and so on.

There is another page of stringent criticism, ending. 'A disappointing paper – you have tackled two deceptively easy religious questions and only disclosed that you are not equipped to answer them – & a third very difficult econ qn – difficult because no one knows the answer. You do much better on a 'straight' question where your fertility of style pays off.' The sum of all the marks was a Beta – a lower second. I must have been somewhat depressed by this – but perhaps it spurred me on to the Herculean efforts I made over the next six months.

The term seems to have been split between English history from the late C18 to the later C19, and my special subject, which was Oliver Cromwell. In terms of English history it is difficult to be sure what I did, but the first essay I have is one which really intrigued me. The title was 'What does one mean by the term 'The Industrial Revolution'? This was one of the essays I most enjoyed and put a huge effort into. It was nearly fourteen pages long (foolscap, by hand) replete with tables etc. It laid out many of the thoughts and questions which I would return to over the following years – particularly the unresolved problem of whether the rise in population of the eighteenth century was a cause or consequence of industrialism. For this essay I took almost 60 pages of notes, many of them typed, from forty books and articles.

What does one mean by the term 'the Industrial Revolution'? (1)

For this essay a purely arbitrary division has been drawn between causes and results of the Ind. Revolution – a division which is patently artificial since such factors as population growth, agricultural change, standards of living were both cause and result of the Industrial Growth.

Beales' 'historical revision' of 1928 has warned us of the danger of placing an isolated emphasis on the events of 1760-1840 by showing that neither was 1760 a starting point nor 1840 an ending to the period of economic growth. All the fundamental characteristics of the so-called revolution – capitalist relationships, division of labour, technical innovations, increasing population and so on were present before 1760. Further, Coleman's article on 'Industrial Growth & Industrial Revolutions' shows that if measured by growth curves, rather than by absolute production graphs, the classic 'Industrial Revolution' was no more a Revolution in the paper industry than the application of water-power to rag-beating processes. He does go on, however, to defend the use of the term and says "the term should not be applied to certain technical or economic innovations in particular industries. It is necessary to go beyond the curves of industrial growth, [margin: conjuncture of changes in which pop' growth,] large scale and extensive industrial investment, and the remarkably pervasive effects of the application of science to industry are amongst the most important in producing industrialisation. In this usage, the industrial revolution means the "take off" into industrialisation, a use which avoids the danger of equating industrialisation itself with industrial revolution, and which reserves the term for the comparatively sudden and violent change which launches the industrialized society into being, transforming that society in a way which none of the earlier so-called industrial revolutions ever did." It is in this sense that the term 'Industrial Revolution' is used here.

Before considering the major causes of the economic growth of this period there are several factors which should be dismissed as fundamentally contributory to the process. Ashton includes these exploitation of colonial peoples, protective tariffs and war. The last of these undoubtedly acted as a short-term stimulus in several industries – such as silk, cloth and iron – and A. John has shown the stimulating effects of war on coal, glass, paper, textile and other industries. But Chambers' detailed study of the Vale of Trent 1670-1800 "gives no great evidence either way", while Ashton's study of the number of patents taken out each year shows that for instance in 1782 when a disastrous war was drawing to an end only 31 patents were taken out as opposed to 64 in the following year of peace. War, bringing higher rates of interest and government borrowing, not to mention insecurity - could have a harmful influence on industry. War therefore might have been stimulating in short bursts - but Nef believes that, since there was little to choose in the rate of growth in industry and population in England in the 1760's as compared to France, it must have been the French Revolution and Napoleonic Wars, in which England was less directly involved than the continent, which helped G.B. to gain a tremendous lead over continental countries in industrial development. War moreover was a major factor in producing growing industrial discontent in the Luddite years by cutting off the supplies of timber and hence preventing an adequate supply of houses in the growing towns.

Various factors played a role in encouraging the industrial revolution in England earlier than in the rest of Europe. Religious toleration played a part attracting Huguenot workmen to England, as also did religious dissent. The Society of Friends, for example, were predominant in the development of corn-milling, brewing, pharmacy, and banking as well as in the iron and steel industries with such families as Darbys, Reynolds + Huntsmans. The 'Protestant Ethic' and 'Tawney thesis' may explain this connection to some extent, and more obvious factors such as the superior education of nonconformists and their greater solidarity which, in days of primitive borrowing facilities, enabled them to raise capital more easily than others, also contributed.

England had certain social advantages over continental Europe. Ashton claims it had a more mobile society which allowed every class to contribute its share of talent and ideas. Inventors and entrepreneur's came from every class and a family like the Peel's could rise in three generations from small Lancashire yeoman farmers, through a great industrialist, to a Prime minister. Connected with the social hierarchy were legal relationships and perhaps most important of the effects of the laws of England was the fact that, since the sub-soil was the property of the landlord, men like the Earl of Bridgewater were directly interested in mining expansion.

Industrial Revolution. (contd) ②

~~Perhaps most import~~ Other factors included the ~~fact that there was a~~ close relationship between land and industry in the ruling families and, further, that "these families" ruled the country. There were no stifling royal regulations. But here we must remember that Nef's study of C16 & C17 France and England showed that government interference could not stifle industrial expansion entirely, tho' it might delay it. Perhaps most fundamental of all, was the complex of political, economic and social factors which had made England into a 'middle-class' nation, tho' there is a danger of in using such a term of the C18, it is true that the national wealth was more widely divided than in France and that, as a result, more was spent on manufacturable and utility products than on relatively wasteful luxuries. This process, as we will see, was increased during the first half of the C18 by the profits gained by the agricultural workers from the agricultural depression.

England had other advantages - one of them being geographical. Habakkuk in his article on the 'Basic conditions of economic progress' stresses the importance of trade in providing the initial capital for industrial expansion - and says of England 'English trade, both internal and external, was exceptionally favoured by geography and less impeded by destructive wars, disorder and political instability than the continent, this "he continues" may well be the crucial reason" (for England's industrial leadership). In this context it is important to remember that unlike France, England had no internal customs barriers. "The breaking down of internal customs barriers" says Thomas, "was the prelude in Italy and Germany to the industrial revolution in those countries."

Finally England had certain mineral advantages. In 1754 Sir John Dalrymple ~~wrote~~ pointed out that "among all the known countries on the surface of the globe it was in Great Britain alone that the coal beds, the iron ore and limestone, which the three raw materials of the iron manufacture, were frequently found together and moreover in close proximity to the sea." This was an essential condition of industrial development, but ~~why~~ in what way may coal have caused the industrial revolution? Wrigley, in a "Conference on the Origins of the Ind'l Rev'n" argues that "as long as the chief raw materials of industry are animal & vegetable in nature (wool, wood etc) there must come a time in a small country like England, when there is competition for land between food and industries." This puts a break on economic expansion – witness the battle between sheep and men in Tudor times. "Once, then," he continues "the change over from wood to iron had taken place, great expansion could begin." Prest denies the implication that the Industrial Revolution was a mere accident following a timber shortage but stresses that it was ~~the~~ superior advantages of coal as a fuel which attracted manufactures. Whatever the cause the results were certainly to be momentous. Not only was greater power provided and the future of the steam engine made possible but as Wrigley points out, it encouraged heavy capital investment in improving transport facilities, for this was justified in moving large volumes of mineral raw materials, whereas it had not been when collecting animal or vegetable raw materials together from over a wide area, since only a small volume will move over any one route. A warning, however, against placing too much emphasis on cheaper fuel as a main cause of the Industrial Revolution is provided by Nef's studies which have shown that both fuel (& labour) were probably cheaper in France than in England in the period 1540-1640 (without any appreciable result on industry in that country) ~~and~~ also by the surprisingly small expansion in the coal industry in the C18, relative to that in the 17 and C19s. In the 17 it increased fourteenfold, in the 19 twenty-three times and in the C18 – only threefold.

Such were, what ~~we~~ may be ~~might~~ called the 'natural' advantages of England. How did these energies find an outlet in economic activity?

The study of two C18 figures gives us an introduction to the problem of how economic expansion was financed. Adam Smith outlined the need for capital accumulation in his distinction between "productive" and "unproductive" labour. Investment (spending on "capital") sets to work productive labour, and luxury consumption (spending on "revenue") merely employs unproductive labour. "The proportion between capital and revenue" he continues "seems everywhere to regulate the proportion between industry and idleness. Wherever capital predominates industry prevails; wherever revenue, idleness." Thus the age of expansion was forced to be one of self-denial and re-investment and we see this process ~~[illegible]~~ clearly displayed in the career of 'Parsley' Peel & his son.

Industrial Revolution (cont'd) (3).

A small excerpt from Norman Gash's book will demonstrate the ~~typical~~ C18 ~~...~~ phenomenon of the growth of the industrial entrepreneur from small beginnings, illustrating both the small amount of capital needed and the methods used to get it, and also illuminating Charles Wilson's article on the importance of the entrepreneur — the man who combined many functions.

"The Peels, like many farmers and cottagers had intermittently combined wool-weaving with agriculture. Peel's brother-in-law Haworth (the son of a 'chapman' a dealer in woven fabric) had been sent to London to learn the mysteries of calico-printing with a Dutch firm in Spitalfields. On his return he proposed to Peel that they should jointly set up a print-works at Blackburn. Peel raised a mortgage on his small freehold estate; further capital was provided by Yates - whose father kept the Black Bull Inn; and about 1760 a factory was estab'd.... tho' the original intention was only to print Blackburn 'greys' the enterprise soon developed into a more ambitious organization embracing all the processes of carding, spinning, weaving and printing.... his son was sent to London to enlarge his experience before returning to the family business. In the early years when capital was short, and tho' competition of the London calico printers still ~~was~~ formidable he worked unceasingly."

Ashton outlines several methods whereby capital was harnessed of which the growth of the country bank - ~~mobilizing~~ ~~banking~~ mobilizing the capital of agriculturalists for the benefit of industrialists - was one of the most important. He emphasizes that banks did not often hold shares in business but played their part by holding mortgages and ✱ bonds for would-be industrialists. Interconnected with this was, of course, the rate of interest which fell and was stabilized ✱ at between 3-5% in this century. It was still high enough to attract a large amount of foreign capital into England - especially from Holland (according to Lord North about 3/7ths of the National Debt was in their hands) - but its fall ~~had~~ during ~~the~~ ~~last~~ ~~fifty~~ the years since 1685 had certain beneficial influences on industry. Mortgages, as we have seen, were the usual method of raising capital for small family concerns - often they were mortgages on the factory buildings themselves - and as the return on investment in public funds fell, a mortgage at 5% became an increasingly attractive security for the neighbouring landowner, solicitor, clergyman or widow. Likewise falling interest rates would encourage investment in capital works - especially large concerns such as ~~re~~ turn-pike roads and canals. Thus, indirectly, industry was benefitted, for instance there was less capital tied up in goods in transit. Both Charles Wilson and Ashton warn us against placing too much emphasis, however, on a direct effect on industry; as the former points out, ~~Indeed~~ ~~the~~ fall did not prevent the decline and virtual extinction of many well-established industries, since firms obtained their resources largely by reinvestment of profits; and * the amount ploughed back, it seems likely, was influenced very little by changes in the rate of interest.

~~The~~ ~~late~~ Professor Nurkse is quoted by Chambers as saying " in ~~the English~~ England in the C18. Everyone knows that the spectacular revolution would not have been possible without the agricultural revolution that preceded it. ~~wh~~ and what was the agricultural revolution? It was based mainly on the introduction of the turnips...." This opens up a new field of causality - how far did agricultural changes - perhaps by creating a hungry, ~~??~~ increasing, expropriated, proletariat, or possibly by providing an expanding, increasingly wealthy and manufacture-consuming ~~tenant~~-farmer population, ~~or even~~ by stimulate the Industrial Revolution? The demographic factor will, of necessity be excluded for a while, tho' it was, of course, crucial to the answer of this problem.*

Among the ~~several~~ problems which this question sets is - how far the enclosure movement of the late C18 - for the first time directed by Parliament, ~~was~~ was a direct and successful attempt to expropriate the peasants and hence provide a labour force for the ~~??~~ growing factories? Such an interpretation is inherent in M.H. Dobb's 'History of Capitalism' which is summarised by Tawney as follows - "A proletariat emerged on the scale required, not primarily as the natural consequence of a growing population, but as a work of political art, manufactured with the aid of peasant evictions, the corporate egotism of exclusive gilds, and the control of indispensable financial and marketing facilities by commercial middlemen." Was this true of the late C18 + early C19?

It seems, emphatically, that it was not. Lavrovsky concludes that 'the English peasantry as a class disappeared before those more extensive parliamentary enclosures." He stresses that the decades from 1640 - 1780 saw the disappearance of the ~~smaller~~ peasantry. E. Davies* agrees and goes further in saying that parliamentary enclosures after 1780 'led to an increase in all grades of occupying owners" and Lindsey supports this with figures - for instance that ~~the total~~ average per village of occupying owners in 18 parishes enclosed 1790-1830 was 10.1 in 1790 and

* "The Small Landowner" 1780-1832 (Ec' Hist Rev' 27-28)

Industrial Revolution. (contd) (4)

27·3 in 1830. Not only was this so, but the number of men employed per acre after enclosure probably increased. Chambers* points out that as well the increased need for labour during the work of enclosing, the lag between new agricultural practices and the technical devices for dealing with them meant that, until the methods of ploughing, reaping and threshing were substantially speeded up in the 1830s and 1840s more men were employed on the land. The Industrial Revolution was not supplied with a labour force drained from a depopulated countryside. Another related problem was? - what were the economic position and relationship of farmers and labourers? - (omitting the self-supporting peasant who, as we have seen, was by 1780 a relatively unimportant figure.)

Miss George in her article 'Some causes of the increase of population in the C18 as illustrated by London' says that the 'Bills of Mortality' show that London shared in the general prosperity from 1700 - 1757/65, which is considered to have been one of the chief periods of English working class prosperity." If this is true it may well have been an important factor in the Industrial Revolution for it would have the double effect of allowing earlier marriage and hence increased population, (as well as better nutrition contributing to longer life etc) and of creating a larger market for the new industrial goods. Others support Miss George's conclusion - Chambers in the 'Vale of Trent' suggesting that the "long period of low prices, the generality of the population became accustomed to the good things of life, and when prices began to rise, and the population also, the people still expected the better conditions to which they had grown accustomed to continue." He goes further than this even and suggests that "from 1782 the outdoor labourers were obtaining allowances in aid of wages to settle married labourers, so that some of the gains by landlords and farmers were channelled off in support of labourer's living standards." Conclusive support is given to the theory that agricultural labourers enjoyed a period of increased real wages, in the years before 1750 by Mingay's article on the 'Agricultural Depression 1730-50'. He shows how the symptoms of the depression was "a slight tendency for rents to fall, the occurence of heavy arrears of rent, and the granting of various concessions by the landlord to the tenants" and concludes that "apart from London, where they were rising, money wages tended to be stable in the 1st ½ of the C18 thus there was an improvement in real wages in an era of low prices

(* Enclosure & Labour Supply in the Ind'l Rev'n Ec.H.R. 1953)

which would have a beneficial influence on the standard of living of the labouring poor. A good harvest increased both agricultural and non-agricultural employment, money wages improved, and the incomes of exporters of agricultural produce rose." This may be, as we have seen a partial explanation of the population increase – but its direct significance for industrial growth is limited in that it was offset by the serious effects of continued depression among the farmers and landed interest. For Mingay also points out that "it may be significant that the quickened pace of industrial development in the later decades of the Century had as its background a farming community that was enjoying prosperous conditions after a lapse into depression of 20 yrs." Finally, agriculture's failure to continue its early expansion during the second half of the C18 – due to varying factors such as the ease with which agricultural profits could be made with older methods, the frequency of bad harvests, and the rise in English agricultural imports during the period 1763-76, – a failure which was perhaps one of the main reasons for the rise of prices, since agricultural output failed to increase in proportion to population① (as John points out), may well have been an important factor in persuading men to devote their resources to industrial and commercial rather than to agricultural expansion.*

* – but this [illegible] merely if [illegible] profits & [illegible] were more worthwhile.

At this point we arrive at the crucial problem in relation to the Industrial Revolution – was demographic expansion a cause or result of the Industrial Revolution? From the answer we give to this is likely to spring our whole ethical evaluation of the Revolution – for if we conclude, with Ashton and others, that population was expanding rapidly anyhow and hence England was only saved from the fate of Ireland by its economic growth we may be prepared to forgive many of the horrors of the change to industrialization – but if, with most C19 historians we see the population increase as a response to industrial labour demand we are likely to view the Revolution as an unparalleled tragedy, even if we admit that statistical tables show that real wages of factory workers were as high or higher in the C19 than farm labourers' had been in the C18.

① John (24) –

Industrial Revolution. (contd) (5)

As this is a long and complex subject and this essay is already overlength I will confine myself to the following approach to the question. Firstly I will give ~~the~~ ~~plan~~ general answer of ~~tea~~ the leading modern writers to two basic questions and then give ~~my~~ my own conclusions in outline.

The first question is - was it increase in the birth rates ~~[illegible]~~ or decrease in the death rate which caused the population explosion and (if they suggest an answer) what was the cause of the change? ~~this~~. It is evident that, since it is fairly certain that whatever improvement there was in medical or nutritional standards in the century this had little part in the fall in the death rate, only the birth rate could have been affected by industrialization - so those who decide for a lowered ~~birth~~ death rate ~~exclude~~ exclude the possibility of industrial expansion causing the rise. Here are the conclusions of the authorities.

	Rising Birth Rate	Falling Death Rate	Cause
1948 ASHTON (Industrial Rev'n)		Completely due to this. ✓	Higher health & living standards.
1958 KRAUSE (Changes in Eng fertility 1781-1850)	✓	(a 50% rise in deaths 1781-1815)	None given.
1957 HELLEINER (Vital Rev'n Reconsidered)	BOTH.	(But birth rate rose as result of ✓	Disapp of plague (rats) + 2nd = mitigation of subsistence crises
1953 CHAMBERS (Enclosure + Labour Supply)	✓		Higher marriage rate; better standard of living.
1960 KITSON CLARK (Making of Vict'n Eng)	✓		Absence of plagues [illegible]; Natural process [illegible] earlier marriage.
1951 CONNELL (Some unsettled problems in Eng & Irish Pop'n Hist)	✓		Change in habits of [illegible]
1922 GEORGE (London - Some causes of incr of pop'n)		✓	Improv't in medical & social (Hanway's etc) conditions
1959 KRAUSE (Some neglected factors in Eng Ind'l Rev'n)	✓		Higher marriage rate
SALTMARSH (On the plague).	BOTH.	(tho' decrease in death prob' most imp) ✓	Change in habits of rats + improv'd living conditions cause plague disappear [illegible] 1680
1955 McKEOWN + BROWN (Eng Pop'n changes in C18)		(with secondary results in the former) ✓	Prob due to reduction of incidence of disease - perhaps(?) living conditions [illegible]
1958 HABAKKUK (Economic Hist of Modern Britain)	✓ BOTH	(this did fall - change in virulence of disease)	Increased marriages - failure of both to fall [illegible]
1953 HABAKKUK (Eng Pop'n in C18)	✓ BOTH	(a definite fall - due to change in age-comp'n due to earlier crises & raised birth rate - cycles of pop'n) ✓	Better economic diet, better nutrition etc.
1929 MARSHALL (Pop'n problem during Ind'l Rev'n - note on controversy)	BOTH.	(Main factors; increased marriage rate - birth rate kept up by economic factors)	
1936 MARSHALL (Pop'n of Eng & Wales - Ind'l Rev'n to 1914).	BOTH.	(Fall in death rate in C18 due to better hygiene etc - not better nutrition)	
about 1937 TREVELYAN (Quotes Griffiths) (Social History)		✓✓	(Better nutrition; Advance in medicine)

Question 2 is simpler and evolves from the first - was economic growth a cause? or response to population growth?

	A cause of pop'n growth	A response to.	~~Cause~~.
1948 ASHTON (Industrial Rev'n)		✓ (tho' not a necessary response of modern India)	
1953 CHAMBERS (Enclosure + Labour Supply)		✓ (tho' in turn it affected inducements to incr' pop'n)	

Cause of.	Response to.
1959. KRAUSE (Neglected factors in Eng Ind'l Revn)	✓ (greater wealth caused greater am't of marriages)
1953. HABAKKUK. (Eng Popn in C18)	✓ (one cannot reject ev' of Malthus etc)
1960. KITSON CLARK (Making of Victorian Eng)	(Eng prevented from fate of Ireland.) ✓

Necessarily this is a bold summary of these author's conclusions and most of them emphasise the complexity of the problem in which there is so much interaction between cause and effect.

My own conclusion is based on a negative approach. Although it is statistically obvious that during these crucial years there was a fall in deaths and a rise in population there is no satisfactory explanation of either. As far as falling death rate is concerned there is no strong evidence for improved medical facilities or improved living conditions either existing or - if they existed at all - having much effect on a fall in the death rate. On the other hand there are no obvious reasons why birth rate should rise - for it, too, was governed by these factors. The only explanation seems to be a much more problematical one -ed to which there were two aspects. One was the long-term population cycle suggested by Chambers in which a period of disease and crisis was followed by a rapid increase in births, a lowering of the age composition of the country, leading to a lower mortality rate, leading to population expansion. This suggestion is strengthened by comparison with Ireland and the continent where this process was in motion. But there were two special factors which applied at this time. One was the change in the virulence of disease hinted at by Helleiner, Kitson Clark, Connell, McKeown and Brown and elucidated by Saltmarsh. This aggravated the population increase. So far, it seems, England would have shared Ireland's fate - tho' different social and political conditions might have restrained it from going as far as Ireland. Thus we can see the population increase as divorced from industrialization.

(6)

and even from the economic expansion of the previous centuries - and therefore as a dynamic cause of the industrial revolution. Though here again one must remember that in C18 Ireland or C20 India population pressure does not necessarily result in industrialisation. Such a view, a conclusion which sees the population growth as largely caused by other than industrial factors is emphasised when we remember that during the steepest period of population growth 1780 - 1815 industry still produced, compared to agriculture, a small proportion of the country's wealth and employed a very limited amount of the country's population. It seems to have been, since country districts were not depopulated as we have seen, a surplus agrarian population which industry employed. But even here we have to be careful to see too close link between population pressure & industrial growth - the pioneering work for the revolution was done in a period when inventions were made largely because of a shortage of labour. When all this said, however, it is still true that industrialisation was a major factor in continuing the expansion of population during the C19 by employing and even enriching the already increased workers. Comparison of Ireland and England in the 1840's shows the value of industry as a factor in maintaining population increase.

EFFECTS. Recent evidence, as Beales in his historical revision points out, has tended to minimise the evils accompanying the revolution, and, as he carefully points out, "it is old evils which the industrial revolution was constantly making conspicuous." A statistical and factual reaction has set in against the romantic interpretation of The Revolution and Hammond, in his "The Industrial Revolution and discontent" is a voice crying in the wilderness. But, while admitting that much of the C19 approach is overdrawn and that, as we have seen, the revolution may have saved England from being another Ireland, yet anyone who has been in the most backward part of an underdeveloped country - India for instance (where the standard of living of a labourer is three times lower than that of a pre-industrial English peasant according to Habakkuk) and also to the slums which still exist in a northern industrial town can hardly fail to admit that statistics give as false a picture of life as did the Romantics. What, then, were the effects of the Industrial Revolution?

As we have seen industrial growth was not the main cause of agricultural crisis in the years 1780-1830. There was no great rural depopulation - in fact Chambers' shows that the number of families engaged in agriculture rose from 896,000 in 1811 to 961,000 in 1831. If there was a redistribution of labour it took place gradually, men no longer dividing their occupations but coming to work full time at the loom or coal face, without, often, moving their households, the surplus population moved gradually to industry as the young people tended to go into industry. Halévy shows that the real wage of country labourers after 1810 went through a decline – this does seem to have been the result of industrial competition, to some extent, of small farmers could less easily supplement their wages by home weaving etc. Kitson Clark argues that though conditions were growing worse in the country this was relieved by industry which was absorbing the increasing population. But he fails to underline the fact that some of the reasons which he gives for worsening conditions were caused by growing industrialisation – among them that "a subsistence economy was being replaced by a money economy" and that there was "a decline in rural industry". As Halévy points out "once Wiltshire and Somersetshire had been like an enormous manufacturing town scattered over a wide area; but now the iron industry had been transferred to the centre and the west, and woollen manufacture deserted the south for Yorkshire". Taking everything, especially population growth, into account, however, industry probably did have a predominantly beneficial influence on agriculture.

~~Considerable work has been done to show that factories were neither the "predominant feature", nor the "unmitigated" evil as they have sometimes been seen. Halévy shows that~~

4 Hutt and others have shown that factories were not an unmitigated evil and this trend has gone so far as to suggest that 'factory hours' acts, by preventing children spending up to 18 hours in 'light work' at the factory both crippled parents economically and increased evil home influences. A comparison is made with pre-factory conditions and it is shown, that conditions in pre-factory workshops or garrets were often worse than in factories – it was in Nottingham, where hosiery was still a home-manufacture, that rioting was worst in the early C19. Again Hobsbawm's article on the machine-breakers demonstrates that it was often not

Industrial Revolution. (cont'd) (7)

the machinery itself which the Luddites attacked, and that, when they did they often had the sympathy of the industrialists themselves. As Halevy points out, as factories began to be made of iron instead of wood and introduced steam-power and expanded in size conditions improved. It is noticeable, however that no significant defence of the early mining industry has been made!

What broadly were the social effects of the industrial revolution? Ashton claims that there was a rise in the position of women and girls who were now economically independent. Again tho' as Halevy points out the revolution widened the gap between employer and employee for a while, in the early revolution there was more opportunity for social advancement – witness, once again, the progress of the Peel family. But more specifically, what were the effects on the standards of living?

Ashton in his article 'Some Statistics of the Ind'l Revn' shows that the real wages of factory operatives rose considerably in the period 1806-1835 (proportion 74:108). From this he concludes that the Industrial Revolution is considered such a calamity largely because "there has been a generalization of the worst instances and a failure to realize conditions in cottage and garrett". A.J. Taylor* supports Ashton's statistics – saying that the purchasing power of the industrial worker rose some 70% in 1790-1850: but he is prepared to admit that the progress of the working class lagged behind that of the nation - but explains this largely by factors outside the control of the much-maligned capitalist exploiters. Again Ashton emphasizes that there are other factors which would have caused misery anyhow - the movement of prices, exaggerated by the Napoleonic wars, bad harvests and interest fluctuations. Again Kitson Clark points out that the largest two groups of working people "were relatively unaffected by industrial changes" being involved in farming and domestic service and emphasizes that only 219,000 were involved in coal in 1851. He also stresses the pressure of Irish immigrants in adding to the misery. Finally an attempt has been made, for instance by Ashton in his article on 'Statistics' to put the blame onto other shoulders, in this case blaming the shortage of buildings (due to chronic shortage of timber) for the

(* Progress & Poverty in Britain 1780-1850) – no – see Article which is much more guarded.

obvious misery. All the above is true, but among the facts that must be remembered are that Kitson Clark's attempt to exclude, for instance, the domestic servants from the evil effects of the Revolution is unrealistic - for as Hutt himself has ~~pointed out~~ says and Hammond endorses, it was not the working conditions but the crowded houses, lack of sanitation, lack of any amenities or occupations and so on which were the preponderant evils of the revolution. These may not ~~have~~ been a necessary result of industrialization - but one cannot get away from the fact that the first effective sand filter was only discovered in 1829, or the first Manchester reservoir started in 1848. To quote Hobsbawm's conclusion in his article on the 'Standard of Living 1790-1850' written 5 yrs ago

'The classical view has been put by Sydney Webb (ie that living conditions positively declined from 1781-1837 ~~1837-1787~~) it may be that further evidence will discredit it, but it will have to be vastly stronger evidence than has so far been adduced.'

Suffering - question of visibility.

Hammond - happiness.

More stress on cotton than on coal.

I then wrote an eight page essay, based on very extensive reading (typed extracts from 37 books and articles) on 'English Radicalism 1760-1830'. Unfortunately there are no marks or comments on this or any these English history essays.

I suspect there may be one or more other essays on nineteenth century politics which I have lost. But the longest and most enjoyable essay I wrote as an undergraduate was undertaken at the end of this term.

The essay is very long indeed, some 28 lengthy paragraphs of text, over seven thousand words in all. Unusually, I typed it rather than writing it by hand.

"VICTORIANISM"

"Ah, what a dusty answer gets the soul
When hot for certainties in this our life!"
(Meredith: 'Modern Love')

"The English", Treischke once said at Berlin, "think Soap is Civilization".

It is now a commonplace that "Victorianism" does not mean a definable set of opinions, a united moral attitude, or a framework of accepted institutions. The scorn or laughter of critics has turned to admiration, or at least to an attempt to break down the rigid over-simplifications of earlier writers. Young asks – "Who are these Victorians? By what mark are we to know them? What creed, what doctrine, what institution was there among them which was not at some time or other debated or assailed? I can think of two only: Representative Institutions & the Family". Take any mark by which one might be able to unite the subjects of Victoria & one will find exceptions. Was it an age of hard work & 'self-help'? It was doubtless a time when official encouragement was given to persuade people to work. "Properly speaking all work is religion" declared Carlyle, "Labour is not a devil even while encased in Mammonism; labour is an imprisoned God, writhing unconsciously or consciously to escape out of Mammonism". But Carlyle & Smiles exhorted not because they smugly approved but because they saw work as one answer to the chaos around them. As Briggs has pointed out, the four main elements of the 'Victorian' gospel, the gospel of work; 'seriousness' of character; respectability & self-help – were often proclaimed, not because they were conspicuous, but because they were absent. "Self-Help" was designed to re-inculcate old-fashioned but wholesome lessons which, in the words of its author "cannot perhaps be too often urged".

Was it then an age of optimism & belief in progress? To a certain extent it was. When the Prince Consort spoke at the Mansion House, a few weeks before the opening of the great exhibition, he used it as the symbol of the forthcoming unity of mankind. "We are living", he said, "at a period of most wonderful transition, which tends rapidly to accomplish that great end to which all history points – the realisation of the unity of mankind". In Macaulay & others there is a confidence that there was in motion a movement towards greater happiness, justice & liberty, an optimism of Godwinian flavour & having a factual basis in a real advance in national wealth & scientific knowledge. Tennyson versified the prosaic dream of Cobden & others &

"... Saw the heavens fill with commerce, argosies of magic sails
Pilots of the purple twilight, dropping down with costly bales;
Till the war-drum throbbed no longer, & the battle flags were furled
In the Parliament of man, the Federation of the world."

But, as Eliot points out, Tennyson was in fact filled with doubt & George Eliot & J.S. Mill were only two of the minds who revolted against this kind of optimism. The disillusionment cannot be dated, though it seems to increase after the turn of the century & is epitomised in two remarks of Ruskin in the "7 Lamps of Architecture" – "the stirring which has taken place in our architectural aims & interest within these few yrs, is thought by many to be full of promise: & I trust it is, but it has a sickly look to me". In the 1880 edition he added – "The only living art now left in England is bill-sticking". Arnold's 'Culture & Anarchy' is yet another example of an anti-Macaulian reaction. Yet deeper than this reaction lay a belief in human progress, a confidence in the ultimate value of individual effort which does seem to underly all Victorian thinkers before 1880. It is likely that George Eliot approved, as Morley approved, of Mill's belief that "All the grand sources of human suffering are in a great degree, many of them entirely, conquerable by human care & effort; & though their removal is grievously slow ... yet every mind sufficiently intelligent & generous to bear a part, however small & unconspicuous, in the endeavour, will draw a noble enjoyment from the contest itself." Even the critics assumed certain values so to be good in themselves & criticism to be worthwhile.

To read too much doubt & underlying unhappiness into the age is as dangerous as to see it as an age of exuberant self-confidence. As Young remarks, the Englishmen knew that in the essential business of humanity – the mastery of brute nature by intelligence – he had outstripped the world, & the Machine was the emblem & the instrument of his triumph. Further, he has compared the man-sided curiosity & competence, its self-confidence & alertness of Late Midvictorian culture to that of Greece. When one becomes absorbed in the underlying tensions of the age it is well to remember that for most of the upper strata of society it was an age of unprecedented enjoyment.

Finally – what of their ethics in its application to art & architecture & life? A picture of Mrs Grote, who "sat with her red stockings higher than her head, discomfited a dead party by saying "disembowelled" quite bold & plain, & knew when a hoop was off a pail in the back kitchen". Or a recollection of the exploits & views of Misses Nightingale, Martineau & Charlotte Bronte will warn us not to generalise about Victorian women. Victorian intolerance as regards sex was only felt by the public figures, & even then the aristocracy were exempt from criticism: Hartington had numerous mistresses, yet Gladstone admired him. St John's Wood was built for mistresses. It was because J.S. Mill was a public figure that he suffered as a result of his irregular private life. The Victorians admired manliness, & hence we find despots like Barrett of Wimpole St, who, as a demonstration of his manhood, cd have as many mistresses as he liked. [note in pencil in margin "Adultery = theft"] But it would be false to dismiss their 'respectability' as a legend. Miss Mitford was publicly reproved for calling a pudding a 'roly-poly' & a Parliamentary Cmtee, who asked a factory woman if she had ever miscarried, brought on themselves the anger of the Times for violating the principles which shd preside over such inquiries – " a dread of ridicule & an anxious avoidance of indecency".

Nevertheless, before an age which covers its shop-window dummies while their clothes are being changed mocks as "typical of Victorian gentility" the clothing of a Cupid on a Valentine of 1840, it might ask why, in an age when the family was the only stable unit and when families were far larger, stricter discipline should have been enforced. Further, Young, quoting from Gogol's "Dead Souls" has shown that much that we think of as "typically Victorian" & English was, in fact, part of an European movement. If English prudery was noted as "Englanderie" as early as 1805, 2nd Empire furniture & American manuals of business, as Young also points out, represent much that we consider 'Victorian'. In fact there is a case for saying that the terms "Victorians" and "Victorianism" have become "masked words droning & skulking about us", to use the words of Ruskin.

If we are to seek for any meaning for the words we must go deeper, catching at various strands & chance remarks as indications of the "Spirit of the Age". As an indication of such an approach, I quote once again two examples from Young – "When Bp Wilberforce was killed, Mr Gladstone passed some hours in silent depression; then he observed, "He was a Great Diocesan", & recovered his spirits at once. This impulse to say the right, the improving thing, is most characteristic of the Victorian temper. Once a servant was sent to meet Sir Bartle Frere at the station. He asked how he was to know him. "Look for a grey-haired gentleman helping some one". And, of course, the Proconsul was duly found lifting found lifting an old woman's basket out of the carriage."

A certain unity & value can be given to the term "Victorian" if it is regarded as the reaction to certain fundamental problems – economic, social, political, mental & spiritual. On one side the Industrial Revolution, on the other the scientific, were shattering the old framework of society & "Victorianism" can be viewed as the attempt to assimilate & order the new elements in society.

In 1801 the population was roughly 9m, by 1851 it had doubled & in another twenty years increased by four more millions. Arnold knew that the old world had been killed by the French & Industrial Revolutions, & in the vast, sprawling democracy which had succeeded he could see no centre of control, no sense of direction, little in fact but the worship of Mammon & machinery, supported by a faith in the virtue of "doing-as-one-likes" & often a complacent belief in material progress. So he wrote "Culture & Anarchy".

Dickens saw the horror in which thousands of families were born, dragged out their ghastly lives & died: the drinking water brown with faecal particles, the corpses kept unburied for a fortnight in a festering London August; courts where not a weed would grow, & sleeping-dens afloat with sewage. He did not need statistics to tell him that the mortality was twice as great in the East End of London as in the West & that in adjacent streets it varied from 38 to 12. Within sight of the Houses of Parlt there were streets where no decent person, except a doctor perhaps, or a Sister of Mercy would venture. If he chanced to pass Deptford on a Saturday night he might easily see under the glare of a gin palace a ring form to watch two women, stripped to the waist, fighting with broken bottles. This "undercurrent of brutality" as Kitson Clark calls it explains many aspects of Victorian life. For instance the Temperance Society was dealing with a very serious evil & an emphasis on a rigid sexual code was necessary when women were not safe in the streets & the life of the miserable poor was, as House says, 'soaked in sex'. In the 1830s only about half the children went to school & even of these few learnt anything. In Hull a close investigation revealed that of 5,000 children who had been to school, 800 could not read, 1,800 could not write & just half could not do a sum. From the marriage registers it would appear that in the thirties about one-third of the men & two-thirds of the women could not.

Nor had there been much progress in the last thirty years. Society was itself being dissolved & the "gentleman, nobleman and yeoman" which had constituted Cromwell's "good interest" was splitting "into a hundred aristocracies & a hundred democracies, button-makers & gentleman button-makers" as Young calls them. Social stratification, particularily the emergence of the middle class obviously explains much of the Victorian respectability philanthropy. "The middle classes know", Ld Shaftesbury once said, "that the society of their lives & property depends upon their having round them a peaceful, happy, & moral population". To induce, therefore, some modicum of cleanliness & foresight, to find some substitute for savage sport & drinking, to attract the children to school & the parents to church, to awaken some slight interest in books was more than pure altruism. Up to 1848 at least there was a real fear of social revolution. Looking back, Kingsley wrote of the years 1815-1848 when "young lads believed (& not wrongly) that the masses were their natural enemies & that they might have to fight, any year or any day, for the safety of their property & the honour of their sisters." Bertrand Russell tells us that his grandfather, lying on his deathbed in 1869, "heard a loud noise in the street & thought it was the revolution breaking out". Even Macaulay predicted a time when "either some Caesar or Napoleon will seize the rein of govt with a strong hand or your republic will be as fearfully plundered & laid waste by barbarians in the C20 as the Roman Empire was in the 5th". Though yhe pressure of fear subsided after 1848 as economic conditions improved any challenged to the order of society – especially to religion – continued to be interpreted as a social danger. Darwin, in the review of his "Descent of Man" (1871), was severely censured for "revealing his zoological conclusions to the general public at a moment when the sky of Paris was red with the incendiary flames of the Commune". As internal tension died away with the economic boom a new type of worry appeared – the challenge of Germany & America. Soon after the turn of the century the "Economist" remarked that Americas's eventual world predominance, tho' it might take time, was assured; & those who went to the 2nd World Exhibition at Paris in 1867 were no [t] so convinced as to the length of the delay. Soon the Prussian invasion of France (1870) was to lend force to Arnold's prophecy that well-meaning amateurism & individualism was not enough.

The disruption of the social hierarchy & the awesome realization that no class had an absolute claim to any position – leaving men to scramble for themselves – is paralleled by another development which also destroyed established &, assumedly fixed, relationships. This was the growth [of] the autonomous personality of woman. The fundamental issue of feminism was growing clearer all through the century, as women, no longer isolated heroines, but individuals bent on a career, drew out into the sexless sphere of disinterested intelligence; a process which Young claims may truly be named 'Victorian' if only for the horror with which Victoria regarded it! "I want", said Bella Rokesmith to her husband in

Dickens, "to be something so much worthier than the doll in the doll's house". Often this movement met almost hysterical opposition, as in Florence Nightingale's youth, for it could be viewed as one more challenge to the old, male-dominated world. Some critics have even seen in the frequent beards & whiskers of the mid-Century a flaunting masculinity, an "excessive hairiness" which was perhaps reflected ideologically in Kingsley's "Muscular Xianity" & was a reassertion of male domination.

The importance of the Victorian family can hardly be overstressed. Here the old hierarchies & values could be preserved; it was increasingly found to be the centre of virtues & emotions which could not be found in completed form outside. Here at any rate was something firm to stand on. In the home so conceived, man could recover the humanity he seemed to be losing. The Victorian home was not only a peaceful, it was a sacred place. As outward religion lost its hold – the living church became more & more the "temple of the hearth". For the agnostics also, the home became a temple. For them the family was the basic source of those altruistic emotions they relied upon to take the place of the Xian ethic. Houghton goes as far as to say that "it might be said that mainly on the shoulders of its priestess, the wife & mother, fell the burden of stemming the amoral & irreligious drift of modern industrial society." The family was also, of course, the vehicle of an increasing class-consciousness – fostered by the increasing stratification of society which we have already noticed. Respectability in 1860 is the dividing line & the sign of respectability is family life & cleanliness. Young observes that as you go downwards into the mass of poverty & wretchedness the home counts for less & less, until it breaks up altogether. The great gulf was between the households where the children are cared for & where they are not. As a channel for self-respect it played an indispensible part.

"Narrowness of education, pride in possession, fascination with ingenuity, & a hankering after 'sublime display'" says Briggs "led most of the mid-Victorians to prefer the ornate to the simple, the vast to the balanced. They liked imposing public architecture with 'pretensions', wanted it to demonstrate wealth, to abound in decorations – even in polychromatic effects & to incorporate the elaborate symbolism of an age of free trade & material progress." The love of detail & ornateness is displayed in the religious symbolism of Worcester chapel & the desire of a new class, made by wealth, to display its superiority is exemplified in Leeds Town Hall. Certain features in the art & architecture are considered to be 'Victorian' – the ethical aim of art being one of the most-noticed features. Hunt, in his "Hireling Shepherd" sought to express by a crowd of intellectual symbols the moralising intention which had supplanted his original lyrical idea. His "Light of the World" was immensely popular & this is explained by its ethical overtones. But it becomes slightly more difficult to account for the worship of the "Monarch of the Glen". It is not so easy now to blame "didacticism" & "puritanism" for the artistic uncertainty of the middle-Victorians. As Young points out, Puritanism could be looked on as one of the prime inspirations of the artistic excellence of the C18 – with its taste for simplicity, its purity & its subordination of inessentials for essentials. In fact, Young concludes that "in so far from making Puritanism responsible for the anti-art bias of the C19", I am inclined to look for the secret in a quite un-Puritan delight in unrestrained extravagance, to which the new development of mechanical ingenuity powerfully contributed" & we would add, with Pevsner, an extra delight in accumulating facts which made this an age of statistics & rapidly growing factual knowledge. Pevsner also points out that the artistic position was not very different abroad, & notes that English architects won both the international competitions for St Michael's, the principal church of Hamburg in 1844 & for the new cathedral at Lille in 1855. It is perhaps significant that the Gothic revival was, outside England, strongest in Germany, where, as we have seen, the old religion was being undermined fastest. Perhaps in the uncertainty, the wavering between different styles, the search for authority in the imitation of old styles, we see another aspect of the growing doubts which underlay permanent truth to be found & what was the style which should convey this? The leaders themselves were uncertain & as we have noticed Ruskin was pessimistic about the attempt. Instead of blaming ethical preoccupations for the supposed failure of Victorian architecture, it might be fairer to see this as another symptom of a deeper uncertainty. As Clark has said in "The Gothic Revival" – whenever aesthetic standards are lost, ethical standards rush in to fill the vacuum." [in margin '& vice versa'] People liked pictures with titles not because they were largely a new & aesthetically untrained class, but because their whole conception of what is absolutely good or valuable was being undermined.

Many of the Victorian movements, though obviously not all, can be interpreted as a reaction to a growing uncertainty as to where real value lay & to where intellectual speculation was leading. It seems paradoxical that as the Bible lost authority the Churches became fuller. The Oxford Movement & the fuller churches (often filled with an aristocracy who had thirty years earlier flaunted religion), the new idolatry of men of letters – epitomised in Comte who attempted to found his own secular priesthood, & finally the willingness of the average Victorian to defer to the opinions of his "elders & betters" rather than to question them or think them out, are all aspects of a recoil to authority from the anarchy which seemed to be opening before their feet. The anti-intellectualism of Carlyle is well-known & this found a more practical outlet in the common disparagement of theory in the name of practice – the preference of amateurism to professionalism. Throughout "Self-Help", genius, talent or native intelligence are minimised & the moral qualities of hard work & persistence are exalted. "It is also to be borne in mind" we are reminded "that the experience gathered from books, though often valuable, is but of the nature of LEARNING; where the experience gained from actual life is of the nature of WISDOM". Macaulay was the great apostle of the "Philistines" & argued that poetry would inevitably decline in a soc' more enlightened & more aware of the nature of "reality as revealed by observation". Other signs of this anti-intellectualism are the democratic theories in both political & religion which exalted natural shrewdness & the virtues of the heart against arid intellectualism & acquired knowledge. Even in the most honest of writers there was a certain reserve, & certain "incapacity to follow any chain of reasoning which seems likely to result in an unpleasant conclusion" as G.M. Young says (rather unfairly I believe) of Tennyson & which we have already noticed in Morley's failure to apply historical relativism to himself.

Victorian dogmatism was, to some extent, exorted not by confidence but by doubt. Carlyle may well have been so raucous & positive because he was so aware of the precariousness of his ideas, perhaps not in his own mind, but in the mind of his age. If we apply this approach too far, for instance to Macaulay's confidence in progress we will be guilty of over-subtlety, but the desire to hear great sages pronouncing their dogmatic assurance is nevertheless a feature of the age. Underlying the whole age is the belief that dogmatism can be justified. They believed that truth, tho' it may, as Coleridge & Mill & Eliot saw, have many mansions, is at least one truth, that it is not only absolute, but that it is attainable & should be pursued &, when found, asserted. When we accuse the age of rigidity & intolerance, often arising from a narrow religion, we have to start making exceptions – Mill, Arnold & Eliot being the most notable. But their flexibility of mind was maintained by a tense balance between conviction & tolerance, & this earnestness mixed with an ability to appreciate other points of view did not last much beyond the 1870s. Hero-worship, patriotism, imperialism, & medieval revival, from the extraordinary popularity of Greek myths, mediaeval legends, Kingsley's heroes & Tennyson's Idylls, as well as the other volumes of Golden Deeds & Ages of Fable, the Gothic revival in art & architecture & even the encouragement of a belief in progress can be seen, in part, as a sort of escapism. Though an oversimplification of such movements to fit into a pattern is dangerous, it is true that this age could revive its faith in man, if not as an intellectual conviction, at least as an emotional attitude, in the contemplation of the supposed serenity of Iseult, or the purity of Arthur. In the Middle Ages, it was thought, though morality was far inferior, "individuality was strong, will was energetic. The spirituality & altruism which were seeming to disappear in the advancing tide of mercantile & social ambition are lamented by Hopkins –

"Generations have trod, have trod, have trod;
And all is seared with trade; bleared smeared with toil;

And wears man's smudge & shares man's smell: the soil
Is bare now, nor can foot feel, being shod." (Hopkins)

Arnold felt the mysterious mediaeval charm of Oxford, in her moonlit fields – & Hopkins once again finds words for its permanence

Towery city branchy between towers;
Cuckoo-echoing, bell-swarmed, lark-charmed, rook-racked, river-rounded;

(& longed for the serenity of Duns Scotus' age –)
....these weeds & waters, these walls are what
He haunted who of all men most sways my spirits to peace;...'

The desire for permanence found another outlet in what G.M. Young calls an "almost nervous craving" for natural beauty. Delicate observation of nature & the power to convey its unchanging, unhasting, unartifical, purity was the prime reason for Tennyson's popularity. Young suggests that this craving was at its deepest level an almost biological necessity. "Tennyson's public was becoming, in spirit, suburban; a country-bred stock, entangled in a way of life which it had not learnt to control was instinctively fighting for breath. And for sixty years its poet was there, flashing on it, in phrases of faultless precision, the "jewels five words long" of the Princess for instance, pictures of the world from which it was exiled & in which it yearned to keep at least an imaginary footing. To take but one example of the peace which the C19 often found in the contemplation of natural beauty we can study Hale White – or Mark Rutherford as he was known to his public. Though like Pascal he knew that we cannot base religion upon Nature alone – he retained a sense of kinship with the "wisdom & spirit of the universe". Speaking of Wordsworth he said – the real God is not the God of the Church, but the God of the hills, the abstraction Nature, & to this my reverence was transferred. Instead of an object of worship which was altogether artificial, removed, never coming into genuine contact with me, I had now one which I thought to be real, one in which literally I could live & move & have my being, an actual fact present before my eyes..." In Nature, especially the "lovely asunder star-light", he found a force which lifted him clean out of his morbid introspection, finding there "for this uneasy hear of ours, A never-failing principle of joy, & purest passion." Willey has pointed out that the Lake District was part of the C19's religious creed. The Lakeland mountains, linked heaven with home & spoke intimately to the disturbed heart. Throughout that "iron time of doubts, disputes, distractions, fears" they remained, for the dweller on the darkling plain, a silent & constant symbol of sublimity. Even without Wordsworthian associations, he suggests it would have had immense importance as a region owing nothing to human contrivance & undesecrated by human hand, which could symbolize permanence, grandeur & joy..."

If anything, the intellectual & spiritual problems were even graver. Nothing 'absolute' was left in the social sphere of society except the family, & when men turned to their minds for comfort & order, for real values with which to harmonise & direct their swiftly changing world they must have often [sic] have cried with Hopkins –

"I cast for comfort I can no more get
By groping round my comfortless, than blind
Eyes in their dark can day or thirst can find
Thirst's all-in-all in all a world of wet."

Many of the intellectual & spiritual crises with which the Victorians were faced were operating before Victorian times. Evangelicism & the Romantic movement had been largely reactions against the neutralisation of nature & the relegating of God to a first cause by Newtonian physics. In the battle to retain spiritual values Coleridge had prepared much of the ground for the struggle between religion & science. The emotional implications of C17 science have been described by Prof. Burt thus "... Newton's authority was squarely behind that view of the cosmos which saw in man a puny, irrelevant, spectator of the vast mathematical system … The world that people had thought themselves living in – a world rich with colour & sound … speaking everywhere of purposive harmony & creative ideals – was crowded now into minute corners in the brains of scattered organic beings. The really important world outside was a world, hard, cold, colourless, silent & dead – a world of quantity, a world of mathematically computable motions in mechanical regularity…"

Descartes & Locke joined in this world view & it was against such a conception that Romanticism protested. Coleridge was convinced that the C18 had "untenanted creation of its God", & this, later, was to be the protest of the arch-Romantic of our own century Lawrence, who avoided the problems of sciences, by claiming that the "… two ways of knowing, for man, are knowing in terms of apartness, which is mental, rational, scientific, & knowing in terms of togetherness, which is religious & poetic", & on these grounds announced triumphantly that the "universe isn't a machine after all. It's alive & kicking & in spite of the fact that man with his cleverness has discovered some of the habits of our dear old earth … the old demon isn't quite nabbed." Coleridge's preoccupation between a living whole or organism on the one hand & a mechanical juxtaposition of parts on the other, became the increasing preoccupation of the more sensitive of the Victorians. And in important ways he anticipated two fundamental answers of the age. Like the Tractarians he discarded all evidential support & laid the foundation of religion in the specific religious experience, in man's need for a God who comes to meet & to redeem him, & like Arnold or Kingsley he insisted that the alleged invulnerability of the bible was a dangerous & rigid superstition, untenable in the face of modern criticisms, & that the way to deal with criticism was not to offer blind resistance but to deepen one's understanding & see the spirit behind the words.

One of the two main challenges to Victorian belief came from the theory of historical relativism, especially in the works of Germans. So fundamental are these to an understanding of later Victorian thought, & especially as a formative influence on George Eliot that a survey of at least Strauss, Hennell & Feuerbach is necessary. In the C18 men asked of an opinion or belief "Is it true?" Nowadays we ask, "How did men come to take it as true?" We are more interested in tracing the history of an idea than in judging its goodness or badness. But a belief which has been historically explained, whose origins & growth have been traced, tends to lose its authority over the mind. Morley, one of those who, like Eliot, realized some of the implications of the "principle of relativity in historical judgement" said of it "The greatest intellectual conversion of this era, as Renan not any too widely put it, transformed the science of language into the history of languages; transformed the science of literature & philosophies into their histories; the science of the human mind into his history, not merely an analysis of the wheel-work & propelling forced[s] of the individual soul. In other words, the …. Substitution of becoming for being, the relative for the absolute, dynamic movement for domative immobility … (as Mark Patterson said) … what is important for us to know of any age, our own included, is not its peculiar opinions, but the complex elements of that moral feeling & character in which, as in their congenial soil, opinions grow." But it is worthwhile noticing that Morley did not take this to its logical conclusion. For him it <u>did</u> matter very much indeed which side one took in the great struggle between "truth" and "error", & it horrified him to realize that his own sort of "truth" might, on the same principle, be explained away as yet another "think-so". He agreed with Pope Paul's remark to the Council of Trent "that belief is the foundation of life, that good conduct only grows out of a right creed, & that errors of opinion may be more dangerous even than "Sin". A belief in <u>absolute</u> value, which George Eliot held to the last, marks the Victorians. When thinkers ceased to search for certitude, to accept relativity, we can say that the 'Victorian' age was over.

This historical revolution can be best studied in three books: Hennel's "Inquiry concerning the origin of Xianity" (1838), Strauss's "Life of Jesus" & Feuerbach's "Essence of Xianity". Hennel's book swept George Eliot off her feet, for it turned Jesus into merely a 'great man'. But Hennel is not out to show the Gospel writers as wilful impostors, his whole drift is to show how "naturally" & spontaneously the myths grew up. Strauss's book has been accused of "saving Xianity by turning it into an unchristian doctrine". For though he claims that he is "well aware that the essence of the Xian faith is perfectly independent of his criticism…", he finally identifies the 'substance' of Xianity with entirely human values. Man is the true 'Incarnation'; the world in him returns in reconcilement to God. For 'Christ', substitute 'Humanity', & you have the ultimate meaning of the great myth. Feuerbach took the process even further stating that "The divine being is nothing else than the human being, or rather the human nature purified, freed from the limits of the individual man, made objective – ie. contemplated & reversed as another, a distinct being. All the attributes of the divine nature are, therefore, attributes of the human nature." He attempts to show that "God" is an ideal substitute for the real world, a wish-fulfilling symbol, which we worship, because we find that easier & more satisfying than improving the real world.

Marx expressed these views as the basis of his dialectical materialism & they found musical utterance in the words of Swinburne's 'Hymn of Man'.

"Thou & I and he are not gods made men for a span,
But God, if a God there be, is the substance of men which is man.

…

Thou art smitten, thou God, thou art smitten; thy death is upon thee, O Lord.
And the love-song of earth as thou diest resound through the wind of her wings –
Glory to Man in the highest! For Man is the master of things."

Not everyone shared Swinburne's or Comte's joy, however!

It is recorded that when Charlotte Bronte had read the Atkinson-Martineau "Letters of the Laws of Man's Nature & Development" she exclaimed "If this be Truth, man or woman who beholds her can but curse the day he or she was born". Well-might the Victorians be horrified by the scientific discoveries of the time. It has been well said that "time was expanding & space contracting". While the laying of the Atlantic cable in 1865 & the yielding of up earth's most mysterious secret (when in 1856 Speke stood on the shores of Victoria Nyanza & saw the Nile pouring northward) made the earth smaller & less strange, growing full of the "light of common day"; men on the other hand found himself increasingly alone in a waste of years. In 1845 John William Burgon [a Worcester man] could sing of Petra as: "A rose red city, half as old as time". For, like most of the Early Victorians, he believed that time had begun less than 6,000 years ago. But in 1857 the 1st remains of Neanderthal man came to light & Darwin's publication of the "Origin of Species" in 1859 put the finishing touch to a movement which had started with Lyell's "Principles of Geology" in 1830 & the "Vestiges of Creation" by Chambers in 1844, which together completely overthrew the Mosaic cosmology, & took away for many the last refuge of the God of Wordsworth & the C18 – 'Nature'. After Darwin, no longer could a relation between science & morality be drawn. The theory of spontaneous "natural selection" seemed to substitute accident – or perhaps mechanism – for intelligent purpose in the world of nature. Sedgwick, once an ardent admirer of Darwin, wrote of him that he had "demoralized understanding" and had done his best to plunge humanity into a "lower grade of degradation".

From a conception of man as a special species, created in a day, & only some few thousand years old, the Victorian mind had to assimilate a picture of the earth as being inhabited by vermes some 450m years ago, jawless fishes some 400 million years, birds 140 million years, marsupials 80 million years & man as a late developer possibly less than half a million years ago. The shock to human dignity & conception of a benevolent providence, in whom all things 'work together for good' can be most clearly seen in the torture of 'In Memoriam'.

'Shall he….
Man, her last work, who seem'd so fair,

Such splendid purpose in his eyes,
Who roll'd the psalm to wintry skies,
Who built him fanes of fruitless prayer,

Who trusted God was love indeed
And love Creation's final law –
Tho' Nature, red in tooth & claw
With ravine, shriek'd against his creed –

Who loved, who suffer'd countless ills,
Who battled for the True, the Just,
Be blown about the desert dust?
Or seal'd within the iron hills?

No more...."

Many others could echo his desperate cry –

I falter where I firmly trod,
And falling with my weight of cares
Upon the great world's altar-stairs
That slope thro' darkness up to God..."

This struggle which Young calls the problem of the "standing of personality, the finite human personality, in an age of flux" was the central one of the age. How did the Victorians react to this double challenge, physical & spiritual? In the practical sphere an indication can be gained from a remark of G.M. Young. "On one side of it, Victorian history is the story of the English mind employing the energy imparted by Evangelical conviction to rid itself of the restraints which Evangelicism had laid on the senses & the intellect. But the Evangelical discipline, secularised as respectability, was the strongest binding force in a nation which without it might have broken up. "Sweet are the ties that bind" chanted a contemporary hymn, sweet indeed in an age when everything seemed to be in flux. Two of the most important of these ties were the Church & the family. In 1818 £1m had been granted for the building of new churches – as the only social measure in an age of unrest & incipient revolt. For a long time after the Revolutionary wars religious orthodoxy & the stability of society were held to be closely interrelated. Thomas Arnold was one of the many who saw the Church as foremost a moral institution – he called it a society "for the putting down of moral evil ... for edification, devotion, consolation & the like are ... means, not ends in themselves." Naturally he deplores the Oxford Movt as tragically irrelevant for in it, it seemed, the 'social character' or religion has been lost sight of, & the ministry has been corrupted into a priesthood. But as Victoria's reign progressed & alarm to some extent died, rigid orthodoxy was allowed to break-down. It dissolved under the influence of new doubts as well as under the relaxation of social pressure & the survey of 1851, showing that 7m could go to church, & that 5 million of these did not, & revealing that the bulk of the potentially most anarchic elements had not, for a long time, been touched by religion, finally made it clear that religion could no longer be used as 'social cement'.

As a final glimpse of the age no better picture could be obtained than a study of three of its central thinkers – Arnold, Tennyson, & George Eliot. All three were pre-occupied with the re-interpretation of the faith of their parents in the light of new scientific criticism – the problem voiced by Mark Rutherford "a childlike faith in the old creed is no longer possible, but it is equally impossible to surrender it" – or in Mathew Arnold's own words – At the present moment two things about the Xian religion must surely be clear to anybody with eyes in his head. One is, that men cannot do without it; the other, that they cannot do with it as it is." In intention they were optimistic, but in conclusion their message was one of sadness, though without bitterness, & resignation, without hopelessness. As Eliot has pointed out 'In Memoriam' is religious not because of its faith but because of its doubt. The melancholy beauty of Dover Beach, like 'In Memoriam' clothed in natural imagery, betrays the weariness of the later Victorian age:

> "…. …… the world, which seems
> To lie before us like a land of dreams,
> So various, so beautiful, so new,
> Hath neither joy, nor love, nor light,
> Nor certitude, nor peace, nor help for pain;
> And we are here as on a darkling plain
> Swept with confused alarms of struggle & flight,
> Where ignorant armies clash by night."

And lastly the 'Mercian Cybil' – George Eliot – who epitomizes the century, starting from evangelical Xianity, passing through doubt to a reinterpreted Christ & a religion of humanity: beginning with God, she ends in 'Duty'. In her life we may see the outstanding attempt to effect a synthesis between the new knowledge & the old & indispensable ethics. "The 'highest calling & ethic' is to do without opium, & live through all our pain with conscious, clear-eyed endurance" – she once wrote. She is an outstanding example of what Willey calls the new C19 phenomena – the religious temperament severed from the traditional objects of veneration, & the traditional intellectual formulations by that Zeitgeist. It was the attempt to turn from God to each other for help & sympathy. "Heaven help us! Said the old religion;" she once said "the new one, from its very lack of that faith, will teach us all the more to help one another." Like all true Victorians she still searched for certainty, for universal values & for absolute truths – because the old traditions were gone all the more reason to build up the new, but this time on an entirely human basis. "Pity & fairness" she once wrote, "embrace the utmost delicacies of the moral life". Like other Victorians she still believed that a cultural synthesis would be made which would harmonize apparently inconsistent truths & have absolute & not merely relative value.

"Oversimplification of the human personality" one of the descendents of a man who did much to shake the Victorian age to its foundations has warned us [in margin 'Aldous Huxley'] "is the original sin of the intellect" & if this attempt to find the Zeitgeist, the coherent thread which holds the years 1830-1880 together has led to overemphasis on the doubts & uncertainty of the age I refer the reader to the first paragraph again. But it does seem that a craving for certainty in an age of unprecedented change is the central core of the age. Young remarks that "Psychologists say that one of the characteristics of the child mind is the capacity for holding contradictory ideas simultaneously. Another I think, & one that lasts longer, is the craving for certainty. The child loves speculation, but when his meditations have issues in a question he wants definite answer[s]. We do not often think of the early Victorian age as primitive. But in many ways it was. It could hold with undisturbed conviction a religious & an economic faith which were incompatible, & it wanted to be sure…" This comparison to the growing child, if it is not presumption, seems valuable. Idealism, romanticism, bursts of self-confidence mixed with periods of morbid self-introspection & even a growing pre-occupation with the relationship of the individual to sex & to society & his concept of duty all seems to be characteristics of youth. Perhaps the change from this search for "ultimate truths" which Briggs describes as mid-Victorian, to a period of flirtation with every form of historical & moral relativism & above all by sheer indifference to the issues raised by both Huxley, Wilberforce, marks the waning of adolescence & a temporary compromise. Tho', as Young points out, man has a troglodyte mind & immediately sought an inerrant system of economics in Marxism, yet the change from absolutism to relativism seems to have been the achievement, if that is the right word for it, of the Victorian era. A change which had started long before & is defined in these words by Christopher Dawson.

"The Western mind has turned away from the contemplation of the absolute & eternal to the knowledge of the particular & the contingent. It has made man the measure of all things & has sought to emancipate human life from its dependence on the supernatural. Instead of the whole intellectual & social order being subordinate to spiritual principles, every activity has declared its independence, & we see politics, economics, since & art organising themselves as autonomous kingdoms which owe no allegiance to an higher power."

*

The other main area of work this term was my special subject. I had chosen to do Oliver Cromwell ('Commonwealth and Protectorate) and have a very thick file of papers related to this. The special feature of the special subject was that it gave us, for the first time, the opportunity to go in depth into original documents. In this case we used sets of Commonwealth and Protectorate papers, and I have several hundred pages of notes from the Clarke Papers, the Letters & Speeches of Oliver Cromwell, Burton's Diary, Thurloe on Anglo-Dutch Relations, Gardiner's Constitutional Documents, Guizot, the Somers Tracts, Ludlow's Memoirs, the Nicholas Papers, the Thurloe State Papers, 'The Case of the Army Truly Stated' from Wolfe's 'Leveller Manifestoes', etc. As well as this there were extensive notes from various secondary sources and lectures, some 155 pages of typed and handwritten notes on about 80 books and articles.

The subject, as I recall, was taught in a seminar with a dozen or so undergraduates. As yet I cannot recall who was our tutor. Each of us presented one essay at one of the seminars. Mine was on 'Financial and Commercial Problems & Policy under the Protectorate'. I remember getting really involved with this and feeling that I was discovering something new, making an original contribution to knowledge. The essay was nine pages (foolscap, handwritten), accompanied with seven diagrams. I seem to remember that it was commended, but there is no comment on it.

In preparation for our final exams, we were tested in two ways. One was a series of Gobbets, where we had to comment on extracts from original sources. I wrote about ten pages on various gobbets, and there are quite extensive notes at the bottom of each, though no mark, to indicate we had personal feedback on them. Either at the start or end of the term we had a set of collections. Here I did a little better than in my English history collections. For '"Cromwell .... Endeavoured to put the whole Baltick sea into the Swede's hands." Is Slingsby Bethel's criticism of Cromwell's policy in the Baltic justified?' I got a Beta plus. For 'Did the Protectorate enjoy the confidence and support of the commercial classes?' I received a Beta Alpha. For 'Does the expedition to the West Indies mark "the decline of the spiritual extasies [sic] of Puritanism and the rise of the mundane sprit"(Gardiner)? I got a Beta plus. And finally for 'How did finance affect the constitutional history of the Protectorate?' a Beta minus. There are quite a few comments on the papers and overall the mark was beta plus question mark plus.

Spring Term 1963

Perhaps not surprisingly, there is almost nothing for this term, either in terms of cards or other ephemera. I was obviously a hermit. There are not even society cards, religious calendars, U.N. or Oxford Union cards.

As far as entertainment was concerned, there is a programme and ticket for 'Noye's Fludde' at the University Church of St Mary the Virgin on Thursday January 24th (price 2/-) with all profits to Oxfam. Also programmes for 'The Voyage by Georges Schehade', and 'A Man for All Seasons' by Robert Bolt, both at the end of January at the Oxford Playhouse.

Nor are there the miscellaneous writings, poems, observations of this and that, which are scattered through previous years. The only exception is a poem in the style of e.e.cummings which is appended at the end of this chapter. In so far as I did have energy for non-work writing, it seems to have gone into a few letters to my parents and numerous letters to Penny.

The only other trace of my life during this period is in the cheque stubs for the term which indicate some of my expenditure.

22 Jan Battells Worcester College £10-8-0 [Battels were the standard charge for meals in College, so I was clearly eating my main meals there, rather than buying food and cooking for myself as I appeared to be doing in the winter term.]
27 Jan R.Martin (Boat Club) £1-10-0

15 Feb Exam fees £8
16 Feb £5

21 Feb Miss Norridge [rent] £12-10-0

1 March £2-10-0
20 March Self (26/- jeans) £7-0-0

1 April £10-0-0
9 April £10
21 April For Lodgings in Burford – Mrs Weir £5
22 April £10

*

Again the letters between Penny and I were numerous. However, though getting a place at York University for the following academic year, Penny was working at Harvey Nichols, so was somewhat less busy, and I was even busier coming up to my final exams, so the ratio of our writing changed. During the nearly four months of the Spring term and vacation, I wrote twenty-four letters and two post cards. Penny wrote some thirty-four letters. Mine tended to be longer, so probably the total words was roughly equal. I have pruned my letters considerably including only more general topics as the romantic aspects of the relationship have been amply covered before. I have omitted the numerous pieces of prose and poetry which were appended to each letter. I have also only selected some of Penny's letters.

Penny, uncle Richard and I drove down from the Lakes on January 10th. Penny went to London and I to Oxford.

The first letter from Penny was on January 11th [Friday]

Have you settled back into your Oxford rut? I have slipped back into my own through with less distress than the last time that I went up to Westmorland. Perhaps the darkness last night disguised the 'agony' of this turbulent city. Today it is bitterly cold, and the wind sucks at one's life blood. If only you were here to keep me warm – I miss you very much, and shall do so even more when I realise fully that I shall not be seeing you for a long time. Oh Tumnus, why do we have to work academically so hard? Why is this type of study the mainspring of progress nowadays?

You left the 'Gita' in the car yesterday, so I have sent it off today. It should reach you tomorrow or on Monday.

Richard and I reached London about 9.30 pm. R had drinks with us, before going on to R & A's. He seemed to size the flat and my mother up quite quickly – it was amusing to watch him. I don't think he liked being organised by mother, when she tried to persuade him to telephone R & A, to tell them he was on the way there. He is witness to the fact that she does not stutter.

I went round to Anne's today with the guitar. [My sister Anne] *I banged, crashed & walloped on the outer front-door for 10 mins but in vain. Nobody came. I shall have to write to Anne, and arrange to meet her somewhere. By the way, her postal address is S.W.5, not S.W.8 as you told me. Do change it in your address book, as letters otherwise take twice as long, as they wander around London.*

I am sending the 'Towers of Trebizond' as a token of my affection, and as a means of having a part of me with you, if only intellectually and spiritually. The days to come will be grey, without you, although I shall be comforted by my dreams of Peru.

Send my love to Erik, Mark & Ralph.

I am sorry if this letter is not very inspiring – I shall write a nicer letter on Sunday.

Love to you, my dearest heart, and look after yourself. Don't exhaust yourself by work, and do eat proper meals. I have been working out a food-hamper for you – not very exciting, but nourishing. I shall concoct an exciting meal when I come down to see you. (Ha-has, I expect on that weekend you will be able to find some money to take us out to meals).

I wrote to Penny on Sunday 13th January

Thank you very much darling for the "Towers.... " I will read it at the earliest opportunity. After grave meditation I have decided that you are ... an absolute poppet (the more so for sending on the 'Gita'). I have sent Richard 'Archie & Mehitabel' as a birthday present. I dipped into it before I sent it and it seemed delightful, I must buy another copy. So far I have spent £4-10 of the book token. Among the books I have bought are – an anthology of 'Rhadakrishnan' (editor of the Bhagavadgita & a foremost Philosopher), Axel's Castle; 'The Once & Future King'; Zorba the Greek; 'Doors of Perception & Heaven & Hell' – Huxley; Individualism Reconsidered & other essays – Riesman; 'The Rebel' – Camus; 'Women in Love'; and 'The desert Fathers' – Helen Waddell. I have embarked on several of them – but whenever I try to read the more serious I get a headache. I just can't pick up 'The Rebel' without my head splitting, perhaps it is my escapism & laziness setting up a reaction?

Today I have written my yearly letter to Ian, saying I may come over to Canada after finals. Earlier in the day I went to St Aldates & then read the Introduction to the Bhagavadgita. Since then I have been doing some 'Serious Thinking' on religious topics – perhaps the cause of the headache? Anyhow I meditated my way along the dazzling meadows to Binsey & had a Guinness & meat-pie in the 'Perch'. It brought back memories & made me feel lonelier than before.

The same day Penny wrote to me:

London Sunday [13th January]

You, who pass over the world lying in darkness, see its rampant agony and distress, and the cruelty which gains strength from night; through whose mind speed the words of Baudelaire;

C'est l'heure où les douleurs des malades s'agirissent.
La sombre nuit les prend à la gorge; ils finissent
Leur distineé et vont veis le gouffre commun;
You, who have seen the rosy dawn, and have flown back to direct the night on its passage into silver-sanctified day – are you well? Are you pleased with your progress? Are you HAPPY ??! Do you miss me? I miss you very much, and am longing for the time when I can next see you. I even felt like coming down yesterday. But don't worry – I shall not in future come down without due warning, or without being invited by you. Meanwhile, I shall keep the memory of you in my heart, until the fire is resuscitated by the sight of you. How sentimental, I sound, sweetheart, but I do mean it?

We have just been in the throes of an electricity power-cut… [description of and reflections on…; lecture by Marguerita Laski and publishing – quite lengthy;] … *I was reading last night some of Christina Rossetti's poetry. Crouched* [sic] *in beautiful terms, her whole theme is sad and tragic… I enclose a sonnet on 'Death', which is the sweetest end to a life of misery and sadness.*

Penny wrote again the next day, London, Monday Evening [14th January]

Thank you for your letter. It is now four days since I have seen you; I think we would lessen the agony of separation if we counted off, not the number of days since we last saw each other, but the number until we see each other again. O, when can it be? I miss you very much and am continually meditating upon the cruelty of Fate, which keeps us apart.

I am glad you received all my parcels. I had to send so many off on Friday that I am glad they reached their respective homes safely. I had sent some delicious cheese sent from Harrods to your grandparents – it was the first time I had ever tasted it, and I was very much inclined to take it home and eat it in a corner by myself. "When I grow rich / Said the Bells of Shoreditch" I shall buy some, with some shrimps and bring it down to Oxford. One day I hope to fulfil all these resolves, about purchases.

I am glad you have bought those books – I noticed 'The Once & future' was out in a paper-back. Read something light, if they are all too high-powered for your present state. I am reading 'Sir P. Sydney and the English Renaissance.' [discussion of] …

I received a sweet letter from Richard today thanking me for my card. He is almost like a guardian uncle – and I think I shall adopt him as this. I don't believe I ever met anyone quite like Richard, combining a gentle wit, with benevolence and kindness.

And she wrote again the next day, London, Tuesday [15th January]

How are you, dearest heart? I hope you are well, and able to lose consciousness thro' your work. I am missing you terribly, and am quite distracted from my History. I guess I shall have to throw myself into Clio's embrace, though I should prefer that it were yours.

I received another letter from Richard today thanking me for a book of verse. Can I therefore assume that you sent 'Archie' as a gift from me too? You are an absolute darling, and have "completely angled" me. I thought at first, that Richard did not know from whom the book came, supposed for some obscure reason, that I was the donor.

I also received a letter from York, asking me to an interview on 24th. This somewhat disarranges my plan of work; however I do hope that I get in.

The first letter from my mother in Assam is dated January 15th.

My dear Alan,

Hope you can raise your nose from the grindstone long enough to read this, as I imagine you will be back by your little electric logs with the tape recorder going and the typewriter tapping. Do hope it doesn't really feel like prison, these are still supposed to be the happiest days of your life don't forget! I'm sending a reply to the letter you copied out, not that I think it will be printed as the letter appeared a good while ago… I'm still wanting to tackle the Moguls, Robert Shaw has seven volumes on them which I was hoping he would be bringing over soon … We're waiting breathlessly for Lord Roseberry, send me all the cuttings on him wont you. I'm glad you got the new Tolkien which sounds wonderful from the reviews and snatches I've read, John is reading the Rings and is bringing them home with him for you. Daddy is deep in "Florence Nightingale" at the moment…

The Croppers party sounded fabulous, how do people afford these riots, perhaps by the time Anne "arrives" we shall be able to too. The other parties Fiona described sounded dull and typical, nothing ever seems to change….. What is Penny going to do now? How was Fiona looking, and Anne if you saw her? … Much love from us both – Mummy

Penny wrote the following day, Wednesday [16th January]

Are you well and keeping warm in your Hobbit-hole? (I have just realised the analogy between the characters and plot of C.S. Lewis's books and those of Tolkien's. Do you think that Mr T. would have been the hobbit, Frodo, effecting his task of overthrowing the Dark Lord of Mordor, and his followers, who had gradually penetrated into every sphere of society). I think a Hobbit might appreciate the enclosed on a cold snowy day though I should have preferred to send him something more exciting – perhaps one of the foods served by Sam Gamgee. It is snowing here in London, and the Zephyr winds are unusually sadistic. I expect the weather is the same in Oxford – so don't catch 'flu. I'm feeling FOUL (Why don't you like that word?) and am not sure what is imminent.

I received a charming letter from Anne today. She asked me to send her love to you. I was surprised how easily her style of writing flowed, considering her shyness. She thinks that necessity might force Felix[1] *and herself over every day for a meal. Poor Mr. Tumnus, I fear that what with Erik's, Richard's, Anne's, and Fiona's (forthcoming?) visits to us, you will be the last of the Macfarlane's to see the M lair, instead of the first. Do come down and see me soon. We should like to have you, and I am sure that you & I could keep out of my Mamma's way, if she need to do some very pressing office-work.*

My spirits have been roused considerably by writing this jovial letter, though I still feel somewhat medically groggy. I had been so depressed today because I was not with you, but now I am happier, though still missing you very much. It has helped to turn my thoughts away from my depression (sounds as if I have grown smaller!) and think of other topics…

PS. Please let me know if you don't have enough food – I hope this token will help out.

I wrote again to Penny on Thursday [17th January]:

I meant to write last night but got caught up in an argument with Mark on the nature of 'Satire' on which he is writing an essay. He wants to see my Essay on 'Victorianism' – after he has read it shall I send it on, since it is dedicated to you? …

Most of my friends have come back – Eric has been round for coffee several times & Paul came round today. Pam isn't back yet, so you can't come down for a little longer. We will have to start planning visits soon, at least that distracts one from the absence a little (as you can see I, too, am missing you very much.) But fortunately, especially with exams tomorrow [Collections I presume] *I don't have much time to think. Good luck in your exams, darling, surely this York interview will cut right into the middle of them? When do they begin so I can pray for you etc?*

I bought a few more books – another 'Don Marquis' to make up for the one I sent to Richard (have you read his article?) 'Archy's life of Mehitabel'; Totem & Taboo – Freud; 'Modern Man in Search of a soul' – Jung & "Notes towards definition of Culture' – Eliot, if only one had time to read them …!

Am just off to have chocolate with Ralph.

My next letter was on Tuesday evening, Worcester College [22nd January]

It is so bitterly cold here, if only we had each other. Sometimes I get really furious at myself for wasting the best years of my life swotting; but perhaps it won't all be wasted. I have done absolutely nothing of interest since you left. Eric comes to soup and toast every lunch time & this keeps me sane. Tonight I went to a mission in 5th week with Alec. Do write to him if you feel like it; and try to keep some time during that week free as I want you to meet John Bowker.

The poem I send is rather like 'Love guards the roses of your lips' … and carries the same image as Burn's 'Banks & Braes' ("But my fair luv' has stolen my rose – but, ah, he left the thorn with me"). But even in 'the

---

[1] Felicity, my godmother's daughter.

honey & the bee' there is a flippancy, & fancifulness & lack of real feeling which seperates [sic] it from the Metaphysicals & Elizabethans (for a background to the Metaphysical poets you must read 'C17 Background' Basil Willey – esp on Sir Thos Browne).

I wrote again on Sunday [27th January] Worcester College

I still miss you very much but am on the whole much more cheerful, and immersed in Existentialism (& in my spare time with Ernle, Nef etc). I have been to see Pam [St Clair; an American girl and part of a group of friends at the time] *etc several times & find it very relaxing. I went to a medieval mystery play on Thursday 'Noye's Fludde' – set to music by Benjamin Britten. It was delightful – especially the procession of animals (school-children) hopping & squeaking their way up to the Ark.*

Here, to give a flavour of the reciprocal letters, though this is an unusually long one, is part of the letter Penny wrote after she heard that she had been admitted to read history at York University.

Monday [28th January] London

I am so happy that I am [sic] scarcely write. I have just written to Sussex Univ. cancelling an interview I was to have there on Thursday, and also to Richard. He wrote another sweet letter to me, telling me about an article of his that the "Times" are publishing in the near future. What a darling uncle he is! He hopes that you are managing to keep warm and healthy in Oxford. He seems to appreciate Archie very much. I find it extremely funny – the sort of wry, semi-serious, throw-away stuff that I particularly like!

By the way, Robert's book, according to Angela, will not be published until Feb. 15th because of the snow. Poor Robert, it must be very frustrating. However, I noticed in the Lit. Supp. today that he is writing another book. "Europe: 1870-1914". Aylmer seems to admire him, and called him a very prolific writer.

Aylmer looks rather like Robert, and is the prototype of a young don – tall, slim, wears glasses, slightly vague, but a brilliant brain. He let me off quite lightly on the interview: he questioned a friend of mine very fiercely. He told me about all the museums and art galleries of York, and about the old Houses. King's Manor, where the interviews were held, was formerly the home of the President of the North…

Oh how glorious is York minster. I first saw it in a haze of late afternoon blue silver light, with the setting sun sending its beams onto the sand coloured towers. Inside the air was cool, and the atmosphere awe-spiring [sic]. On all sides, the windows stretched upwards like coloured stallegnites (?), and I could only distinguish the far end of the minster by a coloured veil of light…

I liked the city of York and its people. I went into a restaurant called Betty's, where every strata of York society were having tea … Oh, isn't it wonderful I've got there; and having Aylmer almost to myself, since very few student[s] are doing History, without any appendices. In some ways, however, I regret giving up my ambition of going to Oxford, which I have virtually done, by doing so little work for the examinations… Also I don't think York will ever have a library to compare with the Bodleian, although it has a large collection of virtually untouched medieval manuscripts, ready for the historical research.

But enough of me, sweetheart, please don't be unhappy. I wish I could be with you more to cheer you up, but so far this has been impossible. You must go around to Pam – she's just like a tonic, good for both you and me (I sent 'A Little Princess' to Carrie & to her, via Paul – I hope they got it). Also, go out sometimes with Erik – he, too, is an extrovert character, and has very few, or no, complexes. Certainly, leave Lord S[udeley] alone – I'm most indignant that he dared to analyse you – the priviledge of analysis is only for you & me. Lord S. may be outwardly very beautiful, but I'm sure he has a larger percentage of grime and carbon soot, of which man is composed, than the rest of us.

I hope you were not offended by my failure to write. I felt so depressed over the weekend, that I do not think I could have written a coherent letter. But, dearest heart, I thought of you a great deal – you and York Univ – rivalled for my thoughts – St Anne's did not have a look in. I miss you very much, and am longing to see you. Do let me know the dates of Pam's opera, and of the mission – I'm too lazy to work out when 4th or 5th week actual falls.

Dearest heart, I hope your introduction to Dick's [Richard Smethurst] *talk went off successfully. I hope you weren't too nervous. Was Dick interesting? Write and tell me what he said. Enjoy tomorrow's party, and send my love to Erik.*

I am sending an article from the Listener on Marilyn Monroe…
Please darling, be happier. I know how depressing work can be, but it makes me very unhappy that you feel so wretched. I love you very much and any time that you want to see me, either come up to London, or ask me to come down – in the future I'll be able to afford both money and time.

Will you type out the essay on Victorianism, for me to collect when I come to Oxford. Aylmer seemed to stress the importance of Victorian History in my interview.

I'm also sending you some variations on the poem you sent me. Janet is studying Wyatt for A-level, and together we tried to find as many versions as possible…

The next letter from my mother was dated Jan 29th:

My dear Alan,

Thank you for a letter which I tore open the wrong way… Money first to get it over – I have told the bank to transfer £30 to your account as soon as our money gets home at the beginning of Feb, and will send another £30 in March. I hope this will see you through the next couple of months, £4.10 doesn't seem much to live on a week and you'll need lots of brain building food this next few months. Hows the Guinness going have you acquired a taste for it? We do not want this paid back out of your grant, you will need every penny of that I'm sure, our financial situation is slowly but steadily improving, the chief difficulty now is the restrictions the Indian government have put on sending it home.

I think the Canada and South America idea sounds wonderful, we will help with your fare of course, in fact could probably manage it all by the autumn. I should let the question of your career ride until after the results of your exam come through as a lot depends on what sort of degree you get. The Bhagavad Gita has some wise things to say about work, Work is Worship is one of its main themes in fact. I'm glad it finally arrived. I'm into Tawney now and find it very interesting, specially with the little bit of "O" level knowledge I still retain, the problem of how to reconcile one's religion with the rat race is almost impossible to resolve. One can see the enormous attraction of the monastic life, and all the Indian saints who spent their lives sitting under trees really never had it so easy.

Here we are still without rain and everything is beginning to look parched…. [news of Assam] …I'm sorry to say I still haven't got down to anything definite, I'm doing quite a bit of drawing nowadays which I find less demanding than writing, I suppose because I know I'm not much good and my standards are lower.

I wonder what Penny is going to do. She seems to have gone down very well with the A.P's [Aged Parents] except they thought how very Frail – but I think that transparent look is probably misleading. Anne seems to be settled and I hope will manage to spend a day with you if the weather allows. … Don't work too hard, please – it's only one spring when you will be twenty one!

Much love from us both, Mummy

My next letter to Penny was headed Wednesday [30 January] – 'brillig time' Worcester College

Thank you for your long and ecstatic letter – all my friends join me in sending their congratulations – especially Ralph, Mark, Erik & Paul (who says he will tell you all about York & also wants to use you so that he can meet Aylmer). It really is wonderful & I'm sure you'll never regret going to York. It has also taken a weight off my mind as I've always been certain that you'd enjoy & profit from university life more than almost anyone else I know. When you write tell me more about your plans between now & October; when you get your job etc. Pam's play is next week (3rd week) & if you can come down on the Saturday let me know & I will book for it. As usual I am torn between a desire to see you and worry that I'm not doing enough work (and also memories of the agonies of parting).

I remember York minster, and many of the other wonders of the city from my several visits. You presumably remember Paul lives there? Do you know anything about the History syllabus – organization of the University etc? (I believe it's on Oxbridge lines – but what, apart from a tutorial system, does that mean?)

… I seem to be busier than ever & for a change have got something to talk about – apart from my work. But all the same I am taking your advice and going to see Pam. She is rehearsing non-stop for the 'Opera', but promises to be in this evening. She thanked you (thro me) very much indeed for 'The little princess' – but is too vague to write. I met Charles the other evening & liked him very much, especially as he kept telling me how sensible I was finding someone as clever & nice as you (and refusing to be disillusioned when I told him the

truth about you – aren't I mean!). Tomorrow evening we have Christopher Hill talking on 'C17 women' in the college society.

The introduction to the speaker at the 'Woodruffe' went off fine. It wasn't Dick, but a Mr Thompson, chief 'Probation Officer' for Oxford. He was one of the best-informed and amusing speakers I have ever heard. He had wanted to be an actor when younger & retained a wonderful flair for impersonation & mimicry. He told stories of the cases he had met (Craig & Bentley were two of his customers) & his impersonations of the 'Colonel bloodshots' who wrote 'flog-them, hang-them, brand-them…' letters to the Daily Telegraph, or of simpering land-ladies & even sluttish prostitutes, were superb. If I can't decide what else to do I might well go into the probation service because it might be the best way of employing the few gifts I have (i.e. ability to strike up a natural personal relationship). But my thoughts have reverted to the population question & I enclose an excerpt from an article. It is so calmly stated and so horrifying that I can't really assimilate the untold misery which will result from the increases. One has always to convert such terms into human lives and imagine the disease, hunger and agony which will ensue. And now to show my <u>complete</u> lack of any feeling such problems, I must reveal that I went to a wonderful dinner last night – Eriks party. (he thanks you for the card).

We had sherry first in Peter Lee's brother's room (you remember Peter? The only one you liked at that 'hearty' party) and then dinner in the place where the jazz band played at the winter dance. It was a sumptuous meal, with oysters, duck, raspberries & a constant flow of wine & then champagne & port! Afterwards we retired to our previous room & for three hours talked & played party-games, and consumed cigars & liqueurs. I left feeling gloriously happy. But am back in the grip of reality, sadly.
My essay on 'Victorianism' is typed and ready for you whenever you want it.
P.S. Could you send the 'population article' back soon?

Penny's next letter to me is from London, Friday [1st February].

I hail thee, my dearest Tumnus, in all your variety – Mister, Hon, K.C.B.V.C, M.A (failed Oxon), Bluebeard, Philanthropist…. Etc etc. neurotic: diagnosed 'Oedipus' complex and sexual schizophrenic… Population Officer – are all these facets of your nature happy? I am glad you are no longer depressed – some of your past letters have seemed as if you were completely bored with your work, but perhaps I have surmised wrongly. I am still feeling fairly ecstatic and longing to start all the reading, that I have postponed for such a time. I have just started again Malcolm Lowry's 'Under the Volcano' and this time I plan to finish it.

I tackled the St Anne's papers in a carefree and careless manner, and consequently have not done too well. However, it does not really matter….

York is going to be similar to Oxford, not only because of tutorial but also because students will be grouped in Colleges, for lodging and/or teaching …

I should like to come to Pam's play, but I don't know if either your time or my money can be afforded for both the play and the mission. It all depends on whether intellectual or spiritual edification is preferable. Perhaps the latter I think, but let me know. But, surely, I don't interrupt your work that much?

I am just dashing off to Harvey Nichols about the job …. [University entrance…] *All these worries must seem to be something of the past for you – though I could not have managed without your sympathy.*

What a superb idea that you should become a probation officer! I thought, anyway, that you might do that, although still like you to work in some remote Asian village on the population problem. Do send me a synthesis of what Mr Thompson said – I should be most interested.

My next letter to Penny was on Sunday [3rd February] Worcester College

I have had an exhausting week since I wrote. Already I had been out two evenings then I went to hear Christopher Hill on Thursday. He was a poppet, tho' rather ferociously attacked by my tutor. The next day I went to the Ford Lecture (Douglas) and there, afterwards, as I was coming out, met Hill & summoned up the courage to say 'Hullo, Mr Hill, how did you enjoy it?' and had a short chat about the terrors of giving the Ford lectures.

The next evening, Friday, I went on Pam's suggestion (with her) to 'A man for all seasons' which was fabulous. The author – Robert Boult [sic] *– was there & gave a short talk afterwards. Sir Thomas is now elevated to my list of heroes & I would like to write a book of case-studies of those who have been killed because they made their age uncomfortable – Socrates, Jesus, More, Ghandi among others. I will tell you all about it when you come down.*

Today I went skating & fell flat (deservedly) trying to show off to some girls. Goodness, don't I sound 'busy'! But my thoughts have been even busier – on tolerance, hate, God, lust, torture & all the usual themes & including the most usual of them – you my sweetie. But enough drivel for now. Look after yourself poppet & come down if you can…

My mother wrote again a week later, on February 6th.

My dear Alan,

…. Thank you for yours, I'm glad you aren't working yourself silly, I should think the time has come to start to digest all the vast files of information you have amassed hasn't it? I am deep in Tawney now and find it quite fascinating, have your read it? The central problem is the one you're facing now in thinking of your future, when does money-making become avarice, when does "enterprise" end and greed begin – and the book deals with the thoughts of the Church & the reformers on the subject. I simply cant come to any conclusions. The fact is that for oneself poverty (as if I've never been really poor, but relatively speaking) means nothing, but money does buy the things one would like for ones children.

This was driven home when Granny wrote the other day saying we were being very unfair on you to keep you so financially insecure. I'm afraid I was very cross and wrote back rather nastily, which I'm regretting, but it was just another dig at Daddy who thinks of practically nothing else but how to get money home – the reason for my crossness too was partly that I knew she was right and that you don't any of you have enough. And yet – in Calcutta I felt that every penny we earned should go towards trying to alleviate in some tiny way the terrifying misery of three quarters of the population. What to do? In my case just muddle & drift on getting psychotic headaches & tired feelings from submerged guilt complexes about you & the starving children of Calcutta I suppose – but in yours a life of helping would probably be possible. I still think a year or two's travel would be excellent, during which you might find a particular place or people you would like to settle down with – and then a course in social organisation to fit you for the practical side. Or you might like to do it the other way round. You would get a grant to cover it at a provincial university I'm sure, I'm always seeing them advertised. Anne seems to be working like several slaves & then wants to go abroad…

Here we have a grey day at last & a few drops of rain… [news of Assam] … I've had my historical sense reawakened by Tawney. I'm not thinking in terms of writing a book for publication, just want to get "involved" in a period and learn some Indian history. I did try Assamese history on "History To-day" but they weren't interested though they wrote a very nice letter saying they enjoyed the article. Do hope the money has arrived, Richard says he'll help over temporary shortages & I'd rather you didn't even discuss the subject with Granny… Much love – Mummy

My next letter to Penny is from Worcester College [Thursday 7th February]

… I am in a mood of rebellion, and consequently haven't done much work this week. I went to a lecture this morning by Isaiah Berlin which was quite interesting & amusing. Going to lectures is a new craze I have.

For the rest of them I have been talking to people – principally to Peter G[oodden] & a neurotic friend from St J's who has just had an awful break with his girlfriend. I went to see Elvis (Girls Girls GIRLS!) on Tuesday with him which he enjoyed. Pam's play, for which I have tickets, appears to be going well. If you come before 4.0 bring a little reading as I must do a little myself.

I went to talk to Alec[1] last night about career, population etc – but with no appreciable result.

The frequent references to Pam in the letters above, are to Pam St Claire who was part of the circle of vivacious girls to whom I had been introduced by Julie. I remember her as a striking blond American, which is confirmed by a photograph I have of her holding a baby, presumably Julie's first son, some years later. She was, among other things, keen on theatre and there are a number of mentions of an opera she was producing in Oxford. A typed card from her with the date stamp, Oxford 6 February 1963, refers to this and to Penny's present of a book.

---

[1] Rev. Alec Graham, chaplain of Worcester

Dear Magic-Maker!

Missing you; come backstage after the Orgy. And then for coffee, etc., and bring that delicious girlette. [Penny] Is she coming for the week-end? Will she want a bed? The method in the madness of this scrawl is to wit: I need her surname, please, so I can thank her for that adorable book. If you can provide me with same haste-post-haste I will have time to re-enforce my invitation for the week-end and congratulate her on York, etc. Do let me know what's going on, how you are, when you are coming. I am in an absolute flap, tonight being firs performance. But I am eager to see lil' you always, and hope you will surprise me one of these eves. Won't be back before about midnight due to perfs. But COME.

Much love, P

My next brief note to Penny was on Monday evening [11th February] Worcester College:

... Oh if only this beastly weather went & spring came I might (and my friends in general) might feel more cheerful. If you ever wonder of a book to get me I would like any of the following –

'The dark Sun' – Hough (Pelican)

'Report from Palermo' – Dolci (if in paper-back)

'To feed the Hungry – Dolci

My mother wrote on Tuesday 12th February from Cherideo.

My dear Alan,

Now I have a form[1] *I've lost my typewriter, it finally got too temperamental for words & has been removed to Sibsager for treatment which will take anything up to six moths. Nothing from you this week but we don't expect too many letters now, just hope the money has arrived..... I spent a bad night & slept a good deal of yesterday but in between read Florence Nightingale so now I no longer want to write History but rush off and nurse the sick under appalling conditions – I'm sure it is the sign of a very weak character to be so swayed by everything you read. I* <u>*will*</u> *study the Moguls though, if I can get the books. ... John Lampitt left yesterday, we shall miss him very much, he's taking "The Rings" back with him for you. I've told Anne & Felicity to visit you one Sunday, they went to Cambridge & loved it. I think they're probably a bit lonely poor pets & have very little money to spend on entertaining themselves. Perhaps Penny could go with them & between you you could show them the sights, do hope Penny will be successful in one of her efforts to get a place.*

Much love from us both,

Mummy

Penny wrote again on Wednesday [13th February] London:

Thank you very much for Raleigh's poems. I was so pleased to receive it, for before I have had only brief looks into Janet's copy. I am sorry that I was unable to send you the book on Lawrence, but I have been in bed with flu for the past two days. Hence the token of my own making. I am afraid that I am still feeling very groggy, so this letter will be more incoherent, and less effusive than usual. By staying in bed, however, I have been able finally to finish 'the Lord of the Ring'. I now understand the allegory behind it, but will explain it when I see you, though I suppose you will know it already. O darling Tumnus, this letter must be very depressing and really I ought not to send it to you; but I feel like writing, so you must bear with me. Actually all I really want is sympathy, so please send me a long & jolly letter soon.

What a marvellous person Danilo Dolci is! Did you hear the programme last night on his recent fast, carried out last Sept to achieve the building of a dam in Sicily? I should love to go and see him when I go to Italy. Why don't you join the Brit organisation which sends out volunteers to help him in Sicily? I suddenly thought last night of doing this, if I don't go to Perugia.

Pam doesn't know when she is leaving Oxford, but she will definitely have gone by the end of the month. Oxford is going to seem very quiet without her.

---

[1] Air-letter form.

Tumnus, I believe Spring is coming! The air seemed pure & gentle this afternoon, and the sun made delicate tracings on the bedroom wall. I hope you will be wondrously happy now, dearest Tumnus, and may you strive towards your ideals, and your spirit towards its goal.

Have a joyful Feb. 14th and pense à moi quelequefois.

My next letter to Penny is from 3, Southmoor Road, Oxford [Pam's house?] [Thursday 14th February]:

I mustn't write much as I have to catch the late post. Pam arrived back at lunch today – she seems a little relaxed. I have been to one of Huddleston's talks so far – pretty good – on the problem of how to deal with property in this unequal world: I am coming to the conclusion that there are only two answers – either to compromise or be completely dedicated & follow Jesus' suggestions to the 'Rich Young Man', but whether I have the courage to give all up as a sacrifice I doubt. I enclose a poem which is a poor echo – as you will notice – of 'Intimations' & some of "4 Quartets" – a rhapsody on 'lost innocence' (please return sometime), weep with me darling! But I am happy – are you darling?

My next letter to Penny is on Friday [15th February] Worcester College:

I have been as busy as ever – doing nothing very important, writing essays etc. The weather is miserable – depressing everyone, even the buoyant Mr Tumnus sometimes.
He was even more depressed when he had a long talk with an ex-tutoress, Lady Clay, who has given him a lovely bowl of narcissi (white) but largely because she wanted to have someone around for her to pour out all her griefs on. I will tell you about the conversation…

I went to tea with 'F' (Lord Franks) today – borrowed a suit from Ralph. Huddleston is tremendous.

My next letter is on Sunday [17th February]

Absolutely recovered from your cold/flu I hope darling. It has been going around Oxford too; I dropped in on Peter this afternoon and he was in bed with a temperature. I expect you will be back selling your mink bathing costumes again at H.N.!

I had a letter from Granny yesterday, Jummy [Next door neighbour] *died on Wednesday/Thursday. I am just about to write to Beryl. I'm sure she would like to hear from you (Mrs Buckmaster, Field Head) if you feel like writing. I don't know really how one should write – perhaps I will send a Donne sonnet. Death is so strange, so distant that it only makes one feel stunned, very small, very unable to give easy comfort – especially in this case where, to use the horrible phrase, it was a "merciful release". The tragic thing is that it brings out all one's own selfishness, one's fear and realization that one cannot enter into another's sufferings. We both echo Donne "it tolls for thee" and realize (as you quoted) that we are unable to enter other's; each other person is a little glass case into which we peer with goggling eyes. But enough; I have been pondering on these subjects for a few days & don't know any answers.*

My next letter is on 22nd February, Worcester College

Huddlestone was tremendous & you will be especially glad to hear that he read quotes from the 'Towers of Trebizond'; three times and said it was one of his favourite books – I must read it sometime. With the last of my book-tokens I have bought "The Human Condition" Miss Arendt; "The Lonely Crowd" & "The Poverty of Historicism" – Popper. I must try to read them, but everyday the work grows more hectic.
… Robert's book does seem to have done well – and I have written to congratulate him.
Do get in touch with Annie if you can, I'm sure she'd like to see you & meet people thro' you. My mother is convinced she is lonely.

The next letter from my mother is on the same date [Friday 22nd February]:

My dear Alan,

A nice long cheerful letter from you which bucked us up no end, I had had a depressing week, not being very well and then having to watch my poor old cat die and also being worried about the money not getting home. However I feel better now and have heard from the bank and got over the first misery that an animal's death always inflicts. We will wire the next lot of money home so that it'll get there earlier in the month.

I was delighted to hear about Penny, a lovely city [York] to study in, perhaps not quite as lovely as Oxford but much better than any other provincial university. Will she be reading History or English? Anne said she was very well, looking much better than in the summer, and earning vast sums writing figures on price tags, really one wonders why one bothers to spend money on giving ones daughters a "training"! …

I've taken up my study of Assamese again and am starting lessons with the wife of our assistant next week… I've been doing quite a lot of history reading too, finishing Fisher as Anne and I stopped with a bang at the end of the Thirty Years War, and also Assamese history. It is annoying that here where I have the time to study, I cant get hold of any books. My Family Planning has also been frustrated for various reasons…

I'm glad you are able to slack off a little in your work, I think your plans for a years travel and then a social science course are excellent, though it means that we shant see you when we come home next year which is rather an awful thought. Unless we come home in the autumn for a winter leave which we are seriously thinking of doing. … Anyway you must make your plans as you think best and go for guidance to your friends and tutors because obviously they're much more in a position to help you.

I agree with Father Huddleston of course, but alas and alack the spirit that took missionaries to difficult and dangerous corners of the world was so often militant, intolerant and arrogant that the good that they did was cancelled out. It would be an interesting subject for study actually, missionary work in India or Africa, and its exact impact for good or bad. The Jesuits wrote vastly as far back as Akbars day & as they were always the first on the scene everywhere it would be fascinating. Another subject that intrigues me is the East India Co. but I shall have to leave all these studies till I get home & can ransack the India Office Files.

Wonder how Roseberry has fared? Granny just said she "liked" it but I hope the critics are more enthusiastic. … are you drinking your Guinness? Much love – Mummy

One of the three surviving letters to my parents for this period from me is from Worcester College on Sunday [24th February]

Dear Mummy and Daddy,

Thank you very much for your letter. I enclose a few reviews of Robert's book – as you can see it seems to have been another hit (as Granny will probably have told you!), despite some catty remarks about Fowler's Usage from Mortimer. When I asked for a copy (to look at!) at Blackwells they said that they had sold out and had had to send for another batch.

Having just looked up in my little book I find that it is your 22nd wedding anniversary on March 1st – many congratulations. I only wish I could send you more than a few newspaper cuttings and my oft-repeated professions of filial devotion (and a spring crocus). It is also 'Mothering Sunday' soon. Oh dear. All I can send is my especial love and affection to you both and remind you how wonderful you have been to all three of us. I will dedicate my first book to you, rather than to any old Earl or venerable statesman! [Which I did. A.M.] I owe you everything (including my life), and although I sometimes feel like digging a hole in the ice and laying my bones among the fishes and sea-fungi, yet it has been the best upbringing one could have. (& today is a beautiful spring day)

You will have heard of Jummy's death, perhaps I have already written since it happened. Anyhow Beryl is going to stay on in the Lakes. Poor thing. I wish I could go up North, to see if I could help; but it looks as if I shall have to stay up at Oxford all the vacation – with a brief spell in London and perhaps a short hike over the Cotswolds.

I have written to the girls inviting them down to Oxford one Sunday, alternatively I will go up to London and take them out. By the way, the money arrived safely, thank you.

It has continued very cold. Every morning it snows thinly, all day the snow melts and the roads are brown, gritty and slushy. By evening there is no snow left and it freezes – and starts snowing again! I have been skating quite a lot; when I feel my brain is going to explode, I go down to the Lake and try to learn how to skate backwards. Today I intend to go down for an hour to Port Meadow; I'm told there's an ice-yacht down there.

Last night I went to 'Mon Oncle' with Jacques Tati. It was delightful, with much boisterous French slapstick, but an element of sadness as well. It fell over backwards trying not to be satirical – for it was about the difference between those who had little money & a family with all the modern household gadgets – which of course all erupted or broke down. The film with it was about the Riviera and I nearly rushed straight to the travel agency and set out for the sun-shaded beaches and summer coolness of the olive groves.

Look after yourselves, I do hope Mummy won't get any more bilious attacks.

All my love, Alan

The next letter is to Penny on Sunday on the same day as my letter to my parents Worcester College

I have been living in a shadow for the last few days, and even my communion this morning was lifeless and dead. I felt the blood and body sink traceless in my arid soul and no new hope or thankfulness sprang up from the waste. But from the above lyrical outburst you can see that I have suffered a 'sea-change'. This is the result of going out, skating and walking, on a warm, almost voluptuous, blue day, when one can almost feel the young shoots being sucked with a popping sound from the hard earth, and can imagine the trees spreading their cold, bony, hands to the warmth of the Sun. For this reason I have included a very famous piece of Spring poetry, which is eminently evocative, breathless with the whispered incantations of pagan ritual [Swinburne – 'When the hounds of spring'] – *Sorry, my words flow on heedless of all grammatical rules. But I feel so happy. If only you were hear to share it. Perhaps it will be nice next Sunday & we can go for a long walk, and perhaps there might be snowdrops?*

Tell me if you can think of anything which ought to be done about Pam's party. Otherwise I will leave everything until you come down.

I went to a delightful film yesterday – 'Mon Oncle' – full of laughter, Paris, and quiet good-humour. Doesn't the sun make all the difference! I envy you going to Perugia.

I must rush off to the hospital [For my Christian visiting and guitar playing.]

Penny wrote again on Monday [25th February]:

How are you sweetheart? Is Spring really coming to Oxford? How wonderful! I am longing to see snowdrops and bluebells, especially along the lanes and in the woods around Binsey Church. I hope we shall be able to go for a walk on Sunday, and to penetrate the first diaphanous veil of Spring. Roll on the weekend, when I can be enfolded in your embraces.

Your two sisters seem to be painting London red. Fiona and a couple of friends came down on Thurs to see several art collections. On Saturday, together with Anne and Felix we all went to see 'My Fair Lady.' We enjoyed the choreography, production and stage sets, but the show seemed to lack "punch'.... Yesterday Anne & Felix spent the day with us. We enjoyed having them so much. Mamma liked them both immensely and they seemed to get on with her very well. I'll try to meet them again tomorrow, and possibly take them over to Janet's... Don't do anything about Pam's party, except to invite people casually... Love to you, dearest heart. I adore you very much. Look after yourself. I'll write properly tomorrow.

Penny wrote, as promised, again the following day, Tuesday [26th February]

Are you keeping well, my sweeting? Please be fit for the weekend, although I should love to nurse you back to health. I am feeling somewhat susceptible, both to love-charms and ailments of sickness...

I have sent some very incoherent, muddled and depressing letters to you. I am sorry about this. Exiguences always seemed to occur, whenever I sat down to write to you, which prevented me from writing other than a 'scraggly' note. Also, I have been too tired to contemplate on the ways of the world, or to reciprocate to your recent wisdom & philosophies. I sometimes feel incapable of reading novels. I must write to Alec soon; but it needs some preparation, so please don't arrange for me to see him this weekend. I wonder if I am being a coward about reconciling myself to the Church. Perhaps only very lazy about thinking seriously. Sometimes the desire to comprehend wells up from every limb, and body and mind unite in a sensitivity to the distress and agony of mankind. But all too soon, this surge fades, like a mighty wave, whose strength disperses as it rolls across the eternal length of golden but arid sand.

I have decided to come down on Friday evening since I have been given Saturday morning off. It is far better that I am around in Oxford on Sat morning, if I am going to arrange this party. Anyway, I want to make the 'Grand Tour' of all my friends in the morning... Don't meet me on Friday evening, if you have 'tuts' etc. I promise I won't disturb you, until Sat. afternoon. (I'll try hard to keep my promise). Also can you invite Erik

over to coffee after lunch on Sat? Will you ask him to bring his car, too, as I want him to help me carry some food?
[other news*] … Afterwards I am meeting Fiona for coffee, until her coach leaves for Manchester at 11.30 p.m.…*

the poem I include comes from a Penguin edition of Durrell's, Jenning's & R.S. Thomas' poetry, which I have just acquired. The poetess speaks of the purity of birth…. Etc. [description] [The poem is attached. Elizabeth Jennings. 'For a Child Born Dead'] …
Now I must flee, reluctantly, from thoughts of you into the chaotic & clamorous world of H.N. Don't worry, sweetheart, I won't be contaminated. …

The next letter to Penny is on 27th February, Wednesday:

Thank you for your two letters. How are you my poppet? Enjoying the wonderful weather we are having down here I hope. Today is the third blue, bright, thrushes' egg day full of the quacking of ducks and bird-song, & just as I write the humming clap of some swans taking off from the canal behind me drowns the shunting of trains for a moment. As you will have guessed I am writing from the gardens, sitting on one of the edging-stones to the Lake with my feet on the ice and the sun slanting down through the bare trees onto the remnants of the snow and onto the long, fine willow hairs which will soon burst with green and then white. There are little shiny birds on the chestnut above me. Lady Clay has told me of a whole list of places where we may find snowdrops – one of them a "deserted village" with the snow-drops growing in the burnt-out manor house. I pray that it may be fine when you come down. I have a 'tute' on Friday evening from 6-7.30 but if you arrive after that let me know. Otherwise come to my room & we can do something in the evening. Would you like to go to Othello? (though it may be booked-up).

I'm so glad you have seen the 'girls'. I had a letter from Anne this morning. She obviously loved her visit to the 'M' household – and would like to come down here – but seems to prefer the idea of coming down with you. Perhaps the last week-end of term (17th?) you might make a joint expedition down. Give them my love if you see them.

This is going to be another short & boring letter. But I will see you soon. Till then this carries all my love and affection to you dearest heart.

Penny wrote again from London, Thursday [28th February]

Thank [you] for your letter – full of joy and vernal ecstasy [sic]. I shall love being in Oxford in early Spring, although London is beautiful when the sunlight filters thro' the silky mist over the parks.

I had lunch today with Annie Felix and Julie Wilcox. Annie really is a darling. Mamma said she wanted to hug her all the time; Annie seemed to get on very well with Mamma, but then, Annie is appreciated by everyone.

Sweetheart, altho' I should like to come to Othello, or go to some flics, I won't be down until about between 8.30 pm or 8.45 (The coach leaves London at 6.00 and the journey time varies from 2 ½ and 2 ¾ hrs). Sweetest, can you meet me, if possible, as I am bound to be embracing countless parcels. 25 hours till I see you again – they will pass so slowly,

My mother wrote again on March 2nd:

My dear Alan,

Thank you for your letter with the cuttings and the crocus which is taking a place of honour on the mantelpiece. I have written to Robert, all the reviews were marvellous (though of course you and I could do better!) and lets hope he will make a nice lot of money, though it seems a terrible price. Thank you for the anniversary wishes too, I must say it doesn't feel like 22 years and yet in other ways I cant remember a time when I wasn't married. We bought a bottle of champagne, had a long look at it, and then sent it back – it was Rs 72. Our only celebration was to take the dogs out tiger hunting after dinner, a beautiful moonlight night but no tigers…

By the way, please thank Penny for her very nice letter which I will answer very soon, I hope getting to York University wont mean we'll Lose her. I got a long letter from Beryl before Jummy died, written very small and rather vague, about you and Penny and then (as I thought) "but now he is in the hands of a woman of 28, however he has a sheep dog puppy which will perhaps win". Couldn't imagine how you could be fitting women of 28 or sheep dog puppies into your present framework but I had missed out a line and it was Martin she was talking about...

I haven't heard from Granny since my sharp letter, not even about Robert, so violent um[brage] *was obviously taken but really its so peaceful not getting her letters. I think you're probably right not to pick yourself and all your files up and go home for Easter but I hope you will at least spend your week-ends walking or boating.*

Wonder if you saw Fiona who was in London I believe, why I can't imagine. Hope F & A managed to come down, they're obviously lonely poor dears. Much love from us both, Mummy

Penny wrote to me from London, Monday [4th March]

This is just a short note to rouse you from the possible depression of starting your work again. I have just held an ecstatic telephone call with Pam – She is in a very happy and joyful mood; do try and see her, when she comes up to Oxford next weekend... She sends her love to you, and thanks you for a wonderful party. Tumnus, it really was terrific; I was only upset that the pxnxch went so quickly.

I have also spoken to Annie this evening and told them the arrangements about coming down. I rang up Paddington Stn and Victorian Coach Stn; the travel and fare situation on Sundays is this: the first train for Oxford leaves London at 10.00 and arrives c. 11.30, and the fare is 16/- day return; the first coach leaves at 9.00 and arrives also at 11.30, but the fare is only 8/9 day return. I think, therefore, that the coach is best all round. Don't worry about sending their fares; Annie was even offering to give you some money. Apparently your grandmother has sent her some extra money thus I thought I ought to tell her about the financial crisis between your parents and your grandmother. Was that O.K? It prevented, I think, further difficulties, because Annie has now completely rephrased a letter she was about to send to your grandma. <u>Please</u> borrow, or have, some money from me if you want it. This letter has helped to clear the dreadful depression that I have suffered throughout today. I was very tired, and hated the noise, insincerity, brashness, crudity and lack of understanding & compassion which, together with the stuffy air, pervades H.N.

My next letter to Penny is on Tuesday [5th March] Worcester College

... You will know how much I enjoyed seeing you over the week-end. I am only sorry that I am always a little too tired and (still trailing the fog of my work in my mind) thus unable to share the wonder of the world with you fully. Apart from being argumentative, or more so than usual, I am not filled with my old joy. On Friday evening I was happier than for a long time – and the last walk was marvellous, with the red sun in the mist and the ice floating down the stream and the solidness of the wet-earth and leaves. Anyhow you will, I hope, one day know me as I really am (if this work hasn't changed me too much!).

The next letter from Penny is on Sunday [11th March] London

As I write on a gentle Sunday afternoon, the pale, honey-coloured winter sunlight gives renewed warmth to the mahogany table before me. From the radio, one of Beethoven's sympthonies streams forth, and its notes are quickly dispersed by the winds, to harmonise with the 'Eternall Musick of the Spheres.' Yet, across the blue sky roll the transient-coloured clouds, sometimes completing the serenity of the afternoon, sometimes portending the fears and dangers of the future. This afternoon is but a beautiful image of the sleepy and often stultifying life which I am presently leading. More and more am I desirous to achieve something unique and purposeful, and not to let my days slip past, and be left bored and resentful of others achievements. O dearest Tumnus, I do not know how much I really feel of the above – perhaps I should go for a walk and thus lose this silly depression. I went to an agonisingly boring party last night, at which there were young people of my own age or older, whose mental age, nevertheless, was half their years. I spent the whole time with three of my school-friends, whom I have known since I was five...

Anne & Felix could not come to the party, fortunately, as I now realise, since they were going to Cambridge to see Nicola, who has just given birth to a baby daughter, Rachel. Isn't that marvellous? ....

I have read several books this week; I finished 'Black Mischief' by Waugh, in which Waugh snaps at New Monarchies, Democracy, and British Colonialism, then I read 'Of Mice and Men', which is an exquisite jewel of lyricism and poignancy, of gentleness and cruelty, of innocence and brash and crude experience; afterwards there was 'A City of Beautiful Nonsense' by E. Temple Thurston to delight me. It is a delicate and quaint fairy-story for grown-ups... Now I am in the middle both of "Potterism" by Rose Macaulay... and of 'Ester Waters' by George Moore. ....

Love to you, my blessed one – I am looking forward to seeing you next weekend. Let us pray that the green grasses of Spring will burst forth , that you & I might admire their beauty during the only spring of your twenty-first year.

Penny wrote again on Wednesday [13th March] London

I hope you are not exhausted, or bored, by reading the fifty books, that you set yourself for this week. I should hate you to collapse into another girl's arms before it's my turn on Saturday. I am longing to see you then, and I think Annie & Felix are looking forward to coming down on Sunday (Don't let all this female worship go to your head!) I do not know by which train/coach I shall be arriving, so I shall just turn up at some point in the afternoon – between 2.30 and 4.30. I have to buy a pamphlet from the bookshop opposite the Union, and may spent part of the afternoon there, if you still have some more work to do.

I bought some velvet ribbons for my hair today; their colours are the fathomless depths of a person's eye, trembling and wavering before the light; the texture of velvet is exquisitely soft, but one hesitates to exert the full pressure of one's fingers and penetrate through the moss surface.

I have been reading some poems by St. John of the Cross, translated by Roy Campbell. Their joyous beauty is like the morning freshness of an early summer's day:

"Sweet day, so cool, so calm, so bright,
The bridal the earth & skie:"

From St John, the soul after 'in darkness up the secret stair I crept" reaches an abode 'enlaced by roses, and where the purest rills run free'; amidst such beauty the soul and its maker will for ever wander together, like a bridegroom & his bride. I was interested by the analogy you found between David 'Erbert & St J; that D.H. believed the complete surrender of consciousness and of the senses, helped the lover to reach the heights of love, and that for a short while, the spirits of man & woman cleave invisibly together, similarly St J says:

I entered in, I know not where,
And I remained, though knowing naught,
Transcending knowledge with my thought.
....

As much as I enjoy, however, writing out these verses in this letter, I must return [to] the task I have set myself of copying out nearly a whole volume of St J's poetry.

I am reading avidly once more, and have just finished a marvellous novel by Eliz. Jennings "The Tortoise & the Hare'. I am, thus, becoming very unsociable, altho I had Annie & Felix over to dinner on Monday. Mamma was out, so we, (or rather, they – I pottered about) concocted our own meal. It was fun; and I think they enjoyed it too.

My mother wrote on 10th March as follows.

Have you read the B[hagavad] Gita yet? Was amused to see the Kama Sutra was a "classic" a best seller at home, it'll be a school book next!

My dear Alan,

A long long postal holiday, so this will be late I'm afraid. It is 'Holi' the big spring fertility festival and it has brought the rain as it usually does (indeed has to, if the gods are good & thoughtful). We've had two days of lovely grey skies and the beautiful drip of drops into the drains...

Had a letter from Fiona, she seems to have made good artistic use of her London trip. Anne & Felicity loved their day with Penny, & thought her mother charming, please thank them both very much for befriending the poor darlings. Anne sounds so much happier now that they're getting out a little. (Cliff Richard singing "Please don't tease" – shades of your first Romance!) ...

I think of you often, in the last stretch of your vast project – are you revising yet? What about a couple of weeks in the Hebrides at the end of the ordeal, you could see what the prospect of buying a croft or two is when we retire. Daddy wants to spend his time & energies on the young when he retires, and we dream of a place we could fill with the displaced & dispossessed – and our own grandchildren of course. I wonder if the reality would be too exhausting, remembering my palpitations just copying for us! We both send our love & thoughts. Mummy

The next letter from my mother is three weeks later on March 22nd:

My dear Alan,

Thank you for your letter and for having the girls, who will have come and gone by now. "Oh to be in England…" although Richard says you are having a wet spring but this is the time of year I feel most homesick, remembering the daffodils and cuckoos and curlews and moss, everything wet and soft and gentle, not that it isn't beautiful here but in a hot hard way that soon wears one out….

I have my Moghuls at last. They turn out to be five volumes of the travels of a certain Peter Mundy in the seventeenth century, only one of which deals with India, but all of which are quite fascinating, have you read any of them? As well there are several other history books which I have started to summarise and am already lost in another world, the India of the first traders, and a shocking lot they were, though brave enough. I don't know whether I will ever write any of it up, or what exactly to choose, if I did write about the Moghuls it would be as seen through the eyes of contemporary travellers, otherwise the whole subject is so vast that I would have to take to my bed like F. Nightingale. I think a Woodham-Smithish book called "The Great Greed" on the colonising of India might be interesting, anyway it is all going to keep me happily occupied for years. I wonder if you could find out if the Hakluyt Society is still going, and if you have time in the vac. perhaps you could browse through old bookshops and see if you can find anything relevant to the early colonisation, Portuguese, Dutch or French as well as the East India Company. I'm particularly anxious to read the descriptions of the Jesuits at the court of Akbar, and the travels of Ralph Fitch, and a book called "English Factories". No hurry for any of these as I have enough to keep me going for months and months, but while you are in Oxford you might be able to find out if these books are still available. My brain is so rusty that I find myself absolutely whacked after a couple of hours reading, I'm taking your tip and making notes on my typewriter which is a great help in remembering. I'm also plodding on with my Assamese…

I was tempted to send for Roseberry but at the price didn't dare. He seems to be selling well still and I got a letter from Granny saying "I hope you are duly impressed". Don't quite know what she meant by that, I'm inclined to read the worst into Granny these days! Awfully sad about Uncle Roy, what a mess Aunt Margery has made of her family with that terrible spurious Christianity of hers, I still get nightmares about the holidays I used to spend with her... Poor Sheila, what a lonely position she is now in, I wish I could help…

I will send some more money at the beginning of the month, let us know when you expect your grant. Perhaps Richard could find you something in America to start you off? Don't think any further than June at the moment, doors always open.

Much love from us both – Mummy

Attached are three Bodleian book order slips, on the back of which are noted the costs of subscriptions to the Hakluyt Society, some addresses in India, and about 30 book titles with prices against them, to do with early travels to India etc.

My second letter is dated Sunday 23rd March 1963 and typed on airmail form

Dear Mummy and Daddy,

Thank you for very much for your letter, posted during the 'Holi'. Sorry to have been so long in replying & for doing so on a typewriter – my work will have to excuse both. I am now at the revision stage – 9 hours-a-day of looking thro' notes. It is difficult to prevent this deteriorating into a mechanical & absent-minded rush thro' pages of jumbled thinking. I seem to have <u>pages</u> of stuff – most of which I didn't understand when I copied it down conscientiously from various books; this means that there is a lot of digesting & re-assessing to be done. I am specialising on the Tudor & Stuart period &, if I have the opportunity, would like to do post-graduate research on some aspect of this age – perhaps the population & plague factors which have neither been studied *adequately nor related to modern problems of underdeveloped societies – problems so similar to those faced by England as it began to absorb new industries & a rapidly increasing population & swept, as it was, by periodic famines & plagues. Tawney, of course, is the pioneer in such a field, & he puts the idea of such a utilitarian approach to history thus –*

"The disorders of Chinese agriculture … are one species of a genus which has been widely diffused, & which is characteristic, not of this nation or that, but of a partic' phase of economic civilisation. The persistence of an empirical technique based on venerable usage & impervious to science; the meagre output of foodstuffs which that technique produced; the waste of time & labour through the fragmentation of holdings; the profits wrung from the cultivator by middleman, usurer & landlord; the absence of means of communication & the intolerable condition of such as existed; the narrow margin separating the mass of the population from actual starvation & the periodic recurrence of local famines – such phenomena, if exception be made of a few favoured regions, were until recently the commonplaces of western economic life … From the Middle Ages to the C19 the social problem of most parts of Europe, in spite of natural advantages of soil & climate, was what in China & India it is today. It was the condition, not of the industrial wage-earner, but of the peasant…." (Land & Labour in China).

This is also true of the problem of corruption of which you spoke during your last letter. As you will know the half century up to the Civil war was riddled with bribery of members of parliament, of judges, of tax-collectors, of the chief officers of State. For instance Yelverton paid James £4,000 to be Attorney General in 1617 or again Roger Manwood – Chief Baron of the Exchequer in the 1590s – awarded himself £7,000 in a series of cases which he brought up himself! Bacon assumed that everybody took bribes. Sir Edward Coke himself became one of the richest men in England. Both Robt Cecil and his father were making a tidy pile from the sale of offices on the quiet & even the 'upright' Strafford has recently been shown to have had dirty hands. The whole society was riddled with graft, tips, extortion etc. The causes are fairly obvious. There were no fixed salaries in the Law Courts & the fees paid to the Crown's officers were very low. They were expected to get the bulk of their income by indirect means. As in France, offices were increasingly sold, & the more they paid the more they had to squeeze from those below them on the ladder. Thus the main causes of corruption are the lack of professional traditions of service, static salaries in a Price Rev'n, the sale of offices & the absence of any really competent & public accountants. The reasons for the death of this kind of corruption seem to have been the rise of accountancy, the rise of a literate public with an opinion & a voice in the running of things (& a Press to inform it), & the bringing of salaries & fees up to the right level. But this, as you will know, is an interminable process – it took about 300 years in England!

Having finished that little lecturette, on to some lighter matters! I am progressing with the Bhagavad Gita & enjoying it immensely. But my reading is limited to a few minutes before bed so I haven't reached the middle yet.

Anne, Felix & Penny all came down last week-end. They all seemed in good health & we had several large meals – on my floor. Needless to say, it was a drizzling misty day & so we seeped wetly round Oxford's dank quads – attempting half-heartedly to visualize what it would be like in Summer. I am going up to London next week-end & will, at last, meet Mrs M.

Today was wonderful, full of rushing wind & dancing sunlight & growing shoots & whirled bird-song. I went for a 7-mile walk over Wytham woods down to Eynsham where I had tea in an old pub. My happiness will be revealed when I tell you that I even wrote some sentimental poetry! My joy is best expressed in the words of a poet who is my present fad – e.e. Cummings. He never, or hardly ever, puts in punctuation etc. Here is something on a lovely day, altho' it is far from being his best.

> "I thank You god for most this amazing
> day: for the leaping greenly spirits of trees
> and a blue true dream of sky; & for everything
> which is natural which is infinite which is yes
> ….

This fits my work-induced-bleary awakening very well.

How are the 'family planning' & 'Moguls' going? I will be very interested to hear the progress of both. No developments on 'graduate service' except that Granny can't find my passport – you don't by any chance, have an idea where all my valuables were put away?

As I am staying up in Oxford all vacation I am afraid I will need a little money – about £2 or so per week – I wonder if you could forward this – or shall I get it from Granny, with whom I would be staying? I will wait to hear from you.

Lots of love to both as ever.

Alan

A day later, on Sunday 24th, I wrote again to Penny.

I wish you could have been with me today. It was blue as a thrush's egg and one could feel the leaves being pushed up by the burrowing bulbs. I went for a long walk to Eynsham. I called for Carry [another female friend] *on the way and she came as far as the 'Perch' with me and we had a drink in the sunlit garden there. She is coming up to London next week and will be meeting Charles – perhaps we might make a four-some to do something. She also asked if you'd left any brown high-heels at the flat? To continue with the walk. I walked up beside the smiling Thames where the swans were swimming on the flooded meadow & then off up Wytham Hill and through the field of rich earth to drop down on the old village of Eynsham. The trees are still stark and buddless, the grass withered white and autumn leaves under one's feet but Spring depthened [sic] in the sunlight and the shadows were awake with bird-song. I can't convey my happiness. I ran down the woodland paths, glades such as Robin Hood and Charles escaping from his enemies must have galloped down. At Eynsham I had a country tea at a lovely little pub. And now back to the slog… (tho' I am still enjoying it immensely .)...*

I enclose a snatch of e.e. Cummings poetry (This is how I felt today, after days of blindness). I am mad on him at the moment. He has the honesty and seriousness of Lawrence and the clarity of vision and faith of Blake. I will bring you his poems when I come.

Cherideo, March 30th 1963 Iris to Alan

A lovely long typewritten letter from you yesterday, thank you very much. I was most interested in what you had to say about corruption, which is very much on my mind these days (the paper never printed my letter, it was too strong I'm afraid, I ended by saying that corruption more than the Chinese was India's national enemy which at a time like this with the C's beginning to pant hot breath down our necks again was not very tactful, even though true). Of course you are right when you say that, as in Tudor England, the chief cause of this kind of society blackmail was the low salaries paid to men in responsible positions – and yet many of the chief offenders here are ministers who get quite reasonable pay – the chief Minister of Orissa owns the Air Line that got the contract for dropping supplies to the Indian army at the time of the invasion, but afterwards it was discovered that half the supplies had found their way into the black market. And so on and so on. But he's still the Chief Minister although the Press have published the allegations against him, even if they're not true fancy allowing the possibility of such a situation.

As you say it takes years to clean this sort of Augean stable but in Tudor times the whole world was run on those lines, England if I remember rightly being rather better off than the rest of Europe – it seems ridiculous that India in the twentieth century should still be in the same muddle when the answers have been found. As I said in my letter the only solution seems to be the setting up of special courts, sort of Star Chamber affairs, with arbitrary powers to strike and punish – but this is not democratic and India is determined to be a democracy in name even if in fact elections are rigged and illiterate masses bribed to vote for somebody's son in law, the somebody having himself been bribed by a more powerful somebody in an endless vicious cycle. I have got to the part in my Indian history where Clive and Co. are in full swing in Bengal, they really got the hang of bribery, Clive got a yearly income of £30,000 from his Indian property and was still amazed at his own moderation when he only took a million home with him. It is fascinating if somewhat depressing reading, the debates that followed the discovery of what the East India Co. had been up to were full of wonderful speeches, "We are Spaniards in our lust for gold, and Dutch in our delicacy of obtaining it" Walpole shouted at one stage, even Clive himself entered the fray against the company, "They thought of nothing but the loaves and fishes" he said, the loaves and fishes being the £4,000,000 a year revenue the company was making, quite apart from private trading. Ah well, human nature never changes, but I don't think I could ever write a detached study of the British in India, I get so angry reading about it I feel my ears pounding, even though I know it isn't fair to judge them two hundred years later. I'm re-reading "A Passage to India" for the third time and finding it as fascinating as ever, of all the books I wish I'd written that is the one I'd choose …

I have told the bank to put £30 into your account for April, I can't think how you were planning to live on £2 a week? I don't want you to have to worry more than possible about money now, and also you must eat nourishing food and will need a few clothes. Yes do do a post graduate study on how the Tudors coped with the problems of poverty and food and then come out here and tell someone. Daddy says he gave your passport to you, if you can't find it you will have to report its loss, but it isn't very difficult to get a new one. We have your birth certificate.

My next letter is to Penny on Tuesday [2nd April] Worcester College

… I am taking your advice & will be going off to the Cotswolds on Thursday. I went for a bus ride to Burford and found a charming woman in the P. Office who will put me up. I will stay there until about the 18th – anyhow a week before the beginning of term. So write to me c/o Post Office, Burford (I'm not sure of the County).

… I won't write any more as I'm writing this in Carry's flat & the girls are talking & asking me questions. It's a wonderful day. Glory be to God for dappled things…

Penny wrote again from London, Sunday Afternoon [7th April]

I hope you are not overworking in the delightful Cotswold town of Burford. This afternoon London is reflecting every face of early Spring, but in the Cotswolds the air must be still fresher, and the skies deeper and clearer. I should very much like to spend Easter with you, but I do not think I ought to leave Mamma alone over Easter. Anyway, you are probably coming to London in a fortnight, aren't you? And I am coming down to Oxford with Erik on the 28th.

I have [been] quite busy during this week. On Tuesday I met Annie for coffee, and after going for a walk, we went back to Angela's for dinner. Robert was somewhat sarcastic, but the women of that household were as charming and delightful as ever. Angela's expecting another offspring in December.

On Friday I went to a party that Babs was supervising for her sister. It was very boring – Babs went to bed, halfway through the party, and Jeremy spent his time making passes at me. God, he is a drip! …. I am going to see Felix off to Scotland. F suddenly postponed her departure to Mon even – I think she wanted to celebrate Scotland's winning a football match against England, and to go mad with the rest of the Scottish barbarian's who have been crowding London streets this week. We took her out to Lunch yesterday…

I miss you very much, even though we do bicker when we are together. I think my moodiness is due to an increasing inward dissatisfaction with my job, and with my inability to take full advantage of the interim period between school & college.

Write to me soon, sweetheart. I will write often, so long as my letters are read & not put in a paper-rack.

My mother then wrote again on April 8th

My dear Alan,

We're sitting in front of a fire with Brahms on the gramophone, nothing could be cosier or less like April… I'm sorry spring is not working its magic on you, one feels terribly restless when young at the passing seasons and youth flying past and so on and never seems able to enjoy things without the desire to "share" which spoils a lot of the time. Still its rather a delicious sadness. I'm waiting to hear from Fiona who was starving in a garret according to Granny but I hope is back by now…

[Assam news] …

I had a very nice letter from my agent yesterday, they are terribly charming people, he said I was not to be discouraged by the publisher not wanting the background, he had liked it and hoped I would write more children's books and would like to see me about them when I come home – all this gratifying correspondence is owing to you of course. The trouble is I don't really like writing for children, it is extremely difficult to work within a tight vocabulary and yet not be boring, makes one realise what marvels books like Alice in Wonderland are. I heard from the Hakluyt, an Assamese friend who is a member of the British council has got a book for me so I am busy for another few weeks…

Did I tell you that the professor who was helping me with my folk stories, last week died of a heart attack – it is slightly ominous the way each time I get in touch with someone he dies shortly afterwards, i.e. Verrier Elwin.[1] *… Much love from us both – Mummy*

I went off to relax and revise in the Cotswolds so my next communication is a postcard of Burford Main Street, postmarked 8th April.

I will write properly in a day or two; this is just to say I am thinking of you and to tell you I'm having a wonderfully relaxing time here. There are a multitude of glorious Norman Churches, a host of picture-postcard villages complete with daffodils & ducks on the pond, and miles of fresh & rolling upland on which the great sheep-flocks of the middle ages used to graze.

The lady who runs the P.O has gone away for a few days so I am alone, but go out & meet 'the locals' at the pub & coffee-bar. At Burford was the Leveller mutiny vs Cromwell in 1649 & in the Church one can still see the signature of 'Anthony Selden, Prisner, 1649' – Selden watched two of the mutineers being shot from the Church tower.

My mother's next letter is on April 11th

My dear Alan,

No letter this week, but don't think I'm complaining, I shant expect you to write more than once a fortnight now as I know you will have a vast amount of reading and writing to do. I hope you wont have to resort to pep pills, more important to you to sleep properly. I gather from Anne that you never got to meet Mrs M after all, she gave the girls a slap up Chinese meal and I must write and thank her, she and Penny have both been very kind.

Such a beautiful day here… Not much headway with Family Planning though… In the afternoons I bury myself with the Moghuls, actually I haven't really got to them yet as I'm having to get a picture of Indian history so as to put them into context. It is fascinating but takes a lot of sorting out… In my spare time I'm reading "the Great Hunger" which is good but I don't like it so much as her other books. I think she has done too much research and the book is one long quotation which tends to become irritating. The facts are appalling of course, one wonders why so much fuss was made about the Black Hole of Calcutta when the Irish landlords forced their wretched tenants to put up with far worse conditions, or at any rate for longer…

Have you read the Bishop of Woolwich's book? [Honest to God?] although I'm sure it is sensible and possibly true, I don't see how he can go on calling himself a bishop and the church really should be firm enough to say so. He doesn't even subscribe to the beliefs of the creed let alone the 39 articles…

I hope the money arrived safely, let us know in good time if you want more, the difficulties the Reserve Bank are putting in ones way these days make us feel we shall have to think of packing up, we have now had to send our passports back to 1936 in order to remit money home… Much love from us both, Mummy

My final letter to my mother was one which is a pointer to future interests and a life of work, written in the still point before I started my last term at Oxford from my Cotswold retreat, the Burford Post Office, on Sunday 14th April. Easter [Day]

Dear Mummy and Daddy,

Thank you for your letter. I hope the various philanthropic campaigns progress well – keep me informed. I enclose an e.e. Cummings – as a late Easter present. I am absolutely crazy on him at the moment. Someone described him as a 'romantic realist' which isn't bad; he is a sort of poetic counterpart of Lawrence, someone who reminds you of all the basic things one tends to forget and reassures one that all the materialism, lies and cruelty which cloak themselves under the words 'common sense' and 'expediency' nowadays are as wicked as they ever were – I think he sums himself up "there's never been quite such a fool who could fail pulling all the sky over him with one smile" and his message "love is the whole & more than all".

---

[1] The date of this letter, and that on May 17th is correct - though there seems to be a contradiction about whether Verrier Elwin was alive. In fact he did not die until 22nd February 1964.

A wonderful week in the Cotswolds & one more week before I return to Oxford. I have been for some glorious walks through these rolling, lamb-haunted uplands. They are very lonely and very old, and one often feels uncomfortably like an intruder when the rabbits scitter away and the pheasants brake from the hedges. There is also a sense of magic and witchcraft, of Puck and Merlin; of distant elfin-laughter and the gloom of evil spells. The stream of jaguars and sports-cars which scream along the roads, the tired business-men & their wives who drift shadowy & pale into the pubs heighten the effect of man's transitoriness. As you can see from the above I have been meditating on lots of 'deep' subjects – brooding over the new, flower-strewn, graves and medieval paintings of death in the churches, and feeling the ritual and primitive growth of Spring. All this blended with Easter and a re-assessment of my Christianity has given me plenty to meditate on as I wander, (like the scholar-gipsy?) with my long [h]air and black duffle coat flowing in the wind & my eyes dream-filled. (this is how I like to picture myself – those in the cars probably see a dishevelled & tattered beatnik with holes in his shoes!). I went to Chedworth Roman Villa yesterday, built overlooking the fields & woods of the Colne valley. It was a day of sun & rain, with glorious rainbow's – one of which spread over the valley while I was looking out from the village – and the earth humming with growth.

I have just heard from Graduate Service Overseas, to whom I applied (did I tell you?) for a job for a year abroad, that they can't have me. My enquires about teaching in Canada have not been answered – so it looks as if I will have to spend the year just wandering about – stocking up with memories & experience for the rest of my life. I am leaving everything open at the moment "Take no thought for the morrow .... Sufficient unto the day is the evil thereof..."!

I have been thinking a good deal recently about something I would like to think, & perhaps write, about, after I left Oxford – a sort of hobby (like Robert's history). This is the relationship between the following – Religion (partic' Eastern) – Anthropology, folk-lore etc – children's stories – poetry – C16–C17 & C19 (Literary) English history. The strand joining them is the process of 'growing up'. This is a very large subject as you can imagine and I won't go into it now – but just mention the sort of things I am on the look-out for.

Wordsworth of course is a prime example – in the prefatory note to 'Immortality' he speaks of "that dream-like vividness & splendour which invest objects of sight in childhood, everyone, I believe, if he could look back, could bear testimony." This, W.H. Hudson calls "animism" – "that sense of something in Nature which to the enlightened or civilized man is not there, & in the civilized man's child, if it be admitted that he has it at all, is but a faint survival of the primitive mind." This struggle to reach beyond everyday experience – to assert that Science has not 'nabbed' Nature as Lawrence said is, perhaps, at the heart of the Romantic revolt in the early C19, & is implicit in the poetry of the Metaphysicals who sought to yoke together two modes of thinking – the old all-embracing, magic-believing, religious temperament of the middle-ages & the new scientific sprit of enquiry. Ultimately it is an attempt to unite all action & all thought into one pattern – for instance as in 'Religion & Rise of Cap'm' to subordinate economic action to higher ends – and also a belief that there is something wonderful & unalysable in the world.

A study of this vast borderland of mystery, romance, 'totem & taboo' etc would entail a research into those people & books who most interest me at the moment – Lawrence, Wordsworth, Donne, psychology – Freud etc., fairy stories, the Grail legend etc. The danger is a) that it is a boundless field – a dream-land where one could easily get lost – to wake up to find life gone & nothing achieved b) that it is merely a temporary attempt at escape but some have suggested that nearly everything we do is such an attempt. As Prof. Murray says in 'Religio Grammaticus':

"Man is imprisoned in the external present; & what we call a man's religion is, to a great extent, the thing that offers him a secret & permanent means to escape from that prison, a breaking of the prison walls which leaves him standing, of course, still in the present, but in a present so enlarged & enfranchised that it is become not a prison but a free world. Religion, even in this narrow sense, is always seeking for soteria, for escape, for some salvation from the terror to come or some deliverance from the body of this death ... some find it in theology, some in art, some in human affections; in the anodyne of constant work ... the permanent exercise of the inquiring intellect called the search for Truth etc...." – this covers most things!

Probably the desire will die out as I come into "the light of common day" but I hope not. The area I would like to explore has been 'mapped out', thou' that is the wrong expression, by Robert Graves & I will finish by quoting him.

Lost Acres

These acres, always again lost
By every new Ordnance survey

And searched for at exhausting cost
Of time & thought, are still away.

Well another 7 weeks or so to exams. Can't summon up much enthusiasm for revision. The nearer they get the less I care & the less work I do.

Look after yourselves,

Much love, Alan

On the same Easter Day I wrote to Penny from Burford.

Thank you stacks for the cats – they are delightful. I hope you have had a wonderful Easter – and perhaps time to meditate a little? This break in the Cotswolds has given me leisure to ponder on some of the things which in the fury & stupefying rush of work I had forgotten – the eternal problems of 'what is it all for' – 'what does death mean?' etc. Easter, of course, is an especially appropriate time for this. I wish I had Herbert's poems with me as I would send you his lovely poem on this subject – instead I send you a snippet from East Coker which is appropriate. It is very stark and harsh – almost cruel (I have also included a little of the famous opening of the Wasteland) or Spring is a savage season. It is full of the primitive savagery, the sweat & agony of new life, the bloody triumph over the forces of darkness, cold and fear. Here in the Cotswold with only a few lambs about, and hardly any flowers, with the warm but strong winds bending the thorn trees over the long fields one feels very close to the old struggle for mastery. In the older churches there are often wall-paintings of death & in many churchyards there are new graves covered with a profusion of flowers – often fading fast. There is a blankness and secrecy about a countryside which only seems to be scratched on the surface by the movement of Spring.

The twisted agony on the Cross, the Crown of thorns and the glorious resurrection when Light triumphed over darkness find expression for the age-long triumph. The borderlands between faith and experience, between one's orthodox religion & one's most inmost & primitive desires & feelings becomes misted over. One walks again in the strange twilight of the 'Wasteland' where forces larger than life move & where the petty doings of man pale to a shadowed dream. Witchcraft and fairies, magic and ritual murder suddenly people the haunted woods and sunny streams. Puck is heard over the distant fields and the sound of nightingales as if the woods were rich with summer. Do you know what I mean? Perhaps I'm babbling; perhaps just trying to escape. But the escape is no less real than the tinsel land from which one flees. The mystery of the old fir-forests and the eternal rivers, of the startled rabbits and the whirr of the pheasant is as real as the brassy women and frightened rabbitty-men who patronise Burford pubs, fear in their eyes, money wedged in their pockets, tiredness on their brows and a jaguar outside. The country people are nice – tho' I haven't met many, but the younger ones are mostly Americanized and loud.   Enough rubbish for now! If nothing else this rest is making me realize how small-minded my work-mania was. I do intend to read some children's stories next term – starting with 'Once & Future King'. Have you read it all?

I also copied out 'Lost Acres' by Robert Graves, which I also enclosed in the long letter to my parents.

My next letter to Penny is on Tuesday [16 April] on Worcester College Notepaper – though still in Burford:

It is indeed wonderful here – and the Churches are fantastic. Every day I find out more about the historical associations of this place – for instance yesterday I discovered A) that Burford was the site of a great battle between Mercia & Wessex in 752 which I was studying that morning. B) That Speaker Lenthall (who answered Charles when he came searching for the 5 members is buried in the Church here). C) That Charles II came here for the racing. D) I went to a delightful & tiny church – St Oswald, Widford – about C11-C12 but built on the site of a Roman villa, of which a few tessellated paving stones (mosaic) remain. Also there is a medieval 'morality' on the wall – 3 kings out hunting meet 3 spectres. After Widford I went beside the winding Windrush to Swinford where a) was buried 'Unity' (Valkyre) Mitford (ask your mother about her if you don't know who she was) & in the Church are the Fettiplace tombs – 6 knights all leaning awkwardly on their elbows in the chancel because there is no room for them to stand upright.

… I have cut down my work-time & am already feeling much refreshed.

I heard from the Voluntary service people today that they don't want me – but can't be bothered to think of anything else.

Penny wrote again on Thursday [18th April]

I miss you so very much that I'm not sure my patience will last until a week's time, when I'll see you. Life seems to go up and down. Sometimes I hate every individual I meet, sometimes this creature is in a fairly affable mood. I lack any stimulus, and am too-lazy, or bored to seek a way of raising my spirits. At times, like these, I think I am one big drip, not revealing a thousand thousand coloured prisms, but fog-hazed over.

We spent a quiet Easter, although we had a number of friends over… … I went to see 'Salvatore Giuliano'. Tumnus! It is a superb film about the life and background of a Sicilian bandit… [long description of] *How I should love to go to Sicily.*

Instead of poetry, I am sending you an article by Laurie[Lee] on spring. Please keep it, since I would like to copy it out when next I come to Oxford….

P.S. In my next letter – no time now – I'll comment on the effect of this prose upon me. Meanwhile, I was interested by the similarity to your letter (or did you listen to LL on woman's hour)

Penny wrote on Saturday [20th April]

How do you like being back in Oxford – I send you some G.M.H. [Gerard Manley Hopkins] *to remind you of its own beauty – after sharing the eternal innocence of the Cotswold hills. Please don't loose the benefits you have gained in order to entertain the rabbling crowd of historical characters, threatening you upon the stage. Work sensible hours (ie don't get up at 6.00 (?) or have lunch at 11.30 am) and be calm and tranquille. I'll be mad if you are tired or depressed when I come down next weekend. Also I shall try to find dozens of childrens' stories for you to read. I hope you have the self-control to be able to settle down to them. Pam and I have decided to try to get down to Oxford for May Morning. This is probably my only chance of taking part in the May-day revels for years to come and I don't intend to be without you, while you prefer to stay in bed.*

Jeremy took me out to lunch after work today. …. I had a card from Erik this morning. Besides imparting the information of where & when to meet him for coming up to Oxford together next weekend, he was very poetic about the mountains – in his remarks about the loneliness he revealed his Norwegian spirit. Erik is a wonderful combination of Slavonic dignity and French vivacity and frivolity….

Love me, darling, as I love you, and care for me a little. My hopes and aspiration go with you till we wander through the 'cuckoo-echoing, bell-swarmed, lark-charmed, rook-racked river-rounded city; which scattered the same white flames of rarity upon G.M.H. in the C19 as upon Duns Scotus in the C14.

My next letter to Penny is on Sunday 21st April – from Burford

… I am a placid, sleepy creature, perhaps a drowsing trout at the bottom of some deep pool like the one described by Kathleen Raine, which is content to swim gently, occasionally rising to inspect a fly, then sinking to his slumberous dream. When you are around I feel as if I have been hooked and am struggling for my sleepy existence – for you are as the young deer, easily startled, pausing a second with uplifted nose on some wild moor & then darting off, leaping fallen trees & streams.

I'm sure the above is an exaggeration and it is not meant to be at all derogatory, most people would far rather be the deer. I just mean that I am no longer eager with the curiosity of a child. Perhaps you think you are losing this when you are 'too bored or lazy' to make any way of raising your spirits; I wouldn't have thought so. But enough of this analysis – it probably irritates you & quite rightly so.

I return to Oxford in about half an hour, blissful and blistered, expecting to feel very superior over my neurotic & care-worn friends – which is very unkind of me. I am looking forward to going back and getting the exam over, I always seem to want to be where I am not. I have lost my concern about the exams so much that I'm getting worried that I'm not worried enough. I spend less & less time working and am spending the new freedom thinking for a change. As I have been rejected (?) by Voluntary Service I will have to think of something else to do next year. Vague ideas 'sink or swim' in my head, including going out to Assam to study Assamese history etc, but nothing firm has turned up. With luck I will become one of life's Wasters – perhaps a sort of scholar gypsy, learned & detached, wandering like a phantom through the autumn woods?

Thank you for the Laurie Lee. No I hadn't heard him when I wrote, but I agree there is a remarkable likeness, I suppose because poets (& pseud-poets) are likely to react in a similar way, especially to something as 'poetic' as spring. I enjoyed the article very much & like his poetry – though I can't help feeling he is rather an inferior Keats or Hopkins, tho' this is unfair.

Finally, I sent Penny a picture postcard of a mosaic "Spring" from Chedworth Roman Village, Gloucestershire, date stamped Oxford 23 April

Please excuse my laziness in not writing properly – but I will be seeing you in a few days. I saw this inconstant nymph while at Chedworth. Thank you for your letter & the by-leaf, and also for the G.M.H. poem – one of my favourites.

Oxford is bright with bird-song and bubbling with spring sunlight which splashes down the roofs and that gathers thickly in the shadows. It is too wonderful – and here am I stuck working. My relaxation regime doesn't start 'till the beginning of term & collections are an added burden, so don't expect to find me too carefree on Saturday.

*

The only poem which I wrote and has survived was written in the Spring of 1963. I was enamoured of e.e. cummings and this is in his style.

actually well actually I don't
come here often so don't bother
asking of course perhaps that's
because I'm not a ballet dancer
nor have I ever written a santa
claus letter my sweet so please
forgive aw why am I always
making excuses

my friends say I must
become a Grown Up Person and
forget the fairies and stars and
dreams and mysteries and realise
that Life is tragic and hard
and decisions must be taken for
instance that I should stop
getting starry-eyed about you
and the way you let the light
make gold out of your hair and
close your rose petal lips
instead I should say to you
hey girl I think you're a
cute chick a real slazzy
hipster or to put it in oxford
terms and more politely i
hope we can be friends i
have no long-term intentions we
can never marry or make love
properly but I like being
with you and isn't it fun
kissing this is o.k this is
fine whoopee but then when
I see you all my good
Resolutions go and I get

All mean and jealous and
Melancholy and go round
Trying to 'emprison your soft hand'
etc etc when you would much
rather I didn't and looking
mournful and getting all
spiritual when my friends really
know that all I want is
to persuade you and me
that we're 'in luv' and also
that I want to possess
your wonderful body but
daren't strange how this
kind of letter-poem drags – all
sorts of things from me –
sorry I can't put an
exclamation mark there tho i
could have a full stop

Academic Work - Spring Term 1963

My plan was to work up to a crescendo in the last Michaelmas and Spring terms – I talk about doing 9 hours a day, with a half day on Sunday – a 60 hour week. I then relaxed somewhat in the Spring vacation, with perhaps seven or eight hours a day, and even more so in the Summer term, with six hours a day, and a few days off before the exams.

In the Spring term we continued with English history into the nineteenth century. We also tackled one new field, a second special subject, in my case 'English Economic History Documents, 1485-1730'. I did this with the noted Tudor economic historian, G.D. Ramsay and vaguely remember the seminars and supervisions in Teddy Hall.

*

A few extracts from the down to earth economic history documents teaching provides a good balance to the intense emotional life I was leading, though the two extracts give little indication of how hard I was working. I have three or four hundred pages of typed (and some handwritten) foolscap pages of notes, extracted from several hundred books and articles on economic history. An immense labour for one paper.

I have four surviving essays in relation to economic documents.

Essay 1: To what extent was the production of wool determined by the progress of enclosures in the C16 & C17?

Essay 2: With what aims and what success did governments attempt to control industry during the sixteenth and seventeenth centuries?

Essay 3: Might it be argued that Co. organization was more a hindrance than a help in English overseas trade in the C16 & C17?

Essay 4: To what extent did the problem of poverty change in character from 1485-1730? (A typed essay).

We were also taught by answering 'Gobbets', of which there are four remaining sets.

Each week we would have been either doing an essay or gobbets. There are no marks for any of these attempts – but quite copious notes from detailed feedback.

I have chosen to include just the third essay I wrote, presumably around the middle or end of February.

Essay 3.

Might it be argued that Co. organization was more a hindrance than a help in English overseas trade in the C16 & C17s?

Many contemporaries did consider Co. organization as a cramping force. Some of the commonest arguments of these men against monopolies in trade are set out in the complaint of the Jt Stock monopoly of the Muscovy Co. in 1604. It is accused of allowing all its business to be conducted by one factor, of constricting the trade so that the unregulated ~~french~~ ~~[illegible]~~ are swiftly overtaking the English, that it keeps the price of Russia commodities artificially high - for instance the price of cordage has quickly gone up from 20/- to 30/-, and that young merchants within the Co. have not the capital to "forbear their stock" for as long as the Co dictates, any anyhow wish to manage their own affairs. More ~~[illegible]~~ contemporary arguments against Co's are to be found in the Arguments against incorporating the Barbary Merchants in 1582, most important of these are the allegations that the Governor & his assistants in London will be too remote from Barbary to have any practical control and that "this Corporation will not bring any possible advantage - it can only limit shipping." If we add to the above the protest of Gypps in 1582 at being arbitrarily excluded from the Barbary trade in which he has already invested heavily because he is not a 'mere merchant', and if we remember the complaint of Hull in 1575 against "Merchants united into Co's, whose heads are in London, who make ordinances benefitting themselves, but hurtful to the local merchants, ~~and~~ which Co's draw all the wealthiest and most talented to London thus helping to precipitate the decay of provincial ports, the arguments against Companies seem formidable."

Secondly if we look at the actual progress of trade in the second half of the C16 with its periodic crises and ~~occasional~~ over-production and then turn to the minutely detailed regulations of the Co's (in which I intend to include the M.A's) it is tempting to see the link of cause and effect. This is the conclusion of Unwin. Basing his case largely on evidence from the M.A activities where he sees restrictionism and stints, limitation of numbers by Gresham in 1564 and the attack on the Hanse, a safety valve for English exports he concludes that "the question whether the M.A were an organ for the expansion of English trade must clearly be answered in the negative. The same, he says, is true of the provincial branches of the M.A which sprang up in Exeter (1557), Chester (1553) Newcastle (1547) and so on. They exclude "all but "mere merchants" and thus restrict fluidity of capital and enterprise. More generally he sees trading Co's as branches of the M.A, indulging in harmful pirating activities and closing huge areas of trade to enterprising activity - thus these new Co's "did not open new channels of exportation or of importation", and like the M.A their parent they interfered with internal production, putting pressure on the government to carry out acts like that against country weavers and the Act of Artificers which Unwin sees as one large concerted act of restriction. He concludes "the prevalence of privateering, the restriction on banking and international credit, the interference with the wool-dealer and clothier, the suspension of the Hanseatic trade, the closing of one region of foreign trade after another by the erection of monopolistic companies, and finally, the attitude of the M.A towards the attempted expansion of their own branch of trade leaves us hardly surprised that the latter half of the decade (1580-90) was a period of great depression for trade in general, and especially for cloth export."

Unwin argues on general grounds and may be attacked with specific arguments. But it must also be remembered that Elizabeth's reign was a bad time for trade for reasons quite unconnected with the M.A. The Low Countries were gripped by Revolt, and the Eastland trade bedevilled by the Hanse. There was piracy in the Mediterranean and Russia's demand was precariously dependent on the Tsar. Wheeler's argument was based on the assumption that foreign markets were strictly limited, and remembering the absence of technical improvement in the cloth industry and the unlikelihood of a rise in the standard of living and hence of consumption per head, it was not such an 'astounding' (Unwin) view. The reign of Elizabeth was a period of transition from an almost single-lane trade to multifarious one, and in this transition, it can be argued, the M.A's and other

(2)

trading Co's played an important and helpful part.

The arguments used to support trading monopolies were usually repetitions of three or four central views, that trade to distant and difficult markets needed skilled merchants; that they needed regulation to prevent under-cutting and friction with the local inhabitants; that those who discovered a new trade should have some advantage and so on. We find one of these arguments employed in the request for a monopoly of the Barbary Co in 1574 which claims that Englishmen, often unskilled, have started trading haphazardly and are so unskilful that they often omit to come back in the ships that they sent their goods in and so are forced to remain stranded in Morocco for several years. More plausibly they argue that these new men carry arms to the infidels often take treasure instead of cloth out of England - charges which we will examine later. The account of the beginnings of the East India Co in 1599-1601 shows a perfectly reasonable grounds for starting a Co - the need to raise a large amount of capital for a difficult new trade. More arguments are put forward against dispersed and unregulated trade in the petition from the M.A to the P.C to suppress Interlopers in 1584. It points out that dispersed trade through Hamburgh inland to Germany and Italy leads to foolish bargains being struck inland when cloth is sold at a loss, shoddy foreign wares bought, and friction created with local German merchants. Negotiations with the Hanse have been undermined by such unregulated trade they maintained. Also English subjects ship cloths and other commodities to Calais, Graveline and Dunkirk as well as food, which all help to sustain Parma.

An examination of an ~~actual~~ trading Companies throws even more light on the pressures behind the formation of Companies. The highly privileged position granted by the Emperor of Russia to the English merchants in 1555 was based on the assumption that the merchants were acting as a concerted group - they had been incorporated two years earlier. This need to act together can be seen even more clearly in the foundation of the Eastland Co. It seems to have been founded largely so that a united attack could be made on the Hanse and also on the piracy which was increasing on the North Sea. The immediate cause may well have been the long and expensive negotiations which preceded the move from Danzig to Elbing and necessitated a strict regulation of trade once the merchants settled at Elbing. Hinton is fairly certain that the privileges offered by the Company more than compensated for the restrictions it imposed. Thus the appointment of shipping times, the strict rules about the toll-bill were all beneficial in the end. He dismisses the accusations that the Co was an oligarchy as "probably not of much importance" and points out that the Company were bound to admit any mere merchant who offered to pay the entry fine of £20 and that a young man could obtain admission to the Eastland Co without payment if he were the son of a member or if he graduated by apprenticeship. He also justifies the exclusion of all but expert merchants, pointing out the difficulty of the trade and argues that the Co were probably right in saying that more competition would have led to a diminution of cloth exports. Again he shows that the ~~ex~~ 'exorbitant' impositions - eg on a short Suffolk cloth in 1618 - worth perhaps £10 the King took 6/8d + the Co 8d, "seem not excessive". He concludes that before the age in which the State could provide these things, the Co ensured that merchants abroad had rights of warehouse, freedom from taxation and security of property, and that "tangible benefits such as these chiefly justified their discipline & impositions". For lack of space, Hinton's arguments must be used to justify the Muscovy, Levant and Guinea Co's, but a swift look at the formation of the Barbary Co shows other considerations at work.

Most of the usual arguments were used for and against its incorporation in 1567, 74 and 82 but Willan has shown that here is a ~~definite~~ case when the incorporation can be seen as against the wishes of the majority of the merchants. It was true, as Elizabeth admitted to the Portuguese ambassador, that arms were shipped to Morocco, tho' Willan points out that the allegations about bullion cannot be proved either way. But he decides that "the Co itself seems to have been imposed on the merchants rather than to have been created by them in an attempt to solve their difficulties in Morocco." The pressure for incorporation, he decides, came from Leicester and a section of the merchants who "having entred into contractes with The Kinge of Barbary to furnish him with iron and other metalls, and dowbtinge lest he might be prevented, if the merchauntes trading thither were not of such thinges restrayned, caused the shippes Then laden with your suppliante goodes, by your Honors order, to be stayed:" this explains the enormous power given to Leicester & Warwick in 1585 and also the rather contradictory arguments used in 1576 & 1582 by the same people for incorporation. It also shows us that a Co' could be just as harmful as any other monopoly.

It is well to remember two other facts. One is that we do not know how effective the Co's and the M.A's were in restraining interlopers and smugglers, on this we can only conclude with Willan that "a consideration of interloping & of the Staple suggests that Elizabethan trading companies were much less monolithic in structure & much less monolithic in practice than their charters & ordinances imply", he supports this with a figure showing that in 1598 the equivalent of 7.8 % of the total London short cloths were carried out by interlopers and pointing out that the provincial branches of the M.A do not seem to have always traded with the current staple.

Secondly it must be noted that the Co was a useful instrument for the government, both in its dealings with other nations and in its growing struggle against smugglers. It provided Loans, like those of the M.A at Antwerp, and maintained embassies abroad. Further it was a means of preventing the growth of Dutch imports which can be seen as a serious threat from 1615 on - for instance in 1615. Considerations of defence and the desire to encourage the exportation of English cloths led the gov't to believe up to the late C17 that England's interest would, on the whole, be best served by trading Co's. They seem to have been right.

At the end of the essay there are half a page of notes of other points and other articles I could read on the subject.

The other way we learnt and were examined were through 'Gobbets', where we commented on a choice of texts. These are not wildly exciting, but to give a flavour, let me reproduce part of the second set of Gobbets.

There are six answers and I shall reproduce the first three.

GOBBETS (2) (1)

If the clothier did pay xij d. for every course clothe insteade of the iiij d. for the Aulnage, it would be more than 10,000 pounds yearly.

(John Hales to Mr Secretary Cecil, 1552)

viii) Until a man growe unto the aige of 24 yeares, he (for the moste parte, though not alwayes) is wilde, without judgement, and not of sufficient experience to governe himselfe.

[Memorandum on Statute of Artificers, 1573]

Though it seems likely that the apprenticeship clauses of the Statute of Artificers were usually enforced - witness the administration of these clauses in the North Riding quarter sessions in 1607-8, this memorandum was called forth by a fear that enforcement was growing lax. The original Statute had said that any householder over 24 might have an apprentice and that anyone owning ½ a plough land might have an apprentice aged between 12 + 24. In fact 24 seems to have been considered the 'age of discretion', just as 21 is the age of legal responsibility now. Thus this memorandum, in its attempt to stabilize society, in its avowed attempt to provide fully skilled apprentices, in its aim to prevent a surplus of semi-skilled independent artificers who would swamp their elders + betters says that the master of an apprentice must be at least 24 and, in the above example, must serve apprenticeship until he is 24, which will prevent his falling into idleness + licentiousness. An example of the enforcement of this clause is given in the proceedings at the North Riding quarter sessions, already mentioned, against a defendant for trading "he being a very young man, unmarried, which is contrary to the statute".

Apprenticeship went want a from early
Not a prosperous period.

ix) The Spanish wool usually brought out of Spain into Flanders and there dressed is now carried over to alicante ... and from thence transported & into Italy, Venice + those parts.

(Argts for maintaining an English agent in Turkey 1587-8)

The purpose of this remark is to refute the wishful thinking of those who argued that if the trade with Turkey was cut off other markets for English cloth could be found in the Mediterranean, especially the Venetian one. It is here pointed out that the Venetians were in fact buying merino wool from Spain & turning it into cloth themselves and even putting heavy duties on English goods going to the

Levant so that their own goods would have an advantage in that trade. This was indeed a serious threat to English markets in the Mediterranean region, but it was bipassed by the growing production of the 'new draperies', brighter, lighter and cheaper than anything that the Italian and Venetian factories could produce, and even at the time that this argument is put forward the Italian cloth centres. At the time that this document was written, the Levant market was of fast growing importance, for the slump in the mid C16 had shown the danger of ~~a~~ restricted, one-track trade to Europe & had turned Englishmen's eyes outwards, to Russia, Barbary, ~~&~~ the colonies, as well as the Levant. This is ~~shown~~ [illegible] ~~shown~~ i.e. by another argument put forward in the same document — that over thirty ships specially built recently will be wasted.

i) Spanish wool not being used in England – enemy wool.

E.H.R. Decline of Italy. Cipolla (Decline in 17C) ii) Also much restriction

42–50 Sella Annales shows Venetian wool & cloth production reaches its climax in 1600 (and later for wool) was brought by Cipolla)

xii) <u>Such a private exercise & use had not been within it, for every one may work in such a private manner, although he has never been an apprentice in the trade.</u>

(Case of the Tailors of Ipswich, 1615)

The Master and officers of the Guild of the Tailors of Ipswich accused Wm Sheninge of breaking guild rules in not presenting himself to the Master & Wardens and they claim they can fine him also for breaking the Statute of Artificers in not having served an apprenticeship. This may be seen as a test case both for the power of a guild and also as to the strength of the Statute – though it would be absurd to generalize from it and deduce that guilds and the Statute were henceforward were of no power for clearly such restrictions were only broken down gradually, but like Tolly's case this is a definite indication of a trend, coinciding as it does with the long hostility to monopolies and more especially with the attack on the Merchant Adventurers monopoly by Cockayne and his colleagues. More generally the judges find Sheninge innocent "saying that "at the Common Law no man could be prohibited from working in any lawful trades & sciences... and therefore the law abhors all monopolies ... if he who undertakes upon him to work is unskilful, his ignorance is a sufficient punishment to him..." (cf. St of Artificers attitude) and more particularly on guild ordinances that they "are against the liberty & freedom of the subject, and are a means of extortion... (the) ordinances for the good order & govt of men of Trades & Mysteries are good..." Sheninge pleaded that he was only working domestically, and in the above the judges uphold his claim, & by so doing leave a loop-hole to individual & practically unrestrained activity. (Unwin)

Lane has shown Portuguese did not undermine Venetian trade (when spices was as high in 1600 as 1500)

Lively connection betw Antwerp & ~~Ital~~ Venice.

There are several lines of cross references and comments at the bottom of the Gobbet, in my hand.

The other three Gobbets, which I answered at equal length were:

xiii. The Clothiers at their will have made their work extreme hard, and abated wages what they pleased. (Petition to fix wages addressed to Justices by textile workers of Wiltshire, 1623)

xx) Gloucestershire must not be pass'd over, without some account of a most pleasant and fruitful vale which crosses part of the country … and which is called Stroud-water. (Defoe: Tour)

xxii) Here is a curiosity in trade worth observing, as being the only one of its kind in England, namely, a throwing or throwster's mill, which performes by a wheel turn'd by the water. (Defoe: Tour)

There are a few more notes by me at the bottom of the Gobbets, noting comments by the supervisor and further references.

*

As well as economic history, I was continuing my British history into the middle and later nineteenth century. I have an immense number of notes on Peel and an essay of over 7 foolscap pages on 'What was "Liberal Toryism"; why did the Conservative party stay together so long?' There is an essay plan and some comments on the essay, but no mark on it.

The second essay is titled 'The Economic Background to English Imperialism 1870-1914', some six pages of writing.

The third essay, was on 'Consider British Policy in Africa as a test case of "Imperialism", 1887-1902. The notes for this, and the essay itself, were shorter than for the others, but the contents interest me, given my imperial past.

Consider British Policy in Africa as a test case of 'Imperialism'. 1870 - 1902

In 1893 the leader of the party which was supposedly the more opposed to imperialism said these words:

"It is said that our Empire is already large enough, and does not need extension. That would be true enough if the world were elastic, but unfortunately it is not elastic, and we are engaged at the present moment, in the language of mining "in pegging out claims for the future." We have to consider, not what we want now, but what we shall want in the future.... we have to remember that it is part of our responsibility and heritage to take care that the world, so far as it can be moulded by us, shall receive an English-speaking complexion, and not that of other nations....". It was a speech of Rosebery, the successor to Gladstone, the man who alone could have led an opposition to Chamberlain's policy and it reveals several assumptions which we consider to be constituents of imperialism - the view of expansion as enlarged by Seeley, of the superiority and responsibility of Englishmen charted forth by Kipling and lying at the heart of Rhodes's desire for the federation of S. Africa and finding expression in many of his conversations - for instance his remark that history had taught him "that expansion was everything, and that the world's surface being limited, the great object of present should be to take as much of the world as it possibly could". Chamberlain echoed the above sentiments frequently, a clear example being found in his words "I believe that the British race is the greatest of governing races that the world has ever seen.....it is a gigantic task that we have undertaken when we have determined to wield the task of empire. Great is the task, great is the responsibility, but great is the honour." These were the views of some of those most deeply involved in S. African politics. They expressed, often, but not always pressures, economic, popular & jingoistic, political or strategic, which came from within England, from Europe, and, as Gallagher & Robinson rightly stress, from the actual situation in Africa. In the light of events in Africa what was the relative responsibility of each of these factors in producing the annexation of vast areas of tropical Africa, in producing intervention in Egypt, and in causing the clash in South Africa?

The very differences of the areas within which British interests were operating in the 1870s on suggests that no single and coherent theory will explain events. As Gallagher & Robinson point out "It seems unlikely that the motives in regions as dissimilar as

Egypt, the Niger and S. Africa can be fitted easily into a (2)
simple formula of imperialism." Thus if we try to apply
any single thesis to Africa it soon becomes untenable. For
example if we seek unity by using the Hobson-Lenin
view of the necessity for new outlets of investment and
new markets for English goods we immediately fall flat." The basis
for the hostile attitude to other powers seems to have been
the extension of European power politics to the African scene; it
it was apparently not fear of economic competition" declares
Wilde and gives as an example the fact that
"Chamberlain in no case indicated on the minute sheets any
concern for special economic interests". It was politics
which dictated economics in S. Africa. There is no proof that
Chamberlain & Thilner were "used" by financial interests or
Rand 'capitalists' in an attempt to bring in a laxer
government. Neither Thilner nor Chamberlain had any sympathy
with "stock-jobbers", the "money-bags" as Chamberlain called
them. To see more than a coincidence between gold and
the Rand the aggressive policy of the government though
attractive cannot be proved except in the sense that
increasing Boer wealth an otherwise impossibly
tange rapid growth of independent nationalism. This is not
to deny Rhodes' own financial interests in the Transvaal not
to suggest that economic motives were completely absent
from Chamberlain's mind. But the government had too
much faith in A/Saxon superiority to want anything more
than fair dealing: given that the British would come out on
top.

Again if we turn to other parts of Africa, apart from the
major consideration that Africa as a whole played a very
small part when compared to the rest of England's formal &
informal empire, we see no direct link between economic
expansion & government activity. West Africa seemed to
offer better prospects of markets and raw materials than
east Africa and the Upper Nile; yet it was upon these
poorer countries that the British government concentrated
its efforts. Finally Egypt is hard to square with a
purely economic or financial interpretation of imperialism,
even with the interpretation of Gallagher & Robinson stressing
the varying methods used by "the imperialism of free
trade".

(3)

~~What light then, do events in Africa throw on other motives for imperial~~

In their book on the Victorians in Africa the above authors stress that "Ministers only listened to the pleas of missionary, imperialist and financial groups only when it suited their purpose." On the whole this seems to be borne out by events in Africa. For long African colonies, especially in S. Africa had been the least popular of British acquisitions. Rhodes' was disappointed in the 1880's at the lack of enthusiasm and interest in imperial expansion. They had colonists, but produced little trade or revenue, attracted no capital and few immigrants. Such a view was expressed by James Stephen of the Colonial Office in the 1850's "If we could acquire the dominion of the whole of the continent it would be but a worthless possession." At the time when public opinion was scarcely interested – indeed when it was believed by many ministers to be radical + anti-imperial, great chunks of Africa were won and mapped out. Chronology alone disproves the simple connexion between popular pressure and African expansion, the enthusiasm for Jameson arose largely *after* his Raid. Politicians had to lead the 'people', and even if it had been the other way round it is unlikely ~~that~~ popular pressure would have changed the policy of the aristocrats in Whitehall. Nevertheless there are exceptions to the immunity from pressure-groups. One example of this was the reluctant annexation of land on the Niger to protect trading and missionary interests. Again none can deny that British opinion in the ~~colon~~ Cape colony was imperialist, or not interested in finance, and it is clear that such opinion did sway the government to a considerable extent. Whitehall officials made the decisions, but they depended ~~to~~ exclusively on their information on men in Cape Town. Milner's power is stressed by Gallagher + Robinson and Wilde has shown the immense influence misinformation – in the case of the mistaken view that the Uitlanders outnumbered the Boers in the Transvaal which this author calls "the greatest single factor in the complex of events leading to the South African war." – could have on Downing Street. The broad outlines were imposed by ministers – thus Chamberlain wished to turn South Africa into another Canada say Gallagher + Robinson, but within ~~that~~ framework it was believed that so long as London kept in line

(4)

with colonial opinion and Britain's collaborator's were upheld in South Africa would eventually turn itself into another colonial dominion. The final exception to the remark about Ministers not being determined by imperialist groups is that they themselves were often 'imperialists', if that word is to have any meaning at all. That is, they believed, as we have seen, in the mission of the A/Saxon empire, they believed that the imperial net-work should be strengthened ad so on. But even such a generalization belies the situation, it may be true of Chamberlain, but not of Gladstone who, nevertheless annexed large territories to secure large territories for the Cape Colony, to keep the Transvaal Republic encircled and to seal off the imagined German challenge. Here we find another broad range of factor entering into the policy towards Africa, a factor which recent historians, for instance R + R and Fieldhouse, lay their emphasis as the determining one in late Victorian imperialism - strategic and international considerations.

Put crudely this view is summed up in R & R's words that "if the papers left by the policy-makers are to be believed they moved into Africa, not to build a new African empire, but to protect the old empire in India." This stress on the importance of the Indian lifelines, threatened mostly by internal developments in Africa, the weakness within Egypt, the crumbling of Turkish rule and the growth of an independent Transvaal is very different from Fieldhouse's thesis that "until the end of the century, imperialism may best be seen as the extension into the periphery of the political struggle in Europe," which therefore stresses Bismarck's action in 1884-5 in announcing the formal control by Germany over parts of West and South Africa and of New Guinea as beginning the new phase of political imperialism; the latter point being contrasted to Gallagher + Robinson's view that it was in the collapse in the khedival régime in Egypt that the new imperialism saw its start - leading them a to say "From start to finish the partition of tropical Africa was driven by the persistent crisis in Africa." Neither view can totally explain African developments; an examination of just one example of African politics shows a failure to account for events. Events in South

Africa cannot have been wholly dictated by the need to protect the route to India in 1895 on. There was another route, and the invasion of the Transvaal cannot possibly be wholly explained by a desire to safeguard Capetown. As for Fieldhouse' view of the influence of German intervention, tho' superficially the Kruger telegramme, German capital on the Rand and the hasty annexation of Bechuanaland seem to support such a suggestion a closer examination of the documents of the views of Rhodes or Chamberlain hardly lend evidence to support such a view. As Gallagher + Robinson have concluded, after Gladstone's annexations "the German challenge was no longer an important factor" in S. African politics. *

In general, then, what light does an examination of African policy show? Above all it demonstrates that the great imperialists, men like Chamberlain, were not following a systematic, predesigned policy of expansion. As Wilde says "Chamberlain + his staff were apparently intent at all times upon solving particular problems and did not reflect upon philosophies with which their acts might or might not be consistent". Again the evidence demonstrates that non-economic factors played a considerable part, in Egypt the canal, in tropical Africa missionary protection and strategic considerations, and in South Africa a vague sort of belief that the whole of the area was a unit and should be federated which might possibly be called "imperialistic spirit" when it finds forceful expression in Rhodes.

Imlah : Schlote : British Overseas Trade.

Péche. 340m (302)
8% Trade / Investment } of S. America.

1787 - Sierra Leone mission: 1st mission.

Finally, there was a typed essay on 8th March on 'Examine & account for the impact of the Irish Question on English politics 1870-1890'.

Summer Term 1963

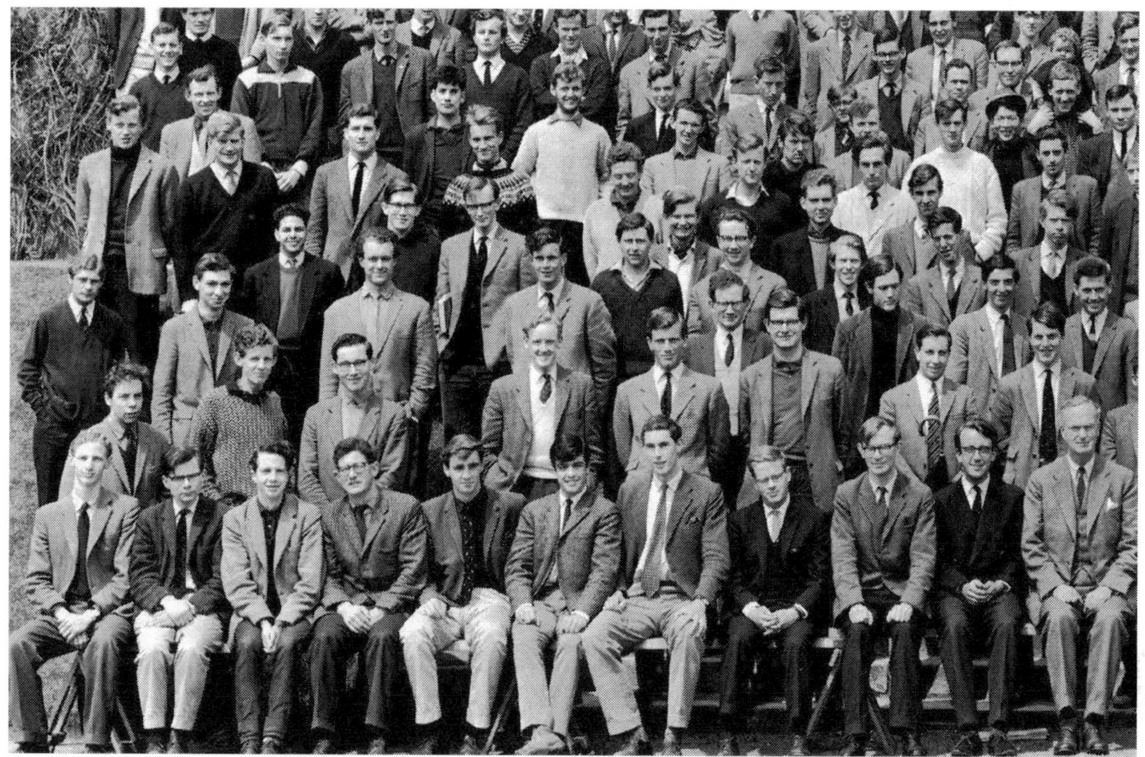

I am third from the left in the front row

EPHEMERA AND REVISION

There is a certificate of Life membership of the Oxford Union Society, on 1st June 1963 and the programme for the summer term.

An invitation card, from St Hughs College.
Maran Liebmann & Jane Piachaud invite you punting birthday party on Friday May 10th. Meet 3.45 p.m. Timms, Bardwell Rd. R.S.V.P.
P.S. Guitar also welcome!

A programme for the Worcester Buskins Summer Production of 'The Dream of Peter Mann' by Bernard Kops. A Play with Music. May 27th–June 1st – 8.30 in the Gardens. I have one ticket for this costing 3/- on 27 May

The last summer term was, of course, peculiar. Firstly, it was effectively only half a term, since we started examinations at the start of June. Secondly, because we were being examined on three years of work, there was a lot of revision to bring three years of essays and readings back into the memory. For both these reasons we did not take on any new topics, except, perhaps rather informally and indirectly, prepare the General Paper. This was the nearest we got to a theory paper, and was a chance to reflect on more general issues, particularly in historiography. So I think that we were encouraged, alongside revision, to read some more general books.

I have a printed Lecture List for Trinity Term 1963 which has a number of lectures. I also went to some final lectures on 'Economic and Social History of England 1000-1300' by Miss B. Harvey; 'The government of England 1066-1307' by H.E. Bell; 'The Post-Restoration Church of England 1660-1800' by Dr. E.A.O. Whiteman; 'Government and Society in France in the Reigns of Henry IV and Louis XIII' by Mrs M. Prestwich and 'Aristotle, Hobbes, and Rousseau' by Mr. K.V. Thomas.

*

I thought carefully about how to prepare for the exams and used various methods. One was to start to continue the system of copying quotations, statistics and other 'facts' onto five by three inch cards cut in half, which I had started in my first year. I had learnt this method from Brian Harrison, and it later became one of my chief research methods during my D.Phil. and also in later years, so that I finally ended up with over 60,000 of these quotations.

For the purposes of the exams I typed out some hundreds of small cards, and over the last term I would carry them round with me and try to learn them off by heart – sometimes also reciting them before I went to sleep. The idea was that my essays would be attractive because they had specifics – facts, quotations – rather than just being run of the mill generalities. It may have helped to pull up my marks a little, as I finally did better in the exams than I had done in my essays and collections over the three years.

A flavour of the sort of thing I was abstracting can be seen from just a very small selection. There is a heading at the top of the card to indicate what the content is. Then there is a quotation or fact in the middle of the card and, if lengthy, this is continued onto the back of the card.

The inalienable rights of a subject. Hobbes.

"a man cannot lay down the right of resisting them, that assault him by force, to take away his life ..."
(same can be said of 'Wounds, Chaynes & Imprisonment'..)
+ also punishment
+ also accuse himself.

'The Obligation of Subjects to the Sovereign, is understood to last as long, and no longer, than the power lasteth, by which he is able to protect them. For the right men have by Nature to protect themselves, when none else can protect them, can by no Covenant be relinquished.'

In the Comm't Manifesto, his ideal is expressed as "An assoc'n in which the free dev't of each is the condit'n of the free dev't of all."

Like Rousseau he believed that freedom was for all – or none.

"Covenants entered into by fear... are obligatory..."
"Voluntary action can arise from fear as from any other emotion (e.g. generosity)"
"fear + liberty are consistent"
(e.g. a man on a sinking ship can either jump off or not: or a man who one holds up with a pistol is taking a voluntary action when he hands over his money.)
[Contemp' law-courts recognize physical but not social or economic pressure.]

"...when therefore our refusal to obey, frustrates the End for which the Sovereignty was ordained; then there is no liberty to refuse; otherwise there is..."

"If a man by the terror of present death, be compelled to doe a fact against the Law, he is totally Excused."

In his 'Utilitarianism' he says if one of 2 pleasures 'is by those who are completely acquainted with both, placed so far above the other that they prefer it, even tho' knowing it to be attended with a greater amount of discontent, + would not resign it for any quantity of the other pleasure.....we are justified in ascribing to the preferred enjoyment a superiority of quality.'

The Communists abandon equalitarianism.

Marx's 'withering away' of the state can only be achiev-ed after the state has grown considerably first, say Stalin & Lenin.

Plato realises that his Rep. is an ideal.

I also used larger cards throughout my time at Oxford to write down quotations that interested me, but not ones which I would learn for my examinations.

> "In every human soul there is a socialist and an individualist, an authoritarian and a fanatic for liberty, as in each there is a Catholic & a Protestant" (R.H. Tawney – Religion & Capitalism, p.212) – November 1961

<u>Philosophy – The Soul</u>

One Nature, perfect and pervading, circulates in all natures.
One Reality, all-comprehensive, contains within itself all realities.
The one Moon reflects itself wherever there is a sheet of water,
And all the moons in the waters are embraced within the one Moon.
The Dharma-body (the Absolute) of all the Buddas enters into my own being.
And my own being is found in union with theirs …
The Inner Light is beyond praise & blame;
Like space it knows no boundaries,
Yet it is ever here, within us, ever retaining its serenity & tallness.

It is only when you hunt for it that you lose it;
You cannot take hold of it, but equally you cannot get rid of it,
And while you can do neither, it goes on its own way.
You remain silent and it speaks; you speak, and it is dumb;
The great gate of charity is wide open, with no obstacles before it.
Young-chia-Ta-shih (Perennial Philosophy – November 1961)

<u>Philosophy – The soul</u>

When a man follows the way of the world, or the way of the flesh, or the way of tradition (i.e. when he believes in religious rites and the letter of the scriptures, as though they were intrinsically sacred), Knowledge of Reality cannot arise in him. Shankora (Perennial Philosophy) November 1961

<u>Systems of life Philosophy</u>

"It requires great energy of mind to create a system, it requires even greater not to become the slave of a creation. To become the slave of a system in life is not to know when to 'hang up philosophy', not to recognise the final triumph of inconsequence; in philosophy it is not to know when the claims of comprehension outweigh those of coherence. (Oakeshott, introduction (xv) to Hobbes Leviathen)

Letters

During my last summer term at Oxford, as I prepared for and took my final exams, the intense relationship with Penny continued, but started to subside. There are hints and traces of a mutual acceptance that things had changed, but also perhaps an understanding that having given Penny so much support during her entrance exams, she would make a last strong effort to support me in these difficult days. The fact that the early urgency was draining away is shown by the fact that within a few weeks after the end of term Penny had left for Italy and we were 'just good friends'.

I shall include just a few of Penny's letters in this final set. In fact she wrote more frequently to me, some 18 letters from her survive with only 13 from me. But many of her letters were just short notes of encouragement. I only give an indication of the poems and prose attached to the letters, and have only included some of the letters I wrote.

There are no letters from me to my parents for this period – I was obviously immersed in exams, and the few letters I probably wrote have disappeared. I shall just give my mother's letters to me, and two from Julie, who had not written for some months and who came up to see me just after exams.

Cherideo May 9th 1963

My dear Alan,

Ten o clock of a hot May morning, I've already been for a long walk with the dogs, had two cold showers and drunk six glasses of water and feel the day ought to be nearing its end instead of just beginning. I should be going to the hospital now but have a tummy upset so am giving it a miss. My work there has achieved some springs on the doors so that the flies are kept out, and five women have been sterilised so I feel I am achieving something though it's only a drop in the ocean of need...

I have been writing round about getting you a job, no answers so far but I am told there would be no difficulty in your getting a lecturer's post at Gauhati University if all else fails, the Vice Chancellor is an Englishman whom I hope to see soon as I'm planning to go to an Assamese wedding if I can face the bus trip to Gauhati. We shall be able to give a bit of help with your passage out as we are being given new cars by the company which means we can sell our old one, won't get much for it but will probably be about £100 to the good.

Apart from the Bish's visit this hasn't been a very eventful week, the tea is piling up so Daddy is more and more involved in the factory and my daily round is much the same. I am half way through Sir Thomas Roe (I see his letters are in the Bodleian) and finding him great fun, he came to India when the position of the factors at Surat was very precarious, and his job for three years was to follow the Moghul Emperor Jehangir around trying to get him to sign some definite contract to protect the English from the Portuguese and the Indian customs officials. He was determined to impress everyone with the dignity of his position, which was pretty hard going as to the Moghuls and in fact Indians generally, traders were only one class above servants and though they were all polite nobody had any intention of taking him seriously. It is all so amusing one is inclined to forget how brave these lone Englishmen were, trekking across India and braving fevers and famines, and then living in Oriental courts so magnificently barbarous that every day must have been a hazard. Roe, who had been a friend of Sir W. Raleigh, had to live in "a house of mud" and the only presents he got were "whyld hogge" though the whole place was dripping in jewels and gold...

Hope you aren't getting nerves & the revision isn't proving too vast, take some tranquillisers if you feel you need them, my little mauve heart-shaped pills are wonderful for about 2 hours & would be just the thing for an interview but you'd better see what effect they have on you first! They make me feel tall, fair & elegant & <u>completely</u> confident though this might be dangerous in an exam! When exactly do you "sit"?

Much love from us both – Mummy

The first of Penny's letters I shall include was written from London on Monday [13th May]

How are you sweetheart? Did you enjoy the party, or did you go to bed early? I really had a marvellous weekend with you, and now am sad that I may not be seeing you for over four weeks. But after your finals are over, we could make whoopee, and visit the places that alternatively one of us has postponed seeing. I found out today that I shall have to leave Harvey Nis earlier than I had expected.... I will have about two weeks free before going to Perugia.

Erick [sic] and I finally arranged where to meet on Tuesday... I'll write to Carrie & Sally tonight, and perhaps Jo too. ...

Look after yourself sweetheart – I love you as much as ever, altho' perhaps we are now both wiser about the future. Thank you very much for the brooch. It is exquisitely beautiful, and was admired last night and thro'out today. I shall always value it as a token of our love and affection.

Tumnus, would you please have some <u>post-card size</u> copies made from the negatives of me? I don't have many photos of me at this young, healthy, age, and should like to posses some. I'll pay you for them when I next see you – oh when will be the day?? – together with the six shillings I owe you.

Darling, darling Tumnus, please don't worry excessively about the finals. And DON'T OVER WORK. You did enough last term, unlike many of your friends, and therefore you don't need to work as desperately as <u>they</u> are doing now. And if you want some relaxation, you know that you can either come up to London or summon me to wherever you are.

My next letter, with its recognition that our relationship had changed, was a day later on Tuesday [14th May]

Thank you for your sweet letter. Yes, it was a nice week-end, tho, as ever, I moped around. Perhaps I will be better company when the cloud has gone. I have been round to thank Geraldine & enclose a letter from Jane

– I went round to thank her this afternoon but she was not in – nor were Carry & Sally when I went round to them.

I enclose a poem by e.e.c [e.e.cummings] – the one you asked for. I will send the whole of his work soon. It makes me sad – as it reminds me of our last few minutes together – perhaps for another 4 weeks? I still love you too my poppet, and I agree that tho' things have changed – there is no need for sorrow.

I am not working very hard at the moment – as you say there's no point in getting hysterical and I reckon that I have paid enough sacrifice for this exam without going mad as well. It has cut me off from many of my friends & what is worse it is precariously near cutting me off from God – for materialism as someone pointed out – is not a disbelief in spiritual things, but a loss of interest in them consequent on an absorption on earthly matters. It will be a heavy loss if I get a good 2nd and lose my soul! I must keep the old flame flickering – even if it it's only by reading poetry & going for walks. Today is leaden, but the purple & white lilacs are still beautiful and I can dream of "the whisper of the seas among the furthest Hebrides" if I get too sated with Oxford.

Enclosed the e.e. cummings poem:

Anyone lived in a pretty how town
(with so many floating many bells down)…

The next of Penny's letters was written on Thursday [May 16th]

Thank you for your letter. It is marvellous that your spirit is so calm and reassured – it is the only way to tackle these damn exams. Don't worry about your soul. The spiritual conflicts may be difficult for you, but I am confident that never, throughout your life, will you stop seeking, nor will you, especially, succumb to materialism.

'I Must Be Talking to my Friends', Michael Mac Liammoir's survey of Irish literature, was superb. He had a wonderful voice range, and he acted as old women, young lovers, and fops with equal verve. Alone, M. M-L held the complete attention of his audience for over three hours, while he savoured the tragedy and comedy of Ireland's progress, lyrical and grotesque, wayward & pitiful, blood-stained and laughing", from an ancient to a modern civilisation. Perhaps this was due to his own poetic genius – I wonder if a volume of his poetry is available.

I hope Erik was not too tired, afterwards, for his interviews the next day. Send him my love, and ask him from me how they went.

I have just written a note to Mark, telling him not to work so hard. Also, would you give the enclosed letter, for the flat-mates, to Paul?

Send my love to all your friends.

The next letter from my mother is dated May 17th, Cherideo:

My dear Alan,

Thank you for your letter describing your visit to London, Mrs M sounds just like Penny and I'm sure I'd like her a lot. There seems to have been a hitch over my letters as Fiona also mentioned not hearing, but I write every week without fail, the only entries in my diary are "Wrote Alan" etc. I haven't had any replies to my enquiries about you here, but nobody ever answers letters for months in Assam. I hope to go to Shillong on June 2nd and will go and see Dr Verrier Elwin then, and also the Vice Principal of Gauhati University. You will probably have changed all your ideas by now, but never mind, can always cancel things. The only snag might be that we will have thrown in the sponge ourselves, we wrote to the Board last week and said unless something was done about our salaries (which have just been lopped by Rs 600 a month due to tax and oddments) we would have no alternative but to resign…

I feel a little depressed this morning after my visit to the hospital, my baby has measles and none of the women are interested in family planning… The Moghuls are more rewarding, I really feel I know Sir Thos Roe well and Jehangir and the lot of them, I will write an article when I've finished which I'll send to you and you can read it and see if you think "History Today" would be interested. I've had no reply to my letter to the Hakluyt Society gent but am still hoping… …

I long to hear you and the coffee cantata … I hope you manage to get to the Cotswolds for a few days before the exam to get that peace and inspiration you need, this is the last big hurdle anyway, you really have had rather an orgy of exams this last few years, one forgets what its like to dread things that much and to have a date hanging over you, but you seem to be being sensible & fatalistic about it. Don't forget to let us know when the exam is will you. I really will answer P[enny]'s letter this week, what are her next moves?

Lunchtime, roast beef & Yorkshire pudding, ug! What wouldn't I do for a salad & a Guinness!

Much love – Mummy

I wrote again to Penny on Sunday [May 19th] from Worcester College

With two and a half weeks to go even the most calm among my friends are beginning to worry – you know that awful paralysed shivering feeling down one's spine and the emptiness in one's stomach! I know that there's nothing really to worry about – but the worry is thoroughly irrational. I am doing less & less work – largely because I don't seem to be able to concentrate. Also feel periodically depressed about other things – which tho' they seem disconnected I suppose will vanish with the cloud – e.g. about the bomb, the death of my soul aforementioned etc. But today feel better and am reading poetry so don't worry for me – thou' you might pray for me? …

I went to the Scala yesterday afternoon. First was 'Through a Glass Darkly' – marvellous as ever. You'll no doubt know the story, but the agony of the girl schizophrenically torn between two worlds – between her husband and God – between her more-than-real dreams and her less than real life was stark & terrible, and for obvious reasons I felt this terrible tension especially. The faces of the girl and her younger brother were exquisite, strong bones yet soft and delicate. The horror of the scene in which God suddenly comes in through the door – and turns into a spider was awful.

The second film – a Polish (?) comedy – "Little Eva- had an adorable sex-kitten in it and some amusing touches – but it's picture of innocence untouchable in the midst of crowds of kindly policemen & crooks was a little overdone. But there, I think I'm in too serious a mood for such things.

I have also been for some walks – one round by the Trout and down beside the 'sparkling Thames'.

Enclosed:

(1st 3 verses of long poem by Charles Causley, 'Survivor's Leave')

'The Song of Samuel Sweet.'

I live in the grassy meadow
Where the little houses lie

Worcester College, Date stamp [Thursday] 23rd May

My brain is quite numb with its burden of facts & theories – I hardly take in the beauties all around – for instance the joys of watching the trout up at Godstow in the warm water lazily chewing bits of floating grass or the strength of a chestnut stallion against the green of Port Meadow.

This afternoon I went to the last ¾s of "Les Enfants du Paradis" & came away dazed but delighted. I won't attempt a trite description with terms such as 'tragic, yet comic, sparkling, yet heavy with grief' etc. You will just have to see it if you haven't. I met Jo afterwards & went along & had tea with her. Christine has just got engaged so there is great rejoicing. I met the boy this afternoon – David someone, he seemed nice…

P.S. One of my favourite of Wordsworth's poems – I often quote the first line & it sums up my present state – yours too?

Enclosed:

The world is too much with us; late & soon
Getting and spending, we lay waste our powers:

… etc.

Penny wrote on Saturday [25th May]:

(Today, I write on pink paper to remind you of my early letters).

How are you, my crxxpy man? Has your wild social life been sustaining your spirits? Wasn't our conversation on Thursday strange? I am sure I was talking a great deal of nonsense, especially when I was encouraging you to flirt with that St H. girl. If you pursued any advantage in that field, I'd be wildly jealous, so you had better remain constant to me (while my eyes meanwhile are wandering this way or that" [small pictures of eyes – 'ho-ho!'] *What has been* [written above 'and still is'] *marvellous about our affair, is that neither of us has ever inflicted any unhappiness upon the other. Really you are a darling man!*

Today has been a very satisfactory day…. [exhibitions etc – at length] …

But now I am getting tired and my thoughts are growing hazy. I am going to tea with Judy Hudson tomorrow, which will be fun.[1]

Look after yourself and carry my love within you. Love to Erik, Mark, Peter etc. Also send my love to Ralph – do go over to see him. I'm sure that he, especially with his optimistic, "poohish' outlook on the world, would keep you happy.

PS Take time off on Monday to read this piece of Dame Edith, at her most bubbling and intoxicated.

My next letter to Penny is postmarked 26th May [Sunday]

I have been dipping into 'Love & Death' as you can see from my quotations. I hope to read it this afternoon when I laze on a punt and drift willow-veiled through the land of Mole and Ratty. I will also take 'The Wind…' with me – which I have borrowed from Ralph. It is a glorious day, with the old ladies basking and your hated swallows glittering from the eaves. It has been <u>*too*</u> *beautiful this week; I went for an agonizing walk on Friday evening to the Victoria Arms & down to the Parks. The young trees and the evening sun and the warm sunlight on the tree-trunks and my shadow against the earth banks and the smell of growing hay and of willow-roots deep in the cool water and the stillness of the leaves and the lakes of butter-cups made me want to cry with delight and sadness. I was in the mood with which Powys is imbued – the bitter-sweet of beauty & mortality. Luckily I met Peter after my walk and talking to him soothed the rawness. Today looks as if it will be another such evening, but if I go walking it will be with Ralph & I am having lunch at the Perch with Peter...*

Mark is very dispirited and will hardly see anyone. Euan held a dinner-party yesterday at the Tudor Cottage – an inn at Iffley about 3 miles from Oxford – and all the gang were there – except Mark who said he was too tired etc. I must go & see him this morning. The party was fun – tho' only Alistair & John Munks were very lively as it was a drowsy evening. We had sherry in Ralph's room – drove out to this 'Ye Olde' place, had a plump meal of sweetbreds etc and then afterwards Peter Ralph and I had a look at the dimly lit Iffley Church. Amidst the darkness of the yews and the graves it was tall and very distant, and as in De la Mare's 'Listeners' we seemed to be intruders into the bat-haunted dusk where the strong Norman carving became soft in obscurity. Then we returned to coffee & brandy.

So the days pass by breathlessly and the fruits and the flowers and the stillness of evening blend into an ever richer harmony and youth flies and the thunder of the waves grows ever louder outside the sheltered reefs of this pleasant lagoon – and we desperately attempt "to squeeze life's grape against our palate fine". And what is left of us my darling?

The above isn't really sad – so don't sympathize – it is just dreamy reverie & clichéd at that – and a lousy letter. But forgive me poppy, look after yourself & love to your mamma.

Enclosed are two quotes.

---

1 . Judy Hudson was the girlfriend, of a limited kind, with whom I had broken up in spring 1962 just before I met Penny.

For our tyme is a very shadow that passeth awaye, and after our ende there is no returnynge, for it is fast sealed, so that no man commeth agayne… The Boke of Wysdom.

'In the house of the moon where I was born
They fed a silver unicorn
On golden flowers of the sun.'
(From 'Love & Death')

Cherideo May 27th

My dear Alan,

You will be very near the Time now, if not already embarked on your ordeal – it sounds like labour the way I've put it and I expect it feels like it too but the relief when it is all over is so exquisite that its almost worth it. As far as we're concerned its of absolutely no importance what sort of degree you get or don't get, my only regret now is that we couldn't have let you have more money at Oxford so that you could have enjoyed the lighter side of life and not been worried about finances all the time, but there it is. We shant expect to hear from you till its all over and you're home, you'll need to hire Pooleys lorry to get you back or perhaps Richard will be able to help.

I cant imagine that any of my doings will be of the least interest to you at the moment, I'm so cross that two of my letters went astray, one in which I sent ideas for jobs you could get here. I think a couple of months in a Kibbutz would be an excellent scheme, if you learnt fish rearing you would be able to give the chaps here a few tips, they have a sort of scheme at Sibsagar but it is very haphazard. I only hope the Chinese don't knock all our ideas on the head, they are making menacing gestures again but its impossible to work out their reasoning. I'm off to Shillong next Sunday 2nd June…

Is it too late for you to apply for a research grant I wonder, Dr Verrier Elwin has been very ill which is probably why he hasn't answered my letter. I had a letter published in the Statesman last week about the burial mounds here… I have finished Sir T. Roe and am on to Peter Munday now, I was so sorry to leave Roe… My hospital work is fairly static now, but I think of F. Nightingale and take heart…

Our thoughts & prayers will be with you, I'm quite sure you have nothing to worry about but that isn't any comfort when one is already worried sick! Life does go on, with or without B.'s! All our love – Mummy

A nostalgic letter from Julie was dated 27th May 1963

Dearest Alikins,

Many thanks for your letter; I was so pleased to hear from you. I should have written to you before now, but I'm sure you know how I dislike the role of Ugly Sister, or Wicked-Step-mother-waiting-in the wings; and did not want to intrude on you until you made it clear that such an intrusion would be welcome. Also, I was very pleased to hear that Penny had passed on my message to you…

I passed thro' Oxford about 10 days ago with Sally and another girl and two boys from the Courtauld. My parents were in Wales, so we drove to Blenheim in Mummy's Wolsley. I did want to stop and see you and our friends, but there was no time. Sally and I both found it heart-breaking to pass through like that. I was driving, and I was so overcome that I had several narrow escapes. When we were passing Worcester, I thought I saw Alistair, and called to him delightedly. It was most unfortunate, because firstly it wasn't Alistair, and secondly, I went straight into a stationary car. He must have thought me dotty, but he said the dent in the car was an old one, so we took his word for it, and hurried on!

Also, I nearly attended May-Morning with Pam, but at the last moment, decided not to, and then regretted it bitterly for days.

Sympathy. I don't know if I deserve any sympathy… I'm not being very successful at the Courtauld… How exciting for you to be going to the Far East! I wish I could. … Sally and I spent a week on Lesbos with a charming and handsome boy… I am glad you are coming to London. I suppose you will stay with your uncle? Of course I shall not try to monopolise you, but hope there will be time for us to see each other a couple of times. I should love to come to Oxford, esp. to see 'Ondine', but I think that will be over. If I did, it would probably be Friday 21st for the weekend, if that's all right with you. I expect Jo Benson would have me. But I don't think it would be very pleasant if everyone will be leaving during those days, would it? I should think the weekend of the 14th would be a much better idea, but only if I can get enough revision done by then, to allow me to lose the 2-3 days before my exam, which is unlikely. If you'd ring me during a lull in the finals (or even just as soon as they are over) I could tell you then. It would certainly be lovely.

.... I shall certainly pray for you, esp. during your exams, tho' honestly, I doubt the efficacy of my prayers right now!

Bonne Chance, and much love. Pusseybite.

Penny wrote again on May 27th from London

Thank you for your exctatic [sic] letter and for all your love – I received both from Pam herself, and from Pam via Judy. I spent yesterday with Judy, and am quite delighted by this enchanting creature (She sends her love to you.) Had you managed to catch her, instead of me, you would have done very well for yourself. However you caught me, and did even better he-he – I wish I was more modest).

I received a short, but nice, note from Mark this morning. I earnestly hope that he manages to pull off the Granada television job... Luckily, sweetheart, I have no such fears for you. Your own tranquillity has sustained me whenever I have been thoroughly neurotic. It is wonderful you are so happy now. Keep it up, my sweeting. PS The enclosed poem may show you, though you've disbelieved me in the past, how difficult it will be for me ever to return to Oxford when you are not there.

Enclosed a poem by Elizabeth Jennings:

Absence

I visited the place where we last met,
Nothing was changed, the gardens were well-tended,
The fountains sprayed their usual steady jet;
There was no sign that anything had ended
And nothing to instruct me to forget.

[two more verses were included]

I wrote again to Penny on Wednesday [29th May]

Thank you for your two letters. I'm glad you're having such a cultured time. I also am indulging in culture of another sort. I have permission to record the records of a friend & spent yesterday evening & the whole of today transferring 10 of Beethoven's string quartets and a quantity of Schubert onto my tapes. At the moment 'Die Winterreisse' is playing – it brings back memories, for I played it constantly last summer. How are things going sweetie? Have your straying eyes alighted on any worthy object? My attempt to carry out your instructions re. Linda were unsuccessful.

I went to the college play on Monday – 'The Dream of Peter Mann' – it was most enjoyable, with some superb acting. Yesterday it was rained off, but Monday was a beautiful evening, with the Lake calm and the trees silent in the evening sun.

I will be going off to the Cotswolds tomorrow – but write to Worcester as usual as I don't know how long I will be away for.

Poor Mark has gone home feeling very depressed I suppose. Peter is morose & very tired. There must be something wrong with this bxxxxy system somewhere to drive so many people to such depression.

I will write at length from the Cotswolds. Look after yourself poppet & think of me. Will be seeing you in a couple of weeks!

Two days later, on Friday (31st May) Penny wrote back about my letter, over-interpreting it as being wretched, which it does not seem to be:

For Christ's sake cheer up!! This last minute wretchedness of yours is fatal, nor is there any need for it. Your recent letters have been so happy, that this morning's epistle almost astounded me. Also don't be affected by Mark's depression. Mark has always been neurotic, and is certainly not typical of most undergraduates. So take

FULL advantage of Burford, DON'T WORK, and read a couple of light novels – at this time they are more useful than poetry, which is often exhausting because of its intensity. Don't forget, either, to go to this party on Sunday. Parties are marvellous just before exams. This is all my advice for the present, tumbling forth in a typical hickedy picked [sic] *manner.*

The concert on Wednesday was superb… [detailed description of] *…Judy and I met for lunch today, and wandered around in the blazing heart of Knightsbridge and Piccadilly – hence my weariness.*

I wrote again to Penny on Sunday [2nd June], postmarked 4th June, from Worcester College

I was meaning to write to you this evening from Burford, but have just missed the 1.0 bus back there after coming down to Oxford for the party last night so will write now instead. First to answer you questions about addresses – Roy Collins, St John's college and Michael Davies (Worcester) both start history schools on the same day as I. Eric thanks you for his letter & says he will be writing soon. Jenny hasn't yet written back about his letter. Eric failed his interview [for a job in the Civil Service] *in part, but has had another & they say he can take method B. which entails taking an almost identical exam to schools a week after he finished proper schools – he's not sure whether he'll do it. I saw Carry today – her exams are not going too badly. She hopes to see you after Wednesday this week. Finally, many thanks for several letters. It <u>is</u> nice to hear from you. I think of you often & miss you.*

As you, even in London, will have noticed the weather has been superb & my Burford excursion is, so far, a great success, and I have lost that depression which you say pervaded my Wednesday letter. I am enclosing a Keats poem, one of his best known, which describes better than I possibly could the lush scenery of the Cotswolds. The change from when I was there last – April with its new-born lambs, bare hedges & fields, cries of curlews and rain-and-sun showers to June with its full-blooded warmth and vegetation, the thick texture of cream and ripening leaves, the glimpses of bluebell lakes and ragged-robin, the smell of warm grass and browsing-cattle, the moss and coolness of the dappled woods is astounding. If only the intoxication doesn't cloud my mind too much over the next week and doesn't make me dream too much of the sleeping woods & fields when I am meant to be writing about Cromwell's Baltic policy! Already I can feel a satisfied numbness creeping over me – an unconcern with the sordid present.

I walked up the delightful Colne valley on Friday. If you remember I went there on Easter Sunday, in the pouring rain, but this time I escaped into the cool, timeless churches with their white walls and rich-wood seats, their mysterious chancels and solid fonts not from the rain but the baking sun. I drowsed in the churchyards and leant, rustic-like & straw-chewing on gateways watching the cattle swinging through the crushed grass. Each bridge I came to I stopped and watched the trout delving upwards to catch flies or swaying like weeds in the pale water. Sorry for all this descriptional gush – but at least it shows I'm happy – tho' I would be happier if you were here to share it all.

I walked back over Wytham woods yesterday evening for the party at the Vicky arms. It was a superb sunset-glowing night and this all helped, but I didn't really enjoy the party terribly as I felt too lazy to attempt conversation or to do anything 'mad'. All I remember of it is a vague impression of faces dancing in the fire-light, of smoke and the distant sound of a tape-recorder, and then the river with dark trees and the moon above and the may-hedges spectral white and cold…

P.S. I am just about to walk through Wychwood – the original from which Tolkein [sic] took his name (Witchwood)

Enclosed two verses from 'Ode to a Nightingale' by Keats, those starting

> I cannot see what flowers are at my feet,
> Nor what soft incense hangs upon the boughs, …
> ….
> Darkling I listen; and, for many a time
> I have been half in love with easeful Death…

The next letter from my mother was from Shillong on June 3rd.

My dear Alan,

I'm sitting in a little wooden hut looking out on green ridged hills very like the downs with big soft English clouds resting on them – 3,000 feet up at a place called Burrapani just below Shillong…
Your poor nerves must be frayed to shreds. I'm thinking of you all the time & wishing I could help in some way, but by this time the worst should be over I reckon…

17 years ago to-day I sent you out of hospital here after your tonsils operation, & started having Anne, strange that I should be back & makes me have long sad thoughts of how I have changed since then when I was full of bright dreams for you all – now I realise how little we have managed to accomplish & how much of the sparkle seems to have gone out of life too. Enough dreary reminiscing, it must be those Readers Digests with their hearty advice to the Over Forties, the most depressing thing about middle age is that your feelings all seem to be carbon copies, nothing quite fresh or authentic. All hormones according to the R.D. [Reader's Digest]! …

I do hope you'll have a couple of weeks of peace & good weather in the Lakes after you've finished, we'll discuss plans in due course, we shall be able to help a bit with your passage – a great deal depends on your finding your important papers! e.e. Cummings arrived safely & very quickly and I love it, wish I had him here. Actually, wish I had some paints too but I couldn't capture these humped monsters of hills…

I won't mention money except to hope that you have enough to get you home, let us know eventually. Do hope you aren't too worn out, discouraged or generally got down by Events, this time last year it was Anne & I in a minor way but it all seems terribly unimportant now.

All our love & thoughts, Mummy

The day after my exams had begun, Penny wrote on Friday [7th June]

I hope everything is whoopee with you. Isn't it hot? I hope you are not being baked in the examination schools. What are the questions like? Interesting? Unstimulating? Do send me some examples of the questions.

Yesterday I went to the flics with Carrie. …

Look after yourself, sweetheart. I am thinking of you.
PS Have a nice weekend – don't work too hard.
PPS. I am sending you one of my favourite Auden poems. I sometimes believe that the sea, which has made for England's greatness, and the sauntering clouds, are part of England's physical solidarity, which remains unchanged in atmosphere and climate, though the character of its people is constantly in flux.

Attached was another poem, which I will include as a scan as an illustration of Penny's handwriting.

'Look, Stranger"   W. H. Auden.

Look, stranger, at this island now
The leaping light for your delight discovers,
Stand stable here
And silent be,
That through the channels of the ear
May wander like a river
The swaying sound of the sea.

Here at the small field's ending pause,
Where the chalk wall falls to the foam, and its
tall ledges
Oppose the pluck
And knock of the tide,
And the shingle scrambles after the sucking surf,
and the gull lodges
A moment on its sheer side.

Far off like floating seeds the ships
Diverge on urgent voluntary errands;
And the full view
Indeed may enter
And move in memory as now these clouds do,
That pass the harbour mirror
And all the summer through the water saunter.

The Final Examinations Summer 1963

We worked for three years, but almost everything depended on the ten days or so at the end of our third year when we sat all the papers, usually twice a day, from 9.30 a.m. – 12.30 p.m and 2-5 p.m. I have most of the papers, though I sent English II and the two General European Papers to Penny and so do not have them. I also kept some of my working notes/plans on some of the papers. In the plans, I divided each answer into four parts, with timings written at the top as to when I must finish that answer. I shall put under each answer what appears in each section/box of my plans.

SCHOOL OF MODERN HISTORY

ENGLISH HISTORY

I

Thursday, 6 June 1963, 9.30 a.m.–12.30 p.m.

Candidates should **complete four** *answers, including at least* **one** *from each section. They should illustrate their answers by sketch-maps where appropriate.*

SECTION A

1. How did the pattern of Anglo-Saxon settlement and land-exploitation differ from that of Roman Britain?

2. Which single source or type of evidence provides the most reliable material for English history between about A.D. 400 and 600?

3. Why is Theodore of Tarsus important?

4. In what ways did the authority exercised by the West Saxon kings after Alfred differ from that of earlier Anglo-Saxon kings?

5. How important was trade as an influence in the development of English boroughs before the Norman Conquest?

6. 'The weakness of the tenth-century monastic revival lay in its failure to act as an intellectual stimulus.' Discuss this view.

7. Can a case be made out for starting a history of Feudal England in 1066?

8. Did the Norman Conquest accelerate the growth of Papal influence in England?

9. Did the Danes make any lasting impression on the social organization of any part of England?

10. 'His circumstances called forth the display of greater constructive power than had been shown even by his father.' Discuss this judgement of Stubbs on Henry I.

3 U 15 **Turn over.**

Section B

11. 'The king was the source of justice and the guardian of order, but he neither created the law nor imposed a system of order.' Discuss this comment upon the government of England in the twelfth century.

12. 'From pleasant France, where I was brought up to the love of learning, I was taken to this land of wretched barbarians.' Had the scholars and courtiers in the service of the Angevin kings any grounds for looking on England in this way?

13. To what extent was the power of the Crown over the English church affected by the murder of Becket?

14. 'A great prince, but an unlucky one.' Discuss this contemporary description of King John.

15. What light does the career of **either** William Marshal **or** Simon de Montfort throw on the conventions and ideals of their contemporaries?

16. 'A time of new ideas and rapid change.' Discuss this description of the thirteenth century as applied **either** to architecture **or** to the study of natural science.

17. Examine the factors governing **either** Anglo-French **or** Anglo-Scottish relations under Henry III and Edward I.

18. Discuss the view that the policy of Edward I as king was deeply marked by his memory of the events of 1258–65.

19. Examine the ways in which the agents of the royal administration during the twelfth and thirteenth centuries were recruited, trained and rewarded.

20. To what extent was England part of a European trading area during the thirteenth century?

Theo. 1. Bede on. – Sit'n in Britain. – Celtic – Roman. – King – Church.	– Sit'n in 664. Whitby & aftermath. plague. Wilfrid. – power of Cant.	character Theo's reforms. – penitential. – synod of Hertford. – bps & clergy.	10.20. 11.0. 11.40. 12.20. later history of Church – power of Cant.
~~Feudal Eng'd 1066?~~ Alfred – A/S kingship. Mercian + N/an kingship – Church. – Economic – financial – geld etc – legal. – local gov't. – central admin'n. – [illegible]	– divisions. ealdorm. unity – military –	– personal Kinship/lordship. [illegible]	
Feudal Eng'd in 1066? 1. Introduction. Stenton's view.	1. Institutions. – Church. Law. Central Admin. Landholding – Overlordship. Military. Financial.	2. Personnel.	3. Synthesis. 1356. [illegible] BAWD.
King source of justice + [illegible] of order. meaning – i.e. he was fount of will – NOT struggle. – e.g. Henry I.	~~Ste~~ Order. – eg Stephen.	Law. ~~eg Stephen.~~ – innovations. – Hen II + Stephen.	1. O.W. Sussex. and he was the first of the A/bps whom the whole Church of Eng'd agreed to obey. [illegible]

My second paper was English History II. I sent the paper to Penny so do not have a copy of it, but I did retain my notes on how to answer the questions as follows:

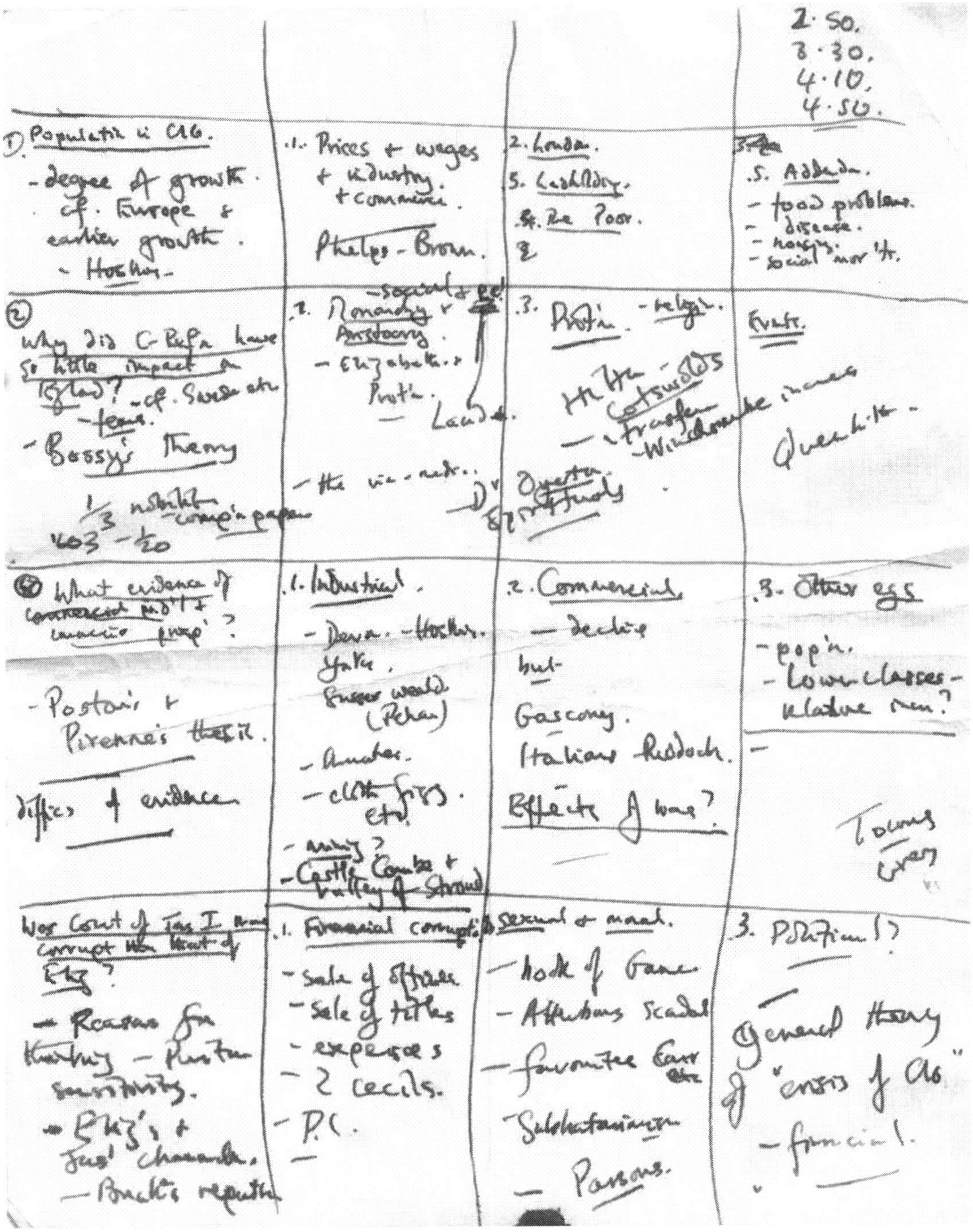

2·50.
3·30.
4·10.
4·50.

1) Population in C16. – degree of growth cf. Europe & earlier growth. – Hoskins –	1. Prices & wages & industry & commerce. Phelps-Brown.	2. London. 5. Cash[illegible]. 4. The Poor.	3. [illegible] .5. Addenda. – food problems. – disease. – [illegible] – social mor[illegible].
2) Why did C-Ref'n have so little impact on Engl'd? – cf. Swedish etc – fears. – Bossy's Theory. 1/3 mobility – comp'n paper. 1603 – 1/20	1. Monarchy & Aristocracy – Elizabeth & Prot'n. – Laud. – the via media.	3. Prot'n – relig'n. Cotswolds. – Transfer – Winchcombe [illegible] – Dr Ogster Eg [illegible] funds.	Events. Queen [illegible] –
3) What evidence of commercial dev't & economic prosp'? – Postan & Pirenne's thesis. diffics of evidence.	1. Industrial. – Devon – Hoskins. Yorks. Sussex weald (Peham) – Amstr. – cloth [illegible]. etc. – army? – Castle Combe & Valley of Stroud	2. Commercial. – decline but – Gascony. Italian [illegible]. Effects of war?	3. Other eggs – pop'n. – Lower classes – relative rise? – Towns [illegible]
Was Court of Jas I more corrupt than that of Eliz? – Reasons for thinking – Puritan sensitivity. – Eliz's & Jas' characters. – Buck's reputation	1. Financial corruption – sale of offices – sale of titles – expenses – 2 Cecils. – P.C. –	Sexual & moral. – Book of Game – Overbury scandal – favourites Carr etc. – Sabbatarianism – Parsons.	3. Political? – General theory of "crisis of C16" – financial.

The following day came the two European General papers which I do not have, nor do I retain the notes. On the Saturday I did a French unseen paper. I did not receive a mark for this, so I imagine it was just an extra paper to make sure that we had kept up with at least one foreign language.

SCHOOL OF MODERN HISTORY

FRENCH TRANSLATION

Saturday, 8 June 1963, 2–5 p.m.

Each language must be done in a separate book

Le paysan est volontiers sentencieux, surtout en prenant de l'âge. Il s'exprime par proverbes et maximes; il ne peut pas se créer à lui-même des idées générales, et il les emprunte à la sagesse traditionnelle. 'Le pauvre père disait' revient très souvent dans la conversation des paysans. Cette tradition est le seul livre où beaucoup d'entre eux aient lu. Or, elle se compose de formules courtes, de proverbes et de maximes. Nous nous étonnons quelquefois que, vivant en pleine nature, les paysans ne fassent pas sur les phénomènes naturels plus d'observations personnelles et neuves: nous sommes dupes d'une illusion. A part quelques grands faits très simples, comme la succession des saisons, tout dans la nature est extraordinairement compliqué. La plupart des proverbes rustiques ayant trait à la vie agricole n'expriment guère que des coïncidences qui se renouvellent de loin en loin, mais comme c'est pour le paysan le seul point de repère, il y tient beaucoup, et il a beau prendre le proverbe en défaut, dix fois, vingt fois: il n'y renonce pas. C'est qu'il résume pour lui un premier essai de généralisation, de science, et qu'il a, en outre, la marque vénérable de la tradition. Voyez ces paysans sentencieux dont les paysans eux-mêmes disent qu'ils ont 'l'air prophète'. On sent que, quand ils citent une maxime, ils croient participer à une sagesse très haute, et qu'ils en conçoivent pour eux-mêmes une sorte de respect.

Au point de vue de la terre, le paysan est très attaché à la propriété individuelle; au point de vue de l'esprit, il aime, au contraire, à confondre sa propre sagesse avec la sagesse indivise de la tradition. Le prix de l'effort personnel, de la conquête personnelle dans l'ordre du savoir ne lui est pas suffisamment connu. Et c'est là une des raisons qui l'empêchent de vérifier et de corriger par son expérience propre les préjugés nombreux qui circulent. (JEAN JAURÈS.)

maxims.
proverbs.
wisdoms.
aphorisms.

2.2.30 read
2.30 – 1 pk.
2.3.0 – 3 lay.
3.0–3.30. fuel up.

①

The peasant, above all, (increasingly? as he gets older) is — governed by folk-lore ? — — — — ?

~~the expres~~ the expresses himself by proverbs and maxims; he cannot form for himself general ideas, and he borrows these from ~~the traditional~~ the wisdom of tradition. "My old (son?) father used to say.... 'very frequently appears in ~~the~~ peasant conversation. Thus tradition is the only book in which many of them have read. On the other hand short formulas, proverbs and maxims, are invented. ~~Thus~~ We often say to ourselves that, living in a natural state? the peasants cannot have more ~~than~~ personal and new (renewed?) novel observations on natural phenomena: but we are mistaken. Apart from several great and simple facts, like the succession of the seasons, everything in nature is extremely complex. The majority of the rustic proverbs being concerned with the agricultural life ('life in agriculture') hardly express more than the coincidences which reappear / renew themselves from time to time, but since it is for the peasant the only point of reference, he holds onto it strongly, there is much truth in it, and he has oft heard the proverb by mistake ten times, twenty times over; he does not renounce / give it up / lose it. It becomes for him a first attempt at generalization, at science, and it has, on the outside, the venerable aura of tradition. Regard these peasant wisdoms which the peasants themselves say have a "prophetic atmosphere / spirit / flavour / presence" One feels that, when they quote a maxim, they believe themselves to joining in a high / elevated wisdom, and that they find in this, for themselves a kind of respect.

As far as the land is concerned the peasant, on the other hand, is attached to individual property; as far as the spirit is concerned he loves to merge / immerse his own wisdom with / in the invisible wisdom of tradition. The price / cost / prize of personal effort, of personal achievement / conquest in the sphere of knowledge is to him not sufficiently / adequately / hardly known. And it is this which is one of the reasons which prevents him from verifying / correcting by his own experience the numerous prejudices which circulate.

We had a day off on the Sunday, when I wrote a letter to Penny, indicating my state of mind with six papers done, and five to come.

Postmarked 9th June (Sunday)

I have pile of letters beside me from you – thank you so much darling, they have cheered me up immensely as I awake into another day of exams. … I know you'll forgive a short & dull letter. I've been scribbling madly too much recently & have the worst to come. …

I enclose the English II paper which might interest you – I did those with rings round them – quite well I hope. I can't make any guess at how well I've done – pretty badly I suspect on English I when none of my prepared questions came up – alright, I hope, on the rest. Everyone is fairly cheerful and the questions have been pretty fair and at least it is a relief to find 6/11 gone. I had a gift question on English III paper – "how did the religious conflicts of the time reflect themselves in Victorian literature" – so that I could woffle on about Tennyson, Mathew Arnold, George Eliot, Wordsworth etc. The only slight catastrophe has been muddling up the order of the papers & hence doing no revision for the first general paper. I enclose the General Papers – though I'm not sure you'll find them of great interests. Could you return the English II paper by Wednesday as Lady Clay wants to see it.

Thank you also for the delightful Lear we had a session after dinner on Friday reading him – Euan, John, Sally and myself. I know you'll forgive a short & dull letter. I've been scribbling madly too much recently & have the worst to come. But before I get onto my troubles – how are you sweetie? Carry said you were a little tired on the evening she saw you. Are you happy poppet? If you've had this superb weather through which I've been sweating even London must have begun to look like Paris. It looks like being by far the most balmy summer term of my time – it would be! ...

Today I take off. Yesterday evening I had supper at Nos. 3. Carrie seems a bit depressed – vacant & purposeless – probably a reaction of tiredness and anti-climax. I expect I'll feel the same. It is once again lovely today and I intend to go up above Godstow with Mathew Arnold. I <u>have</u> liked the passages you sent me, especially the Auden. Bother! When I was just looking for a snippet to send you I packed up the 'Rubaiyat of Omar Khayam' into my essay yesterday. Anyhow here is a snippet – 'Gaudeamus igitur...." There is so much of the sadness, the hopeful bravado of the Victorians in it that I don't know what to include – anyhow you must have a copy so I will just put in a very little.

About next week-end darling. Would it hurt you terribly my sweetie if I said I think it would be better if you didn't come down, but we saved all our celebrations to the following week-end? I will probably be still tired and anti-climaxish and all my friends will be tense and in the middle of their papers still. Apart from this I have an <u>enormous</u> amount to do. For instance I've got to record a lot of music, prepare some reading for before my viva, sort through my notes and books & all my junk of 3 years before packing it, I am having dinner with my tutor[1] and have got to go and see some friends in the Cotswolds for a day & take Carrie to the witch museum another day. My mother wants me to search for books on Indian history for her and I've got to organize my trip to Israel and see people etc about getting a place somewhere next year as well as write a million letter. Please say if this is thoughtless of me – especially after my Wednesday protests – but I'm sure it would be better to be completely free and revived than still worried & involved in 'business'. Anyhow darling I think of you often & will write soon – Look after yourself & love to yr mama,

Enclosed is a sheet:

Yet Ah, that Spring should vanish with the Rose!
That Youth's sweet-scented manuscript should close!
The Nightingale that in the branches sang,
Ah whence, and whither flown again, who knows!

---

[1] I was advised to prepare in case I was asked back to Oxford a few weeks after I left for an oral examination or viva. Vivas were only held for about one in ten students, in cases where the marks indicated a borderline between classes and the chance that through the oral examination the student could be put into the higher class. I would need to take some books and other materials to prepare for such a contingency, particularly as my teachers could see that I might be on the border of a first class degree but was by no means certain of that class.

SCHOOL OF MODERN HISTORY

ENGLISH ECONOMIC HISTORY FROM 1485 TO 1730

Monday, 10 June 1963, 9.30 a.m.–12.30 p.m.

Candidates should **complete four** *answers.* **Questions 1** *and* **2** *must be attempted. Other questions attempted should be answered, as far as possible, with reference to the documents.*

1. Comment briefly on **four** of the following:

(*a*) That no maner of person . . . bye or bargeyn any Wolles, or take promyse of bargeyn of any Wolles, that shall growe in any of the same Shires . . . but onely such persones as of the seid Wolles shall make or doo to be made Yarne or Cloth within this realme.

(*Act reserving English wool for English clothiers*, 1489.)

(*b*) The statute for enclosures and intacks to be put in execution, and all enclosures and intacks since 4 Hen. VII to be pulled down, except mountains, forests, and parks.

(*The agrarian programme of the Pilgrimage of Grace*, 1536.)

(*c*) Ye shal do the King the greatest service that can be devised. For hereby his people and subjects (in the multitude of whom his honour and safty consisteth) shal be encreased.

(HALE's *charge to the juries impanelled to present enclosures*, 1548.)

(*d*) 6. Apprentices.—None to be received apprentice except his father spend 40*s*. a year of freehold, nor to be apprenticed to a merchant except his father spend 10*l*. a year of freehold, or be descended from a gentleman or merchant. (*Considerations delivered to the Parliament*, 1559.)

(*e*) For answer to the first allegacion, the seid merchants doo saye that they neither doo kepe or intend to keepe, nor in any former tyme haue kept, a monopolie in their trafique at Embden or elswhere.

(*The Merchant Adventurers' answer to the criticisms of the Hanse League*, 1582 (?).)

(*f*) It is contrariant to the lawes of this realm and customes equivalent to the lawes written, that a forreiner should be privileged in a free borrow in such manner, and the inhabitantes restrained, And that men shold not convert ther salt pittes and salt cotes, being ther inheritance, to ther best vse.

(*Protest of Boston against the salt monopoly*, April 1586.)

3 U 2 **Turn over.**

(*g*) *Item*, the great charges that have been defrayed by the traders into Turkey, finding out and continuing the said trade unto this day.

(*Commercial arguments for maintaining an English agent in Turkey*, 1587–88 (?).)

2. Comment briefly on **three** of the following:

(*a*) Now the company seeing the extreme malice of the haberdashers, and that the sale of their wares lieth solely in them . . . they have considered to raise them a stock to take in all men's wares when they be made, to avoid hawking, and to encourage men to follow their trade and continue within the corporation, for the benefit of all parties.

(*The Felt-makers' joint-stock project*, c. 1611.)

(*b*) Next to erect and settle an office of assurance, with fit and skilful Iudges, which should determine, and give speedy Execution in their Decrees and Acts, betweene Adventurers, to avoide demurs, delayes, and hindrances, that happen by tedious suites in adventures at sea among Merchants. (ROBERTS, *The Treasure of Traffike*, 1641.)

(*c*) Neither are these heavy Contributions so hurtfull to the happinesse of the people, as they are commonly esteemed: for as the food and rayment of the poor is made dear by Excise, so doth the price of their labour rise in proportion; whereby the burden (if any be) is still upon the rich. (MUN, *England's Treasure by Forraign Trade*, 1664.)

(*d*) It is observable, that in this part of the country, there are several very considerable estates purchas'd, and now enjoy'd by citizens of London, merchants and tradesmen.

(DEFOE, *Tour*.)

(*e*) This town of Sheffield is very populous and large, the streets narrow, and the houses dark and black, occasioned by the continued smoke of the forges, which are always at work. (Ibid.)

(*f*) The county of Essex, a large and exceedingly populous county, is chiefly taken up with the great manufacture of bays and perpets.

(DEFOE'S *account of the wool trade and woollen industries*, *temp*. George II.)

3. 'Local studies have shown that England has not one agrarian history but many.' Consider this view with reference to **either** the sixteenth century **or** the time of Defoe's *Tour*.

4. Why did enclosure arouse less controversy at the end of the seventeenth century than it did in the middle of the sixteenth?

5. Assess the financial achievements of Sir Thomas Gresham.

6. To what extent did the fortunes of the English clothing industry in the sixteenth century depend upon the policies of the central government?

7. Do you consider that the working of the Poor Law had any important consequences for the economic history of this period?

8. Assess and account for the extent of London's participation in English foreign trade in the period 1540–1640.

9. How much importance would you assign to the usury laws of this period?

10. 'The obstacles to expansion seem to have lain in the field of demand rather than in that of supply.' Discuss this dictum with reference to the non-textile industries of the period 1560–1640.

11. What was new about the economic thought of **either** Thomas Mun **or** Sir Dudley North?

12. Did the Navigation Acts achieve their objectives during this period?

13. What light does Defoe's *Tour* throw upon the economic consequences of the state of inland communications in the early eighteenth century?

14. 'The age of internal laissez-faire.' Does the early eighteenth century deserve this description?

1 + 2 by 11.0.
3. by 11.45.
4 by. 12.30.

and all the trade of merchandize ... a ... drawn by hand.
engl

(1) Amount.
- Defend ... Defoe.
- Advice to Steward - Montague

(2) Attitude - Position.
- Other ...s

(3). Population & prices.

(4) Food.
Who was protected?

Assess + account for ... partic... - ... trade.

The ... .
1) Pop'n.
2) Complaint of Hull
3) ... in 1581.
4) Debate in 1604 - 1608.
5) Figs usually given.
- food.
- coal.
- ... diss'n

Local studies -
6. Midlands + Leics.
- enclosure.
- engrossing.
- yeoman
... of depopn. ...

4 Cloth + wool trade.
Reasons given for growth of ... ...

Decline of outports.
Ipswich etc. - Defoe.
- ... ...

(2) ... of West
- enclosure ...

(1) Gov't + Monopo...

(2) Cloth trade.
- ... - Wilts etc.

(3) Re-exports.
'new stuffs'

(3). Lake District.
- ... + ...
- ... in ...
... of ...
(Diss'n of ...)

(4) Med'n trade.
(5) Antwerp.
(6). Baltic + ... trade

SCHOOL OF MODERN HISTORY

GENERAL PAPER

Monday, 10 June 1963, 2–5 p.m.

Candidates should **complete three** *answers*

1. 'The great ambition of the political scientist is to be like other scientists.' What are his chances of success?

2. Could there be a plausible Marxist theory of art?

3. What part did the discovery of nature play in the Romantic Movement?

4. Consider the characteristics of a historical explanation.

5. What differences have **either** sociology **or** economics made to the procedures of the historian?

6. Does history throw any light on the problems presented by under-developed countries?

7. Discuss the importance of slogans in determining the course of historical events.

8. What part does intuition play in historical knowledge?

9. Discuss the place of **either** Stubbs **or** Namier in the development of historical method.

10. Has appeasement ever been the right policy?

11. Were people in general more superstitious in the Middle Ages than in the modern world?

12. Why has Antiquity exercised such power as a model in **either** political theory **or** the arts? Illustrate your answer from any period of European history.

13. What conditions have favoured the development of opera?

3.0.
4.0.
5.0

Any light on problems in under-dev'd countries?

Tawney & China.

1. Similarities & differences - dangers.

2. Corruption, payment & civil service.

3. Leadership.

4. Process of industrialization.

5 Opposition to change - vested interests. superstition.

- change.

Lawrence & nature.

Romantic Nov'l.

1. [illegible] & C18?

- definition of Romantic nov'l.

both more general & more specific.

- idea of growth.

2. Challenges which Romantics sought to face
- religion.
- artistic
- social etc.

3. Weapons
(a) Style
(b) New Objects.
(c) 'Nature' in C18.
(d) The new 'nature'.
(e)

4. Eg. of romantic.
Wordsworth, Keats, Coleridge - Goethe
[illegible] - [illegible], de Sade, etc.
Novelists etc. - Scott, Macaulay

People more superstitious? - external superstition - [illegible]

1. Attempted defin. of superstition.

- explanation of phenomena that cannot otherwise be [illegible]

- eg. Chaucer.
- astronomy etc.
- psychology.
[illegible]

(a) Witchcraft.
- [illegible]

(b) 'Sophisticated superstition'
= religion.

i) War.
2) Moon.
3) T.V.
4)

(c) 'Country' superstition.

(d) Organized religion.

(e) 'Open Society theory'.

SCHOOL OF MODERN HISTORY

POLITICAL THOUGHT

Tuesday, 11 June 1963, 9.30 a.m.–12.30 p.m.

Candidates should **complete four** *answers.* **Question 1** *must be attempted. At least* **one** *question (in addition to Question* 1) *must be* **completed** *in each section of the paper.*

SECTION A

1. Comment briefly on **four** of the following passages, including at least **one** from each of your prescribed authorities:

(*a*) A husband and father rules over wife and children, both free, but the rule differs, the rule over his children being a royal, over his wife a constitutional rule. (ARISTOTLE.)

(*b*) From what has been said it will be clearly seen that all the partisans of different forms of government speak of a part of justice only. (ARISTOTLE.)

(*c*) For, as I must repeat once and again, the first principle of all action is leisure. (ARISTOTLE.)

(*d*) Of Persons Artificiall, some have their words and actions *Owned* by those whom they represent. (HOBBES.)

(*e*) Feare, and Liberty are consistent. (HOBBES.)

(*f*) The end of punishing is not revenge, and discharge of choler. (HOBBES.)

(*g*) La guerre n'est donc point une relation d'homme à homme, mais une relation d'État à État, dans laquelle les particuliers ne sont ennemis qu'accidentellement. (ROUSSEAU.)

(*h*) Ainsi la Loi peut bien statuer qu'il y aura des privilèges, mais elle n'en peut donner nommément à personne. (ROUSSEAU.)

(*i*) Quoi! la liberté ne se maintient qu'à l'appui de la servitude? (ROUSSEAU.)

3 U 22 **Turn over.**

2. How would Aristotle judge one state to be better than another?

3. What did Aristotle consider to be the connection between education and politics?

4. Why is Hobbes's theory of political obligation open to such divergent interpretations?

5. Is there any relation between the economic ideas and the political recommendations of **either** Hobbes **or** Rousseau?

6. With what success did Rousseau solve the problem he set himself in the *Contrat Social*?

Section B

7. Discuss the posthumous influence of the political thought of **one** of the following: Plato; St. Paul; St. Augustine.

8. What effect did the feudal structure of society have upon medieval political ideas?

9. Analyse the relationship between the political thought of Aristotle and that of **either** Marsilius of Padua **or** Hooker.

10. What was new about the political thought of Machiavelli?

11. Assess the impact of scientific thought upon the development of political thought in **either** the seventeenth **or** the nineteenth century.

12. 'Almost all the governments which exist at present, or of which there remains any record in story, have been founded originally either on usurpation or conquest, or both, without any pretence of a fair consent or voluntary subjection of the people' (Hume). Why then did the notion of the social contract prove so enduring?

13. In what ways did the political thought of the English Utilitarians reflect their assumptions about human nature?

14. What moral assumptions do you find in the political thought of Marx?

15. 'Some of the most valuable insights into the working of political society are to be found in the writings of men not usually regarded as political thinkers at all.' Discuss this statement with reference to the work of **one** of the following: Shakespeare; Pascal; Voltaire; S. T. Coleridge.

16. Has the concept of Natural Law any intellectual validity?

17. Are there any good grounds for saying that my moral obligations are greater to my fellow-citizens than to the inhabitants of other countries?

18. Discuss the influence of ideas about primitive society upon political thought before 1800.

19. Why are relatively few contemporary British philosophers interested in political philosophy?

Aristotle education & politics. cf. Plato on education. cf. Rousseau. Hobbes	(1) The overall of political ch[illegible] & state "states originating in the bare existence for the sake of the good life." - leisure - happiness - virtue.	(2). Aristotle's justice. (3). Function of educn. & stability – cf. revolts - it is not the property but the desires of men that needs to be equalized.. by state educn. - the legislator must mould to his will the frames of new-born children mass of one amenable to compulsion rather than reason." "states become in time what their leaders make them."	(4) The good life. - nature - custom - reason. (5) No division state & society.
Rousseau. "such a form of association must be found in which each will surrender to all yet retain all his liberty." cf. Aristotle. Hobbes	(a) R's def'n of liberty' & alienation. "liberté consiste dans la loi qui on s'est prescrite" - cf 2nd Disc. S.C. cf. on inequality "dependence" cf. Hegel – outside him Kant.	(b) His solution.	(c) Criticisms. "l'obéissance à la loi qui s'on prescrit c'est liberté".
Marx. (a) Marx & Hegel & (i) Rejection of complete materialism	(b) Alienation & the worker.	(c) Inherent values (d) His critique of cap't society (e) Dialectic	cf.

SCHOOL OF MODERN HISTORY

Special Subject (7)

COMMONWEALTH AND PROTECTORATE

1647–1658

I

Tuesday, 11 June 1963, 2–5 p.m.

Candidates should attempt **all** *the questions*

1. Comment on **four** of the following:

(*a*) Notwithstanding what was said, Lieutenant-General Cromwell, not for want of conviction, but in hopes to make a better bargain with another party, professed himself unresolved, and having learn'd what he could of the principles and inclinations of those present at the conference, took up a cushion and flung it at my head, and then ran down the stairs. (LUDLOW, 1648.)

(*b*) This mine of his was not wrought with so much privacy but it was observed by some discerning men of the Parliament, especially by those who had the direction and management of the war with Holland. (Ibid. 1652.)

(*c*) The new Chief Justice, before he came to sit on the bench, took care to have this business accommodated with Cony, who lost his reputation by withdrawing himself from a cause wherein the publick was so much concerned. (Ibid. 1655.)

(*d*) Sir Henry did not disown either his dissatisfaction with the present state of affairs, or the publication of the discourse before-mentioned. (Ibid. 1656.)

(*e*) When in the long Parliament, you did by a law confiscate men's estates and lives and liberty, both in England and Ireland, had you any more, nay so much, evidence as in this case, though, I presume, justly too. (MR. BEDFORD, *Burton's Diary*, 6 Dec. 1656.)

(*f*) An Act for taking away purveyance, and compositions for purveyance, was this day read the third time, and, upon the question, passed; and ordered to be offered to his Highness the Lord Protector, for his consent. (Ibid., 12 Dec. 1656.)

 Turn over.

2. Comment on **four** of the following:

(*a*) And if there be any one that makes many poor to make a few rich, that suits not a Commonwealth.

(CROMWELL to WILLIAM LENTHALL, 4 Sept. 1650.)

(*b*) And that there was high cause for their dissolving, is most evident: not only in regard there was a just fear of the Parliament's perpetuating themselves, but because it actually was their design.

(CROMWELL'S SPEECH, 12 Sept. 1654.)

(*c*) The Gentlemen that undertook to frame this Government did consult divers days together (they being of known integrity and ability), how to frame somewhat that might give us settlement. (Ibid.)

(*d*) And therefore I say, under favour: These two Experiences do manifestly show that it is not a *Title*, though never so interwoven with the Laws, that makes the Law to have its free passage, and to do its office without interruption.

(Ibid. 13 April 1657.)

(*e*) The lieutenant general hath behaved himselfe most childishly, not refrayning very poysenous and bitter expressions in publique meetings.

(MR. LLOYD to THURLOE, 13 March 1654.)

(*f*) They told me, when we come to an agreement, that in that I had done my lord protector as much service as in winninge a battell.

(BROGHILL to THURLOE, 26 Feb. 1656.)

3. Comment on **four** of the following:

(*a*) 1st. That by Order of the House the 11 Members by his Excellency and his Army impeached, and charged of high misdemeanors be forthwith sequestred, and disenabled from sitting in the House.

(*Representation of the Agitators presented at the Generall Council of Warr*, 16 July 1647.)

(*b*) There are many thousands of us souldiers that have ventur'd our lives; wee have had little propriety in the Kingedome as to our estates, yett wee have had a birthright.

(MR. SEXBY at Putney, 29 Oct. 1649.)

(*c*) I do again repeat to you this truth, that the now ruling party among the States of the Province of Holland had much rather that the present government of the Rebels in England were well established than that the K. were restored. (NICHOLAS to HYDE, 14/24 April 1653.)

3 U 11

SCHOOL OF MODERN HISTORY

Special Subject (7)

COMMONWEALTH AND PROTECTORATE

1647–1658

II

Wednesday, 12 June 1963, 9.30 a.m.–12.30 p.m.

Candidates should **complete four** *answers. Their answers should be illustrated by reference to the prescribed authorities.*

1. Assess the importance of the *Heads of the Proposals.*

2. Did the Leveller leaders display a lack of political realism?

3. How much political importance would you assign to the land sales of this period?

4. How effective was the use made of sea-power by the governments of the Commonwealth and Protectorate?

5. 'The lunatic fringe of radicalism.' Do the Fifth Monarchy Men deserve this description?

6. To what extent did the objectives of Cromwell's foreign policy differ from those of the Rump?

7. Would you agree that the years after 1653 saw a steady decline in the political consciousness of the Army?

8. 'Emigré gossip, lacking any genuine historical value.' Consider this description of the *Nicholas Papers.*

9. In what ways did financial problems affect Cromwell's relations with the parliaments of the Protectorate?

10. What obstacles stood in the way of complete religious toleration under the Protectorate?

11. Did the rule of the Major-Generals achieve anything?

12. Assess the contribution made to the Protectorate government by **either** Thurloe **or** Henry Cromwell.

The subsequent report on how I had done only emerged a couple of months later, as shown below.

*

My mother wrote again from Cherideo on June 11th:

My dear Alan,

A letter from you just arrived, very calm and relaxed I'm glad to say, by now all will be Over – but not the wonderful weather I hope I hope so you can have some <u>*really*</u> *carefree summer days afterwards. I'm longing to hear what the papers were like, hope you'll send them out. Before I go any further, no I didn't get your letter about reading on the Ahoms, but 2 lovely books have just arrived, the "History of India" and "A Pearl to India". The former is* <u>*exactly*</u> *what I wanted to pull together the threads of my somewhat scattered knowledge, so far I've only read the Moghul chapters but intend to go right through it, it even mentions the Assam Co! Thank you very much for both, I shall consider them as my birthday present, so don't dream of sending anything else.*

When I was in Shillong I rang up Dr Verrier Elwin the anthropologist in charge of N.E.F.A. (or rather advisor to the North East Frontier Agency). He was very nice and asked me to go & see him, but alas I couldn't without transport. He said he didn't think N.E.F.A. was much good to you as no Europeans are allowed passes, but gave me the name of someone who is in charge of a new research institute in the Garo Hills and said he thought this might offer you an opening. Anyway I'll try it. I saw a few days later that according to the local rag "Dr Verrier Elwin's philosophy for N.E.F.A. has failed & he'll soon be leaving". I was almost glad to see in yesterdays paper that 12 N.E.F.A. officials had been killed by the Daflas, one of the wildest tribes. Dr V.E. advocated a very careful approach, with emphasis on not disturbing the tribal pattern, but the Assam Govt. thinks it can charge in and order everyone about willy nilly.

I enjoyed my stay in Shillong very much… There must be somewhere a religion that combines service with wide tolerance, Buddhism perhaps, but I've never seen this in action. Or Quakers? I must learn more about them…

Have a good clear out of all your papers & see of you can find your passport & birth certificate, if not I'll get a copy of the latter from Shillong. We'll be able to help you with your fare to Israel & on here, so hope you'll carry on with the Scheme – unless you get a 1st & then will you stay on at Oxford? Could you please send this to Penny, I've lost her address, it was chewed by a goat!

My next letter to Penny is Friday June 14th, from Worcester College, two days after the final exams were finished.

I am taking it fairly easy at the moment. Writing all the letters that have been piling up – sorting out my notes etc. I don't quite feel like beginning to read yet – though I took some notes from a book on C16 witchcraft yesterday. I bet I was the only historian who went and read a history book in the Bodleian the day after his exams!

Otherwise I have been drifting around, vaguely thinking of my future plans and talking to Ralph etc. I probably won't go to Israel until the Autumn as I must get some money before I go, just in case …. Looking at David's letter I see he thinks of spending September in Perugia, when will you be there? Can you let me know soon as I will be writing to him shortly. He is coming back to England at the end of this month.

I waited for Mark & Peter outside schools with Sally. Then when those two had gone off to dinner (their exams seemed fairly ghastly, but everyone is relieved that things have started) Sally and I went to a film 'The Apartment' with Jack Lemon and Shirley McLean. It was most amusing and Shirley completely (?) won my heart.

You will understand why I have enclosed the Wordsworth – I'm longing to see the Lakes again (& you), Look after yourself darling & write.

Enclosed are lines from 'Tintern Abbey':

These beauteous forms,
Through a long absence, have not been to me
As is a landscape to a blind man's eye: …

From The Tables Turned

Sweet is the love which Nature brings;
Our meddling intellect
Mis-shapes the beauteous forms of things: –
We murder to dissect.

I wrote again to Penny on Monday [17th June] Worcester College

… The weather has been gloomy ever since schools and my spirits reflect it. Its funny – you'd think one would feel happy and relaxed now – but the reaction after the release of tension leads to a mood of vagueness and

accumulated tiredness. I am unable to concentrate for long or get very enthusiastic about all the books I intended to read. I've started Zorba but not got very far into it. Yesterday evening Roy came round when I was about to write to you and we talked for a longish time and then went & had a drink at the 'Welsh Pony'. He seemed cheerful – if dazed – and much appreciated your card – as did all my other friends. I haven't seen Mark or Eric since the first day, but I imagine they are already feeling much better. Mark & Peter end tomorrow afternoon and are having their champagne at Carrie's flat. But I'm having tea with Alec (chaplain) so won't be there. I wonder if they'll suffer from the same feeling of anti-climax and the same conviction that they have done badly which I now feel. I hope we're partly recovered by next week-end, tho' by then we'll probably be getting sentimental at leaving the old place…

There was another letter from my mother from Cherideo on June 19th.

My dear Alan,

I hope by this time you will be a man of infinite leisure with nothing to do but go through your possessions (says she hopefully). Alas the wonderful weather seems to have just lasted through your exam and now broken as it did last year, never mind if you have Penny with you I expect the weather will be of little consequence. Anne said she might be coming up also Felicity and Fiona and Rosemarie so that hunt for Men will be on again as the Lake District never seems to be able to produce anything new in that line.

I'm enclosing a letter I got from this place I wrote to, I will leave it to you to decide if you want to follow it up. Dehra Dun is certainly a delightful place and as she say there are lots of schools there where you could probably get fixed up but of course its rather a long way from here. Perhaps you have changed your mind about the whole tour? But I'm pressing on regardless, the only snag is that we may not be here by then ourselves. We have decided to resign at the end of the year if they don't do something drastic about our terms, this struggling on against financial odds, wearing climate, indifferent health (mine out here) and the dreadfully callous attitude of the people in charge is getting us both down. We should have to work for three years at home until we get our pension but both feel we'd be happier and healthier and more satisfied living on bread and cheese (and Guinness) than banging our heads endlessly against the rocks of indifference, corruption and complacency which is our lot here. As I get older too I find I am physically worn down by the suffering of people and animals all around me, and can seem to do nothing to alleviate any of it as everything needs money of which we never have any to spare. I could continue my study of the Moghuls just as well at home, better in fact as books are easier to get, of course there are lots of things I would miss and I'd carry a million regrets for all I have left undone, but in this particular sphere it is almost impossible to do anything I've discovered. … Even if we do decide to retire though you could still carry on with your tour, spending less time in India perhaps and concentrating on the cities where the need is greatest…

What is your present money situation? I sent £50 to Fiona this month and I don't suppose she has spent it all so get some from there. I feel a little worried about her, Granny and she don't get on…

We went to spend the week end with friends at Mohokutie which was the first garden I came to in tea and is full of memories of you all, the river you fished and fell into, the little pool where you learnt to swim, the tree you fell off, cant think how any of you survived there actually! It's a terribly hot bungalow…

I have nearly finished Peter Mundy and am then going to write an article on S T. Roe and send it to History To-day, could you give me their address? Don't tell Granny or anyone as the shame of having to admit rejection after Roberts successes would be galling! I'm revelling in the Oxford History which is very impartial on the whole though it is rather amazing to read that it is a matter on which the British can congratulate themselves that by 1921 the Indian continent was beginning to stir in its sleep. So many subjects for books occur to one as one reads, for instance the catastrophic Afghan war of Lord Auckland where of 16,000 people who escaped from Kabul (British) one survivor arrived a few weeks later, one could write a lovely debunking Woodham Smithish book on that and on Warren Hastings and on Napier in Sind, in fact most of them. But of course they were handed India on a plate and would have had to be high minded indeed to have pushed it aside and it is always easy to be wise after the event. It is the post Mutiny period when society petrified into the stony superiority of the Raj as revealed in E.M. Forster and as I remember it when I first came out that made the tragedy of modern India. It's a tragedy I've had almost enough of frankly, though I'll never cease to feel guilty.

A dull letter but you must be used to them –

My love to Penny, and everyone, and lots to you, Mummy

The following note from Penny shows that the relationship lasted until the end of the term.

Friday [21st June] 1963 London

Darling,

This is a very brief note to cancel this mornings time-arrangements. Unfortunately I may be running about 1½ hrs late, and so won't be coming with the others. I think I arrive at your room about 2.30 – however I do not know by what means of transport – so don't meet me. Sweetheart, also, do try and look decent for the evening, ie. white shirt.

Love, love, love, Poppy

The final letter from my mother in this period was on June 23rd.

Cherideo June 23rd

My dear Alan,

I was relieved to get your letter and hear that you got through the exam without getting nosebleeds, toothaches or a nervous breakdown, all of which I had envisaged! As you say it is really of no consequence what degree you get, a friends brother is now doing a year of Social Administration at London after getting a 3rd at Cambridge so you could always do that. You sounded as if you were in a slight trough of depression and anti-climax, sheer tiredness I expect and I hope by now you will be feeling revived. I understand the feeling you have of not quite knowing where next, but I'm sure you are doing the wisest thing in taking a year out from life to wander and wonder, and don't worry about the money side too much, we will help you as much as we can and will pay your fare from here to Vancouver, we are now allowed to draw on our Provident Fund for passages and you can count it as a late birthday present. We Can also help you get started as we have the money from the car coming in, so go ahead and make your plans. I suggest you set off in mid-August then if you spend a couple of months in Israel and a month in Calcutta I reckon you will reach us for Christmas. I haven't had much success in getting you a job here but haven't tried the University yet, the trouble is there wont be an awful lot of time if you want to get a job in Canada too, because we hope you will be home again for the last month of our leave next year, and anyway whatever course you take will start in September.

Jack Simpson came back last Monday, and we have new terms so I suppose will hang on after all, the increase in pay wont affect us too much at the moment as so much of it goes in tax, but it will bump up our provident fund quite a bit. It'll mean we can send a bit more home too and save us tearing out our hair in handfuls quite so often. When you have seen how much if anything you get from your grant let us know because its now a subject we can discuss without anguish!

Seem to be having an unusually dull time here and do little but read and write, I have got onto a thing called the National Library where I may be able to borrow books for my Moghuls, I'm half way through my article on Sir T. Roe and finding I know far too much and could really write a book on him and pruning is a problem…

Please tell Granpa I'll write to him to-morrow, are the raspberries ripe & the azaleas blooming & is there honey etc?! Wonder how Beryl is, she seems to go from one problem to another poor dear.

Lunch time again, oh to be eating it in the front lawn, am terribly homesick. My love to everyone and don't do too strenuous a job if you have to do one at all. I'm so glad the ordeals over (or nearly) but I suppose leaving Oxford is a sad moment. Much love – Mummy

My undergraduate days at Oxford were now over, and I awaited my exam results in the Lakes, for which I left on Tuesday 25th June. For a while I would live at home and returned for a viva on 23rd July.

Summer Vacation 1963

Me as Assistant Warden and Jack (Warden) of Glenridding Youth Hostel

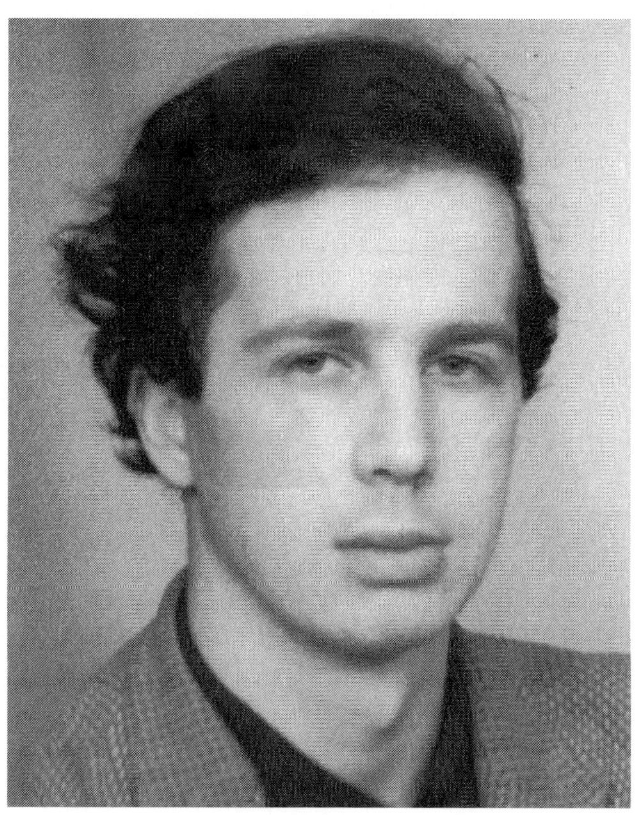

My passport photo

I had been planning to spend a 'gap' year after I graduated in the Summer of 1963. There are frequent references to these plans in my mother's letters and my letters and writings. Various places are mentioned. I was also wondering whether to spend part of the year working for some good causes. Through the summer of 1963 as I worked at the Youth Hostels I tried to finalize these plans – called off at the last minute by getting a State Studentship that would not allow me to defer for a year.

I have a file with some of these plans. Several documents about visiting Israel, including a 'Working Visitors Application Form' for Kfar Hannassi kibbutz. The details on this application are as follows, leaving out personal details and religion. The purpose I specified as 'Learn about fisheries; meet interesting people; learn about communal life.' I was recommended by Paul Hyams. The period of stay was specified as 'Am travelling overland so dates are very approximate – will confirm nearer date. November 1963 – January 1964. (I never sent the application)

There is a travel brochure for Greece, an International Certificate of Vaccination showing my TAB and other vaccinations, and a brochure on 'Essential Information for citizens of the United Kingdom and Colonies who intend to travel overseas'.

Other than this, there are various small cards with addresses of people whom I could contact. These included R. Hamlish, Chief Economics Branch, Fisheries Division, FAO, Rome; Sir Geoffrey Nye, Technichal Co-operation at the Ministry of Agriculture.

There are several short lists of what I might take on my travels: sleeping bag, matches, cycle cape, foam rubber, ground sheet, sleeping bag, torch, mug & cooking set; raisins & nescafe, meths tablets, book, medical – sunburn, fly-repellent, midge ointment, Savlon, plasters, enterovioform (2 tubes), Hallwag – map of Europe; water bottle. A less impressive list of things than those I had taken to the Outer Hebrides in the summer of 1961.

Letters

The deep relationship with Penny seems to have withered very fast, partly because she had gone off to Italy for several months, before returning in October to attend York University.

My mother's first letter of this period was written on July 11th.

My dear Alan,

I cant remember whether I've heard from you this week but it doesn't matter, don't bother to write until your viva is over (except for my birthday!) as you must be sick and tired of trying to express yourself on paper. I have very little to write of except that I'm feeling much better, physically and mentally, got so depressed with the heat and feeling ill and not having anything to take my mind off it but am right back to normal now…

Anne sounds very happy which is also a comfort, it just remains for you to get this last beastly bit of the exam over, how important is the viva anyway? I expect your plans are all in a state of indecision still but don't worry, its much better to be elastic and grab at "handles of chance" as they come along. I am writing to-day to the Principal of Tura College in the Garo Hills as I see he is advertising for a teacher of English, he wants one straight away so it wouldn't do for you but he might have some other ideas. The Garos are the people Dr Verrier Elwin mentioned in his letter, wonderful fishing rivers there, we could visit it even if there isn't a job available. I see Oxfam are starting a project in Naini Tal so it might be worth while enquiring about that.

… I have started on my old round of family planning but am not having a great deal of success, only two more women this month…. Am struck with the Moghuls too as I cant get any more books… Could you give me the address of the Hakluyt Society and I think I will join. Meanwhile I'll brush up my Assamese history which

I've largely forgotten. If I don't get the address of History To-day I'll send my article on Roe to you and you can see if you think its interesting enough to pass on to them. …

I will ask Terry Luscombe if I can buy his guitar off him when he goes, you cant lug yours round on your back but it would be a wonderful ice-breaker here, apart from picking up catchy tunes and learning them. Keep your tour elastic, if you are enjoying Israel you might want to stay much longer, or vice versa…

The next letter from my mother from Cherideo is on July 20th

My dear Alan,

Thank you for your very nice birthday letter which as you see arrived in good time, I wish you hadn't sent me a book, I counted your last books as my present…

I don't see any reason why you should become humourless or bigoted, one is much more inclined that way when one is young and sure one knows the difference between right and wrong, the older one gets the less dogmatic usually, though of course its easy to confuse tolerance with laziness. I'm sure you'll find a job where you can use all your talents and enthusiasm if you don't rush things and don't expect your life's work to be anything but confusion, frustration and just occasional gleams of pure happiness and fulfilment. I don't think that's a cynical attitude, so much of our trouble is expecting happiness as a right, those who don't expect it are patently the happiest people.

I haven't quite got the idea of the fisheries, are you planning to learn about increasing fish production so that you can go to some part of the world where people are hungry? I think it's a jolly good idea and I'm sure Freedom from Hunger or one of those things could advise you. I feel so guilty that I didn't get a letter off to you to cheer you on your way to your viva, I lose all sense of time here but nevertheless it was most remiss. Anyway it'll all be over now for better or worse, I hope the warden thing comes off, it should be amusing, no word about your passport so I presume you have found it… Hope you'll manage to see Felicity again, she is certainly very attractive …

With much love, have a good rest (mental)
Mummy

My grandfather's diary notes that on Tuesday 23rd July I had my Viva Voce examination in Oxford.

The next letter from my mother was from Shillong, [postmarked at Ambleside August 6th, hence written towards the end of July]

My dear Alan,

Perched on the side of my hillside in Shillong I'm thinking of you perched on the top of Ullswater with all your cares and exams temporarily behind you … I came up last Friday through the awful floods… Now we have the Chinese making warlike noises again… [failed to see Verrier Elwin because he was not well] [reflections on poverty etc]

I can't accept any of the religious excuses for the world's unhappiness – i.e. it is man's wilful turning away from god that brings about his destruction, or his payment for the sin's of a past life, this might apply to grown men but don't tell me little twisted starving children are responsible for their lot. If there is a loving god in charge of this mess it is so impossible to understand his motives that it is profitless to think about them. We shall know eventually, meanwhile there is this unfair, unjust, unhappy world into which millions more children are being born daily to become twisted and starve…

Anyway enough of this, the trouble is there are very few people I can let off steam to out here, everyone thinks I'm mad for even thinking about such things, except Daddy who agrees with me but is so burdened with practical problems that he doesn't have much time or energy for metaphysical speculation…

I will send £20 this month and £30 next as I said, I would like you to have £40 in travellers cheques before you leave so let us know at the beginning or anyway middle of September how things stand. You will need some clothes don't forget.

Much love, enjoy yourself, Mummy

The first of my writings, a post-card, is written to my grand-parents a few miles away in the Lake District. There is no date on this but it is from Glenridding Youth Hostel, so must be in late July or early August soon after I went there. The postcard is of Ullswater, with my youth hostel indicated by arrow.

Dear G & G,

Hope all goes well – I will try to get over later this week but it is complicated & expensive (about 10/- return) so will come over Friday or Saturday. Please give my regards to Beryl, Anne J etc. I dream of the strawberries & raspberries – perhaps I will collect some when I come? The job here is not too strenuous and we have had wonderful weather. The hostel is where the arrow points (in the middle of the picture) from my room there is a glorious view down to the Lake. There is good fishing & I caught 2 plump 6 oz trout the other day. Look after yourselves – see you soon. Much love, Alan

In early August, I received the official notification of my result in the History Finals - a somewhat curt acknowledgement on the card (with my writing) I had left to be filled in by the University.

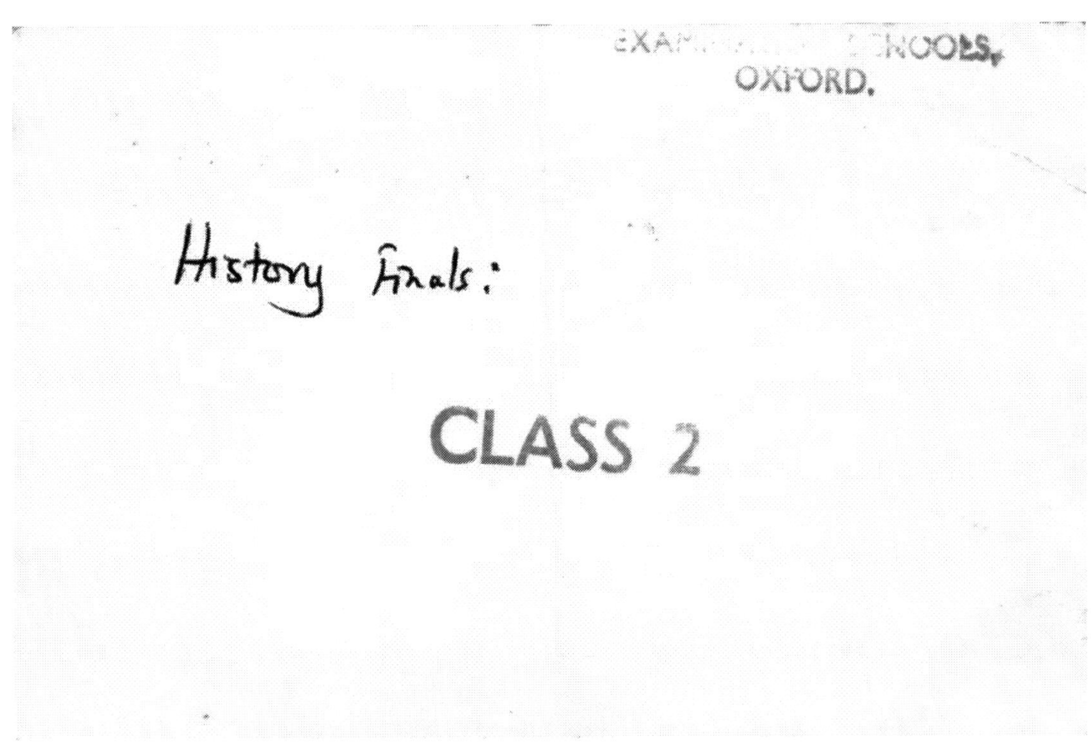

OXFORD.

History Finals:

CLASS 2

The next item is a short letter from my uncle Richard, dated 4 August.

Dear Alan,

May I send congratulations on getting your 2nd in History. I saw the notice of the results yesterday… It was a good reward for a lot of hard work. What new? Maybe some travel. Are you still keen on teaching? I will be interested to hear your plans…. [school news] I hope you get yourself a good holiday, Love Richard

My sister Anne also sent a card from Germany to congratulate me.

The next, undated, letter from my mother was written in early August 1963

My dear Alan,

I thought you would like to have this which was waiting for me on my return, and gave me a great thrill as you can imagine. My first rather unworthy thought was "Snooks to Robert", I thought it was a very nice letter though and sent almost by return of post – don't lose it, it might be the Breakthrough. I owe a lot to you for your interest and encouragement, it is very easy to get discouraged when one is thudding away on a typewriter on boiling hot days in this remote corner of the world, but I now shall take up my work with fresh enthusiasm.

By now you will have heard your results and will either be sunk in gloom or whooping it up, I suppose the long viva meant that you were a border line case, but that doesn't help because one doesn't know which border! It doesn't matter to us in the slightest, or to you really except your pride as you don't intend to get a "good" job in the sense of one bringing in large sums of money where the snob value of a first might matter. You don't need to have your injections till ten days before you leave so needn't worry about that for the present, the situation here is a bit depressing again, many people think this is just a political move on the part of the Chinese, a sort of war of nerves, lets hope they're right. We are to be flown out at the first sign of any real trouble…

I came down from Shillong yesterday and it was lovely to be back… Mind you send me a copy of the paper when it comes out.

With much love from us both – Mummy

I returned to the Lake District after my viva and at the end of July or very early in August started to work at a small youth hostel, high up above Ullswater lake. From there I wrote.

August 5th 1963 Greenside Youth Hostel, Glenridding, Penrith, Cumberland

Dear Mummy and Daddy,

I'm writing in advance of your letter to tell you my exam result. After a week of anxious waiting etc Granny rung up to tell me that a card had arrived announcing that I had got a 2nd. So there it is! My feelings are mixed. On looking through the lists of results in the paper & seeing how many of my friends got 3rds & how few of those expected to, got firsts, I am very relieved. Also, if, as I hope, my viva was between a 2nd & 1st. I must have done fairly well & got a good second – I will now know if this is so until my tutor returns from France; on this depends whether Lancs – or rather the Ministry of Education – will give me a State Scholarship – only a very few are given. So I still have to wait before my plans become reasonably definite. The slight disappointment I felt when I heard my result – one always hopes against all reason – has almost disappeared & I feel far less tense. I hope to get down to some serious reading – but there are more distractions in this life than one expects – eg tomorrow I have got to go into Kendal to see the dentist & the day after Stephen Grieve is coming over. He rang up on the evening of the day on which results were published in the paper to congratulate me. His brother Alistair also got a 2nd at the Courtauld Art Institute & has got a lecturing post at Leeds University. Stephen sounded very husky, but says he is better. He is going back to St Andrews in October for another two years. Apparently the root of the trouble was in the kidneys all the time.

I have just written off to Leonard Cheshire about working in a Raphael home in India. I said that I would be prepared to work for up to a year –depending on any conditions attached to a State Studentship. (If I <u>did</u> get such a Studentship I would only go abroad for a year & then return to do a B.Litt. attached to Worcester – by the way there grant would cover <u>all</u> my costs at Oxford so don't start reaching into your pockets anxious, but as I said, this is a big <u>if</u> since they normally only give them to Ist's). Yes, the fish-farming idea was to study problems of fish culture (?) then apply them to the world hunger problem. I have got some literature from Miss McCormick & a friend at Oxford is putting me in touch with the greatest authority in the world on fish-farming in the far East – Hickling. This would be an alternative to the Cheshire home & would be rounded off – if Lancashire fork out – by a years course in Agriculture Economics at Oxford. If the worst comes to the worst I can always just go to Israel for a year, wandering round the Mediterranean for a few months & then come back to do a Diploma in Education or Social Studies. The latter sounds very interesing & has been expanded to a two year length. I've a feeling that tho' very interested in economics, I am better suited to dealing with small personal problems, rather than large, abstract ones, which require a scientific, rational mind. I can't see myself running a big organization – tho', as you know, I have a mania for filing cabinets & little lists!

How is Mummy's reading going & Daddy's extra work? I suppose it must be the worst of the hot weather now – tho' you don't sound as conscious of the heat as usual. Here the long spell of baking weather has broken

& mists swirl round the toes of the mountains. August bank holiday, needless to say, was flooded out. Loud moans from all the landladies at Blackpool etc, who attribute their losses to the fact that people haven't as much to spend nowadays as they used to have' – but when you see the cars parked outside the little country pub down the road one wonders!

The work is harder than I thought it would be. Not that it is particularly exhausting, just opening tins, washing up, mopping floors, cleaning lavatories, emptying waste-bins & giving orders to pimply youths & maidens. But I work in the morning from 7.30 to 12.30 & in the evening from 5 to 9 or 10 – 7 days a week (about 65 hours per week). For this I get £2-15s per week – also as much food as I can eat and a small ration of fresh fruit. It is extremely difficult to get home. I tried it the other day, and came back absolutely exhausted with a pile of books etc. I had to run down the struggle in twenty minutes – and my bones have been aching ever since. It was a sultry day and I dripped sweat as I tumbled into the bus & then after a gobbled meal and frantic search for possession staggered back up the 1½ miles to the hostel bearing, it seemed, all 26 volumes of the Encyclopaedia Brittanica, but in reality books of criticism on the Romantics, the Metaphysicals etc. Billy etc will be coming up next week as Granny will tell you –I hope to see them over here.

I have just sent Felicity 'The Young Visiters' by Daisy Ashford (aged 9) have you read it? It starts "Mr Salteena was an elderly man of 42 and was fond of asking people to stay with him" and has delightful remarks such as "Then he sat down and eat the egg which Ethel had so kindly laid for him"

Hope all goes well & things don't get worse on the frontier.

Lots of love, Alan

My mother had written to the Raphael Homes on my behalf in May.

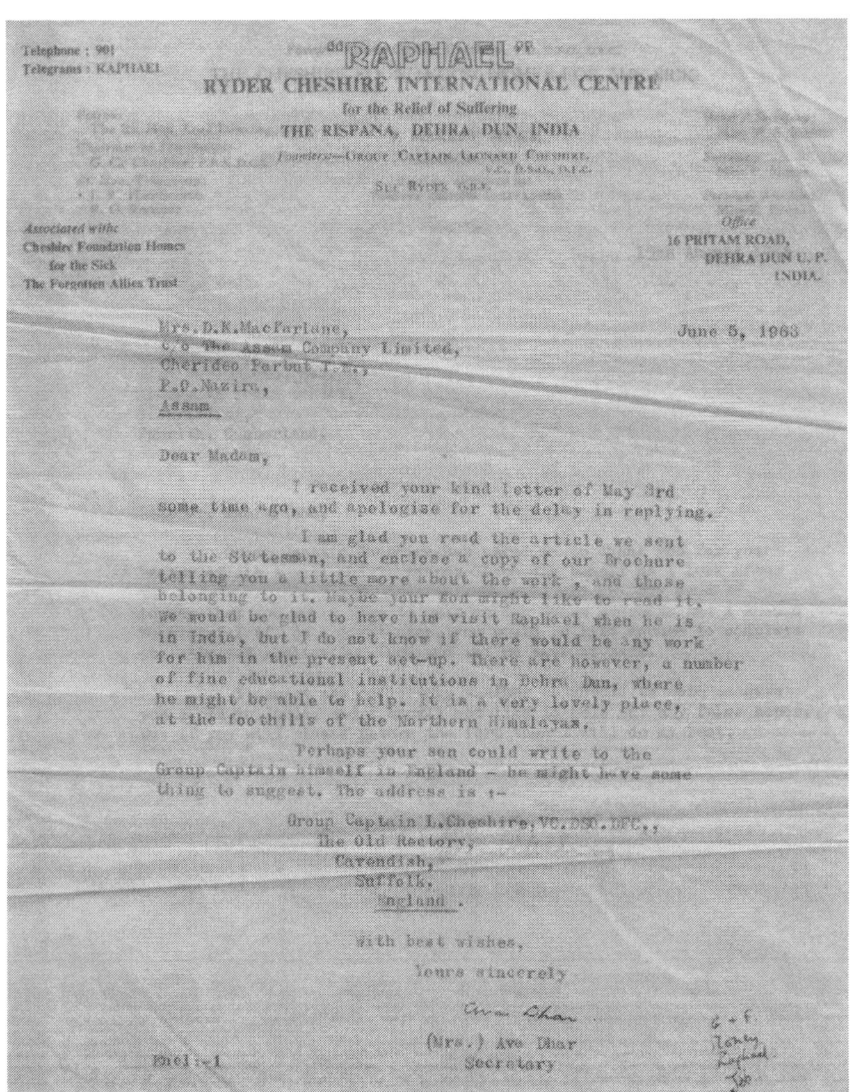

Telephone : 901
Telegrams : RAPHAEL

"RAPHAEL"

RYDER CHESHIRE INTERNATIONAL CENTRE
for the Relief of Suffering
THE RISPANA, DEHRA DUN, INDIA

Associated with:
Cheshire Foundation Homes for the Sick
The Forgotten Allies Trust

Office
16 PRITAM ROAD,
DEHRA DUN U.P.
INDIA.

Mrs. D.K.MacFarlane,
C/o The Assam Company Limited,
Cherideo Purbut T.E.,
P.O.Nazira,
Assam

June 5, 1963

Dear Madam,

I received your kind letter of May 3rd some time ago, and apologise for the delay in replying.

I am glad you read the article we sent to the Statesman, and enclose a copy of our Brochure telling you a little more about the work, and those belonging to it. Maybe your son might like to read it. We would be glad to have him visit Raphael when he is in India, but I do not know if there would be any work for him in the present set-up. There are however, a number of fine educational institutions in Dehra Dun, where he might be able to help. It is a very lovely place, at the foothills of the Northern Himalayas.

Perhaps your son could write to the Group Captain himself in England – he might have some thing to suggest. The address is :-

Group Captain L.Cheshire, VC.DSO.DFC.,
The Old Rectory,
Cavendish,
Suffolk.
England.

With best wishes,

Yours sincerely

(Mrs.) Ava Dhar
Secretary

Encl:-1

I wrote after this encouraging reply and also received a helpful response.

Founder: Group Captain Cheshire, V.C., D.S.O., D.F.C.
THE CHESHIRE FOUNDATION HOMES FOR THE SICK

Patron:
The Rt. Hon. Lord Denning, P.C.
Chairman of Foundation:
G. C. Cheshire, F.B.A., D.C.L.
Jt. Hon. Treasurers:
J. R. Handscomb
R. G. Emmett

7, MARKET MEWS,
LONDON. W.1.
Telephone: GROSVENOR 2655
Telegrams: CHESHOME AUDLEY LONDON

General Secretary:
Miss M. S. Mason
Secretary:
Miss E. Mayes
Personal Assistant:
Miss E. Evans

13th August 1963

Alan Macfarlane, Esq.
Greenside Youth Hostel,
Glenridding,
Penrith, Cumberland.

Dear Mr. Macfarlane,

Group Captain Cheshire has asked me to thank you for your letter of 4th August and to answer it on his behalf as I look after the offers of help the Foundation receives. It is very good of you to say that you would like to help in our Homes overseas and I should be grateful if, as a first step, you would be kind enough to complete the attached application form and let me have it back.

I cannot say definitely whether we should be able to give you a job in India, and I should not like to hold out any false hopes. But if you will please return the form then I will do my best.

Yours sincerely,

H.E. Marking

However the idea of working at the Ryder International Centre petered out. They were already winding up the institution and I was in any case unable, as we shall see, to take off the time before my next degree.

It was at the Youth Hostel that I received notification from James Campbell of my marks.

WORCESTER COLLEGE
OXFORD
Tel. 47251

8. 8. 63.

Dear Alan,

Thank you for your p.c. Your marks were good. Eng I $\beta+?+/\beta?+$, II $\alpha\beta/\alpha\beta$ III $\beta=/\beta++$, Dos. $\beta++/\alpha\beta$, Gen. I β, II $\beta+$, Pol. Th. $\alpha\beta$, SS I $\beta+?+$, II $\beta++$, General $\alpha\beta$. As you see they marked a lot of your papers twice and viva'ed you for a first. All told very creditable though I'm sorry you didn't quite make it.

Yours sincerely,

James Campbell.

I had obviously been viva'd for a First, but not quite made it.

The next letter from my mother is from Cherideo on August 9th

My dear Alan,

We saw the results of your exam in the paper yesterday and were thrilled – of course we knew you would do it but it is wonderful nevertheless. You deserved it after all that hard work, and I hope now you are having a blissful rest with all the tension eased out of your system. We just cant get over our good fortune in having such gifted children, really it is little short of miraculous – anyway thank you for all your work and for making the very small sacrifices we have had to make more than worthwhile. I only wish you hadn't had to scrape so much at Oxford, but I suppose a lot of others do too, its just one of those things. How I wish I could be there to see you get your degree, Daddy is talking wildly of flying me home but I'm afraid its out of the question really, let us know when its to be so that we can visualise it anyway. I shall always remember getting the news, I was watching the efforts of a python in the chicken run to climb out, he had been caught in the tea and was about to be hacked to death when Daddy rescued him and we let him cool off a bit before escaping. He had just reared his eight-foot length and got his head over the edge of the wire netting when Daddy appeared on the back verandah with the paper, I was so glad he read the lists first, I should have been in such a panic I would have missed your name altogether. We celebrated with some cherry brandy and I felt wonderfully relaxed and fulfilled, all the things we had planned for years coming true although there was a sort of sadness too that our "little boy" was finally grown up and on his own! Now you will be able to concentrate on your tour with an easy mind and I hope the Israel thing will work out.

Your birthday present arrived yesterday and looks fascinating, I have glanced through it but not started to read it yet but it just what I revel in as you know. Thank you very much. Assam is one of the strongholds of the "White Goddess", the primitive tribes who first flowed in were all matriarchal, and even when they became Hinduised it was a special form of Hinduism with the worship of the "sakti" or female principal as its main form. One of the things I've often wanted to study but never got round to (chiefly language difficulty) was the strange blending of myth and religion that produced the Tantric cult which was special to Assam…

No more news of the Chinese… am now writing an article on Peter Mundy which I will send to the Statesman… I'm delighted at the thought of getting Robinson by the way, it is the one account of Assam I've never read and seems unprocurable here. I read a D.H. Lawrence in Shillong, three short stories which I'm afraid I found mildly irritating though wonderfully written…

[Daddy] …joins me in love and congratulations, or even might write with luck. Have a good rest & don't worry about anything for a bit – how did your friends do?

Much love from us both – Mummy

One of the letters of congratulation came from my history tutor, Lady Clay, the first page of her letter is below.

Aug 10

121, WOODSTOCK ROAD,
OXFORD.
TEL. 53086.

Dear Mr Macfarlane

I was delighted that you got your II — all your recent hard work deserved it & I hope that you & your family are pleased.

Mr Hyams success gave me the greatest happiness — he must have done brilliantly as Mr Southern told him about it straight off. I was touched that he came round here. He was hardly recognisable, being so much transfigured with happiness that he looked as if he were sort of phosphorescent.

I hope I shall some time see you again.

Paul Hyams got a First.

Next comes a letter from my grandmother at Field Head, dated August 13th

Dearest Alan,

These are the shoes I meant to bring you & enclose a shirt as well as I feel yours must be getting a bit "rich". We so enjoyed our day with you & so grateful for all you did to make it a wonderful outing.

I wish you could get away somewhere nearer & with a pleasanter warden. Fiona came for the day yesterday & after a huge lunch here they all went to Tarn Hows & bathed etc. Robin was terribly sick early evening & luckily Billy & Julia wee here to clear it up …Fiona returns for a few days before hitch-hiking to Cornwall – She left Poochi [dog] *behind this time …. Look after yourself & come nearer or even home,*
Lots of love, Granny

My mother then wrote again.

Cherideo August 22nd

My dear Alan,

Thank you for your letter and the enclosed, how sad you were just pipped at the post for a first, but a comfort to you to know how close you got and as you say may do the trick as far as a scholarship goes. I couldn't quite understand your tutors remarks, which paper was it you didn't do so well on? If you get a scholarship will you give up your tour for the time being and carry straight on? I hope Robert was duly impressed, I don't know why we have such shabby thoughts about him as he has never been cocky or unpleasant about his successes! ….

In a way I would like you to go straight on with your diploma[1] *but don't want to influence you. Sorry to hear about the nose bleeds, its funny how they always come on at this time of year, you might think about having your nose cauterised if you can ever get to see Mylchrest,*[2] *your mountain fastness certainly has disadvantages without transport.*

The only name I recognised from the list was Monks who was that nice boy you went to Borstal camp with I think, was he disappointed to get a 3rd… I am finding "The White Goddess" fascinating, but at least half of it is above my head, such erudition is depressing rather, but I suppose if you spend a secluded life-time of study it becomes possible. I feel I've wasted so many opportunities with all these primitive tribes working here who I could have studied but its too late now, I've contacted someone in Lahore who will help me get books on my Moghal so will be able to carry on with yours and the help of the National Library. I agree there will not be the same interest in my article as Roberts, but if I ever finish a book it might be handy to have the contact with Quennel? …

I hope you're feeling rested, mentally anyway, don't feel you've got to go on and on with your job – though it might be advisable to make it last till the cousins have scattered from the region of Field Head.

With much love, Mummy

I was clearly seriously contemplating trying to stay on at Oxford to do a Diploma or another course at oxford and asked a friend who was a few years senior to me to write me a reference. I had also applied for a State Studentship.

---

[1] A Diploma in Public and Social Administration at Oxford.

[2] My doctor in Ambleside.

WORCESTER COLLEGE,
OXFORD.

13th August, 1963.

TO WHOM IT MAY CONCERN.

Re.-Alan J. D. Macfarlane,
Fieldhead, Outgate, Ambleside, Lancashire.

I have known Alan Macfarlane well for three years as he has been a member of Worcester College, Oxford and we have together been involved in running a number of extracurricular activities.

He came up to Oxford University in 1960 to read History and applied himself diligently to his studies and obtained a good degree (Batchelor of Arts) this Summer. He has, therefore, proved himself an intelligent and able person. He has, during his time in College, also shown himself to be a competent games player, and organiser and he tackles anything he takes on with tenacity.

During last Summer he and I were both helping with a camp for Borstal boys and he showed himself then to be able to get on with most types of person as he is sympathetic and understanding.

I have every confidence in recommending him for the work he now has in mind; he will prove an excellent companion and colleague and give every satisfaction in his work to which he can also contribute in thoughtful approach.

Yours faithfully,

Ralph Johnson.

Dr. R. H. JOHNSON, M.A.,
Schorstein Research Fellow of University of Oxford.

Department of Social and Administrative Studies

40 WELLINGTON SQUARE.
Telephone: OXFORD 58637

APPLICATION FOR ADMISSION
(Diploma in Public and Social Administration)

Name in full..

Home address and telephone number..

....

Name and address of next of kin..

Nationality and place and date of birth..

School...................... University (and college)...................................

Are you, or have you ever been, a matriculated member of Oxford University ?..............

Degrees, etc., taken or being taken ....

Subject of degree course ....

.... Honours class gained.................................

Present occupation...

Previous experience of social work, administration or research (with dates)...............

....

....

....

....

For which of the following do you wish to prepare :

(a) public administration
(b) industrial administration (including personnel management)
(c) social research
(d) child care service
(f) probation service
(g) family casework
(h) group and community work

I was successful in my application for a State Studentship and the formal notification was sent to me on 29th August.

MINISTRY OF EDUCATION
AWARDS BRANCH
13 Cornwall Terrace, Regents Park, LONDON N.W.1
Telephone: HUNTER 1455

Your reference:

29 AUG 1963

Please quote in reply
(addressing to THE SECRETARY) Awds. 4A.
UP 63/9154

STATE STUDENTSHIPS

Sir/~~Madam~~,

I am directed by the Minister of Eduction to inform you that you have been selected for the award of a State Studentship.

You are requested to inform the Ministry, not later than 19th September 1963, whether you wish to accept the award.

--- A pre-paid label is enclosed for this purpose.

I am, Sir/~~Madam~~,
Your obedient Servant,

(D. E. Lloyd Jones)

A.D.J. Macfarlane, Esq.,
Field Head,
Outgate,
Nr. Ambleside,
Lancs.
Form 109UP.(A.1.)

6/2/63 - 1200

I have the rough draft of my reply asking whether I could intermit for a year.

Dear Sir,

~~I enclose a state~~ Thank you for your letter informing me of my selection to a State Studentship which I gratefully accept. I enclose a "statement of Financial Circumstances and undertaking". I have ~~left~~ included alternative dates for the commencement of my award since I would like, with your permission, to postpone my postgraduate study for a year. I believe my tutor Mr Campbell has written to you on this subject. ~~My main~~ reasons ~~I feel that~~ firstly, I feel that since my knowledge of European languages is meagre a year in which to study two languages – probably German – French – would be ~~of fundamental importance~~ fundamentally to my study of C16 – C17 ~~subjects~~ history, especially to the educational topic on which I hope to do my thesis, ~~since educational and intellectual reform was heavily influenced by Continental thought~~. Secondly there are personal reasons, for instance the fact that I would like to see my parents who have been abroad for several years as well as ~~my~~ conviction that a year abroad would ~~[illegible]~~ deepen my somewhat limited experience & thus enrich my work ~~[illegible] which I now lack~~. Could you inform me of your decision on this matter as soon as possible since I must make arrangements accordingly –

I also contacted James Campbell who wrote to me enclosing a general purpose reference for use in whatever I did.

From THE DEAN
TEL: OXFORD 47251

30th August.

WORCESTER COLLEGE
OXFORD

Dear Alan,

Thanks for your note. A letter arrivedt today to say you have a State Studentship, I'm pleased to say. No doubt they've sent to you too. I'm not quite sure what view they'll take of your proposed delay. They may not think the general good of your soul an academic enough reason. I should write off to them asking and linking your proposed trip as closely as may be compatible with reasonable honesty with your proposed research. Tell them they can write to me and please send me a reminder of what sort of research you now propose to do and where you are going. God, or Jehovah, only knows who writes the most effective testimonials for kibbutzes (though you might ask Paul Hyams). Anyway I 've typed out a sort of ticket to anywhere and have put all the signs of authenticity I can find in the Bursary on it. I think the college seal looks rather grander upside down.

Yours in haste,

James Campbell

From THE DEAN
TEL: OXFORD 47251

WORCESTER COLLEGE
OXFORD

30th August 1963.

To whom it may concern:

Mr. Alan Macfarlane is a member of Worcester College whom I have known for three years. He is a man of the highest character.

J. Campbell.
Dean.

WORCESTER COLLEGE, OXFORD.

I have a carbon copy of a letter written at the end of August to Felicity, my godmother's daughter, about my future plans.

My dear Felix,

Thank you very much for your letter. I hope the confusion sorts itself out & you get off without leaving too much behind. I can imagine you reading this at snatched moments, sitting on top of a pile of half-packed cases with clothes etc strewn around & the family downstairs moaning for their next meal. I think this will be the last letter you will get from me until you let me know another address. Why don't you tell me the name of the ship you are going on & where and when it calls & then I can send post to await you – as you did with my mother. Don't you know the address to which you are going in S. America...

Now for my plans. I have just heard that I have been awarded a State Studentship – which means money to do research for 2-3 years. Thus I will either go back to Oxford in October or, I hope, go abroad for about 8 months & come back next spring when my parents come (about May) – spending the winter wandering round the Mediterranean in a D.H. Lawrentian manner...

James[1] says historians are narrow-minded? Let James say what he likes, only narrow-minded people go round saying "so & so are narrow-minded" (you notice I've committed the same fault – but am at least aware of it, like that puzzle – all Chinamen are liars said a Chinaman). From my limited experience at Oxford, I have found you just can't divide people into faculties – though I agree that the conception of the narrow-minded scientist which is held by many is not true. Most of my scientist friends are interested in many things. But the difficulty really is, what is "narrow-minded"? Everyone assumes that "breadth of mind" is a virtue. But most artists are very narrow-minded i.e. their interests are intensely focused on one object & to make any impression they have to exclude many other subjects. By most standards D.H. Lawrence, Yeats etc were very narrow-minded as were most of the greatest musicians. Is depth of understanding worth more than width? I would readily admit myself very narrow-minded if this means that I am much more interested in some things than others, but in the damning sense I suppose it means "shutting your mind to things one should be prepared to allow in". Nowadays it is often more difficult to be narrow-minded than superficially broad-minded. Enough of this rambling. You see my difficulty? ...

I have another week at this hostel. I will be glad of the change as I am beginning to get restless. My reading & writing have practically stopped & I can't be bothered to go on. There are moments of ecstasy, as when I walked down to the village thro' a superb sunrise on Wednesday, the lake & hills glowing with mist and the glory of the early rays or when I suddenly hear a snatch of my favourite music. Again there are long dull interludes of vacancy ...

The final letter in these two months is from my mother from Cherideo on August 31st:

My dear Alan,

No letter from you this week, maybe you are changing hostels or perhaps given up altogether, no letter from Fiona either so maybe it's the post but the paper is arriving… I had another letter from the Principal of Mayo College … [who] said he probably could give you a temporary job if you would let him know when you would be coming. The term starts in January and I imagine you would stay about six months? Anyway let me know as soon as you can what your plans are, … If you could keep yourself for a couple of months in Israel we could save up enough to pay your fare on here, if you haven't abandoned the whole idea by now…

I've finished the "White Goddess", slightly dazed, it was fascinating, though I thought his idea that we should go back to worshipping a lustful and bloodthirsty mother figure instead of a loving and compassionate father rather odd to say the least of it. I am re-reading the Golden Bough to compare it, Frazer also has some odd ideas, such as the dangerous and miserable state of the savage who must quickly be weaned of all his old ideas and education – which makes one wonder if he ever lived in a savage society as the first thing that strikes one is that they are happy and well adjusted. Of course he was a Victorian with all the reforming zeal and intolerance that implies. …

My mother's next letter is from Cherideo on Sept 7th.

---

[1] One of my undergraduate friends.

My dear Alan

A letter from you at last, it seemed ages since we had heard and I was worrying that all your plans were going astray, but we're delighted to hear that you had got your State Studentship, we will leave it to you and your tutor to decide when you start. We will add £100 a year to your grant, that will bring it up to 500 a year which wont be very much but you should be able to manage and of course we shall be able to help out at odd times if you are short.

I agree that something practical would be best now, humanitarian work nowadays is not charity but positive instruction in how to grow two crops instead of one irrigate, drain and fertilise or breed fish – I think you would find this interesting too once you got started – couldn't you find a course that combined social economy with anthropology and then you could spend one of your long vacs out here living with the Garos who are as backward as they come –and could probably pay for your time in articles. Will you be going to Oxford or some provincial university? I agree that there wont be time to do a world tour properly, you could leave that till your course is over.

I only sent £20 this month so that is 60 altogether. I don't want you to start off for Europe penniless so let us know how things stand. Perhaps you could go to Sicily and get some practical experience if you cant make Israel. ….

[sickness of monkey] Your two books, "Mughal India" and "Account of Assam" arrived a couple of days ago and I was delighted with them both… In between my work I'm reading "Sword at Sunset" a novel about King Arthur which I'm enjoying very much… Do hope the cauterisation has worked, its very tiresome having these nose bleeds, does height affect them I wonder as you don't seem to get them in Oxford… Much love & hearty congrats from us both – Mummy

Did you ever get our wire?

My mother's next letter is from Cherideo on September 13th

My dear Alan,

Thank you for your letter yesterday, sorry I was so moany about not hearing, it was just a bad week and I was moany about everything. I hope your present youth hostel is a little less remote, it doesn't sound it! Daddy and I might well throw in the sponge and retire to some mountain fastness, I often feel we would be happier but D. feels he must go on earning to the last moment.

I expect you will have come to some decision about your future by now, don't leave it too long and lose the grant. If you spent your holidays doing social work perhaps you wouldn't feel so bad about spending your time contemplating while the world suffered, but couldn't you use your grant for social science in some form, there is endless scope here for youth club and after care and so on in the cities. I seem to give you contrary advice in every letter, luckily you will probably ignore it all and make your own choice…

I'll see what I can do about collecting folk tales, I mean to try and visit in the villages when it gets cooler… Its been an awful week… [sick monkey etc] … I got a letter from Julia saying Granny had thought I'd got my article accepted on the strength of Robert's name but you had quietly put her right – thank you! Poor Billy is mugging up for a Min. of Education Diploma and selling insurance, a bit dreary.

I've had my depressing week cheered by "Sword at Sunset", a lovely book about King Arthur, you should read it, very moving and though it strips a lot of the glamour off the chivalric story and replaces it with a more likely setting, it is still inspiring. Quite a lot of Frazerish incident too, the ritual sacrifice of the king, the Sin that must be expiated etc. We have such a nice new assistant, your age and half way through his first novel, and a fan of T.H. White… Its odd how much more I have in common with the young lads than my old generation… Write to Anne sometime, I think she's a little homesick, though happy…. Are you a B.A. officially?

From Patterdale Youth Hostel, Sunday 15th September 1963.
[a little of the carbon paper has slipped so parts of the first paragraph are missing, indicated by ...]

To Mummy and Daddy,

....would be ideal for working in & I could go with one or two of my friends & ...working parties; I think I may have discussed the subject before, if I find a reasonable place for £50 or so how do you feel? Still this is far in the future I hope since I will probably be abroad for a year before that. My ... advised me to suggest to the

Min. of Ed. that I ought to learn two languages – probably French, German or Italian – as a preparation for ... and also put forward the personal reason that I would like to come out to visit you, tho' the latter seems unlikely because of the time element. My fate has is now being decided. If I can go away I hope to just wander around, perhaps going to a university like Penny at Perugia, getting odd jobs etc, mostly just talking & reading so as to learn the languages. I must also try to take 'O' or 'A' level in the languages next summer, since this might give me the needed discipline. I'll let you know my financial situation later. So far I've saved about £15 & added to the £60 which should see me until the time when I get a job. the brother of Jack, the assistant warden under whom I am working here, travelled around with a tent for about 2 years in Europe & averaged £1-8s a week in spending money so £75 should see me a fair way. Yes, I would like to go to Sicily & see Danilo Dolci in action but I may let myself get swept by events.

The nature of my job has changed radically since I came to work at Patterdale, & this has outwardly been symbolized by the superb weather we've been having, day after day of strong wind & sunshine with the fells like Heaton Cooper water colours. Apart from the first two days there have been very few people around & consequently there is hardly anything for me to do, I am working about 25 hours a week instead of 70. the 'boss' is very pleasant, a man of 38 tho' in many ways he seems much younger. He is very kind, rather uncertain of himself & a bit restless. He hopes to go to Australia soon to earn a fortune & I can see why the explorers & gold-hunters of the last century appeal so strongly to him. His brother, a few years older, & also a wandering type, one of the slightly dissatisfied drifters, has been staying for the last few days & we have been having endless discussions on art, religion etc.

The brother, Jim, is a committed, tho', so far, unsuccessful, writer. He wrote a travel book, which was rejected, & is just getting over the disappointment. they both read extensively & have an amazing appetite for philosophic discussion. We have swopped plans for changing the world, discussed the vices of the academic way of life, dragged Colin Wilson, Henry Miller & Wordsworth through the critical flame almost ad nauseam.

As I explained to them, somewhat to their surprise, I have spent more time on 'deep discussions' in the last week than three years at Oxford. Partly as a consequence of this my great thesis on Adolescence has hardly progressed. I have dipped into various books, but in this superb weather feel it more profitable to go walking. There will be more than enough time for thought in the near future probably.

Today I walked with them to Ullswater along a cart-track through a pine wood. The sight of the suddenly blue water, the smell of junipers when they had been squeezed, the fluttering greenness & silver of a silver-birch against the reddening bracken were infinitely beautiful. In my mind they blend with a walk I took up to Kirkstone pass on Thursday along the other side of Brotherswater. On this occasion there was no wind & the lake mirrored the rowan trees, the rushes & the converging mountains.

You may be surprised to hear that I actually took some strenuous exercise after weeks of inactivity so I will explain. On Wednesday evening, per usual, we got a girl to help with the washing up etc in our kitchen. She was very giggly & had a broad Lancs accent etc so we offered her coffee. Soon afterwards her friend came in & seeing the coffee demanded some in such a cheeky way that we had to give in. On closer inspection she turned out to be extremely attractive, with turned up grey eyes, nice lips & nose & shapely figure. Thus we did not refuse when they pleaded to have coffee at 10.15 p.m. We talked & talked on every subject & turning away from gazing ecstatically into her eyes I found that it was after 2 p.m.

It appeared that Jean, as I found out the prettier girls name to be, was a nursery nurse, studying for her exams. She lives in Blackburn, has just won a beauty competition & is going down to the South Coast next week-end for the next round. She likes a little classical music – mainly ballet, since she learnt ballet when she was younger; you can see it when she walks – but mostly 'pop'. Through a combination of attractiveness, cheekiness & a candid awareness that 'stars' like to be treated as human beings, she has met & knows most of the current singers – Emile Ford, Marty Wilde & especially 'Cliff' to whom she writes. As you can imagine all this gave her a sort of glamour which was heightened by its distance from the 'intellectual' & 'Aesthetic' virtues which normally attract me.

Anyhow they both came down for breakfast with us, on the condition that they made it, & I had a pleasant walk & a pleasant talk to the top of Kirkstone, with me discoursing on subjects such as King Arthur – which must have secretly amused them. After a picnic at the top we said a sad farewell. I'm not sure why I've gone into all this boring detail except that one day I might find it an interesting record of that momentary clash between two characters, full of promise but blighted by conventions & by iron barriers of upbringing, class etc! I don't suppose I shall see her again, which is perhaps as well, & there are seven girls coming tonight - –who knows?

It was unfortunate that Granny, Richard etc chose Thursday to come over her to collect me for fishing – and didn't phone me. I wonder what Granny thought when she heard I was out conducting two young ladies over the fells – tho' even she must have thought it harmless enough. I went home last Monday for my night off & was immediately submerged under the 'Lemon' invasion.[1] *Actually I like all the family very much. Jean is obviously very sensitive & intelligent, & possibly, rather unhappy? Do you know here well? The children are nice & full of bubble & squeak. I went fishing with Roddy in Black Beck & the trout almost jumped up onto the bank for us – we ended up with 12 plump little fish & Lee caught a few more. Richard, the universal chauffeur, remained in the background a bit, & I feel slightly sorry for him, if this doesn't sound too condescending.*

I hope all goes well & the wealthy cools down.

All my love to you both,

Alan

15th September Palatine Sq, Burnley Sat.

Dear Alan,

Thanks a lot for your letter, I didn't get it until this afternoon, as I overslept a bit! I'm sorry we missed you yesterday but I can assure you, that we didn't deliberately avoid you. … [description of her visit to Youth Hostel near Troutbeck] … If you ever feel inclined to write, please do, as I shall be pleased to hear from you again. Remember me to Jack, and once again thank you very much for everything, you have been "very gallant", "Sir Galahad", no seriously though, I do appreciate your "pack-horse" act.

All the Best, Jean

During my relationship with Penny, I stopped writing love poetry, though I sent her much of other people and my letters were loaded with sentiment. Yet when I returned to the Lake District in late June 1963 and Penny left for Italy and we became just 'good friends', my amorous eyes could turn towards others. I started again to write snatches of poetry which show something of the mixture of yearning, sensuous excitement and restraint of this period. Here is a scan of part of just one of these, written to Jean.

[1] The Lemons were my grandmother's sister Margery's family.

19.9.63.

To Jean: (iii) evoked by J. Sutherland.

My heart flutters, swept on a soprano voice
Tossed helpless up the autumn hillside
Gusted over the bracken & back to you,
To the withdrawing of your lips
And your eyes open in mock surprise
As we sit in a restaurant
And the softness of your side
As we walk linked thro' the
Everyday streets. The dust & grime
The weeping weariness are transformed
And I see no faces pass but yours
And the drift of petals in the sky.
Breaking the heart of the night.
There is a catch in your voice,
A discovered tenderness when you
Say 'fool', but I feel the
Blood's liquid pouring thro'
My throbbing side as the night
Excitement suddenly hits the
Nothing as we emerge from
The restaurant, And now the
Excitement seeps away &

My Lake District idyll ended soon after for I heard back from the Ministry of Education that they would not allow me to postpone my State Studentship, which meant that I only had a couple of weeks to re-arrange my life and prepare to return to Oxford.

MINISTRY OF EDUCATION

AWARDS BRANCH

13 Cornwall Terrace, Regents Park, LONDON N.W.1

Telephone: HUNTER 1455

Your reference:

Our reference: UP 63/9154

18 September 1963

Dear Sir,

With reference to your letter of 14th September, I write to say that after careful consideration of your case, we are unable to approve postponement of your State Studentship. Would you therefore tell us whether you propose to accept our offer for studies commencing this October or to decline the award.

A prepaid label is enclosed and an early reply would be appreciated.

Yours faithfully,

K. Humberstone

(K. T. V. Humberstone)

A. D. J. Macfarlane Esq.,
Field Head,
Outgate,
Near Ambleside,
Westmorland.

I wrote again to my parents from the second Youth Hostel, describing the aftermath of this refusal.

Saturday September 21st 1963 Patterdale Youth Hostel, Penrith

Dear Mummy and Daddy,

Thank you for your letter of the 13th. I'm sorry Ting is still bad, I only hope he can hang on until the cold weather. You ask if I'm a B.A. officially yet – no. One has either to go to Oxford & do it in splendour with dons mumbling latin, or one can do it in absence. I had thought that, if the dates are alright, you might like to come to Oxford for the Encaena or whatever it is. It would provide an excellent opportunity for Mummy to wear her black hat which the lama chewed & I believe it is traditional to have swarms of adoring & admiring relatives cooing round & taking photographs – doesn't that sound superior. Say if you think this would be a good idea. There might be complications, for instance I might have to be an official B.A. before I started my research.

When is your local leave? I hope you manage to get away, & don't spend most of it mending punctures on the way there & back, as seems frequently to happen. I'll be interested to hear if you find any local legends etc; I must start a serious study of anthropology soon. I also want to read "Sword at Sunset", actually someone to whom I told my enthusiasm for Arthurian romances recommended it to me a long time ago. I'm still half way thro' 'The Once and Future King' & will perhaps try to finish it next week. I lent it to the warden at the last Y.H. & he seemed to enjoy it...

There have been continued frantic phone calls & letters this week about my grant. I suggested to the Ministry that I might learn some foreign languages etc, as I think I old you. The final outcome was a letter on Friday which said that after careful consideration & so on they had decided <u>*not*</u> *to postpone it a year (as my tutor said, they're not really interested in the good of my soul) & so I will have to start in October. There are recompenses. most of my friends will still be there; I will still be thinking along the right patterns etc. I just hope that I don't lose touch with the swarming world outside the cloister walls & become a dry worshipper of academic truth.*

As I think I told you, I have chosen a subject which moves me slightly away from 'pure' history I hope, either towards utility or towards literature, we'll see. No doubt practical problems, ie. digs, will crop up. I'll probably be finishing this job on the 27th or soon after & then must go down to Oxford. There is also the question of money. I should have about £70 saved by October, what would you like me to do with it since much of it is the money you have been forwarding? The only things I need are one or two clothes & some working equipment – a filing cabinet, more index cards & other gadgets which are my hearts delight. Sometime soon I would like to re-do my room, put in some book-shelves since my books are spilling over & get a desk at which I can type, but this can wait till you come back. We'll work out other details later.

Last Monday I decided to hitch down to see the girl I told you about in my last letter – Jean. She'd written to say that she was occupied on Monday evening which was my evening off, but I thought I could go on & see Fiona if she was at home at the least. It was a glorious day & I felt rather foolish leaving the Lakes & entering industrial Lancs, but I soon found that on a fine day the Northern cities have a glowing beauty of their own.

I was lucky with my lifts which took me in four hops over the Yorks moors via Settle & arrived in Burnley at about 4.30. I prowled round the town for a while & then rang up Jean from a phone box near to her house. She was surprised but pleased to hear me & we had coffee together. She had a meeting of the Youth Leaders or something (she does a lot of Youth Work – is a guide, leads the Rangers, entertains old people etc) & so we arranged to meet the next evening. Then I caught a bus over to Mancs to see Fiona.

It was a wonderful drive over; one imagines a succession of grimy seats, but in fact there is a high moor in between & the sun was just setting as we climbed out of Burnley. The town lay in a maze of lights below us, while the black moors stretched silent on our right, with the after-glow of the sun making each tuft of grass stand out sharply. then we tunnelled into the mean streets again, with their half-lit shops & evening restlessness, the guttering lamps & the scraps of paper in the wind.

I finally located Fiona's new flat & was let in by a very pleasant girl who lives below. It is in a very pleasant situation, with a park opposite, with good lighting & near to a bus. The flat itself is ideal & looks

unmistakeably bohemian with its collages, weird sculptures etc. Fiona & Janet seem very well & thrilled at their new work. They are preparing for their house-warming party.

I had lunch with Fiona & then went over to Burnley where I spent a very happy evening with Jean. She showed me round Burnley's parks & football ground & then we had a meal at a Chinese restaurant & went to see Gregory Peck in 'To Kill a Mockingbird' – all about the colour bar. I didn't notice much of the film, but I'm not sure it was as good as it is supposed to be. I left Jean about 11.20 & wondered where I could stay the night. But with my first thumb I was given a lift by a nightclub proprietor who gave me a drink in his 'joint' in Bury and then drove me on to Mancs & I returned to F's flat at about 2.30. I hitched up easily the next day.

We that's enough of my doings. By the time I write again I should have left my Y.H.

Look after ourselves & much love to you both,

I wrote to my tutor James Campbell on the same day:

Youth Hostels Association, Goldrill House, Patterdale Saturdays Sept 21st [A typed letter]

Dear James,

I have just heard from the Ministry that they won't let me have a year off. I tried to ring you on Friday evening but hear that you have been away for the weekend. As they wanted an immediate confirmation if I still wanted to accept the grant I have written to them saying I will start in October; I hope this is in order. I am working here until the end of the month, tho' I can get off to come down to Oxford before then if it is urgent. Otherwise I will be coming down in the first week of October to look for accomodation [sic – corrected by James!] etc, & presume I will work out the details of the thesis then. I hope all the regulations of College & University authorities can be settled.

I am just off to sunbathe beside Ullswater as it is another sweltering day & my 'puritan' conscience is partly quietened by the thought of the work ahead.

Yours sincerely, Alan Macfarlane [in red biro]

I also wrote several letters to both Penny and Julie during the summer. Only one survives, because I kept a carbon copy of it. It was written from Patterdale Youth Hostel, Sunday, 22nd Sept. [I have added paragraph breaks]

Dear Julie,

Thank you very much for your long letter. Please excuse this typewritten reply. If you object to such an impersonal way of writing please do say, it is only laziness on my part & also the fact that I can write much faster like this & thus much more.

Poor Pussy, you sound very disconsolate, or rather the contents of what you say sounds very depressing, but the way in which you say it is so resigned & stoical – even self-amused as if you were looking at yourself from outside – that I don't quite know what to make of your state. For instance when you say "I expect I'll be done for in a few months" or "the advent of my long-expected breakdown is nigh" the contrast between the terror of what you say & the casual way in which you say it makes the thing almost ludicrous. I wish I knew what to say to help you, but all I can really do is offer you my sympathy & tell you that I am thinking of you. If I was to start to analyse you in my amateur way I would probably end up in an awful mess, but here are some way-out suggestions.

I think that the truth lies between the two theories you mention, deep-seated causes & environment. Judging from my own experience the deep-seated cause is that you are too sensitive & intelligent. This means that the disease, a kind of religious schizophrenia which I believe to be at the heart of modern life affects you most & brings you more agony than most. I can hear you protesting – "Why bring religion into this" & it may be that I'm just a fanatic, but listen on a bit. Also you may object that you don't have any great soul-wrestling, no great spasms of guilt etc. This isn't really what I mean by religious agony. I am thinking more of a dryness, a feeling of hopelessness perhaps, a disillusion & conviction of purposelessness. It is the dull ache hinted at the end of Dover Beach & Meredith's Modern Love – "Ah what a dusty answer gets the soul when hot for certainties in this our life". It is the realization that your last attempt to impose coherence & order on things, to live by an absolute code & to believe in things above greed & selfishness is failing, that everything is splitting up & losing its relationship; that the mystery & the 'otherness' as Lawrence would call it are only conjured up by the brain

& that reality if there is such a thing is dry & meaningless. I have a suspicion that I am speaking more of my own spiritual struggles than yours, but perhaps it may help all the same.

This whole problem, the fading of coherence & belief, the emergence of an entirely relativistic philosophy & the death of the great dark & light powers which once lived just below or behind the surface of life is the central core of what I hope to turn into my background work for the next ten years. If [you] are sick with this disease, as most of us are, your help would be invaluable, since you are a more than ordinarily gifted & sensitive person. I don't know the cure yet, I just guess that to study the disease itself might provide the answer. I suppose most of us immerse ourselves in some little escapist world, whether it is the common man's busy life or horse-racing, or the intellectual's pursuit of some kind of abstract truth. All I am certain of is that to try to give up the struggle altogether is death, while probably the best temporary solution is to immerse oneself in something bigger than yourself. For me I hope this will be some kind of humanitarian work, that if I pit myself up against some monster of cruelty & ignorance, for instance the giant problem of population of the slums of Calcutta, this may cure my ache and & also help someone.

I doubt whether recommending you to become a nun or something would be very helpful, but I am certain that unless you make a complete break with the rather dilettante life you have led for the last 2 years you will only get worse. I hope this doesn't sound too presumptious [sic], it will I'm afraid, & also it will sound a bit like those of your advisers who say that your state is only the result of being well-off & spoilt. The only truth in this is that even if you were a prostitute you would have to struggle to keep alive & have less time for thought, & probably wouldn't be thoughtful enough to feel as miserable as you do now. I can feel that I'm not helping at all so I will leave the subject until you tell me some more; perhaps after all it is merely that you need to get married & have not found anyone suitable yet. Why do you want to bring Per[egrine] into this bitter world of which you seem tired? As I have said my own long term solution as I see it now is to a) try to keep hold onto my traditional Christian faith b) self-discipline myself and try to help others; immersing myself in some great cause – perhaps something to do with educational reform c) as a hobby & relaxation study the intellectual aspects of the problems which are worrying me & I assume many others.

You ask why I am doing such a badly-paid job which anyone could do. As you may know I have a Puritan obsession about money – I am determined not to let it become a devouring object in my life (which is, of course, just the way in which one drifts into becoming obsessed with it – in a perverted way) and hence the money angle doesn't matter. I would rather do a job I enjoy – & I do enjoy this now that the season is over & things are a bit quieter – than a highly paid & unpleasant job. Anyhow I haven't much longer since I am finishing on about Friday.

I've just heard from the Min. of Ed. that they won't let me go abroad for a year & so I've got to go back to Oxford in October; it'll be nice to see Paul, Alistair, David Izaac etc, but I shall miss those who have gone – including Peter who failed his English exams entirely & Sally (Broadbent) & Carrie at nos 3 Southmoor Rd; also I'm afraid of becoming too dry & academic. Still if I read plenty of Keats I should be alright!

There has been absolutely gorgeous weather here for the last week & I have been sunbathing on the side of Ullswater lake. I could imagine myself beside the Med'n with the ripples kissing the rocks, the steep gorse & bracken hillside away from the water & the smouldering air, just the cicadas were missing.

On Monday I left the Lakes for a couple of days & hitched down into industrial Lancs to see a sweet girl who I had met when she was staying in the hostel here. She is a nurse in Burnley & a good corrective to my pomposity & dreaminess. I also stayed with my sister in Mancs where she has got a very 'arty' flat.

I hope you'll be able to come over to see me in Oxford, I will come to see you if I'm in London. Yes, do write to Penny, she comes back soonish tho'.

Look after yourself Pussy & write soon; don't get too depressed,
Fondest love, Alan

MINISTRY OF EDUCATION

(AWARDS BRANCH)

HUNter 1455

13, CORNWALL TERRACE,
REGENTS PARK,
LONDON, N.W.1.

Your reference:

Our reference: State Studentships
UP.63/ 9154

2 3 SEP 1963

Sir/~~Madam~~,

I am directed by the Minister of Education to refer to previous correspondence about your State Studentship, and to confirm that your Studentship will be tenable from 1st October, 1963, for the period of your approved studies. This award is subject to satisfactory attendance, conduct and progress.

The value of your award from 1st October will be as follows:

(a) approved fees;

(b) a maintenance grant at the rate of £450 per annum, which will be paid in four instalments.

This award is subject to review at any time in the light of changes in your circumstances and is given on the understanding that:

(a) you will be required to devote at least 44 weeks of the academic year to approved full-time study, during which time you will be living away from your parental home. Otherwise, a proportionate reduction in grant will be made;

(b) your total income from other sources, including Scholarships etc., will not exceed £100 in the academic year 1963/64.

~~(c) your total income from other sources during the academic year 1963/64 will be:~~

Any changes in your circumstances as outlined above or, e.g. marriage or a change in your place of residence, should be reported to the Ministry without delay.

In writing to the Ministry on any matter connected with your State Studentship you should quote the reference number shown at the head of this letter.

I am, Sir/~~Madam~~,
Your obedient Servant,

A. D. J. Macfarlane, Esq.

D. E. Lloyd Jones

Form 108 UP.
19/3/63 - 1300

(D. E. Lloyd-Jones)

[From the Worcester College Archives]

A very generous grant indeed. Especially as my parents offered to supplement it by £100 per year.

The next letter from my mother is on September 23rd from Cherideo. The letter was addressed to Patterdale Youth Hostel; forwarded to Field Head', then forwarded again to Worcester College, Oxford. So it heralded the start of my doctoral years.

My dear Alan,

I didn't write last week, it was a bad week as Ting [a monkey] *died on Thursday… I have been terribly bleak since, this is a bad place for trying to get over things as there is no outlet, nowhere to go to, I read and work until I'm dizzy but then there comes a time when I must stop and then regrets and memories rush in. I know it is only a minute fraction of the suffering that goes on everywhere, but one is struck afresh with the pointlessness of it, let us beastly selfish grasping men suffer but why a small innocent animal who has done nobody any harm. One can go on banging ones head and asking why for ever, there seems no answer but acceptance. I don't think I got a letter from you either, by now you will probably have made up your mind about your future and I hope are happy about it. Granny never writes these days...*

Just at present I feel I want to leave India, now, and for ever. I cant take it any more and the helplessness of its suffering – so we shall probably be after that wardens job in the Isle of Arran – how lovely it sounds, the cold sea air, the gulls, no more blindness, starvation and sores. But I doubt if there is really any escape and one will carry the sores and sorrows round with one forever.

I have just read James Baldwins "The Fire Next Time", it is very moving and beautifully written and makes one see more clearly exactly what it is to have a black skin. I think your generation will have a saner outlook on that, it is something ingrained in the older people, so instinctive that it probably dates way back to a primitive world, that despising of colour. Like anti-Catholicism and anti Semitism – really the more I survey the Victorian scene the more unpleasant they seem to be. And yet my grandmother who hated Catholics and despised Jews and thought Black Men were animals was in many ways a pet and spent an awful lot of time and money on charity. Ditto Granpa who is a terrible snob, it seems that people who are intolerant in general are kinder in particulars.

Daddy and I have made a vow that we aren't going to the club any more, at least not unless we absolutely have to, and I hope to visit the villages more and try and paint and collect folk stories. I'm beginning to get the hang of the Moghuls and their administration, and feel I know enough to write several books already but I still haven't decided how to approach the subject from a fresh angle. ….

I hope I'll be feeling more cheerful in my next letter – time is a healer & the stale flat & unprofitable feeling will pass. Much love, Mummy

Her next letter still echoes themes of the summer, so I include it here. It is from Cherideo on October 3rd.

My dear Alan,

Two letters from you last week for which I was very thankful as I was feeling pretty depressed. I am recovering now, though have terrible pangs sometimes. Still I think I am trembling on the verge of some discovery about pain and suffering, something to do with pain being at the heart of happiness (as it always is) and vice versa – I cant really explain but it has a lot to do with Evelyn Underhill and the one-ness of experience, I haven't grasped it yet except in flashes. It's a most interesting and enlightening book, and I now want to read all the references he lists, I think I shall start with the Sufi mystics who I can get here, I cant ever see myself having the time or opportunity to meditate properly!

I am glad your future has resolved itself, as you say there are things in favour of both courses but now it has been decided for you you can relax and make the best of it. You don't say what you are studying for what degree or doctorate. Of course I am longing to appear in my llama-chewed headgear to coo over you – we were both regretting bitterly the fact that we wouldn't be able to see you get your bona fide B.A. – but as you say you might perhaps have to take it now – I hope not though.

I'm glad you managed to see your Jean again, I don't think long absences make the heart grow fonder, short ones do but time is the great eraser and when you cant remember what a persons voice is like even its hard to stay ecstatic.

We got a p.c. from Penny from Perugia which was nice of her, are you still Good Friends? Here it is quite chilly to-day.

I have finished my notes on your Moghul book and have sent off to the National Library in the hopes I'll be able to get more from them, if they cant help I will join in the Hakluyt Society….

It was nice to get your description of Fiona's flat, she did actually send us a scrawl a few days later but told us little except that she was happy…

You can do what you like with the money, you will need clothes, probably a suit, and anything you have over can go to the Croft Fund. We are hoping to go to Geeya (?) [Gigha] where Daddy's uncle was a minister and

find something there, we still owe you a 21st birthday present and that could perhaps be it. I believe you lent Fiona some money, as neither she nor Granny let me know how things stand it is difficult but I thought she had plenty. Do hope you are cosily dug in somewhere with your tapes and filing cabinet and don't feel "stale" – but this time you will be working along different lines presumably without an exam hanging over you?
With much love, Mummy

*

One of the long letters I wrote to my Sedbergh school-friend Ian Campbell in Canada is dated Thursday 26th Sept, addressed from Field Head, but clearly written at Patterdale Youth Hostel. It is a carbon of a typed letter.

Dear Ian,

Thanks for your letter which has galvanized me into action after months of sloth (recognise the word?!) Apologies for this typewritten letter, I get lazy in my old age. I can't remember if I have replied to your last letter or when I last wrote so I will start from my news since I finished at Oxford in June; with luck I'll cover your remarks about career, Joyce (to whom best regards by the way) etc under the usual divisions of sex, religion & vocation. Here goes…

Exams after three years were a nightmare, tho' I was luckier than some of my friends who almost had breakdowns – one of them failing his English finals completely into the bargain. For lack of anything better & for a rest & an opportunity to read I then got a job in a Lake District Youth Hostel on the slopes of Helvellyn. The work was much harder than I expected, cleaning out toilets, preparing meals, scrubbing floors etc for nearly 70 hours a week at about 1/3d per hour. The Warden was rather an aggressive Geordi & there were a stream of Geordi's with whom I reminisced about my brief visit to Jesmond Dene! The great compensation was a superb view down to the Lake and a stream of pretty & friendly girls.

Most of the time I was waiting to hear my results. I had been given a long 'viva' or oral at Oxford after the written exams which meant I was a borderline case, but between which grades I wasn't sure. Anyhow the outcome was that I found that I had just missed a first. Then there was another long wait to see if I had been awarded a State Studentship which would finance me to do research. During this time I planned my world tour, writing off to Leonard Cheshire & beginning to get clued up on fisheries etc. Then I heard I had got the Studentship, so letters flew back & forth from my tutor & myself to the Min. of Educ'n to try to postpone the commencement of the grant to allow me a year abroad – probably in the Med'n region – before I started. I learnt about a week ago that they refuse & I have got to start my thesis in about 4 days. I haven't even chosen a subject – but one can't turn up one's nose at £1500 [£500 a year for three years], however much one harangues at the gross materialism of life etc.

I hope to do a subject which both takes me slightly nearer practical matters & also raises literary topics – since literature has always been my real love – perhaps I will do something on English educational reform in the C16 or C17. I will be off in a couple of days to find digs & will emerge in three years with a B.Litt. or D.Phil. & probably dried up inside. I have been, as usual, thinking along the same lines as you & agree entirely that tho' one cannot underestimate the importance of training there is a constant pressure dragging one away from one's earlier idealism & eagerness to contribute. Financial temptations & the desire for security is one of my greatest temptations; once I was married I think the battle would be lost. And that takes me on naturally to the next topic – sex etc. But before that I must say how sorry I am that I won't be able to get over to Vancouver next summer. Is there any chance that you might be on this side of the Atlantic in the next three years? You know that you would always be <u>very</u> welcome at Field Head. My parents will be home next year. Is Joyce still thinking of coming over to England?

As far as love/lust is concerned I've come to the conclusion that I'm too young to fall in love, & that consequently I might as well be slightly less intense about my affairs than previously, tho' careful not to hurt any girls. This is all very well to say, but I'll idealize & spiritualize each casual affair I have in the future as much as I have up to now.

My affairs are slightly complex. Penny & I are, I believe, just 'good friends'; she has been in Italy at Perugia university for the last two months & starts at York university in a couple of weeks. We had a great row, but parted in friendship with many wonderful memories of a strange but enriching relationship which saved me from a worse neurosis during my pre-exam work.[1]

Since then I have been writing to Felicity, a daughter of my Godmother who I have known since she was about 6. I won't go into details in this letter since I have a suspicion that I've told you about her before. But if I haven't she's very pretty, with turned up green eyes, very gold hair & a nice smile. Also she is very sensitive & intelligent... Anyhow she has gone off to South America & at the time of writing must be a few miles off Buenos Aires where she will remain for about 6 months & then come back to do a nursing course.

In the absence of anyone serious I have flirted gently with various youth hostellers. At the moment I am having an idyllic affair with a girl who I met about 2 weeks ago (I have been at another Youth Hostel for the last two weeks, here there is much less work to do & the Warden is a bachelor & seems about my own age, tho' he is in fact 38 & one of life's wanderers) we talked until about 3 in the morning & I then helped her with her pack over Kirkstone pass (romantic isn't it!) & went down the following week-end & took her out to dinner & a film from her home in Burnley. She is a trainee-nurse, good Lancashire background & very sweet & attractive needless to say (she has been down South on a beauty competition this week-end). She may come up this week-end, but I don't know what will happen then.

Apart from anything else as a student &, I hope, helper of humanity as well as a budding (?) writer it is most valuable to be with someone from such a different environment & to break through sociological & intellectual barriers on the pulses of emotion. Do you still [believe] in keeping away from marriage until your are nearly 30; in abstract I agree more than ever .... But who knows?

I am going thro' my usual spiritual turmoil. Work for exams helped to drug my mind to a certain extent & I was forced to put such questions aside, but it all burst out again when I had time to think. I get more dazed every minute and I expect this is what has made me decide to undertake a course of study, reading & writing, in the attempt to re-impose unity & order on a world which seems to be breaking up before my new knowledge.

It's a bit late so I won't bore you with the details of the plan – anyhow it's probably a fad & won't come to anything. But it is centred on the question of what happens to a child's mind & imagination when it becomes an adult. I would study this on a collective basis in modern history, with the impact of modern science on old religious beliefs; in anthropology, with the impact of new ideas on an old, closed & united, system of beliefs & taboos; in literature – especially in children's stories & of course in psychology. If nothing else it should give me a framework from my reading.

This summer I have been trying to start on the Literature aspect by comparing what happened to the poetic & artistic imagination in the C17 & C19 when there were giant shocks to the older order from the new astronomy, geology etc & all absolutes seem to vanish between an entirely relative world in which the air was too rarefied [sic] for man to breathe. In the next three years I want to study Anthropology, Psychology & Literature. Of course this will be just an introduction to these fields & probably I'll find that my thesis more than drains all my reserves of intellectual energy. My uncle's successes as a writer – he is now an established historical biographer & is reviewing for newspapers, going on the wireless etc spurs me on. My secret ambition is to be asked by Sedbergh civics!

Actually I expect all this study of poetry, the Grail & Arthurian legends etc is probably my equivalent of the scientist's escape into the world of abstract 'truth' & absolute laws – far from the harassing problems of contemporary life.

I've been reading Yeats avidly – do you know any of his poetry? Tell me what you think of the 'Sorrow of Love if you can get hold of it. Not sure what it means but sounds good.

All the very best & write. Regards to all the family. Alan

There is a list of some of the books I was reading over that summer referred to in this letter, and also when I wrote about carrying many books up to the Glenridding Youth Hostel, these are what I meant.

---

[1] Penny and I remained good friends and wrote to each other and kept in contact for some years, and have recently renewed our contact. We each married someone else a few years later.

	I. BERLIN.	The purpose of philosophy
*	D.H.LAWRENCE.	Selected Letters. (Introduction - A Huxley)
*	D.H.LAWRENCE.	Letters.
*	D.H.LAWRENCE.	Love poetry.
*	D.H.LAWRENCE.	Sons + Lovers.
*	MALHERBE	(poem).
	NAMIER.	On 'History'
	MACAULAY.	On History.
	GIBBON.	On History
	THE VENERABLE BEDE.	On History.
	TOQUEVILLE	On History.
	ANATOLE FRANCE	On History.
	ALDOUS HUXLEY.	Introduction to 'The Perennial Philosophy'.
	QUOTATIONS. (Misc)	On History.
	HAYEK.	Capitalism + the Historians.
	CROZY	On 'Individual Responsibility'.
*	LEAVIS.	The Great Tradition.
	QUOTATIONS. (Misc)	On History.
*	BASIL WILLEY.	The C17 Background.
	TAWNEY.	Religion + the Rise of Capitalism.
	J.R.HICKS.	The Social Framework.
*	T.S.ELIOT.	The Four Quartets.
	THUCYDIDES.	The Plague + its effects; The moral results of revolution.
*	SIR THOS WYATT	(Poem)
	TAWNEY	General Conclusions from 'The Agrarian Problem of C16'.
	SIR CHARLES DARWIN.	World Population.
	KAUFFMAN.	Existentialism from Dostoevsky to Sartre.
*	JOHN KEATS.	Letters.
	QUOTATIONS	Perennial Philosophy; Reality + the Soul.
	TAWNEY. (Quotes)	Religion + the Rise of Capitalism.
	OAKESHOTT.	Systems of Philosophy.
	ORWELL.	The Prevention of Literature.
*	T.S.ELIOT.	Blake.
*	T.S.ELIOT.	Swinburne as Poet.
*	T.S.Eliot	The perfect critic
*	T.S.ELIOT.	Introduction to 'The Sacred Wood' (Extract)
*	T.S.ELIOT.	George Herbert.
	ACTON.	On the Study of History.
	STONE.	On R.H.Tawney
	DOLCI + HUXLEY.	Report from Palermo.
	SMETHURST.	Language, Logic + God.
	TREVOR ROPER	E.H.CARR - What is History?

RIESMAN - Some Observations on Intellectual Freedom.
POPPER - Open Society & its Enemies.
HOSKINS - On the Writing of Local History.
HOLLOWAY. S.W. - Sociology & History.
JOHNSON. C. The Mechanical Processes of the Historian.
LEWIS. C.S. The Anthropological Approach.

LEGENDS & MYTHS.

HILTON. R.H.	The Origins of Robin Hood. (1958)	(1)
HOLT. J.C.	The Origins & audience of the ballads of Robin Hood.	(4)
KEEN. M.	Robin Hood - Peasant or Gentleman?	(7)
HOLT. J.C.	Robin Hood - Some Comments.	(8)
CAMPBELL.	Medieval Outlaws.	(9)
KEEN. M.	Robin Hood. A peasant hero.	(10)
BAUGH. A.C.	The Outlaw Ballads in the Middle ages	(11)
ASTON. T.H.	Robin Hood.	(12)
LEFF. G.	In ~~pursuit~~ search of the millenium.	(13)
LEE. S.	Robin Hood. (D.N.B. 1890).	(15)

Thanks and acknowledgements

I would like to thank all those who have read and commented on this volume for their help. This includes Sir Keith Thomas, Julianna Simor Lees, Fabienne Bonnet and Sarah Harrison.

I would like to thank Julianna Simor Lees and Penelope Marcus for their permission to use their letters, and acknowledge their copyright in these.

If any others whose materials I have quoted feel I should acknowledge their copyright, I hope they will get in touch and I will take due notice.

Printed in Great Britain
by Amazon